DOM COLUMBA MARMION
ABBOT OF MAREDSOUS

ABBOT MARMION

RAYMOND THIBAULT, OSB

DOM COLUMBA MARMION
ABBOT OF MAREDSOUS

A Master of the Spiritual Life
1858–1923

Translated from the French by Mother Mary St Thomas
A Nun of Tyburn Convent

THE CENACLE PRESS
AT SILVERSTREAM PRIORY

© 2024 Silverstream Priory

This revised edition, published by The Cenacle Press at Silverstream Priory, incorporates some minor corrections to the text.

Nihil Obstat
Joannes Gray Canonicus
Censor Librorum

Imprimatur
Andreas Joseph, OSB
Archiepiscopus S. Andr., et Ed.

Edimburgi
Die 6 Maii 1932

All reservable rights reserved.

The Cenacle Press at Silverstream Priory
Silverstream Priory
Stamullen, County Meath, K32 T189, Ireland
www.cenaclepress.com

ppr ISBN 978-1-915544-59-9
cloth ISBN 978-1-915544-60-5

Interior design by Kenneth Lieblich
Cover design by Silverstream Priory

CONTENTS

	List of Illustrations	vii
	Author's Preface	ix
1	"As a Chosen Arrow"	1
2	Training for the Priesthood	17
3	Beginning of His Ministry and Religious Vocation	31
4	Monastic Initiation	47
5	The Path of Perfection	75
6	Ascensiones Cordis	91
7	Louvain	129
8	Graces of Union	157
9	Dom Marmion as Abbot	195
10	Christ's Representative	221
11	The Spiritual Director	257
12	Cardinal Mercier and Dom Marmion	307
13	A Spiritual Son of Dom Marmion: Dom Pie de Hemptinne	337
14	Christ's Apostle	355
15	His Written Work	395
16	To Live as a Child of the Heavenly Father	427
17	The Fruits of the Spirit of Adoption	451
18	Spiritus Precum	477
19	To the Father's House	521

LIST OF ILLUSTRATIONS

Abbot Columba Marmion	ii
The Marmion Family	6
Joseph Marmion (Clonliffe, 1876)	16
Brother Columba (Maredsous, 1888)	76
Dom Marmion (Louvain, 1900)	132
Maredsous Abbey	194
Cardinal Mercier and Dom Marmion (1916)	308
Dom Pie Hemptinne	336
Pius x	378
Facsimile of Autograph Page from Dom Marmion's Writings	500
Abbot Marmion In His Last Years	518

AUTHOR'S PREFACE

In the judgment of the most competent critics Dom Marmion's ascetical works reveal him as a master of the spiritual life.

What has notably struck readers of *Christ the Life of the Soul, Christ in His Mysteries,* and *Christ the Ideal of the Monk,* is that such books could only have been published after having been lived; they give the impression of often being simply the echo, scarcely veiled, of an intense inner life.

Therefore, directly after Dom Marmion's death in January 1923 the appearance of a *Life* of an author whose writings are of such depth and so eminently calculated to do good was eagerly awaited and was asked for on all sides.

Would it be possible to realise this expectation? Were sufficient documents available in order to attempt to reconstruct the different stages of Dom Marmion's inner life? For a further knowledge of this inner life could alone satisfy the commendable curiosity of thousands and make for the value of the work.

The reply was soon forthcoming. Amongst Dom Marmion's papers were found two small books of spiritual notes dating from the beginning of his monastic life. Then in his manuscript books as professor of theology there was the pleasant surprise of discovering, intermixed with the outline of his lessons, numerous pages on his intimate life with God during the time he was at Louvain. But above all, we have received little by little the loan of letters written by him and numbering, up to the present, more than four hundred.[1]

---

1 This number is certainly far below that of the letters written by Dom Marmion. Many correspondents have destroyed the letters Dom Marmion wrote to them. "I destroyed all his letters of direction," the Mother Superior of a religious community wrote to us, "one day when I wanted to obtain a great favour from God. I then made a sacrifice of all my treasures." One can only respect such a supernatural motive, but at the same time one can only regret that the sacrifice should have concerned so precious a matter. There are other correspondents with whom we have not been able to come in touch through not knowing their address. Should these lines fall under their eyes, we ask

The documents thus collected have allowed us to retrace, if not in detail, at least in sufficiently sure outline, the story of his soul. With the addition of information gathered in Ireland from his own relatives and friends it became possible to grasp how nature and grace had prepared him for his mission, to follow him in his training for the priesthood, to watch his monastic initiation and progress in the cloister, to contemplate the growth of divine grace in his soul. The theologian, the abbot, spiritual father of monks, the director of consciences, and the apostle are brought before us with the varied gifts of a rich and original nature wholly given up to the breath of the Spirit. Finally it was made possible for us to linger over his last years to behold the wonderful attainment of high virtue and to enter into the sanctuary of the contemplative.

We have undertaken this task. Nevertheless the work we offer to the public is not presented as a complete biography, nor even as a biography at all in the modem sense of the word. It is, in a biographical setting, an essay of which the essential end, at once more restricted and more ambitious, is to find again in the clear light of the documents themselves the bent of the spiritual ascent of one who has spoken so well of Christ's mysteries; to reveal at the same time the genesis, development and extent of his doctrine. To discover in the *life* of Dom Marmion the full import of his ascetical *work:* such, before all, has been our ambition.

The realisation of this ambition has been a comparatively easy matter. Dom Marmion does not hide from us his true self: in his entirely spontaneous notes he does not place between his heart and ours any literary labour; his letters, especially to those who were his intimate disciples, are like a clear mirror which reflect him as he was; it is in these pages that he is most easily to be apprehended. He is his own best portrait painter. He depicts himself better than any other could do; and in order to lay ourselves under the pleasant illusion of having him still present with us, we have truly but to leave him to speak.

> them to be so good as to lend us the letters (which we will restore after reading) or to give us a copy of them; we shall be very grateful for this.

The end and object that in this way we have sought to attain has shown us the plan to be followed. Chronology has only supplied us with the indispensable framework and through every event recorded we have, above all,[1] endeavoured to gain an insight into Dom Columba's spiritual life and work.

Hence we could have no hesitation as to utilising in the largest measure these hitherto unpublished records and thus revealing so much of the inner life of a master in asceticism; it has seemed to us that we were bound to draw out handfuls of these hidden treasures thereby to make souls the richer. Besides, if we were jealously to keep such riches only for ourselves, should we not be frustrating the design of One who so abundantly meted them out to His servant?

Hence again, we could not think of publishing these often fragmentary notes apart from the chronological setting: that would have been to break the living and deep unity which links the work to the man and which constitutes one of the most attractive characteristics of Dom Marmion's personality.

This book will not appeal to readers who like biographies with swift movement. But we are confident that it will be favourably received by all Dom Columba's friends – and they are many; by all those, too, who are interested in psychological problems and ascetical questions; they will watch the development of a doctrine of life in an assuredly privileged soul. We have, above all, the intimate conviction that this book will be welcomed with joy by all who have read and appreciated *Christ the Life of the Soul:* they will find again in it the same teaching, high and acceptable, supernatural and human, under a more spontaneous but not less profound form; not more systematised, but lived from day to day, from year to year, in the complexity of life's vicissitudes: we have the certainty that they will be won over by the simplicity of these luminous confidences, and will always be glad to have read them.

It remains to us to fulfil a duty of gratitude towards all those

---

1 "Above all," we say, for it is quite evident that necessity has more than once obliged us to dwell on such or such event even when, for lack of documents, we could not know Dom Columba's sentiments on the occasion.

who have helped and encouraged us by their counsels in this long and delicate task, often interrupted, often, too, resumed on fresh letters being communicated to us in the course of our work.

But our gratitude goes out, above all, to those who, with a confidence which honours as much as it touches us, have lent us original letters of Dom Marmion. From this precious source was derived the important chapter on the "Spiritual Director" and the best pages on his close and childlike intimacy with God during his later years.

We would wish this work to be such as Dom Marmion himself would have wished it to be: an act of fervent and loving faith in the Divinity of Christ, who vouchsafed to shed in the soul of His servant an abundance of divine lights in order to make of him a herald of His mysteries.

Maredsous, this 8th of September 1929.

. . .

Many of the pages of the notes and many of Dom Marmion's letters are written in English. Dom Marmion had the habit of underlining certain words to bring out his thought the better, or draw special attention to them. We have respected this proceeding by printing in italics the words he has underlined once and in small capitals the words twice underlined. This remark applies to all the original passages given in this book.

Finally, the extracts from letters have only been published with the assent of those to whom they were written, but more than once, out of discretion, we have not given the date.

1   "AS A CHOSEN ARROW"
(1858–74)

Irish on his father's side, French on that of his mother, Joseph Marmion possessed a diversity of natural qualities which gave rare complexity to his character.

To his Celtic antecedents he owed his keenness of intellect, lively imagination, wealth of sensibility, exuberance of life, and perpetual youthfulness of soul. From the French blood which flowed in his veins he inherited his logical mind, clarity of vision, readiness of expression, directness of aim. From these two influences brought together came the glad generosity of his great heart with all the spontaneity and strength, devotedness and delicacy which belong to such great-heartedness.

But – let it be said at the outset so as to be faithful to his own spirit – the best part of his personality, or to be more exact, that which made him what he was, lay elsewhere, and to find it we must, without denying what he owed to his racial antecedents, seek further and plunge into the supernatural.

At the beginning of the book which is his masterpiece, *Christ the Life of the Soul*, he has given as the *leitmotif* of his whole teaching the words of St Paul: *Elegit nos in ipso*, "God chose us in Christ, 'before the foundation of the world, that we should be holy and unspotted in His sight in charity.'" Intended for all God's chosen ones, these words are singularly applicable to Dom Marmion. God had marked him with the seal of His Christ from all eternity. We see nature and grace wonderfully blended in him – and this is one of the great attractions of his character. All his natural qualities were little by little to be sealed by grace which was to find in them pliant and useful allies. The essential unity of this richly endowed personality lay in the wide unfolding and far-reaching influence of one great passion that uplifted and sustained all his energies, namely, the love of Christ, and of souls to be won to Christ for the glory of the Father.

Joseph Marmion was born in Dublin. His father, William Marmion,[1] a gentleman farmer of Kildare, had come to settle in the capital. He there filled the post of head of the shipping department in an important firm of exporters established on the banks of the Liffey, in the mercantile quarter alongside Arran Quay.

The Marmions came originally from Normandy, but settled in Ireland previously to the Hundred Years' War.[2] The name is still attached to an old town in Lower Normandy, *Fontenay-le-Marmion*, not far from Caen, where one of the Lords of Anbon, Robert Marmion, was besieged in the twelfth century by Geoffroy, Count of Anjou.

According to constant family traditions, William Marmion was descended through his mother, an O'Rourke, from a noble and powerful line possessing many branches, as is the case with the greater number of ancient Irish families.

In the absence of conclusive documents it is not easy to trace a genealogy, but there is nothing at all unlikely about such traditions in Ireland. We know that the island was formerly divided into a great number of clans, having kings at their head, and it was from this that the use of family names became general. The Counts O'Rourke distinguished themselves at all times by their attachment to the Catholic Faith and their love of learning and the arts. Under the reign of Elizabeth I they remained absolutely faithful to their creed. Later on, under James II, they had to emigrate, like many of their compatriots, and several entered the French king's army. They are to be found fighting in the Battle of Fontenoy in 1745, where two of them lost their lives. It was an O'Rourke who became the chaplain of Prince Eugène. Other Counts O'Rourke entered the Russian army, and one of their descendants is the present Bishop of Danzig, Msgr Edward O'Rourke.[3] The O'Rourkes

---

1 In Ireland mention of the family is first found at Kilmessan (Co. Meath). There is nothing specifically Celtic in the name, which is much less common in the island than are typical Irish names. Irish works on genealogy tell us nothing of the Marmions who came to Hibernia.
2 Arcisse de Caumont, *Statistique monumentale du Calvados*.
3 Nominated by a Bull of 3 January 1926. It is to the great kindness of Msgr O'Rourke that we owe these details contained in a brochure *Documents and*

had for their device: *Serviendo guberno,* "I reign in serving." It may be that Dom Marmion was, perhaps subconsciously, influenced by this fact when, on being elected Abbot of Maredsous and undertaking the government of the abbey, he chose as motto the sentence from the *Rule of St Benedict: Magis prodesse quam praeesse,* "To be useful rather than to command." A simple variant of the same great idea which, better than any other bond, formed a link with his ancestors, whose history was a series of services devoted to the highest causes.

Like all the Irish race, William Marmion had a lively and practical faith, and in his home circle his children possessed from their cradle the most precious of inheritances. We are insisting upon this point for, as we are about to see, faith was one of the most marked traits of Dom Columba's character. After God, he owed his faith to his race. The faith of the Irish is proverbial, but it must be seen in its own country for all its ardour and intensity to be realised. One must needs see the men, women and children crowding into the churches, kneeling on the flagstones, even out on to the road. Few or no movements: one would say all were absorbed in the contemplation of the Beyond, that Beyond of which the Celt more than any other race has the habitual intuition. Again, one must needs see, especially in the towns, the long files of the faithful of every condition who, on Saturdays or the eves of great feasts, remain on their knees awaiting their turn for confession; countless communions often made late into the morning; the public recitation of the *Angelus;* the placing of the picture of the Sacred Heart in full view inside the tramcars, etc.

What perhaps gives the stranger travelling in Ireland the keenest realisation of this faith, especially in the West, are the "Stations." At Christmas, during Lent, and at Easter the priest goes to the distant and outlying hamlets of his parish. No chapel there; the priest lodges with one of the inhabitants; in the morning the Holy Sacrifice

---

Materials for the History of the O'Rourke Family, Danzig, 1925 (for private circulation). We may add that there has been a branch of the O'Rourkes at Saint-Brieuc (Côtes-du-Nord, France) for several centuries.

is celebrated in a room, often a very poor one, of some particular house, intimation having been given long before the time.

Everyone goes to confession, then all, pressing against each other as far as to the steps of the improvised altar, assist at the Divine Sacrifice, communicating at it with deepest piety. This touching custom, dating back to the days of persecution, recalls how dearly this most precious faith has been safeguarded, and above all, how heroically defended.

Let us add to this the affection, at once respectful and simple, that the flocks bear to their pastor who, in his parish, "is like a king in his kingdom,"[1] the one to whom secrets are naturally confided, the counsellor sought after and obeyed, the supreme arbitrator of disputes.

More particularly in the towns the fact of being thrown amongst Protestants still further accentuates the Catholic's esteem for his faith. From Arran Quay William Marmion saw every day, on the opposite bank of the Liffey, the proud silhouette of the marvellous cathedral of St Patrick, taken from the Catholics by the Protestants; a saddening sight which, while bringing to mind the struggle against heresy, only revived in faithful hearts the love of the old faith.

William Marmion's personal piety is shown in the following anecdote: when the young Joseph had just donned the clerical attire he, in his zeal, ventured to counsel his father to practise the presence of God. He received this simple reply:

"My son, in the midst of my most pressing occupations, I never remain many minutes without making an entire offering of myself to God."

A special devotion towards the Blessed Sacrament characterised this piety. Mr William Marmion was recognised by his attitude in prayer before the tabernacle, kneeling erect, with joined hands raised to the level of his face.

His somewhat serious character, slightly authoritative, early Victorian, as we should say, and a great insistence on moral rectitude along the whole line of conduct, corresponded to his exactitude

---

1 Louis Paul-Dubois, *L'Irlande contemporaine*.

and performance of religious duties. The innate reserve of the parents and the deference of the children gave a certain dignity, with just a shade of stiffness, to the mutual relations and to the family life as a whole.

It was at the French consulate in Dublin that William Marmion met for the first time the one who was to be his life's companion, Mlle Herminie Cordier. A Scotch gentleman, Donald Campbell, connected with a large firm of wine importers established in London, had been called by business to Paris and had there married Mlle Marie Cordier, daughter of a royal bookseller in that city.[1] Commissioned to establish a branch house of the London firm, he came to Dublin for that purpose. Mrs Campbell was accompanied by her younger sister, Herminie Cordier, and this chance meeting at the French consulate brought her face to face with William Marmion. As soon as he saw her he was struck by her beauty, and resolved to ask her hand. A little older than her husband,[2] Herminie

[1] The Paris Printers' and Booksellers' Year Book of 1829 mentions no less than nine Cordiers following this business. In the absence of exact information it has been impossible to identify which of these was Dom Marmion's grandfather.

[2] She was born in Paris in 1820. Her mother was a Claude. We may mention a curious fact in reference to this. At Saint-Gérard, not far from Maredsous, the nuns of the Visitation of Meaux (they have since returned there) had taken refuge at the beginning of the century in an ancient Benedictine abbey. In recognition of the spiritual services rendered to their community by the monks of Maredsous, the Visitandines offered them a letter of aggregation. Seeing among the signatures that of Sister Claude, Dom Marmion exclaimed with surprise: "Claude! The name of my grandmother" (on his mother's side). Some time after this Dom Marmion gave for the first time a conference to the Visitandines. On account of her deafness, Sister Claude – who, moreover, knew nothing as yet of Dom Columba's remark – was placed near the grille facing the preacher. "It is astonishing," she said to her sisters during the recreation which followed, "how much Dom Columba resembles my father." Told of this, Dom Columba wished to go into the matter. He learnt that the nun's grandfather was Joseph Claude and that his wife was Marie Catherine Collin, both well-known names in Lorraine. They lived in Attert where, in those old coaching days, Joseph Claude was postmaster, One day, at the beginning of the Revolution, he received a mysterious mission, which he was to fulfil in person. Had this mission anything to do with the escape of the royal family, to

THE MARMION FAMILY

Cordier joined great simplicity to much charm of manner. Of an old Lorraine stock, a family known for its royalist tendencies, she had received a good Christian education, rather strict, which accorded well with Mr Marmion's character. To the end of his life he kept for her a deep respect that had in it something almost sacred. It was undoubtedly from his mother that the child received as heritage a deep love for France and a great reverence towards God, and all that concerns God's service.

As he could not discover any official record of the baptism of his future bride, William Marmion, through a rather curious scruple, persuaded her to be conditionally baptised on the eve of their wedding-day. They were married in Dublin, in St Andrew's Church, on 21 April 1847.

God blessed this union; nine children were born of it, four girls and five boys: Mary, later Mrs Joyce, who died in 1924; Lizzie, who became a Sister of Mercy and superior of the house of the Institute in Waterford, and died in 1918; John Sebastian, called back to God at the age of two; Flora, likewise a Sister of Mercy, who died in 1892 at Clonakilty, at the age of forty, leaving behind her the memory of a soul high in sanctity;[1] Philip Henry, taken to heaven at the age of twelve months; Rosie, Sister of Mercy.[2] Last of all three sons: Joseph,

---

whom the Claudes were much attached? We do not know. However this may be, in the course of this mission Joseph Claude drove off in one of his own post-chaises, and nothing more was ever heard of him. His wife died of grief, and the impression made upon their children was such that ever after these family reminiscences were scarcely ever touched upon. This was why the nun possessed but few details of Dom Marmion's grandmother, except that it is certain that she married a Paris bookseller, which agrees with the fact that Dom Marmion himself had gathered from his mother's lips.

1 Flora had great affinity of soul with Dom Columba. After her death her brother was shown her spiritual notebook. She had written in it: "At one time before praying I every day as my angel guardian to carry my soul into the bosom of God. Now I have no longer to ask my angel, for my soul rises there of itself, all alone, as soon as I enter into prayer." Dom Columba was the more struck by the similarity of their spiritual attraction, "the bosom of the Father," in that he had never spoken on this subject with his sister.
2 She died in May 1930.

the future monk; Frank, who died in 1896; and Matthew, who became a doctor of medicine and died in 1927.

As we see, death had early visited the Marmion homestead. It had struck the two first sons while, so to speak, they were yet in the cradle, leaving none but girls. The loss, therefore, was deeply felt. In their bitter desolation Mr and Mrs Marmion turned to God. They implored the favour of a son, and this intention was confided to St Joseph.

God wished to test their faith. Yet another girl was given to them, whose coming accentuated, while it tempered, their recent loss.

Their gladness was only complete when, three years later, on 1 April 1858, one Holy Thursday, a son was born.[1] Out of gratitude to St Joseph, who had at last obtained for them their great desire, it was decided to give the newborn babe the name of Joseph, a choice which had no family tradition to support it.

On that same day the parents consecrated their son to God's service, and from that moment he was always looked upon as a future priest. A curious consequence of this act of donation was that the young Joseph in his childhood and during his college years was always dressed in black, while as for his younger brothers and his sisters, they were dressed like other children, in the fashion of their day.

Joseph was baptised on April 6th, in the church dedicated to St Paul, Apostle of the Nations.[2] At that hour of benediction his soul received the seed of that grace of supernatural adoption which made him a child of the Heavenly Father in Jesus Christ – a grace common to every Christian, and constituting the very basis of all inner life; but we shall see how in Dom Marmion this seed was to grow and develop with such fullness as to become the chief characteristic of his spirituality.

There is no doubt that at this hour he likewise received, through the intercession of the doctor of the Gentiles, the yet invisible

---

[1] They were living at 57 Queen Street. A short time afterwards William Marmion moved to Blackhall Street.

[2] Arran Quay. He was baptised by Fr Daniel O'Keefe, the parish priest. The godfather was Denys Brison, and the godmother, Mary Sarah Brison.

first-fruits of that grace of the apostolate which was to make of him a herald of Jesus. During the long years of childhood and youth, the boy's eyes when in church often rested on the picture of the Conversion of St Paul above the high altar, with St Patrick and St Columba depicted on the lateral panels. But St Paul was to be to him more than a mere historical figure. Dom Marmion was to assimilate in a remarkable manner the teaching of the apostle on the riches of the mystery of Christ in order to shed it abroad in souls with the same vehemence and the same glowing language.

Nothing remarkable is recorded of his childhood. It is remembered, however, that his delicate health more than once put his life in danger; it was not until he was turned eight years old that his constitution grew strong enough to give no further cause for anxiety.

Of quick intelligence, and of a loving and lovable disposition, generous, gentle, and obedient, the child never gave the slightest trouble to his parents or to those who had the charge of him; he was thus surrounded by an atmosphere of warm sympathy, and petted by all, especially by his sisters. He liked to share in his sisters' games, except when it came to playing with dolls. He could never bring himself to dress, fondle, or rock a doll. It would not have occurred to us to mention this childish detail if, long years afterwards, it had not inspired Dom Marmion with an original thought quite in keeping with his own manner of seizing on some fact, word, or gesture, and applying it to the interior life. We read, then, in a memorandum book of 1899, this phrase jotted down in pencil: "Self-love is a doll which one nurses. When it is proud one dresses it up finely; when it is sad one dresses it in black, but fondles it all the more. It is a poisonous doll. I have never understood…"

The phrase remains unfinished: a stroke of the bell, or someone coming in had doubtless interrupted Dom Marmion, but it is easy to complete his idea by recalling these reminiscences of his childhood.

Like his sisters, and later on his brothers, Joseph came under the special influence of one of his father's sisters-in-law, Miss Sullivan, who lived in the family under the name of "Aunt," and whose piety was deep and fervent. She seconded Mrs Marmion in the religious education of the children.

Joseph made his first Communion at the age of nine, and after that continued to receive the Bread of Life every fortnight; the girls communicated every week. As to the parents, out of reverence for the august Sacrament of the Altar, they only approached the Holy Table once a month. Never would they, where they themselves were concerned, depart from this rule, the result, especially in the mother's case, of an education which Dom Marmion later sometimes referred to as Jansenistic.[1]

But a no less rigorously established practice was that of assisting every day at Holy Mass. Each morning, the only excuse admitted being that of illness, father, mother, children, aunt, servants, went to church to hear Holy Mass together. It was held that God had not been duly honoured unless the first-fruits of the day were consecrated to Him by the sublimest act of religion.

In this atmosphere of piety Joseph Marmion formed a habit of seeing things from the standpoint of faith. He used afterwards to tell how, whilst yet a child, he was travelling one day during the holidays with an uncle, a gentleman farmer, who, in spite of his Irish faith, was keenly interested in everything that had to do with business. He asked his nephew what he intended to be when he was

---

[1] This strain of Jansenism is to be understood in its spiritual sense, the "religious and moral tone," not in the dogmatic sense. It was to be found in numerous French families at the end of the eighteenth century. What Msgr Alfred Baudrillart wrote of the mother of Msgr Maurice d'Hulst may be applied to Dom Marmion's mother: "She had kept that spirit, that manner which is often styled, for want of a more exact term, as *Jansenist* and which was still at that period the characteristic of the most deeply religious French families: rather too much constraint and severity were compensated for by the firmness of principle, the training of the conscience and the habit of taking very much in earnest even from the tenderest years, all that touches the relations of the soul with God." *Vie de monseigneur d'Hulst*. Nevertheless, Dom Marmion judged this tendency prejudicial to souls become *children of God* by baptism, and he kept a certain grudge against Jansenism on account of the influence this spirituality had gained over his mother's side of the family.

grown up, and talked to him about banks and markets. At length the boy, who had other ambitions, interrupted:

"But after all, Uncle, money is not everything!"

"Ah, my child," he replied, with an air of astonishment mixed with pity, "you do not know what money is. You cannot understand that yet."

"This view of things," Dom Marmion would add, "quite took my breath away. Now," he concluded, "my uncle is in eternity, and thinks much less of money than I do."

In this essentially Christian home, where the ancient Faith was jealously guarded, the divine law perfectly observed, and where, with patriarchal manners, easy circumstances prevailed, seven children grew up healthy, active, and brimming over with life and mirth, as was to be expected of their generous Irish blood. Their fount of joyousness was to last as long as life itself.

Indeed, the contrast presented by an exceptional merry temperament and a reflective mind was already to be marked in Joseph. This contrast was to be further accentuated as years went by; it was often to prove disconcerting to those who did not know Dom Marmion closely, and having heard him spoken of as an interior man, found it difficult to understand how the humorous sallies of his spontaneous gaiety could be combined with an intense spiritual life and a deep spirit of recollection.

Even in this united and happy household there were chosen affinities between certain of its members. It was with Rosie, the youngest girl, though three years older than himself, that Joseph from his childhood and ever afterwards was bound by a special affection. The same meditative character, the same constant zest for spiritual things, later in the case of each to be developed in the cloister, had very early drawn these two together – twin souls despite their difference in age, and of the self-same candour.

Rosie was Joseph's favourite companion in his games and walks, the safe confidante of his sorrows, joys and plans, and it was always her advice he was most ready to follow. When each summer the family went for a month to Kingstown,[1] Joseph's greatest delight was to take Rosie out alone with him in a small boat. Letting themselves be rocked by the monotonous rhythm of the waves, the two watched the varied movements of the numerous pleasure craft full of lively, merry young folks. But what particularly held their attention was the beauty of the sea under its thousand aspects. Their eyes wide with the wonder and dreams of innocent youth, drank in their fill of beauty, and while they exchanged their impressions, telling each other how lovely it all was, the hours glided by. But, above all, their pure hearts and minds were merged in that blissful and harmonious peace which has its wellspring in God.

Joseph Marmion was educated in Ireland. He received his first lessons from the Augustinian Fathers at a day college, called the Seminary of St Laurence O'Toole.[2]

In 1868, when he was ten years old, he entered the Belvedere College in Dublin directed by the Jesuit Fathers and he there received all his secondary education.[3]

He soon won the good opinion and affection of his masters, and for his own part he always kept a faithful and grateful recollection of them. The whole course of his secondary studies was marked by brilliant success, especially in Latin and diction. With his open mind he was naturally keenly interested in the recent discoveries made in the domain of aerostation and electricity.

But his companions found him too much of a "girl." His gentleness and sweet temper annoyed some amongst them who determined to make him come out of his shell and provoked him in every way in the attempt to force him to retaliate. Pains lost were these attempts at "ragging" to which those of his temperament are particularly exposed. One day a school fellow struck him, having no other reason than that just mentioned. He succeeded no better

---

1 South of Dublin.
2 This college has long since ceased to exist.
3 Under the rectorate of Fr Edward Kelly and Fr John Mathews.

than the others. Relating this incident to Rosie, he told her it had cost him all his Irish blood not to hit back, but he had kept a strong hold on himself, so as to imitate the good Jesus in His Passion – certainly a noteworthy remark from a lad of thirteen.

He was soon to follow more perfectly in the steps of the Divine Master by consecrating himself wholly to His service. When old enough to take the matter into his own consideration he had readily fallen in with his father's cherished notion of making him a priest. His great love of religion had besides long since drawn him towards the priesthood.

At the end of his secondary studies he had to come to a decision; it was taken for granted that the youth would enter the episcopal Seminary of Holy Cross at Clonliffe. He passed his entrance examination before Paul Cardinal Cullen, Archbishop of Dublin, and it was arranged for him to enter in the beginning of January.

Joseph was then in his seventeenth year.

At this turning point temptation lay in wait for him, as for so many others. In fact, when the devil foresees God's mighty working in His elect he leaves no stone unturned to thwart the Divine Plan; but perhaps never does he set his snares with more delight and hatred than under the feet of enthusiastic youth brimming over with hope and ready to immolate all to Christ: one altar less in the world, a saint less upon earth, floods of redeeming grace never to flow. When the young Benedict of Norcia, after three years of hidden life in the desert, was called by God to found the monastic order which was to save the Church from barbarism, to civilise Europe and help to establish Christendom, he experienced hell's formidable assault, from which he was to come forth victorious only at the cost of an act of heroism almost unexampled in the annals of saintship.

In our own day, one of St Benedict's sons, Dom Pie de Hemptinne, at the moment of entering the cloister which was to witness his wonderful ascent of soul, was beset by the Evil One till he almost came to believe he was about to entangle himself in an abominable business.

Young Joseph Marmion was likewise to experience Satan's fierce assaults. When the time came for him to cross the threshold of the sanctuary a deep repugnance for the priestly vocation took possession of him: a struggle between nature and grace – nature, which would have kept him in the sweet and pure intimacy of the family circle, and grace, which would have him belong to Christ that he might give Him to souls. "Come, I will make of thee a fisher of men!"

On the morning of the day before he was to enter the seminary he went as usual to Mass with Rosie. His puckered brow had for some days past betrayed the inward struggle. His sister remarked to him that he was less gay than usual. "Oh! Pray for me, Rosie; pray hard," was all his reply.

With the sure instinct of a confidante Rosie guessed the painful drama that was being enacted in her brother's soul, and she kept silence.

In the afternoon Joseph went out to see some of his friends. The farewell dinner, given by William Marmion in honour of his son's entering the seminary and to which relations and friends had been invited, was to begin at five o'clock. At the hour fixed all were present – all except Joe. Ever strictly punctual, the father began to show annoyance at this unwonted absence, but a few tactful words from Rosie dispelled the cloud, and all sat down to table. The meal went on. Still no sign of Joseph. Six, seven, eight o'clock struck. At such a prolonged absence Rosie became uneasy. About nine o'clock a loud ring of the bell. Rosie went to open the door. It was Joe.

"It is all right," he said, radiantly. "I will tell you about it later."

To the general delight, he went into the dining room. At the end of the evening when the moment came to say good night Joseph held his sister back.

"Oh, Rosie, how you must have been praying, and praying well. I was terribly tempted; I no longer wanted to enter the Seminary."

He then told her about his visit to his friends. He had at first spent a long time, but in vain, looking for his friend N—. This failure was no doubt providential. In Joseph's state of mind, and with his impressionable character, the influence of N—, superficial and

worldly as he was, might have had disastrous results. It was W—
whom the future seminarist found after a long search, a young man
in every way to be depended upon, whose intervention on this occasion proved decisive. Joseph confided to him all that was disturbing his peace of soul; they had a long discussion, but W— knew
how to speak the determined words that were needed.

"Look here, my dear fellow," was the substance of the conclusion he arrived at, "these hesitations are all nonsense; now that you
have passed your entrance examination, and your father has paid
the fees, and everything is settled, you can't shirk. Be a man; make
an honest attempt; if it doesn't succeed, well, be a man still and
have the courage to come away."

This sensible reply got the better of the trouble that the spirit of
darkness had stirred up in the young man's soul.

The struggle was to be renewed a year afterwards – again a sharp
one – but once more Rosie's prayers prevailed: the Lord's claim
upon the one He had marked as His own was henceforth undisputed. The Divine Archer – this was an interpretation of the sacred
text which Dom Marmion himself was often to apply to vocations
– the Divine Archer placed in His quiver the chosen arrow that His
mighty hand was later to use for the winning of souls: *In pharetra sua
abscondit me quasi sagittam electam....*[1] *Sicut sagitta in manu potentis.*[2]

---

[1] Isa. 49:2.
[2] Ps, 124:4.

JOSEPH MARMION
(Concliffe, 1876)

2 TRAINING FOR THE PRIESTHOOD (1874–81)

At Clonliffe, a suburb at the extreme north-east of Dublin, there stands in the midst of a large, peaceful park, where the distant murmurs of the city die away, the ecclesiastical College of Holy Cross.[1] The façade would be commonplace if it were not for the high perron dominating the great doorway built in the Doric style of architecture adopted by many of the city buildings. To the left is the church consecrated to the Holy Cross.[2] The façade is a replica of that of St Frances of Rome, while the interior is a reproduction of that of St Agatha; details which show the love of the founder, Msgr Cullen, Archbishop of Dublin, and first Irish cardinal, for all things Roman.[3]

Founded in 1859 for the priests of his diocese, Holy Cross remained particularly dear to Msgr Cullen; it was his wish to have his tomb in the crypt beneath the apse of the church. Another memorial of this great cardinal held in high honour, and hanging in

[1] It is here our duty (writes the author) to express our gratitude to the Vice-President of Holy Cross College, Fr Patrick Dargan, MA, DD; in the absence of the president he received us with great kindness and that simple cordiality which distinguishes so many of the Irish clergy. We were agreeably surprised to see in the college parlour, among the portraits of those who have made Clonliffe illustrious, that of Dom Marmion.

[2] A large relic of the True Cross, given to Cardinal Cullen by His Holiness Pius IX, is enshrined here.

[3] Cardinal Cullen was born at Prospect (Co. Kildare), in 1803; he studied at Carlow College, then at the Propaganda. From 1832 to 1849 he was Rector of the Irish College in Rome, where he enjoyed the friendship of the Sovereign Pontiffs Gregory XVI and Pius IX. Made Archbishop of Armagh in December 1849, he was transferred to the See of Dublin in May 1852, and made cardinal in 1866: he was the first Irish archbishop to be invested with the scarlet. At the Vatican Council he was remarkable for his zeal in the cause of papal infallibility; it was he who was asked to draw up the formula of definition. He died in Dublin in 1878. The Catholic cause owes much to Cardinal Cullen; he was especially zealous in the cause of Catholic education; under his episcopate a real renascence was wrought in piety and devotion. Ecclesiastical discipline and works of charity were also the objects of his constant solicitude.

a prominent place in the college assembly hall, is a fine portrait of him to which the warm tones of the scarlet give life and colour.

At the period when Joseph Marmion entered the college at Clonliffe (January 1874) nearly eighty seminarists were studying there.[1]

On coming amongst them, Joe Marmion proved himself a student of ready intelligence, lively, impulsive as well as impressionable and expansive; apt to flare up occasionally, but still more ready to yield to generous impulses. His temperament still remained at this period very near to nature; he sometimes went rather far in his disregard of forms and ceremonies, and amused himself in trying to find fun in everything. Without any taste for outdoor games and sports, he enjoyed friendly talks, in which he shone by his wit and high spirits. His gaiety was infectious; the others readily gathered round him, and from the group of which he was the centre fresh and merry laughter was always to be heard. Simplicity and merriment reigned amongst these seminarists who, like the legendary Father O'Flynn of the Irish ballad, did not the least intend to

> Is it lave gaiety all to the laity?
> Cannot the clergy be Irishmen, too?

Joseph Marmion's love of a joke found vent on every occasion as his friends knew to their cost. For their part they paid him back in his own coin. They highly amused themselves with the blunders he made in speaking, and especially in spelling, without however succeeding in curing him of his originalities in this respect; according to the remark of one of them, he had not "the saving grace" of suspecting these slips.

With a character such as his, fervent and lasting friendships easily spring up. His two chief friendships were with Msgr James Dunne, now parish priest at Donnybrook, Vicar General of Dublin and

---

[1] The rector at that time was Fr Michael Verdon, later rector of the Irish College in Rome, and then Bishop of Dunedin in New Zealand; the Vice-Rector, Msgr Fitz-Patrick, died Vicar General of Dublin.

Dean of the Metropolitan Chapter, and with Msgr Patrick Dwyer. The latter, who had come from Australia, was afterwards to return there to be raised to the episcopal See of Maitland.

At this time the students of Holy Cross had the habit during their morning walk of repeating to one another the dogmatic thesis which was to serve as theme at the following class; this they called "dogmatising." Every morning Dwyer and Marmion might be seen spending this recreation together in dogmatising. Inseparable in this practice, the two friends were together again in sharing prizes and awards at the end of the school year.

Indeed, Joseph Marmion early distinguished himself in the divers tests in philosophy and theology, but, according to those who knew him best during this time, he never fostered any ambition – which he might easily have gratified – of shining in mental achievements. Without gainsaying its specific value, study already appeared to him – what it was ever to be in his eyes – a help to the love of God.

It was on this latter plane, that of the supernatural, that he asked God to make him excel. Making no secret of what he felt on this subject, he followed retreats with sustained fervour and strove faithfully to keep the resolutions he had taken, in spite of a certain amount of banter that some of his companions allowed themselves at his expense.

His faith was very strong. Already it was evident that the revealed truths of religion were for him something more than simple theoretical theses without any bearing upon the moral life. There was something about him that impressed one with his sincerity; seldom was man less of a Pharisee. The recollected way in which he genuflected before the Blessed Sacrament bore convincing proof of his deep and practical faith in the Real Presence. His faith was such that during the vacations he never passed a church without entering were it only for a few moments, to adore the Divine Guest abiding in the tabernacle.

In this matter of devotion, he, like many of his companions, came under the influence of Fr John Gowan of the Congregation of the Mission. This son of St Vincent de Paul had the fine grave face of an ascetic. It is enough just to stand before his portrait in the great hall of Holy Cross to understand the strong impression he must have made upon souls. A long emaciated face, deeply lined by his austerities and zealous ardour; a determined chin, black, almost melancholy, eyes, still holding in their depths the horrors he had witnessed during the famine of 1846–50, a high forehead framed with a crown of white hair; every feature tells of the virtues of the ascetic.

Born in 1817,[1] John Gowan very soon felt an attraction to the priesthood, and after a few years ministry as a secular priest he consecrated himself entirely to God by joining the Lazarists. In conformity with his vows he devoted himself to missionary work and spent himself without counting the cost. His reputation for holiness, even more than for his eloquence, everywhere followed him. A man of prayer and a most zealous priest, he only sought to be an instrument in God's hands. He was made confessor and spiritual director at Holy Cross from its very beginning. His conferences are still held in high repute. He had the gift of communicating to others his own supernatural spirit. Very humble himself, he continued till the end of his life (1897) to recommend the virtue of humility to those under his direction; he strongly insisted on the necessity of receiving reprimands and corrections well. He had a very special devotion to our Lord's Passion. When he approached this subject he did so in such impressive terms as to move his hearers even to tears.

Fr Gowan's influence on Joseph Marmion was a very real one. It was Fr Gowan who inspired him with esteem for the virtue of humility and above all with fervent devotion to our Saviour's sufferings. He often told him: "If you frequently meditate attentively on the sorrows of Jesus whilst making the Way of the Cross, you will quickly arrive at perfection; you will not lose your fervour and

---

[1] At Skerries (Co. Dublin). He was the fifth of eight children. Educated at Maynooth. Appointed to the district of Glendalough, he spent himself unremittingly in the relief of his parishioners during the famine. On becoming a Lazarist his great achievements were the combating of Protestant proselytism and the creation of the Institute of the Sisters of the Holy Faith, for the instruction of youth. He died in January 1897, laden with years and merit. *Cf.* Fr Ernest Farrell, *Rev. John Gowan*, CM, *(1817–97)* Dublin, 1927.

you will receive many graces." This is the language of the saints. Joseph Marmion readily followed this suggestion, and it may safely be said from that time forward he never failed to make the Way of the Cross every day.

Everything at Clonliffe seemed to echo or to serve as a reminder of Fr Gowan's exhortations on this subject – the name of the college, the dedication of the church, the sacred relic enshrined there and in honour of which the Votive Mass of the Holy Cross is celebrated every Friday: "But it behoves us to glory in the cross of our Lord, Jesus Christ; in whom is our salvation, life and resurrection." Later, after his ordination, Fr Marmion was to be made curate at Dundrum (south of Dublin) at the Church of Holy Cross – and that was on 14 September 1881, the feast of the Exaltation of the Holy Cross – coincidences which did not escape his notice. All these circumstances gave a special tonality to his spirituality which he kept to the end of his life.

The young seminarian was all the while attentive to the work of his perfection and to the inspirations of grace. "In an instruction," he confided one day to one of his spiritual sons, "a holy priest showed us that an excellent form of continuous thanksgiving is watchfulness not to commit infidelities. There were ten of us who then took the resolution not to fail in the rule of silence. Sometimes in the beginning a word would slip out." How could it be otherwise with this young cleric who, as much and more than many of his age, was full of high spirits and light-heartedness? "But," he added, "I then imposed a penance on myself. Little by little I arrived at completely keeping the silence, and I think I may say that during five or six years I did not fail in it."

Sometimes it was what he read that inspired such resolutions, and in his longing to strengthen his spiritual life he had recourse to pious expedients. A fact related in the life of St John Berchmans gave him the idea of making a spiritual "league," as he himself expressed it, with two of his friends. This league, approved by Fr Gowan and duly signed, obliged them to pray every day for one another for three special intentions: to obtain a great devotion to the

Blessed Virgin, true humility, and fervent zeal for souls. Moreover, each of the subscribers promised that if after his death he was, as he hoped to be, admitted into the joy of the Lord, he would ask these graces from God for his survivors. Scattered later by their various vocations, the three friends never saw one another without recalling their agreement. Dom Marmion's life makes us feel how truly their prayer was heard.

He was already serving his apprenticeship to that zeal with which he was later to burn. Out of obedience to his director he once spent all the long vacation together with a companion visiting the poor in the town, lavishing on them, in addition to material help, the spiritual alms of comforting words. On the advice, too, of Fr Gowan, who was particularly drawn to the defending of the faith of children against Protestant souperism, he with the help of two other seminarists and a layman undertook a Sunday school to teach religion to little boys. He put all his heart into these oftentimes very difficult tasks, although, as he had foreseen, the Sunday school was not to have a lasting success.

Thus blindly to give himself in person accorded well with his generous nature, which had, however, severe assaults to undergo on certain occasions. One day during the vacation he learnt that a poor old woman, well known to his family, was threatened with being summoned before the magistrates by an exacting creditor who claimed the payment of a somewhat large debt. The young seminarist possessed an equivalent amount saved up little by little for a trip he had promised himself. A struggle went on in his heart between his generosity and the legitimate desire to enjoy the fruit of his economies. This struggle lasted all night. In the morning charity had gained the day; with his father's consent he generously made over his savings in favour of the poor woman.

It was at this time he experienced for himself the truth on which he was later especially to insist, namely, that a man's love for God is measured by his love for his neighbour. And God, having first inspired his act of charity, rewarded him for it; soon afterwards he heard the call to a more perfect life, a call which, however, was not yet clearly defined.

His steady advancement in love was not to be made without effort. In other matters he had likewise many a struggle. His impressionability at times made him for the moment forget his resolutions, and then his overflowing fun would provoke titters among his companions, which was fatal to discipline; but under the firm direction of Fr Gowan, who did not spare him, even publicly, Joseph Marmion overcame himself. He received these reprimands of which he visibly felt all the force and stringency with true humility.

"You see," he said to one of his friends, "it is a bitter medicine, but wholesome. So I must accept it if I am to be cured."

God, moreover, did His direct part in shaping the generous soul He had chosen for Himself. It was at this time (April 1878) that the young seminarist had the great grief of losing his father. This was a severe blow for him: the revered and beloved head of the family was now no more; his had been a living and practical faith, and in the warm atmosphere of the home he had seen the religious aspirations of his children brought to fruition. Three of his daughters had consecrated themselves to God, the dearest of his sons was ascending the steps to the altar, but he was not to have the joy of seeing him mount the last step.

The grace of trial was presently to be succeeded by a signal favour which had a considerable influence on Dom Marmion's life. One day when about to re-enter the study hall after a brief absence he had all at once, without there being any outward circumstance to account for it, "a light on God's infinity." The ineffable reality that lies hidden behind and is yet at the same time disclosed by the name of *God* seemed to reveal to him a ray of its inexpressible splendours; it was given him to approach the shoreless ocean of infinite perfection and obtain a glimpse of its immensity. This light only lasted an instant, but it was so clear and strong, it penetrated so far into his mind, that he felt an imperious need to lose himself in silent adoration of the Divine Majesty.[1] This grace which, after

---

1 There is a veiled allusion to this fact in *Christ the Ideal of the Monk*. Dom Mar-

God, he attributed to the fidelity with which at this period he was practising silence, left an indelible impression on his soul; it was as it were always present to him, and he referred to this not without emotion and thanksgiving, during the last days of his life.

We must lay stress on this episode: it marks a very important moment in Dom Marmion's inner life. A heavenly and precious seed had been cast into this chosen soil, and it was to grow little by little and produce a hundredfold. We will refrain from searching too curiously into the nature of this experience; let us simply hold to the fact that the vivid light, the powerful inward illumination granted to Dom Marmion was the source to which we must go back – as he himself said more than once – to find the secret of his reverence toward God, especially in celebrating the Holy Mysteries and the office in choir: one might have imagined that on these occasions he was dazzled by the Divine Majesty. This light was likewise the deepest and most tenacious root of his humility, which made him live in presence of the Invisible in utter self-abasement.[1]

Many fresh lights were later to be thrown on other aspects of the divine mystery, but it would seem as if few of these touched him so deeply and were to have so great an influence on his spiritual life.

The young seminarist's steady progress in virtue and marked success in his studies decided Msgr Edward MacCabe to send him to the Irish College in Rome to complete the last years of his theological course.

He travelled there in company with the Rector, Fr Michael Verdon, and they arrived at their destination on 24 December 1879. Joseph was to remain in Rome about two years.

---

mion drew from it the lesson that: "Christ Jesus chooses the moments which, humanly speaking, appear the least favourable to calm and recollection to communicate to us His lights."

[1] See in *Christ the Ideal of the Monk*, the chapter on "Humility." § 3: "Reverence towards God, the source of humility." In these pages Dom Marmion evidently refers to this experience and draws from it the lessons it contains.

TRAINING FOR THE PRIESTHOOD

In a letter dated February 1890,[1] Dom Marmion wrote: "I always look back on Rome as one of the happiest epochs of my life." This is one of his rare allusions to those years spent in the Eternal City. About fifteen years later he went further into detail in a note addressed to one of his young monks: "To be in Rome even without studying there is a real education for heart and soul. I am overjoyed to think of the advantages you will have during these fruitful years which so much affect our life. When I say 'even without studying,' I do not intend to suggest that *you* are not studying. I am sure that you are in the mood to drink in great draughts of philosophical learning to be used later for our Lord's glory."[2]

Failing documentary information, properly so called, about this period of his life, these lines at least give us some idea of what his stay in the Eternal City meant to him. He must have felt a singular fullness of spiritual life in this Rome where beats the heart of Catholicism. The *Christian* sense was doubled in him by the *Roman* sense. The young Irish seminarist's simple, intense and robust faith attached him strongly to the Vicar of Jesus Christ, at that time Leo XIII. All through his life he held the Roman Pontiff in a particular veneration, derived from his first sojourn in the city of the popes.

In the frequent visits that he made with his friend, Fr Joseph Moreau,[3] to the churches and catacombs his whole being was steeped in the entire Catholic past. What fervent prayers he uttered at the tomb of Peter, whose profession of faith in the Divinity of Jesus, the Son of the Living God, he was later to repeat in such tones of conviction; what prayers, too, were his at the glorious tomb of the Apostle of the Nations, who was to show forth to him "the mystery of Christ!"

Cannot we see the hand of Providence in the twofold fact that his last Mass was that of the Conversion of St Paul (January 25th), and that the ultimate lines traced by his hand, also on January 25th,

---

1 Without precise date.
2 Letter of 12 January 1903.
3 To whom we owe these details about Dom Marmion's life in Rome.

whilst he was yet unaware that his death was already imminent, were those of a letter addressed to the Sovereign Pontiff?

For Joseph Marmion this life in Rome was then, according to his own words, "a real education for heart and soul."

He was greatly helped by the exceptional staff of professors whose lectures he followed in the College of Propaganda. The chair of Holy Scripture was then filled by Msgr Ubaldo Ubaldi, who, although he died young, left behind him some remarkable works; the course of moral theology was taken by Fr Antonio Agliardi, later cardinal, and that of canon law by Fr Camillo Laurenti; the professor of Church history was Fr Luigi Galimberti, who was to become Nuncio at Venice, then cardinal, and to enjoy the particular friendship of Leo XIII.

But the one to have the greatest influence on Joseph Marmion was the celebrated Fr Francesco Satolli, professor of dogmatic theology. In his youth Fr Satolli had been distinguished at Perugia by Msgr Pecci: being unexpectedly called upon by his archbishop to preach the Lenten station at the cathedral, Fr Satolli had risen to the occasion to the full satisfaction of everyone. "Therefore, on becoming pope, under the name of Leo XIII, Msgr Pecci, whose love for the teaching of St Thomas is well known, remembered Fr Satolli and called him expressly to Rome to teach the *Summa Theologica* of the Angel of the Schools at the Propaganda.

As in the case of his preaching, Fr Satolli fully justified the pope's expectations.[1] By his penetration of mind, his sure and wide learning, his glowing style, he quickly won the esteem and affection of his students, who pressed around his professorial chair to the number of a hundred. Long afterwards, in the evening of his life, Dom Marmion still recalled those far-off and never-to-be-forgotten lessons of this beloved master. He particularly cherished the memory of a lesson on the Beatific Vision of the elect in heaven. Approaching this

---

1 Cardinal Satolli has left *Praelectiones in Summam theologicam divi Thomae Aquinatis*, I–V, Rome 1884 sq. Doubtless on some points, as on that of the divine motion, Cardinal Satolli does not always follow St Thomas closely; nevertheless, he must be numbered amongst the fervent adepts of the Angelic Doctor.

magnificent subject according to the teaching of St Thomas, Fr Satolli waxed eloquent on the supreme bliss that has its fountain-head in God: full satisfaction for the mind by the possession of the whole truth, and perfect satisfaction for the heart in the indefectible union with the absolute and supreme Good in the bosom of the Trinity. He went so deeply into the subject of this divine beatitude that his hearers were enraptured. They broke out into applause when the master, resuming his exposé and finishing it in prayer, exclaimed like the Psalmist: "Thy children, O Lord, shall be inebriated with the plenty of Thy house, and Thou shalt make them drink of the torrent of Thy pleasure. For with Thee is the fountain of Life, and in Thy light shall we see Light...."[1]

An object lesson by which Joseph Marmion was to benefit. Under such a master, with whom he was besides akin in mind in several ways, he learnt notably how to rest his ascetical teaching on dogma and to make of theology a science "which turns to loving."

He was now deep in the study of the *Summa*, of which Fr Satolli had discovered to him the luminous plan, powerful structure, vigorous logic and marvellous unity. To repeat his own expression, "he drank in great draughts" of this magisterial doctrine of one of the noblest geniuses, now offered to him in such rich abundance.

On his side, Fr Satolli was not long in marking out the enthusiastic and responsive student that Hibernia had sent to him. Sometimes ceding the professorial chair to his pupil, Fr Satolli invited him to sustain the thesis. The academic jousts where the learning of the master and the youthful talent of the disciple met in combat were carried on in the midst of profound silence and general attention. The clearness and sureness with which Joseph Marmion elucidated a doctrine, the facility of his replies to the objections of his rivals and of his master won him Fr Satolli's warm congratulation and the applause of his fellow-students when the theological dispute, which had proved a feast for the mind, reached its conclusion. Coming out first in the course of lectures at the end of the academic

---

1 *Cf.* Ps. 35:9.

year, Joseph carried off the gold medal.¹ Circumstances so befell that the young theologian, having finished the ordinary round of studies, was recalled to Ireland by Cardinal Cullen and left Rome before it had been possible for him to go up for his doctor's degree.²

The memories he took away with him from the Eternal City were to remain so much the more lasting in that they were linked to the different stages passed before attaining the greatly to be desired grace of the priesthood.

The previous year he had, in a few months, climbed all the steps that lead to the altar. On 27 February 1881, he received minor orders, and in the following month, on March 12th, the feast of St Gregory the Great, the first of St Benedict's sons to mount the chair of Peter, he was ordained sub-deacon at St John Lateran.

"It is twenty-nine years ago," he wrote in 1910, "on this Saturday of the Lenten Ember Days since I received the sub-diaconate. The first office that I recited as minister of the Church was that of the second Sunday of Lent: each year I say it with fresh joy."

He must have received an impression of grace on that occasion, for in the days to come, when preaching, he often commented, and that with marked delight, on the two scriptural episodes that the Church has chosen for the composition of this office: the story of Esau and Jacob and the scene of the Transfiguration.

The diaconate was conferred upon him in the same Church of St John Lateran on Holy Saturday, April 15th. Finally, on June 16th, the feast of Corpus Christi, he received in the *Cappella* of the Irish

---

1 The medal is a representation of our Lord surrounded by His apostles, with the text, *Euntes in universum mundum praedicate Evangelium omni creaturae*; on the reverse it bears these words: *Pietati et doctrinae*. Dom Marmion hung the medal on the statue of Our Lady of Perpetual Succour in the chapel of the Redemptoristines of Dublin, to whom he was appointed chaplain.

2 To gain the Doctor's degree it was necessary to go through a course of four years' study in Rome, but as Fr Marmion had already done two years in Dublin and had completed the full course, it was impossible for him after only two years in Rome to enter for the Doctorate.

College the order of the priesthood from the hands of the Rector of the college, Msgr Tobias Kirby, Archbishop of Ephesus.

For two months past he had been preparing himself for this great grace with intense fervour. It was in the Church of St Agatha[1] on the feast (transferred) of St Philip Neri that on June 17th he celebrated his first Mass, served by his intimate friend, Dwyer, who had rejoined him in Rome.

No written record has come down to us of his innermost thoughts and feelings during these great days, but the particular esteem in which he ever held the grace of the priesthood, the great devotion with which he each year celebrated the anniversary of his ordination, help us to realise what acts of thanksgiving rose up from his soul towards Christ who had called him to close participation in His eternal Priesthood.

A letter written several years later (February 1890)[2] and addressed to a young student at the College of the Propaganda, who had just been ordained like himself at Rome, gives us some idea of what had been his own frame of mind.

> I have been for a long time anxious to write to you to congratulate you on the priceless grace God has bestowed on you in calling you to the priesthood. I could not tell you how happy I felt when I heard you were ordained.... A priest can do so much for God, if in offering the Holy Sacrifice he unites the oblation of himself, his life, his love, all that he has, with that of the Divine Victim; he can obtain priceless graces for all mankind, can stay the anger of God and gain powerful aid for the Church, not to speak of the great merit he gains for himself. Let us try to be faithful and loving towards our dear Lord; it is in the heart of the priest He expects to repose

---

1 One of the oldest churches in Rome; situated nearby the Irish College, it was served by the priests of the college. That is why Msgr Cullen, who had been Rector of the Irish College, wished, when he founded Clonliffe, that the interior of the Church of Holy Cross should be in imitation of that of St Agatha. We may add that Dom Marmion had a great devotion to the holy martyr.

2 He was then already at Maredsous.

when He is outraged by sinners, and, alas, He so often finds even there but coldness and ingratitude.

His soul full of memories and freshly embalmed with the holy oils of his priestly ordination, Fr Marmion on 11 July 1881, bade farewell to Rome and set out for the Emerald Isle.

3 BEGINNING OF HIS MINISTRY AND RELIGIOUS VOCATION (1874–81)

At Rome Fr Marmion formed a close friendship with a young priest from Belgium, Fr Joseph Moreau, belonging to the diocese of Namur and educated, like himself, at the College of the Propaganda. During their stay in the Eternal City Msgr Rosendo Salvado, a Spanish Benedictine monk, and abbot of the mission he had founded in New Norcia,[1] Australia, arrived there for a visit *ad limina*. He gave

---

1 Msgr Salvado was born on 1 March 1814, at Tuy in Galicia, Spain; at the age of sixteen he made his profession in the monastery of St Martin at Compostella. Driven out of his country in 1835 by the revolution, he went with a confrère, Fr José Serra, to the Abbey of Cava. Ordained priest in 1839, he passed over to the Cassinese Congregation. Burning with the desire to evangelise the pagan tribes of Australia, he, with Fr Serra, obtained permission to accompany Msgr John Brady (Irish) recently nominated to the bishopric of Perth, Australia. They landed there in January 1846. They penetrated to the heart of the country, and only fixed their place of abode after journeying some 170 miles. They found themselves in the midst of a tribe who, at that epoch, had the name of being cannibals. The missionaries by their gentleness and the services they rendered them, gained the hearts of the savages. A hut made of tree trunks and branches served as dwelling, chapel and school. At the cost of immense efforts they succeeded in making Christians of these cannibals and savages. On 1 March 1847, they laid the first stone of the monastery. In 1848 Fr Serra was appointed Bishop of Port Victoria and Fr Salvado was left alone. In 1849 Msgr Brady sent him to Europe to beg for money and recruit fellow-workers. It was when he was in Rome that he was told of his appointment as successor to Msgr Serra, who had resigned. He was consecrated bishop on 15 August 1849, and only returned to Australia in August 1854. He took with him thirty-nine religious, seven were priests and thirty-two lay brothers. At the moment of embarking he learnt that England had refused to supply subsidies to the colony of Port Victoria. The colonists went elsewhere, Msgr Salvado was left a bishop without a flock. He returned to his foundation at New Norcia, and there laboured at the moral improvement of the natives. In 1867 the monastery was raised to the rank of abbey *nullius*, and Msgr Salvado became its first abbot, and remained in office until his death. In 1887 he was appointed titular Bishop of Adrian. In spite of his advanced age he returned to Europe to attend

a conference to the members of the Propaganda amongst whom was Fr Moreau. The earnestness of the intrepid missionary, the stirring account he gave of his apostolic labours, made a great impression on the young Belgian priest; he was inspired with the idea of joining Msgr Salvado and helping him in his work of evangelisation.

In the course of a conversation with his Irish friend, Fr Moreau confided this project to him. Fr Marmion was at once much struck by it: the vocation of a missionary monk appeared an ideal one to him; his generous enthusiasm saw in it a splendid field of apostolic activity.

This vocation, besides, was well in keeping with all the traditions of his country. The annals of the Church have gratefully preserved the remembrance of those monks of Hibernia who, from the sixth to the seventh century, set out from the Green Isle of Erin for the Continent, there to consecrate their lives to the spreading of the Gospel and the propagation of monasticism: St Columban of Luxeuil and of Bobbio, St Gall, St Folian and St Fursay, St Fiacre, St Kilian, who converted Franconia and Thuringia, St Fearghal of Salzburg, St Fridolin, the first Bishop of Alsace, the saints of Armorica, and so many others; a vigorous and enterprising race, tenacious and devoted, firmly fixed in their ideal and at the same time very adaptable to circumstances, deeply attached to their native soil and yet ready to give up all thought of return and to forge fresh and loyal links with an adopted home and country. During the space of two centuries Ireland, by means of missionaries who traversed the whole of Europe from the Hebrides as far as Germany and the Apennines, thus fulfilled her high calling as an apostle: *Peregrinari pro Christo.*[1]

> the General Chapter of the Benedictine abbots convoked by the primate on the occasion of the consecration of the abbatial Church of St Anselm. At his request the Holy See granted that his abbey of New Norcia should be attached to the Spanish Province of the Cassinese Congregation of the Primitive Observance. Death overtook him in the midst of his preparations for his departure for Australia, 29 December 1900. He is one of the men in the Benedictine Order of the nineteenth century who are most worthy of honour.

1 This missionary migration was repeated in the nineteenth century. In the

It was therefore his Celtic forefathers' wandering instincts which were awakened in the heart of young Fr Marmion; he felt the more inclined to listen to these ancestral voices in that those of friendship were now joined to them; besides Fr Moreau, there was Fr Dwyer, about to set out on his return voyage to Australia....

This idea of becoming a missionary monk long haunted him,[1] but God had other views, and another and no less fruitful form of apostolate in store for him.

Fr Moreau had had to return to Belgium; in June 1881, before leaving Rome, he made an agreement with Fr Marmion that the latter, on his way back to Ireland, should stay at Namur, and from there go to greet his friend who was entering the novitiate at Maredsous in order to prepare himself for the New Norcia mission.

In the middle of July Fr Marmion arrived at Maredsous. At that period the walls of the abbey had scarcely risen above the foundations; only two wings of the claustral buildings were completed, and the graceful towers of the basilica did not yet stand out against the sky.[2]

---

same way as Ireland in ancient times had instructed the nations of Europe in the Faith, so contemporary Ireland founded Catholicism in the Anglo-Saxon societies beyond the seas. She supplied Australia with nearly all its clergy, not excepting Francis Cardinal Moran, Archbishop of Sydney; she watched over the early days of Catholicism in the United States, and supplied nearly all the priests for western America. The list of dignitaries of the Church of Rome in America is almost exclusively composed of Irish names, from that of James Cardinal Gibbons to that of Msgr John Ireland, only to mention those two. Ireland well deserves to be named the mother of all the churches of the Anglo-Saxon world. *Cf.* Paul-Dubois, *loc. cit.*

1 When he was already a monk at Maredsous Dom Marmion again offered himself, in 1896, to that dauntless Benedictine missionary, Msgr Gérard van Caloen, for the missions of Brazil, but his superiors did not allow him to carry out his desire.

2 The foundation of the Abbey of Maredsous (Entre-Sambre-et-Meuse) is due to two eminent religious: the brothers Maurus and Placide Wolter, and to the princely generosity of the Desclée family of Tournai. The Wolter brothers made their monastic profession at the basilica of St Paul-Outside-the-Walls, at the very portals of the Eternal City. In September 1860, Pius IX gave them the charge of restoring the Order of St Benedict in Germany; they founded the

This was not the first time that Fr Marmion had seen something of Benedictine life. When he was living in Italy he had the opportunity of going to Montecassino on the occasion of a visit to Napoli. The wonderful panorama which from that height was unfolded to his gaze, the antiquity of the monastery founded by St Benedict (sixth century), the venerable associations attached to it, the noble simplicity of the monastic observances, all this had keenly struck the mind of the young Irish seminarist. It was there, too, he first heard the secret invitation to the life of the cloister. Dom Marmion recalled this grace in a letter he wrote more than thirty years later, in 1912, when – this time as a monk – the opportunity was again given him of making this pilgrimage.

"We[1] have been overjoyed in making the ascent of the holy mountain. I had not seen it since 1880, when I went up it on returning from Naples. It was there I felt for the first time that God was calling me to the monastic life. It all came back to me with a sense of living reality, as if it had happened yesterday."[2]

It was standing before a picture hanging in the refectory of the monastery and representing the Patriarch of Monks that Fr Marmion received the first notion of his Benedictine vocation.

Nevertheless, his visit to Maredsous, fleeting as was his glimpse of life in the cloister, did not fail to produce a singular impression

Abbey of Beuron, not far from Sigmaringen, on the banks of the Danube. In 1869 there entered at Beuron a young Belgian, an officer in the pontifical army, Félix de Hemptinne; he pronounced his vows there on 15 August 1870. He had kept in touch with an old fellow officer, Lieutenant Victor Mousty, the agent of Jules Desclée, who had a château in the valley of Maredsous, and wished to build a monastery. Mousty served as intermediary. After some preliminary discussions the act of foundation was signed on 15 August 1872, and a colony of monks arrived at Maredsous on 15 October 1872. They were installed at the château whilst the monastery was being built. The first stone was laid on 21 March 1873, on the plateau overlooking the valley; it was only on 25 June 1876, that the monks left the château to take possession of the monastery. Dom Placide Wolter was named abbot on 8 March 1878. The building of the church had been begun in 1877, but it was not dedicated till 19 August 1888.

1 Dom Marmion was accompanied by one of his monks, a professor in Rome.
2 Letter of 7 March 1912.

on him.¹ At the moment of crossing the threshold of the cloister he heard, as it were, an inward voice say to him: "It is here that I want you." A few hours later the abbot, Dom Placide Wolter, said to him point-blank: "You have much more of a vocation than your friend has."²

On leaving the abbey the young priest promised himself to return. Five years passed before he was able to carry out this promise, and when he did return to Maredsous it was to become a monk.

Once more in Ireland, Fr Marmion, on September 14th, was appointed curate of the parish of Dundrum. This small town at the south of Dublin lies in a valley surrounded by the mountains of Wicklow. He there found a friend of his family, Fr Joseph Hickey, who had just rebuilt a handsome church dedicated to the Holy Cross.³

For the space of a year he was there initiated into all the multifarious duties of parish work. His zeal and charity were boundless and his charity has never been forgotten in that town.

To this ministry he added that of chaplain to the convent of the nuns of the Sacred Heart at Mount Anville, some three miles distance, on the coast. Every day he travelled this distance on foot in order to celebrate Mass, and several times in the week to give religious instruction to the girls in the boarding school. Some of his old pupils still remember the clearness and piety of these lessons.

Of a very different kind was his ministry in connexion with the insane criminals in the central asylum which had been built in that parish; but if he could seldom succeed in making much impression

---

1 In an article which he sent twenty years later to the *Belvederian*, directed by his former masters of Belvedere College, in Dublin, he thus notes his impression: "I arrived at the monastery towards evening: I remember how impressed I was by the peace and silence of the vast cloisters, the chant of the Divine Office, and the sentiment of complete separation from the world which reigned there."
2 Later events were to prove the truth of this remark.
3 It replaced the chapel inaugurated on 14 September 1837.

on the poor beings who dragged out their lives within those walls, the pitiable spectacle he witnessed suggested some useful reflections:

"I have seen some very interesting but very sad things: men who had once filled important positions in the world, and whose wits having suffered wreckage, spent all their time in making little mud houses or other childish trifles, as if all the world depended on it. I look upon these poor madmen with intense pity, saying to myself those are very insane, too, who, instead of concerning themselves with their eternal interests, spend their activity on futile and passing things...."

But it was not at Dundrum that all his zeal was to be expended and where his talents were to be given their full scope. In September 1882, the Archbishop of Dublin, Msgr MacCabe, called him to Clonliffe, there to fill the chair of philosophy.[1]

All were happy to have back again in capacity of professor one who had distinguished himself as a student in that house.

According to the testimony of those under his tuition he displayed as professor those qualities of clearness and conscientiousness which were to be characteristic of his teaching; humble likewise, he was never slow nor ashamed to acknowledge an error, but it was not long before he gained a complete mastery of his subject.[2]

Although he was not actually the confessor, he directed some of the most earnest amongst the seminarists who found how ready he was in understanding their spiritual needs. "His direction," writes one of those who confided in him, "was above all marked by its

1 To this he was to add the Greek course.
2 In a document dated 20 March 1907 (we do not know the exact circumstances under which it was written, but it was probably on the occasion of an official mission confided to Fr Marmion in England), His Grace Msgr William Walsh, Archbishop of Dublin, and Primate of Ireland, paid him this testimony: "*Reverendus Josephus Marmion quinque annis hujus nostrae Dioecesis presbyter, primo ut vice parochus per annum adlaboravit et deinde in nostro Seminario diaecesano, per quattuor annos, Professoris munere omni cum laude functus est. Quamdiu apud nos erat, superioribus suis sese commendavit atque zelo eximio, pietateque sincera approbationem eorum obtinuit. Anno 1886, obtenta prius nostra licentia, ab hac dioecesi discessit ut monachus Deo perfectius serviret.*" Dublini, die 20 martii 1907. (s) ✠ Gulielmus, archiep. Dublinien. Hiberniae Primas.

'human' and kindly character; he excelled in solving difficulties and helped one to get out of them."

Thus by a happy combination of the most diverse gifts: the evident liveliness of his faith, an already recognised sureness of judgment, warmth of heart, and the eminent social qualities of a very richly endowed nature overflowing with high spirits and jovial good humour, the personal influence of the young master of philosophy was well calculated to promote joy and unity. The consternation of the students may therefore be well imagined when, four years later, he gave up his chair of philosophy to enter the cloister.

His duties as professor and spiritual director at Holy Cross College did not exhaust all his zeal and activity. In addition to this, Cardinal MacCabe had, in September 1882, appointed him chaplain of the Convent of Redemptoristines in Dublin. The archives of the monastery preserve the memory of his piety, the warmth and persuasiveness of his words, and notably a sermon he gave on St Joseph, in which the young preacher commented very happily and with a marked tone of conviction on the words of Jesus, which he was afterwards so often to repeat: "I bless Thee, O Father, because Thou hast hidden the mysteries of divine life from those who esteem themselves to be wise and prudent, and hast revealed them to little ones and to the humble."[1]

To this ministry, which lasted four years,[2] belongs an incident which concerns his inner life. On 12 August 1884, he had in the absence of the ordinary confessor to help a young and very pure-souled novice, Sister Mary Clare, in her last moments. She pronounced her vows in his presence, and then asked to receive Holy Viaticum. Fr Marmion hesitated on account of her state, for she had not been able to retain the least nourishment. But the dying sister insisted, saying that the good God who had already granted her so many graces would not refuse her a respite from nausea in order that she might keep Him in her heart. Fr Marmion allowed himself to be convinced: the event justified the words of the good sister; con-

---

1 *Cf.* Matt. 11:25.
2 He ended it on 25 June 1886, a few months before entering Maredsous.

trary to all expectation, she quietly prolonged her thanksgiving. The agony which followed was long and painful; Fr Marmion stayed by her until the moment when this soul so recently become the bride of Christ took its flight to heaven.

Fr Marmion had confided to her the distress he often felt on the subject of one detail of the ceremony of his ordination to the priesthood. He asked this sister to beseech God when she was admitted to the Divine Presence that this trouble might be taken from him if the conditions had been regularly observed. Shortly after this holy religious had breathed her last a sense of inward peace took such deep possession of the young priest's heart that from that day forward he never felt the least uneasiness on this account.

If he had the joy of meeting with holy souls and of coming under their happy influence, he was also, in dealing with those who had erred, to come across cases of moral leprosy which aroused in him the sense of merciful compassion. In fact he was at this same time appointed chaplain of the prison for women at Mountjoy, Dublin. He loved these protégées of his and felt a strange consolation in pouring balm from his priestly hands on their wounds; he admired the vitality of the faith which in spite of the corrosive working of vice and misery remained intact in many of his humble penitents.

He had also to devote himself to the political prisoners and others convicted of offences against the common law who languished in the jails of the capital: his relations with them revealed to him the depth of the wounds and the bitterness of the rancour which oppressive measures and persecution left in the souls of some of these unfortunate compatriots of his. Different as all this was from what he had seen at Dundrun, it was no less poignant, and provided yet more scope for his pastoral zeal. No doubt he was sometimes disappointed in his efforts to make certain of these prisoners, exasperated by non-suits or arbitrary condemnations, renounce their feelings of hatred. One of these men, the victim of an iniquitous judgment, had resisted every good suggestion; having come to the end of his arguments, Dom Marmion thought it his duty to bring before him his eternal interests. He received this answer, which throws a

BEGINNING OF HIS MINISTRY AND RELIGIOUS VOCATION

lamentable light on these racial enmities: "Even if I saw hell open at my feet I would not forgive."

Most often, however, he had the joy of seeing his ministry blessed by God. He there came across a poor wretch who had committed a murder. He was a huge fellow, with scarcely anything of the man left in him and ignorant to the last degree. His talks with the young priest made a man of him, and then a model Christian. His conversion was so complete and so sure that when Fr Marmion came to hear his confession he was habitually met with these words:

"Father, since my last confession, there is nothing; but confess me all the same; I want to accuse myself again of my great sin."

And so saying, he burst into repentant tears.

The young chaplain was ingenious in raising and helping these erring souls; he neglected nothing that might revive in them the ancestral Faith. The prisoners often asked him for a rosary. He began by granting their request, until he learnt that the administration provided them with rosaries.

"You have them given to you here," he then told them.

And their answer was:

"Yes, but they are *regulation* rosaries!"

Dom Marmion used this anecdote later to warn those religious who, prisoners of their illusions, might come to esteem only that which is not of regulation or is outside the common life.

So by this coming in contact with different souls, the most wretched as well as the noblest, Fr Marmion penetrated little by little into the deepest recesses of the human conscience. In this way God trained him in the delicate art of spiritual direction in which he was later to excel.

But favourable as were these surroundings to the full developing of his personality, it was not here that his whole life was to be spent.

At that time Fr Marmion read over again the annals of early Christianity in Ireland. "The evangelisation of the island had been followed by a magnificent efflorescence of monastic life: having become the isle of saints and scholars, and the guardian of civilisation, Ireland not only sent her monks all over Europe, but attracted from all parts students, eager for learning, to her monastery schools of Clonfert, Lismore, Bangor, and Clonmacnoise, where Alcuin of York was educated. The solitary ruins of Clonmacnoise still rise on the banks of the Shannon at Kildare, the native place of the Marmions, and this name must have often sounded in the ears of the young priest and professor.

Was it when reading these annals that he felt the attraction for the cloister spring up more irresistibly than before?... Or was it at the time of his pilgrimage to the isle of Iona, held in honour because the holy monk, St Columba, once dwelt there, that the longing for perfection was enkindled more fervently within him?...

We do not know. However it may have been, the call he had heard on the holy mount of Cassino – now nearly five years ago – ever echoed in the depths of his soul, and his mind was haunted by the image of the Abbey of Entre-Sambre-et-Meuse, whither seeming chance had brought him and where this call of God had been more distinct. He little thought then to what this stay of a few hours with an old fellow student would lead. But the impression received on that day had never been effaced.

Then, although he highly appreciated the spiritual advantages that the tutelage of a master like Fr Gowan offered him, he was learning to understand better and better that those in love with perfection, but conscious of their frailty, gain in security, help and merit when they place their perseverance under the aegis of the vows of religion. He had no doubt often read – for he was then and ever remained passionately fond of reading the lives of the saints – those words of St Bernard de Clairvaux calculated to beget total renunciation: "In the cloister one falls more rarely, rises more quickly, advances more surely, sanctifies oneself more fully and dies more joyously."

It was, above all, the idea of obedience, the paramount means of perfection and union with God, which urged him to the life of the cloister. He had naturally been entirely open with Fr Gowan about this. The latter was able better than any other to understand and approve his penitent's aspirations. Had he not for his own part left the secular clergy to consecrate himself totally to God as a Lazarist! And he told the young professor the story of how when he had asked his archbishop's permission to enter religion he met with this retort:

"A religious, a good and excellent priest like you! But you have nothing to gain by such a change."

"Alas! Monsignor, I want to be a religious because here I find no one to reprove and correct me in view of my perfection; when I have religious superiors I am sure of being told when I'm wrong."

In face of so high a motive the archbishop gave in.

A no less supernatural reason, but one which had obedience as its objective, inspired Fr Marmion.

"Before becoming a monk, I could not, in the eyes of the world, do more good than I was doing where I then was. But I reflected, I prayed, and I understood that I should not be sure of always doing God's Will except in practising religious obedience. I had all that was needful for my sanctification with the exception of one sole boon, namely, obedience. That is the reason why I left my country, gave up my liberty and all else."

He confided to someone on another occasion: "I may say that I became a monk in order to be able to obey. I was professor, I had, while still very young, what is called a fine position, success, and friends strongly attached to me; but I had not the opportunity of obeying. I became a monk because God had revealed to me the beauty and greatness of obedience."

The monastic life appeared then to Fr Marmion as the most excellent means of being united to God through obedience, which made of it a holocaust of love. On this subject we have two letters doubly precious. Besides being the first letters of his that we have discovered up to this date, they disclose in the shape of an exhortation to a novice, what he was experiencing in his own soul.

The first is addressed to her on the eve of her clothing.

Holy Cross College, 29 April 1885 – My dear child... I will pray very specially for you that you may receive the grace of resembling your holy patron, especially in the generous oblation she made of herself to her Divine Spouse. Your life at present should be a perpetual oblation of yourself to the Sacred Heart, and as the Holy Sacrifice is being offered at every moment during the day, you can unite yourself with our Lord at every moment and thus be sure your offering will be accepted. When you have got the habit of thus living in a state of perpetual oblation, it becomes a matter of absolute indifference to you, what you are engaged at, as your only desire then, is to accomplish the Will of God, which is manifested to you at every moment by obedience. The more generous you are in endeavouring to arrive at this state of holy indifference and detachment from your own inclinations, the more perfectly you will taste that peace, which is the 'hundredfold' which our Lord promises to those who have left all things for His love.

The second letter goes more into detail and bears further witness to the personal aspirations of this young secular priest; it shows a strikingly well-balanced judgment and highly supernatural points of view; it might have been written by one who had spent long years in the religious life. Already we see him as the zealous apostle and the master who could sum up in a few telling phrases the essential of a doctrine.

Holy Cross College, 27 November 1885 – My dear child, I must not let Advent commence without letting you have a line. I have been so occupied that I found it difficult even to send a line to Reverend Mother and I know that she would let you know the contents as far as they could be of any interest to you. I pray very frequently for you daily at Mass that God may give you the grace to persevere, as I don't think you are suited for a life in the world. You must do your part generously with God and He will not fail to assist you.

Each religious order is like a flower in the garden of Jesus, and just as every flower has its own peculiar odour and beauty, so each order has its own beautiful spirit and characteristic virtues which delight the Sacred Heart. Therefore no matter how good or virtuous we may be in ourselves, if we have not the peculiar spirit and training of the order to which we belong, we are out of joint in the community and can never be good religious, nor truly delight the Heart of Jesus. It was because our Lord saw all the sisters in the little community of Ávila animated with the one, true spirit of their order that he said to St Teresa, 'Daughter, this convent is the paradise of my delights in which my Heart finds delightful repose and protection from the outrages of men.'

But, you may ask me, 'how am I to gain that spirit, how am I to know if I really have it? Well, I answer, this is precisely the purpose of the novitiate; the spirit of the Order of Mercy is handed down from the holy foundress, through the superiors, and all you have to do is to leave yourself *absolutely* in their hands and like wax in the hand of one who moulds it, and at the end of the novitiate the *germs* of that spirit will have been planted in your heart, to bud forth into perfection later on. This, with prayer is the only means of acquiring the spirit of your state.

It is often hard to nature, to be thus cut, and pruned, but otherwise we can never hope to be pleasing to the Sacred Heart. If I were joining religion tomorrow, I would enter with the determination of leaving myself, *absolutely* in the hands of my superiors, to let them cut away *mercilessly*, all the excrescences of my character so that I might be fit to be presented, as a clean oblation on the altar of God's love, and even though nature might repine I would try to bear all for the love of Jesus crucified, and I feel sure that if I were but faithful I would soon acquire the true spirit of my order and thus 'reap with joy, wheat I had sown in tears.' Our Lord makes no exceptions 'if *any one* will come after Me, let him *deny* himself and take up his cross and follow Me.' This is especially true of religious, who try to *follow* our Lord so closely, and consequently, if we reject the cross, if we repine when it presses on us, we are not following Jesus, but ourselves.

There, my dear child, are a few thoughts which strike me when I pray for you, as I know your character so well I think; if you ... and the other sisters might like to know Uncle Joe's views about a novice, well, in a word, my idea of a good novice is this: A good novice is one

1. who enters religion in order to glorify our Lord, by rendering her soul, and those of others as pleasing to the Sacred Heart as possible.

2. who in order to effect this, will spare herself in nothing, and consequently is ready to suffer pain and humiliation and even death itself to please God.

3. who is not content with ordinary Christian virtue, but through fidelity to her Spouse, aspires to render her heart a very furnace of divine love and who does all this under the guidance of obedience, in accordance with the spirit of her order. Oh how the Sacred Heart would rejoice if He could behold such a paradise as this! That Dunmore may be the realisation of this, is my constant prayer.

"If I were joining religion tomorrow..." Evidently this thought was always in his mind. He did not lose sight of this eventuality and regarded it especially from the point of view of its being a proof of the love which gives itself up to obedience. But tomorrow was still far away; another year was to pass – almost to the very day – before his project was to be realised.

Moreover the country of St Patrick had not then any Benedictine monastery: the abbeys which formerly covered the island were suppressed in the persecution which broke out under Henry VIII. Hence Fr Marmion's decision, long matured in prayer, approved by Fr Gowan, consented to by his archbishop, was irrevocably made: he would enter the Abbey of Maredsous.

BEGINNING OF HIS MINISTRY AND RELIGIOUS VOCATION

With the exception of his director and his own family, his sister Rosie in particular, the young professor had not spoken of his intention to anyone, neither to his intimate friends nor favourite pupils. So when the news was spread abroad it caused much surprise and consternation, soon followed on the part of some, by keen opposition. Some were about to lose a master both esteemed and loved, a director already held in veneration; others a colleague whose work and the charm of whose friendship they appreciated more each day. And almost all were astonished: "Why give up a ministry where his zeal was so happily employed for good?..."

Some, and these not the least, almost called it desertion. Writing a few years later (February 1890) to one of his old students then at Rome, Dom Marmion said: "Have you ever seen Msgr Kirby of the *Collegio Irlandese?* You know he ordained me. I have always retained a great veneration for him, as I regard him as a real saint, but I fear he looks on me as a kind of apostate for having left the secular mission. However I heard the words *Magister adest et vocat te*[1] and I obeyed."[2]

Even those who respected the call he had heard and his right to follow it were surprised at the choice he had made of a foreign monastery: "Why leave Ireland?... Had the green Isle of Erin then, whose very soil was steeped in faith, no longer any fervent religious orders?... What was this unknown and distant monastery where he wanted to go and bury himself?... Again, would he with his merry and genial temperament adapt himself to the austere life of the cloister?... Surely not.... It was incompatible.... He would not persevere...."

He listened to all these objections, and impressionable as he was they were all the more painful to him in that they came from friendly lips; but he remained firm. The Divine Master had called

---

[1] "The Master is come and calleth for thee" (John 11:28).
[2] Long afterwards he wrote the same to a young girl who wanted to be a nun and met with opposition: "What if people do treat you as if you were selfish or ungrateful (I too have gone through all that), let it suffice that Jesus sees your heart." Letter of 31 August 1902.

him; he meant to follow Him. And if to do so he must forsake all, the holocaust would only be the more perfect. An obedient and loving response to the heavenly call: that was the whole story of his monastic vocation.

He spent part of the last night with one of his favourite pupils, Francis Wall,[1] making his preparation for departure. He asked Wall what he thought of his decision. Echoing the general opinion, the latter replied:

"O Father, you will come back, I am sure of it: you'll never be able to stand life in the monastery."

"Everyone tells me that," he replied; "but I feel called to the cloister; I must go."

When morning came, Wall served his Mass; then the rector of the college went with him to the quay, together with many relations and friends, to see him embark. A few hours later, the ship that carried him was lost to sight over the horizon.

Obedient to the divine call, the young and brilliant professor – he was then twenty-eight – generously tore himself away from the warm embrace of his kinsfolk, from many a close friendship, his professorial chair, his early prestige as a teacher, the holy joys of his ministry, and from his beloved Ireland. He left his country, his family, his father's house, he went alone to the land which the Lord had shown him, and knocked at the door of a newly founded foreign abbey, there to shut himself up as a simple monk.

It was 21 November 1886, the feast of our Lady's Presentation.[2]

In crossing the threshold of the monastery, Fr Marmion could say like St Paul: "I count all things to be but loss that I may gain Christ." But if he imagined that the sacrifice he had just made was sufficient he was strangely mistaken; he was only at the threshold of a hard career of self-renunciation.

---

1 Now Msgr Wall, PP, Vicar General of Dublin. It is to him that we owe the following details.
2 In a letter of 20 November 1916, he wrote: "Tomorrow, the 21st, it will be thirty years since I entered here, thank our Lord for me and with me."

4 MONASTIC INITIATION
"IF HE IS TRULY SEEKING GOD"
(1886–88)

St Benedict from the first page of his *Rule* represents the monastic life to the would-be monk as a "return to God, by the labour of obedience," and "under the standard of the true King, the Lord Christ."

Elsewhere in the chapter dealing with "the reception of brethren," he lays further stress on this thought. In accordance with the ecclesiastical language of his day, he compares this life to a conversion, whereby one turns away from every creature to cleave to the one supreme Good: it is by this whole-hearted cleaving to God that the monk is true to his name.[1]

Therefore the Holy Patriarch requires, as proof of this conversion, sincerity in the seeking after God: *Si revera quaerit Deum*. Expressive words which indicate the decisive course on which the soul is set. In the eyes of the lawgiver of monks, this "truly seeking" after God is shown by great zeal for the work of Divine Praise and for obedience and by eager acceptance of the humiliations and trials inherent in the religious life.

Care will be taken, he adds, to hide from the postulant none of the hard and rugged things to be met with along the path which leads to God, in order that he may be prepared to go forward with courage in so great an enterprise – the attainment of God.

In completing his instructions, St Benedict ordains that "if anyone in priestly orders asks to be received into the monastery, consent is not to be too easily granted him." Whilst the priestly prerogative is to be respected in the postulant, he is to be given clearly to understand that far from imagining himself exempt from a single point of the regular discipline, he must know he is bound – precisely

---

[1] There is hardly need to recall the etymology of the word *monk*, which comes from the Greek μονος "one, only," on account of this life of oneness of love in God at which the monk aims in detaching himself from creatures.

because he *is* a priest – to give to all an example of greater submission and humility.

Forty years after the event, there are still some who can give personal evidence that those in authority in the abbey did not in fact go out of their way to make things easy for the young Irish priest. On the contrary they applied to him in all its rigour, St John's exhortation, repeated by the legislator of monks: "Try the spirits if they are of God." Might not Fr Marmion have yielded too hastily to a natural movement of unreflecting enthusiasm? Was not this young priest with his lively, sometimes fantastic imagination, his fun-loving character, under some illusion as to the true nature of monastic perfection? Would he truly seek God?

This is what it was important to find out.

The novitiate in every religious order is a period of probation and training. The reality and stability of the vocation, and the seriousness of the postulant's intention of giving himself to God, must be ascertained. At the same time the mind and character of the postulant must be made pliant and malleable, the soul must be freed from its imperfections and from self in order to prepare it to rise to higher things: a probation and formation not to be passed through without effort, struggle and suffering.

Fr Marmion knew this: his letter to the novice – quoted in the last chapter – shows it well enough. But there are not only the sufferings common to the religious life which was not established with the idea of pampering nature. Each one has his own special trials. And generally the suffering touches us at our most sensitive point and where we are the least prepared. God sometimes allows, too, that there should appear to be utter disproportion between the cause of the suffering and the suffering it involves.[1] In this special case, an unusual combination of circumstances made the time of the novitiate particularly trying to Fr Marmion.

In this cloister which he had just entered – above all in this

---

1 Cf. *Commentaire sur la règle de Saint-Benoît*, by the Abbot of Solesmes, ch. 43.

novitiate where the *Rule* was to place him for sixteen months[1] – manners, language, surroundings, persons, everything was foreign to him, and he felt himself to be a foreigner.

The community at that time was comparatively small. Most of its members, the abbot included, were monks from Beuron, come over from the banks of the Danube in 1872, when the persecution of the *Kulturkampf* seemed imminent. Being received in the château of Jules Desclée at Maredsous, they formed the nucleus of the monastery. The abbot was Dom Placide Wolter. We know that in the houses of St Benedict "the abbot is truly the living *Rule*, fashioning to his own image the monastery that he governs.... It is incontestable that the abbot leaves his own impression on the monastery, and casts upon it his own reflection."[2] A man of God, Dom Placide was imbued with great zeal for discipline, and above all things he was solicitous, even to minutiae, as to the exact observance of the *Rule* and customs.

Monastic life at Maredsous at that time accordingly bore the character of a somewhat pronounced rigidity and outward constraint reflected from the personality of its head as well as from its Rhenish origin.

Doubtless this character had escaped Fr Marmion's notice on first passing through Maredsous; on that too-fleeting occasion the visitor had not had the opportunity of realising all the difficulties that a prolonged existence in an environment so contrary to his temperament might hold for him.

This time he was given to learn these difficulties by experience – an experience painful in the extreme.

The almost violent contrast between the life he had hitherto led and that in the cloister at first came upon him with something of a shock. The spacious, easy-going, unconstrained life, seasoned with open-hearted gaiety, understood and shared, a life of gladness such as his education and Irish temperament had created for him, was

---

1 In reality he remained there, according to the custom, two years after his religious profession.
2 Marmion, *Christ the Ideal of the Monk*, ch. 3.

now succeeded by a disciplined existence, ordered in every detail, stable, uniform, formal, apparently monotonous and grey, sometimes severe, almost always grave, without diversion for the mind, and where even social customs were opposed to his ways of seeing and judging. His character was not lacking in adaptability, but his keen sensitiveness made him conscious in spite of himself of an almost perpetual friction.[1]

It was the harder for him to adapt himself to his surroundings in that he only knew the language imperfectly: this necessarily made intercourse difficult and many shades of meaning escaped him, even in the admonitions he received.

Let us add that his companions in the novitiate were few and much younger than himself; the small number limited the opportunity of finding kindred spirits, and the difference in age, joined to the fact of his being a priest, widened the distance between them.

More than once moreover he confesses that his self-love was mortified in having to let a younger novice pass before him and in effacing himself before a less well-instructed brother; he felt humiliated, too, by his occasional awkwardness in doing manual work.

Only pin-pricks, but which loneliness and isolation may sorely aggravate.

[1] Dom Marmion was thinking of his novitiate days when he wrote in *Christ the Ideal of the Monk,* in reference to the mortifications of common life in the cloister: "Without wishing it, we jar upon one another. This is part of the very condition of our poor human nature.... The history of the lives of the saints is full of this want of concord, these misunderstandings and dissensions resulting from temperament, from character, the turn of mind, education, and the ideal formed by each one.... This suffering (of the common life) can be so much more acute in as far as the mind is more and the soul more delicate.... Human nature has at times such weaknesses and deficiencies that even souls who sincerely seek God and are most united together in the charity of Christ, are true subjects of mortification for one another.... Now to endure this friction daily, with patience, with charity, without ever complaining, constitutes a very real mortification...." And he adds: "You may ask: Is not the monastery the ante-chamber of heaven? Assuredly it is; but to stay a long time in a place of waiting, and there to bear monotony and annoyances, can become singularly burdensome and require a big dose of endurance." *Self-Renunciation* §3.

This loneliness was his special suffering. No one more than the Irish Celt is dominated by the social instinct, the need of society. The Irishman loves company and to be in close contact with others. *Better be quarrelling than be lonesome*, says the proverb. "What the Irishman is really attached to in Ireland is not a home but a social order. The pleasant amenities, the courtesies, the leisureliness, the associations of religion, and the familiar faces of the neighbours, whose ways and minds are like his and very unlike those of any other people; these are the things to which he clings in Ireland and which he remembers in exile."[1] For the Englishman, *home* is his own house, comfortable and independent: *ubi bene ibi patria*. For the Irishman it is, over and beyond the house where he was born, "the sense of human neighbourhood and kinship which the individual finds in the community,"[2] with all that Dom Marmion called "sociability." This is why loneliness is the Irishman's worst suffering.

It was so for the young novice. From the first day he entered, there was woven around him by the force of circumstances an intangible curtain of solitude which became ever more opaque as the months went on. Already, quite at the beginning (November 30th, the feast of St John of the Cross)[3] he had had an intuition of this and had been seized by a sense of dismay: "I had the impression on that day that in entering the monastery, I had just done the most senseless thing in the world."

Even happy events accentuated this isolation. On the day he took the monastic habit, as on the day he entered the canonical novitiate, he found himself alone in his cell without any relations or friends to share his joy, whilst his companions' happiness was doubled by the presence of those dear to them.

In hours of sadness, he felt the isolation still more acutely; his friend, Fr Moreau, had left the cloister for another destination; his own kinsfolk were far away; Rosie above all was not there and the

---

1 *Ireland in the New Century*, by Sir Horace Plunkett, cited by Paul-Dubois.
2 *Ibid.*
3 As we have said, he entered on November 21st.

absence of this close confidante was a severe trial for one so hungry for affection.

It was evidently with the kind intention of strengthening the mystic bonds which bound him to his native land that he was given as patron the great Irish monk, St Columba.[1] But this very name brought before his mind all that he had left: the sweetness of the family fireside, numerous and warm friendships, the good opinion of ecclesiastical superiors, his spiritual ministry, and freedom of action: all that hitherto had made sunshine for his soul, or at other times had served to stimulate it, was now no more. He regretted nothing, but lingering memories only made the contrast the greater and the trial harder to bear.

In his case, by the permission of Providence, life in the cloister was seemingly stripped of much of that outward graciousness which it generally radiates. Only one old monk, every time he passed him in the cloister, gave him the consolation of a smile, emphasised by a friendly gesture – but a silent one, out of respect for the precept which forbids the "ancients" and novices to speak to each other. A ray of sunshine for the poor lonely brother, but which could not dispel the chilliness of the atmosphere in which he felt himself to be plunged.

If only he might at least have found in the master entrusted with his formation that understanding which comforts and sustains the soul! Alas! the suffering that awaited him in this quarter was to fill up the measure of human trial.

The Father Master at that time was Dom Benoît d'Hondt. He was a man of rigid character and those who knew him retain a vivid remembrance of him. A native of Waes in Flanders, and entering late in religion after an already long career in the secular clergy, his great spirit of penance and absolute fidelity to the *Rule* were at once remarked in the cloister. His virtues and the necessities of a

---

[1] One of his sisters in religions, Sister Columba, had a strong wish that her brother should bear the same name as herself, but of this she only spoke to those in heaven. The wish became a prayer on the day her brother entered the novitiate. And heaven heard her.

recent foundation numbering only a few subjects had led his superiors to confide the formation of the novices to him. An ascetic saintly figure but of the most austere type; his face was thin and angular, rarely lit up by a smile, grave, stern even to coldness and sometimes even to harshness. He habitually laid stress on the mortifying side of things and situations. Always hard and in every way unsparing to himself, without any self-consideration whatever – to give one example out of many, he endured, during the frequently severe northern winters, the acute pain of an array of broken chilblains without seeking any alleviation – he was a past master in the art of making war on the "old man," and in spite of his real affection for his novices, he did not fail to subject them to the bitterest humiliations. Never did he lose his temper, but cutting home-truths fell hard and fast from his lips. Had not the Divine Master declared, "The truth shall make you free!" One human consolation for the novices was that in matters of discipline they were all served alike. A rather singular contrast lay in the fact that when Dom Benoît explained St John's Gospel, especially the discourse of Jesus after the Last Supper towards which he had a special devotion,[1] he was apt to be overcome with emotion: "How beautiful it is, my children," he would murmur and, in the sight of the astonished and spellbound novices, tears would run down the ascetic old man's furrowed, emaciated cheeks.... But the usual subject of his instructions was self-renunciation, abnegation, death to self; he came back to this unceasingly as to his *delenda Carthago.* The monastic conceptions of this man of God recalled those of the Fathers of the desert, and for him everything was contained in this grand and simple antithesis: the winning of God by setting self at naught, forgetfulness of all created things in order to live only in view of the infinite. A short, dry gesture, whereby he seemed to wave aside some invisible obstacle, demonstrated this solid, exalted, but austere teaching.

Brother Columba was capable of grasping and savouring this *doctrine,* but between the *person* of the master and that of the disciple, understanding was scarcely possible; the contrast between

[1] He had this discourse copied on a card and re-read it every day after Mass.

their temperaments was moreover too pronounced not to become, for the novice, a real suffering which its very continuance was further to aggravate.

In the face of this suffering which came upon him from all sides, to be woven into the fabric of each day, what was Brother Columba's attitude to be? As for the excellent counsels of direction that Uncle Joe had once given – and with such assurance – to the little novice of Dunmore, how was he going to practise them now that he had himself become a simple novice in the cloister? "All that you have to do," he had written, "is to abandon yourself – and he had underlined the word – *absolutely* in the hands of your superiors like wax in the hands of one who moulds it." For him, "a good novice is one who will spare himself in nothing, and consequently is ready to suffer pain and humiliation and even death itself to please God." And he added by way of encouragement: "If I joined religion tomorrow I would enter with the determination of leaving myself absolutely in the hands of my superiors to let them cut away (the word is again underlined) *mercilessly* all the excrescences of my character so that I might be fit to be presented, as a clean oblation, on the altar of God's love."

The moment had come for him to show that he was thoroughly determined and that he knew how to follow the path which he pointed out to others. He was to persevere in it until death. Francis Wall was to be proved a false prophet.

Whether trials came from men, or arose from circumstances, or were instigated by the Evil One – he knew how to hold on. His was a virile attitude. He had besides too much good sense as well as too much intelligence to imagine that the word of command had been given for him to be immolated. If he felt suffering – and he did feel it to the quick – he did not pose as a victim.

The dismay that had seized him at the very outset did not make him turn back. Not only did he submit himself absolutely into the hands of his superiors – in this case the Father Master of Novices

– but it was he who treated himself mercilessly by forestalling trials and humiliations.

In order to overcome himself in the matter of the want of natural attraction he felt towards the Father Master, he had in fact, taken the habit – which amounted almost to heroism – of going every evening to make known to Dom Benoît the faults into which he had fallen during the day; a practice often rewarded with an admonition such as may be imagined. "One day," Dom Marmion afterwards related to one of his disciples, "the Father Master asked me what caused me most difficulty and made me suffer most. Thinking it the most perfect to be perfectly sincere, I answered: 'You, Reverend Father.'"[1]

Dom Benoît allowed the remark to pass without comment, but he did not change his line of conduct towards the novice. Perhaps, too, he understood the generous character of Brother Columba, for when he had to deal with a soul very much in earnest, he threw the thorny path of trials widely open before it.

After all we have just said, it will be easy to understand the full meaning of that prayer which Brother Columba had composed and often repeated: "My Jesus, it is for Your sake that I am here, and it is for You that I mean to stay; You can keep me here, and I have confidence that You will. I have only You on whom I can count, but I trust myself entirely to You."

Long afterwards when he was abbot he spoke of those arduous years to encourage others who had to pass through difficult hours. To one of his monks sent by obedience to a far off mission where he had many difficulties to encounter and found little support, he wrote (12 October 1909):

"I have the intimate conviction that this year will be a very important stage for you in the formation of your soul. You will be forced – as I was during my first years at Maredsous – to throw yourself headlong into God's hands. Try, my dear son, to find *all* in Him.

---

1 Dom Marmion added: "I acted in that way, believing it to be the right thing to do, but I should never advise it to others, it might in the future create a certain sense of constraint with the superior, and vice-versa."

Try to become an interior man wholly submissive to God and accustomed to lean upon Him alone."

This is what he himself was then striving to do. On one occasion, quivering with wounded sensitiveness, his inmost self crushed to its very fibres, he went to throw himself down before the tabernacle, and with tears in his eyes, said to our Lord: "And yet, my Jesus, I know that You want me here. And so I would rather let myself be hacked to pieces than leave the monastery...!"

Thrown into the crucible his soul was strengthened and purified; Brother Columba proved himself to be of those whom the Patriarch of Monks had in his mind when he bids the abbot "so to temper all things that the strong may have something to strive after."

Where did he gain such constancy? Where is the secret of this more than ordinary strength of soul to be found? In the love of Christ and in humility.

St Benedict, in the chapter he devotes to this last virtue, has wonderfully traced the portrait of the monk who, in spite of the difficulties he meets, in spite of the contempt and insults he may have to bear in the practice of obedience, far from growing weary and giving in, knows how to keep silence with heroic patience. A patience which is found in the monk's love for Christ. "To show," says St Benedict, "how the faithful servant ought to bear all things for the Lord, even those most against his inclinations, the Scripture saith: For Thee we suffer death all the day long... and: In all these things we overcome through Him who hath loved us." A wonderful page of nervous conciseness, all telling of endurance and love of God.[1] A page well in harmony with Brother Columba's own manner of thought. Had he not written to the little novice in Dunmore: "Even though nature might repine, I would try to bear all for the love of Jesus crucified?"

---

1 It is remarkable that in this single page, the Great Patriarch heaps up terms signifying endurance: once the words "bear," "not give in," "not weary;" twice he speaks of "patience," and four times of "sustain" *sustinere*.

He must often have pondered over this page in order to find strength and courage. In proof of this we have the first leaves of his private notes, precious documents, for they reveal what were his thoughts and feelings during this period.

Up to the time he entered the cloister we have only a few particulars of his spiritual life. In the too cursory light supplied by two letters and a few scanty details, we have seen a little of his strong faith, the lofty and supernatural character of his piety, and the warmth of his charity and zeal. But the interior life of this future master of asceticism has for the most part escaped us. We have grasped neither its underlying source, nor its intrinsic direction, nor its essential bent. A regrettable hiatus, impossible to fill in for lack of more numerous documents. After his entrance into religious life we are better provided, thanks to his private notes, by means of which we may gain access to his soul's inner sanctuary; we are about to see heavenly grace delighting in continually fashioning his rich nature, and this nature no less generously yielding itself to the chisel of the Divine Artist.

In these *Notes*, the young novice speaks of *lights*, an expression which falls again and again from his pen; whether he means by this the natural outcome of his own meditations or whether it concerns – and this, as cannot be doubted is the most frequent case, for they bear the impress of their origin – inspirations coming down from the Father of Lights from whom is every perfect gift.

But whatever be their character, we reverently gather them up. We shall besides find in them many of those master-ideas which form the substance of *Christ the Life of the Soul* and *Christ the Ideal of the Monk*, works which were not to come to light till thirty years later, after having been slowly brought to maturity in reflection and prayer, and above all fully lived.

In fact – as Dom Marmion sometimes confessed – when he received any lights he strove during some days and sometimes for a whole week to keep his mind illumined by them in order to assimilate as perfectly as possible the truths they contained. The impressions of grace grew stronger in recollection, the truths sunk deeper into his soul until they became an integral part of his inner life. And when the hour came for him to preach, Dom Marmion had simply to give to others of the superabundance of his own soul. We here touch, let us say in passing, on one of the chief causes of the winning charm of his eloquence: between his preaching and his inner personal life, as between action and contemplation, and between nature and grace, there was with him compenetration and unity.

This collection of *Notes* opens in the month of January 1887, with this verse from St John's Gospel: *Pater, clarifica nomen tuum:* "Father glorify Thy name," the prayer of Jesus at the moment when, by His miracle of the raising of Lazarus, He gave the world a new revelation of the mission of the Son of God.

The young novice made this prayer his own. This was no doubt because, according to his familiar and usual expression "this text had struck him"; his soul must have been particularly impressed by it, and having gathered it up like a treasure – a precious pearl of the Gospel – he inscribed it as a watchword of life and action at the head of his *Notes*.

"To glorify the Son, and through the Son, the Father who gave Him to us," no thought could have been better chosen to express the innermost aspiration of Brother Columba's soul, one that was to uplift and sustain him during all his religious life; none other could better have summed up in advance his whole existence: here is truly the light which illumined all his path, directed all his steps, sustained his apostolate and shone out from all his works. All his life – as we shall see – was but a hymn of ardent and practical faith in Jesus Christ, the Son of God, to the glory of the Father.

Immediately after comes the Litany of Humility. And this is no less significant.[1]

---

[1] Brother Columba had evidently taken the original litany from some manual of devotion; it is the fact of his having chosen this litany to place it at the head of his *Notes* that is significant. Let us, however, give the text. (It will be understood that the repetition of the words: "From the desire of being... From the

At this period, Brother Columba had scarcely counted three months of monastic life, but his quick and penetrating mind, of which one of the most marked characteristics was to go to the heart and core of a subject to disengage the essential – had soon discovered, in the divine light, the fundamental points of asceticism as brought forward by St Benedict.

And it is above all in the chapter on humility that the Patriarch of Monks has condensed his spiritual teaching.

This chapter, it has been said, views the spiritual life taken as a whole. St Benedict marks out the stages of the soul's ascent to God, from the renouncing of sin to the plenitude of charity; in his eyes the ascent of the soul is characterised by a deeper and deeper submission of man before God. It is by progress in self-abasement and submission that man raises his soul as by a ladder towards union with God and heavenly exaltation. The more one progresses in true humility, so much the more is one absorbed in God, and raised towards the heights of union with Him.[1]

> fear of being..." is in each case indicated by the semi-colon).
>
> Litany to obtain Humility
>
> Lord, have mercy on us; Christ, have mercy on us; Lord, have mercy on us, Jesus, meek and humble of heart, hear us. Jesus, meek and humble of heart, graciously hear us.
>
> From the desire of being...esteemed; loved; sought after; praised; honoured; preferred; consulted; approved; spared; deliver me, Jesus.
>
> From the fear of being...humbled; despised; rebuked; calumniated; forgotten; laughed at; made game of; insulted; deliver me, O Jesus.
>
> O Mary, Mother of the humble, pray for me. St Joseph, protector of humble souls, pray for me. St Michael, who wert the first to trample upon pride, pray for me. All the just sanctified by humility, pray for me.
>
> Prayer. O Jesus, whose first lesson has been: "Learn of Me because I am meek and humble of heart," teach me to become humble of heart like Thee.

[1] "This theory of humility is, with St Benedict, exactly correlative with his conception of grace. The progress of the soul in God is the progress of God in the soul. The work, which by means of grace, belongs, properly speaking, to the soul, is to open the way to God's action, to open itself to God. To every degree of ascension towards God corresponds a decree of the opening of self

As Dom Marmion himself was later clearly to bring out, "St Benedict has a very sure and at the same time a very wide concept of humility. He does not envisage it simply as a very special virtue apart, linked to the moral virtue of temperance, but as a virtue expressing the whole attitude the soul ought to have in presence of God."[1] This attitude of soul born of the divine light consists of infinite reverence tempered by boundless confidence; it is an attitude wherein are fused the different sentiments that should animate us as creatures and as adopted children; it should, in the opinion of St Benedict, be the condition of the monk's whole existence and the basis of his whole spiritual life.[2]

It has been necessary, although it may appear tedious, to make this doctrinal explanation in order to understand what a singular grace was that of the young novice when he discovered – a practical discovery which was to become a principle of action and source of life – the ruling thought of the Holy Patriarch's asceticism.[3]

> to God. How do we open ourselves to God? By more and more abolishing pride within us; by more and more deepening humility according to the law of the Scriptures: 'God resisteth the proud, and giveth grace to the humble'; and that is why 'Everyone that exalteth himself shall be humbled, and he that humbleth himself shall be exalted.'" *Christ the Ideal of the Monk.*

1 "St Benedict's conception of humility far surpasses in amplitude those that have become classic with moralists; but it in nowise contradicts them." Dom Marmion, *Christ the Ideal of the Monk.* We may add that St Thomas Aquinas repeated – in order to emphasise its truth – the definition by the Patriarch of Monks.

2 "The twelve degrees of humility in the Benedictine *Rule* form an astoundingly penetrating and harmonious whole, showing the blending of fear and confidence, of obedience and energy, of recollection and charity which ought to compose the attitude of the monk who advances in spiritual life," Dom Idesbald Ryelandt, *Essai sur la physionomie morale de Saint-Benoît.* Pages of searching psychological analysis and suggestive side-lights are to be found in this opuscule which places the character and doctrine of the Holy Patriarch in a clear light.

3 He had doubtless been prepared to esteem humility by Fr Gowan's lessons, but here Brother Columba entered further into the comprehension of this virtue as set forth by St Benedict. Doubtless, too, the Litany of Humility rests rather on the element of *abasement,* but we shall see by the following notes that already at this period, the young novice had grasped that this abasement

He was to remain faithful to this grace. Humility in the full sense of the word, was indeed to be – with the merciful kindness which is one of its most delicate manifestations – one of the dominant and particularly outstanding traits of Dom Marmion's moral physiognomy.

And yet in this rich and complex nature, there existed baffling contrasts. His joviality was apt to set people on the wrong track as to his inner life; it was to be the same as to his humility: the superficial forms of this virtue were never to be found in him. His expansive, even exuberant, temperament led those who judged by appearances to form a false idea of it, but those who knew him a little more closely could have no difficulty in discovering the deep reality of a sincere humility.

To the Litany of Humility Brother Columba adds a prayer to obtain compunction of heart,[1] which breathe the spirit of St Benedict. When the patriarch traces the portrait of the perfect monk who has climbed all the degrees of humility, he shows him to us bathed in the invisible light of the Divine Presence, lost in the abyss of his nothingness and the consciousness of his faults.

---

had its source in reverence towards God and that, on the other hand, confidence in divine grace must be correlative with it. When he came to the end of his novitiate, he was in possession of all the elements of the Benedictine conception of humility.

[1] Dom Marmion has himself written that compunction is hard to define. He describes it as an abiding sense of contrition, firm and peaceful, and a source of generosity. (See the beautiful chapter "Compunction of Heart" in *Christ the Ideal of the Monk*). The prayer of which we are speaking is his own composition. It is interesting because after first writing it he later afterwards modified it. This is the text translated from the Latin: "Prayer. We beseech Thy immense loving-kindness, O almighty God, that through the intercession of the Blessed Virgin Mary and all the saints, Thou wilt take away from the heart of Thy servant all that is displeasing in the sight of Thy Divine Majesty and that, purified in mind and body, he may be immolated to Thee as an acceptable victim of penance. Through Jesus Christ our Lord." Later (after his canonical entrance into the novitiate) he added his name of "Columba" to the word "servant," and replaced the words "purified in mind and body" by these: "made conformable to the image of Thy Beloved Son." This modification is significant.

These prayers, transcribed in January 1887, must often have been repeated by Brother Columba; they seem to have satisfied his devotion for a long time, for he did not write any more till three months later. We will take some extracts from these *Notes* which cover the period between April and October 1887. All we need do is to group them together occasionally to avoid repetition; and to note their logical connection or fundamental character. But they should be read without losing sight of the nature of the trials that beset him: it is only in this light that we shall grasp their full import.

8 April 1887, Good Friday – I had the happiness of spending nearly three hours (last night) before the Most Holy Sacrament. I felt a great desire to love Jesus with my whole heart. The thoughts which I had yesterday during the *Mandatum* made a great impression on me, and continued with me today; they threw a great light on the love of Jesus in His Passion. This thought was the unspeakable love and humility of Jesus in washing the feet of the disciples. When the abbot in his pontificals came to wash our feet, I felt how truly he represented Jesus Christ. He (our Lord) desires this ceremony to be repeated showing that He is ready to perform it for even one of us in the person of His priests. As Jesus delights in humility, I felt that He would give me some special grace while washing my feet. I felt that I was Judas, and I felt Him saying to me, 'you must imitate My example and become the servant of all; abase yourself in all things, beneath the feet of all and you will become great in love,' because 'Amen, amen, I say to you, as long as you did it to one of these My least brethren, you did it to Me....'

With humility as with the other virtues, union with Jesus is the sure way, the secret of progress.

"I feel today, the necessity of close union with Jesus, 'I am the Vine; you the branches'; 'he that abideth in Me, and I in him, the same beareth much fruit'; for 'in this is My Father glorified, that you bring forth very much fruit.' But 'unless the Lord build the house, they labour in vain that build it.'"

To this intimate union with God, the union of love, the young novice feels himself, a few days later, called by our Lord Himself; he is thereby to find strength to ascend the degrees of humility:

> *Thursday, Feast of St Anselm (April 21st)* – After breakfast while walking the garden I read the eighth chapter of the *Imitation of Christ*, and felt greatly moved to make Jesus my only friend. I felt that in spite of my great weakness and infidelity, Jesus wished to be my friend above all others. The text 'my delights are to be with the children of men,' moved me much and I felt greatly moved to make every effort to give Jesus this satisfaction. The thought of the Magdalene moved me much, I felt great gratitude to God for having called me to enjoy that *better part*. During the meditation I felt the near presence of Jesus, and felt a great desire to do all things under His eyes.

"To do all things under His eyes." That is the thought of St Benedict in his chapter on humility.[1] According to him this sense of the Divine Presence ought to harmonise with a great confidence in the tenderness of the Heavenly Father. Fear and love – the twofold rhythm which ought to regulate our whole life.

Reading at this time Msgr Charles Gay's *Christian Life and Virtues*, Brother Columba took down this passage which particularly struck him: "*17 August 1887* – Speaking of the fear of God Msgr Gay says: 'that the fear of God if surrounded by those virtues which complete it, *viz.*: simplicity, confidence, what I will call *le sentiment pratique du caractère honorable et paternel de Dieu*, far from casting us into perplexity, minutiae and scruples, corrects any tendency we might have in that direction.'"

Lines to bear in mind, and especially let us notice the care that Brother Columba took to underline the words relating to the practical sense of God's honourable and fatherly character; we here find the earliest written testimony to the most marked characteristic of

---

[1] First and twelfth degrees.

Dom Marmion's spirituality: the consciousness of being, through Christ's grace, the child of the Heavenly Father. We shall often meet with this expression but we must point out that this is the first time it appears under his pen.

Brother Columba added to this passage: "[This virtue] gives great liberty of spirit, because in proportion as the exterior man is restrained, the interior becomes dilated and free."

This interior liberty, the prelude to divine union, is only attained at the price of self-renunciation and obedience, the practical expression of humility for the monk. The young novice notes this on that same date of the octave of St Laurence (17 August 1887).

"The words 'He that will come after Me, let him deny himself' (Communion of the Mass for the day) struck me today. *Abnegare* is the opposite of *affirmare*. We are constantly trying to affirm ourselves (*i.e.* to have our words, actions, etc., approved, our desires accomplished) and the more we keep ourselves in the shade, *abneget semetipsum*, the closer will we follow Jesus."

How far this self-denial can go is shown him a few days later by light from above and it is again a liturgical text which provides the occasion:

> 10 *September 1887* – I was greatly struck today while those words, *Vos qui reliquistis omnia et secuti estis me*[1] were being sung in the Communion of the Mass. I understood that this 'leaving all things' has many degrees. There is (*a*) *material* leaving of all things which is very pleasing to God but yet very imperfect; (*b*) the spiritual leaving of all things which is detachment; (*c*) there is entire leaving of all things which consists not only in abandoning all that we hold dear, but in denying ourselves the joys of memory and imagination in their regard. As spiritual mortification transcends corporal, as spirit transcends materiality, so does this spiritual abandon of all things transcend the merely bodily absence.

This total renouncement finds its summit in obedience which

---

[1] "You who have left all things and followed Me."

is the giving up of the inmost self. Obedience is the most tangible manifestation of humility; when the soul is filled with reverence towards God, it submits itself to God and to those who represent Him in order to accomplish His Will in all things.[1] This is why the Patriarch of Monks could equally well base the spiritual life of his children on humility, and present the monastic life as a return to God by the labour of obedience.

Brother Columba is given to understand this on the occasion of the feast of St Joseph of Cupertino (September 25th). After reading a life of the saint, he notes: "St Joseph of Cupertino allowed himself to be led like a blind man by obedience. 'There is nothing which the devil so fears,' he says, 'as obedience.'"

This ideal was to be his own; he meant to give up all to love for love's sake:

> *5 October 1887, Feast of St Placid* – A thought which consoles me when, on reading the lives of the saints, I feel tempted to discouragement on account of not being able to practise their austerities is *plenitudo legis dilectio*,[2] love without these austerities may be perfect, but these austerities without love are *aes sonans aut cynbalum tinniens*.[3] If I could entirely renounce my own will in all my actions, and perform them solely for God's love, I would soon be astonished with the progress I would make. And after all what did I give up all and enter this monastery for but to arrive at the love of God. If I would but leave all things I would soon receive the hundredfold but the material leaving of all things is but little, as long as our minds and hearts are not detached. 'Where your treasure is there will your heart be also....' *Conversatio nostra in coelis est*.[4]

---

1 *Humilitas proprie respicit reverentiam qua homo Deo subjicitur ... propter quem etiam aliis humiliando se subjicit*, St Thomas Aquinas, II-II, 9, CLXI, a.3, and a.1–5.
2 "Love therefore is the fulfilling of the law" (Rom. 13:10).
3 "As sounding brass, or a tinkling cymbal" (I Cor. 13:1).
4 "Our conversation is in Heaven" (Phil. 3:20). It is the same idea which he had expressed on the preceding September 10th. This example justifies what we said (p. 57) as to Dom Marmion carefully treasuring the divine lights he

This thought, which with good reason consoles the young novice, Dom Marmion was later to share with others when experience had further convinced him of its truth. It is one of his merits to have made many persons understand the hierarchy of values in the use of means of perfection. In his spiritual direction he often came back to these two points, namely, the relative importance of extraordinary austerities (for it is evidently of them he speaks) and the supremacy of love as a source of perfection. Setting souls on their guard against the illusion of seeing a necessary and indispensable means of spiritual progress in exceptional mortifications, he never ceased to recommend doing all for love of God, because in this lies the real secret of holiness.

This is why he insisted so much upon fidelity in little things[1] as in great, out of love. Thus as he wrote much later (January 1918) to one of his spiritual daughters – and it was besides one of his favourite maxims: "Fidelity in all things is the most delicate flower of love to which nothing is little."

The conditional form that he gives to the thought cited above sufficiently shows that he lay under no illusion: "If I could entirely renounce my own will in all my actions, and perform them solely for God's love." The self-detachment thus involved necessitates exceptional virtue and considerable strength of will. But it leads infallibly and quickly to the hundredfold, to perfection of union. This was the high aim that the young novice had in view.[2]

---

received and nourishing himself with them during several days.

1 "'Little things'? Yes, in themselves; but great by reason of the virtue they require, great by reason of the love that observes them, and the holiness to which they lead." *Christ the Ideal of the Monk*, ch. "Self-Renunciation," § IV.

2 This thought of Dom Marmion is dated 5 October 1887. Several months later there entered at the Carmel of Lisieux, one who was particularly to teach the value of the "Little Way" of love. In reference to this, see *St Teresa of Lisieux. A Spiritual Renascence*, by Fr Henri Petitot, OP (translated by the Benedictines of Stanbrook), ch. 1, "First negative character: the absence of any violent or self-imposed mortifications." This is a noteworthy book and certainly one of the best written on the spirituality of St Thérèse of Lisieux. The author's too cursory knowledge (to judge at least from the too simplified explanation he gives of it) of ancient asceticism is to be regretted. This deficiency is of a na-

From the fact that "St Benedict conceived the upward progress of the soul as being characterised by an ever deeper submission of man in the sight of God" it is justly acknowledged that this "conception is the reflex of an essentially religious and contemplative inner life"; it is "the expression of a soul earnestly attentive to the divine mystery and finding in this contemplation the secret of every renunciation as of all spiritual elevation in God."[1]

Is it not in this way that St Benedict would have his sons to realise this ideal, and become – as he himself was – fundamentally religious and contemplative? The monk then becomes a man of prayer, joining his own individual prayer to the duty of public praise.

In virtue of the same conception the holy legislator expects from the novice not only a love of humiliations and obedience but an eagerness for the offering of praise which he calls by the beautiful name of "the work of God."

The high idea Brother Columba has of this work arouses and enkindles his zeal and fervour:

> 1 May 1887 – I find it a great help in saying the office to remember that I am really an ambassador sent by the Church to deliver a message several times daily before the throne of the Most High. This message must be delivered in the words and in the manner which the Church prescribes. When I recollect how dear that Church is to Jesus – His Spouse! His Beloved! For whom He shed His blood, and which He desires so earnestly to present in perfection to His Father, I feel great joy in thinking what joy I am giving to the Heart of God. The various passages of the *Canticle* come before my mind to show how pleasing the prayer of the Church must be to Jesus: 'Let thy voice sound in my ears; for thy voice is sweet and thy face comely. Who is this who cometh up from the desert, flowing with delights, leaning upon her Beloved?' 'Thou has wounded my heart, my sister...' 'My delight is to be with the children

---

ture to lessen the value of his thesis.

1 Dom Ryelandt, *Essai sur la physionomie morale de Saint-Benoît*.

of men.' There is besides the thought that the very words of the office are inspired by the Holy Spirit. All the ceremonies, etc. are the code of etiquette of these ambassadors.

The liturgy not only helps his personal devotion, it widens his horizon: *"Feast of the Sacred Heart (1887)* – I find it very useful to thank God for all the favours both spiritual and temporal which I receive from Him, but also for all those He is constantly conferring on all mankind. I do this especially during Holy Mass at *Ite Missa est.*"

Undoubtedly liturgical prayer is essentially mental prayer; Brother Columba had read in the *Rule* that during the psalmody the mind of the monk ought to be in accord with the words pronounced by his lips.

Nevertheless the Holy Patriarch intends his sons to give themselves up to private and silent prayer, heart to heart with God.

On this very important point of the spiritual life, the private *Notes* contain only two passages, the second of which is a quotation, but they show the spiritual tonality of the young novice. We must especially bear in mind his sense of sharing, through Jesus Christ, in the grace of being the child of God: it is the essential point of his whole piety.

> *Feast of the Sacred Heart (1887)* – I felt today that we are pleasing to God in proportion as we are conformable to Jesus Christ, especially in His interior dispositions. This is why a *childlike* confidence in prayer, in spite of our sins, is so pleasing to God. 'I know that Thou always hearest Me,' said Jesus. We are the adopted children of God, and should always, in all humility and simplicity, treat Him in the same manner. I find it a great help in prayer to look at God, thinking how good He is, and refusing to listen to the motives of distrust suggested by the devil. It was when St Peter looked away from Jesus at the wind and the waves, that he sank. I feel that I thus give great glory to God, *confiteantur Domino misericordiae ejus.* God is pleased during this life to be glorified chiefly in His mercy.

A few months later, he transcribes – underlining the words that particularly struck him – a beautiful passage from Msgr Gay[1] which, he says, "gives great light on the manner of praying."

> *10 September 1887* – Try to understand what is meant by *asking in the name of Jesus Christ*. It is without doubt to allege Jesus Christ as a title to the Father. He is a title of infinite worth. It is further to repose on Him as on a faithful *Intercessor*, whose prayer is always heard; as on a devoted and reliable Advocate who is sure to gain all the causes which He undertakes to plead. It is to present ourselves to the Father under His protection and in His company. It is above all to bear this name of Jesus in our hearts; it is to possess habitually this divine name of Son of God, which divine grace communicates to us, and which causes us to enter into a real participation in the eternal filiation of the Word. It is to be wholly filled with this *filial spirit* which proceeds in us from the generation of grace, and causes us to cry to God in the virtue of this Holy Spirit, by the words of our mouth, the sighs of our hearts, by our actions and dispositions 'My Father, my Father!' And if – as is but lawful and natural to Christians – it is to Jesus Christ in person that we address our prayers, it is also in His name, that is to say, confiding in His words, His sufferings, His merits and the titles He has conferred on us; it is as being His members vivified by His Holy Spirit that we ought to implore Him. And He Himself wishes that it should be thus, as He says in the Gospel: 'If you ask Me anything in My name, I will do it.

"I find," concludes the young novice, "Msgr Gay's chapters on hope and confidence full of light and grace; I hope often to read them.

He does more than read them repeatedly; he drinks in the spirit of this wise teaching; he makes of it a rule of conduct and above all, when his own hour came, he preached, in tones of glowing

---

[1] *Vie et vertus chrétiennes*, ch. "*De l'espérance chrétienne*," 11.

conviction born of inward light and confirmed by practice, this profound doctrine of our supernatural riches in the filiation of Christ Jesus.

At this period of his life, this sense of being the child of God in Jesus Christ deeply impresses him: *"25 September 1887, after reading the life of St Joseph of Cupertino –* [This saint's] manner of prayer was 'as it were to identify himself with the Persons of the Holy Trinity.' As I am the adopted son of God, I should try to *imitate Jesus Christ perfectly in His relations with the Holy Trinity."*

God, however, did not give him only lights. A few days later Brother Columba speaks of trial – and the means of drawing profit from it: *"5 October 1887* – Aridity, temptations, ennui. The only thought which I always find to recall me to devotion is that if I were at present gazing on the face of God, as the saints are, I should be overpowered with love, and forced to break forth into actions of sorrow for sin, thanksgiving, etc. I ought to have the same sentiments *through faith;* this thought often causes me great devotion and *confidence*, especially during Mass."

"I ought to have the same sentiments *through faith*." Let us treasure up this thought: it, too, was to become one of the main points of Dom Marmion's spirituality. *"To live by faith,"* to make faith the root of all Christian justification, the foundation of the whole spiritual edifice, the principle of all activity: how often he commented on this teaching of St Paul which he judged of first importance for the spiritual life! He knew by his own experience its necessity in order to advance in perfection; he likewise knew in how large a measure it is the means of ascent to God.

It was due to this faith that his obedience was without any reservation, and his reverence and exactitude were exemplary in the fulfilment of the worship of God. He truly *saw* God in his superiors. And he perceived, lucidly and practically, that the actions of the liturgy are those of the immediate and as it were domestic serving of God. The virtue of religion, which was at all times one special mark of his spiritual personality, was spontaneously allied in him with love of prayer. The others soon grew accustomed to seeing Brother Columba prelude the recitation of the psalms by a long time spent in recollection, and likewise to seeing him, when the office was over, remain kneeling in his stall, immovable and absorbed, prolonging a prayer solely nourished on the thoughts that the psalmody had left in his mind or that had been poured into it by light from above. More than one confrère struck by his attitude, applied to him, with a smile, that verse of Scripture: *Meditabor ut Columba.*[1]

The last thought that we find expressed during this period of his life as a novice again relates to humility. Divine grace evidently gave him to fathom the sublime doctrine of this virtue, whilst men were meanwhile providing him with the opportunity of practising it in all its bitterness.

"*5 October 1887* – I had the grace to see that a great means of arriving at a true humility is to love my superiors and my brethren *humili caritate.*[2] Humility takes care above all things not to act from self, but to make all things date from grace, in fact give the initiative to God and to grace in all things according to the words of Jesus, *I cannot of Myself do anything. As I hear so I do.*"

But the submission due to God Himself demands, by way of logical sequence, submission to men for God's sake. On reading the clauses devoted to this virtue by St Thomas Aquinas, Brother Columba makes a special extract of these two passages:

"Humility principally regards the submission of man to God, but on account of God, humility also submits to others in the spirit of self-abasement."[3]

"Humility principally deals with the reverence by which man submits to God, and consequently every man *in what concerns himself personally,* ought to submit to *any other man whatsoever in the measure that this other represents God.*"[4]

---

1 "I will meditate like the dove" (Isa. 38:14).
2 "With humble affection." *Rule of St Benedict,* ch. 72.
3 II. II, q. CLXI, a.i, ad 5.
4 *Ibid.,* a. 3 in corp.

Here is his practical and concise commentary on these passages:

> Humility recognises the divine everywhere; hence the inclination which it gives to subject self to all superiors, especially spiritual ones. There is no authority but that which comes from God. No matter what their personal character may be, they possess participation of the divine *in so far as they are* superiors, and humility naturally subjects herself to them. This is the foundation of all those texts regarding authority. 'I have said: You are gods,' 'he that heareth you, heareth Me.' 'There is no power but from God.'
>
> This is true also of all men and humility regards in others that which is divine in them, she searches God in everything in order to render Him homage, regarding in herself only what is her own work. She thus finds no difficulty in regarding others as better than herself. This is especially true in the case in which she perceives that others do not honour in themselves that participation of the divine nature which all possess.

It is with this thought that he closes his notebook as a novice.

In these rare *Notes* do we not find, already lived by him, the whole substance of Dom Marmion's spirituality? At the basis of the inner life, the virtue of faith. It reveals God's great plan: to make us His children by the grace of adoption in Jesus Christ, the God-Man. This supernatural adoption is engrafted on our condition as creatures: the compunction, humility and obedience of the creature ought to be blended in the child of God with a deep sense of filial confidence and generous love.

Does not a novice who is guided by such lights and strives to correspond to them truly seek God?

And yet – in spite of Brother Columba's zeal for obedience and observance of the *Rule* during the whole time of his hard probation – it became evident a short time before his admission that there were some who did not understand him.

As for himself, he was at this period "reduced to powerlessness"; it was almost impossible for him to compose his litanies of profession;[1] his spiritual aridity and sufferings were such that, according to his own expression, his "soul and conscience were all on edge."

Nevertheless he was able to pronounce his vows on 10 February 1888, on the feast of St Scholastica, sister of St Benedict.

When on the day of his religious profession the novice is led processionally from the chapter room to the church, the community sings the Psalm: *In convertendo Dominus captivitatem Sion* – Psalm of gladness celebrating the end of the captivity of Sion. No novice can listen unmoved to this canticle telling of the sowing in tears that is to bring forth the joyful abundance of the future harvest.

Had not Brother Columba himself clearly alluded to this Psalm in the letter he wrote to the little novice in Dunmore while he was yet a young priest in Dublin? "During my novitiate I would leave myself absolutely in the hands of my superiors ... to be presented, as a clean oblation on the altar of God's love.... I would try to bear all for the love of Jesus crucified, and I feel sure that if I were faithful I would soon acquire the true spirit of my order, and thus reap with joy wheat I had sown in tears."

The hour of oblation had come. During long months the novice had truly borne all things for the love of Christ, he had already understood and had striven to live in the spirit of his monastic vocation. Does it not seem as if in receiving this grace of religious profession so dearly purchased, so hardly won, he would be overflowing with that spiritual joy of which the Psalmist speaks?

This was far from being the case. Even on this day, as he afterwards sometimes confessed, for he has left no written record of his impressions on this occasion, he suffered "death and martyrdom";

---

[1] Prayer preparatory to profession, composed by the novice himself according to his attraction, and made up of litanies followed by versicles and a collect. This is recited during the nine days preceding the profession. The one composed by Brother Columba has not been found.

he felt that profession "was sealing a tomb where [he] was wholly buried alive, never to rise again." An impression which was to be intensified that very day. When in the evening, according to custom, the newly professed went to thank the abbot, the latter said to him:

"That is enough! As for your profession I am quite sad about it."

Strange words only to be explained by one of those inspirations which the abbot sometimes thought it his duty to follow (there are other examples of this) in order to exercise and try his monks. But, in this case, he cannot have suspected how particularly sharp and painful a shaft it was.

For Brother Columba the sorrowful sowing was to be still further prolonged, or rather it was the Divine Sower who was burying the grain of wheat more deeply into the ground; but ere long this grain was to spring up and the harvest was to be the more abundant in that the winter had been the more severe and the frost the more rigorous.

5 THE PATH OF PERFECTION
(1881–91)

Henceforth Brother Columba was a monk. The gift he had made of himself to God in the Order of St Benedict was to be a continuous self-oblation during thirty-five years.

These thirty-five years may be considered as divided into three periods, each of about an equal length of ten years, the *decennium* being rather widely calculated. Clearly defined from one another by the outward setting of his monastic life and the position he held in the Community, these three periods were linked together by an essential continuity of intention and spirit.

The first period, from February 1880 to the month of April 1899, was passed at the Abbey of Maredsous, where Brother Columba completed his religious formation in the novitiate until his solemn profession (February 1891). From that starting point his inner life was joined to a rather extensive and dispersed outward activity on which a constant spirit of obedience set the seal of unity. The striving after and the practice of those virtues which detach the soul from self, kept his heart, under the influence of abundant spiritual lights, centred in God.

The second period, extending from April 1899 to September 1909, was spent at the Abbey of Mont-César, at Louvain: a period of full development, in a wider sphere of activity, one more homogeneous, more concentrated and fostered by an intense life of union with God.

Dom Marmion's abbacy at Maredsous (September 1909–January 1923) formed the last period. His life, come to full maturity, yielded its rich and generous fruit.

After pronouncing his simple vows, Brother Columba remained two more years in the novitiate to complete his monastic formation under Dom Benoît's direction.

BROTHER COLUMBA
(Maredsous, 1888)

During this space of time, only a few isolated occasions of pastoral ministry came to break the uniformity of his religious life.

Only his inner life need detain us here. We shall again find in it the same oneness of purpose: his efforts were still especially directed towards the practice of those virtues which empty the soul of self in order to make room for grace.

The *Notebook* opens again in April 1888, on the occasion of the Annual Retreat:

> *April 1888* – I had a thought which I find of *great service* in praying with confidence. This thought may be expressed by the words 'prayer must be made with *resignation*.'[1] I found this thought of immense help, particularly when tempted to distrust by the sight of God's mysterious ways in dealing with His creatures. Then I found that to cast myself down in humble adoration before the Holy of Holies in which God chooses to veil the secrets of predestination, etc., not daring to try to pierce this veil, but humbly trusting God's goodness in pure faith, filled me with reverence and loving admiration and confidence. For example, in praying for humility, not daring to complain at not being answered, but humbly *resigned* to God's mysterious counsel in deferring this gift, determined if it were His Will, to continue asking for a hundred years, because He pleases.

But, above all, he is ever as confident in the merits of Jesus, who makes us by His grace children of adoption, as he is impressed with the sense of his misery as a creature; he constantly comes back to this thought as to the centre of his inner life.

> *Same date* – The more I feel and acknowledge my utter unworthiness, the more do I glorify in me the merits of Jesus and the Divine Mercy, if I pray with confidence. The prayer of the humble pierces the clouds.

---

[1] Under Dom Marmion's pen this term implies the idea of *abandon;* later on he only uses the latter word.

> The more miserable, weak and unworthy I am to be heard, the more should I cover myself with the merits of Jesus; and strong in the faith I have in them, I should approach the throne of God, that infinite mercy of my Father, trusting as firmly to be heard through Jesus, as He did *pro sua reverentia*,[1] when He said, 'I know that Thou hearest Me always.' This is the true spirit of adoption.

From this filial spirit the best of all prayers finds utterance: "I find repeating the petitions of the Lord's Prayer, particularly *fiat voluntas tua,* an excellent form of prayer since it is the Will of God that we should sanctify ourselves."

A little later, new lights bring out more clearly this fundamental attitude which the creature ought to have before the Divine Majesty. The young monk enters more deeply into the supernatural spirit that the Holy Patriarch requires of his disciples.

> Today[2] I had some very useful lights touching compunction, mortification, devotion to St Benedict and stability. *Compunction.* The angels standing before the throne of God veil their faces and, filled with wonder and admiration at the sight of God's infinite holiness, cry aloud without ceasing 'Holy, Holy, Holy is the Lord.' For us poor sinners here below, our *faith* should produce the same effect, but *differently.* Gazing in spirit on this infinite sanctity, we should cry from the bottom of our hearts, 'mercy, mercy, mercy!' This is our *Sanctus,* and the Church adopts this in her daily cry, *Kyrie eleison, Christe eleison, Kyrie eleison.* I found this thought of honouring God's sanctity, by uniting with the angels as they cry *Sanctus,* in crying for mercy, very fruitful. As their cry is *eternal,* so should my cry for mercy never cease in this life.

This thought was in fact very fruitful. The spirit of compunction – little cultivated by modern piety, but dear to the saints, and

---

1 "Christ was heard for his reverence" (Heb. 5:7).
2 Without exact date, but between April and June 1888.

practised by the Church in her liturgy, especially in the Mass – took strong hold of Brother Columba's soul. This virtue was his own in a rare degree; we shall see he was to carry out his intention of never ceasing his cry for mercy during all his monastic life.

Fruitful, too, for souls was this sense of compunction; it was this especially that gave to his spiritual intercourse with others that inimitable depth of strength and sweetness by which he brought back or won so many hearts to Christ.

Compunction, the source of humility, is the principle of generosity and mortification. On the latter, the young monk receives a light that same day:

> *Mortification.* As I am convinced that it is only in so far as my works are united with the merits of Jesus Christ that they are satisfactory and meritorious, it follows that my great aim should be to unite myself *as closely as possible* with Jesus Christ and His sufferings in all my actions, and thus it would matter little what I am engaged at. But how is this union to be effected? St Benedict tells us 'We share in the sufferings of Christ by patience.' This little sentence threw a great light on St Benedict's life. I felt that it must have been a life of great but hidden suffering since St Gregory tells us that 'he could not teach except what he practised.' *Patientia = Sufferentia.*

The monk has one special ground of self-renunciation which is singularly trying to the patience of human nature, with its hankering after change: this is stability. By a special vow, the Benedictine monk is attached to the abbey where he makes profession.[1] "It is one of the miseries of man," says Blaise Pascal, "not to know how to keep within four square walls." No one is more sensible to this misery, common to all, than the Irish Celt with his wandering instincts. It must often have weighed upon Brother Columba, but he generously accepted this mortification for love of Christ:

---

[1] St Benedict was the first legislator to bind the monk by the vow of lifelong stability in the same monastery.

It is relative to stability that St Benedict uses the above words – ['We share in the sufferings of Christ by patience']. It follows that he considers this stability the great act of patience. 'If anyone will come after me, let him deny himself....' This shows that it is suffering which draws us near to Jesus. 'He who does not take up his cross daily and follow Me, cannot be My disciple.' Therefore all other methods which do not include this are founded on error."

Brother Columba was on his guard against this error; his generosity accepted not only all the rulings of Providence in the manifold events of ordinary life, but he strove to give himself up more to that life of obedience which constitutes the summit of self-renunciation. On this theme, lights abound.

Pentecost 1888 – Very fatigued, much tempted, resigned. At Vespers had a good thought from which I hope for fruit: Obedience in its perfection demands that we should try to accomplish not only the wishes expressed by superiors but also their known wishes. Now I know without the slightest doubt that the express wish of my abbot is that we should acquire the highest possible sanctity, and that he regards everything else as secondary to this; he has declared this over and over again. Therefore the more generous I am in my efforts to attain sanctity, the greater is my obedience. I can thus make my life a continual act of obedience, and at the same time a continual progress in fervour. Thus each time I renew my vows or salute my abbot, I gain new fervour, etc.

The longing for perfection in the young professed is certainly strong and ardent; God is urging him to enter further and further into this way of submission, which is, according to St Teresa of Ávila, "the quickest and most effectual means of arriving at perfection."[1]

---

1 *Foundations*, ch. 3.

"I got light[1] to understand that *obedience is everything* for a Benedictine. Mortification,[2] long prayers, Mass, may be impossible or may produce little or no fruit (for example, schismatic monks, bad or tepid priests) but perfect obedience takes the place of all. I always find great peace when I take this view."

To such an extent does the Holy Patriarch wish obedience to be everything for a monk, that he requires this virtue to be practised even in impossible things. The reading of the chapter where St Benedict speaks of this point of his teaching coinciding with the feast of Christmas[3] when we honour the self-abasement of the Word, suggests this beautiful page to Brother Columba:

> *The day after Christmas 1888* – The chapter of the *Rule: Si impossibilia injungantur*[4] – viewed in the light of our Lord's life made a great impression on me. Obedience is the most sublime act of adoration that a man can offer to God. This is the keynote of our Lord's life. All the evils which have afflicted humanity, destroyed God's work, and filled hell, come from one act of disobedience.[5] All the graces obtained for us by Jesus Christ are due to His obedience. 'In the head of the book it is written of Me that I should do Thy will: O my God, I have desired it, and Thy law is in the midst of my heart.' St Paul explains the word *exinanivit*,[6] which is the highest act of adoration, by saying 'He humbled Himself, becoming obedient unto death.' The abasement and renouncement of self, for God's honour, is so great in perfect obedience, that man is incapable of more, for by perfect obedience man immolates, on the altar of God's love, all that he holds most dear,

---

1 Without exact date, but between September and Christmas 1888.
2 In the sense of doing penance.
3 The *Rule* is divided into sections in such a way that it may be read through three times during the year.
4 "If a brother be commanded to do impossibilities."
5 This is the thought of St Paul: "For all by the disobedience of one man (Adam) many were made sinners; so also by the obedience of one (Jesus Christ) many shall be made just" (Rom. 5:19).
6 "He emptied Himself" (Phil. II:8).

all that is, in a word, himself. This is the explanation of the thirty years of Jesus' life summed up in the words 'He was subject to them.' In His holy Passion 'Father, not My will, but Thine be done,' is the very keynote of all.

Jesus' example is powerful. The soul that truly seeks Him is drawn after Him on that path of obedience which He Himself was the first to tread. Brother Columba therefore concludes: "I made the resolution to try to excel in obedience as prescribed in our *Rule*, that is to say, towards all, obeying the words of St Peter, 'Be ye subject therefore to every human creature for God's sake.' I made the resolution: when saluting my superiors, or equals or inferiors, to make interiorly an act of submission to them, and express the desire to obey their slightest wishes."

So great is his thirst for obedience, so high his ambition for perfection, that he wishes to make this virtue, after the example of Jesus, the true spiritual atmosphere of his whole life and the motive power of his whole activity. "I made the resolution, in the morning when I hear the bell to meditate on our Lord leaving the bosom of the Father (to become Incarnate) saying: *Behold I come to do Thy will.* Let this be the keynote of my day."

The same idea of integral obedience again appears among the chief lights received during the retreat given in May 1889.

"Just as Jesus hidden under the sacramental species is a source of grace to those who approach Him in proportion to their dispositions (faith, hope, charity, humility) thus also the graces we will receive from Jesus hidden in our superiors will be in proportion to the dispositions with which we approach them.

"*Resolution.* To reject every thought which would be against the reverence and submission due to our superiors. To renew this reverence and my vow of obedience each time I salute my superiors."

He was to remain faithful to this resolution. Meeting the superior in the cloister and saluting him, according to custom, he completed his act of obedience, by saying interiorly: *Ave, Christe.*

Truly no one could have shown more ardour in appropriating,

whenever possible, what St Benedict excellently calls the boon of obedience (*bonum obedientiae*). Above all, no one could have been more persevering in his desire, or had more of the spirit of faith in practising this virtue: the young monk was certainly among those who "see Christ in the abbot" as the Blessed Benedict wills, and among those who "holding nothing dearer than Christ," are intent on giving God the full homage of their entire faith and absolute submission.

Fervent as is his longing for perfection, he however only bases the expectation of its realisation on humble confidence in Jesus.

> I received lately[1] a light on this subject [of humility] which I find very useful, *viz.* God is at this moment gazing at me. He sees down into the depths of my misery. He knows all things, even *futura conditionata*.[2] He knows perfectly into what crimes I would fall were He to deprive me of His grace. This is true at every moment, even when I feel burning with the desire of pleasing God. I am so changeable! I find that this thought humbles me, and makes me see how good God is to bear with me, and that it is solely in the merits of Jesus Christ that I must hope.

He closes this page with a thought of Bl. Julie Billiart: "You are doubtless aware what use God wishes us to make of our aridities. It is to put ourselves still lower than the state we are enduring. That is our place."

And he adds this thought of St Francis de Sales: "Humility is nothing else than the courage to apply the truth to ourselves with all its rigour and consequences."

God's action was manifestly making itself felt in the soul of Brother Columba; by the lights He was lavishing on him, God willed to deepen his capacity for the grace of union in detaching him more and more from self, through compunction, renunciation,

---

1 Without precise date but after the month of May 1888.
2 Events which take place in such-or-such circumstances.

mortification, humility and, above all, obedience, which for the monk sums up everything.

At the same time, other graces were strengthening his life of union with God and with the neighbour in charity: *"Feast of the Blessed Trinity, 1888* – I find great devotion while reciting the *Gloria Patri* in uniting with the adorable Trinity in that eternal hymn of praise which It is ever offering to Itself with infinite love, and (in uniting) with the whole court of heaven."

We may likewise gather up the following *lights* on the Eucharist, suggesting a practice of devotion to which he remained faithful, and used to recommend in his sermons as being well calculated to foster love towards the august Sacrament of the Altar.

Feast of the Sacred Heart, 1888 – I am greatly struck by some reflections I made on the Blessed Eucharist. I see plainly that it is the great fountain of grace. Jesus brings with Him the Holy Spirit, and all kinds of graces and favours. I see plainly that if I could make my life a perpetual preparation and thanksgiving for Holy Mass that I would receive the most extraordinary graces at Holy Mass, because every little act, aspiration and sacrifice offered during the day in view of Holy Communion, would be there (*virtuali intentione*),[1] at the moment of receiving (next day) and no matter then about involuntary distraction.[2]

The thought (has struck me) also that in giving us Jesus Christ in Holy Communion, the Father has given us all things, and the surest pledge of all that we ask. So that *on His side* there can be no doubt that He is ready to give us all things – 'Hath He not given us all things together with Him?' – the fault must be mine. When God delays to give me some grace,

---

[1] In virtue of the intention previously expressly determined.
[2] A letter of December 1922 proves the continuity of this practice.

the angels adore in silent admiration the reasons which cause this; let me unite in reverence with them!

Besides the sacraments, prayer, particularly the Divine Office, is ever for him a fount of grace because he bases his confidence on Christ's merits:[1]

> I find it a great help in prayer, particularly in the Divine Office, to unite with Jesus in His quality of Head of the Church, and Advocate with the Father. Jesus exercises His *eternal Priesthood* by standing before the throne of the adorable Trinity in heaven and showing His Sacred Wounds. God *cannot* refuse His prayers, He is 'heard for His reverence.' I unite thus as *a member of Jesus Christ* particularly when I fill the office of *hebdomadarius*,[2] and feel great confidence and get much light.

In fact we have more than once seen a text, or a liturgical feast serve as the channel of divine grace to touch his soul:

> *Feast of the Seven Sorrows of the Blessed Virgin and Feast of Our Lady of Ransom, 1888* – I felt a great increase of devotion towards the Blessed Virgin. Our perfection is in just proportion to our resemblance to Jesus Christ. 'This is My beloved Son in whom I am well pleased.' The love and reverence of Jesus for His Blessed Mother were immense. Therefore I must try to imitate Him in this. This is especially true of a priest who is *alter Christus*.
>
> On the feast of our Lady of Ransom I felt great devotion in saying the Divine Office *in persona Beatae Mariae Virginis* addressing my prayers and praises in her name, as she must have done, to the Eternal Father through Jesus Christ, trying to enter into her sentiment of profound adoration and abasement, confidence and joy, at the thought of the triumph of her Son.

---

1 After the feast of the Sacred Heart 1888 and before September 1888.
2 The hebdomarius (*hebdomada*, "week") is the religious who is charged to preside at the office in choir, to sing the conventual High Mass, etc., during a week.

I got light to see that as all praise addressed to Mary is rendered back *entirely* to the adorable Trinity (for example, the *Magnificat*) so when I consecrate myself to her, she receives the gift only to give it immediately to God.

The feast of a martyr suggests to him the following lines:[1]

As regards confidence in God, I find the thought that the martyrs laid down their lives rather than *doubt* the words of Jesus Christ a great aid. The great motive for believing God's word is the same for all His words, and I ought to be prepared to lay down my life rather than listen to the voice of Satan when he would wish to diminish my trust.

I find also a great help in thinking of the heroic trust of the Blessed Virgin Mary in the veracity of the Word made Flesh at Cana, on Calvary, and while our Lord was in the sepulchre. Confidence is a *virile* virtue which must be often reanimated and defended against the devils. I unite myself thus to the martyrs during the office and offer my life to the adorable Trinity in testimony of my absolute trust in the promises of Jesus Christ. I sometimes represent the Eternal Father overshadowing me and saying (in showing me His Son) 'This is My beloved Son, *hear ye Him.*'

If in offering the Divine Praise, he glorifies the Blessed Virgin and the saints with ardent faith, so too his supernatural spirit shows him all mankind as members of Christ's Mystical Body to whom his charity must be extended. The love of Jesus should be radiated. In the following page, Brother Columba dwells on the underlying motive of that essential truth of Christianity, "Love one another," which he was later to develop on grand lines:

May 1889 – The thought that God accepts as done to Himself each action and thought done to my brethren made a great

---

1 After Christmas 1888 and before May 1889.

impression on me. Jesus gives me Himself without reserve every morning in the Blessed Sacrament, and He asks me during the day to prove and testify my love for Him in the person of my brethren.

Resolution. To venerate habitually Jesus Christ in the person of my brethren, placing myself often in spirit beneath their feet, and often thinking that what I think of them or do to them is done to Jesus Christ.

As regards charity towards my brethren, the more I reflect on it, the more I see its importance, and understand why St John was never tired of inculcating it. I find it a most excellent means of practising the presence of God. The thought that our soul is whole and entire in every part of our body, and consequently after Holy Communion we are, as it were, saturated with the Divine Presence, aids me, amongst other things, to venerate my brethren. If we could see a person as the angels do after Holy Communion, he would appear quite transfigured, entirely plunged in the Divinity: 'he abideth in Me and I in him,' and my brethren[1] here receive Jesus almost every day.[2]

In meditating on the manifestation of Jesus to His disciples at Emmaus, the thought that they were not content with offering Him hospitality but 'constrained Him to enter' gave me a vivid light regarding the manner in which I ought to practise charity – looking out for opportunities of aiding my brethren and this at my own inconvenience.

He concludes by making the rays of his charity reach out far beyond the horizons of his monastery: in the same spirit of faith his love embraces all humanity to extend God's help to the ends of the earth. An admirable putting into practice of the dogma of the Communion of Saints, in the Oneness of Christ: "I find as preparation for Mass and office that a very good practice is to place the

---

1 The novices who were not yet priests and amongst whom Brother Columba was then living.
2 The decree on daily Communion was still a long way off being promulgated.

whole world in spirit before my eyes, the poverty, suffering – sin – missions, etc., and to carry them all with me to the altar."

In a note of the same period, he writes down a passage from Msgr Gay upon prayer for one's neighbour. "You may very easily fulfil this divine office of intercession and in doing so with great fervour you will continue to find it perfectly easy. Understand that you can largely pay your debt to your neighbour by simply giving him a share in your life of prayer and especially in each day's liturgical prayer. To do this it suffices to make a compact with God once and for all and to renew it occasionally. Moreover God sees all, Jesus prays and merits for all. United to Jesus, when speaking to God, never forget that to attain the desired end in all this, a movement of the soul is enough, or a look, a sigh, a word, an amen said from the heart to that holy and powerful prayer that the Sovereign Priest Jesus prays within you for all those included in your charity."[1]

Brother Columba made this compact in thus setting down his intentions for each day of the week:

Monday: Souls in Purgatory.
Tuesday: Order of St Benedict.
Wednesday: Relations and those to whom I am under any obligation.
Thursday: Sovereign pontiff, bishops, clergy, religious orders.
Friday: Missionaries, sinners, heretics, infidels.
Saturday: Spiritual children.
Sunday: Abbot, community, my own perfection.

We see how wide his charity was. In these notes full of zeal for souls and God's glory in them, the apostle stands confessed. The moment has not yet come – but will not long be delayed – when he will be enabled, under the aegis of obedience, to preach in glowing language the riches of the grace of Jesus. But first must be sealed

---

[1] *Vie et vertus chrétiennes: la charité fraternelle,* § 2.

that compact of mutual and definitive union between himself and the monastic community which is solemn profession.

He has left us a beautiful page showing how deep and lofty were his thoughts and feelings on the subject of this great action of his life as a monk.

9 February 1891, Eve of my Solemn Profession – I am filled with gratitude to God for His wonderful mercies towards me. Last Sunday (*Quinquagesima*) I celebrated Holy Mass in thanksgiving for all God's mercies, in reparation for my sins and for the grace that my sacrifice might be complete and agreeable to God. I made a good confession, after many acts of contrition, and feel that God will be merciful to me. I am in great peace. The great thought which fills my mind at present is that solemn profession is a holocaust, a complete *tradition* of self to God, the most perfect imitation of Jesus Christ. In the temple at the Purification He offered Himself *absolutely* to His Father and from that moment of His *official* oblation, every instant of His life was *quae placita sunt ei* until on the cross He could say *consummatum est*.

I resolved to try to imitate this perfect offering, by making my profession a holocaust of faith, hope and charity.

Of faith. On the day of my profession I give up all rights over myself into the hands of God, *believing* with firmest faith, that as I abandon all that I am and have to Him, and renounce the right of directing myself, so He will inspire my superiors to lead me in all things by the path most pleasing to Him. I realise that this absolute abandonment is very pleasing to God, and a source of great glory to Him. It honours His fidelity and goodness, and is an heroic act of faith.

Of hope. I give up all things in this world, and protest solemnly that *Dominus pars haereditatis meae*. It is also an heroic act of hope because I expect *blindly* all things from God through depriving myself of all power of directing myself or choosing my future.

Of Charity. I abandon all things and all inclinations even the most holy, leaving the choice of my occupations entirely to obedience, sacrificing my tastes, and undertaking solemnly, if obedience should so require, to employ all the remainder of my life in actions which have no charm for me, and for which I may have a great repugnance.

We may imagine with what intense fervour an act inspired by such high ideals was accomplished. God was to accept this holocaust *in odorem suavitatis.*...

6 ASCENSIONES CORDIS
(1891-99)

The total self-oblation made by Dom Marmion in solemn profession was to be manifested by a more and more absolute obedience to those who, for him, represented God.

Dom Placide Wolter, elected Archabbot of Beuron in 1890, had been replaced at the head of the Abbey of Maredsous by Dom Hildebrand de Hemptinne. Born in Ghent of a family in which the love of Roman traditions was particularly cherished, Félix de Hemptinne in his early youth – he was scarcely sixteen – was enrolled in the service of Pius IX in the pontifical army. His health obliging him to give up his military career, he exchanged the *zouave's* uniform for the monastic habit, and made profession at the Abbey of Beuron.[1] He was later appointed Prior of Erdington Abbey. The monks of Maredsous recognising his virtue and talents elected him as their second abbot.

Noble minded and great hearted, a born organiser, Dom Hildebrand was especially distinguished by his spirit of faith and his aptitudes for governing; having an inherent need of high ideals and wide horizons, and being at the same time of a reflective and resolute turn of mind, he was firm of will and tenacious of purpose, authoritative and prudent. In 1893, Leo XIII, with the aim of uniting the different Benedictine congregations into one confederation, chose him as primate – the first in date – of the Order of St Benedict, while leaving to him his Abbey of Maredsous.[2]

1 See p. 33, note 2.
2 Dom Hildebrand received the abbatial blessing at Montecassino. On his return, he stopped in Rome and was received in audience by Leo XIII, who at once discerned in him a man of superior capacity; therefore when the Sovereign Pontiff wanted to establish the Benedictine confederation of all the monasteries, he chose Dom Hildebrand de Hemptinne to preside over it. Dom Hildebrand was not only a man well fitted to govern, he was talented in art and architecture: the abbey of the Benedictine nuns of Maredret is a notable example of his work, and the international *Collegio Sant'Anselmo* in Rome, his

It was under his guidance that Dom Marmion was henceforth to live. In Dom Hildebrand, as in Dom Placide, faith showed him the lieutenant – *locum tenens* – of Christ, and above all the *Father* of the monastic family. We have had the good fortune to discover a letter written by Dom Marmion at this period, the first so far that we have of his as a monk. It is dated Maredsous, 8 January 1891,[1] and is addressed to his abbot, then at Montecassino. Dom Marmion recalls how Dom Hildebrand had told them that the abbot on the day of his election receives as a special grace from above a very tender and very fatherly love for his sons, a grace which is, as it were, a reflection of the divine Fatherhood. And he goes on to say that though he feels himself to be unworthy to be numbered among Dom Hildebrand's sons, he wishes to act towards him as he tries to do towards his Heavenly Father, and to love him with that sincere affection of which St Benedict speaks.

The divine light which had so often shown Dom Marmion the good of the monk in obedience was henceforth to bear much fruit. Not only would he be at the disposal of his new abbot, but he would leave everything to his decision.

From that day forth, his activity was to be exerted in many and various directions, but obedience and zeal for souls were to ensure its unity, whilst the very diversity of its nature contributed towards that total detachment which gives full inward liberty and prepares the heart to rise to heavenly things.

In the offices first of all confided to him Dom Columba met with failure. Necessities of organisation in a college so recently founded obliged his superiors to entrust him with the function of prefect during the school year 1891–92. But the fact of his being a foreigner, his accent, his fun-loving character, the blunders to which

masterpiece, is one of the finest monuments in the Eternal City. A *Life* of Dom Hildebrand has recently appeared.

[1] Dom Columba dated it 1890, but this is evidently an error such as is often made at the beginning of a new year.

his imperfect knowledge of French inevitably led, were not conducive to the maintaining of discipline among mischievous and headstrong boys. Here he was not to be a success.

He stayed in the college as professor of English, a charge which he kept until 1897.

He found himself especially in his element in teaching philosophy and theology. At first this consisted in giving a few courses of philosophy to the young Desclées, to coach them for their university degrees.[1] His pupils, struck with the clearness and the ease with which he delivered his lectures, were loud in their tutor's praise. It followed from this that the regular course given to the young monks at the abbey was confided to him, and soon, owing to his extreme natural facility for speculative studies, he had in addition to give lectures in theology.[2]

Later on, when at Louvain, he was definitely to occupy the chair of theology. In the next chapter we shall have occasion to speak of the original qualities which distinguished him as professor. For the moment we extract a page from his private notes, the only one of the kind, written in 1891, which already shows how he drew spiritual profit from his doctrinal teaching.

> For the last few months I have been teaching the treatise *De Deo*. I have received many lights on the nature of God. Meditating on the words *Ego sum qui sum*, 'I am who am,' I saw that our duties towards God are all resumed in adoration. Faith is but the adoration of God considered as supreme Truth; hope as supreme Fidelity and Power; charity as infinite Goodness; submission as incommensurable Majesty; and as in God all these (perfections) are but one Being – God,

---

[1] From 1890 Dom Marmion went every month from Maredsous to the "Pedagogy" at Louvain to prepare the students for the examinations.

[2] "I have today begun the course of philosophy, and this evening I shall begin that of theology; but I do not know if, with my classes at the college and other occupations, it will be possible for me to continue these courses in a satisfactory manner. Nevertheless I will try." Letter of 9 January 1891 to Abbot Hildebrand.

supreme adoration contains all these acts *in radice,*[1] or implicitly. I find absolute submission to God's Will a sovereign remedy in every trouble, and when I consider that in reality God's Will is God Himself, I see that this submission is but the supreme adoration due to God, due to Him in whatever manner He may manifest Himself.

During the eight months that elapsed before he left for Louvain he was given, in addition to his charge as professor, that of second master of ceremonies. He excelled in this important office: with the help of a memory which served him to perfection, he lived the ceremonies with true liberty of spirit; faith showed him the virtue which went out from the symbolism of the liturgical rites and his devotion was happily fed thereby.

Finally, a charge which brought him abundant merit was that of zelator of novices which he filled for four years (1895–99). The right hand of the Father Master from whom he has often to take his lead and whose action he must always second, the zelator is entrusted with all that concerns the exterior training and material needs of the future monks. Living with them in the novitiate, he shares their daily life in many points, notably as to their walks and recreations. Obedience thus caused Dom Columba to go back into this novitiate where he had suffered so much and which he had left several years before. He again found Dom Benoît there and once more lived side by side with him. Certainly he was no longer personally under the Father Master's spiritual direction, but his position as zelator did not release him to the same extent from the mortifying experiences resulting from Dom Benoît's austere teaching and stern guidance. It more than once happened that the latter with fine impartiality meted out the same treatment to both zelator and novices.

This charge gave Dom Columba the opportunity of exerting, often unawares to himself, a very happy influence. His filial submission to the Father Master, whose authority he always upheld with perfect loyalty, set a most effectual example to everyone concerned.

[1] In germ.

But above all, in this field of asceticism, his genial, open countenance – in direct contrast with the frigidity of Dom Benoît's emaciated face – and his infectious gaiety relieved the tension and brought into the atmosphere that life and warmth essential to all growth and development.[1]

As we see, the confidence his superiors had in him led them to entrust him with many charges; with the exception of that of prefect, the varied resources of his rich nature, as adaptable as it was zealous, made him equal to them all.

It was not long before his zeal reached out beyond the cloister walls. How his pastoral ministry as a monk first began is worth recalling. It was shortly before his solemn profession and whilst Dom Placide was abbot. The priest of a neighbouring parish[2] being unexpectedly disappointed of the preacher on whom he had been relying came to ask help at the monastery. As it happened to be the eve of a great feast, all the available monks were already in request.

"I am exceedingly sorry," said the abbot, "I have no one likely to be of any use to you. There certainly is a young foreigner, but I do not quite know what may be expected of him; he only speaks French imperfectly, and I fear he would lay you open to disappointment."

"Let me have him all the same, at any rate it will be a change for my parishioners."

"Take him if you will have it so, but at your own risk."

---

[1] Abbot de Hemptinne perfectly well knew the rigid character of the Father Master and the chilly impression he had on the novices; he purposely encouraged the gaiety and the amusing remarks of the Irish zelator which sometimes proved so disconcerting. Still better, Dom Benoît had received instructions to let this gaiety have free course at recreation, and with his spirit of obedience he fully submitted to this ruling. At the end of a letter without precise date, but in 1896 or 1897, Dom Columba wrote to Abbot Primate Hildebrand, then at Rome: "I have nothing to add on the subject of the novices. The Father Master and I live in closest union, and a very remarkable spirit of charity and holy joy reigns in the novitiate."

[2] In the village of Graux.

The priest took Dom Columba with him. Three days later he brought him back himself:

"I never had such a preacher in my parish," he declared, "nor one who so moved the people."

The *curé* told others, as he had told the abbot, of the great good produced amongst his flock by the warm conviction and picturesque originality of Dom Columba's sermon, and they in their turn wanted the "Irish Father" to preach for them.

Such was the beginning of a ministry which, under the aegis of obedience, rapidly became a very active one, where the young monk's enthusiastic fervour found wide outlet.

We need not follow Dom Columba throughout this ministry. It is enough to say that it was very varied, and not confined to preaching in parish churches; very different classes of hearers hung on his words; at Tamines it was the workman's circle; at Braine-le-Comte, the college students; at Bouvignes, the *Association des dames chrétiennes*. The little city of Dinant was the special theatre of his zeal. The great good he did there is still remembered. Each time he arrived in the city the confessional placed at his disposal by the dean of the parish[1] was literally besieged. Obedience required Dom Columba to leave for the monastery every evening by the last train, and more than one penitent, who would confide in none other, finished his confession whilst accompanying him to the station, or in a corner of the lost-property office.

It was also at Dinant that his work in relation to priests first began. Every month the clergy of that town and the environments met together at *Collège Bellevue* for a day's retreat; this was the prelude to a form of pastoral zeal which was ever afterwards particularly dear to Dom Marmion.

God's blessing visibly rewarded this zeal. The reason was that Dom Columba's outlook was altogether supernaturalised by faith and piety. His celebration of the Christmas Mass and office in a

---

1 The archpriest, Houba, a most upright man, of rare energy and burning with boundless zeal. "I am terrible," he would say to his parishioners, "but I love you terribly."

parish[1] nearby the abbey has not yet been forgotten. His outward beating expressed such devotion that the people told one another: "He could scarcely have greater devotion if he saw the little Jesus in person in the crib." It is good to treasure this spontaneous testimony of simple folk; it exactly describes the deep impression he produced in the exercise of his ministry; the vivacity of his faith always made the great realities as it were visible.

The secret of the blessings with which God crowned his zeal was that he never acted except by obedience. Every work of his was marked by that totally supernatural obedience which safeguarded the unity and soundness of his inner life in the midst of much outward and apparently widely dispersed activity.

Of this inner life we have only a few glimpses. Scarcely twenty pages are to be found in his private *Notes* bearing on the eight years of this period. Many of these notes are in reference to the annual retreats; it will serve a useful purpose to quote some of them, showing, as they do, how intent the monk was on the work of his spiritual perfection and how generously and perseveringly he laboured to this end.

The first retreat he records was in May 1891. Given during the octave of Pentecost, it had for theme the comparison of the religious life with the life led by the first Christians after the coming of the Holy Spirit. With great originality of thought the preacher brought out how the monastic life is linked to the life led by the faithful in the primitive Church, the tradition of which is handed down in the Acts of the Apostles as an eternal example to Christians of all times.

Of these remarkable conferences,[2] Dom Columba especially

---

[1] In the village of Flavion.
[2] They were preached by Dom Germain Morin, monk of the Abbey of Maredsous, and were afterwards published under the title, *The Ideal of the Monastic Life found in the Apostolic Age*. This volume bas been rightly named a "little masterpiece of spirituality."

notes those which best corresponded with his own aspirations: compunction, obedience, and simplicity.

Directly after the first instruction, on compunction, he takes this resolution: "While living in a holy joy and even gaiety, to correct and banish all that is too trivial and dissipating as being the sworn enemy of compunction."

It is especially the conference on obedience that impresses him. "*Beautiful* conference on obedience. The vital principle and starting-point of the monastic life. It is obedience which gives to our life that unity which we lost by Original Sin."

He immediately takes the resolution: "To try to do all my actions from *obedience;* let this be their motive power: this is the *forma substantialis*[1] of a monk's actions, giving unity to everything and elevating all things."

After the address on simplicity, he writes: "A beautiful conference on simplicity: *Si oculus tuus, etc.*[2] This *oculus* is the intention which makes the whole body lightsome. We must be simple with our neighbour, especially by avoiding suspicions. Let us not be surprised by his miseries and faults, *but let us consider him not as he is but as we hope to have him during all eternity in heaven."*

As conclusion to the retreat he comes back again to obedience:

> To endeavour to increase in *faith* in my obedience. 'My just man liveth by faith.' The more I live by faith the more abundant graces will I receive. Our abbot will be to us Jesus Christ in proportion to the faith with which we believe *eum vices Christi in monasterio agere.*[3] How beautiful it would be could we have Jesus Christ amongst us as the apostles had to address in our doubts, etc., and yet if we have but faith, our abbot is all this to us. Besides we have the merit of faith: 'He

---

1 Substantial form, that is to say, the principle which gives cohesion and value to our actions.
2 "The light of the body is the eye. If thy eye be single thy whole body shall be lightsome" (Matt. 6:22).
3 "That in the monastery the abbot holds the place of Christ." *Rule of St Benedict*, ch. 2.

that heareth you, heareth me.' Peter sank even in the presence of Jesus because his faith wavered; our abbot never fails to sustain us except when our faith ceases to behold Jesus Christ in him. I understand now the immense treasure contained in [the orders of] our abbot, *obedientiae bonum*,[1] and see also the necessity of absolute simplicity in my relations with him, as though dealing with Jesus Christ.

From one retreat to another these private pages are almost silent. Dom Columba's life of activity was becoming full to overflowing and no longer left him the leisure necessary to note down the lights from above and the experiences through which his soul was passing.

We will, however, here give the complete text of a letter to one of his sisters, dated about this period (17 October 1891). It is one of the earliest letters that we have of his, and so much the more precious that it has escaped the lamentable destruction of a copious collection of several hundred letters, extending from the time he entered the monastery until his death.

In these lines coming from a young priest of thirty who counted only a few years of religious life, we already notice that knowledge of the things of God, that sureness, that maturity of judgment, as well as that discretion which was to characterise all his direction.

> It is a real pleasure to aid anyone to love our dearest Lord, and nothing conduces more to this than peace of soul. As regards your questions, your being a professed religious need not in any way hinder you from making the act of offering for poor sinners, which is very agreeable to our Lord. When a religious makes such an act, the condition is always understood 'as far as my obligations as a religious permit.' So that, in practice, you make this act once for all and renew it from time to time, and then go on just offering your actions for the intentions prescribed by obedience and for your own wants,

---

[1] "The good of obedience." *Rule of St Benedict*, ch. 71.

etc. ... just as others do, who have not made this act and our Blessed Lord will arrange the details, that is He will reserve in your actions what obedience and your obligations towards yourself and others require and apply the rest to sinners.

In one word, act in this matter without *any anxiety,* make the act with your whole heart and then just go on as before.

As regards your intentions in prayer, there are many souls who find that great precision and nicety in specifying various intentions in prayer interferes with the *unity* of their prayer and is a cause of anxiety and distraction. For such souls the best thing is to specify these intentions only from time to time, for example, *once* in the morning and then a *simple glance* of the soul is sufficient to recall them at the beginning of prayer. However, in all this, my dear sister, follow the *attraction of the Holy Spirit* with great peace, as all anxiety is the mortal enemy of that disposition which the Holy Spirit wishes to find in that soul which He calls to a great union with Him. If there is anything you don't take in in what I say write when you like, and I will answer *when I find time.*

Your 3rd question is regarding the sister with whom you like to be at recreation. Well my dear sister, your attraction to speak of God and to be with those who are fervent, and to go often to choir is an excellent sign of the state of your soul and shows that the spirit of God is guiding you and calling you to an intimate union with Himself, however I don't like the idea of your searching out special sisters to be near during recreation, even though the motive be most excellent, unless it be only from time to time. In a community charity is *so delicate,* that any preference shown to others is sure to wound it, and then the eye of love is so quick that with the utmost precautions your secret will get out in the end, and you will have wounded our Lord in the apple of His eye by saddening the heart of some sister, who thinks herself less loved and esteemed by you than others, and this would be specially the case with less perfect sisters.

I don't mean to say that you may not love in Jesus Christ some sister more than others, or find more pleasure in the company of those who are edifying and kindred spirits from time to time, but it is certainly more perfect, more pleasing to out dear Lord to associate yourself freely with those whom you find yourself with, and this practice will have a great power of detaching your heart from all merely human consolations and fixing it in the Sacred Heart.

However in all this there must be nothing strained or violent, no closing yourself up in yourself, but every day as you advance in love of Jesus Christ and in union with Him your heart must expand more and more in love towards all your sisters. I would like you to read this portion of my letter to Reverend Mother, if you like, as what I have said depends in a great measure on the manner in which recreation is taken in the community.

Understand me well. What I have said does not mean that it would be against perfection to be united by a *spiritual* affection, or even to enter into a league of pious practices and prayers with sisters who had aspiration and desires similar to yours – St John Berchmans had entered into such a league – but it would be contrary to perfection to do anything which would lead any of your sisters to suspect that they occupied a lower place in your affections and esteem than others.

As regards your desire and attraction towards a more intimate union with God, for a spirit of prayer, I feel, from the various points you indicated, that it is the Holy Spirit who has inspired the desire, and that if you are faithful and patient, He will in His own good time work in your soul what is for His greater glory and your perfection. Theologians teach us that when God inspires us with an ardent desire of some gift, such as that of a spirit of prayer and that we often feel, when praying for it a great peace and confidence, it is a certain sign that He means to accord it. Your habit of frequently turning to God during work, and of purifying your intentions are excellent aids towards the formation of this habit, in so far as it depends on us (for never forget that a spirit of prayer is a *gift* of God). You must be very careful to possess your soul in peace, as the evil one will probably make great efforts to prevent your acquiring this spirit of prayer. As a general rule, you ought to regard as coming from the enemy any thought which agitates you, throws you into perplexity, which diminishes your confidence and narrows up your heart. The best thing in such cases, is just to put the matter which perplexes you out of your mind, saying, 'when I have the opportunity I shall ask the solution of this difficulty from some priest,' then go on in peace as you were before.

And after having dwelt on this special advice, he rises to the principle of all good and concentrates his correspondent's mind on Jesus Christ, the only Way that leads to the Father and the only Source of perfection: the ruling thought which becomes more and more dear to him:

Finally, my dear sister, never forget that Jesus Christ is *everything* and we are agreeable to the Father just in proportion as we are united to Him. When celebrating Holy Mass lately I was greatly struck while reading the *Preface,* with the thought, that the seraphim and cherubim and angels and archangels, in all their perfection burning with love as they are, can praise the Divine Majesty only through Jesus Christ (*per quem majestatem tuam laudant angeli,* etc). He is the golden bond of union between all creation and the adorable Trinity; as our dear St Gertrude[1] says, He is the harp through the

---

[1] This thought is very familiar to St Gertrude. We cannot refrain from quoting this beautiful prayer: "For all Thy gifts to me, my God, and all that memory can recall, in thanks to Thee I give Thee what is Thy own, namely, Thy Divine Heart; to the sweet music of which, resounding through the power of the Holy Spirit, the Paraclete, I sing to Thee, Lord God, adorable Father, praises and thanks on behalf of every creature, of those in heaven, of those on earth and in the depths, of those that are now, or once were, or shall ever be." From *Prayers of St Gertrude and St Mechtildis,* translated by Fr John Gray (Sheed *&* Ward).

cords of which all praise must resound in order to be an agreeable harmony to the adorable Trinity. This is why the *Canon* of Holy Mass ends with those mysterious words *per ipsum, et cum ipso, et in ipso* etc. 'through Him, and with Him, and in Him is *all* honour and glory to Thee Eternal Father,' etc.

Therefore my dear sister, in every action try to unite yourself intimately with Jesus, who is ever in your heart, with His dispositions, His designs on you and on others, etc. And you will thus raise your actions to a value they would not otherwise have. I have the habit of uniting myself thus by repeating very frequently in the depths of my heart 'My Jesus mercy.' However in all this follow the attraction of the Holy Spirit.

Pray for me, as I have many miseries of soul and body. Yours in Jesus Christ.

In August 1892, Dom Columba again took up his pen on the occasion of the retreat given by Fr Étienne Leplat, of the Discalced Carmelites of Brussels, who seemed to him to be "very holy and united with God." In writing these words, Dom Marmion was not mistaken. This religious was indeed a saint; his words full of warmth and apostolic unction bore much fruit. We can understand from Dom Columba's notes the impression they made on him.

The following points struck me.
1. I saw that in order to teach with unction and touch our hearers, we must be in intimate union with Jesus Christ. He is the 'Author and Finisher of our faith' and it is in proportion as He speaks and acts in and with us that we produce fruits of salvation.
2. I saw also very plainly that the entire absence of reproach, bitterness and personalities gives a sweetness and grace to a retreat which speaks to each heart and prevents our thoughts from resting on our brethren. The man who

preaches 'Jesus Christ and Him crucified' is always understood and his words bear power and grace.

3. What struck me most in the meditations were the ones on the perfection of our ordinary actions, on the Blessed Virgin and on charity.

In the meditation on the Blessed Virgin Mary, he dwelt especially on her quality of mother. He told us that St Gertrude had the habit of asking our Blessed Lord to address to Mary in her behalf the words: *Mulier, ecce filius tuus.*

In the meditation on Charity he made a beautiful commentary of Ps. 132: *Ecce quam bonum....* In a monastic family the abbot is the *head* on which God pours all the benedictions for the family. This perfume poured on the head descends to the uttermost limits of the sacred garment, or like the dew poured on the summit of the mount descends to the deepest valleys and most hidden nooks. But as a garment not united with the head on which the perfume is poured receives none of it, or a valley separated by some chasm from the summit receives none of its dew, so all the members of a community must be intimately united with the head, and with each other, in order that the benedictions of heaven be poured out on it. But when brethren are united, oh, how sweet it is: *Illic mandavit Dominus benedictionem:*[1] *i.e.* in such a family the Lord causes His benedictions to flow, and fills every member with spiritual life.

Dom Columba was not the only one to be touched by these words of a saint. The impression left by Fr Étienne on all his hearers was so strong that the superiors wanted to have him again to preach the retreat the following year. The eminent religious yielded to these friendly entreaties, and his words, filled with the spirit of God, moved minds and hearts alike. Dom Columba notes this:

> Very beautiful retreat. The chief fruit was a great desire to make Jesus my only love. I remark more and more in this

1 Ps. 132.

Father a wonderful goodness and largeness in his dealings with God and souls, and I see that this is the true spirit of Jesus.

His meditation on the Blessed Virgin was very beautiful and filled my heart with confidence and desire to become a true child of Mary. My three resolutions were:

1. To try to perform all my ordinary actions with all the perfection I can for God's love alone.
2. To try to become the servant of all (*servus servorum Dei*).
3. To be perfectly obedient.

To make Jesus my only love: this fruit of the retreat was to ripen. The thought of Jesus took greater and greater hold of him; it was little by little to take full possession of the monk's soul so generously given up to the Divine Action. At this period of his monastic life, the lights that visited him were more and more directed towards the thought that Jesus is the Alpha and Omega of all spiritual life. Among the rare pages in his notes of this period, other than those that deal with his retreat resolutions, figure the following. We shall find in them some of the essential ideas of Dom Marmion's ascetical doctrine to which he was most often to return:

Between August 1892 and September 1893 – I have been greatly struck by the words of our Lord to St Philip: 'Philip, he that seeth Me, seeth the Father also.' Jesus Christ is the *revelation of God* to man. 'No man hath seen God at any time: the only-begotten Son who is in the bosom of the Father, He hath declared Him.' When we try to think of God in His divinity, we are often dazzled by His brightness, and at times these thoughts can be a temptation and a trouble to us. God is so far above us, in a sphere so utterly beyond our ken, that it is impossible for us to understand His dealings with His creatures. We must then gaze on Jesus. He is *God revealed* to us; by humble faith in Him, we have the solution to all difficulties. When we would penetrate into the sanctuaries of God's secrets, He says to us, this is my beloved Son, *hear ye* Him. This is the solution of all. Jesus stretching out His little arms to us in the crib *is God*. Jesus eating with publicans and sinners – *is God*, Jesus weeping over Lazarus – *is God*. Jesus giving us His body and blood – *is God*. If we want to know what God is, let us look on Jesus. *He is God*. As we gaze on Jesus we have no difficulty in understanding that God is love.

If God is love, this love will be poured out in abundant blessings on His creatures and there is no grace we may not hope for and expect, above all when the soul rests on the words of the Son in whom He is well pleased:

After September 1893 – J E S U S. I see more and more that Jesus is *all* for us, and that his riches are unspeakable (*inénarrables*). He is true God and true Man. As God, He is the Word. 'The brightness of [the Father's] glory, and the figure of His substance,' containing in Himself the whole *substance* of the Father and of the Most Blessed Trinity. He dwells within us 'by faith' and when we pray or act thus united with Jesus our prayer becomes that canticle which the Word is ever singing to His Father, and in which the hymn of creation is offered to God.

He has said, 'If you abide in Me, and My words abide in you, you shall ask whatever you will, and it shall be done unto you.' I like then in the light of this promise to put before my eyes some word of our Lord and strong in faith to make my petition. This kind of prayer I find easy and very efficacious. For example this word of Jesus, 'Ask, and it shall be given you: seek, and you shall find: knock and it shall be opened to you. For everyone that asketh, receiveth: and he that seeketh, findeth: and to him that knocketh, it shall be opened.' To cast myself down in spirit before Jesus, and hearing those words proceeding from the mouth of the *Verb* I adore the infinite Truth *fortis in fide*, by His grace.

The secret to obtain God's gifts is "to abide in Jesus," for in Him we form but one mystical body of which He is the Head: Dom

Marmion was later to develop this doctrine in all its magnificence; for the moment, he lives by it. He notes, at the same date, this beautiful page of the Bl. Jean-Gabriel Perboyre which is so thoroughly in accord with his own inmost thoughts:

> If our sins render us unworthy of being heard, the holiness of Jesus and the fervour with which He prays for us, makes His Father forget our unworthiness, and He only considers that One whom He has made to be our Advocate. Besides, by our baptism, we have become the members of Jesus Christ; in consequence of this union, our needs are in some sort the needs of Jesus Christ Himself; we cannot ask anything that refers to our salvation or the perfection of our soul that we do not also ask it for Jesus Christ Himself, for the honour and the glory of the members is the honour and glory of the body.[1]

As lights the more abound, the more readily Brother Columba perceives in his soul any obstacles to union with God. And with that humility which bears the stamp of sincerity, he does not spare himself nor make little of his imperfections. It is true that those who, like himself, only see their soul in a supernatural light, judge themselves with severity; we must remember this in reading these lines set down with all simplicity at the end of a retreat of September 1894.

> 1. The first and it seems to me the principal fault [which prevents my union with God] is a want of perfection in the performance of my ordinary duties, both as regards intention and execution. I aim more at my own satisfaction than the accomplishment of duty, and in the manner of accomplishing them am the slave of the feeling of the moment.
> 2. The second is excessive sensitiveness, craving for

---

[1] Between September 1893 and September 1894. This thought must have particularly struck him, for he returns to it ten years later, in a letter of 22 April 1906. He likewise at that time recommends the reading of the life of the Bl. Perboyre.

approbation, and a too human fear of displeasing my superiors. A deliberate indulgence in such reflections and imaginations.

3. A want of fidelity to my resolutions as regards distribution of time, following whims rather than sense of duty.

We must see the saints as they really are; they are not born saints, they become so; that is their greatness. And "it is an encouragement for us, so ready to suffer defeat, so slow in rising up again, to realise that the saints, they too, have known our fluctuations."[1] But, like the saints, Dom Marmion was little by little, by his daily generosity, to attain that total detachment where he would no longer see anything but God alone and would be possessed by one love alone – the love for Christ and souls.

God moreover was Himself working during all this period at purifying him. Must not the branch of the vine be pruned that it may bring forth more fruit?

The state of Dom Columba's health left much to be desired: "Pray for me," he wrote on 5 December 1894; "I am better but I cannot yet follow the common life, which in my weakness is an occasion of slackness."

He suffered especially by long insomnia which exhausted him. He notes on this subject a thought of Fr Xavier de Ravignan: "One day when he was asked if he was wearied by his sleepless nights, he replied: 'Never do I feel weariness; the time does not even appear long; I pray; I think how good our Lord is, that it is well in heaven, and that consoles me for being bad and ill on earth.'"

This state continued for a long time; to bodily fatigue was added spiritual trials, but for these, too, his generous soul knew likewise how to draw profit. Dom Columba learns notably at this time by his own experience how necessary is the life of pure faith, and this experience, as we shall presently see, was to be fruitful:

17 February 1895 (Octave of St Scholastica) – I had been ill for several months; besides some physical suffering, *e.g.* sleeplessness

---

1 *La mère Jeanne Deleloë*, Preface.

etc., I was greatly troubled in mind, and seemed at times quite abandoned by God. On the feast of St Scholastica, anniversary of my profession, the clouds passed away, and I understood that my trials and temptations had done much good to my soul, and especially I learned what it is to serve God through *pure faith,* and that those who have not passed through such trials cannot know what it is to believe and hope in God through faith alone.

During meditation the words: *Spiritus est qui vivificat, caro autem non prodest quidquam,*[1] made me clearly see that the acts which proceed from a motive of faith are alone supernaturally pleasing to God, and that sensible devotion (*caro*), although it may aid us to produce these acts more easily, is of itself useless; and acts whose principle alone is sensible devotion are of no supernatural value in God's eyes.

Since the 10th (February) I enjoy a quiet union with Jesus through faith, though often without any *sensible* pleasure. I find little difficulty in remaining with Jesus nearly all day, and this in no way interferes with my duties, but rather aids.

The devil often tries to hinder my devotion and union with God by suggesting theological subtleties and scruples. I recognise the presence of Satan by the trouble and darkness of my spirit. I find it a great help to invoke my guardian angel often with great faith and to despise these tricks.

Providence had been holding in store for him the joy of a visit to his own country at this period. The occasion was the celebration, in June 1895, of the centenary of Maynooth. One of the greater if not the greatest of the seminaries in Christendom, Maynooth is in some respects the ecclesiastical centre of all Ireland.[2] The cele-

1 "It is the spirit that quickeneth: the flesh profiteth nothing" (John 6: 64).
2 Ireland numbers twenty-eight dioceses for a population of nearly four million Catholics scattered all over the world. Some of the dioceses have no seminary of their own; the Irish bishops therefore founded a central seminary at Maynooth, a short distance from Dublin. It was founded in 1795, and a number of French priests, driven out of their own country by the Revolution, contrib-

bration of its centenary was moreover an almost national festival, for the Irish Catholic makes scarcely any distinction between his church and his nation.

The Order of St Benedict and the Abbey of Maredsous had been asked to send representatives to Maynooth for the centenary. "Pray for me," wrote Dom Marmion on 5 April 1895, to one of his spiritual daughters; "there is a question of my going on a visit to my country; ask our Lord to arrange all things for His glory, for I only want it in so far as it pleases Him."

Reading between these lines, it is to be seen that this "visit to my country" is no ordinary event for Dom Columba. This is because he was particularly attached to his native land. Some years later when his superior wished him to be naturalised as a Belgian, he declared it was one of the greatest sacrifices that obedience had yet required of him.

Every son of Erin has indeed the love of his country deeply rooted in his heart: a virtue which becomes a source of suffering in the case of those obliged to emigrate. "I have spent years in America and made a fortune there," said an ex-emigrant on returning to his own country, "but I have never *lived* anywhere except in Ireland."[1]

Travel over the island, and everywhere both in towns and country, when you meet an Irishman, to whatever social rank he belongs, as soon as he sees you are a "continental" he is sure to greet you with this question, "How do you like Ireland?"

How can anyone help loving this fascinating country with its

---

uted to implant sound instruction and good discipline there. These two factors were further accentuated as time went on and Maynooth prospered beyond all expectations. This seminary counts on an average six hundred young men intended for holy orders; the greater number serve in Ireland, the others go to England, Australia, and the United States. Maynooth sees about eighty priests ordained every year; seventy out of every hundred of the Irish secular clergy come from this seminary. These celebrations were the occasion of an extraordinary gathering of the Irish clergy; more than eleven hundred priests took part in it, and the cardinal archbishops of Armagh and Westminster – Michael Cardinal Logue and Herbert Cardinal Vaughan – presided over it surrounded by forty of their colleagues in the episcopate.

1 Quoted by Paul-Dubois.

manifold beauties a hundred times described? It was eight years since Dom Columba had last seen it. True he had kept in touch with his own kith and kin by means of letters; circumstances had often carried his thoughts in the direction of the beloved isle. But now he was about to look upon it again. In June, he and a confrère reached England and embarked at Bristol.

While the boat was bearing him to Cork where he was to land, all his childhood's memories rushed back upon him. He recalled the scenes that had met his gaze as a boy and young man: the strange Giant's Causeway, the shores of Wicklow the garden of Ireland, on which his eyes had so often rested in his excursions with his sister Rosie; in imagination he once more followed the course of the Blackwater, the most beautiful of the rivers of Hibernia, in its setting of woods and meadows and country seats reflected in its waters, earning for it the name of the Rhine of the Emerald Isle. He saw again Killarney and its lakes, Glengariff with its fragrant forests: marvellous landscapes which stand out like radiant and verdant oases in this western Ireland so poignant in the poverty of its inhabitants, the desolation of its plains strewn with grey, gaunt rocks, its bogs covered with heath and whin, or rent by pools of black stagnant water like great gaping wounds – bogs which often extend till lost to view in low-lying tracts, dreary and monotonous. Further to the north and most desolate of all lies Connaught, a name well known to Dom Columba in its relation with Irish history, for during the years of persecution it was held as synonymous with hell. *Hell or Connaught!* At the heart of this region dark lakes of austere beauty are encircled by bare solitary hills from whence human and even animal life appear to be banished. On the coast, high jagged cliffs dominate the ocean; magnificent bays with numerous inhospitable islets, rough fjords, the impressive grandeur of nature wild and strong, where the waves beat against the rocks in age-long contest. And yet here again, by a caprice of nature, flourishing oases of exuberant vegetation are to be seen: thick groves of giant rhododendrons, holly trees of luxuriant foliage, high thickets of azaleas with blooms of richest colour, brakes of tall reeds and rushes, hedges of fuchsias bordering the roads, and rising above this extraordinary and almost tropical vegetation, every variety of coniferae from the Scotch pine to the majestic araucaria.

It is generally a pale light which bathes this grandeur and beauty, but on sunny days nature's most changing moods have play under an ever-restless sky, and the sunsets on the Atlantic are of a glory to be the despair of the most skilful artist. In this island nature seems to delight in every contrast.

However, another beauty transcends and envelops that of nature: an altogether spiritual beauty no less attractive and the inmost splendour of which is unimpaired by the very faults, apparent though they be, of this people: a beauty flowing from the legends of the saints, the religious festivals, the constant thought of the supernatural and of the World Beyond; in a word, the beauty of the Faith, of which Fr Columba, like the greater number of his compatriots, was particularly conscious. His devotion to his country did not consist in a merely natural attachment to his native land; much more than this, it was a conception of all that Ireland stands for in the history of Christianity and the spread of Catholicism.[1] On the same ship which carried Dom Columba to Cork were three young Irish soldiers on their way home from the Transvaal. Sitting on the bridge they were chatting together in high spirits. As soon as the coast of Hibernia was to be dimly discerned, they at once sprang up and devoured with their eyes the Emerald Isle rising from the ocean. And one of them, breaking the almost religious silence that held them, burst out: "There it is … the holy land!"

For her sons, Ireland is indeed the thrice holy land: the land of heroes sung by her bards on harps of gold; the land of monks who, from the sixth to the eighth century, were the saviours of civilisation and carried the Good News to the continent; above all, the mother-country of the martyrs who, throughout three centuries of persecution, suffered misery, nakedness, hunger, fire, prison, exile and

---

1 We are speaking of the Catholics of the south of Ireland, not the Irish of the north (Ulster), who are for the most part Protestants, and besides much less numerous.

death, to guard the Faith of their fathers. A faith loved and lived, defended and propagated: it is this ineradicable faith that explains the attachment of the Irishman to his country.

It was then not without emotion that the young monk once more set foot on the soil of his beloved Ireland.[1] From Cork to Clonakilty, at Waterford, Dublin, and Belfast, he again beheld his native land as he had known and loved it in past days. In the space of a few weeks he was to live over again his whole childhood and youth, simple and tranquil, enthusiastic and joyous. At the Convent of Mercy at Clonakilty he saw Rosie again; it is easy to imagine the joy of those hours spent with that confidante after his own heart; together they went to kneel in the little cemetery nearby the convent where their sister Flora had been laid to rest in October 1892. At Dunmore, in a convent of the same institute, he saw another of his sisters, a saintly soul who was later to die as superior at Waterford; once again he looked upon his home and relatives, although his mother was missing from the family circle, having been called to God in April 1893. In short, the celebration at Maynooth gave him the opportunity of reviving the fervour and joy of old and unchanging friendships.[2]

This visit to Ireland was, however, but a passing incident; on his return to Maredsous Dom Columba at once took up again the course of regular monastic life, for him active and absorbing, yet whatever his outward activity he did not neglect the work of his own perfection. Coming anew into touch with the land of his birth had brought back the thoughts and feelings which had marked the various stages leading towards his monastic vocation; his clear and faithful memory had enabled him to live over again those years when

[1] A graphic account of this journey was given by Dom Columba's companion in *Le messager de Saint-Benoît* (1902–04).
[2] We may add that at Maynooth, Dom Marmion again met Msgr Désiré-Joseph Mercier, at that time president of *l'Institut Léon* XIII, sent to represent *l'Université de Louvain*.

as a young priest God's call had made itself heard in his heart. In the light of those memories of eight years ago he was able to take into account how far he had advanced since then. Generous as he had been, he had not yet reached the mark; he must continue his spiritual ascent, rhythmically governed by that twofold sense of humility and confidence which we have already mentioned as characteristic of his spirituality.

During the course of the preceding years he had never lost sight of the virtue of humility. In February 1890, he begs one of his old pupils, then studying in the Irish College in Rome, to send him an opuscule on humility published by Leo XIII when Archbishop of Perugia.[1] In a letter of 16 March 1891, he advises an English convert who was thinking of the religious life to read *The Groundwork of the Christian Virtues* by Bishop William Ullathorne. "Read it; it is a fine treatise, and very deep, on the virtues, especially on humility."[2]

But not satisfied with studying the subject of this very necessary virtue, Dom Marmion was resolved on steeping his life in it. A letter written to an Irish nun soon after he himself had entered the cloister is interesting from this point of view: it discloses one of his most usual ascetical practices.

> *11 September 1895* – Your letter was a joy for me, for I see that despite your unworthiness God is guiding you, and is full of mercy and love in your regard. Your great object ought to be, to become very humble, this is the sure road to God's love, for He is so powerful that He can change even our corruption into the pure gold of His love if He finds no obstacle, and the great obstacle is pride. Believe me my dear child, if you are sincerely humble God will do the rest. To become humble a practice I have may aid you. It is to make three stations every day.
>
> First station. Consider what you *were*. If you have once

---

[1] In reality it is only the translation of a work by the celebrated *Feuillant Sans de Sainte-Catherine*.

[2] This great work is certainly remarkable; it contains particularly searching analyses, and has become almost a classic.

sinned mortally in your life you have merited to be cursed for all eternity by Him who is infinite Truth and infinite Goodness. And that curse would have brought with it, separation forever from God, eternal hatred for God and for all that is just and beautiful; and to be trampled for all eternity beneath the feet of the demons. And this punishment would have been just, and have been pronounced by Him who is Goodness itself. Oh my dear child, we have perhaps merited all this, and if we be not there now it is an effect of God's infinite mercy and of the sufferings of Jesus Christ. Can any thing be bad enough for us, can any one do us injury in despising us?

Second Station, what *we are*. It is *of faith* that we are incapable of a good thought without God. 'Without me you can do *nothing*' that is we cannot make one step towards God without Him. Then our daily infidelities, our sins, our ingratitude, our best actions are very miserable indeed.

Third Station, what we may *become*. If God takes away His hand from us, we are perfectly capable of becoming what we were before and worse. God sees this, He knows what depths of treachery we are capable of. How can we be proud?

Certainly no one could show more forcibly than he does here the nothingness of the creature and of poor human misery, but faithful to his habitual mode of thought, Dom Marmion at once adds the counterpoise:

But after these stations we must never forget another, and it is this. We are *infinitely* rich in Jesus Christ and God's mercies are to our miseries what the ocean is to a drop of water. We never glorify God more than when despite the sight of our sins and unworthiness we are so filled with confidence in His mercy and in the infinite merits of Jesus Christ that we throw ourselves on His bosom full of confidence and love, *sure* that He cannot repel us: 'a humble and contrite heart, oh God, Thou wilt not despise.'

In a note dated a little later (Second Sunday in Lent, 1896) he reveals the source of this confidence. God sees us in His Son Jesus. The history of Esau and Jacob is read in the canonical office for this day. It may be remembered that this was the first office that he recited as a priest; he was strongly impressed by it, and each time that the liturgical cycle brought round the reading of this episode he seems to have received new lights on the subject. The following lines bring home to us, to say it in passing, how Dom Marmion used to apply an incident in the Old Testament to the religious life and make all converge to Christ:[1]

> On the second Sunday in Lent, I understood how all the promises made to Jesus Christ as the Only-begotten Son of God are also made to His sons by adoption.
>
> The more one is united to Jesus Christ by faith and love, the more one is a child of God: as many as received Him He gave them power to be made the sons of God: this receiving of Jesus has several degrees – the more God's promises are fulfilled in us.
>
> When we go before the Heavenly Father in the name of Jesus Christ, and firm in our faith in Him, the Father says: *Vox quidem est vox Jacob, manus autem sunt manus Esau.*[2] That is to say we are so 'clad in Jesus Christ that the Father sees only His merits' *'manus'*, and ravished by the sweet odour of His virtues, *flagrantiam vestimentorum ejus,* He forgets our unworthiness: *Ecce odor filii mei sicut agri pleni cui benedixit Dominus,*[3] and He pours His blessings upon us, not earthly blessings like those which the Patriarch Isaac called down upon Jacob, but heavenly blessings.

---

1 He develops the same thought in *Christ the Life of the Soul,* ch. "Christ the Only Model of all Perfection," end of § 3.
2 "The voice indeed is the voice of Jacob; but the hands are the hands of Esau."
3 "Behold, the smell of my son is as the smell of a plentiful field which the Lord hath blessed."

This conviction of how rich he is in Christ is so clear and vivid that he returns to it a little later in a letter to the same Irish nun.

2 July 1896 – Every day I live I see more and more that there is but one thing which is worth living for and that is God's glory. In all that He does, He seeks His own glory, (to do otherwise would be contrary to His sanctity and an imperfection) and for us what can be nobler than to unite our will with His in seeking His glory purely in all we do. In seeking His glory, He seeks out good, for God's glory as regards His creatures consists in communicating His love and grace and joy to them. And we can glorify God by our actions, for although in themselves they are very little and mean, united with those of Jesus Christ, they give an infinite glory to the Blessed Trinity. And all the infinite riches of His Sacred Heart *are ours*, more truly than anything we possess in this world, if we are united to Him by divine grace. Oh, my dear child, I would wish to engrave on your heart in letters of gold this truth, that no matter how great is our misery, *we are infinitely rich in Jesus Christ,* if we unite with Him, if we lean on Him, if we realise constantly by a firm living faith that all the value of our prayer, and of all that we do comes from His merits in us. All this is contained in two texts: 'Without Me you can do *nothing*' 'I can do *all things* in Him who strengtheneth me.' Try then to become a saint by acknowledging to yourself the full extent of your past miseries, present unworthiness, and the possibility of future infidelity, and at the same time honouring 'the Father through Jesus Christ' by reposing with a most absolute confidence on His infinite merits. 'By Him, and in Him, and with Him' as we say daily in Holy Mass, all glory is given to the Blessed Trinity. And even the praises of the angels do not ascend to God except through Jesus Christ as we sing daily in the preface of the Mass '*by whom* the angels praise Thy Majesty.' Therefore the acts of praise, of oblation, of adoration, and of acceptance of humiliations and contempt, made in union with Jesus, especially after Holy Communion, are infinitely agreeable to the Holy Trinity.

There is a postscript to this letter where we see Dom Columba give way to that irrepressible Irish sense of humour, where homely and unexpected illustrations intermingled quite naturally with high and serious thoughts. He felt besides all the more at his ease in that he was writing to a compatriot to whom he was never anything else but Uncle Joe. *"August 4th* – This letter has been interrupted for more than a month, we have been up to our ears in examinations, university etc., etc., so you must excuse."

And in reference to a recent ordination of some young priests under his direction, and which coincided with the name day of his correspondent, he continues:

> They are full of fervour and as they came here quite young they know very little of the world's wickedness except from books. What a joy for Jesus to enter into such pure hearts entirely consecrated to Him, knowing no other affection and yearning to make Him known and loved by others. We old fellows after our long years of priestly life are nearly dried up like old cabbage leaves, but their young hearts are full of unction and fervour, so I'll get them to pray for you and for dear Dunmore. From what I hear I am to have very little to do next year, these young people will take up some of our work. The old pots will be laid up on the shelf as rare specimens of antiquity, so I will bury myself in the Sacred Heart and try to make some little progress in prayer and the interior life. Pray for me, for that intention.

He is clearly exaggerating or under an illusion; his prognostications as to lack of work were not to be verified; and his life was still to remain a very active one. He was only just beginning to show all he was capable of and it was at Louvain, as we shall soon see, that his talents reached their height.

The last retreat of which there is any mention in the *Notes* before he left for Louvain, was one given in 1897 by Dom Basile de Meester, Prior of the abbey. A man of duty and regularity, Dom Basile set forth the obligation of the religious life with a methodical clearness and spirit of analysis which was further emphasised by his grave and firm manner of speech. Dom Columba must have been impressed by these instructions, for, contrary to any previous custom of his, he made a rather lengthy résumé of eleven of the conferences and noted his impressions and resolutions. These last conferences alone bear directly on his inner life, and we only give the conclusion.

> Thanks to the good God I have made a good retreat. I am in peace. With an utter sense of my great misery, I have great confidence in the goodness of God and the merits of Jesus Christ.
>
> *Lights.* 1. Obedience is the most perfect sacrifice, the most sublime holocaust that man can offer to God;
>
> 2. Our imperfections, when wilful, can lead us far astray; they are quickly and terribly punished by a God who is jealous of hearts consecrated to Him;
>
> 3. For the religious whose heart is wholly consecrated to God all merely human affection diminishes his joy, weakens his heart and may lay the door open to many miseries.
>
> *Resolutions.* To keep guard over my eyes and imagination, without however being scrupulous. I will never voluntarily seek to satisfy myself with the sight of any human beauty. This sacrifice is: (*a*) an act of homage given *in fide* to God's infinite beauty, a homage which will be richly compensated; (*b*) a good mortification; (*c*) an act of the virtue of purity, since 'we may measure the progress we are making in any virtue by the care we take to avoid every occasion of transgressing it' (St Pierre Fourier).
>
> I will practise this particularly in the exercise of my sacred ministry when I am dealing with souls, so as to remain a true

representative of Jesus Christ *infinitely* removed from all that is natural. Jesus gave as a proof of His love for His Father all that He did for the salvation of men: *Ut cognoscat mundus quia dilgo Patrem et Sicut mandatum dedit mihi Pater sic facio.*[1] And what is this commandment? To give His Blood for mankind. 'Then I will exercise my ministry only for love of God, and to co-operate with Him in His designs of love towards men: for each one of them He gave His Son, and Jesus gave the highest mark of His love: *Majorem hac dilectionem nemo habet.*[2]

Others were to benefit by the abundant graces Dom Marmion received during this retreat.

The *Notes* of this year (1895) contain the "Plan of a retreat to nuns."[3] It is a very broad outline but it is a very precious one for in it is to be found the whole pith and marrow of his masterpiece *Christ the Life of the Soul,* published more than twenty years later.

Christus mortuus est propter peccata nostra – et resurrexit propter justificationem nostram.[4]

The retreat to be divided in two parts:
 I. To die with Jesus to sin, to imperfections, to ourselves.
 II. To rise with Him to a new life.

Quod mortuus est peccato, mortuus est semel; – quod autem vivit, vivit Deo. Ita et vos existimate: vos quidem mortuos esse peccato – viventes autem Deo in Christo Jesu.[5]

Peccata nostra ipse portavit im corpore suo super lignum – ut peccatis mortui, – justitiae vivamus, – cujus livore sanati estis.[6]

---

1 "That the world may know that I love the Father, and as the Father hath given me commandment, so do I" (John 14:13).
2 John 15:13.
3 We have not been able to discover who these nuns were.
4 "Who was delivered up for our sins, and rose again for our justification" (Rom. 4:25).
5 "For in that he died to sin, he died once; but in that he liveth, he liveth unto God: So do you also reckon, that you are dead to sin, but alive unto God, in Christ Jesus our Lord" (Rom. 6:10, 11).
6 "Who his own self bore our sins in his body upon the tree: that we, being dead

Here the whole equipment for his fundamental work is to be seen clear cut and simple, strong and powerful. It is certainly borrowed from St Paul, but we know with what mastery Dom Marmion understood, assimilated and developed the thought of the Apostle of the Nations.[1]

The divine light helped him besides to enter further and further into the depths of the mystery of Christ:

> During the octave of the Epiphany, I understood that the great fact, the great truth, the pre-eminent truth is that Jesus Christ is the Son of God.
>
> 1. God the Father solemnly proclaimed this truth on two occasions: the Baptism of Jesus and the Transfiguration. *Hic est Filius meus dilectus in quo complacui...*[2] *Clarificavi et adhuc clarificabo...*[3] *Ut in nomine ejus omne genu flectatur...*[4] The glory of His Son – (who humbled Himself even unto death for the love of His Father: *Ut cognoscat mundus quia diligo Patrem*)[5] seems to be the Father's great preoccupation.
>
> 2. Jesus Christ Himself proclaimed it solemnly before His judges and it was for this declaration that He was crucified: *Confessus bonam confessionem...*[6] *Adjuro te per Deum vivum ut dicas nobis si tu es Christus, Filius Dei benedicti? Tu dixisti...*[7] *Debet mori quia Filium Dei se fecit.*[8]

It was around this great truth, this pre-eminent truth, that Dom Columba's whole inner life gravitated, as did all his preaching. During the years now approaching which he was to spend in Louvain,

---

to sins, should live to justice: by whose stripes we are healed" (1 Pet. 2:24).
1 See note at the end of this chapter.
2 "This is my beloved Son, in whom I am well pleased" (Matt. 17:5).
3 "I have both glorified it, and will glorify it again" (John 12:28).
4 "That in the name of Jesus every knee should bow" (Phil. 2:10).
5 John 17:23.
6 1 Tim. 6:12.
7 "I adjure thee by the living God, that thou tell us if thou be the Christ the Son of God" (Matt. 26:63).
8 "He ought to die, because he made himself the Son of God" (John 19:7).

his close union with Christ brought home to him this living and life-giving truth.

The last pages of his notebook referring to this period of his life contain some reflections of Holy Scripture, extracts from the spiritual writings of St Catherine of Siena, St Teresa of Ávila, Blosius and Jean-Jacques Olier; and from the life of St Pierre Fourier, and the first Oratorians, etc. All deal with humility and obedience, the spirit of adoption and the condition of intimate union with God.

It would take too long to repeat them here. We will simply note how in a letter Dom Columba[1] wrote to the Abbot Primate he says that Dom Prior had given him permission to read the works of St John of the Cross and he had found them "a perfect flood of light" for his soul. He adds that he begins to understand what the life of faith is and what it is to pray the prayer of faith and not to take any account of changes of weather, or moods; at the same time he sees more clearly than ever what a danger those run who trust in their own judgment and let themselves be guided by any other light than that of the Church and the revealed word.

Putting this teaching into practice, Dom Marmion strove especially to live in a spirit of self-abandonment. "This spirit is very evident on the eve of his departure for Louvain: "In reading Genesis, I have been very struck to see how God employs men for His ends, and men are never so great nor so powerful as when they abandon themselves absolutely to His Wisdom and Providence."

And he brings forward the example of Abraham and especially that of the Patriarch Joseph, then he concludes:

> We ought not to regard each little circumstance of life as an indication of some *special design* on God's part, that would be going to an excess which might lead to superstition, but when we place ourselves entirely in God's hands to be employed

---

[1] Without precise date, but in 1896 or 1897.

as He wills, God often uses the smallest circumstances for great designs.

We should then abandon ourselves entirely to the guidance of Providence, and avoid taking our own future in hand by substituting our own ideas, will, etc., for those of divine wisdom. When no indication of the Divine Will is manifested by obedience, we should occupy ourselves with all the perfection and diligence possible with the work entrusted to us, and wait, as for the rest, for the indication of the Divine Will. In this way all our life glorifies God, who should be the primary mover in all things; we become *sicut sagitta in manu potentis*.

This last image taken from the Psalmist had long been familiar to him. In his earlier notes he had expressed these forcible thoughts: "In the epistle for the feast of St John Baptist, the Precursor is compared to a chosen arrow which the Divine Archer hides in his quiver. It is the image of the religious during his noviceship. During the time he is made *sagitta electa,* the arrow is polished; it is made straight, light, well balanced. The superior hides the religious like an arrow in his quiver; then he *lets it fly where he will*: against a wall, to break it; into the air without apparently serving for anything; against a foe, in a glorious encounter, etc."

During his whole noviceship and long afterwards, Dom Marmion had lived up to this image by perfect obedience founded on absolute self-surrender.

Self-abandonment became so much the dearer to him in proportion as the divine light continued to reveal to him the beauty, greatness and fruitfulness of this virtue.

> On the feast of St Joseph 1899, I had a vivid light on the nature and value of self-abandonment. St Joseph was the shadow, the representative of the Eternal Father. His mission was to do here upon earth, in a visible manner what the Heavenly Father did; and he was so perfect because he perfectly fulfilled this mission.
>
> This mission was to manifest in every occurrence the will

and designs of the Eternal Father concerning His Son Jesus and the Blessed Virgin Mary. To carry out this mission, Joseph had to follow exactly, without delay or staying to reason, each indication of the Divine Will ('manifest will,' *voluntas signi*); and where this Will was not manifested, Joseph had to keep himself in a loving state of waiting, *attente* ('will of good pleasure': *voluntas beneplaciti*). St Joseph accomplished this perfectly; at each manifestation of the Divine Will we see him obey it without delay or hesitation, and when this Will was hidden from him, do his best to learn what it was.

Thus arriving in Palestine on his return from Egypt, as God did not manifest to him to what place he was to go, he did all that prudence suggested to him: he avoided Judea and went to Nazareth. Having thus with a perfect love, placed himself in God's hands like a responsive instrument, he perfectly accomplished God's every Will and reached that sublime holiness which has made him the patron of the Universal Church. *Hic vir perfecit omnia quae locutus est ei Deus.*[1] That is perfection.

I have taken the resolution to abandon myself unreservedly into God's hands, having no other desire than to do the Will of God manifested by His commandments and the orders of my superiors, putting all my strength of body and soul at the service of this Will, and keeping myself habitually, as regards the will of good pleasure in a state of loving *attente*, desiring definitively only what is manifested as the Divine Will by obedience or the inspiration of the Holy Spirit. (See *Treatise on the Love of God* by St Francis de Sales, Book IX).

When Dom Columba wrote these lines and took this resolution, his departure for Louvain was imminent. (April 13th). Such dispositions in the soul of the monk prepared the way for a large outpouring of those divine gifts which were to bear much fruit for God's glory.

---

1 "This man hath fulfilled perfectly all that God commanded him."

NOTE

We have already seen the plan of a retreat given by Dom Marmion in 1895 and which forms the doctrinal nucleus of *Christ the Life of the Soul*.

This plan was embodied, developed and made more explicit in the retreat given in December 1898, to the Benedictine nuns of Maredret.

Introduction: The Transfiguration. "This is My Beloved Son; hear ye Him." Application of this episode to the retreat.

PART I: DEATH TO SIN

1. On perfection.
2. On sin – mortal – venial.
3. The Sacrament of Penance.
4. Death. Hell.
5. Scruples.
6. The spirit of compunction.
7. The Passion of our Lord.

PART II: SPIRITUAL RESURRECTION

1. On the supernatural life: Baptism.
2. Obedience.
3. The Divine Office.
4. The Eucharistic Sacrifice.
5. The Bread of Life. *O sacrum convivium.*
6. Faith.
7. Humility.
8. Mental prayer.
9. Love one another.
10. The Mother of the Incarnate Word.

As we see it is the plan of *Christ the Life of the Soul*, blended with certain more specially monastic conferences which, for their part, were to form some of the chapters in *Christ the Ideal of the Monk*.

In two other retreats (January 1899), Dom Marmion makes all converge towards the idea of supernatural adoption in Jesus Christ (I) and towards the Person of Jesus Christ as Model and Source of all holiness (II). In this lies his whole teaching.

I

God predestinated us to become His adopted children through Jesus Christ.

To love and honour the Father, obey Him as Jesus did. We ought to be by grace what Jesus Christ is by nature.

Love: (*a*) to destroy sin; (*b*) to seek God.
Honour: prayer, praise, Mass.
Obey: obedience, humility, vows.

II

"Let this mind be in you, which was also in Christ Jesus." Conformity to the dispositions of Jesus Christ.

1. The Word took the "form of a servant," *Formam servi accipiens*.
2. Jesus Christ emptied Himself.
3. "He humbled Himself" *unto death*. To die to sin.
4. He became *obedient*.
5. Obedient "even to the death of the cross."
6. "God hath exalted Him." Our elevation through Him in grace.
7. God "hath given Him a name which is above all names," "that in the name of His Beloved Son we may deserve to abound in good works" (Collect for the Sunday within octave of Christmas).
8. Prayer.
9. "And that every tongue should confess that the Lord Jesus Christ is in the glory of God the Father." Zeal for God's glory.

This second retreat formed a commentary on the words of St Paul applied to the Christian life.

The retreat given in September 1900 at Maredsous lays down the definitive plan and whole substance of *Christ the Life of the Soul*.

7   LOUVAIN
    (1899–1909) OUTWARD ACTIVITY

To the north of Louvain rises a solitary hill from which a full view may be obtained of the whole of the university city ensconced in a vast hollow. From the confused mass of houses and labyrinths of ancient roads emerge the steeples and spires of the numerous churches and convents of the town. In the foreground the gaze is arrested by the graceful spire, pierced by ornamental openings, of the Church of St Gertrude from whence at regular intervals the bells' clear tones peal gaily out. Farther on in the heart of the city is the majestic nave of the college chapel of St Peter; facing it the town hall, a gem of Gothic art. Yet farther off, *les Halles* and the new library of the university, a fine modern example of the Flemish renaissance. Here and there, humbler and older churches, a little dwarfed – as if in the course of time the soil had sunk under their weight – retain in their weather-beaten condition a massiveness not devoid of grace. Occasionally genuine Gothic gables of Flemish renaissance lift their heads above the other houses. In places the shady green gardens of the ancient pedagogies gladden the scene with bright splashes of colour.

Against the horizon, beyond the boulevards, the eye rests upon the undulating lines of the hills of Kessel-Lo or on the wide extent of the forests of Héverlé.

A picture peaceful as is serene learning, but disfigured by the ugly chimneys of factories and the commonplace buildings raised by modern industry.

This hill is rich in historical associations. It was here, about the end of the tenth century, that the dukes of Brabant built a castle which was their usual residence up to the fourteenth century, the epoch when they settled at Brussels. This castle saw the birth and upbringing of St Albert of Louvain, martyr (1192); Emperor Charles V lived here, and under the guidance of Adriaan Florensz – afterwards Pope Adrian VI – devoted himself to the study of letters.

In memory of this stay of the great emperor the humanists called the hill *Castrum Caesaris*, Mont-César, an appellation retained to this day. At the end of the eighteenth century, Emperor Joseph II decreed that the ancient princely residences of the Low Country should be demolished. Consequently the castle of Mont-César was put up for sale in 1873; the massive towers, the castle keep, the seigneurial buildings and the chapel were soon razed to the ground; of the old feudal manor the foundation walls alone remained and may still be seen at the present day.

Quite near to this castle and upon the same hill is, moreover, a residence of the Knights of Malta: the commandery of St John, the chapel of which is dedicated to St Gregory the Great. In 1607 the Knights rented their house to the English Jesuits who had been driven out of their country by the persecution; these established a novitiate here, and the first novice to be professed, Bl. Thomas Garnet, died a martyr for the Faith on 23 June 1608, at Tyburn (London). Shortly afterwards the Irish Dominicans succeeded the Jesuits and remained till 1650. At the time of the French Revolution the property was sold as national estate and the chapel demolished.[1]

On this hill, Dom Hildebrand de Hemptinne decided to build a Benedictine monastery to serve as a school of theology for the young clerics of the Congregation. On 13 April 1899, feast day of Bl. Ida of Louvain, a colony of monks from Maredsous was established at Mont-César under the direction of Dom Robert de Kerchove.[2] The monastery was dedicated to the Mother of God.[3]

---

1 Is it not in fact one of the traits of genius to distinguish in the confused mass of notions and details, in all that *impedimenta* of erudition, the essential of a theory or doctrine?

2 Later Prior of Maredsous. Residing at Louvain from 1889 to 1899 as director of the house of senior students educated at Maredsous, Dom de Kerchove patiently prepared the ground for establishing the monks there, transacting the business of buying, piece by piece, the whole site of Mont-César – then cut up in small-holdings – directing the first work of construction and supervising the more preliminary arrangements.

3 To make this dedication more tangible, a large statue of the Blessed Virgin and Child was raised on the very foundation of the ancient castle of the Dukes of Brabant; it represents the Queen of heaven petitioning her Son to bless the city

Dom Columba was here to spend ten years of a life fruitful in good. To his charge of prior was added that of professor of theology and of spiritual director to the young monks. A new and wider field of action better adapted to his natural capacities was opening out before him; his original personality and masterly talents were, in a more homogeneous activity, to be fully revealed.

The prior in a Benedictine monastery is as the right hand of the abbot, who, whilst in principle retaining all powers, has to leave to the foremost of his "officers" a large share of action and influence. St Benedict requires from the prior a particularly supple and ready submission to the commands and wishes of the abbot in order to secure union of mind and peace of heart; being moreover especially entrusted with the maintaining of discipline and the observance, the prior owes to all an example of the greatest regularity. A position of confidence, as is clear, but also a delicate one: he must at the same time obey and command, give proof of obedience and act with authority.

This position – held during the abbot's good-pleasure according to Benedictine traditions – was confided to Dom Columba during the whole ten years he stayed at Louvain.

The obedience of which he had given proof up to that time as a simple monk remained absolute. And that is saying a great deal. Monastic obedience, such as St Benedict would have it, is not only of boundless extent; it still more especially reaches down as far as the deepest fibres of the soul with the aim of destroying self-will and self-judgment at their very roots; the psychological inwardness of an obedience carried to this degree calls for rare abnegation from the one who tries to practise it. The merit of this virtue was the greater in that Dom Columba, now Prior of Mont-César, was at this time at the zenith of his energies, and saw on all sides his talents recognised and others depending on his power of initiative.

Some of his notes during this period show the intrinsic principles of which the panorama lies unfolded below.

DOM MARMION
(Louvain, 1900)

which actuated him in this matter: "The religious order to which we belong resembles a tree: *qui* MANET *in me hic fert fructum multum*, we make a part of this tree especially through obedience. The great means is our affective union with the inward dispositions of the obedience of the Heart of Jesus. I have seen that it is very important, before going to a superior, to stir up one's faith and to venerate in him the person and authority of Christ."

"I feel more and more the need," he writes to one of his spiritual daughters, "to give myself to souls, but at the same time Jesus makes me understand that, as a monk, all my activity ought to be regulated by Him, through obedience.[1]

These clearly defined principles, taken from the *Rule* itself, make obedience integral. Dom Marmion's obedience was that of a child. He submitted to his abbot every step that did not enter into the ordinary course of his charge. If he went on a journey he took care that the least detail of his comings and goings should be regulated in advance.[2] If some demand was made on his zeal in the exercises of his ministry he left the decision entirely to the rulings of obedience.

The superior of a community earnestly begged him to undertake the direction of her soul; he replied: "In spite of the great desire that our Lord inspires in me to help souls to attain perfect union with Him, I do not like to accept the direction of souls at a distance, not only on account of my very numerous occupations, but because my Very Reverend Father Abbot does not wish me to increase my already extensive correspondence."[3]

To another nun, he writes these lines: "I regret that circumstances do not allow me to go to M— this month. I have to give my course of theology, do many other things which take up my time,

---

[1] Letter of 25 February 1903.
[2] When going to a place beyond Liège, knowing he would have to wait two hours for his train, he asked permission, before taking advantage of this opportunity, to visit a convent in the town, where there was some matter to arrange concerning the Carmelites.
[3] Letter of 1 November 1908.

and Father Abbot agreed, as long ago as last April that I should give a retreat to the pupils at Jupille and another at Erdington next month."[1]

Some business matters brought the superior of a convent in England to a house of her institute in Flanders. Most anxious to speak of her soul to Dom Marmion, to whom she had confided it, and not being provided with the authorisation to extend her journey beyond the convent of her order, she begged him to come to see her. It would be so easy for him, and it was such an exceptional occasion! He replied: "It is a real sacrifice for me to know that you are at X— and not to go to see you... Yet I am powerless, as I am under obedience and may do nothing but what I am told. If our Lord sees that it would be useful He will arrange."[2]

An event of an episodic character more than once served to emphasise this obedience. In the afternoon of 14 May 1906, a violent cyclone beat down over the town of Louvain; the memory of it still lingers in the minds of those who witnessed it. At the moment when it broke out Dom Marmion was confessing the Carmelites, whose convent is situated rather less than half a league from the abbey. When he had finished hearing their confessions the prioress, being sure that he could not then return to the monastery, suggested that he should at least wait; she offered him hospitality for the night, which was fast approaching. In this way besides he would give them the longed-for satisfaction of assisting at his Mass on the morrow and receiving Holy Communion from his hands as they were so seldom able to do. It was like a repetition of the last conversation between St Scholastica and St Benedict. But he would not listen to this suggestion: the instruction of obedience was to return. The storm was raging, overthrowing the chimney-pots and sending the tiles flying off the roofs; in spite of rain, hail and the

---

1 Letter of 20 November 1907.
2 Letter of March 1907. The Reverend Mother of a community in England informed him that she had written to the abbot asking the latter to allow Dom Columba to preach their retreat; he replied: "I don't know what answer Father Abbot gave to your letter, as he hasn't said a word to me. Let us leave that to our Lord." These are but a few examples out of a hundred which may be found in his letters.

tempestuous wind, Dom Columba set out. Keeping close to the walls of the houses, he with difficulty reached the end of the road where the broad stone pavement leading up the abbey branches off. A stranger who was passing by, cried out:

"Father, don't go any farther. Turn back; it is dangerous."

Dom Columba, indeed, had only to look in front of him to see the danger. The violence of the cyclone had thrown down a great part of the wooden enclosure wall bordering the pavement. From the sloping ground beaten by the rain a part of the garden had given way, and an impetuous torrent of earth, stones, wood, trees, debris of all kind poured down from the landslip all along his path.[1] This time Dom Columba was forced to go back. Retracing his steps, he recrossed the town and came, not to Carmel, where they would have been so happy to welcome him, but to the clinic of the Franciscan Sisters, whose chaplain was a friend of his. He could at last take shelter from the deluge. On the morrow he went to say Mass and give Communion to the "Scholasticas."

This absolute and exact obedience struck all who came near him. Canon N—, a close friend of Désiré-Joseph Cardinal Mercier, one day expressed his astonishment on seeing such prompt and entire obedience, which he considered extraordinary – as indeed it was.

"How do you contrive to obey so easily in matters so opposed to your own way of thinking?"

"It is quite simple. I look above the head of my abbot, and there I see Christ."

Simple in very truth, but only on condition that one is a model of obedience.

"I thought this a splendid answer," his interlocutor added later, when recounting this incident; "I was much struck by it, and have made use of it in the confessional and elsewhere to lead souls in the way of submission."

When, after spending ten years at Louvain, Dom Marmion was elected Abbot of Maredsous, an eminent prelate of the university,

---

[1] It was in consequence of this event that the municipality obliged the monks to have the wooden palisade replaced by a stone wall.

one whose friendship he highly valued, congratulated him, and then added:

"I regret your departure; it is a great loss for us, but I understand; you are obeying."

"Thank you, my dear friend," Dom Columba immediately replied; "as for obedience, you know it is my very life. There is nothing greater; that is why I have always tried to obey."

Dom Marmion was indeed well able to bear himself this testimony, which was later to be confirmed by others.

The self-abnegation which such absolute obedience supposes was only equalled in the Prior of Mont-César by the self-forgetfulness which went together with his charity.

The monastery was at that time in its period of foundation, that is to say, a time of special and abundant grace, but likewise a time of special and continual sacrifice for the generous members of such a community. The monks of a foundation are in many points a generation ready for self-sacrifice; that is their greatness and nobility. In a like undertaking opportunities for self-forgetfulness are multiplied; privations are more frequent and at the same time more felt; on account of the limited number of religious several charges often fall on the same shoulders, and the burdens which accumulate on the same head make the weight of responsibility a heavy one.

Besides all this the monks were sometimes requisitioned to take on themselves supplementary fatigue duty, particularly trying to men who, being more accustomed to intellectual labour, found this a severe tax on the regular routine of monastic life: one week it would be to work in the garden, another to clear the cloister precincts of enormous piles of bricks that had to be carried elsewhere; on another occasion – a tragic one, since they were living in the midst of troublous times occasioned by political events and the streets of the city were running with blood,[1] – it was necessary on account of the isolated position of the monastery to organise exhausting night watches.

---

1 In April 1902 the troops of the civil guard had to fire on the ringleaders, and many were killed or wounded.

In all these circumstances, as in the usual trend of life in the cloister, Dom Columba generously took his share in the labours, crosses and difficulties; he further lightened those of others, ever stimulating them by his example and heartening them by his charity, which especially took the form of unflagging and infectious good humour. His love for the brethren and for his monastery was on a par with his obedience to the abbot.[1]

Soon after Dom Marmion's death the abbot under whom he had lived at Louvain, one therefore who knew him closely, bore him this testimony in a conference given to the nuns of Maredret: "I had him as my prior for ten years; I was always edified by his charity and by his devotedness to the monastery and to everything I confided to him. As to his obedience, I can say that I never had a more obedient monk."

Coming from the lips of one who is now Primate of the Belgian Congregation, this concise and seemingly simple testimony supposes, over and above all we have been saying, singularly high virtue in the one to whom it was rendered.

To his charge of prior, Dom Marmion joined that of professor of dogmatic theology.

Theology, the knowledge of God and of His works, according to the revelation He has Himself vouchsafed to give us, or, to put it more briefly, the supernatural knowledge of divine things, holds the highest rank in the hierarchy of learning. Accepting the revealed

---

[1] In 1903 Dom Marmion fixed his *stability* at Mont-César; from being a monk of Maredsous he became a monk of the Abbey of Louvain. Writing on May 23rd to Abbot Primate Hildebrand, he says that when some months before he had been asked to fix his stability at Louvain he had done so unhesitatingly because he was persuaded it was God's Will and that of his abbot, but it was one of the greatest sacrifices he had ever made for the love of God. He goes on to say that he is sure that as primate, Dom Hildebrand will still allow him to continue to consider him as his father. Until then Dom Marmion had signed his letters to Abbot Hildebrand "your child," henceforward he signed them "your son."

truths contained or expressed in the Holy Scriptures, ecclesiastical tradition, the definitions of the Councils, the works of the Fathers of the Church – the theologian studies them in themselves, compares them in order to analyse their elements, establish their point of agreement, link them together, grasp their accordance, and determine their practical repercussion on human lives. A science of unequalled amplitude since it embraces the whole of reality in the highest meaning of the term: God and His works, the creature and its perfections, Christ the God-Man who, by Himself and by His Church, brings back and binds the creature to God.

Dom Marmion had previously acquired this science, but at Louvain he reviewed it once more in all its parts; he especially availed himself of the advantages that the university city offered him of submitting his personal conception to the most competent authorities. This period of Dom Columba's maturity, profitable for those who received his teaching, was also the crowning point of his own intellectual culture.

Henceforward, according to the expression, he "possessed" his theology thoroughly; he even possessed it so fully that subsequently the ever available nature of this knowledge, which he retained to a remarkable degree, was to furnish him on every occasion, and in the most exact terms, with the dogmatic interpretation and the full ascetical commentary on the Scriptural text.

We must here try to discover from what angle Dom Marmion chose to envisage this divine science, which he had so well assimilated, for his interpretation of the spiritual life is moulded on dogma, and we should have to give up the attempt to grasp one of the most salient characteristics of this conception unless we first understood how Dom Marmion taught theology; for, in his case, the ascetic was in close affinity and dependence on the theologian.

So lofty a science is not to be ventured upon without a guide. From among the different masters and doctors who have distinguished themselves in this domain and have claims to our preference, Dom Marmion did not long hesitate. For more than twenty years, Leo XIII, then gloriously reigning, had never ceased to extol the singular merit of St Thomas Aquinas as the guiding light of human thought. These pontifical rulings sufficed to determine Dom Columba's choice. But other more personal reasons urged him to take his stand under the guidance of the Aquinate. Initiated in the reading of the *Summa Theologica* by Fr Satolli at the College of Propaganda he had since experienced for himself the value of this masterpiece. Furthermore, he had too much affinity of mind with the searching thought, powerful logic and philosophical rigour which characterises that wonderful sum of theological doctrine not to attach himself to it. Finally – and this is perhaps the most fundamental motive of his preference – in St Thomas far more than in St Augustine, Dom Marmion once more encountered St Paul:[1] under the scholastic formulas of the *Summa* he found again that Pauline doctrine so familiar to him.[2]

In his teaching the professor of Mont-César held before all things[3]

[1] "The Church in her teaching lays down the fundamental equation: St Paul = St Augustine = St Thomas." Adhémar d'Alès, quoted by Fr Réginald Garrigou-Lagrange, OP, *Dieu*, 4th edition.

[2] It is not only in doctrine, but also and above all in piety that Dom Marmion strove to follow the Angelic Doctor. "How worthy of the master," writes Thomas Coconnier, OP, "would such a one be who, not content with following St Thomas in the path of doctrine, trod yet more generously in his steps in the path of virtue; who reproduced his humility and gentle benignity, his detachment from the world, his perseverance in prayer, his apostolic zeal, his fervent love for God, the God of the Cross and the Eucharist, his tender devotion towards the Mother of the Incarnate Word! Certainly, he would be a perfect disciple and we should unhesitatingly recognise and hail him as the true Thomist." Of course, Dom Marmion's preferences had nothing exclusive about them. He wrote to a student: "As it is God's Will that you should apply yourself to philosophy, do it *with all your head: aetatem habes!* It is not necessary to embrace the physical premotion if it does not appeal to your mind." – Letter of 18 January 1901.

[3] "Before all things," we say; for it is very evident that a professor who is conscientious and careful for the good and real formation of his students ought first of all to set before them what strictly speaking constitutes the object of his teaching; otherwise he would be preferring the secondary to the principal and would be betraying his mission. Read on this subject Fr Garrigou-Lagrange's pages, so full of truth, in his beautiful book: *Perfection chrétienne et contemplation*, ch. 6, art. III, q. 1, "*la matérialisation de la vie intellectuelle et de la vie intérieure*."

to the essential of dogma, to the traditional elements which, strictly speaking, constitute doctrine: that was why he was continually reading – in addition to Holy Writ and the testimonies of the Fathers of the Church – the definitions of the Councils, wherein the Church, the living interpreter of revealed truth, has condensed the gist of theology.[1]

To a student under his direction, who had submitted to him the plan of his thesis before going up for his doctor's degree, he replied: "I have carefully read the plan of your doctoral thesis: it pleased me very much because you follow the traditional procedure in choosing one of the great theses of the School which are the necessary basis of serious theology."

And after having suggested the authors to be consulted, he adds: "Try above all to go deeply into the thought of St Thomas. It is so fruitful."

The revealed truths, the certitudes of the divine ordering, the knowledge of which constitutes the primary basis of theology, inevitably imply, by the very nature of their object, some degree of mystery. Here the human mind can give itself free course within the limits of dogma. In many points – such as reconciling divine omniscience and divine causality with man's free will – discussions between theologians, schools spring up, striving to elucidate the obscurities that arise from dogma and to solve apparent contradictions.

If Dom Marmion was persevering in fathoming, as far as possibility allowed, questions where dogma and the teaching of the Church are strictly speaking concerned, he, on the other hand, in the domain of controversial propositions observed discretion as to certain theories advanced by the schools, and on which revelation throws less light.

But this moderation did not arise from the fact of his being too easily content with a little; his reservations were adopted after due

---

[1] Dom Marmion had constantly on his study table the collection of the conciliatory definitions and doctrinal decisions of the Church known under the name of *Enchiridion Symbolorum* of Heinrich Denziger, and, thanks to his excellent memory, his knowledge of it was seldom at fault.

reflection and were at least authorised by the most conscientious personal investigation. This attentive study of supernatural problems, the analysis of proposed solutions, the examination of controversies, had convinced him that if the field of holy curiosity stretches out before the theologian to the infinite, the field of certain conclusions is restricted when, from the starting-point of the revealed word, the series of rational deductions lengthen out and distinctions become more subtle. Thus reflection and history inclined him to think that upon more than one debatable question the human mind has long since reached its limits, beyond which intellectual contests, noble as they still may be, no longer avail to the real progress of truth. After having set forth these problems before his pupils and the different solutions brought to bear upon them, he concluded: "Let us confess, without any beating about the bush, that in these cases we have reached the point when man has something better to do than to persist in straining after the mystery, and this is to adore." And he repeated the Scriptural precept: *Altiora te ne quaesieris,* "Seek not the things that are too high for thee," or again the cry of St Paul: *altitudo divitiarum scientiae et sapientiae Dei...* "O the depth of the riches of the wisdom and of the knowledge of God! How incomprehensible are His judgments, and how unsearchable His ways." And often, too, his advice to those whose souls were left restless after speculative effort was to seek peace in the simple and sublime prayers of the Church so full of holy affections.

And then side by side with the individual turn of mind of the *thinker* there is another element to be taken into consideration which cannot be passed over here, so closely does it concern Dom Marmion's case.

One point of view is that of purely scientific and speculative research pursued at leisure by men who have no other aim; quite another is that which has to deal with the regular training of students for the priesthood, which must necessarily correspond with the plan and inspiration of an ordinary course of theology. And seldom was a theologian more imbued with his mission as an *educator* than the professor of Mont-César.

This mission he fulfilled to perfection, as those who had the great privilege of following his lectures can testify. Extensive knowledge of ecclesiastical science, sureness of doctrine imbibed at the best sources, a keen and complete sense of orthodoxy in conjunction with certain conclusions of modern research in matters of erudition or exegesis, a professional conscience in the preparation and method of his lectures: all these qualities combined would already have sufficed to render his teaching noteworthy.

But what particularly distinguished him and gave him a personal and unforgettable style was, on the one hand, his extreme clearness, and on the other his happy and fluent application of doctrine to the inner life.

His teaching was luminous. If he owed to his Irish descent his penetration of mind and swiftness in mental work, with that gift of insight eminently belonging to poets and thinkers, it was from the French blood flowing in his veins that he owed his clarity of ideas and limpid ease in stating propositions.

He had the remarkable gift – and to a degree approaching genius[1] – of always being able to disengage the essential of a question from the accessory, of making this essential stand out, then, having placed it in full light, of showing how all, to the most far-reaching consequences, is subordinate to or linked with it. Whether it concerned the mystery of the Trinity or that of the Incarnation, the delicate problem of the liberty of Christ in His Passion, abstruse questions of grace, or one of the great heresies which throughout the centuries have moved the Christian world, his intellect penetrated to the heart and core of the subject, drew out the central ideas, and hence threw light on all the conclusions. What charm, what security, too, to turn to this master, even apart from the course of theology, on any dogmatic question whatsoever, and to hear him at

---

[1] Is it not in fact one of the traits of genius to distinguish in the confused mass of notions and details, in all that *impedimenta* of erudition, the essential of a theory or doctrine?

once, without having recourse to any bookish research, give you, in a few luminous points, the whole essential of a doctrine.

Conceived with clearness, his thought was stated with ease. In limpid Latin, unstudied, but not always lacking elegance, the professor developed his subject. The fundamental principle being laid down, he unfolded the doctrinal thesis, first of all sketched out in vivid, simple and clear outlines, to attain with remarkable logic to the most intimate and most diverse applications. There was strength in this simplicity, and a dominating unity of thought stamped the whole statement with singular force.

This strength did not exclude warmth. Inspired with strong conviction, the exposé was generally besprinkled with familiar comparisons which for less well-endowed minds facilitated the comprehension and solution of the problems, for nothing could have been less doctoral or less solemn than these theological lectures; they were simple, animated, full of life. Sometimes, even, flashes of wit springing from the professor's native fluency aroused and sustained attention.

Nothing more was needed to make the mind grasp the truth and revel in it.

Complete and luminous as was his teaching, the master's ambition was not, however, limited to forming the judgment and disciplining the minds of his disciples: it was his intent to make their souls live in and by the mysteries he set forth to them. And we have here the most characteristic note of his teaching.

Was it not Cardinal Newman who said that theology ought not to be devotional? Dom Marmion, for his part, only considered he had fully carried out his theological teaching if he applied it to the spiritual life.

That knowledge is sterile which does not turn to loving; and Dom Columba wished that theology should not only be the highest knowledge, but furthermore should become supreme wisdom and a fruitful source of life for his disciples. Not that he taught theology in view of piety, nor regarded philosophy solely as the servant of dogma; he knew too well that each science has its own domain, as likewise its formal principles and particular method, but he could not make up his mind to treat revealed truths like mere theorems of geometry having no bearing on the interior life.

The theologian who is not only learned and erudite *in* the things of God, but is scholarly and wise *according to God and in the sight of God*, is one who perseveringly asks for grace that he may obtain understanding;[1] who, through his long night watches, often escapes from the labour of human reasoning in order to adore, and, having reached the truth at the end of his deductions, finds the consummation of this same truth in loving contemplation. He would have these speculations on the divine mysteries and his teaching on them to be, for his own soul and for the souls of his hearers, something more than a remote intellectual preparation: he would have them to be the incentive to mental prayer and, as it were, give the *motif.*

Such was the ideal at which Dom Marmion constantly aimed. As he once wrote: "Theology, being the evolution of faith, is normally only learnt in prayer."[2]

He loved to recall St Bonaventura's question to St Thomas: "Where then do you obtain this superhuman knowledge?"

---

[1] In this he is again a disciple of St Thomas, or, rather, he is truly a theologian. The Angelic Doctor envisages in fact theology "as an impression of the divine knowledge itself" (*Summa Theologica,* I, q. 1, a. 3) as a participation in the heavenly knowledge of God and of His saints. He therefore declares that he wished to write the *Summa* "trusting in the divine help" *cum fiducia divini auxilii,* so much was he convinced that the human intellect needs a very special help to grasp, to assimilate and to explain theology, the *sacra doctrina* (*cf.* Msgr Martin Grabmann, *La somme théologique de Saint-Thomas*). Cardinal Satolli, who was the master of Dom Marmion, brought out in his *Praelectiones in Summam,* T. I, the thought of St Thomas on the necessity of divine help in the study of theology. In this twofold school Dom Marmion had learnt the importance and power of supernatural factors for understanding divine mysteries, as far as that is possible here below. This was besides only a special application of the principle laid down by Christ: *Sine me nihil potestis facere,* and so often recalled by Dom Columba in the words of St Paul: *Non quod sufficientes sumus...* Of St Benedict: *Quidquid (agendum) inchoas bonum, a Deo perfici instantissima oratione deposeas* (Prologue to the *Rule of St Benedict*).

[2] Letter of January 1902.

And St Thomas replied, pointing to his crucifix: "In this book I have learnt more than in all the others."

As Fr Garrigou-Lagrange writes: "Christ gave to St Thomas that most eminent degree of wisdom which revealed to him the harmonies existing in the mysteries and in the life of our souls."[1]

Inspired by this example, Dom Marmion tried to correspond – and to make others correspond – to the aspirations of sacred learning, to bring about their realisation in his own soul – and in the souls confided to him. Such was his faith in the Word of God! Such his zeal for souls!

In the same way as his lessons in theology were prepared in prayer – persevering and earnest prayer – so they often ended in some short pithy saying that found its way straight to the heart and uplifted the soul: some sidelight thrown on asceticism and apt to be all the more effectual, in that it was felt to be the more truly spontaneous. For in this there was no striving after effects, no singularity. It came about quite naturally, and it was because the professor had himself first lived the doctrine he expounded that from it flowed applications to the life of the soul. All the master did was to point out and stress these applications; *Videtis ergo, fratres carissimi:* "You see then, dearest brothers..." Yes, it was true, they did see. A firm and sure bond linked the suggestion, the ascetic exhortation, to the doctrinal exposé; but in what penetrating tones of communicative conviction this was expressed! It was no longer the master who, with authority and power, was setting the truth before the minds of his disciples; it was the apostle who was persuasively drawing their hearts to the love of virtue.

In this way the conception at once sober, deep and supernatural,[2]

---

1 Fr Garrigou-Lagrange, *loc. cit.* To a student in theology Dom Columba wrote: "Christ is our wisdom, and it is in studying Him with reverence and love that we shall always find the key to most theological difficulties." – Letter of 5 August 1902.

2 "When reason, enlightened by faith" – the Vatican Council defines – "pursues its researches with care, piety and sobriety, it reaches, with the help of God, a very profitable knowledge of the divine mysteries: *Ratio quidem, fide illustrata, cum* SEDULO, PIE, SOBRIE *quaerit, aliquam* DEO DANTE *mysteriorum intelligen-*

which Dom Marmion had on the subject of the teaching of dogma, facilitated and furthered the part which the Church would have theological studies to play in the spiritual progress of apprentices to the priesthood. His method guarded souls from the danger of finding scarcely more in scholastic dissertations than a mental exercise, foreign both to the heart and to piety. It helped them to keep in the quickening atmosphere of the supernatural; it prepared them to pass more easily from intellectual speculation to affective prayer and at the moment when the human voice ceased speaking, it left them attentive to listen in silence to the inward Master who ultimately defines and determines the hidden meaning and sanctifying power of His words.

Was it then surprising that a lecture on theology from such a master was transmuted, in the case of many, into prayer, and ended upon the prie-dieu in the cell or at the foot of the tabernacle...?

Those who have understood, by means of this analysis, the manner in which Fr Columba was accustomed to teach theology will have grasped at the same time one aspect of that spiritual art – of

> *tiam eamque* FRUCTUOSISSIMAM *assequitur* (*Concil vatic.* Denzinger, n. 1796)..
> "Dogmatic theology, moral and mystical theology, are but one and the same eminent science, a participation in that of God and the blessed. In the obscurity of faith, sacred doctrine treats of the same object that the saints contemplate in heaven: God, the works that proceed from Him and the return of creatures to Him. Hence, progress in theology must be made much more by unification than by extension. Documents newly come to light, or fresh applications, useful as they may be, remain very secondary; the important point is to draw near in *spirit* to the very science of the saints, to grasp better and better the connexion that the revealed truths have to each other and especially with the supreme mystery, the vision whereof constitutes our last end. Theology tends essentially to contemplation or it ceases to be a 'participation in the knowledge of God and the saints' to become a sterile collection of texts, where the revealed mysteries remain without bond of union and where the sacrament of penance is of as much importance as the Blessed Trinity. True progress is not directed towards the time to come, but towards the eternity where the unification of knowledge is consummated," Fr Garrigou-Lagrange, *Dieu* 11, ch. 5, n. 67: "*Harmonie progressive des perfections en apparence opposées, dans la vie de la grâce, la sainteté.*"

which we shall have again to speak – by which he so happily opened out to many Christians, by word of mouth and the printed page, the treasures of dogmatics.

These treasures he shared in a more explicit manner with the young monks placed under his direction. Twice a week he gathered these around him to impart to them, in spiritual conferences, that divine wisdom with which he was filled. He loved to repeat the words of Scripture on the excellence of wisdom: "She is an infinite treasure to men, which they that use, become the friends of God... now all good things came to me together with her... and I knew not that she was the mother of them all. Which I have learned without guile, and communicate without envy, and her riches I hide not."[1] Familiar discourses of a character at once simple and deep, original and traditional, doctrinal and fatherly, the whole possessing a powerful and efficacious unity. Christ in His person, in His mysteries, in His union with the soul: that was, with the explanation of the *Rule of St Benedict*, so closely attached to this subject by its eminently Christian character, the whole ground of his conferences; the substance of them was to pass, some twenty years later, into his spiritual works. The form, often graphic and racy, and above all his tone of warm conviction gained the hearts of his young monks. The life of one of them, Dom Pie de Hemptinne, has been written. Further on we shall give a short sketch of this spiritual son of Dom Marmion; it will suffice here to say that we shall be able to see in him the great influence of these conferences on a docile soul; they opened out large horizons to hearts ambitious for divine things; they truly constituted the revelation of love.

The extraordinary efficacy of the master's words depended on yet other causes: to words Dom Columba joined example.

We have spoken of his obedience to the orders of the abbot; his faithfulness to the *Rule* was not less absolute. Never, for instance, would he lighten his heavy charge and exhausting labours

[1] Wis. 7.

by obtaining the dispensation, which would have been quite legitimate, from the Lenten fast and abstinences. In one of those intimate talks in the course of which, when abbot, he used to speak of his own spiritual experiences to his sons who came to open their hearts to him, he said familiarly on this subject:

> People are too ready to believe that they cannot fast without injuring their health. There are certainly persons who could do so if they tried. I am speaking from experience; until I became a monk I had never kept Lent; everyone told me: you must not even attempt to fast. And yet, since I have been a monk, I have done so every year, except when I had the influenza. That means it is more than twenty years that I have fasted, while taking classes in theology, etc., and it has done me no harm. It is a strain, it costs something; the first five or six days one thinks one is going to die; but one does not die at all. However, if the superior does not permit fast or abstinence, then we must obey with great liberty of heart. At Louvain, one year when I had kept the whole of Lent, I had influenza during Holy Week, and the abbot had meat served to me on the Friday. It was a … trial, after having kept all the Lenten observances, but I had to accept it. One sometimes feels a certain satisfaction in being able to say: 'I have kept all *my* Lent.' We have no *my* or *mine;* we have nothing of our own, not even *my* Lent. We must accept what God gives or permits.

Severe as he was towards himself in this matter, Dom Columba knew how to be indulgent to the weaknesses of others.

We may add that Fr Columba was likewise of exemplary assiduity in his choir duties.

It is true that this master only led his disciples along the same path which he himself trod: such is the unanimous testimony of those who knew him.

The renown of Dom Marmion's talent and virtue was quickly to travel beyond the walls of the cloister, and the monastery of Mont-César laid no claim to keep the activity of its theologian and prior for itself alone.

The near vicinity of the university was to create for the monastery uninterrupted relations with the most distinguished masters of the *alma mater* and of the theological colleges of the religious institutes grouped around it.

These relations were manifold. At the end of the scholastic year Fr Columba was often invited to advance the objections in the sustaining of the thesis required from the candidates for university degrees.[1] Those who heard him could never forget the part he played in those academic jousts which were held in the *aula maxima* in presence of the professorial staff, students of the faculty of theology, and an audience consisting of members of the numerous religious bodies of the city.

Dom Marmion's learning, his wide knowledge of the different Protestant sects and their historical and exegetical protests against the dogmas of the Church, the vigour of his argumentation – for he was a sturdy logician, habituated to all the procedures of dialectics – would have made him a formidable adversary, if it had not been known that his essential goodness withheld him from bringing out all his weapons and pushing the new competitor into his last corner.

Sometimes, however, he unhorsed his candidate with a sudden thrust, an unexpected sally, but only to help him at once to recover himself. As ever, faithful to his custom, he went to the heart of the thesis; as soon as the competitor had discovered the crux of the objection and pointed out the principle of the solution, Dom Columba required nothing further and declared himself quite satisfied. He never went as far as quibbling.

The engaging ease that he displayed in these intellectual combats would never have allowed one to suspect the over-fatigue that

---

[1] In a letter of June 1899, Dom Marmion wrote: "I have been invited to object to the 'thesis' at the university. This is not much to my taste, but it is impossible to evade it."

they brought upon him. Not choosing to leave the essential to the spur of the moment, Dom Marmion carefully prepared what he had to say, and this repeated labour, added to those of his own professorship, became very exhausting for him. It was often with steps heavy with weariness that, after these occasions in which he had displayed such brilliancy, he took his way back through the town to regain the abbey and slowly mounted the hard stone pavement under the implacable heat of a July sun.

From the theological plane, the relations between Dom Columba and the little world of Louvain quickly passed into the ascetical domain. Msgr Paulin Ladeuze, today bishop of the titular See of Tiberias – at that time president of the *Collège du Saint-Esprit* and since, in the capacity of *Rector Magnificus*, the highly competent and wise director of the destinies of the celebrated university – asked Dom Marmion, on several occasions, to give the retreat to the students in his institute; moreover, during several years Dom Marmion was deputed to give the monthly retreat. Therefore many were the priests – both professors and students – who confided their spiritual direction to the Prior of Mont-César. On the Friday of each week groups of priests were to be seen valiantly making the ascent of the little hill which separates the town from the abbey, climbing the two flights of stairs which led to Dom Columba's poor little cell, to ask, like Dante at the monastery of Avellana, light and peace.

Or else it was the prior himself who, likewise every week, went down to the town to the *Collège américain de Louvain* to hear the confessions of the students.

Thus in the centre of Louvain, with its invigorating intellectual life and spirit of fervent piety, everyone felt that Dom Marmion was quite in his right place; one grew accustomed to see his qualities of mind and heart exhibited there under various forms.

His talents, his store of gifts and virtues gained him universal esteem and sympathy, and, in the case of a great number and those best able to judge, a confidence and attachment expressed by the frequent recourse they had to him.

Amongst those who honoured him at this time by their friendship must be counted in the first place Cardinal Mercier – then president of the *Séminaire Léon* XIII – who chose him as his confessor; Msgr Ladeuze, Msgr Jules de Becker, the venerated president of the *Collège américain de Louvain;*[1] and the learned theologians of the Order of St Dominic, Fr Antoninus Dummermuth (✠1918) and Fr Marc de Munnynck.[2]

When, after ten years, he left Louvain to return to Maredsous as abbot, one of the highest academic authorities could truly declare that "Louvain was losing its best theologian," and the unanimous regrets manifested on this occasion, from the highest to the lowest in the university and in religious communities of every order, spoke eloquently of the place he had won, a place which may almost be said to have been unique.

His ministry was not confined to the young monks of the abbey and the priests of Louvain; he was also the ordinary confessor of the Carmel there. Having accepted this charge on his arrival at Louvain in 1899, he continued it until his departure in 1909, and each week Dom Columba traversed on foot the long distance which separates the two monasteries to give a conference to the nuns and hear their confessions.

This apostolate was dear to him for two reasons. In the same way that his functions as professor gave him occasion to review theology as a whole, so the obligation of leading contemplative souls to perfection made him go deeply into the spiritual works of St John of the Cross and of St Teresa of Ávila. This was for him the foundation of a wealth of ascetical and mystical lore whereof other souls were to benefit. The knowledge gained in this matter was so much the more valuable in that, from day to day, he was able to put to experimental proof the theoretical notions brought before him quite

---

[1] Msgr de Becker and Dom Marmion had known one another at Rome at the College of Propaganda; at Louvain their friendship grew to close intimacy.
[2] Now professor at *l'Université de Fribourg*.

naturally by his contact in this cloister with souls who had reached a high state of prayer and had confided their direction to him.

Every month, too, he went to Brussels to give an instruction to the English colony of which the spiritual centre was the church of the Servite Fathers; or again, at Cardinal Mercier's request, to preach the monthly retreat to the priests of the parishes and colleges of the capital: this last form of ministry lasted the two years of his stay in Louvain.

Not content with spending himself after this manner during the course of the year's studies, Dom Marmion took further advantage of the weeks when the theological classes were suspended to preach Jesus Christ in England. When, after the well-filled scholastic year he might have laid claim to a well-earned rest, he devoted the time of his "vacation" to preaching retreats to religious communities. The number of the retreats he gave was considerable.[1] It may be said there was no intermission to the output of his zeal. The English Benedictine monasteries of Douai, Ampleforth, Ramsgate, Erdington, Fort Augustus, the nuns of Stanbrook and of Princethorpe, the Augustinian canonesses of the priory of Haywards Heath were visited in turn and on different occasions, for no one ever wearied of listening to his warm, convincing words as he unfolded to them the greatness of the mysteries of Christ. In Belgium, the Benedictine nuns of Maredret, to whom he was extraordinary confessor during the whole of this period, as he was to the Adorers of the Sacred Heart at Koekelberg, the Benedictines of Liège, the Canonesses of Jupille and Lede as well as their pupils, and the nuns of the English Convent at Bruges particularly had the happiness of benefiting by his theological learning and ardent zeal.

Beyond these regular forms of apostolate, how many times, too, he was called upon in unforeseen circumstances! The establishing

---

[1] "You are no doubt wondering at my long silence," he wrote to one of his spiritual daughters; "I have been really overwhelmed with work, for besides my heavy office of prior and professor I have had to give four retreats within a few months, and I am preparing at this moment to give another." – Letter of 13 November 1901.

in the town of Louvain of medical centres often brought to the clinics invalids from afar, amongst whom were often to be found young English girls educated in Belgian *pensionnats*. Dom Marmion's thorough understanding of the numerous sects of the so-called Reformed Church and the well-deserved reputation he had, quite naturally marked him out as well fitted to help these souls to find the path of truth. What joy for him to prepare the way for their return to the Catholic Church, and sometimes, too, when medical art proved to be in vain, for their entrance into heaven!

In this way he found splendid occasions of devoting himself for the glory of his Divine Master, and of outpouring the treasure of the exquisite tenderness of his heart on those who were all the dearer in proportion as it cost him more to win them.

We see the wide extent of Dom Marmion's field of apostolic action.

And yet it would be a great mistake to dwell only on his outward activity at this period of his life. It is true that this activity was astonishing: regular courses, of which the preparation at times demanded hours of uninterrupted labour; frequent ascetical instruction to the young religious or to the entire community of which he was prior; written or oral consultations, sometimes long and delicate, asked for by the ecclesiastical authorities who had recourse to him as being particularly competent;[1] numerous retreats; various forms of spiritual direction;[2] an enormous correspondence: manifold and incessant duties of social life due to his office of prior or his numerous relations with the outer world; we may ask ourselves how one

---

1 "I have been nominated by His Eminence a member of the vigilance committee. I must tell you it is a great joy and consolation for me to have been chosen to watch over the purity of faith in this diocese" (Letter of 7 January 1906, to the Primate of the Order). In a letter two years later he wrote: "I am on the commission of vigilance for this diocese, which means: work, work" (Letter of 8 January 1908).

2 "There are so many priests and laymen who come to me for one reason or another that I cannot find a moment for myself" (Letter of 12 June 1906).

man – bound as he was to the office in choir and other often-prolonged exercises of the conventual life and to all the detail of the regular observance – was able to successfully further such diverse and often absorbing works. Trite as the expression has become, it must be repeated in reference to him, for with him it was fully realised: during those ten years, Dom Marmion showed what he was worth by spending himself without counting the cost.

No doubt a richly endowed and supple nature, rare penetration of mind, extreme facility for work, a memory singularly receptive and faithful in all directions, a special gift for adapting himself to circumstances, a yet greater gift for sympathy to the point that each might imagine that he or she was the only object of this sympathy, and that the subject in question was the only one in which he was interested, all these qualities of mind and heart may help to explain how he was able to perform so much.

But the secret of the power and fruitfulness of his labours lay elsewhere. For, as must be said again, the true life of this monk was not in these things; it was within – an intense life. It was the life of a soul which, before being thus given to the neighbour, was given to God in the most complete self-surrender out of obedience and in intimate union with the Saviour. With Dom Marmion the glowing focus whence escaped so many warm and luminous rays was that "life hidden in God with Christ" of which he has so admirably spoken and of which this would only have been possible after his having completely lived it.

> You can imagine how my time is *eaten up*. I say *eaten up*, for every morning I place myself on the paten with the host that is about to become Jesus Christ; and in the same way that Jesus is there in order to be eaten by all sorts of persons – *sumunt boni, sumunt mali, sorte lamen inaequali* – so I am eaten all day long by all kind of people. May our dear Saviour be glorified by my destruction, as He is by His own immolation…![1]

Of his spiritual life during this epoch – extending over ten years

---

[1] Letter of 19 January 1905.

– Dom Marmion has only left some scant notes, jotted down on the spur of the moment, and scattered without method throughout various exercise books dealing with his courses of theology and even intermingled with the rough drafts of his professorial lessons.[1] This unexpected mixture of study and piety gives a striking impression of unity and strength as regards his inner life.

These precious fragments of a spiritual treasure are to be reverently gathered up; we may see from them with what abundant lights he was inundated and at what high and pure sources the soul of this master of asceticism was nourished.

---

[1] The very fact of these notes being thus scattered proves that Dom Marmion wrote them without any thought of publication, but merely to "note" the lights he received. Notes on his inner life are to be found, too, in his pocket-book.

8 GRACES OF UNION

In pages full of truth and wisdom, which tell of personal experience, Dom Marmion has pointed out the different stages of the interior life. "Although these three stages are real," he says, "they are not in contradistinction to one another; there exists between them a reciprocal penetration, a certain affinity; these denominations result only from the predominance of such or such an element – a predominance which cannot go so far as to exclude the other elements. Thus a soul who is in the way of purification likewise accomplishes, and it may be often, acts of the illuminative way and acts of union.... We cannot then in this matter assign such or such impassable limits, or rather, we cannot geometrically fix souls in one state distinct from another; these stages are not separated by fixed boundaries passed once and forever; they more truly comprehend and sustain and complete one another."[1]

These lines might well be applied to their author himself.

During the first years of his monastic life at Maredsous, grace had drawn Dom Marmion to keep himself especially in the realm of humility, of compunction of heart and obedience, which detach the soul from creatures and from self; we have seen how generously the young monk had corresponded to these calls of grace. Consequently lights had abounded, increasing the spirit of faith in his soul, urging him on to an ever deeper humility, to more perfect obedience, leading him to the threshold of the way of self-abandonment.

At Louvain the call was more particularly to intimate union and this call was accompanied by vivid lights. These all converged towards the Person of Christ and shone on the many aspects of the ineffable mystery of the Incarnate Word. The gentle as well as powerful action of these graces were to lead the monk by a special act

---

[1] *Christ the Ideal of the Monk,* ch. 15, "Monastic Prayer." In reality, these pages are rather an application of the "three ways" in the domain of prayer; Dom Marmion gives a more general view of them in the chapter (in the same volume) on "The Instruments of Good Works."

of consecration into the way of love and abandon, where truly, it is no longer the soul that lives but Christ who lives in it. The interior graces which reveal the secret of the supernatural fruitfulness of all Dom Columba did, kept pace with the exterior activity opening out before him, but above all they mark out a new and decisive stage in his spiritual life. For this period was an important one in his life, and one on which it behoves us to linger.

The following numerous quotations throw a clear light on this development: taken from letters and private notes, used according to their chronological order, they help us to grasp what was the bent of Dom Marmion's spirituality; revealing as they do the inner life of a great soul, we should assuredly have laid ourselves open to reproach if we had left these luminous confidences in oblivion.[1]

However, it is important to note – and the attentive reader will already have noticed this in the preceding chapters – these pages do not contain subtle analyses of the soul; they are rather communications of lights upon God, the mysteries of Jesus, the spiritual life: hence, in many of them, a singular value and depth. What is strictly personal is the response of the soul to these divine suggestions, a correspondence which fixes it in a state of union.

It will likewise be seen how often, with Dom Columba, these lights are in close dependence on the liturgy: the interior life which flows from it receives from this fact a character of simplicity giving spaciousness and freedom to the soul.

At the very beginning of 1899, a few months before his departure for Louvain, he had written, in a pocket-book, these lines which were to serve him as the keynote for this whole period:

> The Church begins the year with the name of Jesus. Let us place this name on our lips and in our heart. Our efforts are weak, but united with Him and His merits, they are of great

[1] In order to accelerate the reading of these pages we have for the most part translated the numerous Latin quotations from Holy Scripture placed by Dom Marmion in the text. If the thought loses in force it may gain in clearness.

value in the eyes of God: By Him, and with Him and in Him, be to the Father all honour and glory.

Merchants and business men draw up a balance sheet at the end of the year in order to see their way for the future. Let us do the same. *Expenditure:* 365 days. Physical and moral forces. Sufferings. *Receipts:* God, and what is done for God: 'Their works follow them,' all the rest is lost.

For this year, let us do all for God. However, our best works are so imperfect! In the eyes of God, says Holy Scripture, all our justices are as filthy rags.[1] The more light we have the more we see our imperfections: 'in many things we all offend.'[2]

But Jesus Christ supplies for us. He is ours. He came down from heaven for us and for our salvation. His riches are ineffable and innumerable. He dwells in our heart. Let us do all in union with Him. He has sanctified all our actions. This is why St Paul tells us to do all things in His name: 'Do all in the name of the Lord Jesus Christ' and—

The sentence, as often happens, is left unfinished.

Dom Marmion has just referred to St Paul, his favourite author. At this time he was assiduously reading the epistles, of which he fully assimilated the meaning. It is notably to the apostle that he owes the characteristic note, already mentioned, of his spiritual physiognomy: absolute confidence in the merits of Jesus allied to entire humility. This trait appears vividly in a page which he has left on St Paul. On his arrival at Louvain (April 1899), he consented to act as confessor to the Carmelites of this town and to give them ascetical conferences. We have had the good fortune to find the notes of the first instructions. At the end of June, on the feast of St Paul, he interrupted the regular order of his instructions to speak of the great apostle; he had drawn up the rough draft.

---

1 Isa. 44:6.
2 Jas. 3:2.

St Paul, June 1899 – Gladly therefore will I glory in my infirmities, that the power of Christ may dwell in me.

1. Interrupt the course of instructions to say a word on St Paul, that great lover of Jesus Christ, so full of His spirit.

2. St Paul is one of those generous souls who do not bargain with God.

Love knows no measure. This is why God tells us: Thou shalt love the Lord with all thy heart, with all thy mind, etc.

Such was St Paul, persecuted, beaten with rods, betrayed, suffering cold, hunger, shipwreck, exposed to all sorts of dangers, and finally bound with chains in prison. And yet he says: 'I exceedingly abound with joy in all [my] tribulations.' From whence comes this superabundant joy? From his love. 'For I am sure that neither death nor life ... shall be able to separate us from the love of God.' He had ever before his eyes his crucified Jesus. 'The charity of Christ presseth us.' He 'loved me, and delivered Himself for me.'

3. The spirit of St Paul. A great consciousness of his nothingness, an extraordinary esteem for the merits of Jesus Christ. 'Not that we are sufficient to think anything of ourselves, as of ourselves, but our sufficiency is from God ... I will glory in my infirmities.'

St Paul sees in himself as it were two men. He recounts his ecstasies, graces received, labours: 'For such a one I will glory; but for myself I will glory nothing, but in my infirmities.'

Infirmities: from without ... [word illegible], suffering from his eyes, humiliating malady, temptations: I will glory in these things.

Wherefore? 'That the power of Christ may dwell in me.' He had received the mission to reveal the innumerable riches of Christ. Description of these merits.

Nothing glorifies Jesus Christ so much as confidence in His merits, in spite of our infirmities. 'For when I am weak, then am I powerful.' Those amongst you whom the good God afflicts ought to be filled with this spirit of St Paul, that they may do great things in themselves and for others. For example, in saying: 'Hallowed be thy Name,' the *Gloria Patri*, in union with Jesus Christ, one does great things for God in the supernatural Kingdom. St Paul in his prison did as much for God's glory as during his missions.

The thought of our riches in Jesus Christ should give us a holy boldness to draw near to the Father.

When we are filled with this spirit of St Paul, the sight of our miseries does not discourage us, for we lean on Jesus Christ alone. When a soul tells me: 'All that is useless for me… I am too full of miseries…' I see that it is a soul who has never understood the greatness of our riches in Jesus Christ, who has never understood these words: 'God so loved the world, as to give His Only-begotten Son.'

The Only-begotten Son is given to us as Model and Means of perfection. On this beautiful theme lights abound for the attentive soul. We have only to quote from the spiritual *Notes*.

July 1899 – Holiness in God consists in the perfection with which He glorifies Himself.[1]

The Word is the substantial glory of the Father; this is why we say of Jesus: 'Thou only art holy,' for He alone perfectly glorifies the Father.

The more we are united to Jesus, the more we glorify the Father.

This thought is stated in a less general manner a few weeks later:

August 27th – Today, during prayer, I had this thought in reference to the text: 'Mary hath chosen the better part.'[2]

---

1 See the development of this thought in *Christ the Life of the Soul*, ch. 1.
2 These words were spoken by Jesus of Mary Magdalene; the Church applies them to the Blessed Virgin Mary on the feast of the Assumption. Dom Marmion received this light during the octave of this feast. See Dom Bernard Capelle, *Revue liturgique et monastique*, 1925, upon the choice of this Gospel for this mys-

God's *essential* glory consists in the intimate life of God, by which He loves and glorifies Himself infinitely. The *accidental* glory is in creation.

In the same way, the essential glory that God requires from each soul is in the interior life by which it glorifies God in itself. The accidental glory is in the works which it performs and which derive all their value from the interior life.

In God, this glory is in the *uncreated* Word. The accidental glory is the created word – the creation.

The same with us, the essential glory is realised by the Word, by Jesus living in us; the accidental, by Jesus given to others. All the glory of the soul, the King's daughter, comes from within.[1]

The more we are the image of Jesus, the more we glorify the Father.

Jesus is at once the Son of God and the Saviour of men.

1. As Son of God, He is the splendour and the glory of the Father. 'I do not seek My glory,' He says in the Gospel, 'but that of My Father who sent Me'. At the head of the book (of My life upon earth) it is written: 'Father, may I do Thy will'.[2] May Thy name be hallowed.

2. As Saviour of men. 'That the world may know that I love the Father,' I fulfil the precept that He has given Me (to deliver Myself up for men). I came not to do My will, but that of My Father who sent Me. The will of My Father is that whoever sees the Son and believes in Him, shall have eternal life. There is no greater love than to give one's life for one's friends. We too ought to give our life for our brethren. All those who have this hope sanctify themselves through it in imitation of Him who is Holiness.

He received another, more concentrated, light a short time afterwards, converging on the same subject:

tery of the Blessed Virgin.

1 Ps. 44:14.
2 Heb. 10:9.

September 29th – Today I received a particular grace. I understood that all my perfection should consist in the closest union of myself with Jesus Christ as Son of God and Saviour of men. I clearly understood this after Mass. In this manner, my thanksgiving is divided between the acts of Jesus in regard to His Father and towards my soul and that of others. St Teresa says that one must love oneself in God.

And as he had at this time to give a retreat, he at once in this clear light sketches the broad outline:

Plan of Retreat.
    Perfection: to imitate God.
    Jesus Christ, perfect image of God.
    Jesus Christ, Son of God, Saviour of men.
     1. Son of God: duties towards God, negative and positive.
     2. Saviour of men: duties towards oneself and one's neighbour: to love oneself and the neighbour in God.

He continues to have a vivid sense of the effect of these lights in his soul:

This very day (*mid-December 1899, Octave of the Immaculate Conception*), the good God made me see that the great object of my life ought to be the glory of Jesus, as it is His own: this is also the object of all Mary's desires. I was very struck by these words: 'God so loved the world, as to give His Only-begotten Son.' The gift of God is worthy of Himself: it is His own Son. Oh! 'if thou didst know the gift of God!' From all eternity, the Father finds His delights in the Son, 'the only-begotten Son who is in the bosom of the Father.'

This same Son is 'in our bosom' by Eucharistic Communion and by faith. Christ, says St Paul, dwells in our hearts by faith.[1] By faith, we ought to find all our delights in Jesus, as the Father finds them in Him: 'This is My beloved Son, in

---

1 Eph. 3:17.

whom I am well pleased.' But it is by faith that we do this: 'According to your faith be it done unto you.'

4 January 1900 – At the beginning of this year I feel a strong attraction of grace to take as the aim of my life that which God has established: the glory of His Son Jesus. I offer myself to the Father and to Mary with this intention.

The same strong attraction of grace some weeks later:

25 February 1900 – Today, while meditating on the faith of Abraham, I felt a strong movement of grace urging me to consecrate all my life and all my energies to the glorification of Jesus Christ in myself and in others, imitating in that the Father who gives us His Son: He tells us to hear Him.

I understood that through faith we identify ourselves in some way in the Holy Spirit with Jesus Christ, that we may obtain, as He has said, all that we ask. It is, moreover, His promise. But, as we see by the history of Abraham, we may have to wait a long time for the realisation of this promise.

He finds everything in this union, for in Christ are contained all the treasures of knowledge and wisdom:

On the Feast of St Joseph, 1900 – The text for the little chapter for None *Justum deduxit Dominus per vias rectas* '[wisdom] guided the just in right paths,'[1] has struck me greatly. These words were spoken first of all of Jacob. In meditating on these words and their application to St Joseph, I felt a great desire to abandon myself entirely to the direction of this eternal wisdom. Christ, says St Paul, has become, in God, our wisdom.[2] Hear ye Him.

25 March 1900 – On the day of the Annunciation I received a strong light on these words: *Fiat mihi secundum verbum tuum.* The whole of Mary's life was *secundum Verbum*, who is infinite

---

1 Wis. 10:10.
2 1 Cor. 1:30.

wisdom. I felt a strong impulse to abandon myself to this wisdom, to substitute this wisdom for my own: 'Christ Jesus, who of God is made unto us wisdom,' under the guidance of His Spirit. Jesus, infinite wisdom, did all under the guidance of this Spirit *vivificantem,* and we have (through grace) this same Spirit: 'The spirit of adoption... whereby we cry: *Abba* (Father).'

The Paschal season, which contains so much of the pith of Holy Scripture and the liturgy, is the occasion of many clear lights being thrown on the mystery of Christ.

The reader will forgive us for lingering, but we cannot sacrifice these beautiful texts which reveal so much of the inner life of a great soul.

Easter 1900 – I was much struck by grace while meditating on these words of St Paul: 'who was delivered up for our sins, and rose again for our justification.'

Jesus Christ is infinite and eternal wisdom, and He chose, as the means of expiating our sins,[1] His sorrowful death. Exempt from death *de droit* (since sin, by which alone death came, *per peccatum mors,* could not touch Him), He *freely* accepted death for us, in our place. I felt the great efficacy of this death, and I untied myself to Jesus in His death, that I may die with Him to sin. I had a great sense of abandonment, of gratitude, etc.

Resurrexit propter justificationem nostram. The end and aim of the risen life of Jesus is our justification. I understood very clearly how much Jesus has our holiness at heart and how the union of our life with His is efficacious to sanctify us: 'For if, when we were enemies, we were reconciled to God by the death of His Son; much more, being reconciled, we shall be saved by His life.'

---

1 Heb. 9:28.

April 18th, Easter Tuesday – Many lights in reflecting on these words: 'Christ liveth unto God.' I have felt the intensity of this life of Jesus *all of God*. The union of our life with this life is the highest form of perfection. Without Him, we can do nothing, but it was just to communicate this life to us that He came: 'As the Father hath life in Himself, so He hath given to the Son also to have life in Himself.' 'I am come that they (My sheep) may have life and may have it more abundantly.' The resurrection is the mystery of this life, and Jesus communicates it to us especially in Holy Communion: 'Except you eat the flesh of the Son of Man, and drink His blood, you shall not have life in you.' This bread is 'the life of the world.' I feel more and more the desire to associate myself with this divine life, so that Jesus may be glorified in me. For that is the *aim* of His glorious life: He 'rose again FOR our justification,' and He ever continues this action: 'always living to make intercession for us.' This life of Jesus is the love of His Father, whence comes the flowering of all the *human virtues* divinised in Him. There is our model. I have taken the resolution of trying to unite my poor life to this intense and divine life.

Dominica in Albis, 1900 – Everything today speaks to us of faith: 'Blessed are they that have not seen, and have believed.' 'It is the foundation and root of all justification.'[1] It is by a living faith, the conviction of the divinity of Jesus Christ that we live the divine life.

1. It is by faith that this divine life begins: Those who believe in His name ... *are born of God.*[2] 'Whatsoever is born of God, overcometh the world.... Who is he that overcometh the world, but he that believeth that Jesus is the Son of God?' This intimate conviction of the divinity of Jesus Christ makes us throw ourselves at His feet like the man born blind: 'The

---

[1] Council of Trent.
[2] John 1: 12–13.

just man liveth by faith.' 'He that believeth in Me, although he be dead, shall live.'

2. By this faith, we identify ourselves in some way with Jesus Christ:

(*a*) *In our thoughts:* 'He that believeth in the Son of God, hath the testimony of God in Himself.' We have the same thoughts as those of Jesus Christ: 'He who is joined to the Lord is one spirit' with Him.

(*b*) *In our desires:* 'Let this mind be in you, which was also in Christ Jesus.'

(*c*) *In our words:* 'If any speak let him speak as the words of God.' Christ becomes the mainspring of all our [projects]: That Christ may dwell BY FAITH in your hearts.'

(*d*) *In our actions:* 'All whatsoever you do in word or in work, do all in the name of the Lord Jesus Christ, giving thanks to God and the Father by Him.'

Then comes to pass the: 'I live, now not I; but Christ liveth in me.... I live *in the faith* of the Son of God, who loved me, and delivered Himself for me.'

To act *in the name* of Jesus Christ: 'For Christ therefore we are ambassadors.' 'As the living Father hath sent me, and I live by the Father; so he that eateth Me, the same also shall live by Me.

These abundant lights produced ardent aspirations in Dom Columba's soul towards the Supreme Good dimly perceived. The insistent call to union marks out this epoch of his inner life. It is to the letters of this period that we must specially turn in order to see how intense were the touches of the grace of union with God in Jesus Christ. He writes to the Primate of the Order[1] on 1 June 1901:

Our Lord continues, I believe, His work in me. My interior

---

[1] At this date, Dom Columba, although residing at Louvain, remained a monk of Maredsous, of which Primate Hildebrand was abbot.

life tends more and more towards a great simplicity. I have learnt that the precious pearl of which the Gospel speaks, is Jesus Christ *qui factus est nobis sapientia a Deo et justitia et sanctificatio et redemptio.*[1] I see that to abandon oneself to our Lord without counting the cost, and then let oneself be guided in all things by His Will manifested by obedience and by His inspiration, is the whole of sanctity.

In prayer, our Lord draws me to identify myself with Him, to abide in Him and He in me, and then, He urges me: 1. to make acts of love to His Father, in union with Him; 2. for myself, to abandon myself entirely to Him; 3. to love my neighbour as He has loved him. It is, above all, this last point which has drawn me for some time past. I feel a *great increase* of love for the Holy Church, the Bride of Christ. I have, as it were, an habitual sense that the neighbour is Christ, and I feel urged to a great charity towards all. I see very clearly that true charity embraces all the virtues and requires continual renunciation.

As interior practice, I feel more and more urged to *lose myself in Jesus Christ.* May He think and will in me and bear me towards His Father. In the *Pater,* the only petition that He teaches us to make to God for our souls is *Fiat voluntas tua* SICUT IN COELO. I try *to love* His Holy Will in the thousand little vexations and interruptions of each day.[2]

And a few days later:

I am again in great peace, and it is in our DEAR Saviour that I find this peace, and more and more all in Him. The feeling is very strong in me that our Lord will be all in all for me: 'wisdom, justice, sanctification,' everything, if I have constant recourse to Him, and if, without neglecting the ordinary means [of sanctification], I depend much more upon Him than upon

---

[1] "Who of God is made unto us wisdom, and justice, and sanctification, and redemption" (1 Cor. 1: 30).
[2] Letter of 11 February 1902.

my own endeavours. Our Lord urges me more and more to this *simple* self-surrender which includes everything.[1]

You have no idea of the *absolute* solitude in which I live... I feel more and more drawn towards complete abandon, and it seems to me that the more I give myself up to *Him*, the more He sees to everything.[2]

Pray for me. Our Lord gives me great desires to belong wholly to Him, but that is not yet![3]

Is not this union which Christ wills to consummate with Him, and to which he feels himself so irresistibly called, the supreme end of all our Saviour's work? On Holy Thursday of the same year, Dom Marmion writes to one of his intimate disciples:

I have just made my Easter Communion, and after speaking with our Lord, I come to say a little word to you also. In the silence of prayer, I see more and more clearly, and especially today, that the great object our Lord had in view in giving Himself to us in the Holy Eucharist was to *incorporate* us in Him as in His mystical body, so that with Him and in Him, we may perfect the great work of the Father: our sanctification and the salvation of the world: *Opus consummavi quod dedisti mihi ut faciam.*[4] I feel myself more and more invited by our Lord to give myself up to Him without reserve and without plan or desire, except that of doing His Will as far and in the measure that it is manifested to me. Thanks to God, I have been able to keep Lent without any dispensation or exception, and I have rarely been so well in health, or so happy and full of peace.[5]

You will be happy to know that I am *very united* to our Lord: more, I think, than ever before in my life. I feel as if I

[1] Letter of 28 February 1902.
[2] Letter of 10 March 1902.
[3] Letter of 14 March 1902.
[4] John 17: 4.
[5] Letter of 9 April 1902.

had made a long retreat and am so united with God and in such great joy and inward peace. More and more I feel myself drawn to lose myself, to hide myself in Jesus Christ: *Vivens Deo* IN *Christo Jesu*. He Himself becomes, it seems to me, the eye of my soul, and my will is blended with His. I am drawn to desire nothing *outside* of Him, that I may abide *in Him*. So much for my soul.[1]

These calls to union found their echo in the pages of St Francis de Sales' *Treatise on the Love of God*, which he was then reading. After the Holy Spirit, the Divine Guest of the soul, he could not have come across a better guide in the ways of love. Certainly, this was not the first time that he had met with the works of the "eminent doctor of the inner life," as he himself calls him – he had known them for a long time. In 1892, he took numerous extracts from these works; in 1895, he recommends the reading of the *Treatise*[2] to one of his spiritual daughters; at the end of a page dated 19 March 1899, where he finds a light upon self-surrender, he himself goes back to Book IX of the *Treatise*. But at the time where we are, he takes up this book again to plunge deeply into it; for two years he studies the *Treatise,* savours it and makes its teaching his own, with so much the more ease that he finds in these pages, set forth by a master and a saint, the doctrine of love on which he inwardly feels himself called to live.

> I have lately been reading Book IX of the *Treatise on the Love of God,* by St Francis de Sales, all our own ideas are there.[3]
>
> I strongly recommend you, he writes another time, the practice of *abandon*. If you could read, *at leisure,* Book IX of the

---

1 Letter of 28 October 1902.
2 "If you have the *Treatise on the Love of God,* by St Francis de Sales, read the 15th chapter of Book IX, where you will find the dispositions you ought to have at this time of trial" (Letter of 13 January 1895).
3 Letter of 30 January 1902.

Treatise on the Love of God, by St Francis de Sales, you would find there *just* what I would say to you.¹

And again later:

I have read, and re-read, and gone deeply into the sublime doctrine of St Francis de Sales in Books IX and X of the *Treatise on the Love of God,* and I have understood that here is the last word of love, and the basis of a profound peace and great liberty of heart. Once it is thoroughly understood that the Will of God is the same thing as God Himself, we see that we ought to prefer His adorable Will to all besides, and take it, in what it does, in what it ordains, in what it *permits,* as the one *norm* of ours. Let us keep our eyes fixed upon this Holy Will, and not upon the things that cause us pain and trouble.²

Thus, after such long contact of mind and heart with the masterpiece of the holy Bishop of Geneva, he justly concludes:

I have the conviction that of all the mystical authors it is St Francis de Sales who has most of the spirit of St Benedict and after having studied other authors, I shall return to his *Treatise on the Love of God* as to my book of predilection.³

---

1 Letter of 14 March 1902. He does not restrict himself only to the *Treatise:* the same year, 1902, writing to a Mother Superior, he cites a long extract from a letter (CXLIII) of the saint.
2 Letter of 4 August 1903.
3 Letter of 28 February 1904. This affinity of spirit between the two great saints has recently been brought out by Dom Ryelandt: *Essai sur la physionomie morale de Saint-Benoît,* ch. 3, "Saint Benoît et Saint François de Sales." Those who are interested in ascetical questions will profit by reading the original and suggestive pages, corroborating Dom Marmion's opinion, and which have received the approbation of another writer of renown, Dom Cuthbert Butler, late Abbot of Downside. They serve indirectly to point out the daring and extravagant theses set forth by the Fr Francis Vincent in his book: *Saint François de Sales, directeur d'âmes, l'éducation de la volonté.* See the serious criticisms launched against this book by Fr Paul Doncœur, SJ, in *Études,* 1923, T. CLXXV; and again by Paul Herbaye, in *La Croix,* 29 May 1924: "The doctrinal physiognomy of St Francis de Sales stands out from these pages, if not falsified, at least altered." See likewise the sharp criticisms made by Fr Henri Brémond in his

The letters of this period clearly bear the mark of this contact with the teaching of St Francis de Sales. He writes on 26 December 1902, to the Primate of the Order: "I am very happy. It seems to me that my inner life becomes more and more simple; it tends to unify my will with that of the Eternal Father through Jesus Christ, and I feel inwardly invited to cut off every desire, except that of fulfilling the *known Will of God*, with all the energy of my soul; and as for the good pleasure of God that *I do not know*, to abandon myself, without plan or desire, to His wisdom and goodness."

There cannot be union with Jesus without union with His members: Christ is not to be divided. In pages which count amongst the most forcible of his spiritual works, Dom Marmion has shown magnificently the substantial identity of a one and only love, which reaching out to God, necessarily flows back again upon creatures.[1] However, at this epoch, the intimate *experience* of this phenomena becomes particularly vivid:

> Our Lord has united me much more with Himself lately, and I see better the nothingness of creatures. In prayer, one ought to place oneself before God in the most complete submission to His holy and all-lovable Will; and then let Him do what He pleases. It is a curious fact that since I have given myself more to God in prayer I have received a very lively sense of my union with all the members of the Church, and with *some* in particular. It seems to me that I bear the whole Church in

---

Histoire littéraire de sentiment religieux en France, T. VII.

[1] One who most closely followed Dom Marmion's teaching, Dom Pie de Hemptinne, notices the *experience* of this phenomenon: "Our well-beloved has much enlightened me these days," he wrote in October 1901. "He has spoken eloquently to me of charity. Until now, I contented myself, in some way, with the first part of this precept (love of God) and I thought only very little of the second, the *mandatum novum* (love of the neighbour). One thing has appeared clearly to me, it is that, in the interior life, the soul cannot be abstracted from the exterior world which surrounds it, in order to love Christ alone hidden in the soul.... We ought all to unite ourselves in one love alone, so deep that it banishes egoism from amongst us, as amongst the Persons of the Blessed Trinity." *Une âme bénédictine*, ch. 4, "La révélation de l'amour."

my heart, especially at Holy Mass and during Divine Office, and in this way I have no more distractions as in the past. It seems to me the Divine Office prepares me for prayer, and prayer for the Divine Office. Another phenomenon: since I have thought more of union with God, our Lord sends me souls who need encouragement and direction in this matter.[1]

The soul drawing near to love sees its horizons widen and the flame with which it burns cannot but radiate more brightly:

> Our Lord gives me more and more a great confidence in the Holy Sacrifice and in the Divine Office. It seems to me that when I celebrate or when I say the office, I bear the whole world with me, all the afflicted, the suffering, the poor, and all the interests of Jesus Christ. When I give myself to Jesus Christ, it seems to me almost always that He unites me with Him and then with all His members and that He asks me to do like Him, of whom it is said: 'Surely He hath borne our infirmities and carried our sorrows.'[2]

Another truth which he then experienced more fully than of yore, is that love is inseparable from sacrifice. Although love ought to be the mainspring of all activity, sacrifice is often, at the same time, the safeguard and manifestation of this love. God only reigns totally in the soul if it is emptied of created things. And the innermost work of casting off self is not wrought without struggle, nor yet without suffering:

> Thanks to the good God, I am *very happy* here. The good God gives us the grace of *perfect* union and peace, and I think that this is the best sign that our dear Saviour finds Himself 'at home' in the midst of us. However, I will tell you that, although the higher part of the soul, the extreme point is at

---

1 Letter of 20 January 1904.
2 Letter of 23 February 1903.

peace, it is night in the rest of the soul, and almost always complete desolation. *Lux et tenebrae benedicite Domino.*[1]

I have some extremely painful things to suffer; at this moment I am weighed down by them, but our Lord sustains me. Ask Him to give me the grace of an immense confidence in the guidance of His wisdom and His love.[2]

This confidence in Jesus is for Him a source of peace and joy:

However, I am under no illusion, I know it is not possible to be closely united to our Lord without sharing in His sufferings: *Passionibus Christi per patientiam participamus.*[3] I have had, in fact, a hard inward struggle during these days as regards the return of my cross. The reality, as ever, has been less hard than the anticipation. It is however always a cross... *Fiat!*[4]

He was likewise to meet the cross in the domain of obedience, towards which he feels himself so strongly urged: "Today [22 January 1900] I have felt a great desire to give myself up to entire obedience."

A letter to Abbot Hildebrand, Primate of the Order, reveals the underlying motive that made Dom Columba feel called to this virtue, and exemplifies how closely his inner life was linked to the lessons of dogmatic theology which he was then giving, and to the abundant lights God was granting him in prayer:

I have been explaining lately in theology the treatise on Original Sin, and I have been much struck by the relation that St Paul establishes between disobedience of the first Adam and the obedience of Jesus Christ, the second Adam.[5] I feel myself almost continually drawn, during these last weeks, to meditate on this truth and I have understood as I have never understood before, that the beauty and strength of our

1 Letter of 7 June 1899.
2 Letter of 10 March 1902.
3 "That we may by patience share in the sufferings of Christ." *Rule of St Benedict*, Prologue.
4 Letter of 9 April 1903.
5 Rom. 5: 4 *sq.*

monastic life consists in our union, as His members, with Jesus Christ in His obedience. I see more and more, that the more we embrace entirely and perfectly, with Jesus Christ and after His example, every manifestation of the Divine Will, by a very perfect submission to superiors, the more closely we become members of Jesus Christ and have a share in the fruits of His redemption. I have always been persuaded of this truth, but recently God has given me to see it with so much light that it seems to me that I knew nothing at all about it before, and I now find that great sweetness and docility of heart in accepting what is even the most humiliating and the most repugnant to nature. I tell you this, Very Reverend Father, because you have been so good as to tell me that what concerns my soul interests you, and also that you may know that, by God's grace, you will find me absolutely ready to acquiesce, not only exteriorly, but also with entire docility of heart and of judgment, in all that you may find well to lay upon me for the future. I feel great detachment of heart from all the persons and gifts of this world, and I have only one desire, that of belonging to God unreservedly, occupying myself only with Him *alone* with the persons and labours which He wills to confide to me, ready to leave them and to occupy myself with other persons and other things, according as He makes this known to me by obedience. Such is, truly at present, my disposition of heart, and I consider it as one of the most precious graces that God has ever given me.[1]

Faithful to the inspiration of this grace, Dom Marmion every morning after Mass united his obedience to that of Christ by this prayer:[2] "Lord Jesus, in union with that intention and that love with which You became obedient unto death, and the death of the cross, and ever did that which was pleasing to our Father, I wish to do

---

[1] Letter of 2 June 1902.
[2] We translate from the Latin.

all things today in Your name and in the spirit of humility, obedience and submission."

Then he renewed his religious profession. But this virtue cannot be practised without sacrifices at times hard to bear. "To lay down our activity," he writes in 1905, "our will and our judgment at the feet of a superior, and that for all one's life, is a very great and immense sacrifice, the greatest we can make. I feel it every day, but I am very happy to be able to offer this sacrifice to our Lord."

Even with the most resolute souls, sensitive nature sometimes takes alarm at this prospect of incessant obedience which embraces the whole life down to the smallest details. With the saints, men of flesh and blood like ourselves, nature shrinks before the trial, but with them generosity responds to grace.

One day (in 1905) – as Dom Marmion himself related to one of his spiritual sons – he was in his cell before his crucifix; he was experiencing great difficulties; he was assailed with all kind of fears for the future, and the thought came to him that it was much to be wished that matters might be arranged in a certain way. But immediately, looking at our Lord on the cross, he said to Him: "No, my God, rather as You will it!" And, he added: "If Christ had said to me: 'I give you *carte blanche,* arrange your life and all that concerns you as you wish it, take your pen, write out your plan and I will sign it,' I should have answered Him: 'No, my Jesus, I do not wish to plan my life; I want only your plan, because it is divine; it is for You to guide me; You are for me the *Alpha* and *Omega,* and I abandon myself entirely to You.'"

An admirable state of soul which was again brought out in the face of trial. Obedience having laid upon him a very hard sacrifice which affected at the same time a person he directed, he opens out his heart to her in the following letter, where we see the supernatural height of view to which he rises, and the delicacy with which he tries to prevail upon his correspondent to enter into his way of thinking, that so she may share with him the recompense of a like self-conquest.

After having explained the nature of the sacrifice, he adds:

You will be happy to know that our Lord has given me a very great grace; I think the greatest of all my life. He has given me the grace to submit myself *without any reservation*. During prayer, I understood that all consists in this: *To receive Jesus Christ such as He pleases to present Himself to us*; as gardener, as pilgrim,¹ but to receive Him not by halves, nor coldly, but entirely, loyally, frankly. The more He strikes us the more we ought to bow down. I could not describe to you the delightful peace which I enjoy and the perfect liberty of heart. The only thing that costs me is that perhaps you have not yet entered into these sentiments. I do not often give you the occasion of practising obedience, but now I tell you that I *want* you to try to conform yourself perfectly and generously to this way of acting and seeing. We must not carry our heads high; but, 'if anyone takes your cloak, give him also your coat': let us be good little children, that is how we shall please Jesus; and do we wish anything else?²

He certainly possessed the patient and inward endurance required by St Benedict³ in the practice of obedience, in the midst of the clash of circumstances most trying to nature. And according to the Great Patriarch's counsel, in this trial which made him suffer deeply he kept at the time the joy springing up from an unshaken confidence in this God whom we love and to whom we have abandoned all.⁴

Some months later, quite unexpectedly and without his having done anything to hasten its term or having sought any alleviation, the trial came to an end. In telling his spiritual daughter of the decision, he writes these admirable lines which reveal what intense love of God was constantly maintained in his soul:

---

1 This letter was written during the Paschal season, hence the choice of these comparisons.
2 Letter dated 1 April 1902.
3 *Rule of St Benedict*, ch 7.
4 *Rule of St Benedict*, ibid.

> When we give ourselves up entirely to our Lord we do Him a great wrong in troubling ourselves about whatever it may be. I have relinquished all to Him, and I have told Him a hundred times with all my heart that I have no other desire than that of doing His Holy Will in everything, and of giving myself to others in the measure and the manner that He wills. Certainly I have withdrawn nothing of my consecration (to Him), nor diminished anything of my affection (for you), but I have left to Him *without reservation,* the power and the manner of acting in all things *solely* according to the designs of His wisdom and the glory of His Father. And now that the sacrifice is made, He gives back to me by the way of obedience, all that I had relinquished to Him. My very dear daughter, this is a lesson for us that we ought to abandon ourselves more and more to His wisdom and to His love. You have been disheartened and so have I; for some weeks the chanting of the office in choir has been an almost insupportable penance; but as I well see, to live in this state, to work, to pray, and to be gay is worth more than the greatest austerities. You will be happy to learn that I have not had *one instant* of sadness or discouragement, although I have been tried in every way.[1]

To moral trials, physical sufferings were at times added. In 1906 Dom Marmion had to undergo an operation in a clinic. This was the occasion of some confidences and lights which we have gathered together: it is ever the same generosity of soul, the same intimate union with Jesus.

> I have had little experience of physical suffering; I always dreaded it; and although I offer myself daily at Holy Mass in union with the Divine Victim, *without reserve* to the love and wisdom of my Heavenly Father, yet I never *asked* for suffering. [During these days] I had no consolation, save the unfelt one of being united to God's Will and a glance at the

---

[1] Letter of 10 August 1902.

GRACES OF UNION

crucifix.... I am *so* glad to have suffered a little, I feel it will do a great good in souls.[1]

In another letter written at this time he speaks of his suffering and want of consolation being for his jubilee year[2] and the realisation of St Paul's words: I fill up in my body "those things that are wanting of the sufferings of Christ" (Col. 1:24).

He had no trouble in using the enforced leisure left to him by the days of convalescence; following the bent of his soul, he especially consecrated them to prayer: "I have long hours all alone with God. The more I gaze at Him, the more I see that He is the Source of *all* good, and that it is infinitely better to look at Him than at ourselves."[3]

All these trials, by stripping Dom Columba's soul of self, served to deepen his capacity for union. During the last years of his stay in Louvain, particularly from 1905, the calls to union, while becoming more urgent, take a special form and are expressed by a more personal tone. It is no longer the simple desire to be united to Jesus in everything that he does, but the deeper one of laying down self at the feet of Jesus, and losing himself in order to live in entire dependence on His Spirit to the glory of the Father. At this time he had been named professor of exegesis, and he chose as his subject the Gospel according to St John.

While studying the pages written by the beloved disciple, he is above all struck by the texts which emphasise the perfect dependence of Jesus upon the Father; he even sums them up on a page of his private notes.[4] This thought of the dependence of the soul of

[1] Letter of 29 November 1906.
[2] It was the 25th year since his ordination to the priesthood.
[3] Letter of 29 November 1906.
[4] [22 May 1906] "I much love to consider Jesus in his perfect dependence on His Father: 'I cannot of myself do anything. As I hear, so I judge: and my judgment is just; because I seek not my own will, but the will of Him that sent Me' (John 5:30). 'I am not come of Myself: but He that sent Me, is true, whom you know

179

Jesus becomes henceforth predominant, and it marks with a special character the notes of this period, so rich in doctrinal and scriptural substance.

> *1 February 1906* – For some time past our Lord has been making me see very clearly:
>
> 1. That we are only pleasing to the Father in so far as He sees us *in His Son:* 'He hath graced us in His Beloved Son ... predestinated us into the adoption of children through Jesus Christ.'
>
> 2. We are in Jesus as His members: 'Now you are the body of Christ, and members of members.'
>
> 3. The more we cease to be members of the 'old man,' children of Adam, the more we become members of Christ: 'stripping yourself of the old man with his deeds, and putting on the new, him who is renewed unto knowledge, according to the image of him that created him.'
>
> 4. This 'old man' is the natural self spoilt by Original Sin and by every sin, vice and imperfection of my life. What comes from this source may have a certain natural goodness; but, in fact, there is so much darkness in the intellect, so much weakness and perversity in the will, such a lack of capacity in supernatural things, that I ought thoroughly to despise this ego, to distrust it, and continually to efface it in order to substitute Jesus Christ for it.
>
> 5. 'Who is he that overcometh the world but he that believeth that Jesus is the Son of God?' The whole occupation of my life ought to be to lay down this ego at the feet

---

not' (7:28). 'Jesus therefore said to them: when you shall have lifted up the Son of Man, then shall you know that I am He, and that I do nothing of Myself, but as the Father hath taught Me these things I speak' (8:28). 'Amen, amen, I say unto you, the Son cannot do anything of Himself, but what He seeth the Father doing: for what things soever He doeth, these the Son also doth in like manner' (5:19). 'For from God I proceeded, and came.... For I have not spoken of Myself; but the Father who sent Me, He gave Me commandment what I should say, and what I should speak' (8:42, and 12:49).

of Jesus and continually to see Jesus *as God, in me,* according Him with all my faculties. He says of Himself: 'I am the beginning, who also speak unto you. He must become the *beginning* of all my activity. To do this we must deny ourselves that we may follow Christ.[1] This continual immolation of self for Christ's sake is the fulfilling of the great desire of the Father: 'Thou hast subjected all things under His feet.' 'Adore Him, all you His angels.' 'This is the work of God, that you believe in Him whom He hath sent.' Our Lord said: 'If any man minister to Me, him will My Father honour.' The essence of the ministry is to lay down all one's faculties at the feet of the Master, that they may be employed according to His judgment and His Will. My Divine Master has said: 'All power is given to *Me* in heaven and in earth.' It is for me to execute His orders, to carry out His designs. He is wisdom, power, love; without Him, I am foolishness, weakness, selfishness: 'Without Me you can do *nothing.*'

I have understood that this is only possible by a life of recollection and continual recourse to the Divine Master.

During this period Dom Columba's prayer is all imbued with this thought:

During my prayer, I love to cast myself at the feet of Jesus Christ and to say to Him: I am very miserable, I am nothing, but You can do all: You are my wisdom, my sanctity. You behold Your Father, You adore Him, You say to Him ineffable things. O my Jesus! that which You say to Him I would say to Him also; say it to Him in my place. You behold in Your Father all that He wills of me, all that He wills for me; You see in Him if I shall have sickness or health, consolation or suffering; You see when and how I am to die. You accept all for me, as for me, I will it with You, because You will it.

---

1 *Rule of St Benedict,* ch 4, the tenth instrument of good works.

From 1906, his lights become particularly clear and abundant.

1 January 1906 – The Church imprints the adorable name of Jesus upon the whole year: 'Thou shalt call His name Jesus.' I feel a great desire to imprint this blessed name upon my whole being, upon all my actions, that I 'may deserve to abound in good works in the name of the beloved Son.'[1]

I see more and more that the Father beholds all in His Son, loves all in His Son; for He is altogether His. We are pleasing in His eyes in so far as He sees us in His Son: 'He that abideth in Me, and I in him, the same beareth much fruit.' A small thing done in the name of Jesus is greater in God's eyes than the most remarkable things done in our own name.

I will strive to disappear so that Jesus may live and act in me: 'He must increase, but I must decrease.' St Paul was filled with this spirit: 'I count all things to be but loss' – the actions done in our own name – 'that I may gain Christ: and may be found in Him, not having my justice, which is of the law, but that which is of the faith of Christ Jesus.' This is why he tells us: 'All whatsoever you do in word or in work, do all in the name of the Lord Jesus Christ, giving thanks to God and the Father by Him.' That is to say, to act as members of Christ, in the same dispositions, according to His designs.

The same thought is reiterated a few days later, but this time with a singular fullness of detail. In the divine light Dom Marmion envisages the life of the soul in its relations with each of the adorable Persons of the Blessed Trinity. This page, written like all the others, without laying down his pen and without erasure, may be cited in full: it forms, as it were, a vigorous doctrinal and ascetical synthesis of the mystery of the intimate life of God and the life of the soul in God:

20 January 1906 – I have received a strong light upon the manner of honouring the Blessed Trinity and of acting in such a

---

1 Collect of the Sunday in the octave of Christmas.

way that our whole life may be a perpetual *Gloria Patri*. These reflections serve me as outline.

The *Father* is the Principle, the Source of all life, *Fons vitae*. The Word and the Holy Spirit proceed from Him, and all creation comes from Him through the Word, in the Holy Spirit.

We honour Him as the First Cause by laying down at His feet our whole being, our plans, our desires, in order that He may take the initiative in everything concerning us.

In this way we imitate Jesus:

(*a*) Who proceeds *entirely* from the Father.

(*b*) Who thought, desired and acted in absolute dependence on Him: 'Amen, amen, I say unto you, the Son cannot do anything of Himself, but what He seeth the Father doing.' 'My doctrine is not Mine, but His that sent me.' During His whole life, He did at each instant, 'the things that please the Father.' He remained in the obscurity of the Nazareth workshop for thirty years, and only began His public mission at the hour fixed by His Father. He limited Himself to preaching to the Jews, because He was sent only to the lost sheep of the house of Israel: 'All things must needs be fulfilled which are written in the law of Moses and in the Prophets, and in the Psalms, concerning Me.' 'One jot, or one tittle shall not pass of the law, till all be fulfilled.'

I have understood that without this absolute dependence upon God the most brilliant actions have little value in His eyes, although they may, of themselves, dazzle men. We are in our true place as creatures and children of adoption when we leave to our Creator and our Father the full disposal of our person and of our whole activity. This is particularly true of the religious, and above all of the monk.

The *Son*, not only proceeds entirely from the Father, and therefore depends[1] absolutely on Him, but being the perfect Son, He is the perfect image of the Father: 'the image of the

---

1 Not a dependence of time nor of authority but, in the divine processions, the Father has a priority of nature of origin.

invisible God.' He is the wisdom of the Father and perfectly fulfils all the will of the Father, all His designs.

We honour the Son as being like Him – Truth and Wisdom – by perfectly fulfilling the Father's every Will, His manifest Will, by a perfect fidelity in accomplishing all the *known Will of God*. Known by His commandments, His counsels, His inspirations, and by obedience. And of His hidden Will, by leaving all to Him. He accepted for Himself and for His members all the Father's Will, and we honour Him by uniting ourselves to Him in this acceptance, by asking Him to take away from our heart all desire or wish to do the least thing that is outside the design of His Will. [We may meditate on the life of Jesus Christ in the light of this thought, and this meditation will bring much peace and union with Him.] It is thus we shall perfectly carry out this precept of St Paul: 'All whatsoever you do ... do all in the name of the Lord Jesus Christ.'

For we do only in His name that which He sees to be the Father's good pleasure for us. Thus is realised these words: 'He must increase, but I must decrease; then we become the object of the Father's delight, from whom comes down every best gift, every perfect grace. These actions become great, because they are done in God.

The *Holy Spirit* is the mutual love of the Father and the Son. He returns unto the bosom of the Father and of the Son with an infinite love which is Himself.

We honour the Holy Spirit by uniting ourselves humbly through Jesus Christ to this love by which we return to God as our last end. It is this love which gives all the value to our actions. This love proceeding from the Father and the Son bears us towards God in dependence and in love. All our life thus proceeds from the Father in the Son in order to return to His bosom, in the Holy Spirit.

Thus united to Jesus Christ in His Spirit, our life becomes a sacrifice of love for God and for souls: 'Christ, who by the Holy Ghost offered Himself unspotted unto God.' If we turn to the Holy Spirit with love and confidence, He will not fail to fill us with true divine love. For He is the 'Father of the poor,' 'Hope confoundeth not: because the charity of God is poured forth in our hearts, by the Holy Ghost, who is given to us.'

This synthesis once established, we can understand how under the divine light he takes up again some of the particular aspects of this ineffable mystery of life in God. An intense and most holy solidarity is established between Jesus and the soul entirely surrendered to Him by faith and love. This deep thought obtains a strong hold on Dom Columba's soul:

> *February 1906* – Our Lord's words: 'This is the work of God, that you believe in Him whom He hath sent,' makes me see still more clearly that we have all in Jesus Christ. He who yields himself up unreservedly to Jesus Christ through faith:
>
> (*a*) Fulfils perfectly with Him, in Him, and by Him all His duty towards the Father. Jesus is *one* with the Father: 'I and the Father are one. He is 'in the bosom of the Father,' and he who is united, by faith, to Jesus, does, *in unity,* what Jesus does for His Father. The member does according to its function what the body does: 'You are the body of Christ and members one of another.' When we are united by faith with Jesus Christ and, in the darkness of faith, lay down our intellect at the feet of Christ, accepting with love all that He does in our name in the full vision of His Father, our prayer is of a high degree, and made 'in spirit and in truth.' Sometimes at these moments the Spirit of Christ draws us to rest in silence and in adoration at the feet of Jesus; at other times He urges us to unite ourselves to His oblation, to His submission towards His Father. We must follow these movements.
>
> (*b*) Jesus is ever united to His Church, for this union is the type of every union: 'The sacrament of marriage is a great sacrament; but I speak in Christ and in the Church.' 'They shall

be two in one flesh. Jesus loves His Church and is united to her, because He contemplates her in the love of His Father. 'I pray for them ... *because they are Thine.*' He who is united to Jesus in truth is also united to all the members of His Church, and in Him and by Him performs all his duties. Jesus comes before us in the name of His Church, bearing *as His own* all our infirmities and all our sorrows, *vere languores nostros ipse tulit et dolores nostros ipse portavit.*

In another page of the same period, Dom Columba, under the inspiration of grace, lingers with more marked delight than before over the ineffable mystery of the life of the Son "in the bosom of the Father" *in sinu Patris,* using, to illustrate the application to the soul, a comparison as true as it is beautiful. A grand page which helps us to penetrate into the secret of his life as a child of God:

> *22 April 1906, Low Sunday* – After a week of dryness and powerlessness, I have had a moment of union with Jesus.
>
> St Paul tells us: Christ 'hath raised us up together, and hath made us sit together in the heavenly places.' Each state of our Lord works in us, like a sacrament, according to our faith, and produces the effects corresponding to this state. But there is a *fundamental state* of Jesus which underlies all the others: 'The only-begotten Son who is in the *bosom of the Father.*' That is His sanctuary which He never leaves. In the manger, at Nazareth, upon the cross, even at the moment when He cried out: 'My God, My God, why hast Thou forsaken Me?' He was always in the bosom of the Father.
>
> At the banquet of the King, the servants stand; they receive wages. These are the Christians who serve God out of fear or self-interest.
>
> The friends are seated at the King's table; He gives them choice dishes, but they are not always with Him, nor in the closest intimacy of His love. These are the pious people who serve God out of love, but who have not God as the *one* object

of their love and who do not try at every instant to do all that is most pleasing to Him.

Finally, the bride leans upon His bosom, *in sinu*. This is the closest intimacy of love, which supposes perfect love, confidence and oneness of will. Thus St John at the Last Supper. One with Jesus. We are *in sinu Patris*. This is the life of *pure love* which supposes the effort of doing always what is most pleasing to the Father: 'He hath not left me alone: for I do always the things that please Him.' Our weaknesses, our miseries do not prevent us from being *in sinu Patris,* for it is the bosom of infinite love and mercy, but it supposes a deep abasement and contempt of ourselves, so much the greater in that we are so near to this infinite holiness. It supposes, too, that we lean upon Jesus, 'who of God is made unto us wisdom, and justice, and sanctification, and redemption.' All that is done *in the bosom of the Father, with the spirit of sons of adoption,* is of immense price. But this state supposes the absence of all deliberate fault, and of all refusal to follow the inspirations of the Holy Spirit. For if Jesus takes upon Himself our infirmities and our miseries, He does not accept the least deliberate sin: 'Which of you shall convince Me of sin?' In this sanctuary graces are received, and often the repose of contemplation.

At times the thought of our weakness, of our stains, of our unworthiness may come to alarm us. This thought ought to humiliate us and make us abase ourselves before God, but not frighten us, for if we are *in sinu Patris,* it is with Jesus and in Him that we are there, and the greater our miseries the more our faith and our confidence in Him, *honour Him*. For Jesus identifies Himself so much with us that, in us, He is sick and feeble, and even clad in our miseries, and when, in the strength of our faith, we come before God in the *name of Jesus,* it is His beloved Son whom He sees poor, weak and miserable (such as He was in His Passion,) in us.

At other times, it is the mystery of the sacrifice of Jesus which he throws in relief:

> *Pentecost 1907* – I have understood that Jesus who is, by essence, all AD PATREM chose the most perfect form of giving Himself to His Father as man, that is to say as *Victim*. This is why at the moment of His Incarnation, He became 'priest forever.' St Paul reveals to us His first movement at the moment of the Incarnation. Entering into the world, He casts His gaze on the Old Testament and He sees that all those sacrifices are only 'weak and needy elements,'[1] which could not worthily glorify His Father: 'Sacrifice and oblation Thou wouldest not: *but a body Thou hast fitted to Me.*' At that moment He offers Himself as Victim: 'Then said I: behold I come.' From that moment Christ is Priest: 'who by the Holy Ghost offered Himself unspotted unto God.' He offers Himself *out of love:* 'That the world may know that I love the Father.'
>
> The apostle exhorts us to imitate Christ in this oblation: 'I beseech you therefore, brethren, by the mercy of God, that you present your bodies a living sacrifice, holy, pleasing unto God, your reasonable service.' We share in Christ's Priesthood and in His state of Victim. For He says: 'Present your bodies.' This is the function of the priest; but what we offer is ourselves *corpora vestra,* and as a living sacrifice, etc. As priest, we ought to imitate Christ's reverence towards His Father: He 'was heard for His reverence,' and above all because we are so unworthy, while He is 'a High Priest, holy, innocent, undefiled, separated from sinners, and made higher than the Heavens.' As intermediary between men and God out attitude ought to be one of adoration, lowly abasement, before the majesty of God. As sacrifice, we ought to give ourselves up to God, to His every Will, like the 'lamb standing as it were slain,' before the supreme Creator unreservedly yielded up to the sovereign goodness.

1 Gal. 4:9.

This sacrifice of Jesus Christ never ceases, for He is ever immolated on an altar, and He ever remains Victim in the tabernacle. Our life ought always to be united to this life of Jesus Christ as Priest and Victim.

It is by the Holy Spirit that Jesus offers Himself to His Father. This same Spirit dwells in our hearts, 'He shall abide with you, and shall be in you.' He proceeds from the Father and the Son, and He bears with Him the whole creation (which He loves in His procession) unto the bosom of the Father and the Son.

The more we yield ourselves to this Holy Spirit of love, the more all the tendencies of our being are directed towards the Father. Three spirits tend to take possession of us: the spirit of darkness, the human spirit, and the Holy Spirit. It is very important to distinguish between the action of these spirits, in order that we may give ourselves only to the Spirit of God.

As we have said, all these lights, which he himself received with so much reverence in order to make of them principles of action, converged towards the same end: to lead the soul to make a total donation of self so as no longer to live save by the life of Jesus – and of Jesus only – to the glory of the Father. The "great thought of the Father," as Dom Marmion called it in 1905 – a thought taken from St Paul (Eph. 1:22) which is to subject "all things under His feet"[1] – becomes a veritable *Leitmotiv* of his life at that time. We shall soon see to what an important act this was to lead.

"Our Divine Lord inclines me more and more to live in an entire dependence on Him and the movements of His Spirit. The Father has placed all things beneath the feet of His beloved Son, and

---

[1] The Psalmist understands this in the relation of creatures to man, king of creation; Dom Marmion applies it to Jesus the supreme King of redeemed creation and to all that which, in man, ought to be subject to Christ.

I feel more and more drawn to live in a state of habitual adoration and annihilation before Jesus in my heart."[1]

At the same time he declares himself unworthy of this grace and very far from attaining this high ideal; he confesses it with great humility and begs those whom he directs to help him with their prayers:

> Ask for me that Jesus may become absolute Master of my inner life and that nothing in me may stir except by His impulse. That is the object of all my desires, but I am yet *very far* from this.[2]
>
> For me Jesus is *all*. I can neither pray, nor celebrate nor carry out my holy ministry except in total dependence on His action and on His Spirit. The good God gives me a great desire to make Jesus the supreme Master of my inner life and the one and only Source of my activity. I am no doubt *very far* from this ideal, because of my self-love and my numberless infidelities. However, I have great confidence that one day I shall be able to say in truth: I live, no, not I, but Christ lives in me. Then according to His promise He will reveal to me the secrets of His divinity: if anyone loveth Me, He has said, 'I will *manifest* Myself to him.'[3]
>
> Pray much for me, that Jesus may become the supreme Master of my spiritual life, and that I may live more and more in great dependence on His Spirit. I see that that is my way, and in spite of my great misery, if I reach this point, Jesus will make use of me for His glory.[4]

A few days later: "Ask for me that I may become the humble and faithful servant of Jesus, that all in me may be *subjected* to Him:

---

1 Letter of 1 Jan 1907.
2 Letter of 1 Nov 1908.
3 Letter of 2 Dec 1908. He added: "This manifestation is the very high, very fruitful and very sure grace that our Lord is now giving you."
4 Letter of 15 December 1908.

omnia subjecisti sub pedibus ejus, and that He will bear me there where He is: *in sinu Patris."*

These lines are dated 21 December 1908. Four days later, on Christmas Day, he made an act of consecration in which he gathered up all these lights, where are resumed all the aspirations arising from these lights, and which is the response to so many divine calls. This act of consecration truly crowned a whole period of his inner life and fixed his soul in intimate union with Christ Jesus:

> O Eternal Father, prostrate in humble adoration at Thy feet, we consecrate our whole being to the glory of Thy Son Jesus, the Incarnate Word. Thou hast appointed Him King over our souls; subject to Him our souls, our hearts, our bodies, and may nothing in us move without His orders, without His inspirations. United to Him, may we be carried in Thy bosom, and consummated in the unity of Thy love.
>
> O Jesus, unite us to Thyself in Thine all holy life, all consecrated to Thy Father and to souls. Be 'our wisdom, our justice, our justification, our redemption, our *all.*' Sanctify us in truth.
>
> O Holy Spirit, love of the Father and of the Son, be as a furnace of love in the centre of our hearts, and ever bear, like glowing flames, our thoughts, our affections, our actions, *on high,* even unto the bosom of the Father. May our whole life be a *Gloria Patri et Filio et Spiritui Sancto.*
>
> O Mary, Mother of Christ, Mother of holy love, do thou thyself form us according to the Heart of thy Son.

Such acts, when they are not the result of an isolated sense of passing fervour, but of the inspirations of grace, leave a deep and lasting impression on the soul.

More than one echo of this impression was to make itself heard, and Dom Marmion was to return to it himself in many circumstances.

Some months later, indeed, Providence granted him the grace

of a retreat at Paray-le-Monial with Cardinal Mercier whose confessor he had been for ten years.

The retreat took place from the 18th to the 26th of March. These were for Dom Marmion days of peace.

Without doubt, the monk's soul thrilled in response to the monastic associations of the past called up by the marvellous Benedictine basilica raised in the eleventh century by the abbots of Cluny, St Majolus and St Odilo; he had the joy of keeping there the feast of St Benedict (March 21st). But what above all attracted him was the little sanctuary where the Incarnate Word revealed His love to a humble Visitandine. In this blessed and privileged spot, all reminiscent of the divine promises, Dom Marmion's soul entered more than ever into the Master's intimacy. He has, however, left us only a few lines on this subject, but the last of them recalls in precise terms the special donation made a short time previously:

> Retreat at Paray-le-Monial, 19 March 1909. Great peace.
>
> *March 20th.* In a meditation made today on the text of St Paul (Eph. 1: 11), I have seen that Jesus is our *all*. My heart *united* with His becomes the object of the delight of the Father. His Heart is the *human heart* of God. This Heart, being the Heart of the Word (to which He is personally united) is entirely *ad Patrem* and, *being created acts in absolute dependence on Him.*
>
> I have seen so clearly that this dependence gives divine value to our activity. I have understood that we must cultivate this dependence and ask for it.
>
> I have resolved to read the Holy Scriptures, usually an epistle at one reading, if possible; this will be a source of light and peace.
>
> *March 22nd.* I have celebrated the Votive Mass of the Sacred Heart with special collects, so that I may make a good confession. Then, the Way of the Cross. Then general confession with great peace.

March 25th. Omnia subjecisti sub pedibus ejus.[1]

So, on the day when the Church celebrates the ineffable mystery of the Incarnation, Dom Marmion renewed the consecration that he had made a few months before on the feast of the Nativity.

Providence was soon to recall him to his monastery where he had made profession, there to be invested with the abbatial dignity. The interior life which he had lived at Mont-César, during ten years – we have just seen with what intensity – gained for him that spiritual "wisdom of doctrine" which St Benedict requires for the head of the monastery, that "knowledge of holiness, gained in prayer, assimilated and lived by the one who is to transmit it to souls... a knowledge enlightened by the rays of the Eternal Word and fructified by the Holy Spirit."[2]

God placed him for the last period of his life (September 1909 – January 1923) in the midst of a community as "a beacon-light of truth, enlightening the hearts of his monks with the pure rays of heavenly doctrine."[3]

---

[1] The same day he was enrolled in the Guard of Honour of the Sacred Heart; his hour of guard was from seven to eight o'clock in the morning.
[2] *Christ the Ideal of the Monk*, ch. 3.
[3] *Idem.*

MAREDSOUS ABBEY

9 DOM MARMION AS ABBOT (1909–23)

On 28 September 1909, Dom Marmion was elected Abbot of Maredsous.

This election was not altogether unexpected. For many years past, Dom Hildebrand de Hemptinne had combined the functions of Primate of the Order with those of Abbot of Maredsous. His frequent and prolonged stays in the Eternal City and his distant journeys interfered with his abbatial charge.

As far back as 1905, there had been a question about Dom Hildebrand resigning the abbotship in order to devote himself exclusively to the general interests of the order; Dom Columba's name had at that time been mentioned as one of the possible candidates to the office of abbot.[1] It was however only in August 1909 that Dom Hildebrand, at the desire of Pius X, was established definitely in Rome in the capacity of primate. Hence an election was rendered necessary. It was to take place at the end of September.

In a letter dated the sixth of that month Dom Marmion, who could not but be aware that his name had again been brought forward, wrote to the Mother Superior of Tyburn:[2]

> As for what concerns the affair of my election, I am quite at peace. In our congregation, a monk cannot accept the charge of abbot *in another abbey*[3] without the consent of his abbot (unless the higher superiors insist).[4] I need not ask you to recommend the affair to our Lord especially from September 19th. As for me, I sincerely believe that the whole thing

---

1 Letters of 12 May 1905 and 14 July 1905.
2 The Very Reverend Mother Marie de St-Pierre (Adèle Garnier) who died in 1924. A close spiritual union existed between this holy nun and Dom Marmion.
3 Although he was a professed monk of Maredsous, Dom Marmion had, in 1904, fixed his "stability," as it is called at Mont-César. He therefore depended on the abbot of that monastery.
4 The Archabbot of Beuron and the Primate of the Order.

is beyond my powers and my talents, but if obedience speaks, *non recuso laborem.*[1]

And some days later, to the same:

The election of the new Abbot of Maredsous will take place next week (the 25th or 28th I think). If I am elected, which is not improbable, and if my abbot authorises me to accept it, which is very doubtful, I shall be free to undertake the office of extraordinary confessor to your children at Koekelberg,[2] without ceasing in any way to be their father. Otherwise, it would be necessary to find another, for my Father Abbot does not wish me to accept it, on account of my manifold occupations. We will leave all that in God's hands. But pray much for me these days, that my dispositions in either hypothesis may be such as our Lord would have them.[3]

The election took place on September 28th, and the monks voted in favour of Dom Columba.

On the morning of that day he had offered the Holy Sacrifice in the chapel of the Carmelites of Louvain and had chosen the Votive Mass of the Passion. At this Mass he inaugurated the new tabernacle of repose in the grille which separates the chapel from the nuns' choir; he had wished to be the very first to place the Blessed Sacrament in it. On this occasion a parchment was slipped under the tabernacle there to remain forever. "The parchment bore the text which was so dear to him and on which he had often commented: *Omnia subjecisti sub pedibus ejus,*[4] and on the reverse, his signature and that of all the nuns; to his own he characteristically added the word *Peccator.* He thus closed, without suspecting it, his functions at the Carmel after ten years' ministry.

On his return to Mont-César he received notification of his election.

---

[1] Letter of 6 September 1909.
[2] Convent (daughter-house of Tyburn), transferred since to Bierges, near Hal.
[3] Letter of September 20th.
[4] "Thou has put all things under His feet."

What were his feelings on this occasion? A few laconic lines in his private notes tell us:

28 September 1909 – Received the news of my election as Abbot of Maredsous. My Right Reverend Father Abbot, Dom Robert de Kerchove, imposed the acceptance of it on me *ex obedientia*.

29 September 1909 – During the night, great struggle and temptation to discouragement. After the Mass of St Michael, great peace and confidence. I understood that the archangel would be my protector.

That same day Dom Marmion set out for Maredsous. Confirmed in his election by the archabbot, put immediately in possession of the keys of the church and the seal of the abbey, as symbol of the jurisdiction with which he was invested, he next received the homage of obedience from his monks.

Dom Marmion wished to have some days of retirement before the abbatial blessing. At Cardinal Mercier's invitation, he went to *l'Hermite*, the archbishop's country house, there to spend in his company those days of retreat.

The date that Dom Marmion chose for his blessing was October 3rd, Holy Rosary Sunday. The ceremony took place in the church and before the altar where twenty years before he had pronounced his monastic vows. By a special privilege of the Holy See, the Primate of the Order, Dom Hildebrand, gave the blessing to the abbot-elect. Numerous prelates and friends came especially from Louvain to bring the new abbot their good wishes and homage.

Dom Marmion noted a short time afterwards: "Since my blessing, I have received the grace of a sense of assurance and an absence of fear when it has been my duty to speak or act. I feel myself urged to great dependence upon God and great directness in my relations with men."

He took as his motto this maxim which St Benedict gives the abbot to direct him in his government: *Magis prodesse quam praesse:*

"To be useful rather than to command."[1] We shall presently see how he found inspiration in this sentence.

Dom Marmion was the third Abbot of Maredsous. A special mission had fallen to each of his predecessors. Dom Placide Wolter had been the organiser and initiator of the observance, the constructor of the church and college. He had placed the institution on an active basis and set upon it the lasting impression of his own deep religious spirit.

To the work of Maredsous thus constituted, Dom Hildebrand de Hemptinne had given further impetus; the school of arts and crafts and the foundation of the Abbey of Mont-César at Louvain were due to him. While he was abbot, the direction of the Greek College at Rome was confided to the sons of St Benedict, and Dom Gérard van Caloen undertook the Benedictine restoration in Brazil. But above all by his position as Primate of the Order and the creation of the *Collegio Sant'Anselmo,* he "internationalised" the Order of St Benedict in some manner and greatly furthered its expansion.

The role which fell to Dom Marmion was rather of the doctrinal order. Gathering up all he had learnt during his priesthood of nearly thirty years and concentrating in his mind the treasures of theological science accumulated during as many years of study and teaching, a consummate master in dogmatics and asceticism, an experienced spiritual director, and a contemplative who constantly searched into the mysteries of God, Dom Marmion was now about to give the matured fruits of these years and to be above all among his own monks, the exponent of the Christian and monastic life in its fullness.

On returning to Maredsous Dom Columba found the abbey much as he had left it ten years previously, except that the number of religious had increased and new works had risen up. He had

1 *Rule of St Benedict,* ch. 44.

a hundred choir monks and lay brothers to direct; activity flourished in the College of Greek and Latin humanities, in the School of Arts and Crafts, and in literary and scientific works such as the *Revue bénédictine;* to which may be added, on the material side, a farm and various workshops: it was then a little city that he found he had to govern.

When he took the abbot's crozier in his hand, Dom Marmion was fifty-two, with an outward appearance of physical vigour. But outward appearances are sometimes deceptive. We must not overlook the fact that for the new Abbot of Maredsous it was not only in a figurative sense, but in the most realistic acceptation of the word, that he felt the heavy weight of years. Increasing stoutness rendered many of the duties of his charge very difficult to him.

Nevertheless, Dom Marmion devoted all the strength he possessed to his new mission, and after barely thirteen years of government – it is true that the years of the Great War may be reckoned as double – his constitution, prematurely worn out, was nearing a state when it would be unable to offer any resistance to ill-health.

During his government the third Abbot of Maredsous kept up and brought the existing institutions of the monastery to perfection; he set the different works on a firm basis, and always encouraged initiative when of a nature to promote God's glory and the good of souls; like his predecessors he maintained a very wide and cordial hospitality, carrying out to the letter, in his spirit of faith, the bidding of the holy legislator: "Let all guests that come be received like Christ Himself."[1]

His ideas on the subject of the concourse that his monastery should lend to the diocesan or general enterprises was such as could only have been inspired by his generous nature and supernatural spirit. He set no bounds to the spiritual aid asked for by the clergy of the neighbourhood, or that might be suggested by circumstances. One trait of this episodic activity will show how open he was to every form of Christian charity. While he was in Great Britain during the war he learnt that, in the midst of many difficulties,

---

[1] See in *Christ the Ideal of the Monk,* the chapter "Good Zeal," § 7.

a day-school had been opened at Maredsous to allow the boys of the neighbourhood to continue their secondary studies and to save them from depressing inaction. He writes to his prior: "I am so glad about what you have done for the youth of the diocese. This work is very pleasing to our Lord."[1]

Dom Marmion consented to his sons exercising their ministry outside the monastery, provided that this was commanded or permitted by obedience. Several of these monks were members of the professorial or administrative staff of the *Collegio Greco di Sant'Atanasio* and of the *Collegio Sant'Anselmo* in Rome; others were attached to the pontifical work of revising the Latin text of Holy Scripture (the Vulgate); others, again, were evangelising the negroes of Katanga (Belgian Congo).

He himself gave the example, in his own monastery first of all, of fidelity to the observance. He made himself, in the eyes of all, the servant of the *Rule* which governed their life. He said one day to the nuns of Maredret:[2]

> I was consoled, to read that phrase in our constitutions, concerning the abbot: Let him do all things in the fear of the Lord; in such a way, that by most faithful submission to the Divine Will, he may carry out his part of the vow of obedience. For I see, he added, that I can still practise my vow of obedience; I am not dispensed from it. I even added to it, on the day of my blessing, the promise to make the *Rule* and the constitutions observed.

It may be said that Dom Marmion was faithful to his promise to the full extent of his power.

His example gave stress and fecundity to his words. By his ascetical instructions and spiritual conferences, Dom Marmion wonderfully carried out the ideal proposed to the abbot by St Benedict,

1 Letter of 15 March 1915.
2 During November 1916.

who would have him to be "learned in the law of God that he may know how to bring forth out of this treasure new things and old" – that is to say, traditional maxims and fresh views upon them, calculated to direct souls towards perfection. Whether it was to explain some mystery in the life of Christ, to echo the voice of the Church in some liturgical solemnity, to bring out the lesson of the Gospel for the day, to show the part played by the different virtues in the spiritual life, he did so with a knowledge, a depth, a simplicity, and above all with a conviction that illumined, delighted, arrested, enlarged and calmed. A true regaling of the mind, an abundant feast for the heart were these ascetical conferences.

These conferences dwelt especially, it goes without saying, on the explanation of the *Rule of St Benedict*. Dom Marmion was most emphatic as to the sanctifying value of this code of spiritual life:

> When I was a novice, he sometimes recounted, the abbot gave me a copy of the *Rule,* telling me: 'You will find everything in that.' I had difficulty at that time in believing it. But now, having made experience, I am thoroughly convinced of it. The *Rule* is truly the mirror of the Gospel; one simple phrase, one remark of this little book often contains a principle of action, an orientation leading to great results. The *Rule* is extolled in heaven by the multitude of saints whom it has brought to the most intimate union with God.

We may imagine from this with what fervent attention he studied these pages, with what success he brought out the depth of meaning and set their supernatural and Christian character in a clear light; with what insistence, too, he urged his sons to that sole seeking after God in Christ's steps, in which, according to St Benedict, all consists for the monk. These instructions, so full of warmth and light, were to furnish the matter of his volume, *Christ the Ideal of the Monk*.

The liturgical cycle and the systematic course laid down for the explanation of the *Rule*[1] brings the orator inevitably back to sub-

---

[1] A section of the *Rule of St Benedict* is read aloud each day, and so arranged that the whole is read through three times a year.

jects already dealt with. No matter. Dom Columba approached them resolutely, because he unweariedly found original aspects to the eternal questions. Such were, moreover, the light, warmth and picturesqueness of his language, that it was always listened to with the same interest and the same profit. It may be granted that in his latter years, when his malady had already undermined his health, he was apt to return rather more frequently and more willingly to certain subjects: the Divine Filiation of Jesus, our supernatural adoption, unshaken confidence in Christ's merits, the necessity of faith, compunction and humility as bases of the interior and monastic life, utter self-abandonment of the soul to God's fatherly mercy. But if he repeated himself, at the same time his conviction grew more intense, his tone more familiar, and his words sank deeper into the heart; if he was more simplified, it was because he was mounting to the summits and already, as he himself loved to repeat, "the splendour of the eternal hills were beginning to cast their rays upon his soul."

Dom Marmion's sons were not alone in profiting from these conferences; every week he went to give an ascetical conference to the Benedictine nuns of Maredret. This part of his ministry was dear to him, and he fulfilled it almost to the day of his death.

But, as at Louvain, his zeal was not to be confined within the boundaries of his monastery and the immediate outskirts. The relations which, under the control of obedience, Dom Marmion had formed, before being elected abbot, with several religious communities or institutions, created moral bonds which he could not break. It was not possible for him to evade the pressing entreaties made to him. He is therefore to be seen once more as preacher at the theological *Collège du Saint-Esprit* or the Carmel of Louvain, at the Canonesses of Jupille, the Benedictines of Liège, or the English Convent at Bruges. Great Britain especially made frequent demands on him; the abbeys of Ramsgate, Erdington, Downside, Ampleforth and Woolhampton; the Benedictines of Stanbrook and Ventnor, the nuns of Tyburn and of Haywards Heath, the Trappists of Roscrea and of Melleray in Ireland, the Poor Clares of Cork, and many others listened to his enthusiastic and convincing words.

The renown of his talents and virtues was such that he was often asked by different bishops to preach retreats to the students of their seminaries: His Excellency Francis Cardinal Bourne invited him more than once to give the retreat at Westminster and at St Edmund's College.[1]

It is in connection with this spiritual ministry that we must link the part he played in the celebrated conversion of the monks of Caldey.[2] About 1906, some young men of the Anglican church gathered together in the isle of this name, near Tenby in south Wales, and little by little had formed a community of some thirty members. They lived there in a monastery and followed the *Rule of St Benedict*, under the direction of a superior. Not far from Caldey, but on the mainland, at St Brides, Milford Haven, a community of women, comprising forty sisters, pursued the same ideal under identical circumstances. A strange but sincere essay to implant in Protestantism the monastic life according to a Catholic rule.

This attempt was so abnormal that, sooner or later, these "monks" and these "nuns" were bound by the force of circumstances to examine their position in relation to the Anglican church. Was it possible to be Benedictines outside Roman Catholicism? Was the recitation of the Divine Office in Latin and in the Romano-Benedictine liturgy, besides other exercises of devotion, compatible with the official belief of Anglicanism? The question was carefully gone into and soon became acute.

We need not repeat here in detail the proceedings and negotiations entered into between Dom Ældred Carlyle, Superior of Caldey, and the Bishop of Oxford, who in this matter was the official delegate of the Archbishop of Canterbury, Primate of the English

---

1 Old Hall, Ware. Among others may be added the seminaries of Wonersh, Southwark, and of Metz and Tournai.
2 In his *Fils de l'Église*, René Bazin has given a circumstantial and moving story of this event.

church. Begun in December 1911, these negotiations came to an end in February 1913. The embarrassment and then the hostility of the religious authorities had led the monks to explain exactly how they stood. In the middle of February 1913, the whole correspondence exchanged between the abbot and the bishop was submitted to the community, and each one was invited to give in writing his opinion on what ought to be done. On February 18th, the "brothers" assembled to read their decisions, which were practically unanimous. They decided that their consciences would not allow them to remain in the Anglican church; the Church of Rome alone possessed the authority necessary to assure the vitality of their work.

On February 21st, Dom Ældred notified the decision to the Bishop of Oxford. The separation of the Caldey community from the church of England was thus complete, as well as that of the members of St Bride's Abbey, who had followed the monks in their decision.

On the morrow, the feast of St Peter's Chair at Antioch, Dom Ældred begged Dom Bede Camm, OSB, of the Congregation of Beuron, to come to help them in the great step they were taking. The son of an English clergyman of the "established church," Dom Bede had been converted at Maredsous in 1890, and in this conversion Dom Marmion, at that time a simple monk, had been closely concerned.[1] At the time of these happenings at Caldey, Dom Bede, who had taken the habit of St Benedict at Maredsous soon after his reception into the Church, was residing at the Abbey of Erdington (Birmingham), and it was there that Abbot Ældred's touching appeal reached him. In his turn, Dom Bede invited Dom Marmion to come to preach the retreat to the converts of Caldey preparatory to their abjuration and reception into the Catholic Church. Arriving at the end of February, Dom Columba at once began the retreat with this text, which he applied to the community: *Cantate Domino canticum* NOVUM, *laus ejus in ecclesia* SANCTORUM: "Sing ye to the

---

[1] Dom Bede himself has given the story of his conversion in pages full of freshness and simplicity; it has been translated into French by Charles Groileau, under the title: *"De l'anglicanisme au monachisme," Journal d'étapes d'un converti.*

Lord a *new canticle;* let His praise be in the *Church of the saints."* On March 5th, the Catholic Bishop of Menevia, Msgr Francis Mostyn – the Isle of Caldey was in his diocese – celebrated Holy Mass in the oratory of the monastery, then received the abjuration of the members of the community. The next day it was the turn of the nuns of St Bride's, to the number of thirty-seven, to make their profession of faith in the Catholic Church.

The great stir aroused by this event, unique in the religious annals of England, may be imagined.

Later on Msgr Mostyn presented a petition at Rome in view of obtaining the faculty to erect Caldey as a Benedictine monastery. The ceremony of the erection took place on June 29th, the feast of SS Peter and Paul. On arriving at Caldey, Dom Marmion celebrated Mass in presence of Msgr Mostyn, then, at the end of the Holy Sacrifice, the bishop gave the Benedictine habit to the convert monks and canonically established the house as a monastery of St Benedict. The communities of Caldey and of St Bride's already received into the Church, thus entered by the true door opened by the only one who holds the keys, into that Benedictine family of which they had until then borne the name and habit without being its living branches. The Divine Gardener now engrafted them on the old monastic stock. This was a cause of deep joy to Dom Marmion.[1]

More than once, as we have been seeing, the necessities of the apostolic ministry took Dom Marmion to Rome. It was at the time of a stay in the Eternal City that he had the longed-for occasion of going to Subiaco. He had received authorisation to spend several days in the grotto where St Benedict had lived. From this blessed and privileged spot, steeped in the memories of the Great Patriarch's life of solitude and contemplation, he wrote to one of his sons:

> How can I describe the *Sacro Speco* to you? It is truly a paradise of prayer: an absolute solitude in the midst of wild and grand nature. Everything in the monastery invites to prayer

[1] Since 1926 the community of Caldey has been attached to the Cassinese Congregation (Primitive Observance), and has left the Isle of Caldey to establish itself at Prinknash (Painswick), in Gloucestershire.

and recollection. One could remain for whole hours before the grotto sanctified by our blessed father. I have prayed much and said Holy Mass for you all.[1]

He must have received great graces there, as is shown by these lines – unfortunately too brief – of a letter written two months later: "My soul is in peace, for I have given and abandoned myself without counting the cost, I think, in the holy grotto of Subiaco...."[2]

The journey to Rome was repeated more than once, either in response to the invitation of Cardinal Mercier, who wished to have Dom Columba as companion, or for the affairs of the order.[3]

---

1 Letter of 12 March 1912. And two days later to another of his monks: "I have passed four delightful days in prayer and solitude. There is a goodness and a charity here which touches me deeply."
2 Letter of 3 May 1912.
3 Many other reasons, furthermore, actuated Dom Marmion. Beyond his numerous engagements, the renown of his virtues caused him to be much sought after to preach retreats; there were, too, the calls made upon him by the bishop of the diocese, who confided more than one delicate mission to him and, above all, the orders of his higher superiors, all of which obliged Dom Marmion to be frequently moving from place to place. He himself felt the burden of this. Having received instructions one day from Cardinal Mercier, he writes to his prior: "To my great regret I find a telegram here conveying the order from the Right Reverend Abbot Primate for me to go to..." (Letter of 27 September 1911). To the Reverend Mother of a community who had asked him to give a retreat, he replies on 6 February 1912: "This year is already very filled up: General Chapter at Beuron in July; retreat at Haywards Heath in August; Liturgical Congress here the same month; Marian Congress at Maastricht with Cardinal Mercier. I have already had all sorts of invitations which I shall have to refuse. I will reserve myself for you in 1913." From St Edmund's Seminary, where Cardinal Bourne had invited him to give the retreat, he writes in the same strain to his prior: "As for myself, I am really distressed and quite sad at not being at my monastery, now you know that I am obliged to set out for Rome on the 14th of this month" (letter of 5 September 1912). This last journey was doubtless undertaken at the mandate of the General Chapter, for he had written from Beuron, 26 July 1912, at the moment when the sittings of this assembly terminated: "The General Chapter wanted to send me to Rome on a very important affair. I think I have succeeded in avoiding this journey." We may add this detail, which once more reveals Dom Marmion's supernatural spirit. When, after the war, the Belgian Benedictine Congregation was consti-

Each visit to the Eternal City was an occasion for Dom Marmion to quicken his faith at the very fountain-head of Catholic thought.

Under the wide and generous guidance of Dom Columba, who set the example of prayer and zeal, the works of monastic peace had thus been carried on for several years when, like a colossal and devastating cloudburst, the German invasion broke over Belgium in August 1914.

Irish by birth, Dom Marmion had, however, personally contracted with his country and home of adoption moral links of wholehearted loyalty, further supplemented by legal naturalisation. He therefore keenly felt the shock of the injustice which overwhelmed the entire country. Directly hostilities were declared he deputed a number of his sons as volunteers to the military ambulances.[1]

A few days later the abbey was literally surrounded by a circle of iron; guns were rumbling, roaring, raging all day, were silent in the evening, and broke out again next morning. Namur was first to fall beneath a storm of shells; next, in the north, the enemy passed over the Sambre after a magnificent resistance from the French troops; to the east, the Meuse could no longer hold out with the too slender line of troops that covered it at Dinant and had to surrender its banks to the enemy with the control of its bridges. Not far from the monastery, on the broad plain of Saint-Gérard, the fighting went on desperately. On August 23rd, under the walls of the abbey, a stream of French soldiers went by, the first eddy of the great battle; it was soon followed by the whole fourth division of the Belgian army, which had held the position of Namur till compelled to retreat by force of overwhelming numbers.

The ark of St Benedict remained peaceful in the midst of the

> tuted under the presidency of Dom de Kerchove, Abbot of Mont-César and senior dean, Dom Marmion, although independent as to everything concerning his apostolic ministry, submitted to the Abbot President all the requests that came to him to preach retreats.

1 As we know, religious in Belgium at that time were not bound to military service under any form.

tempest. Dom Marmion opened wide the doors of his monastery to the fugitives, who arrived in crowds, one scarcely knew from whence, and to the civilians who, swept along the road by the wind of fear or thrust forward by the German outposts and finding themselves thus stranded, gathered confidently under the protecting shadow of the Holy Patriarch.

Soon, the college and the school of arts and crafts, transformed into ambulances, sheltered the glorious wounded of the battle of Saint-Gérard. And while, under his direction, his sons fulfilled their duty of charity, the abbot learned of the tragic death of one of his monks,[1] shot without trial by the invader in a village of Luxembourg.

In the midst of these sad events and the anguish to which they gave rise, the supernatural soul of Dom Marmion was lifted up to Him who holds the hearts of kings in His hand and directs all things according to His impenetrable designs. At this time, he said to the nuns of Maredret:

> Today more than ever, let us seek support in the words of Holy Scripture, in communing alone with God. Sometimes, when we are living united in this way to Him, He raises our soul above earthly contingencies, and one feels strengthened afresh. Assuredly you cannot be disinterested in the grave events passing beneath your eyes nor be absorbed in a kind of contemplation which would make you forget everything else. No. Look at Christ Jesus. He shed tears over Jerusalem, His native country. And why? Because He foresaw for it evils identical to those now overwhelming us. Stoicism is not piety, it is a pose. As Moses prayed upon the mountain that the victory might be won by the people of Israel contending against the Amalekites, so pray fervently for those who are fighting. Keep united to God and in adoration of the designs of His Providence: Providence has its views and will bring them about. And remember that all our support, all our confidence rests on God: *Hi in curribus et hi in equis; nos*

---

[1] Dom Bernard Gillet.

autem in nomine Dei nostri invocabimus: Let our enemies trust in their chariots and their horses; as for us, we will call upon the name of the Lord our God ... may He save the king and hear us in the day that we call upon Him."[1]

After the first upheavals and the establishment of the German occupation, the difficulties of providing food[2] for a large number of monks grouped in a semi-solitude, as was the case with the community of Maredsous, obliged Dom Marmion to seek a place of refuge for a part of his community. It was decided that he should undertake this mission in person, his relations with English monasteries enabling him better than anyone else to find a sure shelter on the other side of the channel.

Passing through Holland under cover of disguise, he soon reached Great Britain. Not having been able to procure the necessary passport, he saw that he would probably be refused entrance into the country. In fact, scarcely had the ship touched at Folkestone than the custom-house officers came on board to verify the passports. Dom Marmion had to acknowledge that he had none; in consequence, they refused to let him land. But the idea struck him that among the officers there might perhaps be an Irishman, and the Irish cannot hold out against a joke.

"I am Irish," Dom Marmion told them, "and the Irish never have a passport ... except for hell, and ... it isn't there I am wanting to go."

This sally provoked a burst of laughter, and he was allowed to pass. Evidently one does not always get out of a tight corner so successfully by means of a joke; that no doubt only happens among Irishmen.

Dom Marmion immediately set about finding a shelter capable

---

1 Ps. 19: 8–10.
2 It is now known that, even after the work of the commissariat had been organised by America, the spectre of famine more than once loomed on the horizon before the eyes of the authorities, but the people remained in ignorance of the danger.

of receiving those of his sons who had already crossed the channel, and busied himself with ensuring the necessary resources for their maintenance. He met with great charity in several abbeys, notably at Ramsgate, Downside, and among his own friends, but material means were far from sufficing, and he was literally forced to undertake a begging tour. A thankless business, which obliged him to make numerous applications often unsuccessfully. He wrote to his prior at Maredsous on December 1st: "Since my arrival in England, I have worked *hard* to find a refuge for my sons and the necessary resources. I have succeeded beyond my hopes for the first,[1] but for the second, in spite of much generosity on the part of my friends, I have not yet enough to gather my sons around me."[2]

He had to continue his efforts to procure what was needed: an arduous and wearing task which, joined to the difficulties of the hour and repeated attacks of illness, gradually undermined his health. He wrote from London to one of his sons in Ireland: "I have been suffering *greatly;* the influenza has taken a dangerous turn. My weakness is such that I can scarcely stand. In spite of everything I am trying to collect some funds to support you. I cannot tell you how my heart is crushed and my soul bruised by all these disappointments."[3]

Besides questing for money, he devoted himself to the work of preaching either in England, notably at Haywards Heath, Westminster and Ventnor, or in Ireland at St Kevin, Clonliffe, and at *La Trappe* of Mount St Bernard; in October 1915, he preached the retreat to the students of Dublin University, in the Church of St Stephen. Zeal for souls was in this way joined to charity for his own sons.

This stress of work and the frequent going from place to place, above all the worries that were continually arising, occasioned him

---

1 At Edermine, Co. Wexford, Ireland.
2 Letter of 1 December 1914.
3 Letter of 18 January 1915. And again, a few weeks later (January 30th): "My task as beggar is very painful to me, but I do it for love of God." He wrote in the same strain to his prior at Maredsous on February 19th: "I have been suffering *much* in body and soul. I have been without resources and have had, like our father founders, to do a lot of begging. In consequence of so much anxiety and fatigue my heart has more than once failed me."

much pain and difficulty, but he ever remained submissive in God's hands, happy to bring his share to the tribute of expiation Providence was asking: "I have seldom suffered more *in every way*, than for some time past. I feel we have to take our part in the general expiation, which is being offered to God's justice and sanctity. My soul, my body, my senses, God Himself, all things seem to combine to make me suffer. May His holy name be blessed."[1]

Whilst, without counting the cost, Dom Marmion was spending himself in his efforts to assure the upkeep of his sons in England, his mind and heart were not separated from that part of the monastic family remaining in the invaded territory. But his relations with Maredsous were confronted with difficulties. On the Dutch frontier, the only frontier not under the firing line, the meshes of the German net were made tighter and tighter, and nothing was any longer allowed to filter through. Perilous stratagems had to be used in order to get the smallest note through; people had to disguise their style and camouflage any news. In the incessant ferment of this troubled period many letters were lost or only reached their destination after considerable delay. Some – by miracle – arrived safely, telling the sons of how their father was thinking of them. On 5 March 1915, he wrote to his prior:

> I have just received your dear letter dated January 20th. As you make no allusion to a preceding letter I suppose that all the others are still on the way. I am so distressed that none of my letters addressed to you and the Benedictines of Maredret has arrived. I ask my good angel to see about that... I bless you *all* from the bottom of my heart.[2]

Ever since May 1915, Dom Marmion had been hoping to return:

---

[1] Letter of 15 June 1915.
[2] This letter of March 5th arrived at Maredsous on 24 October 1915, and several weeks later: "I have written ever so many times to Maredsous; in your letter you never mention having received these letters; I suppose they have never arrived" (29 March 1915).

"My dear nephew," he writes to his prior, using the terms agreed upon, "now that I have put in order all the business of our factory here,[1] I am constantly looking forward to returning; I have received official information that this return cannot be effected without exposing me to great danger. However, I have written to Désiré[2] for advice and help. For I will not have recourse to such protection as I might perhaps have procured *via*....[3] When you see my children tell them that I am counting the hours to the moment of my return."[4]

He was to be counting them for a long time, for this plan was frustrated on all sides. Nevertheless, he held to it tenaciously: "I am doing all I possibly can," he writes on 8 November 1915, "to come back before Christmas; I shall soon be able to fix the date. Pray much for me. God alone knows how I have suffered in *every way* since I left you."

Christmas passed without it being possible to carry out his wish; he met with most unexpected obstacles imposed by his higher superiors:

> I had made *every arrangement* to come back to the dear monastery, and I receive a letter from the Father Archabbot[5] who tells me not to return; I am *distressed* about it. I have just written to him to insist, for *hei mihi! Quia incolatus meus prolongatus est.* I have suffered a great deal. I bear it for you.[6]

He gained his cause.

> I have been moving heaven and earth to obtain a passport.... I have just received a letter from the Father Archabbot, in which he recognises *at last* that I ought to return. N— writes to me from Rome that if I come back I shall be at once taken

---

1 The place of refuge at Edermine.
2 Cardinal Mercier.
3 German intervention.
4 Letter of 1 May 1915.
5 Of Beuron (Germany), on which Maredsous still depended at this epoch. We are not aware of the reason given by the Father Archabbot.
6 Letter of December 1915, without indicating the day.

prisoner.¹ I find that difficult to believe. As soon as I have got my passport I shall start. I think of you *all without ceasing.*²

His efforts were successful; he was about to embark at the end of February, when he was attacked by illness which kept him for several weeks in London:

Dominus est! Sit nomen Domini benedictum! I had made all my arrangements to set out and had announced my return at Maredsous for March 21st at the latest. And here I find myself unable to move with severe bronchitis, complicated with asthma and heart weakness. I have no breath; that is why I am writing this to you with great difficulty. [The writing is in fact very bad]. I kiss the hand of our Lord that strikes me and I offer my sufferings for my sheep. As soon as I can I shall set out, in spite of all the danger.... I constantly pray for you and for all.³

It was only on April 5th that he was able to take the boat for Holland, where new and wearisome formalities awaited him.⁴ Finally, after many hindrances, delays and disappointments, he returned to Maredsous on 16 May 1916.

A few days after his return (May 21st), Dom Marmion told an

1   As coming back from Great Britain. In reality Dom Marmion, as we have said, was a naturalised Belgian. That is why he was sceptical on the subject of this threat.
2   Letter of 8 January 1916.
3   Letter written at the end of February without any exact date being given. On March 16th following: "I am better, but have not yet been able to celebrate Holy Mass. I am very weak. I receive this (attack of illness) as part of the designs of Divine Providence for me, for God alone knows all that I have suffered during these long days and nights of inaction."
4   "I have just arrived in Holland after meeting with great obstacles. I shall be at Maredsous *as soon as possible.*" Letter of April 14th, to his prior: "I have been patiently waiting a fortnight for the result of my efforts. All that can be done has been done. I am *in haste* to see you again. We must pray much" (Letter of April 28th, to the same).

intimate conference of the Benedictines of Maredret:

> I cannot tell you the joy and the peace that I feel in finding myself once more in the abbey in the midst of my sons. I have suffered much during my stay in England; the trials that our Lord has sent me are beyond counting. The conviction I have drawn from them is that God wills to be glorified by the union of our weakness with the infinite strength of Christ. Christ is the *virtus Dei;*[1] but He has deigned to take upon Himself our human weakness, and the whole earthly life of Jesus is the revelation of this weakness. This union of human weakness with the divine strength gives glory to God. Hence St Paul's great cry, *Libenter gloriabor in infirmitatibus meis ut inhabitet in me virtus Christi:* 'Gladly therefore will I glory in my infirmities, that the power of Christ may dwell in me.' This thought has always followed and sustained me in all contrarieties and difficulties, but now it is so engraven in my soul that it, as it were, makes part of myself. I am convinced that I am nothing and can do nothing, but that, on the other hand, I must have unbounded confidence in the strength of Christ, and that in Him I can do all things.

Dom Marmion's joy in his return was redoubled the following month by a visit to Maredsous from Cardinal Mercier, who came bringing noble proof of his old friendship.

But these joyful days were but a passing gleam. It seemed as if Providence had been awaiting this return to permit fresh trials to fall upon the abbey and its head. Soon, in fact, frequent and obnoxious requisitions were made on the monastery by German secret police in the payment of the military administrators. *"Canaille,"* one of the German authorities named them, "but indispensable *canaille."* Some acts of charity to Irish and French soldiers fallen behind in the rush of battle, the discovery of arms left in the precincts of the abbey, in August 1914, by the retreating troops and other "crimes" of equal gravity proved the signal for a prolonged series of vexations.

[1] "The strength of God."

These reached a climax when ten monks, amongst whom were the Prior[1] and the Father Master of Novices,[2] were imprisoned in Germany, condemned to penalties varying from four months of simple detention to two and a half years of forced labour. Dom Marmion never relaxed his efforts to obtain some alleviation in the lot of his sons in captivity, but the blow fell heavily on the heart of their father.

The news that reached him of those at the front was no less harrowing; he hears that one of his sons is grievously wounded; that another, a volunteer stretcher-bearer,[3] has fallen before Dixmunde in May 1916, his head blown to pieces by a bullet at the moment when he is carrying some wounded men to the back of a trench.

Those terrible years of occupation, marked out by so many unforeseen and often tragic happenings, and the incessant alternations of fear and hope weighed heavily on Dom Marmion. The joy of deliverance was for him not to be unmixed with suffering; his health, already affected since his stay in Ireland, besides being secretly undermined, began rapidly to decline. Death brushed him with its wing. He was not long to survive the liberation of his adopted country.

The year 1918 saw the dawn of this deliverance; then at last victory sounded. The final triumph was preceded by some months of inexpressible anguish, provoked by the proximity of the front of operations.

And now might be witnessed the first movements of the immense German army thrown back beneath the onslaught of Ferdinand Foch's battering-ram, the invasion and congestion of all the ways of communication, and the prodigious transporting, during long weeks, of seemingly endless hordes of humanity, of disbanded troops in every fantastic kind of equipment; all this under the blast of defeat which blew vehemently and irresistibly from Flanders and

1 Dom Robert Cornet.
2 Dom Idesbald Ryelandt.
3 Dom Olivier Deroitte.

France. Dom Marmion saw his abbey and all its precincts again submerged by baggage-wagons of the enemy; but these were only passing in haste, and soon the flag of the old Brabantine colours was floating over the towers of the monastery, whilst, in the valley the Teutonic tide, dejected and lamentable, continued to flow on in the direction of the German frontiers.

On November 11th, all the abbey bells – the greater ones silent since 1914 – at last announced the final victory.

Dom Marmion saw his sons who had been scattered by the tempest one by one restored to him: some from the marshes of Flanders, others from German prisons, yet others from exile. His fatherly heart joyfully saw them return to the monastery, like homing pigeons long held back by the storm and now released by the lull. Gradually the monastic family was once more gathered together.

The year 1919 was made memorable for Maredsous by a visit from Her Majesty the Queen of Belgium and His Royal Highness Prince Léopold. The Queen came to follow the offices of Holy Week, which she did with touching attention. On that glorious Easter Sunday a throne was raised for her on the epistle side of the choir; having the Duke of Brabant on her right, she assisted at the liturgical festival as it unfolded itself; in her the wife, the mother and the sovereign joined in spirit with the joyous *Alleluia* of Christ's resurrection.

Just then, as Dom Marmion was absent on pressing business, it was impossible for him to do the honours of the abbey to Her Majesty, Élisabeth of Belgium.

After her visit the Queen wished that the abbey should possess a lasting memorial of the days she had passed there with the monks. On 9 June 1920, the patronal feast of Dom Columba, she herself brought a chalice of great beauty, encrusted with rubies and enhanced with delicate workmanship, in which red roses and golden shamrocks were intermingled. Dom Marmion was deeply touched by this royal and gracious token.

The cataclysm had left behind it a Europe in a state of upheaval, and nations whose respective positions had no longer anything in common with that of pre-war days. It was not possible, even in religious families, to make complete abstraction of outward circumstances and think only of pure love and the supernatural. Rome at once recognised that the position was a delicate one and prepared to take measures which had become inevitable. By a decree of 20 February 1920, the Sovereign Pontiff authorised the monasteries of Maredsous and of Mont-César at Louvain to separate themselves from the Congregation of Beuron, of which they had hitherto made part, and to form, with the monastery of Saint-André-lez-Bruges, a new Benedictine congregation. This was placed under the title of the Annunciation; the choice of this name had been suggested by Dom Columba, happy to honour the mystery of the Incarnation, towards which he had such great devotion.

Thus Maredsous particularly fell under the counter blast of the political and military events of 1914–18; it lost its juridicial bond with an international and numerous group, grown strong with years; but, on the other hand, it became the member[1] of a new, more homogeneous federation; one more closely bound together and full of promise for the future. With his supernatural instinct, Dom Marmion saw the hand of Providence in this event.

We may observe, besides, that a like event, although hastened, and it may even be said precipitated by the war, was not thereby less in conformity with the natural evolution of things. The history of the Benedictine Order contains many analogous facts of segmentation. The separation from Beuron had been, moreover, foreseen by the founder of the Beuron Congregation, Dom Maurus Wolter,[2] himself. It left intact certain spiritual bonds, and on the

[1] But a member rather peculiarly situated, at least quite at its beginning, since the two other abbeys of the Belgian Congregation – henceforward its "sisters" – were, originally, the one directly, the other indirectly, its "daughters."

[2] "When the fruit is ripe," he said, "it will separate itself from the tree." In a recent article which appeared on the occasion of the centenary of the birth of Dom Maurus Wolter, one of his sons, Dom Nicolas von Salis, of Beuron, writes: "The separation of the Belgian abbey from Beuron was an inevitable consequence of the war. It is interesting to remark that, from the beginning of the foundation of Maredsous, the possibility of a Belgian congregation was already foreseen."

part of Maredsous feelings of gratitude towards that Archabbey of Beuron which had, in times past, supplied its first monks.[1] In drawing up the constitutions the new Belgian Congregation was intent on retaining, by means of several adaptations, the spirit and principles of the Beuron Congregation which the three Belgian communities had inherited.[2]

Little by little the monastery took up again its normal tenor; the various activities suspended by the invasion were resumed and the atmosphere of the abbey was again one of peace.

But the health of its abbot had been shattered during the war; Dom Marmion had the presentiment of his approaching end; death was not to be long before striking the decisive blow.

God, however, still held in store for His servant a twofold joy on earth: the first was the appearance in 1922 of his volume *Christ the Ideal of the Monk*, which, with *Christ the Life of the Soul* and *Christ in His Mysteries* completed a luminous triology whence the Divine Figure of Christ radiates. The echo which from every side reached Dom Marmion of the great good wrought by these pages was a deep source of pure spiritual consolation for his apostolic soul.

Secondly, God gave him to see, on 15 October 1922, the celebration

---

[1] It is not superfluous to add that the Abbey of Maredsous has kept an affectionate remembrance of the various German lay brothers, formerly numbered amongst its devoted sons; now, in consequence of the decision of the Belgian military authority, they had, in August 1914, to return to their native country.

[2] Dom Marmion held the constitutions of Beuron in high esteem. To a religious of his abbey who asked to pass into another congregation of the order, he replied: "Your letter has not *hurt* me; I like you to speak candidly and to express exactly what you think, but it has *excessively* pained me, for I have always had the deep conviction – continually confirmed by a rather long experience of our own monastery and other abbeys – that the constitutions of Beuron are the most perfect adaptation of the *Rule* and the spirit of St Benedict to the needs and aspirations of out era.... Doubtless, I admit, changes in the detail might be made in view of adapting it to the national climate and temperament, but the constitutions themselves are excellent." Out of discretion we do not give the precise date of this letter, written before the war.

of the golden jubilee of the foundation of the abbey. Cardinal Mercier had consented to preside at this celebration; Msgr Thomas Heylen, Bishop of Namur; Msgr Amleto Cicognani, representing His Excellence Msgr Sebastiano Nicotra, Nuncio at Brussels; numerous abbots of the Orders of St Benedict and of St Norbert, and delegates of the principal religious institutes in the country likewise assisted at it. The assembly included the Baron de Gaiffer d'Hestroy, Governor of the Province of Namur and numerous notabilities, amongst whom was Madame Desclée, a venerable octogenarian, the sole survivor of those who had signed the act of foundation. The Pontifical Mass was sung by Cardinal Mercier. In the course of the ceremony the autograph letter addressed by His Holiness Pius XI to Dom Marmion was read.

> It was with particular satisfaction that we learnt that the Abbey of Maredsous, confided to your wise government, was preparing to celebrate the fiftieth anniversary of its foundation. The news of this event was so much the more gratifying and we were so much the more desirous to associate ourselves with the joy of your monastic family in that we love to recall the visit we once made to your abbey and the hospitality we there received.
>
> This jubilee is certainly well worthy of being solemnly commemorated: modest in its origin, the institution of Maredsous has taken, in the course of this first period of its history, a development and growth which testify to the blessings and favours that have been showered upon it.

The Sovereign Pontiff next outlined the monastic life and activity of the abbey, then continued: "The very consoling results obtained during these first fifty years of the existence of your abbey are the pledge of the always more salutary fruit that we like to hope from it, for the past is a happy presage of an ever more prosperous and fruitful future. We rejoice and thank God for it, beseeching Him to continue to shed the abundance of His blessings on your abbey, that it may be a focus of learning and holiness."

In the course of the fraternal agape that followed in the great hall of the college, where nearly two hundred guests were gathered together, Cardinal Mercier began by recalling in felicitous terms the close friendship which had long bound him to Dom Marmion; then he evoked the remembrance of beloved and vanished forms who had embalmed the cloister with the perfume of their virtues. Other speakers, particularly the Bishop of Namur and the governor of the province, recalled the part played by the abbey during the last fifty years, and voiced the good wishes of fervent friendship coming from all parts to the venerated father of the monastery.

That day, lit up with the beams of an autumn sun, was one of incomparable radiance, but it was to be the last of its kind for Dom Marmion. Three months later God called him to Himself.

It now remains for us – and from the viewpoint we are taking in this work, it is a question most important to emphasise – to discover in what light Dom Marmion revealed himself in the intimate government and spiritual direction of his monastery.

Until his election as abbot, his life had been that of a simple religious; even as prior at Louvain, any initiative he had been able to take was completely under the control of obedience, and that was absolute. How then did this monk, whose whole activity until then had been set in motion by the will of another, conceive the art of government?

No one will expect that the fundamental principles of his life were changed; but, placed in this sphere, in what manner did he act up to them? To what practical morality were they subjected in their application?

The reply to these important questions will give us the opportunity of fathoming more deeply the soul of this master of asceticism. We shall see how his supernatural spirit and ardent love of Christ ruled all his dealings with the souls entrusted to him; what pure and fruitful results were produced by his close union with God.

10 CHRIST'S REPRESENTATIVE

It follows from the very data of the *Rule of St Benedict* that the monastic community – with its members bound to their abbey by a special vow of perpetual stability, with its superior elected for life and invested with an almost universal authority – presents a special analogy with the natural and most fundamental institution, the one which comes most directly from the hands of God – namely, the family. It may be said that each little cenobitical society, local and closely bound together, is a supernatural transposition of the family.

However, it would be a mistake to suppose that in saying this we have given the whole purport and the primary concept that St Benedict formed of cenobitism, and on which he based its organisation. The correlative ideas of family and paternity have their source, according to him, in a higher and in some manner unconditional principle which he truly makes the cornerstone of the monastic edifice. This principle, which he expresses with a clearness and insistence which leaves no room for doubt as to his meaning, is as follows: "In the monastery, the abbot is deemed to hold, is believed – by others and by himself – *to hold the place of Christ in person*.[1] And it is because he is considered as vice-Christ, that he has the right to bear the names – which are synonymous and belong to Christ[2] – of *Abba* (abbot) *Father*. Do we change Christ? Do we change our Father? It seems as if the idea of making it one of the rules of the cenobitical organism to have a new superior periodically did not even occur to the holy legislator's mind.

The reader may ask why we mention these questions here. It

---

1 *"Abbas Christi vices in monasterio agere creditur,"* Rule of St Benedict, ch. 2.
2 It is certainly the first Person of the Blessed Trinity whom our Lord teaches His disciples to call by the name of Father. But did He not speak to them as "My children"? Did He not say to them: "I will not leave you orphans"? Above all, did He not veritably hold amongst them – for instance at the Last Supper – the position of the father of the family. Hence the name of *father* was originally given to the pope (signifying "father") to the bishop, and the abbot, as to those who hold the place of Christ.

is because the clear understanding of them is indispensable for anyone who wishes to discover in its true light what was the moral physiognomy of Dom Marmion as head of the monastic family. He, in fact, was the personification of cenobitical fatherhood such as it is depicted in the Benedictine *Rule,* and this to such an extent that the *Rule* truly furnishes the lines and colours necessary to the portrait of the man.

But, above all, Dom Columba had completely made his own the principle laid down by the Patriarch of Monks as the basis of cenobitism. There was no monastic doctrine on which he laid more emphasis than this: "In spite of all the human imperfections of the abbot, it must be believed, and he himself must believe he is *the authentic representative* of Christ in the monastery."

> St Benedict says in his *Rule* that the abbot ought to remember the name he bears and to consider that he represents Jesus Christ: *Christi vices agere in monasterio creditur.* He should therefore endeavour to manifest in his life and actions the Person of Christ; if he wishes to do good to souls, he must try to be 'Jesus' and to be 'Christ.' Our Lord is called *Christus* because He is anointed by the grace of the hypostatic union. He is so united to the divinity that there is in Him only one Person, that of the Word. The abbot will only see his action on souls bear good result if he remains closely united to God. He must, moreover, represent Jesus; now this name signifies 'saviour.' The abbot ought, then, to be entirely given up to the souls confided to him by the Divine Shepherd. I wish my whole life to be given up first of all to God in an act of total self-abandonment, and next to the souls whom God requires me to lead to Him.[1]

And when a conviction of this nature enters into the inmost heart and soul of a man, to the point of being his hourly strength and support, it is clear proof that this man is animated by a very lofty spirit of faith. We shall find again and again in the whole sphere of Dom

1 Conference to the Benedictine nuns of Maredret.

Marmion's pastoral activity that supernatural attitude which we have already met with and which forms one of the most remarkable traits of his personality.

We know then that within his soul a flame was burning which shone with a steady light on every aspect of his mission as abbot, and in every direction where his influence was exerted over the monastery of which he was the head and permanent centre: temporal interests and spiritual interests, administration of property and government of men; authority and affection; public relations with his sons in community and private relations with each one of them; finally the very diverse circumstances of common and daily life, from the most familiar and the most ordinary, such as the hour of relaxation and friendly talk, to the highest in the intellectual and religious order, such as doctrinal teaching, the direction of souls and his priestly and pontifical functions.

In unfolding to view the width and variety of action to which an abbot is called to devote himself, it is not to lose ourselves in any detailed analysis. Our intention in casting a glance on this vast field of action is to specify some of the occasions – however slight in themselves – which best serve to reveal the individuality of Dom Columba and to gather in passing a few traits best calculated to give a true impression of him.

Let us say at the outset, without beating about the bush, that neither nature nor his studies, almost exclusively speculative, had fitted Dom Marmion to take in hand the government, and more especially the temporal affairs, of a large abbey.

We have here a singular contrast difficult to understand:[1] this man who in a speculative discussion could state the question with wonderful lucidity, and then lay his finger on the crux of the problem, he who was so skilful in settling intricate cases of conscience and in giving clear and sure advice, one of such astonishing intuition in

[1] It may be partly explained by the centuries of persecution that had thwarted the spirit of initiation in the Irish.

the things of God, often found an uncongenial and therefore eminently meritorious task in the sphere of business affairs, by which we mean that whole amalgamation of various and unforeseen matters, harassing and complicated, and of daily occurrence.

He however devoted himself to these things without any respite, and the way in which he carried out his duties of administration with all his energies until his death was a continued proof of his virtue. Under his wise rule the prosperity of the abbey was kept on a high level, and it fell to Dom Columba to make important improvements in material matters.[1]

He had moreover the wisdom and humility to surround himself with zealous "officers" who seconded him in his labour. In this he followed St Benedict's direction, bidding the abbot to choose aids in order to free himself as far as possible from material cares and to devote himself particularly to the spiritual guidance of the monks.

In this sphere of government Dom Columba did not cling to his own point of view; he was moved solely by consideration for the common good, and the welfare of souls; in short, he had no other care than to follow the Divine Will and judgment. Here again he placed himself in full accordance with the counsels given to the father of the monastery by the Holy Patriarch.

> The abbot holds the place of Christ; he ought to endeavour to be able to say with Jesus: 'I always do that which is pleasing to my Father in heaven.' His duty is then to try to learn at every moment what God wills of him. And to this end he ought to live a life of prayer and union with God; as the constitutions prescribe for him, he ought to strive 'to abide in the sublimity of prayer and of the Divine Presence;' to have a sure knowledge of the doctrine of the Church, and of the *Rule*, to consult his Council, to take every means of knowing God's Will, then to fulfil it perfectly.[2]

---

1 The installation of electricity and central heating. We may add that after the crisis of the war, divers activities (school, publications) were again quickly set on foot.
2 To the nuns of Maredret, November 1916.

One of his sons, then at Louvain, consulted him on some important questions regarding his future:

> What you tell me as to your submission to God's Holy Will manifested by your abbot is a great consolation to me. You may be sure that I shall decide nothing for you until I have spoken of the matter to our Lord in prayer, and this not only from duty, but because I love you with a very pure and sincere affection in Jesus Christ, and because with all my heart I have for you all the devotedness and confidence that you show to me.[1]

This spirit of faith always ruled his line of conduct. "The further I advance in life," he wrote a few years later, "the more I try to discover in every happening what is the Will of God. Any supernatural undertaking which has not this adorable will for its principle is doomed to failure."[2]

He endeavoured not to deviate from this line at the most difficult junctures: "Let us try," he writes in a particularly painful circumstance, "let us try to know God's Holy Will, to keep our soul and our intention fixed on Him, and let men talk."[3]

Sometimes in the hope of being more sure of success, an attempt was made to influence his decision by appealing to his most susceptible point – his goodness of heart. He had had to send one of his monks on a mission far from the monastery. The mother of this religious intervened – as was very natural; we remember the mother of the sons of Zebedee – and had evidently complained (for we have not the letter by us) at seeing her son sent so far away from his own country. Dom Marmion remained firm, while couching his reply in the warmth of his charity:

> I understand the cry of your mother-heart and I should be happy to be able to respond to it by revoking the order I have given to your dear son to go to the post of honour at.... If I

1 Letter of 13 February 1910.
2 Letter of 19 December 1912.
3 Letter of 5 July 1915.

had followed the impulse of my heart, I should have told him to stay at Maredsous. But it is a very dangerous thing to go against what one believes to be the Divine Will for reasons of the natural order. When a monk forsakes the way of the Divine Will, it often happens that God leaves him to himself, and his monastic career is spoilt. However, when things have been organised over there, I will reconsider whether I can substitute another in place of your son.[1]

For what concerned the material part of his work Dom Marmion was very considerate about asking for help or service: he spared the time of others. He showed the same discretion when it was a question of distributing charges. St Benedict wills that the abbot "should accommodate himself to each one in such a way that the strong may have the occasion of generously forgetting themselves, and the weak may have nothing to discourage them." When, therefore, the moment came to appoint one of his sons to an employment, Dom Marmion carefully calculated the strength of the one he had in mind before imposing the burden. He also made a point of appealing to the most supernatural motives, and so obtaining the most unhesitating good will.

Finally, a rare qualification – the exercise of power is easily apt to have a contrary tendency – he respected the dignity of others. In the tone of his orders, whether intimated verbally or by letter, nothing needlessly imperative, nothing harsh or peremptory, but always temperate and measured, the gentleness of a father, that gentleness which finds its way to the heart and gains the will: never was a superior less inclined to exert authority.

As for that which was uncongenial to him in his office of administrator – which in the eyes of St Benedict is the least important and the least noble in the life of a superior – Dom Marmion consoled himself by *his spiritual mission as abbot:* contact with men reconciled

[1] Out of discretion we do not give the date of this letter.

him to his material duties as steward of the house of God – on condition, however, that he could treat these same men *as sons*.

He has himself stated in a masterly manner[1] – after having often besought God to enlighten him on the matter – the essential role of the father of the monastery; he has shown marvellously well what St Benedict requires before all things of the abbot: to be the *pastor* who leads to God the flock confided to his care, to be the *pontiff* whose mediation with God fructifies action in souls.

He was excellently prepared for this twofold task by his theological and ascetical knowledge, as well as by the experience he had gained in guiding souls. Here he was on his own ground, and finding himself at home on it he acted with incomparable ease.

And to begin with, he devoted himself to the special duties of "high priest in the house of God."

In spite of super-abounding occupations, he was always present at Matins until the day when, after the hard times of the war and attacks of illness, physical incapacity often obliged him to leave his stall empty, much to his regret. But then the conventual Mass and the singing of Vespers became all the dearer to him.

The fulfilment of his liturgical task had become so much a second nature to him that the bell which called him to the church awoke within him a need – one of which he was keenly conscious – to go to refresh his soul at the living waters.

And if we wish to know one of the reasons why he had it so much at heart to preside in choir and himself direct the official and collective prayer of the community; if we wish to have one of the secrets of the fervour which animated him when on the great days of the Church's calendar he pontificated at the sacred functions, having around him the whole crown of his sons, it is this. He had to a high degree the sense of the supernatural from the social point of view in the Church, the understanding of the nature of public worship, the perception of the privileged greatness and efficacy that the exercise of sacred magistracy has in God's sight. Quite naturally these convictions which he held so strongly were applied in a

---

1 In *Christ the Ideal of the Monk,* ch. "The Abbot, Christ's Representative."

particularly concrete and active form to the supernatural family of which Providence had made him the head.

"Do you know," he said to one of his sons, "what costs me the most when I have to be absent from the abbey? It is the privation of the conventual Mass. I find it such a grand thing to offer up *all together* to the Heavenly Father the immolation of His Divine Son!"

In his abbey church he felt himself to be the high priest, the authorised representative of his sons, their spokesman, powerful with God, the bearer not only of their words but of their prayers. He felt he had the collective right to praise in their name and the privilege to intercede on their behalf. And in this consisted for him one of the highest prerogatives of his charge as abbot.

For this reason – and it is the only one – he loved to sing the Pontifical Mass himself in his abbey church; it was to him that Christ had given the grace and mission there to represent his sons in God's sight. For the one same supernatural motive he loved his insignia. In everything we find the logic of his faith.

There was yet more: "I am so convinced," he said in a conference to the nuns of Maredret, "that the Holy Sacrifice is the great Source of sanctification, that I have established the custom in my monastery of having the conventual Mass celebrated every Sunday and every Thursday for the community."[1]

Words worthy to be borne in mind because they manifest that spirit of faith which – as we shall see more and more – was one of the distinguishing traits of Dom Marmion's personality.

Dom Marmion found no better way of concluding his beautiful chapter on "The Abbot, Christ's Representative," in *Christ the Ideal of the Monk*, than in showing how sublime a charge is that of mediator and pontiff which belongs to the head of the monastery.

---

[1] He added, by way of a logical extension of the same supernatural principle: "At least once a week, I myself celebrate the Holy Sacrifice for my monks, for I well know that I am incapable of sanctifying them, but I ask our Lord to sanctify them, to make of us all *munus perfectum*" (These last words refer to the *Secret* of the Mass of the Holy Trinity).

CHRIST'S REPRESENTATIVE

On this subject the following lines where he allows to transpire all that lay within his heart find a fitting place:

> Nothing more vividly translates all this admirable and fruitful supernatural doctrine than the conventual Mass celebrated by the abbot surrounded by his sons. Vested in the insignia of his dignity, the head of the monastery offers the Sacred Victim to God, or rather, through his ministry, Christ, the supreme High Priest and universal mediator, offers Himself to the Father. The abbot offers up to heaven the homage, the vows, the very hearts of his monks, whence arises a perfume of sacrifice and of love, which the Father receives, through Christ, in the odour of sweetness.
>
> In this solemn moment of the holy Oblation, when voices are blended in one and the same praise, hearts uplifted in the same spirit of adoration and love towards God, the abbot worthy of the name can repeat the words uttered, in the presence of His disciples, by the Divine Pastor when He was about to give His life for the sheep: 'Father, Thine they were, and to me Thou gavest them.... I pray not that Thou shouldst take them out of the world, but that Thou shouldst keep them from evil....' May they be one among themselves and with me, as Thy Son is One with Thee ... may Thy love abide in them, and to all may it one day be given to contemplate the glory of Thy Christ, and to be partakers of Thy blessed fellowship with Thy beloved Son and the Holy Spirit!

To complete the abbot's mission of "pontiff" must be added that of shepherd of souls.

It need scarcely be said that this equally high and holy mission was extremely dear to Dom Marmion; he would gladly have given his sons more of that time on which during his later years such a large demand was often made by force of outward circumstances.

St Benedict tells his successors that their essential work consists in directing and governing souls, and he further defines the monastery as "a school of the Lord's service," thus giving the very reason of the cenobitical institution. This subject affords the opportunity of gaining further insight into Dom Marmion's soul.

The abbot's task of directing souls may be considered under two forms – namely, the teaching of ascetical doctrine to all his monks whilst illustrating it by his own example, and the giving of spiritual direction in the stricter sense of the term. The first is obligatory, the second is facultative, for each monk is left to chose his own director of conscience.

Under its primary and general form the abbot's action on souls goes far beyond that of the ordinary director. The latter gives advice and guidance in the way of perfection to persons living in the world who come to him either in passing or at shorter or longer intervals for this definite purpose. The abbot, on the contrary, lives in the midst of his monks and can act upon them by word and by example, both at stated times and on unforeseen occasions, such as arise in community life; now on all the brethren together, again on one of them individually in the way of practical advice and sometimes reprimand; in the case of a private interview, more often by a simple and affectionate talk.

The abbot has therefore the opportunity of exerting every kind of influence corresponding with his name and quality of doctor of theology, educator, friend and counsellor, permanently sustaining and tempering all things, and it is precisely from the synthesis of all these names and qualities that he derives the greatest and noblest of all; that is to say, the one of father of the monastery. It is this that in the eyes of St Benedict places him at the height of his mission.

How did Dom Marmion exert this supernatural art of guiding souls to God, both in its general form – the spiritual paternity of the abbot – and in its special form – spiritual direction properly so called?

We will leave what formally concerns spiritual direction till the next chapter, when, in the light of some letters of direction, we shall be able to see at a glance the different characteristics which distinguish Dom Marmion in this domain. We will first envisage him in his capacity as abbot, the spiritual father of monks. Of what aptitudes of mind and heart, what qualities of nature and grace did he not give proof in the sphere of paternal conversation with the members of his monastic family?

We need not go back upon his eminent qualities as doctor; we have said enough of the extent, sureness, and depth of his theological and ascetical doctrine, and of the example he gave in fidelity to what he taught. We are here considering the character of his relations with his sons.

It was Dom Marmion's noble simplicity, his frankness verging on childlike candour, which people remarked in him at the outset. St Benedict, in this again inspired by the Gospel, requires the monk "to speak the truth with heart and lips."[1] Faithful to this precept, Dom Columba uttered his thoughts with simplicity.

"I cannot express to you," he writes to one of his intimate disciples, "the happiness I feel in having a soul and heart to whom I can say *everything*, without danger of being misunderstood. When I write to you, I think aloud. I show you the bottom of my thoughts and of my heart. In eternity it will be the same; we shall be filled with the light of truth and all in us will be true: the *telling* and the *understanding*. What happiness to have it so even in this world!"[2]

He liked this frankness in others as much as he cultivated it in himself: "You will ask me," he writes to one of his spiritual daughters, "why I was pleased with your letter. Well, just because you speak to me just as you think, and that is *so* rare I can't say how much I value it."[3]

To another person in a letter of several years later: "I like your letters because you write to me as you think – simply and frankly."[4]

He kept this simplicity until the end of his life. He wrote on 7 July 1922:

I do not know how to tell you the pleasure your way of

---

[1] *Veritatem ex ore et corde proferre*, Rule of St Benedict, ch. 4.
[2] Letter of 9 July 1917.
[3] Letter of 22 November 1906.
[4] Letter of 17 December 1913.

writing, so simple, so much a child with her father, causes me. With you there is nothing folded away. The word 'simplicity' comes from that: *sine pliqua* (*'sans pli'*) without fold.[1] You must suffer as I do, for the world is not worthy of being treated with simplicity. Better, however, to be deceived sometimes than to be wanting in this virtue.

That is the opinion of the saints.

Like all high-souled people, Dom Marmion held distrust, and all species of suspicion, in abhorrence – not that his psychology or prudence was at fault, for his judgment was often very shrewd – but, as was right, he credited others with goodness of intention and purity of motive. He believed hearts to be true and faces free from dissimulation. Certainly he was wont to esteem his neighbours as better than they really were, and there were occasions when his confidence was abused. One has known him disconcerted at the moment of seeing how his usual absence of suspicion was repaid, but then no vexation on his part, simply sadness – on account of "the other" who had failed in the rules of fair play. Is not a man whose nobility of nature subjects him to such disappointments, one who was never skilled in detecting anything but the good in a person, worthy of all honour?

However, entire as were Dom Marmion's frankness and simplicity, they were surpassed by his eminent goodness of heart. And speaking of this we come to the dominant part of his personality. It is a fatherly heart endowed with great sensibility and exceptional power of sympathy of which we have now to tell.

His manner of coming into contact with anyone for the first time generally made an impression. No ice to break between him

[1] A fantastic derivation such as is often to be met with in the fathers and the writers of the Middle Ages, but the idea is just. Of the two roots which form simplex, the first signifies "one," "once" (*semel*); the second, "plier" (*duplex, triplex*). *Simplex* means, then: folded once, or more exactly, all in one piece; that is to say, "unfolded," "without fold."

and the newcomer, whoever he might be or to whatever social rank he belonged; on occasion, all ceremony reduced as far as possible, perhaps too far reduced in the opinion of some people; no paving of the way by conventional remarks, but, immediately and spontaneously, the word and gesture which with wholehearted simplicity gave the tone to the situation, and the stranger, a little astonished at the first moment, felt it behoved him to accept the diapason with a good grace. Dom Marmion was thus always ready to make the first advance; his was the gift, metaphorically speaking, of going more than halfway to meet anyone *in occursum ire*. He had the frank bearing, the ever-open heart, the hand ready to outstretch, and his direct regard which spoke of singleness of purpose, said as plainly as words: "What can I do to render you service or give you pleasure?"

The fact was that this man possessed a treasure of inexhaustible affection – that treasure which divine love gives. As soon as he felt that the one he had just come in touch with was seeking God, he was ready to sign the pact of friendship in order to help that soul to find God.

The simple, natural and gentle style of his usual relations with those who came near to him may easily be imagined. He welcomed them in the fullest sense of the word, fixing attentive eyes straight upon them, delighted to listen, ready to oblige. On the properly speaking moral plane, that exceptional cordiality which was his may be expressed as an habitual state of goodwill, and of active goodwill, towards his neighbour; his friendship readily offered was, once accepted, equally ready to perform.[1]

This attractive cordiality may be attributed both to his natural qualities and Christian virtues: to an affectionate, expansive and generous temperament, a rich and communicative nature, but above all great purity of intention, the absence of all self-seeking, a love of giving, and then to the supernatural which was especially apparent in the fact that he was equally accessible to all – the most

---

[1] It is true that in Dom Marmion's later years a multiplicity of affairs, and above all a decline of physical health, limited his powers of action, but the goodness of his heart remained ever the same.

wretched soul and the most privileged felt alike that he was altogether at their service.

There was one hour of the monastic life when Dom Marmion's social qualities found full scope and at the same time the opportunity of most happily promoting close fellowship: this was the hour of recreation. And it is not without interest to notice how here again his natural gifts were put at the service of grace.

The duty of presiding regularly at recreation where all the members of a religious house take part is one which many superiors – we are simply stating a known fact – feel a strain; for Dom Marmion this duty was a pleasure. He himself experienced the need of a short break in the midst of the day's close application to prayer and work, and he never failed to be the life of the recreation. We shall be forgiven if we linger over a matter which in itself appears of small importance. We may "recreate" ourselves with tracing a few details of the case in point, besides learning something from them.

We must not forget that Dom Marmion was an Irishman. Despite the accumulated tragedies and disasters of years of persecution, the Irish soul, wistful and mystical, retains an imagination ever on the alert, the sense and instinct of fun, the love of a joke and of familiar and good-natured drollery.[1] In these things Dom Columba was altogether one of his race. He remained so until the end of his life, although in his latter years the slight shadow of a cloud dimmed his old gay vivacity.

In recreation, then, the good humour, the gaiety – the frank gaiety of Dom Marmion – and his flow of words, were inexhaustible. His play of imagination and jovial enthusiasm almost constrained those around him to laughter and merriment. If there were no more events, great or small, to relate, anecdotes came to the fore, and they would have lost much of their interest, and power to amuse, if the story-teller's gestures and play of countenance had been suppressed; there were some which no other save himself would have

[1] *Cf.* Paul-Dubois, *loc. cit.*

known how to repeat; many, too, which were forgotten as soon as heard. In the course of the telling it sometimes chanced that the narrator would drop the thread of his story for an instant to aim the most unexpected shaft at one side or the other; now at the young religious who were thoroughly enjoying themselves, now at some veteran slow to unbend. His witticisms were at times disconcerting; certain monks of colder temperament would have wished for a little less exuberance, the Irish salt has not always the savour of the Attic salt. But how could one take umbrage when all was felt to be so spontaneous, so much the outcome of such a transparent and innocent intention. Besides, did not their author himself plead the extenuating circumstances of his Celtic temperament.

Then, again, where is the psychologist of any discernment on the subject of asceticism who can mistake the nature and legitimacy of this banter, this frank laughter belonging to community recreations? What observer could be superficial enough to count as levity those flashes of wit of which the spark is set alight by one signal of the bell and is extinguished by another. No moralist would be slow to understand that the moments accorded to relaxation – so necessary to give fresh vigour to the nervous forces on which the interior life makes such demands – moreover serves a very useful purpose in conducing to good fellowship and the interchanging of tokens of courtesy and charity.

Besides – and it is on this that we must especially dwell – Dom Marmion's apparent exuberance on these occasions must not lay us open to any illusion. Under his fluent speech, under his spontaneous and genial hilarity, he kept entire possession and control of himself. One quite realised that his jests were not meant in earnest, but were rather after the manner of a pleasant word uttered without premeditation.

Then without its appearing on the surface – but not escaping observant minds – the shepherd of the flock never for an instant lost sight of the end in view: to maintain and further the conditions of his sons' well-being. As an astute psychologist he knew in fact that joy is a tonic – that joyful souls are the best servants of God – that the atmosphere of fraternal cordiality is likewise the most favourable atmosphere of grace; finally, and this especially, that in the habitual easy courteous relations between the father and his sons a certain familiar *abandon* in the form of these relations are, for the sons, a simple and pleasant school for learning openness of heart and confidence, whilst these relations give the father an affectionate hold on those whom he has, before all and above all, the mission of leading to God.

Let us add – and this remark will complete our object lesson in confirming it – that if during the time of recreation Dom Marmion loved to spread joy around him by amusing conversation, as soon as the bell rang for the end of the "exercise" he at once appeared in a different character: the sense of monastic gravity again entirely possessed his outward bearing.

Readily bestowed, Dom Marmion's affections were never afterwards taken back. He had the most faithful memory of the heart, and when long years had gone by still concerned himself about persons with whom he had had a few intimate talks.

"Dom Columba," writes a Carmelite monk who had been helped in his vocation by him, "ever carried in his heart those who had given their confidence to him, and he kept them in religious and faithful remembrance. Although I was really of very small consequence to him, never did he forget me; in the rare circumstances when I had the happiness of meeting him again, as soon as he saw me he came up to me and gave me a fraternal *accolade*. A few weeks before his death, after an interval of nearly twenty years, and though I was in the East, he still took an interest in me."[1]

Many others could pay Dom Marmion the same testimony.

If it was thus with persons whom he had encountered only a few times on life's crossroads, how constant were his friendships with those amongst whom he lived – those friendships which had been supernaturally contracted with him through religious profession!

1 Letter of 25 January 1928, to the author.

Nothing on his side could trouble these friendships, none of those clouds which the uprisings of rivalry or envy, of touchiness born of vanity or of wounded self-love – that ever-circulating small change of egoism[1] – so often cause to pass over worldly friendships. It was because with him that inward enemy, the inordinate and anti-social ego had been reduced to silence. His humility accepted courteously and straightforwardly every remark and observation. He gratefully acknowledged the least service done to him.

But it takes two to form a friendship – two to spoil it as well as to maintain it. The idea that he could have personally displeased anyone did not make Dom Marmion hold aloof in any manner: it only bound him to do his best to remove whatever in him – and in spite of him – seemed to create a grievance. If, without its being in any way intentional, words happened to escape him which hurt anyone's feelings, as soon as he perceived the fact, he was full of regret and sought in every way to dispel the impression produced.

As for any hurt done to himself, it made no difference to his affection. If he was the object of those offences which St Benedict himself calls "thorns of scandal," and which are inevitably to be encountered in every society of men, he forgave promptly and fully; he was incapable of retaining the least vestige of resentment against anyone whomsoever, and in this his high virtue shone out as well as nobility of soul, for, like every Irishman, he had quicksilver in his veins. To the very end he cherished a warmth of charity which nothing could diminish, a freshness of soul which long intercourse with men had been powerless to impair.

"I have just received your good letter, he wrote to one of his disciples. I had already forgiven you from the bottom of my heart. If I did not love you sincerely your attitude would have been indifferent to me.... Let us think no more of it. Our Lord forgives us so easily and so *fully* that we ought not even to think of a difference once it is passed."[2]

1 We are here employing the term in the restricted sense given to it by French moralists, not in its original acceptation (every form of selfishness).
2 Letter of 25 November 1916.

To one of his spiritual daughters who asked forgiveness for being cross, he replies: "The child of God ought to imitate his Heavenly Father who forgives *divinely;* that is to say, completely, without going back on it or thinking any more about it. It is the same with me. Your little fit of crossness – which besides only pained me because I am so much yours, is forgotten."[1]

"All is forgiven and forgotten," he writes to another person who had this time gravely offended him and had asked pardon: "I only see you in the Heart of Jesus which is a furnace of love where everything is consumed and rises up as a perfume to the Heavenly Father."[2]

What supernatural and generous charity is manifested in these lines.

With those nearest to him his heart absolutely refused to admit the possibility of coldness or even to be resigned to indifference.

Indeed, in Dom Marmion reigned that real affective love which makes a man count as his own all the good or evil which befalls those given him to love. He espoused the interests of others, sympathised with their moral or physical state, shared their joys, their troubles, their anxieties, their family losses. And the moment having come, the occasion being given, this love was translated into self-forgetfulness and gift of self.

"I am so sorry," he writes to one of his sons who was away from the monastery, "to hear the bad news about your family. For now that our Lord has given you to me as a son, those who are yours are also mine. You can count on my prayers. I bless you *ex imo corde.*"[3]

And a few months later to the same, with a spontaneity this time which reveals the memory of the heart: "I always pray much for your dear people."[4]

On other occasions, his joy was undisguised: "It was for me true

---

1 Letter of 12 April 1917.
2 Letter of 29 November 1920.
3 Letter of 12 October 1909.
4 Letter of 28 December 1909.

happiness to be able to prove my affection by receiving those belonging to you as if they were my own."[1]

"I am *so* glad," he writes to one of his sons, whose state of health detained him far from the abbey, "that you faithfully follow the doctor's orders. I beg our Lord to bring you back to us quite cured. I pray for you *ex imo corde* every day."[2]

Mere conventional phrases some may say. No, not with him. What he wrote, he thought; what he thought, he lived.

In all these extracts do we not find to the very letter a living example of that Christian affection the variety and shades of which St Paul has traced in exquisite terms: "to rejoice with those that rejoice, to weep with those that weep; not considering the things that are his own, but those that are other men's; bearing the infirmities of the weak and striving to please his neighbour unto good, to edification?"[3] Truly this father found his happiness in that of his sons, in their ambitions, their labours, their success; in fact everything which, on whatever head, made for their welfare.

The spiritual naturally came first, but the temporal was not neglected. On this last point the years immediately following the Great War furnished some episodes of a rather naïve originality. The decorations, medals, honorary diplomas, which usually no one looks to receive in the cloister, this time found their way into the Abbey of Maredsous, as elsewhere, in consequence of events in which the monks had been concerned. On these occasions, it was certainly the Father Abbot who was more pleased than anyone, and found much more satisfaction in them than did those directly interested. And there were some cases when his delight was so keen and expressed with such emphasis that one would have been tempted to smile if it had not been so touching. Let us not interpret this attitude as a manifestation of delight which, although certainly quite permissible, yet went a little beyond the simple *esprit de corps* and monastic solidarity; no, they were the spontaneous expression of a

---

1 Letter of 4 December 1911.
2 Letter of 25 June 1920.
3 Rom. 12: 13; Phil. 2: 4; Rom. 15: 2.

sentiment which in him was never exaggerated: a love in which the impetuosity of youthful freshness was ingenuously blended with the benignity of an elder. With all the instinct of his generous nature, Dom Marmion was intent on restoring around him that fellowship of supernatural affection which the early Christians had formed in Jerusalem, and where the placing of all their temporal possessions in common was but the result of the perfect communion and communication of souls.

But with a too noble heart does not the reality cause it to run the risk of being one day wounded through its own ideal, of finding, at least occasionally, that suffering lies at the very root of its ordinary joys? Providence does not permit – did not even grant it to the Christians of the early apostolic age, those whose memory, as preserved in the *Acts of the Apostles*, we have just been recalling – that spiritual harmony should be maintained without any false note or any falling away amongst men whom the selfsame will of serving God has yet brought together as brethren. And if Dom Marmion gave his affection readily and fully; if he was incapable of closing his heart against others in coldness and indifference, he felt the need of being loved in return; he really suffered when the heart of another did not respond to the affection and advances of his own. This was, moreover, the quite natural effect of the logic of love; it wrung passionate complaints from St Paul and inflicted the deepest wounds on the Heart of the Divine Master.

It must be added that Dom Marmion, who had so sane a judgment on the conditions of our poor human nature and was so well-versed in the lives of the saints, could thank God for having spared him, much more than others – except in the years following the war – from the above form of suffering which would have been to him – and was so – particularly cruel.

For as we have already said, he was of an impressionable temperament. In this, again, he was of his race – his "mercurial race," as Canon Patrick Sheehan calls it in one of his novels.

Dom Marmion himself wrote one day: "The Irish character is difficult to understand, containing contrasts so absolutely opposed: seriousness and gaiety, love and vengeance, laughter and tears, often at the same time."[1] Dom Marmion keenly felt conflicting events, his ardent imagination laid on the colours rather than softened them, and his whole temperament reacted to them strongly and suddenly.

However, this sensibility – it is important to note this – was not in any wise that always more or less cultivated intellectual sensibility of the poet and the aesthetic; it was, in its purity and simplicity, a sensibility of the affections. When it was a matter only touching himself, no movement of impatience was to be perceived in him; he sought peace in prayer, confiding all to God. But when it was as friend, pastor or father that some circumstance or news came as a blow to his heart, he felt the sometimes irresistible need of sharing his first thoughts, impressions and anxieties. In this eagerness there yet entered the endeavour to control his own feelings and to take counsel before acting, but it was a necessity for him to find someone to confide in, someone to share his fears and hopes, his cares or his joy.

Some may perhaps be astonished at such moral sensibility, and at this need of having a friend and confidant in hours of anxiety. We are trying to sketch a portrait, not to compose a panegyric. It may readily be conceded that a man simply engaged in business, administration or government may envy and emulate the impassible attitude of the chess player. But the question is not the same for a man of moral action, one set apart for dealing with souls.

More than once in a similar case, Dom Marmion based his plea on St Paul. During the German occupation his master of novices was for long months imprisoned beyond the Rhine. His being set at liberty was the occasion for Dom Marmion to recall all the anguish he had suffered since his arrest, and then to give public vent to his joy: he did so in appropriating the words of St Paul. "But God who comforteth the humble, comforted us by the coming of Titus": *Qui consolatur humiles consolatus est nos Deus in adventione Titi.*

1 Letter of 4 April 1902.

Dom Columba had good reason to quote the great apostle. St Paul did not hide his generous emotions away in his breast nor cover them with an imperturbable mask. "There are saints," writes Cardinal Newman – the man who in our own day has best seized and set forth the distinctive feature of this physiognomy[1] – "there are saints," he says, "in whom grace supplants nature. That is not the case of the great apostle. In him grace only sanctifies and elevates nature; it leaves him the full possession and the full exercise of all that is human, without being guilty.... Astonishing! He who found his repose and his peace in the love of Christ had need of the love of men; he who sought his highest recompense in the approbation of God, was by no means indifferent to that of his brethren. He loved his brethren, not only for the love of Jesus, according to his own expression, but for the love of themselves. He lived in them; he associated himself with their feelings and their interests; he was anxious about their condition; he lent them assistance, and he expected aid from them (he embraced them and blended his tears with their tears). His soul was like a musical instrument, a harp or a viola, the cords of which, without being touched, vibrate in unison and in harmony with other neighbouring instruments."

"A rare and precious gift," adds Fr Prat, in quoting these words, "which presupposed a generous, devoted, self-forgetful soul, raised far above the petty preoccupations of self-interest and vanity, and knowing how to unite two things which are not easily allied – the power of pouring out affection and of winning it, of diffusing it over others, and of drawing it also to oneself. This marvellous gift, which St Paul possessed to an eminent degree, permitted him to surround himself with an atmosphere of sympathy, and to exercise over his fellow creatures a kind of magnetic attraction."

Fr Columba likewise possessed this gift. He put his rich affectionate nature at the service of grace; he found in it a singularly valuable help in the winning of souls to Christ. Above all, his extraordinary readiness of sympathy made him vibrate to the call

[1] Fernand Prat, SJ, *St. Paul*, translated from the original French by John L. Stoddard (Burns, Oates & Washbourne).

of those hearts that came to open out to him their miseries and needs; it quickened in him his gift of intuition; and if he was able to understand and consequently aid, uplift, console and give new strength to souls, it was in a great measure because the heart of a *man*,[1] in the fullest and noblest sense of the term, beat in his breast and because nothing is so comprehensive and active as love. "God has willed," says Henri-Dominique Lacordaire, another *grand cœur*, "that one can do no good to a man unless one loves him, and that insensibility is forever incapable either of enlightening him, or of inspiring him with virtue."[2]

According to the notion of St Thomas, the emotions are in no wise an evil or an imperfection in themselves. When a soul suddenly vibrates under the touch of reality like a stringed instrument beneath the bow of the musician the sound given back by its chords is precisely the fundamental sound of a human personality. With the vast number of those who are still far from Christian perfection, the emotions, both in kind and object, testify to the degree of self-love and egoism still sealed up in the heart; with others, they are the pledge of the divine charity that fills them. This test may safely be applied to the memory of Dom Marmion.

There is yet one special trait in connection with Dom Marmion which will further emphasise our conclusion and even bring it out more clearly by making it enter into the order of social experience and in the light of an object lesson: this is the effect that Fr Marmion produced on his hearers or interlocutors when he happened to speak of himself out of the abundance of his heart.

He, of course, shared the opinions of moralists, unanimous in pointing out the temptations and failings to which we are exposed

1 St Francis de Sales, with whom Dom Marmion had, as we have already said, great spiritual affinity prided himself on "having a man's heart," and would have nothing to do with "that imaginary insensibility of those who will not allow that we are men"; he declared it "a true chimera." Cf. *La vie spirituelle*, January 1927.
2 *Œuvres*, T. VII, "Discours à Sorèze."

in speaking of ourselves. A man accustomed to indulge his pride or vanity scarcely ever opens his mouth without offering some incense to himself, and even one who has been grounded in humility by long practice has still to keep vigilant guard against the subtle promptings of vain complacency when led to relate anything that refers to himself. However, is this vigilance to go so far as to banish as far as possible, every subject of discussion in which, by the very nature of the case, one of the speakers would have to bring himself into conversation? Common sense replies that prudence – a prohibition – carried to this extreme would do violence to nature, and take away all spontaneity, all pleasant freedom, all charm from social intercourse; in particular there would be no further possibility between men either of a frank and refreshing chat, or of intimacy, or of saying what lies in the heart. Dom Marmion, therefore, faithful on this point to the ordinary inspiration of his spirituality, sought to apply to human vanity a remedy that went beyond prohibitive measures based on mathematical lines. "Let us keep ourselves united to God, and then, the intention being upright and pure, let us say what we have to say with evangelical simplicity." That was his way of thinking.

It was necessary for us to repeat this. Having done so, let us come to the trait we wished to stress. We shall see it under varying aspects whether it concerns Dom Columba's public conferences to his monks or that of his private interviews with them. In one as in the other, this superior, with a heart both so affectionate to others and so eager to meet with friendly hearts, easily gave his confidence, and it was often when he disclosed his own inward thoughts and feelings that he did the most good.

The conferences given by an abbot to his community do not all bear the same character; some of rarer occurrence and following more method, are especially spiritual; others, ordained to be given on days fixed by the *Rule* and more or less austere, deal with points of claustral discipline; others again also coming under the *Rule*, but more familiar and free, gather the monks each Sunday around their superior to listen to him as he speaks to them in a fatherly manner about what concerns the monastery, and this leads quickly to supernatural or doctrinal viewpoints which necessarily predominate in all public conferences in the house of God, and justify the name of "spiritual conferences" being extended to them. This is a hasty glance at what is done in the cloister, which will suffice to place the facts of the case before the reader.

Dom Marmion's spiritual conferences were far from being impersonal. Very free in style, leaving wide scope to the inspiration of the moment, they quickly forsook the didactic explanation to go direct to the audience. Might they be said to take the form of a meditation made aloud? The expression would be scarcely a happy one. Such a meditation might be cold or borrowed from someone else. Dom Columba's words burst forth from the depths of his soul; warm and living, they spoke to other souls. But, and it is this that we have here to remark, there were instants when Father Abbot almost laid bare his own soul. One might then ask oneself if he was not praying aloud in good earnest. It has befallen the hearer – the spectator if you prefer – involuntarily to conjure up the image of those priests and deacons whom the Church generally allowed to give improvised discourses during liturgical functions in the course of the first centuries. It is evident that in discourses of this kind the personality of the speaker would come out strongly.[1] And experience goes to prove that, far from finding this any drawback, his hearers were conscious of the happiest results from these moments of sometimes touching vehemence and pathos.[2]

Under another form the same result ensued in the private intercourse that the Abbot of Maredsous had with the friends he loved, or in the letters he wrote to his disciples. It easily came about that he responded by opening his own conscience to his correspondents

---

[1] It is, moreover, a characteristic of his race, as we have said in the chapter "The Apostle of Christ."

[2] Is it not, *si parva licet*... such as is to be remarked in St Paul's epistles? In them "I" comes out so often and so impetuously! We hear (it is a notorious fact) people in the world who, having read the epistles once, say: "With his strong personality he does not give one the impression of being humble!" And yet how these conferences of the great apostle touched the hearts of his disciples!

or to his sons who came to open their minds to him or simply to chat affectionately with their Father. He then spoke to them of his own inner life, his own spiritual experiences, his successes and his joys, with a rare *abandon*. And on these occasions again, the moments when, without premeditation and beyond expectation, he poured out his own heart, were the ones that made the strongest and most beneficial impression on those thus privileged.

In Dom Marmion, the "I" was not the detestable "I" spoken of by the bitter moralist who takes his examples from amongst worldly egoists; it was the lovable "I" well known by those who study the life of the saints or are acquainted with deeply virtuous and detached Christian souls.[1] "Dom Marmion," writes the Reverend Mother of an English convent, "had the very rare gift of being able to speak of himself without a shadow of egoism."[2] With him, in fact, the ego was free from those characteristics which contract and separate hearts, but was endowed on the contrary with those that enlarge and attract – an ego of disinterestedness, humility and altruism: an ego truly worthy of being loved.

Such is the object lesson, all to Dom Marmion's honour, which from their familiar relations with him many of his disciples deduced.[3]

Noble and simple frankness, kindness, generosity, goodwill, altruism: when such dispositions are innate in a soul it may be said that it bears within it the seed and life-giving principle of all the virtues that have the neighbour as their object.

And yet the soil in which they are to grow differs in each

[1] These two forms of the ego dispute their claim in most of us.
[2] Letter of 22 August 1927, to the author.
[3] Every richly endowed personality is a world infinitely complex. In carrying our analysis still further, it will be discovered that in the ego of Dom Marmion there was something of that of an ingenuous child, an ingenuity that surprised, but without displeasing; the candid ego of those childlike souls who are subject neither to self-love nor vanity, but to a very keen sensibility and are conscious to a rare degree of the reactions of their emotional temperament. A legacy doubtless inherited from his Celtic and Irish ancestry.

individual soul. That which is true of the saint is true also of every Christian; each one has his privileged virtues. What were – and we shall thus finish tracing the portrait of Dom Marmion, as father of his monastic family – what were the forms under which he showed his supernatural kind-heartedness and consideration for his sons? We will mention chiefly three: respect for the liberty of souls – liberality – mercy.

What then was this extreme *respect for the spiritual liberty* of souls that those under Dom Marmion's direction especially remarked in him? Is it not to be seen merged, by being supernaturalised, into that delicate and attractive attitude which takes the finest shades of the affection of the father, the solicitude of the educator, and of humility? It is unfortunate that in seeking for a name to describe his consideration and respect for the highest part of the personality of others, we can only find – whilst rehabilitating it – a word which will be apt to have a bad sound in French ears, namely, liberalism.

Neither in the intellectual domain did Dom Marmion depart from the noble liberalism which (as we are about to see) he made a guiding principle in matters of piety. It is certain that this experienced theologian had the clearest sense of his duty as guardian of orthodoxy and, speaking more generally, of rectitude of thought in his monastic family; from time to time he would remind himself of the heavy responsibility which rested upon him as its head; but he none the less loved and respected liberty of mind in others in every case where it could be justified – and notably in the domain of the sacred sciences wherever the Church has given no decision nor shown a preference. It is true – the very life of the intellect exacts this – he would when occasion demanded, like every thinker sure of his convictions, plead one side of a question, but at no price would he take advantage of his authority as abbot to impose a thesis of the schools, still less his own personal views; he never made an assertion without showing whence it originated and what were its only true titles to credence. It would be difficult to find a firmer, more uncompromising faith, and the outspoken repudiation of all that savoured of narrow-mindedness, more sincerely allied in a

Catholic soul. Even when it concerned heretics, whilst having the inflexible faith of the true Irishman, he always remained extremely tolerant in regard to individuals.[1] A scrupulous uprightness is evident in all this; the will ever to render justice; the understanding that a conjectural problem may frequently intricate the question of a soul; but, over and above these moral virtues and raising them to higher issues, a delicacy of heart showing a noble liberalism in regard to the minds of others.

It is not at random that the modern word "liberalism" and the old word of "liberality" are closely akin in etymology.[2] The first calls upon liberty to further the cause of liberty; and the second signifies that it is to the honour of liberty to give largely. The heart that is nobly liberal in the first sense, cannot fail to be liberal in the second. Such was the case with Dom Marmion. We have seen how on the day of his abbatial blessing he took as his motto in his government this maxim of the *Rule:*[3] "Let the abbot know that he ought to be useful rather than to command." It may be said that Dom Marmion was constantly inspired by this sentence. In his case to command was to serve; to serve was to love; and to love was to give; to give himself. Liberality was with him only one form of service and an expression of love.

In the material order, it is true, monastic rules strictly limited the exercise of this liberality in regard to his monks and he kept to these rules scrupulously. He however never lost an opportunity of practising liberality when in his power and, on such an occasion, his act was one of rare spontaneity. You had to be careful not to

[1] To one of his friends, an English writer who had published a letter on the conduct to be observed in relation to our "separated brethren," he sent this note: "I was delighted to read your beautiful letter in the *Catholic Times:* it is the true spirit of our blessed father, St Benedict, who says *oderit vitia, diligat fratres.* Yes, *let us hate* heresy in every shape, but *let us love* our brethren, even when they are in error." Undated, but between April and September 1899.
[2] *Liberalis* also means *generosity.*
[3] Ch 44.

express your admiration at the sight of an object, of a holy picture for instance: if he could, he would immediately offer it to you to give you pleasure.

In the spiritual order, when his hands were not tied by the vow of poverty, he opened them willingly to give a permission or some gratification. When he did so in writing, it was often only "a little word" dashed off in haste, but "this little word" was weighty with meaning and charged with charity. He loved to have affectionate attentions and forethought for others.[1]

When away from his abbey, he thinks of the feast days of his sons: "I prayed a great deal for dear Fr W— on his feast day, but I was too much occupied to write to him."[2]

At the end of a long business letter, these two lines slip in, a bright and warm ray of pure kindness: "I am praying our Lord to give fine weather to our dear students for their holiday."[3]

To one of his sons whom obedience kept at a distance from the monastery, he allows his fatherly solicitude to make itself heard: "A little word to send you my love and to assure you that I never forget you before God. My wish is that *abbatis melota*[4] may cover you

---

1 At all times he strove to remove the difficulties under which anyone might be labouring. One of his old pupils at Louvain had just taken his academic degrees at the *Collegio Sant'Anselmo* in Rome, and it was a time of hard work. He opened his heart to his old master. Dom Columba replied to him in a few lines manifesting strong supernatural charity and exquisite delicacy: "I had no intention of writing to you, for you are so nearly ending the year of studies, and you and I are in the midst of theses, etc. However, I thought I noticed a little shade of sadness or gloom in your letter; that is why I send you *a word*. Once we have given ourselves unreservedly to our Lord, we ought to be persuaded that not the least thing can befall us without His permission: CAPILLUS non peribit.... When one is tired, without inclination for study, and one has to prepare for examination, it is an opportunity of making acts of self-renunciation and *obedience* very pleasing to our Lord: *Imposuisti* HOMINES *super capita nostra*. It is a sacrifice which we make only for God" (Letter of 12 June 1905).
2 Letter of 15 September 1915.
3 Letter of the month of August 1915.
4 *Melota:* the sheepskin worn by St Benedict. An allusion to an incident in the life of the patriarch. The little Placid had been miraculously saved when he had fallen into the lake of Subiaco by Maurus, who had been sent by St Bene-

everywhere and keep you safe from the fatal influences of the world. It will be so as long as you remain, as at present, in dependence on your father in Jesus Christ."[1]

The jubilee was approaching of another of his monks, who was away on a mission; out of the fullness of his fatherly heart Dom Columba writes him this note, *ultima verba* for they are dated only a few weeks before his death: "United to you with all my heart, I wish you all the grace of your jubilee. Full remission of anything that may have been imperfect and an abundance of graces and blessings for the future. I pray for you every day of my life from my heart of hearts. May God bless and love you as I do from my heart."[2]

He had a propensity for granting the wishes submitted to him; sometimes he forestalled them by even encouraging the expression of them. Read these lines, full of comprehensive charity, to one of his sons whom he had sent to repair his shattered health with his own family. "I had meant to send you a little word for your feast – it was however only belated a few days – but I have been overwhelmed with work. I have been thinking of you and praying particularly for you – as always. I rejoice that you find peace and calm with your holy sister. If you think that, for the sake of your health, it would be better to wait till the end of September before returning and make your retreat afterwards, I give my consent."[3]

When reason obliged him to refuse a request, it cost him an effort: "When I do not grant something to one of you," he said, "I feel it more than does the one whom I have to refuse."

Nothing truer. However, he knew how to resign himself to it, whether he refused absolutely, or whether he laid down conditions in granting the request made to him, and his course of action was

---

dict and had walked on the waters. A friendly discussion had ensued between the saint and his disciple: the latter attributed the miracle to the merits of Benedict, the patriarch regarded it as the result of Maurus's obedience. It was little Placid who decided the question: "Whilst I was being pulled out of the water I saw the *melota* of my abbot above my head."

1 Letter of 12 December 1911.
2 Letter of 4 December 1922.
3 Out of discretion we do not give the date.

always justified by supernatural reasons: "The Superior of X— has asked me to allow you to give her nuns a conference each week. I have consented but *with difficulty,* for I wish you to remain *solus sub oculo summi inspectoris.*[1] I have made one *condition:* after the conference leave without staying to go in the parlour or to talk. I bless you with all my heart."[2]

One of his monks whom obedience had entrusted with the office of superior in a house of the order, having asked for some reinforcement and mentioned the name of the confrère whom he wanted to have with him; Dom Columba replies to him: "It is for me" – the words in italics were underlined by himself – "*a real pain* not to be able to give you Fr X— as aid, but my conscience is opposed to it."[3]

We have seen above, in a letter to the mother of one of the religious, with what supernatural firmness, instinct with charity, he knew how to maintain a refusal. To another person who, on the occasion of the priestly ordination of her son – a monk of Maredsous – begged a favour which would have created an unjustified precedent or would have appeared as a privilege, he told how much it cost him not to be able to grant what she asked.

But when he could satisfy your desire, it was "a happiness" for him. Read these lines, dated the last year of his life,[4] where the bright gold of charity is enhanced by an exquisite sense of humility:

"A little word to tell you that everything is granted. I understand a little the happiness that our Heavenly Father has in giving us what we ask of Him by what I feel in giving you pleasure: *Si vos,* CUM SITIS MALI, *nostis bona data dare filiis vestris…*"[5]

These lines disclose the underlying motive to which Dom Columba was obedient. His liberality was not only a liberality finding inspiration in itself, a simple leaning towards giving bountifully,

1 "Alone under the eyes of the Supreme Beholder."
2 Out of discretion we do not give the date.
3 Letter of 22 December 1911.
4 Letter of 31 March 1922.
5 "If you then, *being evil,* know how to give good gifts to your children, how much more will your Father who is in heaven, give good things to them that ask Him?" (Matt. 7:11).

it was a liberality with end and object put at the service of a very high intention. He had the taste, the passion for giving pleasure, he found happiness in sharing his own happiness; his formal and explicit end was to make happy; his final end, to bring others and himself nearer to God: in two words, to gain hearts so that he might give them to God. The sight of a beaming countenance, the thought of a contented heart, of a soul above all with wings outspread to soar higher, were for him a delicate recompense.

If kindness tends to become liberality, in face of a simple desire or of a simple need, it becomes necessarily mercy, in the face of weakness, poverty, illness, suffering, failing, every kind of physical and moral misery that form the common lot of humanity. Is not the Gospel in one of its most divine aspects, the science of our miseries, the skilful means to cure them, the code of our duties in regard to the miseries of others? And is not the character of a shepherd of souls shown in a wide measure by the attitude he takes in respect to human shortcoming? As abbot, Dom Marmion was full of mercy.

St Benedict makes the abbot particularly accountable before God in two points: integrity of doctrine and the obedience of his disciples.

Never did kind-heartedness lead Dom Marmion to attenuate or disguise in anything whatsoever the vigour of the Gospel or of the *Rule*. In his spiritual works – which are those of a master – are to be found pages of exceptional gravity on fidelity to the inspiration of the Holy Spirit, on the necessity of penance and of renunciation, on fraternal charity, on the supernatural character of obedience, on the bane of murmuring, on regularity in monastic observance, and on many other points. These pages are but a weak echo of the exhortations he gave to his religious.

As to the obedience of his disciples, Dom Marmion insisted that it should be absolute, but animated by love. Whilst he strove to lead souls to entire submission, he put them on guard against Pharisaical exactitude which makes all perfection to consist in the merely material and outward observance of the rules and customs, at the same time he wished love to be the motive-power of all activity and the guardian of all fidelity, In this lies one of the characteristic points of his government.

But if he exacted perfect obedience from his disciples, he studied constantly, on his side, to realise the ideal of a father who loves his sons and, out of this very love to render obedience according to the saying of St Benedict,[1] "sweet to men."

In practical life, as we have said, suspicion was repugnant to Dom Marmion, and leaving his prior, whose first mission it is, to supervise, he sought for his part, to enlarge hearts; he liked to see them expand in supernatural joy. Did he recall the words of the holy founder of Beuron, Dom Maurus Wolter: "The role of the abbot is to spread joy around him"? However that may be, he was certainly guided by this principle.

"The beautiful words uttered by the patriarch in reference to the administration of the cellarer[2] are first to be verified in the government of the abbot: 'Let no one in the monastery, which is "the house," "the family," of God, be troubled or grieved: *ut nemo perturbetur neque contristetur in domo Dei.*'"[3]

This is why he always strove with great care, to found on truth and equity, and to temper with benignity the judgments he had to pass on his sons or their actions.

In a letter to the superior of a community, Dom Marmion thus summed up his thought: "Try and become more and more motherly and loving. We can govern souls by force and authority, but it is only by meekness and love that we can gain them to God."[4]

A golden maxim, faithful echo of the *Rule,* and moreover bearing the stamp of experience, for Dom Marmion believed he could set himself no more noble or fruitful mission than that of winning souls in order to give them to God.

But kindness is not weakness, and shortcomings necessitate

1 *Rule of St Benedict*, ch. 5.
2 The religious charged with the material administration of the monastery.
3 *Cf. Christ the Ideal of the Monk*, ch. 3, "The Abbot."
4 Letter of 10 January 1907.

correction. Dom Marmion did not shirk this duty, he was sometimes even vehement in his reprimands; he showed insistence, but without passion or anger: "When the superior," he would say, "wants to take off the corners and round off the angles, that is to say, shape the soul and bend it to obedience – he ought to take a file and not a sponge." In this matter, however, he again drew his inspiration from St Benedict: "In his correction [thus speaks the *Rule*], let the abbot act with prudence and not go too far lest whilst scraping off the rust he break the vessel; conscious of his own frailty let him remember not to break the bruised reed."[1]

Such was truly the ideal, constantly followed by Dom Marmion. And doubtless he was sometimes conscious of going far in this way of mercy and clemency. He appropriated to himself the words of St Odilo, Abbot of Cluny: "If I have to be damned, I prefer to be so for excess of mercy than for excess of justice." Was he not besides urged to mercy by St Benedict himself? Are there not in the *Rule* maxims – besides those we have just quoted – where the patriarch's tone, elsewhere severe, takes almost maternal accents. Dom Marmion had before his eyes those striking words fallen from the pen of the legislator of monks – the one justly acknowledged to have been a wonderful adept in the art of knowing how to balance strength with sweetness, and to ally strength of principles with flexibility in their application: "Let the abbot ever prefer mercy to justice that he may obtain a like mercy.... Let him study to be loved rather than feared."[2]

Sentences taken directly from the Gospel. There we see God's treatment of us measured by our attitude towards our brethren, the merciful are there declared blessed, and the child of God in his relations with others is to imitate the mercifulness of the Heavenly Father. Indeed it is only the saints who know how to be compassionate.

If, however, any scruple still disquieted him, Dom Marmion did not hesitate to turn to God with the simplicity of one of the just in the Old Testament, and to find his argument in that divine

[1] Ch. 44.
[2] Ch. 44.

loving-kindness, which because it remembers that we are made from the dust of the earth, never wearies of stooping to human misery. And his humility furnishing him with a plea, he brought himself forward as an example: "Lord, am I not the continual object and as it were the manifestation of your mercy?"

These last remarks throw a touching light into the most hidden recesses of Dom Marmion's soul; they truly reveal its supernatural depths. The ardour of his spirit of faith was there blended with the principles of his spirituality. He knew himself, he felt himself to be through Jesus, the child of the Heavenly Father, and the object of infinite mercies. But on the other hand, he knew that he was likewise a father – and father of a supernatural paternity, directly derived from that of God and which belonged to him as Christ's representative in the monastery. Hence like the Good Shepherd, after the very example of God, "the Father of mercies," he had bowels of compassion for all those confided to him by Providence.

All the characteristic features of Dom Marmion as abbot have been placed, we think, under the eyes of the reader.

A very rich nature in spite of certain limitations. If he fell short in several qualities of a man of administration, at least he was always actuated by the most lofty and supernatural intentions. A fine clear intellect, steeped in the light of faith. Frankness and simplicity of character, an open heart, a more than ordinary sensibility; warm and faithful in his affections, ever ready to set you at your ease by the gladness of his welcome, his active goodwill and fund of gay good humour. True humility, despite some appearances to the contrary, disinterestedness, noble forgetfulness of the wrongs done him by others. A heart that felt the need of giving itself, and also of drawing other hearts in order to give them to God. Generosity and mercy.

And although he retained certain pronounced traits of his Irish temperament, one is struck to see how excellently nature and grace "got on together" in him, to what a degree nature knew how to keep all its spontaneity, whilst subjecting itself entirely to grace; and to what a degree grace, for God's ends and for the good of souls, knew how to impress its inward signature on nature, without in any way constraining or impeding its resources and energies.

This happy harmony made, as in the case of the saints, by the higher powers of his soul, and which is one of the most attractive charms of his personality, will be still more evident when we come to speak of the essentially supernatural virtues of Dom Marmion's inner life. But it behoves us first to complete his portrait as a director of souls and see, by referring to his spiritual letters, how he regarded that high and delicate mission in which he excelled. This yet remains to be told.

11   THE SPIRITUAL DIRECTOR

The term *spiritual direction* is one always to be held in particular respect by Catholics. Indeed is there any art surpassing in dignity that of guiding souls towards perfection and leading them to the heights of union with God?[1] One of the greatest popes that the Church has known – St Gregory the Great – calls it "the art of arts": *Ars artium regimen animarum.*[2]

Dom Marmion excelled in this art, and on this subject we find in his letters some instructive pages which may well be borne in mind. They will help to complete the portrait we are attempting to trace.

But here our field of vision widens out as does also the sphere of action open to our consideration. It is not only the abbot acting in regard to his sons living in the cloister that we have to envisage, it is the ministry of a master in spirituality in relation to every category of soul. An abundant supply of letters, so indispensable in this matter, have been generously placed at our disposal; we shall not use them in their chronological order, but according to the logical sequence necessitated by our subject.[3]

As a master well versed in things of the interior life, Dom Marmion first of all lays down the necessity of spiritual direction:

1   "To rule a soul is to rule a world," said Pierre de Bérulle, "and a world that has more secrets and diversities, more perfections and rarities than the world which we see. One single soul counts for more in God's sight than the whole world" (*Mémorial pour la direction des supérieurs*).
2   The holy pope himself in his *Pastoral Rule* has treated this subject of spiritual government so thoroughly that his work, "a masterpiece of prudence" according to Jacques-Bénigne Bossuet, is the perfect manual for all those who have charge of souls.
3   It is scarcely necessary to repeat what we said in our preface that the extracts from these letters are only given with the full authorisation of the recipients and that, in these extracts, the words in italics were underlined by Dom Marmion himself.

It is according to the order of our Lord's adorable Providence," he writes to a young girl, "that we are to be guided not by visions or by angels, but by the men whom He has deigned to give us for this purpose and through whose lips He wills to speak to us.

Dom Marmion then recalls the well known example of our Lord refusing to reply to the questions of Saul, on the road to Damascus, and sending him to the disciple Ananias. Then he adds:

> So in this matter so important for you, I want you to follow only the light of faith, that is to say that you will beg Jesus, with all the fervour of your heart, to enlighten you, to strengthen you, to tell you by the mouth of those whom He has appointed to take His place, what He wills you to do, and that having done this, you will put yourself in His hands without expecting any extraordinary manifestation of His Will.[1]

He lays further stress on these words a few months later:

> You know that God chooses to lead us in the path of perfection by the light of obedience and, often, he deprives us of any other light, and leads us without letting us understand His ways. During a trial such as this, we must remain in complete submission and in an unshakable conviction – in spite of all that the devil or our human reason may suggest to the contrary – that He knows how to turn everything to His glory and our spiritual advantage in a manner quite different from that which you would have chosen for yourself.[2]

Twenty-five years later, he taught the same to a Carmelite:

> God wills that souls should feel not only their physical weakness, but also their powerlessness to *see* and to understand, in order that they may remain in great poverty *without possessing in themselves* what is necessary to settle their doubts. St Francis de Sales writes [to Madame de Beauvilliers, Abbess

---

1 Letter of 12 September 1894. This is the first of a series.
2 Letter of 19 March 1895.

of Montmartre], that however intellectual or enlightened a woman may be, God, according to the ordinary rulings of His Providence, wills her to be directed by a man who is His minister.[1]

This way is besides the only one which leads to the light of life and brings peace: "Our sole means of knowing without danger of illusion the adorable Will of God is to submit ourselves to the direction of those who represent Him."[2]

This is why he does not consider that one should have several directors. He regards this ministry with such natural disinterestedness that he does not allow himself "to interfere with a soul who has a director, for that only causes complications and prevents the soul from living by faith."[3]

He did not disguise from those who confided themselves to his direction that they must apply to themselves the above wise rule which, safeguarding the unity of direction, allows the soul to attain the end more rapidly: "I regard it as important for you that you should not lay open your soul to others, unless you have the certainty that our Lord wills it, for there are contrasts of character in you that everyone would not understand."[4]

And again, later, the same warning: "Although prepared to withdraw if X— had wished it, I am persuaded that he does not know you as I do and that he sees only the irradiation of Christ in you,

[1] Letter of 29 January 1920.
[2] Letter of 19 November 1913. Like every experienced director, Dom Marmion had come across souls of a Protestant mentality, or with a strain of illuminism, the sport of their illusions, who accepted no other authority than that of their imagination, often unbalanced or with an inordinate estimation of their own excellence. We know that illuminism does not lie "in a too great fondness of visions or in some childishness more or less ridiculous; these are inevitable miseries"; but much more in the fact "that one poses as inspired, as a prophet" who has received a mission and "is moved only by the Holy Spirit, and places private inspiration before the decisions of the Church and hence is led straight to schism or heresy" (Fr Brémond, *Histoire littéraire du sentiment religieux*).
[3] Letter of 1 November 1922.
[4] Letter of 4 April 1917.

without knowing, as I do, those depths which ever remain exposed to the deceits of the devil and self-love."[1]

But as soon as it was for the good of any soul under his direction, he himself did not hesitate to suggest to such a one the advisability of having recourse to another guide. To a much tried soul, separated from him by a long distance and to whom he could not give at once the necessary counsels, he writes: "In your present trial you need a director to whom you can have recourse when you want. I advise you to choose one at N—. For all that, I shall not cease to take a great interest in your soul and to pray much for you."[2]

During the war and the German occupation a person who had a strong desire to consult him and benefit by his spiritual advice travelled on foot (for many of the ways of communication had been destroyed or cut off) the distance of sixty kilometres, in order to reach the abbey. Dom Marmion gave all the help which under the circumstances lay in his power, but gave the advice to go for the future to a monastery near at hand.

As for direction itself, Dom Marmion had a broad and generous idea of it.

He knew that, according to the words of Jesus, the inward Master is pre-eminently the Holy Spirit: "I will ask the Father, and He shall give you another Paraclete, that He may abide with you forever,... He will teach you all things, and bring all things to your mind, whatsoever I shall have said to you ... when He, the Spirit of Truth, is come, He will teach you all things."

Dom Marmion often supported this teaching on these words of Jesus. However, to understand thoroughly all that was in his mind it must be remembered that many of those whom he directed were, by their vows, seeking perfection in the religious life. For these

---

[1] Letter of 1 October 1917.
[2] Letter of 25 February 1895. The choice having been made of Fr Adolphe Petit, Dom Marmion writes: "I am so glad that you go to Fr Petit about your soul" (letter of 19 March 1895).

persons whose ideal is clearly specified in their rule, who are under the obedience of superiors and enlightened by their frequent exhortations, who daily find light as well as stimulus in the good example of their companions travelling the same path, spiritual direction ought to be characterised by more width. "I am not a great partisan of much direction," he writes to a contemplative nun. "I feel that the Holy Spirit is the one director who is capable to give the true light and inspiration. Yet it is God's way to direct us by His ministers."

Then, again quoting the words of St Francis de Sales on the necessity of the woman being guided by Christ's ministers, he repeats with insistence: "It is God's way. What is necessary is that the director know the soul *perfectly,* and that once done, he must indicate the way she is to follow and then leave her to the Holy Spirit. From time to time, at long intervals, he must control her progress, and if anything out of the common way should happen, he must know it, but in my opinion, long and *frequent* letters of direction do more harm than good."[1]

In a letter to another cloistered nun, he is more precise: "The Holy Ghost alone can form souls, and the director has merely to point out to his spiritual child the road by which God is leading her, give her some general rules for her conduct, and control her progress, answer her difficulties, if any, at *distant intervals.*"

He adds this remark, which reveals the director's psychological skill and experience: "This is specially true of religious whose interior life is based on the liturgy, for the source in which they find the food of their souls is so pure that their souls are much less liable to error and hallucination than those who elaborate their whole spiritual life out of their own conscience."[2]

Elsewhere, writing to a contemplative nun, he defines his role as director: "Our Lord gives me more and more immense reverence

---

[1] Letter of 21 November 1919. The Sister Cornuau states that Bossuet declared he had no other role than that of "making her listen to God and follow His holy inspirations: that was all his charge."
[2] Letter of 1 May 1906.

for His infinite wisdom in the guidance of souls. He contemplates in His Father all the Divine Plan as regards them. He alone knows what this plan is, He alone can lead them towards it. My part only consists in praying much for you, pointing out to you the pitfalls which even the best intentioned may encounter, advising you in difficult cases, and finally in urging you to give yourself unreservedly to Jesus."[1]

It is what St Paul says: *Dum formetur Christus in vobis:* "Until Christ be formed in you."[2] What Dom Marmion especially endeavoured to do was to place the Divine Figure of Christ before the eyes of the soul in order that she should yield herself to Him, and to reveal the mysteries of Christ that so she should live by them.

Can we be astonished that, regarding the ministry of directing souls in so pure a light, Dom Marmion should have had a rightful horror of its being abused or caricatured, and that in expressing this horror he should have spoken with some warmth? In a letter of 3 December 1921, he says he detests what is commonly called *direction* and direction *à la mode,* because there is often very little of God in it and a great deal of ourselves. For the penitent, it often means only discouragement and misery, and a loss of time for the one who directs.[3] St Benedict tenderly loved his sister Scholastica; he went to see her *once* a year; both spoke of God, of His love, of heaven. They prayed much for one another, they spoke *little* of themselves....

"Most persons do not think of the Holy Spirit, and yet it is to Him that God has confided the direction of souls. Many think a detailed direction is needed, they make endless analyses of soul, write pages upon pages, but the great director of souls is the Holy Spirit. When the priest has been told all that he ought to be told, the necessary direction is given, and the shortest is often the best."[4]

1 Letter of 11 February 1902.
2 Gal. 4:19.
3 In a letter dated 1 May 1906, he had written in the same sense: "I am the mortal enemy of what is called direction."
4 Conference to the Victims of the Sacred Heart at Bomel (Namur).

One of the reasons why Dom Marmion did not like long and complicated directions was because he had known certain persons who put much self-seeking in these directions, speaking at great length of "self," causing the director to lose much precious time, and above all ending in the belief that their spiritual advancement was due to themselves and the man who directed them much more than to God. This last notion, so contrary to one of the fundamental principles of his spirituality, was insupportable to him. Hence, with one of his sudden reactions, that warmth of tone when he touched on this point.[1]

It may readily be gathered from what has been said above that Dom Marmion carefully avoided substituting his own conscience for that of his penitent; he sought rather to awaken and form the conscience so that the soul might mount of itself towards God: such was the respect he had for the liberty of souls and the Divine Action in them!

> The director is not a fabricator of the conscience, but a guide, an enlightener, a helper; he ought therefore never to substitute himself for the conscience of those he directs. When it comes to the point, the latter – after God and with God – must work out their own salvation and perfection. They must necessarily learn to walk alone, at least on broad lines, only having recourse to the director in the most difficult cases and

[1] Another master of the spiritual life, Msgr Gay, speaks in the same way: "One much to be dreaded cause of illusions is the abuse of direction. I mean to say, the frequency or length of spoken or written communication with the director. Besides the fact that, even if the priest lends himself to it out of charity, it may be a serious indiscretion on account of the time he risks losing through this excessive recourse being had to him (time so precious and truly sacred), it fatally inclines the soul to be too much wrapt up in self, it feeds egotism and vanity, the danger of taking a wrong step in virtue, of raising up something more than dust between God and herself, finally of losing sight of Him and wandering away from Him, which is the supreme evil. Then if you wish to go straight on in the truth and not to weaken grace within you, be moderate, very moderate in regard to direction. What a director does not the Holy Spirit often become to a simple, poor and solitary soul!" (*Instructions en forme de retraite*, ch. 4, "*Des illusions*.")

most troublous moments. People in the world often need a closer direction for their more active lives; persons consecrated to God, living in a monastery, under a rule and obedience, ought to become capable by degrees of resolving their own problems in a general way because they are continually in contact with Divine Truth by means of mental prayer, spiritual reading, and instructions, and because God works more directly in them. There is danger in having recourse to a director for things that one ought to be able to decide for oneself: the conscience thus becomes atrophied, and this evil is a hindrance to rising to God in peace of heart.[1]

We have just seen what were the qualifications Dom Marmion required from a spiritual director from the more or less theoretical point of view. Now we may learn the practical lines on which he would have this ministry carried out.

These are the instructions that he gave to one of his monks; under their general form, it will be seen, he only taught what he himself practised:

In the confessional the priest is the minister of Jesus Christ, and the more he identifies himself with his Divine Master, the more he enters into His dispositions as regards his Father and souls, the more too will his ministry be blessed. It is very important:

1. Before beginning to hear confessions, to humble himself deeply in God's presence whilst acknowledging he is incapable of doing the least good to souls without Him: *Sine me* NIHIL *potestis facere.*[2]

2. To offer up this holy action as an act of love to our Lord, who has said: 'As long as you did it to one of these my brethren, you did it to Me.'

---

[1] It was in this sense that he sometimes repeated this sentence of Bossuet: "The aim of direction is to teach how to do without it."

[2] Without Me you can do nothing" (John 15:5).

3. To efface himself as far as possible so that Christ alone may act: *Illum oportet crescere, me autem minui.*[1] To speak, to act, in the name of Jesus Christ, and in great dependence on His Spirit. *Si quis loquitur, quasi sermones Dei, si quis ministrat quasi ex virtute quam administrat Deus* UT IN OMNIBUS GLORIFICETUR *Deus per Jesum Christum.*[2]

4. Not to wish his penitents to be attached to him, but to direct them towards God alone, in great detachment from every creature.[3]

In February 1899, having been asked to undertake the spiritual direction of the Louvain Carmel he wrote two letters of a more personal nature which further explain each other. They throw a valuable light on the subject.

The first is addressed to Dom de Kerchove, who was soon to become Abbot of Mont-César, and had expressed the wish to see him take over the charge of this work.[4]

> I very willingly accept the offer you make me and to undertake the direction of the Carmelites at Louvain.
>
> I know that this charge comes to me directly from God, since holy obedience imposes it upon me. What goodness and condescension on our Lord's part to entrust me, so unworthy, with these souls who are so dear to Him! It will be a fresh motive to give myself with more generosity to my Divine Master, so as to make myself more worthy of the graces and lights I shall need for this work.
>
> There is nothing dearer to me than to be occupied with souls who seek God with generosity and sincerity; but I have always held the Carmelites in particular esteem because of

---

1 He must increase, but I must decrease" (John 3: 30).
2 "If any man speak, let him speak, as the words of God. If any man administer, let him do it, as of the power which God administereth: that in all things God may be honoured through Jesus Christ" (1 Pet. 4: 11).
3 Without exact date, but about 1902.
4 At present time [*c.* 1932] still Abbot of Mont-César and president of the Belgian Benedictine Congregation.

my devotion to St Teresa, and also because of the particular devotion her order professes for the mystery of the Incarnation – which is my attraction.

I will very gladly give a spiritual conference once a fortnight. Please say to these ladies [*sic*] – if you think well to do so – that I accept them from now as my spiritual children for whom I consider myself under obligation to pray daily. I ask very humbly that, on their part, they will pray for me, that our Lord may give me all the graces and lights we shall need.[1]

In the second letter, written to the Carmelites themselves, the future director specifies what was in his mind:

I accept the direction of your souls as a command from Him to whom I owe everything, and I will try by my poor prayers and ministry to help you to reach that sublime perfection to which your Heavenly Bridegroom calls you.

In days gone by, our dear Saviour said to your glorious mother, St Teresa, that when His Sacred Heart was weary and crushed by the crimes and ingratitude of the world, He came to take His repose in the hearts of His dear daughters of the Carmel of Ávila as in a garden of delights. It will be my ambition to make your little Carmel of Louvain, in so far as that depends upon me, a garden where the Divine Bridegroom will find His delights.

When your seraphic mother was named Prioress of the Convent of the Incarnation, she installed the Blessed Virgin as the sole superior of the house, and, through her, she wrought wonders. Well! I want Jesus to be the sole director of the Carmel of Louvain. It is He who has bought you with His Precious Blood; it is He and He alone to whom you belong; it is for Him to sanctify you; and if He deigns to use me in this work so important for His glory, it will be on condition that I depend in all things on His Spirit, that I renounce my own views to follow those of Jesus in all things, that I

---

1 Letter of 12 February 1899.

seek in His Sacred Heart the light to understand what His designs are for each one of you. But as I am *very far* from this union with my Divine Master I want you to ask this grace for me in your prayers.

Please accept, with my respectful homage, the promise of the sincere devotedness of your Father in J.C.[1]

At the period when he sketched out this high ideal, Dom Marmion, then at Maredsous, was continuing in obedience and humility to bring his inner life to maturity, before being sent, a few months later, to the university city. A wider field, as we have said, was about to open out before the holy ambition of his apostolic zeal. So whilst only envisaging the direction of the Carmelites, his letters in reality expressed the general plan he followed throughout his work of spiritual direction; they interpret the supernatural motives that actuated him at this date in his relations with souls, and which were to remain his until his death, twenty-five years later. In going through his correspondence at this time we shall see with what constant generosity he practised the virtues of a director after God's own Heart.

Worthily to discharge a mission which appeared to him so great, Dom Marmion sought first of all to place and keep himself on a thoroughly supernatural plane in regard to those under his direction.

As God's instrument he aimed at undertaking and exercising this holy ministry only in full dependence on the Divine Will and action, on that condition alone would his work in souls bear fruit.

In allusion to the words of St Paul, he writes: "We may plant

[1] Letter of 20 February 1899. See at the end of this chapter, the outline of Dom Marmion's first conference to the Carmelites of Louvain. All his views on spiritual direction will be found summed up there. We may compare with these letters one he wrote more than sixteen years afterwards to the Carmelites of Virton, at the time of undertaking their spiritual direction: "I feel that our Lord confides your little Carmel to me, and I take it with love from His hands. May I one day present it to Him as His little garden! You will help me, will you not, that I may not lag behind!" Letter of 14 November 1916.

and water the ground with our labours, but it is God and He alone who by His blessing gives the increase."[1]

Whilst yet a simple monk living under obedience, he was begged by the superior of a religious community, to which he was bound by great affection, to act as extraordinary confessor. He left the decision, which did not depend upon himself, entirely to Providence; bidden to accept it, he writes:

> I have been striving for some time, in prayer, to place myself in a state of holy indifference in regard to your request, and our Lord has truly given me grace to conform my will entirely to His. I have been drawn for some days to say to Him: 'I wish *nothing* except what you wish, but if you will to use me in helping and consoling your dear spouses, here I am.' I have the *certainty* that it is He who wills it, and this gives me great joy and peace, not only because I thus have the certainty of doing His Holy Will, but because I have now the certainty that this ministry will be blessed and bear fruit. Oh! My daughter, I see *so clearly* that we are NOTHING and that we only do good in so far as we are an instrument, and even we may happen to spoil God's work.[2]

For him, then, to take the direction of a soul was to respond to a divine command. So when by means of obedience or any other means God confided a soul to him he found it an unparalleled joy of which in his humility he judged himself unworthy: "There is no greater joy on earth than to be chosen by our Lord to co-operate with Him in the sanctification of souls. St Paul tells us that God loves to be served by what is weak and miserable 'that no flesh should glory in His sight': *Ut non glorietur omnis caro.*"[3]

It is for him "such great happiness to be able to offer to the

---

[1] Letter of 10 April 1899.
[2] Letter of 28 October 1902.
[3] Letter of 20 November 1916.

THE SPIRITUAL DIRECTOR

Sacred Heart of Jesus so little loved, a soul who, although weak and very ordinary, wishes with all her might to love our dear Saviour."[1]

Appropriating to himself the words of St John, he declares he has no greater joy than to see his children walking in truth.[2] "My greatest joy," he writes again, "will be to help you to reach that perfect union with God in Christ, that union which is your dearest wish." And he adds:

> I feel more than ever that our Lord has given you to my keeping to help you to arrive at perfect union and the perfect accomplishment of His Will. It is not that I am any better, or as good as many of those who have come in contact with you, but I feel that I have been *sent,* that our Lord has said to me when confiding your soul to me: *Ego ero tecum.*[3] I try to answer this call of the Divine Master by *daily* prayer for you.[4]

Thus, in exercising this ministry, he begged before all things help from above. Faithful to St Benedict's counsel, he had recourse "in the first place" to "the Father of Lights," to the word of wisdom, to the Holy Spirit, "with most earnest prayer."[5] It was "under the eye of God," "in the presence of God," that he studied "with great attention" the communications of his correspondents: "After having read your letter, I went to our Lord and besought Him to show me what He would have me say to you."[6]

Such phrases as these fall again and again from his pen, but his recourse to God is intensified when an important matter is confided to his care: "I have implored the Heavenly Father to take entirely away from me my own opinion, so that I may decide only

---

1 Letter of 2 October 1894. The same thought is expressed in a letter of 21 November 1922.
2 Letter of 26 December 1916.
3 "I will be with thee." Said by God to Moses when sending him to deliver the Hebrews.
4 Letter of 8 December 1913.
5 Prologue of the *Rule of St Benedict.*
6 Letter of 12 September 1894. St Francis de Sales said the same to Madame de la Baume: *"Plaise au Saint-Esprit de m'inspirer ce que j'ai à vous écrire."*

what He has determined in His infinite wisdom. After Holy Mass offered for you I laid down before God all my own will and judgment, and I have tried to see God's intentions *solely*."[1]

An attitude of soul altogether supernatural and rooted in humility. For by temperament he was intuitive, but this gift of his did not exclude reflection in which he examined by the light of experience the problems submitted to his judgment. Reflection and intuition only to be confirmed and made fruitful by help from above: hence his constant recourse to eternal wisdom.[2]

If he prayed for himself, he considered it as a real obligation to pray likewise for those confided to him. In his eyes, this frequent prayer for those under his direction formed one of the most imperative duties of his ministry as spiritual director.

Is this surprising? Are not the destinies of souls in the hands of the Lord? *In manibus tuis sortes meae.*[3] "Unless the Lord keep the city, he watcheth in vain that keepeth it." It is in vain to labour at building up the city of the soul if God Himself does not uphold it.[4] And it is above all by prayer that we touch the Heart of God.

Dom Marmion is convinced of this, his prayer is constant for the spiritual children whom God has given him. He says to one: "I

---

[1] Letter of 29 January 1913.
[2] "Let us turn to God and often invoke Him: for in this humble acknowledgment and invocation consist the principle of this art and guidance (of direction): an art founded upon humility, whilst other arts and sciences are founded on self-sufficiency.... This art is a science not of study, but of prayer; not of contention, but of humility; not speculation, but of love; and the love of Jesus who gave Himself up and was forsaken, who was forgotten and spent himself for the salvation of souls.... This science is the daughter of prayer, the disciple of humility, the mother of discretion.... The science of Jesus, of His mysteries, is the science whereby men become the labourers of Jesus" (Bérulle, *loc. cit.*). Did Dom Marmion know this beautiful passage? We are not sure; at all events it is singularly applicable to him!
[3] Ps. 30:16.
[4] Ps. 126:1–2.

THE SPIRITUAL DIRECTOR

feel our Lord has given you to me to prepare for union with Him."[1] After St Paul's example, he does not cease to repeat to them that he bows his knees to the Heavenly Father that their hearts may understand the greatness of the mystery of Jesus, of which he is the herald: *Oro ut carnis vestra magis abundet in omni sensu et scientia.*[2] "He never forgets his dear children;"[3] "our Lord urges him to pray more and more for them";[4] "he makes all their intentions and interests *his own* in our Lord's Heart"; "he feels that this manner of praying for those one loves is most efficacious."[5] "Daily he brings them in his heart to the altar, that united with our dear Lord they may be accepted by the Father";[6] "may our Lord bless them, and make them always to walk according to His Holy Will";[7] "he offers them every day at the altar on the paten with the Host, that they may be *consecrated* and *transformed* like the bread, in Jesus Christ."[8] It is not only during the Holy Sacrifice, but again, "at the Divine Office and during the day that he feels drawn to recommend them to God, that they may not lay any obstacle to His plans for them."[9]

These multiplied and varied phrases which abound in his letters are something more than simple expressions of charity; they not only betray the tender delicacy of his fatherly heart, they express above all a most clear and supernatural conviction from which spring, for him, an imperious duty. The fulfilment of this duty is besides a joy for him, for it is in no wise a detriment to his own union with God. Such is his understanding of the greatness of the

---

1 Letter of 30 December 1912.
2 Philip. 1: 9.
3 Letter of 12 December 1909.
4 Letter of 2 December 1908 and of 6 September 1909.
5 Letter of 6 December 1913.
6 Letter of 12 December 1909.
7 Letter of 21 May 1895.
8 Letter of 2 December 1908. He says again: "It is especially at Holy Mass that I am united to those I love and I ask our Lord to be for them their All, as He is each day more and more for me." Letter of February 6th, date of year not given, probably 1920.
9 Letter of 3 September 1909.

mission confided to him, such is the extent to which he sees souls only in the divine light!

"It is striking with what precision since sometime past, all my spiritual children come before the eyes of my soul, all together and yet absolutely distinct, especially when I recite the Divine Office or celebrate Holy Mass. And far from being a distraction, it is a stimulus to prayer. It seems to me I see them all there, united with me, each one imploring and praying according to the needs of each one's soul."[1]

In return for the large share he gives them in his intentions, Dom Columba, again like St Paul, expects his children to remember him in our Lord: a spiritual "bargain" according to the expression of St Francis de Sales, made between the director and souls in virtue of "the law of their alliance."[2]

> I pray much for you. I feel that God has confided your soul to me as long as you are to remain in the world; there I must guide you in the midst of darkness, and as long as you remain obedient and submissive, I have *no fear.* On your side, pray for me, for my path is not strewn with flowers, although in the cloister I have so many graces and helps.[3]

> I pray for you every day and I shall not cease praying until I can offer you to the Sacred Heart of Jesus as a pure Victim, burning with love for Him. For your part, you will be bound to help me by your prayers to come to a perfect love of God! That is my one and only desire.[4]

He claims this reciprocity of prayers by reason of the grave

---

[1] Letter of 3 February 1904. This is a rather interesting psychological fact. Unfortunately up to the present moment we have not been able to find any other reference to this subject in his letters.

[2] "Pray hard for me I beg you.... You owe me this charity by the laws of our alliance because I pay my share of this bargain by the continual remembrance I have of you at the altar, and in my poor prayers." Letter of 22 July 1603, to Mlle de Soulfour (*Œuvres*, 12: 202).

[3] Letter of 19 March 1895.

[4] Letters of 2 October 1894, and of 27 November 1894.

responsibility that lies upon him in the sight of the supreme Pastor; faithful in this to the spirit of St Benedict,[1] he knows that God will hold him accountable for the progress of the soul in virtue:

> Be convinced that for the love of my Divine Master, I shall devote myself to you; I shall do my best, by my prayers, my instructions, and if needs be by trials, to make of you a good and holy Carmelite. On your side do not forget that in accepting you for my daughter I take the responsibility of your soul before God. Begin now to take the custom of recommending me fervently to our Lord that I may belong ALTOGETHER to Him, and have no other desire or pretension than that of doing His Holy Will perfectly.[2]
>
> As I pray much for you and as I take the responsibility of your soul, you ought also to pray for me, that Jesus may become the supreme Master of my spiritual life and that I may live more and more in great dependence on His Spirit.[3]

When, after many years, circumstances oblige him to be separated from a soul, he still retains his affectionate devotedness and a constant remembrance in his prayer: "God confided you to me, and I have formed and brought you up *for Him*. It seems now that He wishes to separate us, but I always remain your father, and every day I bear you to the holy altar to offer you with Jesus to our common Father. Live for Him, be more and more filled with the spirit of Jesus your Spouse. Give yourself up to souls, Christ's members; live in this sublime communion through Jesus, with the Father and the Holy Spirit, and with the Church."[4]

---

[1] "Let the abbot be ever mindful that at the dreadful judgment of God there will be made a severe examination of the doctrine and directions given to his disciples. However small be the detriment suffered by the flock of the Father of the household let the abbot know he will be held responsible for it." *Rule of St Benedict*, ch. 2.

[2] Letter of 31 August 1902.

[3] Letter of 2 December 1908.

[4] Letter of 23 December 1909.

The generous share that Dom Marmion gave in his prayers to the souls God entrusted to his care was the outcome of his heart's warm and overflowing charity towards them. For them he was ready, like the apostle, to spend and be spent: *Impendam et superimpendar pro animabus vestris.*[1] Neither trouble, nor weariness, nor any difficulty deterred him, once it was a question of coming to their aid. The interest that he manifested in these souls was extreme, and his solicitude was ever on the alert. It was above all in hours of suffering that this love shone out. Again like St Paul he could truly say: *Quis infirmatur et ego non infirmor,* "who is weak and I am not weak?"[2] To this love so wide, so comprehensive and, to say everything, so Christian, we owe some beautiful pages where the most compassionate tenderness is wonderfully wedded to the holy demands of the most supernatural love.

> I do not like to leave you without a word, especially as you are suffering. When one gives oneself to God unreservedly and in *all confidence* one falls into the hands of infinite wisdom and love. From that moment, not a hair of our head falls without His knowledge, without His permission. He ordains *everything* to this great end: our union with Him. This is why I can only desire what His love disposes. We must love in Him, and with Him, and like Him. I pray for you with all my heart that this trial may lead you to perfect union.[3]

To a nun overwhelmed with trial: "I suffer, my dear daughter, with you in what you suffer, but I would not take you down from this cross on which you find your Spouse; He is for you a *Sponsus sanguinis.* Be sure that in prayer I do not leave you, and often every day I place you in His Sacred Heart."[4]

Indeed, it is always towards Christ that his charity, so enlightened and so pure, directs the thoughts and the hearts of his suffering

---

1 2 Cor. 12:15.
2 2 Cor. 11:29.
3 Letter of 14 March 1917.
4 Letter of 24 June 1916.

children: union with Jesus is alone the source of that inward peace which he wishes for them before all things:

> I learnt yesterday that you have been suffering very much. I asked the Sacred Heart of Jesus to take upon Himself your sufferings and to make them His own. He has said: 'As long as you did it to one of these my least brethren, you did it to me.' For we are the members of Jesus, and you are a suffering member. The Father looking upon you sees His crucified Son in you. Your *state* is a continual prayer. I am going to ask Jesus to unite as closely *as possible* your weariness and suffering to His.[1]

We find this expression of strong and gentle charity and of understanding and sympathy in many pages: "I feel great compassion for you according to nature, but when I look at you *in God,* in whom alone I desire to find you, I cannot separate myself from His adorable Will for you. May Christ be your strength. I want you to be weak, so that your weakness, in drawing down His compassion, may fill you with His strength: *Ut inhabitet in me virtus Christi.*"

See to what heights he calls the soul to rise:

> United to Jesus, we enter by right into the *sanctuarium exauditionis*[2] where all petitions are heard. My daughter, when you are weak and suffering, you are like Jesus *in sinu Patris,* but upon the cross. Jesus on the cross, in agony, in weakness, forsaken by His Father, was ever *in sinu Patris* and never dearer to the Father, never nearer to the Father. I leave you there: it is the tabernacle of the Carmelite here on earth. In heaven

---

1 Letter of 19 July 1922.
2 "The sanctuary where requests are heard," and which is "the bosom of the Father." We do not find this term in the Scriptures, but the idea is taken from St Paul (Heb. 5:6–7; 6:19–20; 7:25; and 9:11–12). This thought is dear to Dom Marmion: we find it expressed notably in a letter of 29 July 1914, and in another of May 1922. St Bernard employs the term of *Sacrarium exauditionis* but to designate the Heart of Jesus. (*Sermo 3 de Passione*).

she will sing; *Secundum multitudinem dolorum meorum in corde meo, consolationes tuae laetificaverunt animam meam.*[1]

Such testimonies might easily be multiplied, revealing a heart of fire, but a fire divinely enkindled and of which Dom Pie de Hemptinne, one of Dom Marmion's holiest sons, said that it was "chaste as flame," God alone being "the seal, the strength and the guardian of this love":

> As our hearts are only one in Christ, I suffer what you suffer and yet I could not wish it otherwise. I have placed you in His Heart, I know that not a hair of your head falls without His love. *Nonne* OPORTUIT *Christum pati et ita intrare in gloriam suam.*[2] Our infirmities are our glory, *ut inhabitet in me* VIRTUS CHRISTI.[3] It is the only strength that I desire to see in you. Jesus calls you to the nuptials with Him, but with Him crucified; it is necessary that you suffer, above all as you suffer now, with *pure* suffering, suffering that no one knows, and in which no one compassionates you.[4]

But let the soul keep confidence: if the acuteness of sorrow makes her powerless to do anything, and especially to fulfil her exercises of devotion, the warm tenderness of the spiritual father will try to supply for her: "Since you cannot pray much, I will do so in your place; at Holy Mass, in the Divine Office, I am the mouth of our two hearts to sing the praises of the Blessed Trinity and to plead in your favour. Take courage! *His qui diligunt Deum,* OMNIA *co-operantur in bonum.*"[5]

One of the dearest of his children was in her agony and far away from him. The German occupation was in full force and the long

---

[1] "According to the multitude of my sorrows in my heart Thy comforts have given joy to my soul" (Ps. 93:19). Letter of 20 July 1914.
[2] "Ought not Christ to have suffered these things, and so to enter into His glory?" (Luke 24:26).
[3] "That the power of Christ may dwell in me" (2 Cor. 12:9).
[4] Undated.
[5] "To them that love God, all things work together unto good" (Rom. 8:28).

tedious formalities of the enemy administration made it difficult, even when possible, to get letters through; communications of any kind were consequently few and far between. Dom Marmion contrived to send his child these lines coming much more from his heart than from his pen: "I have just been celebrating the Holy Sacrifice for you and for myself this morning, without knowing if you were yet in life or already *in sinu Patris*. I have been praying *much* for you since receiving your letter telling me that the last sacraments had been administered to you. As I love you in the Father, it is in His Heart that I place you, knowing that He loves you more and better than I do. I can only want and ask for you what He desires."[1]

The agony was prolonged, and to physical sufferings were added still worse moral trials which nothing could alleviate. At this news, Dom Marmion's fatherly heart was deeply moved; his expression of this charity was at once lofty and human:

> If I did not know that your soul is in the hands of Jesus Christ, and that *nothing* can befall you without having passed through His Sacred Heart I should be in anguish after having received your card. For our souls are so much one in Christ that your sufferings are mine, and I know *by experience* what cruel suffering is that through which you are passing. St Teresa had similar trials and so had Sister Mary of the Incarnation and many others. I have the conviction that it is a part of that crucifixion through which our Lord wills that you should pass.

Then the cry *Sursum corda,* as full of hope as of self-surrender:

> Although everything seems to tell that the end is near, and although I have already committed you into the hands of the Heavenly Father who loves you, I cannot persuade myself that it is the end: *Deducit ad inferos et reducit.*[2] We are nothing in His hands and He can use us as He chooses. If He chooses to unite us to His Son like victims (*hosties*) that He breaks, it

---

1 Discretion prevents us from giving the exact date of this letter and of the following.
2 "Thou leadest down to hell, and bringest up again" (Job 13: 2).

is too great an honour for us. Remain in a state of complete self-surrender full of faith and love, and if anguish wrings your heart, say with Job: Though he kill me, yet will I trust in Him.

In turning over the pages of this copious collection of letters one never tires of lingering over the numerous pages where the golden ray of the gentlest charity transforms the uncompromising demands of perfection into appeals full of confidence:

> It is by successive detachments that He ends by becoming *our all,* and at times this separation from all human solace is almost like death. I have gone through it, and know that poor human weakness could not bear it, were it to last; but little by little God becomes our *All,* and in Him we find again what we seem to have lost.
>
> I have been praying much for you, first because I believe God has given you to me to cultivate and prepare for perfect union with Him, and then again because I *feel* how you are suffering. Such trials are often for souls like yours *le point de départ* of a very perfect life. For souls like yours God wants to be all *Deus meus et omnia,* but as long as they could lean on any human aid, how legitimate and holy soever it might be, He could not be their *all.* This is the perfection of the virtue of poverty, it is perfect hope, to have lost all created joy, and to lean on God alone.[1]

This "perfection of the virtue of poverty" which is absolute detachment from every creature is so much the more necessary to a spiritual director, in that the domain of his activity is the more sacred and the aim to be secured the more elevated. How are souls to be brought to God if the director keeps them for himself? How is he to reverence what is divine in them, if he does not possess true liberty of heart? Would it not be to risk, sooner or later, laying a sacrilegious hand on living tabernacles?

1 Letter of 26 May 1908.

THE SPIRITUAL DIRECTOR

In one of his private notes, Dom Marmion wrote on Easter Sunday, 1900:

> The end of the risen life of Jesus is our justification: *Resurrexit propter justificationem nostram.*[1] I have understood very clearly how much Jesus insisted on this holiness, and how the oneness of our life with His is powerful to sanctify us: *Quanto magis salvi erimus in vita ipsius.*[2]
>
> I have felt a great detachment and have understood that I ought to say like Jesus to Magdalene when even for the good of souls a too natural thought arises: *Noli me tangere, nondum enim ascendi ad Patrem meum.*[3] I find that when I have to occupy myself with souls, this is the only means of remaining in supernatural union with God. I have understood too that it is very pleasing to Jesus Christ for me to interest myself in N—, but I must be very faithful to seek only God's glory and the good of our souls, not the pleasure of recalling past memories. And I understand that my efforts will be so much the more fruitful in divine blessing if we are faithful to immolate what is natural. God, who is the fount of all true tenderness and affection, will Himself bring about a holy and supernatural dilection which coming from Him will be exempt from all trouble and will be a source of great graces.

It is certainly not an easy thing to reach that entire liberty of heart which is the secret of heavenly benediction, but Dom Marmion worked generously to attain it:

> On the feast of the Espousals of the Blessed Virgin, at the end of my prayer, which had been altogether dry, I received a *very clear* light on the love of Mary and Joseph. Never did two creatures love one another as did this espoused pair, and never was love so purified from all human element. I saw, but with great peace and calm, that my affections are

---

[1] "And rose again for our justification" (Rom. 4:25).
[2] "Much more ... shall we be saved by His life" (Rom. 5:10).
[3] "Do not touch Me, for I am not yet ascended to My Father" (John 20:17).

> supernatural, and that I am very detached, but there still remains much progress for me to make before arriving at perfect purity, and I have taken the resolution of striving for it with calm and generosity.[1]

He was to keep his word; two years later, he wrote to the same nun:

> There is a limit to all things human, and therefore to our austere silence. We have just been singing the magnificent antiphon of St Agnes, and I have examined my conscience on the subject of my affections. I have observed a phenomenon analogous to that which I remark in my love for God – whence flows my affection for souls – namely, that my sensible devotion has much diminished, it has almost gone, but it has become deeper, more spiritual, more holy.
>
> Yes, my very dear daughter, I am always entirely yours in Jesus Christ, but nature has totally ceased to trouble the delightful peace of holy dilection with which our Lord has filled my heart for you. I place you *several times* every day in the Sacred Heart of Jesus, especially at Holy Mass, praying Him to take you entirely to Himself, to make you see the depths of His perfection and the depths of your nothingness, that so nothing may be opposed to complete union. For, my very dear daughter, this life is so short, and we have only one; and to what does it serve if it is not to love our *great God* and to prepare ourselves a place very near to Him in heaven?[2]

Detachment from self and from the creature, allied to warmest charity for souls, close union with God and total dependence on His action: great as are these virtues they are not sufficient for a spiritual director. Learning is no less necessary. In this connection we know St Teresa's opinion. It is not with impunity that one who

---

1 Letter of 30 January 1902.
2 Letter of 20 January 1904.

wishes to advance in the spiritual life relies on an ignorant, inexperienced or presumptuous guide.

Dom Marmion's learning was extensive, deep and of a high order. The professorial and monastic charges he had successively filled had familiarised him with the different branches of sacred letters: Holy Writ, dogmatic and moral theology, canon law, ascetical and mystical writings, to which must be added his studies in psychology. In these matters his natural mental penetration enabled him to acquire a sure and thorough fund of learning kept steadily up to the mark and to which he might ever have recourse. For he was endowed with an extraordinary memory. He had in a rare degree all the advantages of this faculty: quickness in apprehending, exactitude and faithfulness in retaining. What was perhaps the most striking was the almost ever-present character of his knowledge. Instantaneously, as it were, knowledge acquired long years before was ever at his service, and that without effort of mind or memory. We may imagine the great advantages he derived from this.

But learning is of small account if not combined with wisdom. Dom Columba's learning had been very early matured in the school of experience. We have seen him as a young priest in Dublin coming into contact with souls of every kind, the most degraded as well as the noblest. Although his daily ministry brought him more often into touch with certain categories of souls – converts, sinners, priests, virgins consecrated to God in the cloister – it remains true that his experience reached out to every condition, to every state of life.

Providence, in this respect, was generous to him; the treasury of his experience of souls was continually being enriched, whilst his judgment became ever keener and finer: a valuable addition to the spiritual art is this skill gained by practice as constant as it is varied.

It may be added that psychological intuition was in him doubled by saintly penetration – "the spiritual point of view is the test of everything" – and you will understand its being said that he could read souls.

Such was, moreover, the confidence he inspired in this domain that, more than once, parents until then unyielding, had allowed their daughter to enter a convent on learning that Dom Marmion was the confessor there.

Let us quote in this connection some proofs of this maturity of judgment which enabled him to diagnose souls surely and rapidly. A mistress of novices furnishes us with some small but significant facts.

"A postulant inspired me with uneasiness for the future; I consulted Dom Marmion, who had had a talk with her. He said: 'Postulants' dowries ought not to be taken into consideration when there is question of their admission;[1] besides, it cannot be considered a healthy sign to swallow everything indiscriminately; one must know how to reject what is poisonous!' I understood, and some time afterwards the postulant left us; the course of events proved that this departure was for the good of the monastery. And yet at the time when the venerated father spoke in this way, the community was delighted with this postulant who was very talented. On the subject of another novice, likewise endowed with certain qualifications, the Right Reverend Father said to me after the first interview: 'What are you going to make of this person?... it is as if when wanting to make a vestment you took a piece of leather instead of satin.' Time was to prove the keen-sightedness and wisdom of Dom Marmion's judgment. On the other hand, we were doubtful about a rather timid and reserved postulant. On being consulted, Father Abbot reassured us that we might trust her and need have no fear about receiving her. This young sister has in fact persevered and is now the joy of her community; always modest and retiring, she seeks only to attain to the perfection of divine love and forgetfulness of creatures. Another novice attracted Dom Columba's attention. From first speaking with her he recognised a chosen soul and promised to help her; he recommended me to try her by mortifications and humiliations, assuring me that she was able to bear them. There, again, his foresight was amply justified."

Dom Marmion expressed his opinion about persons in charming words. Of one of his monks who had just died, and whose rather

[1] Was it not St Jeanne de Chantal who said to some of the superiors of the Visitation: "If you seek monied daughters, you will never have golden ones."

rough exterior veiled the beauty of his soul, he wrote: "His soul was *very united* to God, but very hidden, like one of those beautiful clouds of which all the glory is turned Heavenwards."

But the quality which in this ministry (of directing souls) was so evidently a gift from above that it verged on the extraordinary – a quality which supposes and crowns all the rest and may well be considered to constitute the very form of direction – was discretion.

"This discretion in no wise consists in a rigid uniformity – an idea as false as it is dangerous. Discretion does not confine itself to preventing excess: that is an incomplete idea; we can sin against discretion by defect no less than by excess."[1]

What are we then to understand by this term? Speaking generally – these are Dom Marmion's own words – "it is the supernatural art of discerning and measuring all things in view of the end; of adapting every means, each according to its nature and circumstances, to the attaining of the end. This end is to bring souls to God." It is more especially "that wonderful tact which is the first requisite for distinguishing the needs of the powers of the soul, its strength and its weakness, its resources and its deficiencies, what it actually gives and what it is able to give; and consequently the means to be employed to draw from that Soul all the profit possible for God, its brethren and itself."[2]

Dom Marmion was in a good school for perfecting himself in this virtue – that of St Benedict, who, according to St Gregory, was

---

[1] Dom Morin, *The Ideal of the Monastic life found in the Apostolic Age*, ch. 10, "Discretion and Breadth of View."

[2] *Christ the Ideal of the Monk*, ch. 3, "The Abbot": "Discretion is above all a virtue of the judgment; it predisposes a man to judge in all fairness in order that he may adapt principles and commands to the concrete possibilities of the individual. It must not be connected with the cardinal virtue of temperance which is the moderating of the will, but with the cardinal virtue of prudence which is an habitual uprightness and penetration of judgment having in view the right ruling of moral conduct" (Dom Ryelandt, *Essai sur la physionomie morale de St Benoît*).

a masterpiece of discretion. He had but to read the chapter on "The Abbot" where, with a fine and sure hand, the legislator of monks has traced the portrait of the ideal spiritual director.[1]

"We see how many qualities are hidden under the simple name of discretion, and how wisely the Lawgiver calls it the mother of virtues.... It requires, first of all, a breadth of thought, feeling, and action, extremely rare in our days; it implies, in fact, that we should appraise each thing according to its value in the eyes of God, entering closely into the science and Providence of God. He alone is supreme Discretion; none can equal Him in the art of dealing with each soul according to its needs, leading it to its supernatural end, whilst respecting its free will."[2]

It may be said of Dom Marmion that he had received, and in an eminent degree, the gift of knowing how to imitate this divine discretion in his dealings with souls; in his case the term *discretion* takes on a singular fullness of meaning.

To begin with, he laid stress on the necessity of this virtue. It was one of his favourite maxims that in our supernatural life we must keep our personality as to what is good in it. This was a part of that truth, of that sincerity which, in his eyes, the life of grace demands.[3]

---

[1] In speaking of this delicate and arduous art of guiding souls, the Holy Patriarch says that the abbot must accommodate himself to diversities of character. Strength must be allied with gentleness, authority tempered by love. He must know how to be zealous without anxiety, prudent without timidity; loving the brethren, but hating sin; using prudence even in correction lest "in seeking too eagerly to scrape off the rust, the vessel be broken"; showing the severity of a master to the disobedient disciple; to the upright soul seeking God, the tenderness of a father. One – it is still St Benedict who is speaking – must be gained by kindness, another by reproofs, yet another by persuasion and force of reasoning. And summing up his teaching the great legislator gives the lapidary formula dictated by his great experience of souls and his distinctly Roman genius so skilful in the management of men: "Let the abbot so temper all things that strong souls may give rein to their holy ambition, and the weak need not be discouraged" (*Rule of St Benedict*, ch. 2 and 14).

[2] Dom Morin, *Ibid*.

[3] "Holiness is not a single mould where the natural qualities that characterise one's personality have to disappear so that only a uniform type may be represented. Far from that. God, in creating us, endowed each of us with gifts,

"In the same way," he said again, "that we do not find two faces absolutely identical, so there are no two souls exactly alike, and each one of us ought to treat with our Heavenly Father according to our character and the attractions of the Holy Spirit."

"The attractions of the Holy Spirit": for in the realm of grace there is no less diversity than in the realm of nature, and it is especially on this plane that discretion has to be exercised.[1]

And each soul has to respond to the divine idea in the manner proper to itself; each following the direction given to it, has to trade with the talent freely bestowed; each has to produce the "features of Christ in itself by a co-operation which has its own special character. "Thus," he concludes, "is realised that harmonious variety which renders God 'wonderful in His saints.' He finds His glory in them all, but one can say of each of them, with the Church: None has been found like unto him who kept the law of the Lord."[2]

Commonplace and ordinary truths, some may say. No doubt. But

talents, privileges; each soul has its special natural beauty: one shines by depth of intelligence, another is distinguished by strength of will, a third attracts by breadth of charity. Grace respects this beauty as it respects the nature on which it is based; it will but add a supernatural splendour to the natural beauty, raising and transfiguring it. In His sanctifying operation, God respects His work of creation, for He has willed this diversity: each soul, in translating one of the divine thoughts, has a special place in the Heart of God" (*Christ the Life of the Soul*, ch. "The Truth in Charity").

[1] "God," he writes, "freely distributes His supernatural gifts in accordance with the designs of His wisdom. "To everyone of us is given grace, according to the measure of the giving of Christ." In the flock of Christ, each sheep bears its name of grace (known by the Good Shepherd) just as the Creator knows the multitude of the stars, and calls them all by their name, for each one has its own form and perfection" (*Christ the Life of the Soul*, ch. 5. "The Truth in Charity").

[2] "In each of the saints, the Divine Spirit has respected particular natural characteristics; grace has transfigured these natural characteristics, and added gifts of the supernatural order to them. The soul guided by what the Church calls *Digitus Paternae dexterae*, has been responsive to these gifts, and has thus attained to holiness. It will certainly be a true rapture for us to contemplate in heaven the marvels which the grace of Christ has caused to rise from so varied a foundation as that of our human nature" (*Christ the Life of the Soul*, ch. 5. "The Truth in Charity").

what is far less ordinary is to be so thoroughly convinced of these truths that the director is always guided by their light. This was, as we have said, Dom Marmion's eminent gift. To discover in the souls that came to him what was God's thought for each of them, and the special attraction of the Holy Spirit, to make them docile, with generous and constant fidelity to this Spirit who "does not deform nature, but conforms it to Christ; sometimes subdues, but never crushes; transfigures without disfiguring,"[1] and continues this work until God's design is completely wrought out – such was his aim.

His discretion – in which intuition, learning, experience and holiness had their part – was evinced by a twofold respect: respect for the elections of grace, and for the spiritual liberty of souls; this latter he carried to a point of extreme delicacy. He sought, as though instinctively to distinguish what were the aspirations, the elemental affinities of each one in order to take these things into account in judging what was best for them. He hesitated about giving advice of an onerous or restricted nature, choosing rather to take the indulgent side in prohibiting, counselling, dissuading or recommending. Rarely has a guide in ascetical matters better understood the relative unimportance of material actions in comparison with the intention with which they are done and the motives that suggest them. If he was satisfied as to a person's spiritual docility, that was a reason for him to leave such a one a wide measure of freedom. Very generally, in optional cases, he refrained from influencing the will of another and from putting a rein on individual initiative when he had no cause to suspect sincerity and singleness of purpose. Nothing would have been more repugnant to him than to exercise the least restraint that was not fully justified; to lay, however lightly, in the scale of the balance the weight of his authority as director in favour of a devotion, a method or any spiritual undertaking whatsoever, which might have had his personal preference, but which of itself was not of obligation.[2] What did it matter to him, provided

1 *Cf.* Dom Morin, *loc. cit.*
2 For instance, as to the devotion of the Way of the Cross always so dear to him and from which he reaped so much spiritual profit. He suggested it, he spoke

that the "one thing necessary" was safeguarded; this "one thing necessary" which, in his eyes, was infallibly guaranteed by the sure token of humility and filial love towards God? Therefore his one care was to subordinate and adjust his own intervention according to the workings of grace, to put himself truly in the "rear" of the supernatural; in case of doubt or any lingering uncertainty, he preferred to suspend his reply and to wait in prayer rather than to be in any haste to give advice before having received the sign from God.

Whilst he was prior at Louvain he numbered amongst those he directed, a priest who made his daily meditation according to the method of St Ignatius. After two years under Dom Marmion's direction he learnt, through a third person, that in the Order of St Benedict no such rules are followed in mental prayer. He came then to Dom Marmion and asked him why, being a Benedictine monk, he had not made him change his method: "Because," Dom Columba immediately replied, "the method is a comparatively small matter. You are advancing in perfection; is not that the essential?"

The same discretion and the same width of view in questions of vocation. Thus, in the case of a young man who had at first thought of the Order of St Benedict, he advised him to become a Carmelite "as being more in accordance with his real vocation."[1]

On this subject of discretion his solicitude was so watchful that he neglected nothing to ensure the ways of a soul being respected by others: "I fear that after your departure," he writes to the superior of a community who was being changed to another house, "the little N— may not be understood. Hers is a truly holy soul, but of a very special mould. Before you go, tell her (unless she is going with you) that if she is in any distress or difficulty, she must write to me."[2]

---

of its great value, but he never imposed it.

[1] We have this fact from the religious himself. He writes, "Dom Columba's direction was characterised by a great respect for souls, a great dependence on the Holy Spirit, and it was in prayer, especially at the Holy Sacrifice, that he sought light to give to souls. It was thus that he directed me to Carmel as being more in accordance with my real vocation, although I had thought of becoming a monk of St Benedict" (Letter of 25 January 1928, to the author).

[2] Out of discretion we do not give the date of this letter.

The supernatural prudence that he brought to bear in spiritual direction, he would have persons observe on their own account, and know how to keep out of grooves, however good they might appear, but which were not according to the way marked out for them:

> A soul that has reached the point that yours has ought not to ape and slavishly imitate another: that would destroy liberty of spirit and *the liberty of God's action within it*. The soul is too supple to enter into any frame whatsoever.
>
> If, then, when reading the life of a saint, you find something that you admire, but that *does not lead you into the* PEACE *of the Holy Spirit*, it would be a mistake to strive to imitate it. If the Holy Spirit wants this imitation, he will operate it in you in great peace.[1]

This does not mean that when the good of the patient required it, the physician was incapable of giving a prescription in unequivocal terms. He knew how to do so. Whatever it cost him, he at times gave serious warnings; he extracted from those under his direction much that was lofty and supernatural; further on[2] we shall have occasion to give abundant examples of his zeal in inspiring and fostering in them the desire for real perfection.

Let us only mention here one case in which he was always most resolute. If any came to him seeking God, but "restless, embarrassed by the complication of their personal methods," made the prisoners of their illusions and artificial methods of piety, cramped and distrustful, then he judged it necessary "to free them from their self-bondage" by exerting his authority, in order to restore to them the liberty of the children of light, and to "facilitate for them, by rendering it more attractive, their ascension towards God." The expressions just employed are from the preface that Cardinal Mercier consented to write for Dom Marmion's first book; the point he especially brings out in terms of highest praise is the influence

---

1 Letter of January 29th. The year not given.
2 In the volume in course of preparation, *La vie intérieure d'après les lettres spirituelles de dom Marmion*.

exerted by the Abbot of Maredsous on every class of Christian – an influence which the illustrious Primate of Belgium knew, appreciated and extolled long before the publication of Dom Columba's spiritual conferences on Christ was begun or even contemplated.

In prescribing a remedy a little bitter to self-love, Dom Marmion, while remaining firm, never lost his affectionate fatherly manner and the gentle persuasive tone which found its way to the heart. He always said: "Try ... make the attempt ... I wish it ... I want you to try...." Never was a director less tyrannical or less *oracular*.[1]

With regard to the weak he practised those three virtues that Bossuet extols in St Francis de Sales and which he declared "absolutely necessary for those who direct souls: patience that he may be able to bear with their faults, compassion that he may pity them, indulgence that he may cure them."[2] Dom Marmion remembered, as St Benedict would have it, the example of the Patriarch Jacob who would not have his sheep over-wearied by long and painful stages; he was well aware – to repeat St Benedict's words – that all are not called to the same degree of perfection and that more indulgence must be shown to those with whom the ascent is slower and more difficult.[3] He therefore knew, too – a great art and a great science – how to be patient and to bear with a soul as long as needs be; above all he knew how to pray, and to wait God's good time, for, said he, "even from a sinful heart a magnificent flame of pure love can burst forth, when grace so wills."

What was very justly written of St Anselm, one of the most winning of spiritual guides, may be well applied to Dom Marmion: "He speaks to each soul the language it is capable of understanding, and takes it delicately in hand at the propitious moment when it is most pliable. Thus, not disdaining any means of approach, he finds a way to reach this soul, that he may make it understand what is the Divine Will for it in particular, and having won it, he

---

1 The expression is that of Fr Brémond. *Histoire littéraire du sentiment religieux*. "The two go together," the discriminating critic justly adds.
2 Panegyric of St Francis de Sales, *Œuvres oratoires*.
3 In *Christ the Ideal of the Monk*, conferences "The Abbot" and "Good Zeal."

finally makes it docile to grace and to the Holy Spirit: and oftentimes the victories won by his gentleness are the victories of a very exacting divine love."[1]

For the full success of a like ministry it is indispensable that the one directed should be quite open with the director. "Treat him with an open heart," says St Francis de Sales, "in all sincerity and fidelity, manifesting clearly to him the good and the ill which is in you without fear or dissimulation, and by this means your good shall be tried and more assured, and your ill shall be corrected and amended."[2]

Such was likewise Dom Marmion's way of thinking. But, it is to be understood that when he speaks of the opening of the conscience, he does not mean to *oblige* those under his direction to consent to it. This "opening" he always considered as a very sure means – but one that should be free – of sanctification and progress: it was in the person's own interest that he suggested it.

Occasionally, to help persons to attain liberty of spirit, especially when he had known them a long time, he invited them in an affectionate manner to open out their souls to him. "By my tone of voice," relates a religious, "he guessed I had something on my conscience: 'Come, my daughter, say it in all simplicity.... Something is the matter, and I am your father.' And all the difficulty I had in speaking out was taken away."

"You tell me," he says in a letter, "that I don't know you well enough; there is some truth in that. I know what is good and what is bad in your character, but I only know your soul in a general and perhaps erroneous manner, not knowing your past. When you come to ... have the courage to speak quite openly: I shall be able to help you more.[3] During the coming retreat give me an *humble*

---

[1] *Lettres spirituelles de Saint-Anselme,* Paris, 1925. Introduction, xxxix.
[2] *The Devout Life,* 1, ch. 4.
[3] Letter of 14 March 1902.

history of your past, and I will tell you, with God's help, what He wants from you."[1]

And again:

> It is a great consolation for me to see that you are acting towards me with great filial simplicity. You should always tell me with perfect openness and simplicity what God does in your soul. Having accepted to direct your soul out of love for our Lord, I wish to be in a position to judge of the spirit by which you are led, which I cannot do unless you tell me *everything* that I ought to know. I feel, in fact, that our Lord gives me special grace and light to guide you, but on condition that you always continue, as you have done up to now, to open your soul to me without any fear.[2]

His joy was therefore great when, confidence being established, it was possible to take the soul in hand in order to lead it to God: "I have been very pleased to see with how much simplicity and frankness you already deal with me. There is no illusion to be feared for a soul perfectly open with him whom our Lord gives her as guide."[3] "I am charmed by your letter," he writes to another nun; "it is so frank, so open; I will use the same frankness and the same simplicity in regard to you, and we shall understand one another."[4]

This opening of heart could be quite complete in his opinion without writing daily or making any interminable analysis of soul:[5] "In your life which is so simple," he writes to a young girl, "you

---

[1] Letter of 1 May 1906.
[2] Letter of 6 September 1909. He could have repeated to each of those under his direction what St Francis de Sales wrote to St Jeanne de Chantal: "Believe two things about me: the first that God wishes you to make use of me and to have no doubt on the matter: the other, that in what concerns your salvation, God will come to my help by giving me the necessary light in order to serve you, and as to the will, He has already given me so much that it could not be greater."
[3] Letter of 21 November 1900.
[4] Letter of 3 December 1921.
[5] See above, p. 261.

would have difficulty in finding anything with which to blacken your paper. Write to me about once a month; simply, like a little child to a father she loves, and who loves her very much. Let us pray much for one another, in order that we may greatly love the good Jesus and His Mother."[1]

The same counsel to another correspondent: "Write to me about once a month a *short* letter to give an account of your fidelity, temptations and spiritual dispositions."[2]

To a superior of a religious community, after the first time she had opened her heart to him, he writes: "I do not think that many letters will be necessary, for I see that our Lord is leading you by a very simple and very sure way."[3]

This entire opening of the heart is often a difficult thing; the holiest souls have experienced this. "My interview with Fr [Almire] Pichon," writes St Thérèse of Lisieux, "brought me great consolation without the extreme difficulty I generally find in speaking of myself." On the other hand, for the director to attempt to force the entrance of the sanctuary would be to risk seeing the soul draw back into itself and be ever afterwards closed against him. For his part it needs tact, and Dom Marmion was gifted with it.

He had besides a docile and powerful ally in his own nature, with its depth of feeling, exceptional sensibility, cordial manner, and, above all, ready sympathy. The first interview often took place in the parlour. Certainly, for one who did not yet know him, the encounter was a little disconcerting; the spiritual man had in him a very material exterior; nothing of the emaciated type which some people are fond of looking for in the ascetic. But his look as it fell upon you revealed so much gentleness and kindness; his countenance was so simply frank and open; and above all his desire to come to your help and do you good was so transparent, that after the first

1 Letter of 1 October 1904.
2 Letter of 4 October 1900.
3 Letter of 1 November 1908.

moment of surprise you gave him your confidence without delay. Without ever displaying the least indiscreet inquisitorial curiosity, he inspired such trust that the interview seldom ended until the most hidden recesses of the conscience, the darkest and most secret niches had been yielded up to him and brought to light. His experience of the human heart, his intuition of the things of God and the spiritual life made him see quickly into your soul, but he continued to listen to you for he had the charity of the ear. He would not, as he said, "forestall the Spirit"; he hurried nothing; moreover, having humility of judgment, before suggesting any advice, forming a decision or pointing out any course of action, he recollected himself for a moment, without any affectation however, and less in order to reflect than to beg help from on high. Then without taking the air of an oracle, but with all the persuasive authority which might have been expected from such a man of God, and generally in a few lucid words which said much – for there again he excelled in discriminating between the essential and the accessory – he summed up the whole situation, laid down the principles and gave the solution. And as the Irishman in him never lost his rights, he quite naturally, with charming spontaneity carried his point home with an unexpected sally, an innocent joke, a picturesque reflection, or flash of wit which, calling forth a smile, ended by gaining the heart. You had gone to him with a soul that was listless, sad, wounded, restless, troubled, oppressed; you left him with a heart once more serene, unburdened, restored to light, confidence and peace. Happy those who have come under the influence of his great soul or have met him as a guide on the crossroads of life!... Happy those who lying half-dead by the wayside have found in him the compassionate Samaritan!... Happy above all those who have been faithful in following him: they have advanced with rapid steps in a sure path!

An English writer has said that "to be simple and loving is to be born a king."[1] The incontestable empire that Dom Marmion exerted in the world of souls was partly due to the irresistible ascendency of his lovable simplicity.

1 Quoted by Dom Morin, *loc. cit.*

A page, a true fragment of autobiography, which a young girl who afterwards became a Carmelite was so good as to send us will add some further touches to the portrait that we are attempting to trace.

It was only in June 1921, that I had the happiness of knowing Dom Marmion personally, and yet the conversation I had with him bore a great influence on my inner life and left a lasting impression. It is always intimidating, especially for quite a young girl, to present herself alone before a person of high dignity; and I own that it was not without some trepidation that I entered the great parlour at Maredsous. But I was quickly won by the paternal kindness of Father Abbot, who besides having noticed my nervousness, hastened to set me at ease. At the beginning of the conversation I remarked the foreign accent, the confusion of genders, etc.,... but very soon leaving the more or less conventional enquiries, the Right Reverend Father appeared in a different light, and I felt I was in the presence of a saint. From that moment the conversation took quite an intimate turn, and it only needed a few words for Father Abbot to see clearly into my soul. My director had confided to Father Abbot my desire to enter Carmel. Dom Marmion put several very simple questions to me, then recollecting himself, he told me that he distinctly saw what God's views were for my soul; he spoke to me a long time about my vocation, and responding, without being aware of it, to the most secret aspirations of my soul, he gave me the beautiful religious name of X—. My emotion was very great: it was truly God who was speaking to me by the mouth of His minister. The father's glance was so deep, so luminous, whilst he was speaking to me of identification with Christ, of the life of total immolation in love which would be my lot. To encourage one who wished to give herself fully to God, he showed her all the beauty and greatness contained in Christ's offering to His Father. The *Ecce venio* became a light for me henceforth.... Indeed, the soul cannot express what she, however, felt so deeply.... I had never come into contact with Carmel, it was therefore through the Right Reverend Father who so thoroughly understood our vocation that I came to know its spirit. He expatiated on the apostolate of our order, an apostolate of prayer and sacrifice, particularly for the clergy. And to stimulate my ardour, he spoke in sublime terms of the priesthood... but, alas! also of the numerous quicksands that the priest encounters. The tone of his voice showed he was deeply moved as he spoke of the doubts against faith which may assail the celebrant even at the moment of the consecration. 'Certainly,' he continued, 'your apostolate will be hidden, unknown; perhaps you may have the impression of labouring in vain.... The Carmelite prays and suffers in silence; she immolates herself, and sees no result. It is faith that guides and sustains her. But in heaven you will cry out in joy and gratitude to God in seeing the numberless souls, especially of priests, that you have helped.'

The *Angelus* rang; at once the Right Reverend Father, with charming simplicity, knelt down and recited aloud, with me, the salutation to the Blessed Virgin. Then, with his fatherly blessing, he promised to remember me at Mass, in consecrating 'the little victim,' in union with Christ. 'But,' he continued, 'I count upon your prayers, for the Carmelites have the purity and simplicity of doves; they take a rapid flight to rest on the Heart of the Beloved, whilst we Benedictines,' he added smiling, with that Irish humour peculiar to him – 'we are more like ravens!'

Every fresh interview with Father Abbot while I was staying at Maredsous strengthened my soul and brought it nearer to Christ, the ideal of the life of Victim. Dom Columba insisted above all on the life of intense faith, on union with God, on the total forsaking of created things, on generous self-abandonment to the divine good pleasure, on constant faithfulness in all things. A few words were sufficient to make him immediately understand the state of the soul. In short, it is impossible to express the exquisite simplicity, the delicate kindness and extreme condescension with which he deigned to concern himself with a poor little soul....

The first time he saw me at Carmel, he asked me: 'When are they going to give you a proper habit, and when are you going to take off these...*friponneries* (fripperies)? He had consented to preside at my clothing and seemed in a hurry to fix the date, as if he had some intuition of his approaching end. Alas! scarcely had he arranged everything for the month of March [1923] when God took him far from us. But he is still watching over my soul, and, from above, he continues his work in it: the little Carmelite has ever felt for him the warmest gratitude and will only be able to say in heaven all that she owes to him.

This simple testimony of personal experience gives us a glimpse of Dom Marmion's ascendency over souls; it is valuable, too, as revealing another aspect of his direction. When he had to do with determined souls – the special attraction of the spirit having been discerned and the vocation recognised – he urged them resolutely to keep in the path of perfection which was his own. This discreet director had a very clear sense of his responsibilities, and zeal for the sanctification of souls for God's glory devoured him; he therefore often reminded those who truly sought God of all that was exacted from them by their state. His discretion in relation to those under his direction was never expressed in mere platitudes: "I have been praying much for you during your retreat, for my desire for your perfection always goes on increasing. None but our Lord could make you understand how much I want to see you become a saint."[1]

"Your kind letter has filled me with a very strong desire," he writes to a future Carmelite; "I sincerely desire your perseverance in your good resolutions and your progress in the love of God."[2]

1 Letter of 16 December 1902.
2 Letter of 17 December 1901.

He plainly warned persons in advance that the work of perfection is hard, and that he himself would be firm in taking his share in carrying it out: "If the good God gives me the happiness of being your father during some years, all my efforts will tend to subjugating your very ardent nature to grace. For what comes from a purely natural movement has no value for our perfection."[1]

"I should be very happy," he writes to a nun, "to complete God's work in your soul, by yielding you up entirely to our dear Lord, 'who has regarded your lowliness' and wants you to be wholly *His* (without any accounting for taste)."[2]

"You tell me," he writes in a letter to a Carmelite superior, "that you wish to belong *altogether* to Jesus. I promise to help you with all my heart by my poor prayers and by my *obediences*. May Jesus live in you and by your docility may you become an instrument in His hand. It is the fault of our resistance and our unyieldingness that hinders the Holy Spirit from producing holiness in us."[3]

We read at the beginning of this chapter the two letters wherein Dom Marmion traced out in 1899 his plan – the lofty ideal he proposed to realise as spiritual director to the Carmelites of Louvain. Soon after his death, which befell at the end of January 1923, one of those whom he had guided from the beginning of her connection with that monastery, paid him the following tribute. Filial piety plays a very legitimate part in these lines, but there is no mistaking their simplicity and sincerity.

> I have consulted our mothers and sisters, and their unanimous testimony is the same as that which exists in my own soul: Dom Columba was never anything to us but a man of God. No one here can recollect that he ever approached a soul except in the name, in the place and on the part of Jesus. And he drew no soul to himself, but he drew all *in showing them*

[1] Letter of 4 October 1900.
[2] Letter of 1 January 1907.
[3] Letter of August 4th (without date of year, but after 1909).

Jesus, and all were given with Jesus and by Him to the Heavenly Father. He was venerated as much as loved, and he loved his daughters as much as he respected them, as he venerated in them the spouses of his Divine Master. He wished them to be beautiful for Him, and rejoiced – he often said so – to be able to embellish and enrich them for Him. His words by which they profited, his lights that he shared, his gifts that he distributed open-handedly, from the abundance of his heart, were to adorn his daughters with jewels which would eternally rejoice the Divine Bridegroom, and which the Bridegroom would point out to him throughout eternity, saying to him: 'It is through thee that I have thus adorned them.'

He always spoke to us *in nomine Domini*. No one would have thought of dealing with him on a human footing, of reasoning as equal to equal. He was, and always remained, the man of God. And sent by God, he always spoke to us the word of God. Never, then, any familiarity: that would have been a falling away, for himself and for his daughters, but an exquisite simplicity: 'Father'…'daughter.…'

As director of our Carmel, he was the Church's representative. He so well understood that, being delegated by the Church for the spiritual direction of a Carmel in a town where there was no convent of Carmelite fathers – the authorised directors of Carmelite nuns and generally delegated for this ministry – he ought to guide his spiritual daughters as the Church wills, and as the order has the right to expect, *in the spirit of Carmel.* Certain people said: 'He will make the Carmelites semi-Benedictines.' With our fathers-provincial we protest. He wished us to be, he kept us Carmelites, even exaggerating the fact in the precautions he took, such was his respect for the diversity of vocations. He held the principle that the religious is a perfect Christian; that having made his vows in such or such an order, he ought to live his life as a perfect Christian in the lines marked out by the holy founders.

He was an apostle; he only taught us eternal life: 'To know

Thee, O Heavenly Father, and Jesus Christ whom Thou hast sent.' He applied everything to our kind of life. He had a very high idea of the vocation of a Carmelite, and he kept his daughters at the height of this ideal of spouses of Christ, helpers of Christ's Church.

A father he was to all. Each might have believed herself – and each was so in reality – his only one, because the only one of Jesus. In spiritual direction, in the confessional, and especially during the retreat, he truly showed himself what he was; he took an interest in everything, controlled everything in *the character of a father.* He never forestalled grace, he waited, guided, sustained, then his gladness was evinced at the meeting of the Bridegroom and the bride. It might have been said of him, in all truth, that in regard to the souls he directed, Dom Columba was the friend of the Bridegroom, and he rejoiceth because 'He that hath the bride is the Bridegroom.'[1]

As the servant of God in the spiritual direction of Carmel, how well he kept his place and sustained his position! A servant with so supernatural a spirit that he neither asked nor desired any human reward. He loved to say to God: *Deus meus es tu, quoniam bonorum meorum non eges.*[2] We might have applied this verse to him: 'You are a true Father, because disinterested. You never ask anything for yourself.' He expected the prayers of his daughters, but again only for the interests of God, that He might be glorified in him and in the souls who had recourse to him from all sides.

So when the hour of separation came, at the time when he was elected Abbot of Maredsous, we could sing the *Te Deum:* God's servant had been called to serve his Master in a wider field. However, God alone could know the wound made in all hearts, great in proportion to the very disinterestedness that the faithful servant had taught them. But God will not

---

1 *Qui habet sponsam sponsus est,* John 3:29.
2 "I have said to the Lord: Thou art my God, for Thou hast no need of my goods" (Ps. 15:2).

separate His minister from the souls who are, by their vocation, the bounden helpers of His friends and apostles. Dom Columba was no longer, except very seldom, to give *them* his words, but as he bore them spiritually with him, he would give *them* in giving *himself*. He took for granted their power of intercession over the Heart of Jesus, to whom he had affianced them as to one only and divinely jealous Bridegroom.

This tribute paid by a whole community of fervent religious to Dom Marmion's memory, after so many years of spiritual relations with him, is the most beautiful commentary, it appears to us, that we could wish for in the research we have undertaken.

Out of this abundant documentation – for we have seen Dom Columba in relation with a great variety of souls – it remains for us to point out, by way of conclusion, what were the leading ideas that guided him in this important and delicate matter.

For in speaking of any master of spirituality this question, belonging to the very notion of the spiritual art of guiding souls, arises: What was his conception of the fundamental relations which ought to be established between the soul and God? And, as the immediate consequence, what were the dispositions – thoughts and sentiments – which he strove to cultivate and to render habitual and dominating, prompt and vigilant, in minds and souls, and which were to be wellsprings of prayer and motives of action? As we see, this is a question of the fundamental attitude proper to Christians in so far as they are Christians and from the very fact of sanctifying grace, and, consequently, of a general attitude, capable of perfectly and pliantly adapting itself to a diversity of individuals, states, circumstances and degrees of advancement in virtue.

Of primary importance in order to learn how souls are shaped and the path by which they are led, this question is of no less essential interest when it is the personality of the guide himself that one would analyse. There is in fact no master of spirituality worthy of the name who ought not to be capable of teaching his own ideal to others, of finding in his inmost self the counsels of perfection which he is to pass on to the conscience of his neighbour.

True of every leader of souls, this last remark was strikingly exemplified in Dom Marmion, for he – as we have already seen – easily spoke from his own experience on the occasions when he instructed or counselled, and his counsels were sometimes equivalent to confidences about his own inner life.

We shall have the opportunity later on[1] to reply in detail to this question. We however owe it to the reader to point out here, in broad outline, the main ideas that guided Dom Marmion:

Holiness, in man, is only possible according to the Divine Plan: to know this plan, to adapt oneself to it is the whole substance of holiness.

This plan consists in calling the human creature to participate by the grace of supernatural adoption, in God's own eternal life.

At the centre of this plan is established Christ, the God-Man, in whom dwells the fullness of divine life, the life which He comes to communicate to mankind.

Man enters into participation of this divine life by sanctifying grace, which, whilst leaving him in his condition of creature, makes him truly, by adoption, the child of God: the Heavenly Father encompasses all Christians in an extension of His fatherhood in relation to His own Son Jesus Christ.

This grace of adoption, transcending, as it does, the rights, powers and strict requirements of our nature, has therefore an essentially supernatural character. Whilst keeping its nature in what is noble and good, the soul is to strive to live as a child of God, through union with Jesus Christ, under the action of the Holy Spirit.

In consequence of these fundamental doctrines, Dom Marmion required of the soul he directed a twofold essential attitude: the humble submission of the creature and the loving faithfulness of the child. He would have the soul, conscious of the rights of God,

---

[1] In a volume in course of preparation, on *Les lettres spirituelles* of Dom Marmion.

the supreme Master, acknowledge these rights, honour and respect them by perfect conformity of the will with that of Jesus. But being the child of the Heavenly Father, all this work of conformity must be rooted in constant filial love. Dom Marmion unceasingly invited the soul to come and ever to keep in contact with God by looking upon Him in faith, turning towards Him in confidence and in impelling love. On every occasion to lift up the soul to God, the one Fount of life and a Father full of loving-kindness, and at once to imbibe from this ever-living and ever-accessible Source the light that illumines, the strength whereby temptation is resisted, obstacles are overcome, victory is won over self, and whereby sacrifices are accepted, humiliations welcomed, trials received and, finally, the duty of the present moment is fulfilled.

And all this through Jesus Christ, the one and only way that leads to the Father; by having recourse to His merits; by constant union with the interior dispositions of the Incarnate Word, the God-Man, the living Model of all perfection; and, by the action of His Spirit, the Author of all holiness.

Dom Marmion would have the soul endeavour to steep its whole life and activity, even in the smallest details, in the supernatural, and to learn from a lively faith, from a filial and confident, humble and generous love, the secret of all progress.

Let us remark that Dom Columba was ever actuated by these principles: that he had embraced their supernatural inspiration and magnificent simplicity; and that it would be difficult to find a man who, by Christ's grace, felt himself with more confidence and candour to be "the little child of the Heavenly Father," and to find a director who, with more warmth and persuasiveness, sought to imbue those under his direction with the deep conviction which was so intense in his own life.

Such was Dom Marmion, described by himself, we might almost say. Throughout these pages where we have left him to speak – who will complain of that? – he comes before us in the simple light of a very high and very humble human personality, and also, without being aware of it, in the splendour of that close union with God which was the secret of his fervent and enlightened zeal for souls. We see him a ready and responsive instrument in his Lord's hands, remaining near to us by his radiant goodness and ever widening hearts by uplifting them towards the summits.

NOTE

Outline of Dom Marmion's first spiritual conference to the Carmelites of Louvain in 1899. We give the text of it because, under a very simple and somewhat unfinished form, it condenses the principles that guided Dom Marmion in this sacred ministry.

When your glorious mother, St Teresa, was named Prioress of the Convent of the Incarnation she installed the Blessed Virgin in her place, declaring that she was to be the sole superior of the house, and we know what fruits of benediction followed this step. Well! I declare from this very first day that the sole director of this house is Jesus Christ. You belong to Him; He has bought you with His Precious Blood and with His sufferings. You have all given yourselves to Him without reserve by your holy profession, and it is for Him and for Him alone to form your hearts, to sanctify your souls, to lead you to that intimate union with Himself which is the object of all His desires: *Haec est voluntas Dei sanctificatio vestra.*

He is wisdom; He knows the dispositions of your hearts thoroughly, etc.

He is holiness itself: *Tu solus sanctus,* and it is for Him to lead you. To give oneself up entirely to His Spirit.

Only by a decree of His wisdom, He wills that here on earth we are to be led by men. St Paul and Ananias, Cornelius whom the angel commands to go to St Peter.

This direction will be so much the more blessed by God and profitable to your souls if it is given and received with the most absolute dependence on Jesus Christ.

1. The director, instrument of Jesus Christ. The more he is one with Him, the more he renounces his own ideas to follow in all things the inspirations of Jesus Christ, the more his ministry is efficacious. For my part, I shall try to act in absolute dependence on Jesus Christ. I shall try to learn His designs upon the souls of each one of you. I shall try humbly to follow His Will and the direction of His Spirit. I ask you to pray for this intention, etc.

2. For you. (*a*) I recall to you a golden saying of your glorious mother: 'If in the director you look for the man, however learned or however holy he be, you will find the man.'

It is Jesus who does *all* in the sanctification of souls, we are only obstacles: *Omnis homo mendax. Vos cum sitis mali. Sine me nihil.* See, then, by a strong faith, Jesus, and Jesus only, in the one who represents Him on your behalf for the moment. If this one helps you, give all the glory of it to Him to whom alone it is due: *Soli Deo honor et gloria.*

(*b*) Be very open. The director must see into the depths of your soul. As the Father sees His Son. The more open you are, the more faith you will have in the one whom God sends to you – the more will God give His minister the power to help you.

(*c*) Do not be astonished if he is sometimes severe, etc. During prayer, Holy Communion, etc. When you ask our Lord: *Domine, quid me vis facere?* Jesus will say to you: Go to My minister; I have put My words in his mouth, he that heareth him, heareth Me. In the Old Testament, God spoke to men through angels, but since His Son Jesus was made man, He speaks to them through the intermediary of men.

The shepherd ought to begin by knowing his flock. *Cognosco oves meas et cognoscunt me meae.* It needs a little time to do that. I am a father. I have seen all sorts of miseries. My power to do you good depends on the openness with which you act with me. *Beatus qui non fuerit scandalizatus in me.* Blessed is that one who does not lose confidence in me!

In spite of your good will, God will permit, in order to try your faith, that it may seem to you that my words do not contribute to your advancement. *Durus est hic sermo, et quis potest eum audire,* you may think. At those moments, it is needful to walk resolutely by faith and rest firmly persuaded that God will guide you if you place your confidence in the one through whom He is speaking to you at that moment.

The director ought to take Jesus Christ as Model. Now, Jesus Christ is goodness itself and holiness itself.

You will find in me a father to whom you can open your hearts in all confidence, or rather a mother to whom you can come, in all simplicity like children, and the more you are open and simple, the more power I shall have to help you. Your blessed Mother says that her children ought to speak of all that concerns their souls with their director.

But Jesus Christ is also holiness itself, and I ought to represent Him in that. That is to say: Jesus, in spite of the great love He bears you, punishes our smallest infidelities. St Gertrude was deprived for some time of all consolation in consequence of a movement of self-complacency. That is why the director ought to exact great fidelity in the spouses of Jesus Christ, whilst taking into account the progress and perfection of the soul.

Your glorious mother says in one of her letters that it would be a great misfortune for a community of Carmelites if the director allowed his affection for the community to prevent him insisting on great fidelity, etc.

'There are so many signs of God's action in a soul,' says St Teresa, 'that she cannot in my opinion be unaware of them. However, this is the surest line of conduct to follow; there is no danger in it and it offers many advantages, and we women who are strangers to learning ought above all to act in accordance with it. It is to make our whole soul and the graces we receive known to an enlightened confessor and to obey him.

Our Lord Himself has bidden me several times to do this; I put it in practice, and otherwise I should not have any peace.'

12 CARDINAL MERCIER AND DOM MARMION

Foremost amongst those who confided the direction of their soul to Dom Marmion is to be found Désiré-Joseph Cardinal Mercier.

As has been widely recognised, his exceptional gifts and his power of initiative, almost unique in history, made the Primate of Belgium the greatest figure of his day.

A deep thinker, he approached philosophical and scientific questions with equal mastery; the revival of Thomist philosophy – of which the far-reaching benefit will be long felt in the realm of thought – hails in him one of its most fearless and tenacious promoters.

Raised to the episcopate, this thinker showed himself to be a man of action and apostolic zeal. A vigilant pastor of indefatigable activity, he devoted himself during a quarter of a century to the interests of his vast diocese. By his pastoral letters, of which many will long serve as models, he guided the thoughts of men, aroused their energies, encouraged the taking of every initiative calculated to extend Christ's Kingdom.

A cardinal of Holy Church, he enhanced by the prestige of learning, by the highest nobility of character, and by the loftiness of his virtues the eminent dignity with which he was invested.

An intrepid defender of the invaded city, he declared in stirring language, in the face of an unjust aggression, the invincible predominance of immutable right over the brute might of a day; embodying the soul of the nation by his pen, by word of mouth and by example, he upheld patriotism and encouraged an oppressed people to endure.

An apostle of Christ, he radiated goodness and kindliness, making himself all to all that he might gain all to Christ. Everywhere, with the humble as with the learned, his goodness lent itself to all with that exquisite simplicity which is the greatest charm of genius.

An austere ascetic beneath the splendour of the scarlet, he has

CARDINAL MERCIER AND DOM MARMION
(1916)

left, together with the shining and winning example of the highest virtue, spiritual writings which will long be the guide of souls in love with perfection.

His end of wonderful serenity and touching saintly simplicity fittingly crowned a long, full and singularly fruitful life.

The immense impression made by his death, as well as the unanimous and truly unprecedented admiration and praise which from one end to the other of the civilised world accompanied him to the tomb, was but the tribute paid to the eminent place filled during his life by this prince of the Church to whom greatness came as it were naturally.

One might say that he was given to the world to show to what summits a man may rise when God has marked him with His sign of election to bring about the great designs of His eternal Providence.

How did Cardinal Mercier's relations with Dom Columba first begin? They date back to the year 1899. As we have said, the renown of the talent and virtue of Dom Columba, on his first coming to Mont-César at Louvain, quickly travelled beyond the walls of the cloister: close bonds were knit between the most distinguished master of the *alma mater* and the prior of the new Benedictine abbey. Msgr Mercier was at that time president of the college of higher philosophy, founded in March 1894 by Leo XIII. One day Msgr Mercier said to a colleague:[1]

"It is tiresome.... I have just lost my confessor.... I am not quite sure whom to choose."

"For some time past," returned the other, "I have confided the direction of my soul to Dom Marmion, and could not wish for anyone better."

Msgr Mercier decided to see Dom Marmion. With his customary keen sightedness, it did not take him long to realise the Father Prior's great qualities of mind and heart; although the latter was seven years younger than himself, he chose him definitely for confessor, and made him one of his habitual counsellors.

The intimacy was quickly established and grew ever closer.

---

[1] Now canon of the metropolitan church. We owe this incident to him.

No doubt there was more than one contrast between these two men. Msgr Mercier was distinguished by a rare power of reasoning and took pleasure in solving philosophical problems; he was likewise the leader in the intellectual life and the man of action entering into all the problems of his day, with aptitudes for the most diverse tasks, endowed with a will of iron, possessing perfect and serene self-mastery. Of an intuitive and penetrating mind of extreme vivacity, Dom Marmion possessed a profound knowledge of theology, and his mystical spirituality and great wealth of sensibility gave him a special attraction for the direction of souls.

Despite these contrasts still further accentuated by differences of temperament and qualities of race, these two minds were well made to understand one another. In the sphere of ideas they shared the same love for the teaching of St Thomas, but it was above all on the plane of the moral and spiritual life that they came into close or total accord. Simplicity of character, straightforwardness, love of the truth, a sense of humour more witty in Dom Marmion, finer and more restrained in Cardinal Mercier, kindliness, humility and boundless confidence in Providence, the supernatural spirit – these were the common traits which shone out in the character of each. Both, at the same time very interior and very human, were zealous and generous apostles, gifted with the persuasive language that finds its way to the heart and mind. Both felt the pure flame for all that is good burning within them; both felt urged by the same ambition for an intense inner personal life and the extension of Christ's Kingdom.

Of the intimacy which from the year 1899 was formed between the president of *l'Institut Supérieur* of philosophy and the Prior of Mont-César there are but few written records. We should like to have seen these two great minds pour themselves out in their mutual correspondence. But, especially during the first period of their friendship, until Msgr Mercier's nomination to the episcopate, they saw each other frequently; each week Dom Marmion went to *l'Institut Léon* XIII,[1] and Msgr Mercier often climbed the hill on which the abbey stands.[2]

In February 1906, Msgr Mercier was named Archbishop of Malines.[3] Dom Marmion wrote on this occasion: "I have lost a friend who was very dear to me; I mean Msgr Mercier. For several years we have been so intimate that we scarcely had a secret from one another. Now his high position will make our meetings much less frequent. He is so holy and only seeks God and God's glory. He will do great things for souls."[4]

This last prediction was to be fully realised. The happy influence exerted by Cardinal Mercier in the world of souls by his doctrinal writings as well as by the example of his great virtues is beyond calculation.

Where Dom Columba's humility made him a false prophet was in his imagining that his friend's elevation to the episcopal dignity would create an impassable gulf between them. Friendship fills in such gulfs, as it makes naught of distance. The link that bound them together was, moreover, too holy in its origin and too noble in character ever to be weakened by outward circumstances. Under

---

[1] Later on, Cardinal Mercier, when with intimate friends, sometimes laughingly recalled memories of this period: "I was in my study. All at once, I heard in the corridor heavy, rapid steps: thud, thud, thud.... Ah, I said to myself, that is Dom Columba...." The interview sometimes lasted a long time, then before Dom Marmion left, Msgr Mercier knelt down on a prie-dieu of maple wood, covered with black damask, now in the museum at Malines; Dom Columba sat on a chair and fulfilled his office of confessor.

[2] "One day" (it was about 1902) relates the witness we have already quoted, "I went to Mont-César for a three days' retreat. I wanted to be quite alone, And behold at the abbey I found myself suddenly face to face with Msgr Mercier, who had come for the same object, and with the same intention. Mutual astonishment. We wished to have several instructions. Dom Columba offered to give them to us, and proposed addressing them to the two retreatants at the same time; this idea was accepted. He gave us three conferences: first on prayer, text, *Beatus vir qui in lege Domini meditatur die ac nocte;* second on the Divine Office; third on the Mass. They pleased me so much that I wrote a summary of them.

[3] He was consecrated the following March 25th.

[4] Letter of 30 April 1906.

the purple and very soon under the scarlet, Cardinal Mercier's heart continued faithful; his high dignity only enhanced the often exquisite tokens of his affection.

In November 1906, Dom Columba was obliged to undergo an operation in a clinic. On this occasion the archbishop showed most delicate thoughtfulness for his confessor. "Msgr Mercier has written me a charming letter, saying that he offered Holy Mass and his whole day for me. He has written, too, to the doctor to thank him for the care he lavishes on me."[1]

Is not this last trait particularly characteristic?

This friendship was so deep that the cardinal introduced Dom Marmion into the intimacy of his family.[2] At the ordination of one of the cardinal's nephews, Dom Columba was invited to the *déjeuner* which followed the ceremony: the guests at table only numbered six, and the Prior of Mont-César was the only guest who was not one of the family. The *déjeuner* was in the great *salon* of the archbishop's house, where hung the portraits of the archbishops. In the course of this family repast, which was a very gay one, the party amused themselves – an innocent game – in discovering likenesses between these pictured personages and each of the guests.

"You want to see my portrait?" said Dom Columba; "there it is!"

And he pointed out a stout and rubicund prelate, the Archbishop of Berghes. This sally greatly amused the cardinal.

On other occasions it was rather his confessor's ardent piety which edified him. One day he conducted a pilgrimage to Ittre, there to venerate the head of the great Flemish nun, St Lutgarde. According to his custom, Dom Columba put such faith in his devotion that on their return the cardinal could not refrain from relating the fact to his friends:

---

[1] Letter of 17 November 1906. Later, in a letter of 10 January 1907, to Primate Hildebrand, Dom Marmion wrote: "The archbishop has been very kind and has several times celebrated Mass for me during this time, he writes himself to the doctor to ask news of me and commends me to his special care."
[2] We may add that Dom Columba was the director of several of Msgr Mercier's near relatives.

"It was extraordinary to see how Fr Columba kissed the relic of the saint whilst watering it with his tears."

Another day, Dom Columba (he was then abbot) and another monk were to be seen arriving at *l'Hermite*, the cardinal's country house, each carrying an enormous package. These contained two statues, one of St Benedict, the other of St Scholastica, which the cardinal had wanted for his chapel. The visitors themselves fixed the statues on the wall of the oratory.[1] In the afternoon the cardinal took his two friends for a walk in the country, and on the way, finding some blackberries, he gathered them and offered them to his guests out of the palm of his hand.

We cannot be surprised at the cardinal's devotion for the Patriarch of Monks and his sister Scholastica. The friendship with which he honoured Dom Columba had given him the opportunity of coming into close contact with the Benedictine life; it was not long before he grew to esteem and appreciate the depth of its charm. Over and above the historical interest of this order, dating back to the sixth century, what attracted him was the noble simplicity of the cenobitical life seeking to realise Christianity in all its plenitude, the width of view of monastic concepts, their long and peaceful fecundity. All this impressed the cardinal the more in that in his time there was a remarkable revival of the order, and this efflorescence owed its impulsion to the great Pontiff Leo XIII, so beloved by him, and whose special predilection for the sons of St Benedict he well knew.

For these reasons Msgr Mercier, at that time president of the institute of philosophy, felt himself strongly drawn to the cloister. On different occasions he opened his heart on this subject to his confessor. With the most supernatural broadmindedness Dom Marmion dissuaded him from this intention.

"God has other designs for you," he said each time the subject was broached.

[1] These statues are still there.

The future was fully to justify the wisdom of this intuition. More than once Msgr Mercier returned to the charge, but his confessor remained unshaken in his opinion: it was not until his nomination to the episcopate that he ceased to urge his point.

Failing to carry out fully his secret and inmost aspirations towards the monastic life, Msgr Mercier ever kept a special and affectionate esteem for the children of St Benedict, and gladly took every occasion of manifesting what he felt.

In 1907, Msgr Mercier was created cardinal and went to Rome. On this occasion he was invited to the *pranzo,* at the *Collegio Sant'Anselmo,* on April 21st, the feast of its holy patron. During dessert the Primate of the Order, Dom Hildebrand de Hemptinne – he was at the time Abbot of Maredsous – complimented and congratulated the new cardinal:

"I had a dream," he said; "and it seemed to me that St Anselm came himself to celebrate the feast in our midst.... And it was not a dream, for we have a prelate, a philosopher, a friend of monks, if not a monk himself...."

Cardinal Mercier took up these last words:

"Yes," he replied; "a friend of monks, out of gratitude." He began to speak of the Belgian monasteries; then he added: "All that I am I have become through a son of St Benedict." And those who knew had no difficulty in recognising Dom Marmion himself in this eulogistic reference to an anonymous Benedictine.

The following year, in response to Dom Hildebrand's invitation, the cardinal consented to come to Maredsous, on August 2nd, to confer the priesthood on some young monks from the diocese of Malines, several of whom had been students under Dom Columba. The latter, invited from Louvain by the delicate forethought of Dom Hildebrand, assisted the cardinal in the sacred functions.

The high dignity of the prelate, the deep and impressive symbolism of the rites of ordination, the marvellous setting in which the liturgy unfolds the fullness of its splendour, the solemn and religious chanting of a large choir of monks, an *élite* attendance – notably a strong contingent of old students of the college, whose coming together had been fixed for that day – all combined to make of this religious ceremony a never-to-be-forgotten solemnity; a fact to which the cardinal drew attention a few hours later at the banquet which followed.

To the toasts proposed in his honour by the president of the old students and by Dom Hildebrand, the cardinal responded in words of exceptional kindliness and spontaneous cordiality.

> One sentiment is deeply engraved in the depth of my heart: that of gratitude. My soul overflows with it when I have the happiness to come to this abbey. How much and with what delight I feel all the charms of the beautiful motto of the Order of St Benedict: *Pax*. Yes, peace reigns here, with its exquisite and austere sweetness. It shines out triumphantly in the harmony of the singing and the majestic ordering of the religious ceremonies.
>
> Impossible not to fall under the spell of such great impressions. It is because God reigns here and the restful picture is here offered us of the tranquillity of order. I thank you for having given us such strength and consolation and being for us an unfailing source of the purest inspirations. At this morning's solemn office what spiritual joy did I not feel. It seemed to me that your religious family had increased. No; such joys can never be forgotten.

Then turning to the young men, the cardinal addressed them in these vehement words, which so well depict him:

> And now to crown this feast, I have the happiness to find myself once more in the midst of the old pupils who were amongst my good students at Louvain, I hail in them the best hopes for the future. Yes, I love youth with all the fibres of my soul, and I am not afraid to say that in the distresses of the present hour it is our most powerful consolation, our most solid support.
>
> For my part, know that you have won all my devotedness....

I am tall enough in stature for you to know me again. Have confidence in your archbishop; at every meeting with you he will put out his hands to grasp yours affectionately....

Ceremonious visits and public testimonies such as these are not of a nature to be of common occurrence.

Apart from these occasions the cardinal often visited the cloister in a friendly way, in particular when he went there to make his retreat. Each year, it might almost be said, he chose a Benedictine abbey for this purpose. For several days he lived this life which he had dreamt of sharing for always.

It was beautiful to see this prince of the Church gladly and with exquisite simplicity fall in with the order of the monastic day; assiduously follow the Divine Office in choir; sit down at table with the monks, edify them with his piety. During those days he denied himself to all visitors, seculars as well as religious, so as not to be disturbed in his recollection and his communings with God. The only one with whom he spoke was his friend and confessor.

It was even particularly at the time of these spiritual retreats that the cardinal felt the special need of having Dom Columba near him. At such times, when the soul, all absorbed in God, places itself in the atmosphere of eternal things, seeking renewed strength and fresh impetus in the race for perfection, the archbishop made a point of conferring on his spiritual interests with his confessor. And these two souls, illumined with the same ray of vivid faith, upheld by an equal ambition for holiness, were well made to open out to one another in the solemn and pious watches of the night. But no echo of these confidential talks has reached us.

In October 1907, Cardinal Mercier chose the Benedictine Abbey of Maria Laach on the banks of the Rhine as his place of retreat, and took with him Dom Columba. At Cologne the two travellers were the guests of Cardinal Fischer, then they stayed ten days at the monastery on the Rhine. Concerning this stay, the letters of Dom Marmion contain only three lines, but they form a complete picture: "The cardinal makes himself quite at home, we go in a boat on the lake; His Eminence takes off the pectoral cross, then takes up the oars...."

In 1909 it was at Paray-le-Monial that the cardinal wished to have his confessor with him. He had just returned from Rome with his vicar general, Msgr Jozef van Roey,[1] and had decided to stay eight days at Paray in solitude. Wishing to spend them under Dom Marmion's direction, he sent for him from Belgium. In a letter dated March 7th, Dom Marmion wrote:

> I daily get marks of His [God's] loving care. I had a great desire to make a good retreat, but have been prevented for some years from making my annual retreat, and even when I can make it I am so often interrupted I cannot fully recollect myself. I also longed for years to visit Paray-le-Monial, and now the cardinal has just obtained permission from my Lord Abbot[2] for me to accompany him to Paray-le-Monial during his retreat, which he will make there this month on returning from Rome. I shall let you know the date in order that you may accompany me by your prayers.

And a few days later (March 20th): "Here I am at Paray in peace and retreat. His Eminence and I arrived here on Thursday the 18th, and we are to leave on Friday the 25th; I know that you are praying for me, and I bear you every day in my heart to the holy altar with all your intentions."

Some months afterwards, Providence called Dom Marmion to take up the government of Maredsous. On this occasion the cardinal made the gift of a pastoral ring to his confessor as a token of affectionate esteem.

The distance separating the ecclesiastical metropolis from the

---

1 Who has succeeded him as Archbishop (and now as cardinal) of Malines. Msgr van Roey and Dom Marmion closed their stay at Paray with a visit to the celebrated Abbey of Cluny.
2 Dom Marmion was at that time prior at Louvain. On the subject of this retreat at Paray, see above p. 192.

Walloon abbey no longer permitted Dom Columba to act habitually as Cardinal Mercier's confessor, but this made no difference to their friendship.

It was, therefore, not until February 1912,[1] that the cardinal took his friend and counsellor with him to Rome in his pilgrimage *ad limina*. His Eminence stayed at the *Collegio Sant'Anselmo* and there made his retreat. This sojourn in the Holy City was prolonged until March 21st.

When the cardinal did not take Dom Marmion away with him he came to visit him in his abbey. This was notably the case in March 1914.

"His Eminence is at present here in retreat," writes Dom Marmion at this date. "He is a real saint."[2]

Even the war, when it broke out some months later, with all its troubles and upheavals, its anguish and anxiety of every kind, with the extreme difficulties that it brought in the way of communications, did not prevent many proofs of this noble friendship being shown. The sorrowful and tragic circumstances made it all the more precious.

In 1916, the cardinal tore himself away for two days from the absorbing cares of a superhuman task; he brought to Dom Marmion, just returned from England, a fresh mark of faithful friendship, and to the people of Entre-Sambre-et-Meuse the supreme consolation of his presence and words. Having arrived at the monastery on August 14th, he next day celebrated Pontifical Mass of the Assumption.

How different from the visit he had made on the same date, eight years previously, when he came to the abbey to preside at a ceremony of ordination to the priesthood! He himself had then expressed in glowing terms the never-to-be-forgotten impression that this ceremony had made on him. He had lauded the peace that

---

1 To one of his sons residing in Rome, Dom Marmion writes (4 December 1911):
"I am to go to Rome with His Eminence Cardinal Mercier in the month of February; we expect to leave Belgium on February 25th and to be back for March 11th. I should like to make a pilgrimage to Subiaco; I have never been there. Then a visit to the Irish College."

2 Letter of 14 March 1914.

finds its most natural place in the cloister; speaking to the young men whom he had before him, he had exhorted them to devotedness to the noblest causes.

And now war was reigning; youth, obedient to the call of the king, was defending the last shred of national soil with a heroism of which the king himself, who was at that time truly the personification of the country, offered the highest example. But those who sustained in silence the heavy yoke of an arrogant enemy looked for a word to help them to raise their hopes: this word the cardinal brought to them. On coming from the Divine Office, clad in his pontifical vestments, he advanced to the entrance of the choir and addressed the multitude who had hastened from the surrounding district. With all the authority attached to his words, especially under these poignant circumstances, in a clear articulate voice which made itself heard even to the confines of the vast nave, he spoke first of all of Belgium's attitude during the present events, and of patriotic hopes. The emotion was indescribable; a wave of righteous indignation uplifted all present on hearing this defender of freedom express aloud, with noble pride, all that they had felt and thought, yet had scarcely dared to utter: the certain hope of the final victory of eternal right.

Occasionally, in spite of the distance and the almost insuperable difficulty of covering it, to such an extent were the communications blocked by the hostile occupants of the country, the cardinal asked his counsellor to come to him.

"Yesterday," writes Dom Columba to a mutual friend, in a letter dated 1 October 1917, "I spent a beautiful day in the country, which has done me good – body, heart and soul. It was a gift from the Heavenly Father. I went to *l'Hermite*. A good hour's walk through fields brought me from Waterloo to the cardinal's house. His Eminence was never more cordial or more confiding, and we chatted about everything with entire *abandon*.... I admired once more in him the work of grace."

About this date the volume, *Christ the Life of the Soul* was published. Dom Marmion ventured to ask his eminent friend to write some lines of introduction. No one was better qualified than the cardinal to do so. For long years he had lived by the teaching contained in these pages, and he highly appreciated it. The value and import of this work appeared to him so evident that at Dom Marmion's request he at first replied: "But... good wine needs no bush" – and these words are worth a whole preface. Then, immediately being carried away by a movement inspired by friendship and esteem, he promised to present his confessor's work to the public. All the readers of *Christ the Life of the Soul* know in what terms of conviction he described this work.

We should never finish if we brought forward all that testifies to this holy friendship. The last time it could be publicly manifested was on the occasion of the golden jubilee of the foundation of the Abbey of Maredsous in October 1922. As we have said, the cardinal willingly presided and by his presence enhanced the celebrations which marked the event. On this occasion he took visible and cordial satisfaction in emphasising before all the old friendship that united him to the head of the monastery, "hoping that it might become, if possible, closer still." Therefore his fervent wish was that heaven would yet long spare to him his bosom friend. Providence was to dispose otherwise; three months later, in fact, on 30 January 1923, Dom Marmion was called to God: his death broke the earthly links of this saintly friendship.

The close union of these two souls easily allows it to be seen what great confidence the cardinal had in his confessor. The latter had often to play the part of counsellor. It therefore came about that Dom Marmion was often sent for to Malines. On several occasions, moreover, the cardinal sent to Dom Marmion persons who had come to consult him on serious matters:

"Pray," he would tell them, "reflect, then go to see Fr Columba."

To enter into detail and measure the extent of this influence of Dom Marmion is, in the absence of documents, out of the question. The Abbot of Maredsous made it a duty to destroy the cardinal's letters, which were almost always of a confidential nature, and the Primate of Belgium declared, shortly after his confessor's death, that he had no letters of Dom Marmion.[1]

It would be useless under these conditions to waste time with conjectures; only perhaps the publication of their correspondence with others may throw some light on this subject.

We will, however, mention one example, the only one we have been able to find so far amongst Dom Marmion's correspondence, but it is interesting. It has to do, in fact, with a movement which stirred the religious and intellectual world during several years – namely, modernism – and more particularly with the person chiefly responsible for the movement, Fr George Tyrrell, SJ. This correspondence shows at the same time Msgr Mercier's confidence in Dom Marmion and his great charity towards souls.

At the moment when it came to the fore Msgr Mercier had just been consecrated Archbishop of Malines (25 March 1906). At that epoch the modernist movement had reached a height of boldness and found one of its most prominent representatives in Fr Tyrrell, a man of fine, versatile and supple mind, a brilliant and well-read writer, but the impetuosity of whose audacious ideas was bearing him along to the abyss. He had just (February 1906) been expelled from his society, and by this fact was suspended.[2] Sad indeed is the situation of a priest who sees himself banished from the altar! But likewise a situation well calculated to move an apostolic soul, like that of the pastor who had just taken as the motto of his episcopate:

---

[1] This is the explanation furnished by the cardinal himself: in summoning his counsellor to him, Msgr Mercier often informed him, by writing about the affair on which he desired to consult him, in order that Dom Marmion might think it over; Dom Marmion only replied by a note announcing his arrival.

[2] In January 1906, the *Corriere della Sera* of Milan published some extracts from a *Confidential Letter to a Professor of Anthropology*, of modernist tendencies, attributing the writing to an English Jesuit. Eventually Tyrrell was recognised to be the author of this letter, but refused to retract it. It was then that the general of the company decided on his expulsion.

Apostolus Christi. Msgr Mercier, as soon as he heard of Fr Tyrrell's situation, resolved in his great heart to do all he could to save him.[1]

The enterprise was a delicate one. In an extremely grave and painful conflict, not without complexity, it was needful, whilst allowing the greatest indulgence, to safeguard the rights of doctrine and at the same time to avoid being involved in insoluble difficulties.

Circumstances favoured the first proceedings. More than once the name of Tyrrell had been brought up in conversation between Msgr Mercier and Dom Columba. Tyrrell was of Irish nationality,[2] like Dom Columba; moreover, the latter was aware that a nun in an English convent which he knew well had for a long time past been in regular relations with Fr Tyrrell and, out of charity, still continued to correspond with him. It was this nun who was to serve at the beginning as intermediary in the advances made by the archbishop. This is the letter which Dom Marmion wrote to her in the archbishop's name:

> *Confidential 2 April 1906* – I saw His Grace the archbishop yesterday. He begs me to treat a very delicate and confidential matter with you. He has always taken a great interest in poor Fr Tyrrell, SJ, and his large loving heart suffers at the thought that that rich nature and brilliant intellect should be in danger of being lost, and also at the thought of his being deprived of the happiness and *grace* of daily Mass. His Grace's first thought was to offer him a place in his archdiocese; on the condition that he would neither preach nor hear confessions, nor publish anything without permission. However, after chatting

---

[1] Did someone suggest this to the Archbishop of Malines, or was it he himself who first had the idea. We do not know. In his work in favour of the Modernists, *L'affaire Tyrrell* (Paris, 1910), Raoul Gout writes that Msgr Mercier acted in concert with Domenico Cardinal Farrata, but he gives no proof of this. Perhaps Msgr Mercier knew that Fr Tyrrell had appealed without result to two bishops to be received into their diocese. In any case, the letters here published exonerate Msgr Mercier from the imputation of "being scarcely sincere in his friendship for Fr Tyrrell."

[2] He was born in Dublin in February 1861, of Protestant parents, and was converted to Catholicism in 1879.

the matter over with me, he came to the conclusion for *several grave* reasons, that it would not be prudent to do so.[1] His Grace could have him accepted in some other diocese (Liège or Namur) on the above conditions, but he wishes to be assured of his orthodoxy and actual dispositions, and for this he has recourse to you. Please try and find out his actual dispositions, and if you are satisfied, you could let him know – without speaking of the archbishop – that there could be found in Belgium an *episcopus benevolus* who would be willing to give him an opportunity of celebrating Mass and of living in retirement. His Grace thinks also of putting him in relation with me, which might be useful to both.

Please let me have your opinion as soon as possible, as I am to see His Grace towards the end of the week.

Pray for me as I do for you, and believe me with sincere respect, yours devotedly in J.C.

The nun's reply was evidently favourable, for on April 6th, Dom Marmion wrote to her again:

Confidential – I have just received the archbishop's reply. I transcribe the part which regards our case. 'The important point is to know if T. still believes in the Real Presence. What does he mean by *absolute secularisation?* If he is prepared to live in retreat, to refrain from taking any initiative, and only to *second* those which I take or suggest to him, I will do my best to help him. I do not see any difficulty in receiving a visit from him; I will make him understand in advance that the fact of receiving him in no wise binds me or him. It would be merely a means of knowing him and seeking to understand him. In a month's time for example.'

Dom Marmion added: "It appears to me that you would do well to acquaint him *very confidentially* with the benevolent dispositions of His Grace, and the conditions which he insists on. He should

[1] The course of events was to show, as we shall see, the wisdom of this ruling.

however keep this strictly secret for the present. Recommending myself to your prayers, I remain yours most devotedly in J.C."

Then in a postscript, these lines which show Msgr Mercier's high-toned and supernatural charity: "His Grace says that, having been asked by a religious community permission to expose the Blessed Sacrament for several hours the first Fridays of the month, he has accorded the permission, but on condition that one hour's adoration should be made for His Grace's intention which is 'to obtain light, strength and humility for F.T.'"

Henceforward, for the sake of saving time, the conversation was established directly between Msgr Mercier and the nun, but the result hoped for on Fr Tyrrell's side was not attained. In fact, he thanked the archbishop, adding that he did not wish to leave his country and his friends. Hence Msgr Mercier's charitable proposition became objectless.

Moreover, Fr Tyrrell's subsequent publications, notably his famous opuscule: *A Much Abused Letter* (September 1906), which made a considerable sensation, and his revolt against the encyclical *Pascendi Dominici gregis* (8 September 1907), which condemned modernism, no longer left any doubt in his case. In February 1908, Cardinal Mercier called the attention of his people to this encyclical in a pastoral letter on Modernism.[1] Having seen it, Fr Tyrrell responded in May 1908, with an opuscule: *Medievalism: A Reply to Cardinal Mercier* in which he went – as the cardinal expressed it[2] – "so

---

[1] He said in it: "The one who is searching the furthest into the movement and is the most attentive to mark its tendencies and who has his mind most involved in it and is, perhaps, the most deeply imbued with it is the English priest Tyrrell. In the numerous writings published by him, in the course of the last ten years there are, side by side with pages of touching piety – which we for our part have read with edification and for which we are truly thankful to their author – there is often even in the breath that animates these pages, the fundamental error of Ignaz von Döllinger, that is to say, the root idea of Protestantism."

[2] In a letter to the same nun (we quote the letter in full): "You have doubtless heard of Tyrrell's new book, *Medievalism: A Reply to Cardinal Mercier*. The book is frankly bad; the author roundly denies the infallibility of the pope, insults in the grossest way on several occasions all those who represent the authority of

far as to be guilty of the indiscretion of mentioning the private correspondence that he had exchanged with the Archbishop of Malines through the intermediary of a third person, and to make a crime of his charitable advances." We see how wisely the cardinal and his companion had acted in surrounding the spontaneous impulse of their great charity with prudent measures.

It is perhaps in the strictly speaking spiritual domain that Dom Marmion's influence is most easily to be discerned.

No doubt great divergences mark the ascetical works of the cardinal and Dom Columba. Of a more personal and outstanding character and a more distinctly modern appeal, Cardinal Mercier's works are of a less theological nature; neither do they apparently present such synthetical unity, Providence not having given to the cardinal, as to Dom Marmion, to see his writings brought to the consummation of which he had dreamed. In dogmatics Cardinal Mercier

---

the Church, and treats your servant with rare impertinence. I wonder if it is needful to reply to him. If so, should this be done in a few lines, or in an article in a review, or in a brochure? On this point I shall consult those who, in England [the cardinal was on the point of making a flying visit to London], will be best able to decide as to the effect produced by poor Tyrrell's work. In his first chapter, he is guilty of the indiscretion of mentioning the private correspondence that he has exchanged with me through the intermediary of a third person, and he has the affrontery to make a crime of my charitable advances towards him. It is on this question I want to consult you. Have you kept a copy of the letters you wrote to him, and in the affirmative case, may I see them? I have kept the notes you have written or transmitted to me, at the time of the negotiations which you were so good as to undertake. Eventually, I shall be able to affirm, shall I not, that neither the third person nor myself have authorised him to bring this intimate correspondence before the public? Personally I am inclined to reply by a dignified silence to the insults and proceedings by which the unhappy man has degraded himself. But the public might perhaps place a wrong construction on my refraining from replying and the liberal papers here would perhaps take it as an argument against the cause I ought to defend? How does it seem to you? Accept, my good Mother, the respectful expression of my very cordial devotedness."

refers rather to St John, Dom Columba to St Paul; the cardinal is more didactic, Dom Columba displays more tenderness of devotion.

However, different though they may be, these works are not without points of contact. Such constant intercourse between these two men of God must necessarily have led to frequent exchange of views on questions of spirituality.

There is one domain where this influence of Dom Columba is assuredly tangible: we mean the liturgy. Throughout his episcopate Cardinal Mercier ever showed himself a zealous and fervent promoter of liturgical devotion. He multiplied his pastoral instructions, his *monita* to his clergy, notably on the Mass and the rites of the sacraments; he had at heart the restoration of the Gregorian chant and he inaugurated congregational singing in the metropolitan church itself. How many times, too, in his pastorals, in his retreat instructions, he appealed to liturgical texts! And to demonstrate, by a significant action, in what deep esteem he held the Church's public worship, he chose to crown the celebration of his sacerdotal jubilee in 1924 with a congress in view of promoting this cause. Finally, the last letter to his clergy, written on his deathbed, still reveals this preoccupation – a touching page written to the glory of the Mass, the centre and focus of the whole liturgy.

It was from coming in close touch with Benedictine life that the cardinal "discovered" the liturgy; his intimate conversations with Dom Marmion revealed to him its sweetness and savour and its primary role in the spiritual life. Dom Marmion's influence in this domain is undeniable.[1]

---

[1] It is true that it was especially from 1910 that the cardinal publicly manifested his practical esteem for the liturgy, under the impulsion of the movement set on foot by one of his intimate friends, Dom Lambert Beauduin. The latter must be regarded as the real initiator – one with wide views and of searching intuitions – of the contemporary liturgical movement; in the congress at Malines in 1909, he gave a masterly review of the liturgy which impressed Msgr Mercier. But the ground had been prepared by Dom Marmion and the seed had long ago been cast. We may add this detail, known by few, that it was Dom Hildebrand de Hemptinne who had counselled Msgr Mercier at the beginning of his episcopate to establish congregational singing in his churches.

Would it be possible to discern Dom Columba's influence on the plane of spiritual doctrine strictly so-called? It is true that even while he adopts or makes his own an original thought of Dom Marmion, the cardinal's personality remains too distinct, he gives a too special turn to his thought for it to be easy to recognise the inspiration of another.

We are not, however, without those who can bear testimony on this subject. We have heard the cardinal himself declare, at the time of his reception at St Anselm, that he "owed everything to Dom Columba." And assuredly this assertion must be understood, first of all, in reference to that which concerns the spiritual life. Later, in a conversation with the professors of the *l'Institut Saint-Louis* in Brussels,[1] the Primate of Belgium declared with exquisite simplicity that he was much indebted to Dom Marmion. Notably we have it from one of his intimate friends that the pages written by him on divine adoption were inspired by his talks with his confessor. Although Cardinal Mercier was deeply versed in this doctrine, the tone, the insistence, the warm conviction with which Dom Marmion frequently spoke of the Heavenly Father greatly impressed him: "How often Dom Columba speaks of the Heavenly Father! does he not?"

Besides, it would not be difficult to discover in Cardinal Mercier's spiritual works the thoughts which are fundamental in the teaching of his director and confessor, and which Dom Marmion clearly brings out again and again.

There are harmonies between their works that are visibly due to something more than coincidence. In his pastoral letter on *Devotion to our Lord Jesus Christ*,[2] the cardinal writes:

> Christ is the *exemplary* cause of the supernatural order, that is to say the *personal* type on which all holiness is modelled....
> He is the *meritorious* cause; that is to say, in substituting Himself for us, He has expiated our sins and reintegrated us in the

---

[1] We owe this fact to one of these professors.
[2] April 1915.

supernatural order from which we had fallen.... He is the *efficient* cause: the whole effect of grace, whether it concerns men or angels, the Old Testament, the Church on earth or the glorious Church in heaven, the whole effect of grace or of glory has the God-Man for its author.

We cannot but see the relations existing between these lines and the titles of the three chapters at the beginning of Dom Marmion's *Christ the Life of the Soul:* "Christ is the Only Model of All Perfection – The Author of our Redemption and Infinite Treasury of Grace – The Efficient Cause of All Grace."

The cardinal writes in his beautiful book: *À nos séminaristes:*

> Those who while they hope in God yet hesitate in their hearts have not reflected enough on the fundamental motive of Christian hope. The sole condition of the infinitude of Divine Mercy and the rights that it gives us is that we believe in it; our confidence must find its sure and unshaken support in the merits of Jesus Christ. Did not our Divine Wonder-Worker invariably lay down this same condition to those who asked Him to work a miracle. Hast thou faith in Me; that is to say, have you the firm inward assurance that I can heal you, restore your sight, give movement to your paralysed limbs, raise your brother to life?

And in the epilogue of this same book he writes these lines by way of conclusion: "Never separate these two sentiments in which are summed up all aspirations towards holiness – namely, humble distrust in yourselves and the utter self-surrender of filial confidence in Him whom we have the right and joy of calling our Father."

In these passages Dom Columba's disciples will recognise the most characteristic ideas of his asceticism expressed almost textually.

Ejaculations such as these: "O my Divine Jesus, God has given You to be all to us.... Be all for us with God.... Surrender yourself utterly to God, and God will give Himself fully to you," are constantly found under Dom Marmion's pen.

In his volume, *La vie intérieure (5e entretien)*, Msgr Mercier wrote these remarkable lines:

> On us, priests and pastors, another duty is incumbent, we must preach *the Christian life*. Christian people have a right to the fruits of our contemplation....
>
> The moral of our sermons and of the confessional is too often the moral of duty, of the virtues, too little of the supernatural charity, shed abroad by the Holy Spirit in souls.... It is Christ whom we must give. It is Himself, His Gospel, the riches of His grace, His presence and that of the Holy Spirit in the soul, the inward prayer of the heart, the peace of might and power in divine union; that is what must be preached.
>
> But you do not preach that, or you preach it scarcely at all because that is dogma, and you seem to be afraid of dogma. And hence a generation is growing up whose ideal is an irreproachable respectability, the respectability of gentlemen retaining a few religious practices. You do not preach dogma.
>
> You speak of God, but it is ... the God of human reason.... But the God of our revealed truth ... when and with what precision and what warmth do you speak of Him?
>
> Christ, yes, you speak of Him; that is to say, you make known the history of His life on earth; so many events which announce the foundation of the Kingdom of God; but this Kingdom itself which dates from Pentecost.... His supreme Priesthood ... the manifold aspects of the glorified Christ ... what place do they occupy in your personal piety and in your pastoral preaching?
>
> And the Holy Spirit? How many out of the mass of Christians know Him, invoke Him, live in intimacy with Him?... Am I wrong in saying that you do not preach dogma?

We shall be forgiven this long quotation, but it expresses too well the familiar thoughts of Dom Columba for us not to hear in it the direct echo of the cardinal's intercourse with his confessor.

And it was precisely in order to teach his priests how to preach dogma by means of a living object lesson that, in 1907, Msgr Mercier asked Dom Marmion to give the monthly retreat to the priests of the capital.

It is true that two of the ascetical works of the cardinal *À mes séminaristes* (1908) and *Retraite pastorale* (1910) were given to the public before Dom Marmion's books appeared. But, in the case with which we are now concerned, the priority of date of a publication merely creates an illusory point of view.[1]

It must in fact be noticed that at the time when the cardinal confided the direction of his soul to Dom Marmion (1899), the latter was in full possession of his Pauline doctrine; that in 1903, and on other occasions, he gave the retreat at *l'Institut Léon* XIII directed by Msgr Mercier; and that their intimate conversations on questions of spirituality were frequent.

Moreover, from 1898 – when a retreat was preached by Dom Columba to the nuns of Maredret and taken down word for word by their diligent hands – manuscript copies of the spiritual instructions given by Dom Marmion were passed about under the cloak of secrecy; the retreat conferences – notably those in which he summarised his original and fruitful teaching – were taken down, copied, passed from one to another of his spiritual children and spoken of as treasures eagerly sought after. Dom Marmion was aware of this, and with most absolute detachment left each one free to use these notes as seemed good to him or her, for, as for himself, he never thought of publishing his conferences.

More than once the cardinal asked the Benedictines of Maredret to lend him Dom Columba's retreat conferences, notably in 1914. At that date, as we have said, he made a retreat at the Abbey of Maredsous. At the end of his stay he went to visit one of his relations, a Benedictine nun at the Abbey of Maredret. In the course of the conversation the cardinal asked to see the retreat notes of Dom Columba, in view of drawing up an analogous piece of work.[2]

---

1 *La vie intérieure: Appel aux âmes sacerdotales,* came out after *Christ the Life of the Soul;* we there see the cardinal quote Dom Marmion textually.
2 According to a communication made to us by the Abbess of Maredret, a sim-

This is in fact the note he wrote to this relative on the eve of his departure: "*Maredsous, 23 March 1914* – My dear child, I think it well to let you know that I expect to leave, alas! the abbey tomorrow morning at 8 o'clock. If then you have arranged the spiritual notes as you gave me to hope, it is today they must be sent to me. If, on the other hand, they are not ready, do not hurry in any way; I shall receive them at Malines."

The transcribing of the notes asked for was not quite finished, but, in the meantime, another manuscript book of Father Abbot Columba was sent to the Primate of Belgium. The cardinal replied the very next day, the 24th, before his departure:

> My dear cousin, the precious MS. book, the selection of artistic holy pictures and your very kind letter, safely received. I thank you with all my heart. I have not yet looked at or read anything; I wait to regale myself with it at Malines.
>
> Do not hurry with the retreat notes; if I asked you for them it was because I thought they were already written out. I have been indiscreet without knowing or meaning it.
>
> I am counting on your prayers that the good God will help me in this work of redaction and also that he will help me to bear the sometimes heavy burden of my responsibilities. These days of solitude have rested and provided me, unless I am mistaken, with a store of fresh strength.
>
> I bless you.
>
> ✠ D.J.

The work of transcribing being completed a few weeks later, the abbess had the text of these notes forwarded to the cardinal. He replied:

> What am I to say of the words of our dear Father Abbot? Your daughters have given me a surprise in letting me have the written text of Fr Columba's retreat. It seems to me, when I

---

ilar request had already been made at a much earlier date, and with the same end in view, by the cardinal.

read these pages, that I am listening to my confessor speak to me of our Lord and encouraging me to concentrate my mind and heart on His adorable Person. I expect spiritual benefit from reading this, and, unless I am unfaithful to grace, part of the merit will be for the *causae instrumentales* of the divine motion.

Recently a pious and intellectual man said to me that no one knows as well as the Right Reverend Fr Columba how to realise the presence of God and the action of grace. Is not what he says very true? He makes us touch God. It is the return to sane realism in piety.

In these last words the cardinal depicts himself. More than any other he laboured, like Dom Marmion and with him, for this return to "sane realism in piety" which he admired in his director; like him, "he made one touch God."

On 30 January 1923, as we said, Dom Marmion was called back to God; three years later, almost to the very day, the cardinal followed his confessor to the grave; in uniting their souls in Christ eternity sealed forever their holy and indefectible union.

Other noble friendships are to be met with in Dom Marmion's life.

He held the principle – expressed it publicly – that the closest union ought to reign between the secular clergy and the regular clergy. He had it at heart that his monks should, in the measure compatible with the religious life, always lend a loyal and devoted concourse to the parochial clergy. It is not astonishing then that, moved by the same supernatural spirit, he maintained the most friendly relations with Msgr Heylen, the head of the diocese where the abbey was situated. This revered president of the Eucharistic congresses confided delicate missions to him more than once. At the celebration of the golden jubilee of the abbey he mentioned the title of Coadjutor Bishop of Namur that some had conferred on Dom Marmion.

"May God long preserve this coadjutor to me!" he added. He himself consented, at Dom Columba's request, to come and preach the retreat to the monks of Maredsous in 1918.

Cardinal Mercier had put Dom Marmion into relations with one of his dearest disciples, Msgr Amédée Crooy, who was to be raised to the see of St Eleutherius at Tournai and to die on 27 November 1923. A close union was quickly established between these two interior souls.

A letter of Msgr Crooy to Dom Marmion gives us an idea of this close intercourse that he kept up with him:

> Your book, *Christ the Life of the Soul*, is at present serving to facilitate my prayer, and thanks to God, it helps me to come nearer to Him. It is in this way that the contact in which the Divine Master has placed our souls is continued afar off, and I have only one desire: it is to come to spend a few days with you. At this moment especially my soul is so weary, it often needs a very big effort to do the least thing. Happily your good book helps me to find in Jesus the strength so specially necessary to those who have charge of directing others.
>
> Have the charity, too, to ask Him to make the Bishop of Tournai equal to the charge of which he feels himself so unworthy. If your Reverence will allow me, I hope to come before long to be edified at Maredsous. It would be a joy for my soul to see you again. In Jesus I am all yours.
>
> Amédée Marie. *Évêque de Tournai*.
>
> 27 January 1919.[1]

Among those who, beyond the boundaries of his adopted country, honoured Dom Marmion with their friendship figures His Excellency Francis Cardinal Bourne. The Primate of England held him in

---

[1] And several months later, on July 25th: "I am using *Christ in His Mysteries* to nourish my soul in my daily meditation. You do me good. Thank you! I hope that in a short time I shall be allowed to come to see you and talk quite intimately with your Reverence of this Jesus whom I want so much to love with all my heart, In union of prayers, I like to say to myself: All yours in our Lord. ✠ Am. M. *Évêque de Tournai*."

veneration and invited him more than once to preach the retreat to his clergy. In the preface he wrote for the English edition of *Christ the Life of the Soul,* he testifies to the esteem in which he held the teaching he had often had the opportunity of appreciating. After having recalled the approbation of the Sovereign Pontiff Benedict XV and that of Cardinal Mercier, Cardinal Bourne adds: "I very gladly advise all those who seek in the English language a work that will surely help and guide them on the path of closer union with their Maker to read and study this translation of the extremely valuable treatise which is the outcome of long thought and labour on the part of the Abbot of Maredsous. Those who have been privileged to make retreats under his guidance will know what to expect from his pen, and they will not suffer disappointment."

Yet other friendships of Dom Marmion must be mentioned: such as that of Msgr Peter Amigo, Bishop of Southwark, who showed the Abbot of Maredsous particular and most confidential affection; and that of Archbishop Alban Goodier, SJ, then of Bombay, who kept up the most intimate correspondence with him.[1]

To these names must be added those of Msgr Paulin Ladeuze, rector of *l'Université de Louvain,* and since Bishop of Tiberias; the venerated president of the *Collège américain de Louvain,* Msgr Jules de Becker; and many other personalities. Dom Marmion's great heart, his absolute self-forgetfulness, his boundless devotedness, had made for him a large circle of friends, and the misfortune of those who possess such a number of friends is that they have to relinquish the attempt to count them.

What we may gather up and lay stress upon, in this as in all that concerns Dom Marmion, is the supernatural principle on which his friendships rested and to which they owed their unfailing faithfulness. The following extract from one of his letters clearly brings out this point:

It is a long time since I heard from you, or you from me.

---

[1] Dom Marmion greatly appreciated Archbishop Goodier's opuscule *A More Excellent Way.*

Friendship founded on God is independent of time or distance, for it partakes somehow of God's own eternity, and so I have no fear that your friendship for me has in any way changed or diminished. Mine has not in any case. For that place which I have given you in my heart is ever yours, and you accompany me daily to the altar where we meet in that *Communion* of which Jesus is the centre and the bond.

And in regard to one of those incidents which almost inevitably arise and sometimes put the most noble friendships to the test, he writes to one of his friends: "This little incident shows us that the devil will never manage to destroy that union which God established between our souls, for we are too straightforward, too true in our mutual relations for any misunderstanding to be able to subsist. Nothing remains of this incident except that the security of our union in God is made stronger than ever."[1]

---

[1] Letter of 26 April 1918.

DOM PIE DE HEMPTINNE

13 A SPIRITUAL SON OF ABBOT MARMION: DOM PIE DE HEMPTINNE

In October 1922, as we have said, Maredsous Abbey celebrated its golden jubilee. At the fraternal agape that followed the religious ceremonies Cardinal Mercier, referring to the past history of the monastery, recalled the memory of several of those who had especially embalmed the cloister with the perfume of their virtues. Among them the eminent prelate signalled out the angelic figure of Dom Pie de Hemptinne as revealed by his writings, and declared before the numerous guests that this young monk's beatification merited to be introduced at Rome.

None of those who had lived in intimacy with Dom Pie or had simply come in touch with his work felt surprised by these words of the holy cardinal. But discretion had forbidden the Primate of Belgium – speaking as he was in the presence of Dom Marmion – to mention one important point – namely, that it was in the school of the latter that Dom Pie had been formed to the inner life.

We have seen what a life-giving doctrine Dom Marmion gave to souls. This doctrine contains in itself all the qualities calculated to ensure its supernatural efficacy.

In an autograph letter which His Holiness Benedict xv deigned to address to the author of *Christ the Life of the Soul,* he said: "Having recently perused, as far as our occupations permitted, the two books which you have kindly sent us, we readily appreciate their praiseworthiness as being singularly conducive to excite and maintain the flame of divine love in the soul." And His Holiness continued to point out how the teaching there set forth "concerning Jesus Christ, the exemplar and cause of all sanctity ... is capable of fostering the desire to imitate Christ and to live by Him 'who of God is made unto us wisdom, and justice and sanctification and redemption.'"

Such exalted testimony suffices to commend this teaching. Nevertheless, should we not be glad to see its value fully demonstrated and to grasp what its repercussions would be in a concrete and living example? This is exactly what is to be found in the case of Dom Pie;[1] indeed, the chief characteristic of this life was an immense love of Christ going as far as the utter gift of self, as far as complete sacrifice, as far as the joyous acceptance of every suffering.

Let us, then, stay some minutes to sketch the outlines of the life of this son of Dom Marmion. It will be, moreover, an easy matter, thanks to the private notes left by Dom Pie himself in his spiritual writings published under the title: *Une âme bénédictine*. "The memoir of a life all too short but very harmonious and full," wrote Fr Henri Brémond, a rather exacting critic, "this book deserves to be meditated upon slowly. Nothing resembling the loquacious poverty, the cheap sentimentality of so many an analogous collection, either in the biographical introduction written with a simplicity and an emotion perhaps too fearful of letting itself be seen, or in Dom Pie's spiritual notes. In truth ... some of the phrases such as those we have of his are at first sight nothing beyond the ordinary. Other writers have employed them, but with him there is something – I know not what – very searching and very sure, making us feel that the expression is far surpassed by the experience itself. Always true to its depths, the soul is seen gently and in serious earnest being won over by divine love. It is this which makes the book so interesting and so illuminating."[2]

Dom Pie's writings have besides afforded a clue to his biographer[3] enabling him with delicate discernment to follow the trend

---

[1] It is true that none of Dom Marmion's works had yet appeared when he took the direction of Dom Pie's soul (1900), but even before that date Dom Marmion was fully in possession of his ascetical doctrine, and the conferences of the retreat of 1900, which gave the impulse to the higher spiritual life of the young monk, are precisely those which were later to develop into *Christ the Life of the Soul*. Chronologically, this chapter ought to come after the period when Dom Marmion was at Louvain but we have preferred to place it in its logical connection with the chapter on spiritual direction.

[2] *Annales de philosophie chrétienne*, T. 158.

[3] Dom Pie's own brother, Dom Jean de Hemptinne, monk of Maredsous, at present apostolic prefect at Katanga (Congo Belge).

of these upliftings of the soul to God. We scarcely need repeat or emphasise the fact that the reader will find again and again under Dom Pie's pen the faithful echo of Dom Marmion's spirituality.

The son of a former pontifical *zouave*, Yvan de Hemptinne possessed an inestimable jewel from his cradle: this was more than a great military, political, or literary name, it was the precious pearl of the Gospel, the purest supernatural ideal. His childhood was passed in a patriarchal household and was seen ever to tend towards God. An old aunt characterised the whole psychology of her nephew in these rather strong terms: "That child breathes out the good God."

Placed at the *Collège Saint-Benoît de Maredsous*, Yvan there felt an attraction for the cloister, where he sought above all "a place where it would be easy to love," and as soon as he had ended his studies at the college he entered the novitiate.

His first monastic formation was given him by that rugged manipulator of souls, Dom Benoît,[1] who hammered away on the golden anvil of the *Rule* at the refractory ego until a malleable and ductile metal was produced. Dom Pie pronounced his religious vows on 21 March 1899, on the feast of St Benedict. Nevertheless, despite his docility, the young monk remained, even after his profession and until the end of his course of philosophy, inwardly ill at ease; he was conscious of a false restraint; success did not attend his efforts. In the spiritual atmosphere surrounding him at that period Brother Pie seems to have felt cramped – something was lacking to him. But in spite of this trial, his generosity was still absolute:

"Let us do everything with the aim of pleasing God, cost us what it may; let us make a brave fight and keep our eyes open to learn the Divine Will.... Let us hold our hearts in readiness to receive light in every place and at each moment; let us strengthen our will, without ever letting it slacken. Let us be very faithful, and we shall live."

In fact, his faithfulness and confidence did not fail him: God prepared his soul to soar high.

[1] See p. 52.

In September 1900, Dom Marmion preached the retreat at Maredsous; with glowing conviction he revealed to his hearers all the riches of the mystery of Christ.

The light of life that Brother Pie had awaited now shone upon his eyes; a new path was opened out before him. Full of joy and confidence, he went and threw himself at Dom Marmion's feet. "I surrendered myself utterly into his hands," he writes, "and I asked him to give me that divine love which alone can fill our souls."

He felt himself in the presence of one who in the order of grace was to be his true Father.

Looking into the heart that had just given itself to him, Dom Columba could not withhold a cry of admiration: "The more one knows of this dear lad, the more one loves him. Divine wisdom dwells in his pure soul; his prudence astonishes me and the freshness of his affection delights me."

From that moment Brother Pie was, as it were, captured by grace and drawn along in a course of holy folly till his strength utterly failed him; or rather, it was that his wings were at last unfolded to their full extent, and there began for his soul that undaunted flight through regions of divine love, which in seven years was to bear him away to heaven.

Novel reading has accustomed our present generation to psychology. Many have a passion for fictitious soul-tragedies. Nothing, however, attracts like the real drama of the wooing of a generous soul by divine love. Dom Pie gives us that wonderful spectacle of which Fr Columba was to be not only the first beholder, but the quickening spirit. The history of this soul is the record of those daily and mysterious invasions of eternal love until the total conquest is gained.

The very day after his meeting with Dom Marmion, Brother Pie wrote the first lines in the *Carnet du bon Dieu*, which lays open his soul's innermost sanctuary and takes us into an altogether mystic sphere. It is the heart speaking, the heart alone with its beloved, never growing weary of repeating the song of love.

A SPIRITUAL SON OF ABBOT MARMION:

"O Jesus, I surrender myself into Your arms, as the Holy Spirit directs me; do with me all that You will, either directly or through my superiors or my brothers, and I will try to *obey perfectly*. I will do everything, O Love, not to place any obstacle to your action."

In these lines, where Brother Pie lays down the plan he resolved to carry out, is found again the whole essential of Dom Marmion's direction: "Fidelity is the most delicate flower of love to which nothing is little."

A year later, on 12 October 1900, Dom Pie, with a group of young confrères, set out for the Abbey of Mont-César at Louvain; he was to spend four years there studying theology under Dom Columba's direction.

In this school, of which we have already noted the distinctive spirit,[1] the intellectual bent of the young monk was to be clearly defined: he was to take his stand in the realms of the ascetic. With mind widely open to a variety of interests, he yet made all converge to the science of the saints; the problem that captivated him and on which he concentrated all the powers of his heart and mind was that of perfection. Apart from this absorbing question, he writes – echoing the words of his master – "theology itself is nothing more than a metaphysical science very apt to dry up the soul."

Dom Pie especially drank in the spiritual teaching then being given to him in such rich abundance. None amongst Dom Columba's disciples could better grasp and carry out his direction; it might be said that at twenty-two years of age he already possessed its

---

[1] See p. 137. During part of his stay at Louvain, Dom Pie was charged to draw up the annals of the monastery. In 1903 we come across this item: "The *clericat* numbers twenty members. Dom Columba the Prior, presides over them as prefect and wonderfully inspires them with real monastic piety and his direction is full of that confidence and holy liberty which love of Christ gives. His jovial character keeps up a great spirit of joy and there is not one but seeks God gaily and willingly. He himself teaches dogmatic theology. Life flows on very happily, although sometimes one feels the fatigue of the well-filled days.

whole gist; he condensed in his notes the leading ideas which were to be a light for him throughout his life.

> God is love. The love which our Heavenly Father bears to us is the primary cause of our sanctification. The whole question of the dealings between God and man is a question of friendship.
>
> To cast fire upon the earth, to give the Holy Spirit, the Word became Incarnate; Christ is the necessary sacrament of the mystical alliance.
>
> I have learnt that Jesus is for us the sum-total of everything. The desire to possess Him is the one and only prayer which should find utterance in the soul, because all others naturally flow from that, as all heavenly blessings naturally flow from Jesus Himself.

The soul's whole endeavour in presence of Jesus and His Spirit should be to aim at not paralysing the energies of grace, but at corresponding actively and faithfully to them. Dom Pie speaks of the infinite delicacy of this adaptation to the Divine Action, and of the care necessary to protect "the spark enkindled in the soul."

Inundated with light, he at the same time gives full vent to love.

> Man's *raison d'être* is to love; his one need is to love; his only strength, his sole joy is to love. But it is to love You, O my God, that man exists; the need that urges him is Your love; he becomes strong in loving You: the rest he takes in You alone gives him joy. Therefore he does not give up seeking until he finds himself forever lost in You, O uncreated love. A nature without love is a springtime without sunshine.... Jesus has decided for me that He will never give me anything else to do except to love.
>
> I am resolved to be converted to the love of Christ. I am indifferent to all else; I wish to love Him madly; men may break and crush my will and understanding, all that you will,

but I do not intend to let go of the sole good, our Divine Jesus, or rather I feel that it is He who will not let go of me.

Brother Pie's soul vibrated beneath the hand of God who possessed, stimulated and sustained him; he was wrought upon by a mysterious and powerful action. God dwelt in him. Closing his eyes to outward things, Dom Pie's inward gaze was full of faith; he enjoyed a vision surpassing the wonders of nature: "It is Yourself, O infinite beauty," he writes, "that my soul contemplates; it is You, O devouring love, who draws and captivates it in the bonds of incomparable charity."

Plunged in the silence and recollection of self-surrender, he communes with the Blessed Trinity, with Christ, with the Blessed Virgin, constant guests in the sanctuary of his soul, where he leads an intense and hidden life. The *Notebook of the Good God* contains some fragments of these heavenly communings, pale reflections of an ideal love whereof human words can give no true idea.

The twofold character presented by the young monk's love of God at this period is a further proof of its reality – namely, its efficacy to purify the soul and its extreme delicacy. Dom Pie tells us himself that he "had a silly habit of dogmatising on everything. It will need very serious efforts," he added, "to get rid of this wretched habit, for it is rooted in a wicked nature." He wanted with all his heart to have in his dealings with others that love and attention with which he would have tried to act towards Jesus Himself." These serious efforts were not likely to dismay his generosity; he strove and, moreover, successfully, to attain what he wanted. Dom Marmion was presently able to say jokingly to Dom Pie's mother: "Your son was born with the tiara; he now wears only the mitre."

This was still too much; he knew how to rid himself of it.

Dom Pie also learnt by several experiences that the Divine Action in the soul is infinitely delicate. God is jealous of consecrated hearts, and a too natural impulse is enough to wound divine friendship: "The apprenticeship of love," he was yet to write, "requires the soul's constant attention to the pursuit of its end."

In the lives of great souls we come across a mysterious turning-point where love, after having set them free from the world and from themselves, becomes their cruel and happy torment: "the thirst of loving is their uninterrupted suffering."

Dom Pie was to meet with this suffering which, according to his own expression, "spread over his soul like burning liquid on an open wound." He felt torn asunder by the infinite good which was drawing him with irresistible force and at the same time was hidden from him in the cloud of faith: "My God," he cries, "you have given me a heart of fire which unceasingly tortures me either by the excess of its yearnings towards You or by the privation of Your presence."

These spiritual tortures increased in proportion as he came nearer to the object of his desires; he was painfully oppressed by them. In that dark night his soul yet resolutely clung to the divine good pleasure: "I know not what God has in store for me, nevertheless I beg Him to make me attain to true love, however arid may be the way that leads to it."

The pronouncing of his solemn vows on 4 March 1902, may be considered as the beginning of the sufferings that encompassed all the remainder of Dom Pie's life. About this time he had the impression that the progress he had already made was as nothing in comparison with what he had yet to make, and that, on this higher plane, man no longer walks, he is carried by God; he seems to have gone as far as he could go; he had sacrificed all, "and yet he feels that he still does not love."

> When we have given all to You, O my God, and when the soul seeks in vain for something more to give You; when Your divine charity has melted the ice of our selfishness; when we believe we have done everything, or at least, have left nothing undone whereby to gain Your holy love and when we think we love much, then only is it given to us to see that we are but beginning to love.
>
> O Jesus, You have taught me to desire; fulfil now my souls

one desire. You stir up in me hunger and thirst for Your divine love; but when, Lord, will You satisfy my heart?

O my God, is it not time to touch my soul and enkindle in it the fire of love, for I no longer know what to give You, and I feel that I still do not love You!

From that moment Dom Pie's life underwent an essential change. Outwardly, this was scarcely perceptible; there was ever the same recollection, the same charity, the same regularity of observance. But his private notes and letters bear witness to this mystical evolution. Dom Pie enters with rapid strides into the solitude of God, he exults, he suffers: "When love finds its way into a generous soul, and asks for everything, one thing after another, until it is entirely emptied of all... the soul then learns its utter powerlessness, but it begins to feel strong in God."

So he could let this cry escape him: "Strong soul, let suffering, then, penetrate thine inmost recesses; drink of this life-giving wine and lose not one drop of it. And if at times thou art inundated with suffering, if thou art able to slake thy thirst with that generous patience that preserves deep peace in the heart, thou shalt learn the sweetness of suffering, for its bitterness is changed into mysterious delight only at the moment when the soul tastes all its gall."

Interior solitude grows deeper and deeper; the soul feels dismayed and pines with long waiting:

When, then, good Jesus, is to arise for my soul, that day a thousand times longed for and blest, when You will manifest Yourself, when You will take possession of a heart which belongs to You? I cannot think that this day is still very far off, for the intensity of my longing tells me of its near approach. However, the waiting is long... my beloved and merciful Saviour! I know that from the moment You take possession of my soul Your love will torture me unmercifully; I am not unaware of the searching depths of this divine suffering; yet I tend to it with all the energy of my being....

To these bitter trials were added temptations and troubles which stirred him deeply; waters of affliction gathered in his soul.

"The sky is black; no star guides his course; his passions, like the countless waves, lift him on their high crests that they may cast him down again and again into frightful abysses from whence they draw him only to fling him back once more. Scarcely does he find any remaining strength of will wherewith to overcome and hold back this revolt of his whole self that it may not overpass the limits of God's law."

In spite of everything, his sole desire for God ever grew the greater; suffering became for his soul a condition of growth, an essential element of his vocation. Dom Pie is happy to have left the world that he "may run in the path of great love."

Soon ordination to the priesthood placed the seal on this mysterious work, making his soul share even more in the sacrifice than in the Priesthood of Christ: "To become a priest is to be chosen by the Holy Spirit to follow Jesus Christ to His agony and to Calvary.... The priest filled with the spirit of his state is a man of sorrows; he bears the burden of souls; that is to say, their griefs, their miseries, their sins."[1]

For him, indeed, the priesthood was to be the power of bearing the cross with Christ.

The day after his ordination he writes: "My blessed Saviour, now that I am a priest I feel much more keenly the extreme misery of my sinful soul.... It seems to me, beloved Master, that You wish to plant and nourish it in the solid ground of suffering. Do so, but sustain my weakness...."

This entirely mystical life was shortly to be joined to one of a more active character. A year after his ordination Dom Pie was placed at the *Collège Saint-Benoît de Maredsous* as prefect. To this turning-point of his life is attached a twofold interest for those who have followed the ascending course traced by his generous soul.

---

1 See also *Une âme bénédictine*, Pensées LXXXI.

What was to become of the monk thrown into this noisy arena, far from the master who had guided him up to that day? What was to become of this adorer lost to earthly things in his choir stall, offering himself at the altar with Christ, this solitary wrapped in contemplation in his beloved cell? Would not the perfume of this double sanctuary be allowed to evaporate in the inevitable turmoil of a college? If the one Divine Object continued to subjugate him, what would become of his supervision over his pupils? And how easily all this turbulent boyhood might escape the vigilance of eyes lost in distant visions!

Quite the contrary befell. In this life of his everything wonderfully harmonised: creator and creatures, contemplation and action, under the law of obedient and triumphant love. It was soon proved that Dom Pie was an unparalleled teacher, that his zeal embraced everything, neglecting nothing, and that he gained an unexpected and irresistible influence over these young souls. The secret of the union of the active and contemplative life in him was that he acted in concert with Christ: a simple and single movement drawing him towards Christ set the seal of unity on the multiplicity of his functions and revealed the underlying principles of his whole existence.

Under the diversity of his activities Dom Pie's hidden life remained in fact the same. He wrote to his holy mother in May 1906:

> When we strive to lead an active life of which the centre and principal movements abide in the innermost soul, oh, then how often things change their aspect! The tendency towards good possesses, in one and the same soul, so great a variety that never, as it were, do we find ourselves again in the same dispositions through which we have already passed. And yet this one and very simple turning towards God, taking an ever greater and greater hold on the soul, disperses the multiplicity of other thoughts and feelings: it sums up the whole life and reduces it to its most simple expression. It is truly in this wonderful simplicity that we find that unchanging happiness which, however old it may be, is revealed to us under ever

new aspects. These ideas make a strong impression on me. I find in them the explanation of my happiness and the powerlessness of my words. One word suffices to say everything; you well understand what this word is, this desire that God alone places in the heart and on the lips....

Surprising contrast! It was almost at the very time he wrote this letter that Dom Pie jotted down the following lines in his *Notebook:*

I am working hard, perhaps harder than I can do normally. They tell me I am doing good, and this reaches me from different quartets. Nevertheless, this appreciation does not touch my soul. Thou Thyself, my God, dost show me so clearly the nothingness of what I do and the unpardonable negligence with which I do this nothing, that for the moment I want to weep. I feel terribly overwhelmed and good-for-nothing in God's sight. I believe that God is preparing for me a still greater and more crushing trial, and this not only in my inward consciousness, but in the sight of men. As it appears to me, this crushing trial will be hard and terrible.

Dom Pie was tossed about between joy and suffering. Even physically he showed this twofold state of soul. Although only twenty-six years old, the last years had remarkably aged him. His mother, who had come to see him, was quite struck by this; she no longer saw in her son that freshness and youthfulness she had been accustomed to find in him; but in his countenance and his eyes she read heavenly things; she marvelled at a beauty that was to be without decline.

A page of the *Notebook of the Good God,* entitled "Great Graces," sets before our eyes the memorable dates of Dom Pie's life, or rather the long succession of divine favours whereof he was the object. It ends with this entry: "Haemorrhage, 27 June 1906." On the evening of that day Dom Pie had just finished seeing his pupils off to bed and had withdrawn to his little room at the end of the dormitory, when suddenly stooping down, he was seized with a violent haemorrhage. Nevertheless, overwrought as he was, he kept silence until next day, when he was still able to go to the altar.

Obliged to declare his state, Dom Pie was at once sent to the infirmary of the abbey, but he kept his peace of soul: "I rest so entirely in Your hands, my Divine Master, that I do not want to concern myself with what is to be decided about me, nor with what is to befall me. May my love for You, my beloved, feeble though it be, turn all things to my good; that is to say, to Your glory in me."

That Mass of June 28th was to be his last. The deprivation of the Holy Sacrifice marked the first stage of the work of despoilment that death had taken in hand.

On July 3rd Dom Pie was taken home to his parents; the hope of a more speedy cure, which might allow him to take up his charge at the college in the month of October, was the reason of this change.

Now that he was at home again Dom Pie felt himself an exile from his monastery and jotted down on a scrap of paper these lines of sorrowful ardour inspired by the Psalmist: "As the water-brooks flow into the valleys, as the flower raises its head to the light, as the timid hart seeks the deepest solitudes, so, O Lord, my soul ever pours itself out in Thee; that ceaselessly it may be satisfied with Thy splendour, that it may plunge and be forever lost in the divine solitudes that Thy presence creates within it: *Ecce elongavi fugiens et mansi in solitudine.*"

After mature examination, the doctors declared it to be a case of serious congestion of the lungs, and prescribed that their patient must remain lying on his back. He was put to bed, and there he was to spend six long months until the day when his soul, rending its frail bonds, took its flight to heaven.

Dom Pie sent for his theological treatises, his dear treatises from which he had already derived such profit at Louvain under Dom Columba's direction. On the threshold of eternity it might be said that he savoured more than ever those mysterious dogmas of which he was soon to contemplate the glorious reality. He assiduously read the Holy Scriptures; the best spiritual authors: St Augustine,

St Jerome, St Gertrude, and St Mechtilde, for whom he had a great devotion. St Teresa of Ávila and St Francis de Sales succeeded one another at his bedside. Often whilst reading he became absorbed in prayer, his hands joined, his face lit up with heavenly serenity. The two infirmarians who nursed him both declared they had never seen anyone pray as he did, and they found great help in their talks with their patient.

The time passed between recurring attacks and respites, but all hope vanished of any return to Maredsous to take up his classes again: one more link to be broken, one more sacrifice. More than ever after six months of illness Dom Pie felt that: "Nothing, neither place, nor occupation, nor person nor anything can content or fill the heart save the love of God and the neighbour."

Through the casements of his room he saw the sun, the rain, the snowstorm, succeed one another, whilst none of them could reach him. And the thought came to him that it is thus with the soul fixed in God's love and peace, with regard to the world's vicissitudes. Earth slipped farther and farther away from him; not only its vanities and its attractions, but with all that it can offer that is most holy: the august Sacrifice of the Mass, the monastery, the activity of obedience and the joys of devotedness. Only two things remained to him: "A devouring need of possessing God, and the sense of being nothing in the sight of the Divine Majesty."

For years past this twofold disposition fostered in him by Dom Marmion had ever been increasing; the supreme trial brought it out still more strongly.

If we are to believe the last pages of the *Notebook*, Dom Pie on his bed of pain was assailed by temptations more grievous to bear than his bodily sufferings.

In all his life he had never committed any grave sin, but it did not need as much as that to alarm him. At the thought that he had perhaps offended his God he was oppressed with grief, his heart sank, his eyes filled with tears: "Believe me, I am not speaking to you as if I were just a novice, but with my heart weighed down, justly acknowledging my true state. This humility is forced upon me by facts: so many miseries would make me unsupportable to anyone who saw them."

He was therefore not surprised at the dryness in which God left him. On 5 December 1906, he wrote a long letter in pencil to Dom Columba;[1] we quote the principal passage, where again we find the master in the disciple:

> I am in nowise astonished that the Divine Master does not yet open His Heart to me; I very sincerely feel myself altogether unworthy, and this feeling keeps me in great peace.
>
> My soul tastes no consolation, my sins are ever before my eyes, and yet I have no other desire than Christ. I would suffer all my life if God so willed. But when will that one come for whom we suffer and after whom the soul sighs unceasingly? God gives me courage, peace, compunction; when will He give me Jesus?
>
> I pour out into your heart these thoughts which ever press hard upon me and pursue me. After all, I find no reply except in self-abandonment....

Finally, on 1 January 1907, Dom Pie opened for the last time his collection of *Pensées* to write in it these touching words: "Here upon earth the great mysteries of love are deep abysses of suffering. Love, in the soul, only becomes truly a mystery on the day when it probes the deepest recesses, and without painful burning the sacred fire does not reach these depths."

At the hour when he traced these final lines he was already at death's door. A serious complication had just arisen: a keen-sighted doctor pronounced beneath his breath the word meningitis; events were to confirm the prognostication.

On January 12th, Dom Pie fell into a state of lethargy and prostration. Violent headaches, frequent sickness and other symptoms caused it to be feared that in a few hours he would be in a state of

---

1 The original of this letter is unhappily lost.

unconsciousness. The same evening Dom Pie received the last sacraments with great devotion, at the hands of his brother. Holding his crucifix, he kissed the Saviour's wounds and drew from them that generous wine of which he had been so long deprived: "It is," he said, "as when I drink of the chalice of the Precious Blood."

Dom Columba was able to go to him, writing on 16 January 1907, to one of his spiritual daughters, a relative of Dom Pie:

> Yesterday, during the thanksgiving, I asked our Lord, if He so willed, to send me here to Bockrijck to see the dear patient.[1] The Right Reverend Father Abbot told me of his own accord to go there. To tell you frankly my opinion, I think we shall lose our dear Dom Pie. Unless our Lord works a miracle I think the malady is gaining the upper hand. However, *nondum statim finis*. Yesterday I gave him the blessing of St Maurus on the feast of that saint, and this morning Holy Communion. Dom Pie is suffering *greatly* in his whole body, but especially in his head; meningitis is feared. He was so happy so see me. He is wonderful in his patience and submission, but without a ray of consolation or sense of God. He is a saintly soul.
>
> I am happy to be here with Dom Jean.[2] The cross is the root of all fecundity. We have got this cross. *Deo gratias!*
>
> Truly yours in the love of Jesus Christ.

Six days passed by in great suffering. At times the dying monk said aloud, all unwittingly, what he had at heart; he spoke out of its abundance and revealed his beautiful soul, to the great edification of those around him. On a certain day, for instance, someone remarked to him that the Church was celebrating the feast of the Holy Name of Jesus. "Intimacy with our Lord, that is what is very necessary for us…. We need to always live with Him…. Too often this intimacy is represented in a sugary, insipid manner; our devotion ought to be sincere; we must unite ourselves to Christ by vigorous and altogether spiritual faith."

[1] Dom Columba was then prior at Louvain.
[2] Dom Pie's brother and, like him, a monk.

Then after a short silence, he added: "When a soul is united to our Lord, our Lord pursues it; He persecutes it in order to possess it. How I have felt that!…"

Love at length triumphant, was about to fall upon its prey.

Dom Pie was, however, to have again the consolation of seeing Dom Marmion.

"Yesterday, writes Dom Columba, on January 22nd, "I received a telegram from Dom Jean, begging me to return here. I thought it my duty to come, for Dom Pie being by obedience outside his monastery, has a right to every care and spiritual consolation we can give him. His bodily powers are rapidly failing him, but his soul is in God's hands. He had some moments of consciousness yesterday, and I was very well able to confess him. The paralysis extends to his whole organism; he is slowly sinking."

On January 24th, after the doctor's visit, Dom Pie suffered much physical distress and was aware that he was nearing his last hour: "I feel so truly," he said, "that all this is beyond one's own control!"

Then raising himself, he slowly uttered these words: *"Quae placita sunt tibi, volo semper facere."*[1]

No one understood at the time the true bearing of these words to which Dom Pie seemed to attach so much importance, but later on the act giving the explanation was found: that short formula, inspired by the words of Jesus and so dear to Dom Marmion, was his renewal of the immolation of religious profession.

On Septuagesima Sunday, 27 January 1907, three bad attacks, complicated by internal haemorrhage, occurred at short intervals. About ten o'clock in the morning, after the prayers for the dying, Dom Pie twice raised his head and then quietly expired.

The same day Dom Marmion wrote this note to one of Dom Pie's relations:

> *Justus germinabit sicut lilium et florebit in aeternum ante Dominum.*[2] The Divine Spouse who 'feeds among the lilies' has

[1] I want to do always what is pleasing to You.
[2] "The just shall spring up like the lily and flourish eternally in the sight of the Lord."

taken our dear Dom Pie, a very beautiful soul, pure and loving, still more purified by long and cruel suffering, and that without consolation or any sense of God's presence. I am sure that he will be very powerful in heaven! It is a terrible blow for us all. These trials detach us from earth and fix our hearts *ubi vera sunt gaudia*.[1]

The disciple had shown himself worthy of the master.
Soon after Dom Columba's death it could be written in all truth: "Had Dom Marmion done only that – given a saint to the cloister – it would have been enough for his honour and glory."[2]

If the soul of the young monk has afforded us the spectacle of spiritual heights surely and speedily attained, it is because he had entirely understood and perfectly lived the mystery of Christ as revealed to him by Dom Marmion. *Une âme bénédictine* is the adequate and touching illustration of *Christ the Life of the Soul*, and of *Christ the Ideal of the Monk*.

At the crossroads of the spiritual life Providence had brought about the meeting of Dom Columba and Dom Pie: their names, like their souls, are henceforth inseparable.

---

[1] "Where true joys are to be found" (Collect for the Fourth Sunday after Easter). When the Life of Dom Pie appeared, Dom Marmion wrote to Primate Dom Hildebrand: "The *Life* of the dear Fr Pie has done me so much good; it is very well done and brings before our eyes the living image of one whom I loved greatly in Jesus Christ" (Letter of 29 January 1912).
[2] Msgr Joseph Schyrgens, *Revue générale*, February 1923.

14 CHRIST'S APOSTLE

Cardinal Mercier and Dom Pie de Hemptinne rank first among those spiritually directed by Dom Marmion. But Dom Marmion's zeal excluded none from the benefit of his wide charity. For he was an apostle of unwearying zeal; that was one of the most salient traits of his character and it is fitting to dwell upon it here.

Dom Marmion wrote with great justness: "The soul that truly loves God is enkindled with holy zeal for the interests of His glory, for the extension of Christ's Kingdom in hearts; it burns with that fire which Jesus Christ came to cast upon the earth and so ardently desires to see kindled within us."

And he gives the definition of zeal: "A divine ardour which burns and is communicated; that consumes and is spread abroad."[1]

From his youth upwards Dom Marmion had felt this ardour enkindled in his soul; he therefore took delight in reading the letters of St Francis Xavier;[2] the incident in the life of that great apostle where he is to be seen making himself an ordinary merchant to enable him to enter Japan and there to preach Christ filled him with enthusiasm; he would gladly have done the same. We may recall how, when a young student at Rome, he had dreamed of going to evangelise Australia under the direction of the great Benedictine missionary, Msgr Rosendo Salvado. But Providence had other fields of action in store for him. At Dublin, then at Maredsous as a simple monk, and again at Louvain, he spent himself without counting the cost in the very wide measure granted him by obedience. On becoming abbot he saw the field of his zeal extend still further.

We do not intend to sketch here a complete picture of Dom Columba's apostolic zeal, but only to find the mainspring of his zeal and to give a more distinct idea of what his ministry was.

---

[1] *Christ the Ideal of the Monk*, conference, "Good Zeal."
[2] "He read and re-read them; moreover, he got others to read them, finding these letters well qualified to stir up apostolic zeal.

Because he was near to God Dom Marmion was near to souls, and when he came in contact with them he was at the same time full of divine charity and of the milk of human kindness. Only saints know how to love. And that is the secret of their influence. "The saints have, in fact, a way of speaking to others which stretches out arms to every misfortune, adopts all distress, restores dignity to the fallen; they have a way of not thinking of themselves, and of creating a void in their souls emptied of self which opens out abysses of disinterestedness where our miseries may be engulfed. They act less by what they do than by what they are; it is their radiating charity which urges us on even into the arms of Christ. They are irresistible, like omnipotence, because they have become, in the image of God, pure love."[1]

St Bruno, the austere founder of the Carthusians, called those men "divine" in whom kindness dwells. Dom Marmion was one of those. Indeed, where souls were concerned, his kindness was unwearying; he had the understanding, the will, the taste for kindness. The goodness and kindness and mercy of His Divine Master appeared in him.

And this goodness and kindness was extended to all. According to the picturesque expression of an intimate friend of Cardinal

---

1 Dom Bonaventure Sodar, *Une mystique bénédictine du xviie siècle, confidente du Sacré-Cœur, la mère Jeanne Delaloe.* Introduction. The author justly adds, "He who has no fellowship with the saints lives solitary upon earth; he who is not attracted by them knows not the worth of friendship. He who wishes to know himself and learn more than ancient wisdom can teach him, should yield to their attraction. Far better than any analysis or study, their sympathy reveals to us our own soul. Whilst our restless heart longs to experience the mystic joys, the struggles and triumphs of fair love, let us remember that never was love sung, wept and lived as by these heroes.... It is not prudent to enter alone upon the rugged paths of perfection: lest we stumble we must put our hand in theirs; for fear of falling we must think of their holy enthusiasm and forget our weariness, and if we would not go astray we must follow in the track of those flaming torches which in the chaos of this vain and empty world *inanis et vacua*, throw their beacon light upon the high way of salvation and make order and security to reign."

Mercier, "Dom Marmion had a heart as big as a cathedral."[1] It should be added that this cathedral always remained open and that, in its sanctuary, the lamp was never extinguished.

Whoever came to him, and under whatever circumstances, Dom Marmion put himself at that one's disposal as if none other existed. He saw only that one soul, and in that soul he saw only Christ. He made no distinctions of persons; like St Paul, he acknowledged himself the debtor of all: *Omnium debitor sum;*[2] according to his usual expression, "he let himself be eaten" by every soul hungering for light and peace. He made himself all to all – "a Jew to the Jews, a Greek to the Greeks" – according to the expression of the great apostle. Not that he cut down the exigencies of his faith, but he widened his compassion. In this domain perhaps nothing is so remarkable in him as that ease, innate as it were but supernaturalised by virtue, with which he adapted himself to each and all in order to gain them to God.

Extended to all, his kindness took every shape and form. "Never," writes a superior who had known him for long years, "did he depress a soul by bitter reproaches; never did anyone come away from him discouraged or humiliated. He certainly made them see the light of truth, but the rays of kindness prepared the way for this light to reach them and softened and fructified it."

Especially, wherever he found trouble or sadness, Dom Marmion was resourceful, ingenious. Once he was on the point of setting out on a long journey. Someone sent him word of the distress she was in; at once, of his own accord, he suggested to her that he would alter the arrangements already made for his journey so as to bring her light and help.[3]

The same delicate thoughtfulness in similar circumstances: "I am very pressed for time, having to start tomorrow for Ireland, but I

[1] He had himself jotted down in his notebook (1903) this text of Scripture which had struck him: *Dedit ei (Solomon) Dominus latitudinem cordis quasi arenam in littore maris:* "And God gave to Solomon largeness of heart as the sand that is on the sea shore" (3 Kgs. 4:29).
[2] Rom. 1:14.
[3] Letter of 27 February 1911.

was so glad to receive a word from you that I must write you a few lines. I feel great compassion for you, because you have suffered so much.... It is not forbidden to shrink from such trials. Jesus in the Garden of Olives felt all the anguish of our troubles. I pray for you and should very much like to be able to comfort you."[1]

This kindness was one of his charms and one of his most striking virtues. It is in this kindness giving itself utterly to others without reserve or thought of self that we must look for one of the secrets of his irresistible ascendency over souls. Long months after his death a young Canadian girl wrote these significant lines: "I only spoke once with Dom Marmion, but he left upon me such an impression of supernatural goodness, deep, wide and comprehensive, that all I recall of him brings me nearer to the good God. It is as if the grace that accompanied his presence still clings to his memory."

We may have cause to refer again to this touching testimony.

Whilst still a simple monk at Maredsous, Dom Marmion was begged by a poor woman of very humble state of life – she was in service – to take the direction of her soul – an interior, delicate soul, but inclined to have scruples. Dom Columba directed her with extreme kindness and opened out to her the path of the spiritual life. Treating her truly as if he were her father, he kept in touch with her wherever the chances of life took her, without ever losing sight of her. Grown old and infirm, with no one belonging to her, and without resources, she was able, in 1912, thanks to the material assistance Dom Marmion procured for her, to be admitted into the hospice of *Saint-Servais,* near Namur. Dom Columba had entrusted one of his spiritual daughters in that town to pay a visit sometimes to his dear protégée. "All that you do for H— ," he told her, "is as if you did it for me ... it will make me happy too."

And when he wrote to this spiritual daughter he added "a little word" to give to the sick woman. For his part, during more than ten years, every time he passed through Namur he went to see her. For the poor infirm woman, paralysed from head to foot, blind in one eye, and, at the end of her life, her right side eaten away with

[1] Letter of 31 December 1913.

cancer, how beautiful to see Father Abbot sitting familiarly beside her, bringing her some sweets to console her! Above all, what a joy to hear the great theologian talking to her of heavenly things, with that exquisite simplicity full of the balm of sympathy of which he knew the secret, for she was one of those "little ones" to whom God had revealed the mysteries of His love.

Even priests who knew her wondered at the greatness of her inner life, and were edified by the courage and patience wherewith she bore all trials, offering up everything to our Lord and uniting her painful suffering to the sorrows of Christ on the cross for the salvation of souls.

It is easy to understand that she was inconsolable when Dom Columba died, but Providence shortened this fresh trial; a few months later this simple soul, so united to God, went to contemplate in her turn those mysteries on which, for thirty years, the abbot had nourished her.

If Dom Columba embraced all souls in his solicitude, if he refused himself to none, there were some categories of souls towards whom, after the example of the Divine Master, he felt particularly drawn: priests of God, consecrated virgins and sinners.

Very early in life he had to occupy himself with the chosen portion of those whom Christ deigns to call His friends. At Dinant he gave every month the retreat to the priests of the town and its environments; the same at Louvain, at the theological *Collège du Saint-Esprit*, where his conferences on the virtues of the Sacred Heart – virtues which the priest should imitate – were noteworthy; still later, at Cardinal Mercier's request, to the parish priests and teaching institutes of the capital. On becoming abbot he continued to preach retreats to priests, either at the monastery or at *l'Université de Louvain*, where he was more than once asked to return, or again at Le *grand séminaire*. His strong faith revealed to him in the divine light the high dignity of the priest, and the instructions he gave to the Lord's elect were filled with the purest zeal for their perfection. After reiterated entreaties he consented to put together and to show in *Christ the Ideal of the Priest,* the principles of these numerous conferences. This collection will doubtless one day see the light and once more eloquently testify to the depth of the doctrine he taught and the warmth of his zeal.

In regard to consecrated virgins who form the most delicate and radiant portion of the Divine Shepherd's flock, Dom Columba's zeal was most vigilant and earnest.

The extracts we have given of his spiritual letters show to what a high perfection he invited them. Many were the monasteries and convents that had the good fortune of listening to him at regular intervals; to the Benedictines of Maredret, Liège and Ventnor, must above all be added the Carmelites of Louvain and of Virton (to whom he likewise bore a special affection, for, said he, "like Jacob, I have begotten your Carmel in my old age"); the Canonesses of Jupille, of Lede; the English Convent at Bruges and the priory of Haywards Heath; the Adorers of the Sacred Heart of Tyburn and Koekelberg, without counting Irish convents. The Ladies of the Sacred Heart of Jette, of Linthout, of Antwerp, and of La Haye also had the privilege of listening to his apostolic words.

In this ministry he met with some beautiful souls whom, with a zeal full of charity, he loved to spur on to spiritual heights. We may be allowed to pause here to consider one of them, on whom Dom Marmion himself has left an unpublished notice, pages of a contemporary *Golden Legend,* from which we will mention some characteristic details.

She was named, in the world, Clotilde Clément. Born at Termonde (East Flanders), in 1842, she had been formed to piety from her childhood by a Benedictine monk of that town. She very early felt an attraction for the religious life and entered the Carmel at Louvain, where during more than thirty years she fulfilled the functions of mistress of novices and of prioress. Providence, which had guided her first steps in the interior life through the instrumentality of a son of St Benedict, gave her, in another son of the Patriarch of Monks, a guide to lead her to the consummation of holiness.

Endowed with gifts of a high order, she joined a rare broad-mindedness to great delicacy of conscience. God had granted her abundant gifts. "I have found her," writes Dom Marmion, "very enlightened on divine mysteries and of very sure doctrine."

From her childhood she had felt drawn to beg our Lord unceasingly to make of her His true spouse. After her religious profession her director bade her cease this prayer, since her vows had made her the bride of Christ. In that, adds Dom Marmion, the director was in fault, for there exists a closer union with Jesus than that of profession. Nevertheless, as she was perfect in obedience, she ceased this prayer, but the inward attraction ever remained. Once, during Vespers, she felt overwhelmed with mortal sadness. She asked herself: "Have I perhaps offended my Divine Bridegroom in something?" Suddenly in the depths of her heart she heard a voice saying to her: "My daughter, there are some souls that I lead to the perfection of My love by extraordinary ways; there are others that I lead to the same perfection by ordinary ways. It is by these that it is My will to lead you. Be faithful."

And faithful she was, adds Dom Marmion, and perfectly faithful. She made a vow to accept without resistance all manifestation of the Divine Will, however difficult it was, and never to take joy save in God alone.

Much beloved by her community, she was held in high esteem by the superiors of her order. Fr Étienne Leplat, provincial of the Carmelites, who was knit by close friendship to Dom Marmion[1] declared this Carmelite nun to be the most perfect in his province. "I asked her," writes Dom Marmion, "if all the testimonies of affection and esteem of which she was the object did not arouse some feeling of self-complacency. She replied that she had not known even an involuntary feeling of that kind." A very clear and constant light shining in her soul, writes her biographer, showed her all her nothingness in sight of God's greatness. She saw herself as a tiny atom before His immense majesty. But such an apostle as Dom Marmion could not fail to put such sentiments to the proof. "More than

---

1 See p. 103.

once," he writes – knowing besides with what a chosen soul he had to do – "I reproved her sternly, when she was not expecting it, and in matters which could not fail to touch her, and I always found her humility and serenity greater than the humiliation."

The last years of her life were marked with the cross of long and cruel suffering. During the illness before her death Dom Marmion was authorised to see her twice a week. "She was," he says, "reduced to a state of extreme weakness, her only nourishment during some weeks being a little water. And yet, scarcely did I mention a truth of our Faith than she was filled with love and enthusiasm; the colour rose to her face, which became transfigured, and all trace of weakness seemed to have disappeared. I have many times witnessed this sight.

"Some time before her death she said to me:

"'I am *quite* submissive to God's Holy Will, but I want so much to go to my Divine Spouse! Father Provincial has forbidden me to die. Perhaps you could give me permission?'

"Quite decided to uphold the prohibition of the provincial, I said to her rather sharply:

"'First of all make your confession....'

In the course of her confession I was conscious of a complete and irresistible change of mind. When she had finished her confession, she said to me:

"'*Now,* my Father?'

"'In so far as it depends on me,' I told her, 'I give you permission to go.'

"Transported with joy, she added:

"'And on what day, Father?'"

To such simplicity, which he knew to be that of the children of God, Dom Marmion could not refrain from replying:

"Let us see what feast have we coming soon? The eighth of September, the Nativity of the Blessed Virgin. What a beautiful day that would be."

"Very well, Father." And that was the end of the subject.

Accustomed with a simplicity full of faith to consider the least words of her director as an indication of God's Will, the sick nun lived in joyous expectation of the divine meeting, but she did not confide to anyone the permission received. During those days her life was but one long martyrdom, through which her patience, kindness, serenity and union with God shone out. On September 8th she was still able to receive Holy Communion. After her thanksgiving, radiant at the thought of the happiness now so near, she said to the nun who was nursing her: "What a beautiful day to die on!" The infirmarian had so often heard her speak of the joy of dying that she paid no heed to these words. During the morning, after she had been dozing, she all at once woke up, and with an undefinable expression of beatitude she said:

"Oh, now I have seen Him!"

"Whom have you seen?" demanded the infirmarian.

"The Beloved... but I had to run fast to overtake Him."

A simple dream? The ultimate invitation of the Bridegroom to come to Him? Whatever it might be, a heavenly never-to-be-forgotten smile suddenly lit up her features. In the evening at nine o'clock the eager soul escaped its mortal bonds and took its flight to God. Christ's spouse saw her desires fulfilled on the day chosen by the servant of Christ.

Dom Marmion, who had thought no more of that conversation they had had together, was not then in Louvain; he had gone the evening before to Maredret, where he was to assist next day at the blessing of the abbess; but on the table of the dead nun was found the wording of a telegram to be sent to him to announce her death.

"Our Lord," wrote Dom Marmion, humbly, "did not consider me worthy to assist at the last moments of this pure and holy soul. May she obtain for her dear daughters and their most unworthy father the grace to do in all things God's good pleasure."

Dom Marmion often exhorted those consecrated to God to use their efforts to merit for him this constant and generous fidelity. For his own part he left no stone unturned to help them to go forward in the love of God. In this Carmel, among the old lay sisters, he found that some of them were Flemish, who only spoke French with difficulty. Dom Marmion had at first the idea of taking one of them as his professor in Flemish. The professor had neither brevet nor diploma, but the pupil was of good will: they would understand one another. Each time he saw her Dom Marmion was ingenious in picking up some of the expressions of his improvised professor.[1]

The pupil in return for the lessons he received applied them to the spiritual life. On one occasion he learnt that "to chatter" is *klappen* in Flemish.

"Ah," he immediately said with a mischievous smile, "in the convent one must not *klappen, klappen*. I believe there is in some part of Flanders a village where no doubt everyone chatters, for it is called *Klapdorp*. This convent must not be made a *klapklooster!*"

In giving direction – for the apostle almost naturally became spiritual director – he kept the lay sisters longer than the others.

"I suppose," a nun said jokingly at recreation, "that Fr Columba teaches the lay sisters how to do the cooking."

"Oh, no," returned one of them, "he explains to us how we ought to love our Lord very much; he has done us so much good, and taught us so much for our souls!" And to give more weight to her testimony, the old sister let fall this racy Flemish expression:

"*Hij gaf het ons in met een pollepel.*"[2]

He excelled in making them esteem and love the practices of their state. In place of the Divine Office the lay sisters recite the

---

[1] As may well be supposed, misunderstandings and mistakes were apt to arise at the beginning. He had recommended to the prayers of the Carmelites a young girl of his acquaintance who died in a clinic in that town. The day after her death, meaning to announce the sad tidings and to ask anew for prayers, he said to his professor, unintentionally mistaking the right term: *"Ik kom van het hospitaal; die juffrouw is gedood!"* Consternation of the sister! for he had told her in so many words: "I have come from the hospital: the young lady is...killed!" Evidently Dom Marmion did not cling to these too rudimentary lessons, and he had soon recourse to the good services of one of his confrères: "I hammer away at the Flemish," we read in a letter of June 1899, "because it is necessary here. One of my penitents in the convent speaks only Flemish, and as, according to all probability, I shall be obliged to spend all the rest of my life until my death in this dear country of adoption, I ought to know the language."

[2] Literally: "He thrusts it into our mouth with a ladle."

Pater a certain number of times. "You ought to thank the Lord for giving you the office to recite in this way," he told them, "because the *Pater* is the prayer of Jesus, the words He Himself uttered."

His zeal for their perfection equalled, moreover, his kindness. According to the expressive remark of one of them: *"Vader Columba doet er geen doekjes rond."*[1] He is quite ready to say to us: "It is because you are lacking virtue." But these observations were made with so much kindness that they were always well received.

His devotedness as an apostle knew no weariness. As we know, in Carmelite convents each nun in her turn has to make, beyond the common annual retreat, ten days of retreat in private, at the end of which she may speak with her confessor. During all the time he spent in Louvain Dom Marmion went regularly to the Carmel for the sake of this one retreatant – without prejudice to his ordinary weekly visit to hear the confessions of the community. He would arrive on the day and at the hour fixed, however manifold and numerous his occupations might be. And when during the winter the prioress said to him: "But, Father, why come so far in such bad weather? We should quite well have understood your staying away," he interrupted her: "What do you imagine then? For *souls* we can never do too much!"

These words betray the burning zeal of the apostle. And it was from this supernatural dilection which Dom Marmion bore especially to the spouses of Christ that came forth that little work of great elevation of thought and exquisite delicacy of feeling, published a few months after his death under the title: *Sponsa Verbi, the Virgin consecrated to Christ*. Commenting on a passage of St Bernard on the *Canticle of Canticles*, he shows how the virgin becomes, by her religious consecration, the bride of the Incarnate Word. Pages of high inspiration, where Dom Marmion seems to have put all that was best in his heart as a priest and an apostle.

With privileged souls upon whom the Divine Master heaped

---

[1] Which may be rendered: "Fr Columba does not mince matters."

special graces in order to draw them more closely to Himself Dom Marmion rightly showed himself exacting; towards those who had fallen away he overflowed with merciful indulgence.

If he understood all the nobility of human nature, he understood, too, all its weakness: "In the world of souls there are heights of holiness and depths of degradation."

With what keen and anxious solicitude he stooped down to these depths! Sinners, great sinners especially, how he loved them! "They are my dear children!" he could have said of them, like St Thérèse of Lisieux. He fully agreed with those words of Fr Frederick Faber: "Kindness has converted more sinners than either zeal, eloquence or learning; and these three last have never converted anyone, unless they were kind also." It is the manifestation of this kindness in apostolic men which draws sinners to them and thus leads to their conversion.

To lead them back to Christ, Dom Columba spared himself in no way. He did not fear, like his Divine Master, to be a cause of pharisaical scandal. Again like the Good Shepherd, he left the ninety-nine faithful sheep in order to go after the sheep that had strayed. He was preaching the retreat to a community of nuns in England. He was touched by a letter from Belgium begging him to go to a sinner who would not give his confidence to anyone but him. It was serious, it was urgent, there was no time to be lost. Without hesitation, after having arranged with the superior, Dom Columba interrupted the retreat, crossed the Channel, travelled all night, fulfilled his ministry of peace and love, then, never resting on his way, he recrossed the Channel and was back at his post: the retreat had only been interrupted for one day.

As to sinners, he had the second sight of kindness that, with the poignant view of evil, knows how to see in the lowest or most degraded specimens of humanity all that is left unmarred, the good yet remaining, the yet "smoking flax" – and at the same time, the possible remedy, the hope and supreme resource, for when there is nothing else there is God.

"When I was a young priest, I thought it was easy to convert souls. I tried over and over again – I talked, I argued, but all to no purpose. It needs God to speak to souls and touch them, and this grace can only be obtained by prayer, by the holy life of souls closely united to our Lord."[1]

So it was for sinners that he prayed the most earnestly; and most earnestly too he besought the prayers of his spiritual children.

To prayer, to supplication, he added penance; he undertook supererogatory mortifications. One of his sons at Maredsous was trying to bring an old hardened sinner back to God. On learning this Dom Columba encouraged his zeal and said to him: "I will take the discipline for this poor sinner."

In his ministry towards sinners as well as in the conversion of Protestants, his favourite and almost always invincible weapon was kindness:

> I am convinced, and that from experience, that it is not only by controversy, but by kindness, that souls are won or brought back. It is not in trying to convince someone that he is wrong that he is won over, but much more in showing him the truth with gentleness and charity. The truth is beautiful enough to attract of itself. I have never succeeded in converting anyone by argument; as soon as opposition is felt, self-love comes into play, the heart closes, and there is no more of that sweetness of unction which the Holy Spirit uses wherewith to touch hearts.

Therefore what joy for him, when, the hour of grace having struck, the soul of the sinner opened to repentance! It was not only among the angels of heaven, but upon earth that joy then abounded. Never perhaps did the apostle in Dom Marmion know such gladness as that which he felt at the time of the conversion of a priest, wrought whilst he was staying in England. We owe the details of this account to a monastery connected with the event.

It was in a large city during the course of the recent war. A poor

---

[1] Letters of 21 December 1908 and 23 January 1909.

priest who had been losing his faith for some time past in consequence of spiritualistic practices was at death's door; besides an infirmity which kept him a prisoner to the house, he was suffering from heart disease. A Catholic housekeeper who knew him went one evening to a convent to beg for earnest prayers for his soul, for she feared a fatal ending and knew that no priest would be allowed near the sick man.

It happened that next day – it was at the beginning of November – Dom Columba arrived in the town for a rather long visit. He went to say his Mass in this convent. Reverend Mother, deeply moved at what she had learnt, recommended to him the poor priest who was known, moreover, to the community.

Immediately the zeal of the apostle was aroused.

"Where is he? I will go to him."[1]

They did not know the address, but they gave him that of the housekeeper, and after saying Mass Dom Columba, without delay, set out to find her. She was not at home; he waited for her until ten o'clock in the evening.

The following day Dom Marmion went to the house to which he had been directed, wondering within himself if he would find the sick man still alive. On his ringing the bell, a maid came to open the door. The person who received him appeared in no wise disposed to let him enter to see the invalid, her pretext being the necessity of avoiding any emotion. Besides, a slight improvement in his state gave hope that the danger was past. However, Dom Columba desired it to be announced that he had called. Although he had not been asked to come again, he returned more than once to the house, and was at last received. Evidently, the subject of great importance was not approached at the first interview. They had some friendly talks; the improvement in health continued; they came to taking tea together. When Dom Marmion at last approached the question he only received evasive and negative replies: "I have consulted ... I am happy as I am ... I do not wish to change."

---

[1] "I am going to find a poor apostate priest who is dying, God grant he will listen to me!" (Letter of November 10th).

One morning, on November 20th, after Mass, Dom Columba asked the community to redouble their supplications, and to stimulate the nuns' zeal he himself confided to the superior, who was one of his spiritual daughters, that he had offered himself up for this soul: "Lord, do with me what Thou wilt, but I want this soul!" The cry of an apostle echoing that of St Paul, wishing to be an anathema to save his brethren. It is the supreme argument of the saints, as it was that of Christ when He would save those whose hearts were closed against Him. God accepted this offering. A violent fit of asthma complicated by eczema and other ills took Dom Marmion unawares and made him suffer cruelly during several weeks.[1]

As soon as he had recovered a little he went to see the one who had so pitiably gone astray; the latter was touched by what he had done for him, thanked him for it, but still argued like one who was not ready to give in.

"I will write after I have reflected," he said, as Father Abbot left him.

A few days later, in fact, Dom Columba received a letter from him. Alas! it expressed the intention of making no change in his life.

Intensely grieved, but not discouraged, Dom Marmion made a last attempt, and in the letter he sent in reply his apostolic heart overflowed with supernatural importunity and burning charity.

It was the hour of mercy. A note soon arrived from the poor priest.

"You have gained your point.... Come, I await you."

We may imagine how touching was the interview. There still remained much to set right. Dom Columba took all the necessary

[1] "I can only write you a word," he tells one of his sons, on November 21st. "I am very weak and have had to interrupt the retreat I was preaching at X—. In the same way, the retreat to the clergy of Westminster has had to be put off." And again a few days later, on November 27th: "I have been suffering a great deal; fever, heart-weakness, complete loss of appetite, running eczema over the whole of my back.... I am so weak that I am only able to be up for a few hours every day." And on December 3rd, "I am suffering from great difficulty of breathing owing to the asthma." And to another: "I have suffered death and passion" (Letter of December 6th).

steps and had at last the joy of reconciling this soul with God. It was Christmas Eve, the hour when the Church, in her first Vespers, sings, "The goodness and kindness of God our Saviour appeared, not by the works of justice which we have done, but according to His mercy He saved us." For Dom Marmion, so attentive to the passages of the liturgy and Holy Scripture, these words were especially full of meaning, and were illustrated by this conversion in which the Redeemer's immense goodness and kindness shone out.[1]

Presently Dom Marmion was forced by circumstances to leave the town. Before coming away he entrusted the spiritual care of the soul so happily restored to God's grace to the parish priest.

When, at the end of a certain time he was able to return, he found the priest happy, full of a sense of growing confidence in the merits of Christ and of the liveliest gratitude to the one who had been the unhoped-for instrument of his return. This gratitude showed itself in a touching and graceful manner: in spite of his errors, the priest had kept the chalice of his ordination; now that his state of health made it impossible for him ever again to celebrate Holy Mass he wished to make a gift of this chalice to Dom Marmion; he deemed that this precious memorial of a still more precious grace could not be in better hands than in those of Father Abbot. Was it not through him that God had restored to his soul the intimate splendour of the dignity of the priesthood?...

A short time afterwards Dom Marmion learnt that the sick man had breathed forth his soul to God in the most sincere repentance and love: it was for Dom Marmion a fresh occasion to magnify the mercy built up forever in the Heavens: *Misericordia aedificabitur in coelis.*[2]

---

[1] In a letter of January 3rd, he wrote: "My convert is going on well."
[2] An English nun much interested in this conversion wrote to Dom Columba a few years afterwards: "I cannot end my letter without telling you how much I was consoled by the happy death of poor X—. Oh, how many times I have thanked you in God for all you did and suffered for him" (Letter of 9 July 1919).

CHRIST'S APOSTLE

The same intense zeal was displayed in the conversion of those who came to him out of the darkness of Judaism or the frozen regions of heresy. It was above all at the time he was living in Louvain that he had the occasion of giving free course to this zeal. In January 1903, he had the joy of bringing into the Church a young English Protestant of sixteen years of age, Ethel N—, educated at the *pensionnat* of X— (Belgian Limbourg); she was ill and had been brought to the university city in hopes of a cure. It is difficult to describe the exquisite and unwearying solicitude with which he surrounded this soul, assisting her in her agony and arranging all the details of the funeral.[1]

Ethel had two young sisters. In relating the story of her death to one of his spiritual children, Dom Marmion added: "The parents have decided to send their second child to the same *pensionnat*. Pray that the good God will help me to gain her too."[2]

This joy was to be given him two years later almost to the very day: "Ethel's sister, Beatrice, has just died at the age of sixteen, at X—, and I had the great consolation of receiving her likewise into the Church and of giving her the last sacraments, which she received like an angel, and of laying her in the same grave as her sister, here at Louvain."

And this zealous apostle adds: "There is a third little sister, Dorrit, of a decade of years; pray that I may have the happiness of giving her, too, to Jesus. This is a little present that you ought to gain for me by your prayers."[3]

To this conversion of Protestants he devoted the keenest solicitude. A little English Protestant jockey wished to change his religion,

---

1 At the request of the parents, he had a tombstone raised over her grave in the cemetery of Parc, near Louvain, with these lines of John Ellerton engraved upon it: "Saviour in Thy gracious keeping! Leave we now our darling sleeping." Hymn on the verse of Ps. 30, "*In manus tuas, Domine commendo spiritum meum.*"
2 Letter of 16 February 1903.
3 Letter of 13 February 1905.

in view of marrying a young Catholic girl who had made this the condition of her consent. He was frank and straightforward,[1] but a rough diamond and totally ignorant. Nevertheless, although Dom Marmion's time was very full – he was then prior at Louvain – he made a point of undertaking his religious instruction himself: a touching sight was that of this learned theologian accustomed to the highest speculations, making himself into a simple catechist with indefatigable patience and zeal, After a few instructions he wanted to discover how far his pupil had advanced.

"Is there only one God?"

"There is only one God."

"Very good. Are there not several Persons in God?"

"Yes."

"How many?"

After a moment's reflection:

"There must be three."

"Very good. Can you name them?"

The little jockey hesitated.

"Think of the *Credo*," said Dom Columba, who had taught him the Creed.

"Oh, yes... the Father." "The Father" naturally suggested "the Son."

"And the Third Person?"

Renewed hesitation.

"Think again of the *Credo*." And as he delayed to answer, Dom Columba made a motion with his lips with the idea of prompting him. But with a resolute gesture the jockey stopped him.

"No, I know... I know... The Third Person?... Pontius Pilate!"

It needed all the patient zeal of the catechist to complete the instruction and win for this soul the light of pure faith.

Such examples might easily be multiplied. Those that we have just recorded are enough to reveal the ardent zeal, the thoughtful and persevering goodness of the apostle in the gaining of souls.

---

[1] Having come to the conclusion that the practice of his religious duties was not compatible with his life as a jockey, he sought another avocation.

In the course of this ministry it is the supernatural character of his apostolic intention and action that especially shines out in Dom Marmion. He saw only souls – souls redeemed by the Blood of Jesus – and hence he knew no respecting of persons: he took the same care in instructing the little jockey in the first elements of Christian truth as in enlightening and guiding the Carmelite who submitted the control of her way of prayer to his light as a theologian and mystic.

Thus with boundless charity he made himself all to all, distributing bread to the strong, milk to the weak; to all the same Jesus Christ.

Prodigal of himself, he was so, too, of his spiritual goods; for "a heart naturally noble and good, if furthermore it is rich and happy, knows not how to be so all alone."[1] Not content with spending himself in every way to spread abroad the good tidings of the Gospel of love, he gladly seized every occasion that offered to extend the warmth of its rays and to multiply its kindly influence.

The success and extraordinary diffusion of his works was the signal for a great number of persons, almost all unknown to him, to ask to have these sent to them gratuitously: Poor Clares or Carmelites, Little Sisters of the Assumption, seminarists or priests lacking means to buy them; here a Jesuit of Madagascar, there a Capuchin in some out-of-the-way part of the Indies, or a lonely missionary in the Marshall Islands – from all points of the horizon came the plea for the spiritual alms of his teaching condensed in his books.[2]

---

[1] Msgr Gay.
[2] Some were of the most touching kind. "It is a little Carmelite nun in France," we read in a letter, "who comes very humbly to you and this is the reason that brings her. I should like to give to our Reverend Mother a surprise on her feast-day by offering her your three volumes, for I know how highly she esteems these precious works which do our souls so much good to read. We have one copy, but it is not enough to content all those of us who want to find food in it for prayer. Our mother's feast falls on...; she is called X—. It is by means of selling the snails I pick up in the garden that I intend to pay for my feast-day present, but the time is drawing near and the drought has made the

On these occasions the apostle applied to himself Christ's precept: *Quod gratis accepistis, gratis date:* "Freely have you received, freely give." Therefore no request of this kind was ever refused, and the copies of his complete spiritual works thus generously distributed may be counted by the hundred.

When a monk in Poland asked his permission to translate and publish his works in Polish without paying for the copyright, urging as motive for his request the fall in monetary value under which his noble country was then suffering, Dom Marmion did not hesitate. "Provided that good be done, what did it matter to him!" Like all souls of high ideals, he had a royal contempt for money; he had read in the Gospel the Master's words, the same which St Benedict repeats to the abbot on this subject: "Seek ye therefore first the Kingdom of God and His justice; and all these things shall be added unto you." And Dom Marmion, having regulated everything in accordance with his vow of poverty, generously granted to the translator all the authorisations requested.

Let us add that, like all apostles, he was an optimist; of an optimism, however, which was not fostered on illusions. Had he not, in the course of his long experience of souls, sounded all the abyss of human weakness? Did he not know that it is not well to count too generally upon men's justice and gratitude? He was an optimist by nature, by reason of his healthy mind, above all by his sense of confidence in God, by force, too, of charity. With all his heart he could repeat the words of Mother Julian of Norwich: "All for love.... All shall be well...." Not because man is born good, but because God is pure wisdom, omnipotence and unfailing love, and because Christ's merits are of infinite value and efficiency.

> snails scarce, all the more so as I have already collected a good many, and our enclosure is quite small. I very humbly ask you, then, if it would be possible to help me a little to give my surprise to our Reverend Mother by granting me a good reduction. I should be most grateful if you would be so good as to tell me the minimum price, including postage, for which you could send me the three volumes so that I may see if I can attain what I desire." As we may imagine, the reduction was complete, and the little Carmelite had not to look for any more snails.

And this optimism was to be read on his whole countenance: Dom Columba radiated joy; he was one of those of whom it is said that "love had a face of its own"[1] and that "they witness to God's friendly presence in mankind."[2] For those who knew him his name conjured up the cheering picture of an atmosphere of light, confidence and spiritual gladness. Wherever he passed he enlightened, uplifted, calmed, comforted; he left the heart more fervent, the will more strong, the soul more holy.

"The announcement of his coming to us," wrote the Reverend Mother of a convent of the Ladies of the Sacred Heart soon after Dom Marmion's death – "made every face light up with joy, even before his glowing and inspiring words illuminated our souls."[3]

"When Dom Columba has passed this way," we read in a letter received from a monastery of nuns, "he leaves us for a long time with a sense of joy and peace; one turns to God with renewed fervour after having seen and heard him."

So radiant in its effects is the goodness and smile of the saints![4]

Indeed, this overflowing charity, this kindly ardour of zeal, as

---

[1] Msgr Gay.
[2] Fr Léonce de Grandmaison, sj, "*La religion personnelle*," in *Études*, 5 May 1913.
[3] Letter of 4 February 1923.
[4] We cannot refrain from quoting here the following lines of Elisabeth Lesseur, which so well apply to Dom Marmion: "Great and holy ideas and deep convictions have often as a means of reaching souls the charm and personal influence of those who represent them; you know the tree by its fruits, our Lord says; by its fruits of devotedness, of charity, of radiant faith, but also by its flowers which appear before the fruit: these flowers are called gentleness, grace, nobility, and outward distinction of manner and bearing, serenity, an equal temper, the charm of accessibility, of the smile, simplicity. A soul of depth and holiness which, through divine grace, has the body and the obstacles it opposes under absolute control. Such a soul, without ever working actively, radiates outwardly and offers to all the delicate perfume of these flowers of which He speaks. It draws all hearts and prepares them by its gentle influence for the coming of the Master which the soul obtains for them by its prayers."

well as his firmness of faith and the power gained by his experience of souls, gave a singular persuasive force to his words.

Those who spoke with him, even in passing, of spiritual things soon became aware of that particular quality which only holiness can give and which touches more than any eloquence. The direct echo of the Divine Word, the utterances of the saints penetrate to the inmost being.

A cultured layman passing through Maredsous, after having spoken of the state of his soul with Dom Marmion, said to one of the monks who was a friend of his:

"I have been talking with your Father Abbot; he said substantially the same thing to me as several priests have done to whom I have gone, but he is the only one to say it in so searching a manner: it is impossible not to be indelibly impressed by it."

A distinguished priest well versed in spiritual matters made his private retreat at the abbey. At the end of the exercises, he expressed a wish to see Dom Marmion, but the latter, being engaged that day in important and urgent business could only, in spite of his good will, spare him a few minutes:

"It was a very short time, alas!" the retreatant said later, "but his words did me more good than the whole week's exercises, so much conviction did I feel in them and found such light: he struck just the right note and said the appropriate words with the most sympathetic understanding."

All circumstances were propitious to him to raise up the soul; whether in his cell or travelling, with strangers or friends, his apostolic zeal seized, with rare aptness, every occasion that presented itself to lead the thought of his companion to God. "Many of those who had the good fortune to come in contact with Dom Marmion" – writes a well known ecclesiastic, who was also an intimate friend of Cardinal Mercier – "have been struck, as I was, by the happy, enthusiastic manner in which he aroused zest and made one feel an intenser need for the supernatural, even mystical life. As long as I live, I shall remember an excursion we made together by bus in London, where we had been brought by the International

Eucharistic Congress (1908). We passed along the wide thoroughfares dense with traffic and full of hurrying crowds feverishly bent on business or pleasure: the Strand, Oxford Circus, etc. During the whole journey our conversation turned on the love of God and on the means of stirring it up within us more and more. This conversation, in accordance with his custom, my venerated travelling companion embellished with racy, not to say extraordinary, anecdotes. His Irish buoyancy allowed him to join good-natured jests, often when least expected, to heights of spirituality which at moments touched the sublime."[1]

Fruitful as they were in the simple unconstraint of personal conversation, Dom Columba's words were not less so in his conferences and sermons. To his race he owed the gift of oratory. There is one talent indeed which none can contest with the Irish, and that is the talent of oratory. "The Irish orator, the Irish writer, is fluent, musical, graphic; he engages the eye, he delights the ear, and strikes the imagination at least as much as he takes possession of the intelligence. Also, and for the same reason, he moves to feeling, and this further wins the mind to his theme.... When he thinks, he does not cease to imagine the sight and sound, nor does he cease to feel. On the contrary, the more intense his thought, the more does all his intellectual and emotional being react with it; not, however, to distract, but to support. Hence the music of his periods, the vitality of his illustrations, the brightness of atmosphere, the high spirits and personality expressed at every turn."[2] "Whether or no he be of the craft (*du métier*) it comes naturally to him to put his whole individuality into his oration: he has the feeling for expression and colour."[3]

It may be said that Dom Marmion was "of the craft" at the same time as he was of his race. No doubt his eloquence was not under the discipline of academical rules; we do not find in him classical

[1] Letter of 24 January 1929, to the author.
[2] Mrs Sophie Bryant, "Celtic Mind" (*Contemporary Review*, 1897).
[3] Paul-Dubois.

method. But he had incontestably all the qualifications that make the orator: extensive knowledge, strong convictions, intensity of speech, the passion for all that is good, the gift of sympathy and large-heartedness. He possessed to a rare degree what Jacques Monsabré called the "power of affirmation,"[1] kept alive in him by a strong faith. His voice, strong, resonant, vibrating, served him to perfection; brief but expressive gestures and a very mobile countenance gave emphasis to his words.

As an orator he had, above all, the art of dramatising the subject he was presenting. When he described a scene in the Old Testament – Esau and Jacob, Moses prevailing upon the Lord to stay the chastisement of the idolatrous people, or praying upon the mountain whilst the army of Israel fought with the Amalekites in the plain below; Saul rejected by God; the prophet Nathan standing before David and reproaching him for his crime; or, again, when he commented on a parable out of the Gospel: the Sower, the Prodigal Son, the Wise and Foolish Virgins, the Pharisee and the Publican; or when he related an incident in the life of Christ: Jesus with the Samaritan woman, Magdalene in the house of the Pharisee, the Transfiguration, and so many others – what power of conjuring up the scene! What readiness of expression, and above all, what intensity of conviction!

In elucidating a doctrine he made all that bore on it converge round a central thought which, with rare ease, he excelled in placing in a clear light. He was fond of using the means of oppositions and contrasts; his comparisons, spontaneous and helped by a very lively imagination, had at times something so unexpected about them as to be disconcerting.[2] But the point carried, penetrated, and engraved the truth – oftentimes for long years – in the mind of the hearer. Even when preaching the loftiest truths, he remained,

[1] *Conférence de Notre-Dame*, 1880.
[2] Speaking one day of the "inebriation" of the elect, he said: "If we were to see God here, all of a sudden, we should all begin to...dance!" Of souls who do not really seek God, he said: "They wander idly round God without ever finding Him." And again: "A spiritual life without the spirit of mortification is like a human organism without a backbone."

like all true masters, very simple and accessible; the interest never flagged, so animated were his words, at times relieved by a sally of wit, and above all, so full of life and ardent sincerity was his tone. Impossible to escape the persuasive influence of those glowing and inspiring words: *Nec est qui se abscondat a calore ejus....*

Here, as in every case, Dom Marmion placed his natural gifts entirely at the service and on the dependence of grace. What he sought was much less to please than to enlighten and uplift souls. He was ready to say with St Paul: I do not come seeking to convince you by "the persuasive words of human wisdom."[1]

From a work on the epistles of the great apostle[2] he made an extract in his notebook, in 1896, of these lines which were ever afterwards to inspire him: "In a few words worth more than all the treatises on sacred eloquence St Paul sets forth the essential characters of the preaching of the Gospel, which requires virtue much more than talent: *Non sumus sicut plurimi adulterantes verbum Dei sed* EX SINCERITATE, *sed sicut* EX DEO, CORAM DEO, *in Christo loquimur:* "For we are not as many, adulterating the word of God, but with sincerity, but as from God, before God, in Christ we speak."[3]

Dom Marmion remained faithful to this line of thought. More than thirty years later he wrote to a son of St Dominic who had sent him a work on his order:

> From the bottom of my heart I thank you for the beautiful volume you have sent me. I shall hold it dear, not only as a remembrance of your novitiate [where Dom Marmion had preached a retreat], but also because it is the kind that delights me. There are some words in the preface referring to your holy founder which find a response in my soul: 'He went about on earth ... like the Word of God ... it was the utterance, the preaching, the Word ever in action....' What a magnificent ideal! Samson (a figure of Christ who is the wisdom and the power of God) overcame the Philistines with

---

1 1 Cor. 2:1–4.
2 Jean-Baptiste Mérit, *Les épîtres de Saint-Paul.*
3 2 Cor. 2:17.

the jawbone of an ass. Samson was more powerful, more formidable with this primitive weapon than any other would be with the most perfect weapon. I wish to be this weapon in the hands of the Word, for the instrumental cause acts, above all, by virtue of the power of the principal cause. Let us pray for one another that we may reach this divine and sublime ideal.[1]

Dom Columba had read, as he sometimes related, that Fr Jean-Jacques Olier, at the end of his life, had become so closely united to our Lord that it was evident to all that it was our Lord who preached through his lips. And Dom Columba begged the prayers of his spiritual children for the intention of obtaining this same grace. Those who have heard him preach may well believe that it was not refused to him.

The high and supernatural concept he had of preaching, quite as much as did his simplicity, deterred him from quoting from profane authors. It would have been an easy thing for him to do, for he was gifted with an extraordinary memory. Sometimes, but very rarely, he happened to take a quotation from this source. The last Sunday of the liturgical year 1922 (November 26th, only a few months before his death) he gave his monks a remarkable conference on the passing of time and the need of using it to come constantly nearer to God. On this occasion he quoted from memory Horace's beautiful lines:

> *Vivendi qui recte prorogat horam*
> *Rusticus exspectat dum defluat amnis at ille*
> *Labitur ac labetur in omne volubilis aevum.*[2]

The appropriateness of this passage gives an idea of how happily he could have turned his knowledge of the classics to account. But this he renounced without regret. Was he not drawing abundantly at other and purer sources?

This same way of seeing everything through the eyes of faith

[1] Letter of 16 December 1917.
[2] "A man who puts off the hour of his conversion is like a peasant who waits for the river to run dry. But it glides on and on, flowing on forever."

made him consider as a choice grace the special blessing that the holy Pontiff Pius x granted him in view of his apostolic ministry. One day when Cardinal Mercier was going to Rome he asked Dom Marmion, then prior at Louvain, what memento he would like to have brought to him. Dom Columba replied: "I should be very happy if Your Eminence would deign to ask the pope's blessing on my ministry."

The cardinal promised to do so, and with his usual delicacy he fulfilled his promise in an exquisite way. He bought a portrait of the Sovereign Pontiff, beneath which he himself wrote these lines, which he knew would be in close accord with what his confessor had most at heart: "Dom Columba Marmion, OSB, prays His Holiness Pius x to deign to accept the offering that he is making to God of his energies and actions to contribute as far as may be to the end proposed by the Holy Father: *Instaurare omnia in Christo*."[1] In the audience that followed he asked Pius x to affix his signature beneath the request, in token of his august approbation. The Holy Father very willingly consented.

Did Pius x remember this approbation when, some years later, he received Dom Marmion himself, now Abbot of Maredsous, in a private audience? We do not know. However that may be, at the end of the interview, and without Dom Marmion having asked it, the Vicar of Jesus Christ laid his hands on the head of the one kneeling before him and said:

"Lord, I beseech Thee to bless all the retreats and all the instructions that Father Abbot shall give throughout his life."

Dom Marmion always considered this blessing as a very special grace, a pledge of the fruitfulness of his apostolic work. He saw in it, too, a mission confided to him, whereby he was called to be a herald of Christ, and, in relating this incident, he recalled the words of St Paul: *Quomodo praedicabunt misi mittantur?*[2] How shall the words of the preacher bear fruits of salvation, if he has not been sent by Christ or His successors? He may dazzle his hearers, but if he has

---

1 "To restore all things in Christ."
2 Rom. 10:15.

not received this mission from above he cannot give that *verbum dei* which alone touches the heart.

It was not often that Dom Marmion faced large audiences. He did not refuse to do so when God's glory or the good of souls appeared to be involved. In Dublin at the time of the beginning of the university term in October 1915, he preached the opening sermon before 1,300 students assembled in the Church of St Stephen (associated with Cardinal Newman's name); he set forth, in a discourse of rare elevation of thought and well-sustained literary style, the ideal of the Christian university as opposed to the university without God.[1] In November 1919, Cardinal Mercier, on returning to Europe after his triumphal tour in the United States, stayed in London, and his passing visit to this city coincided with the first anniversary of the armistice. On this occasion His Eminence presided at the side of His Excellency Cardinal Bourne at the great service held in Westminster Cathedral and Dom Marmion was asked to preach the sermon in presence of a numerous and distinguished congregation. In September 1922, at the request of Msgr Heylen, Bishop of Namur, presiding over the diocesan pilgrimage to Lourdes, he preached there several times.

These sermons on set occasions ill accorded with Dom Marmion's temperament. Even when he had simply to encounter an unknown audience it sometimes befell that he did not feel entirely at ease. In 1898, while still a young monk at Maredsous, he was commissioned to preach a three days' retreat to the students of the theological *Collège du Saint-Esprit* at *l'Université de Louvain*. On the morning of the opening, relates Msgr Ladeuze, at that time president of the college, "he was trembling like a leaf, and I had to reassure him." We can understand how he, a stranger, called upon unexpectedly to take the place of a preacher who had been prevented, and to address, in a language other than his mother tongue, an audience

[1] This beautiful discourse was published in full in a supplement of *The Freeman's Journal* of Dublin.

before whom he stood for the first time, may well have felt some apprehension.[1] However, in spite of his accent and incorrect language, this retreat was noteworthy, and more than one of his hearers kept a very vivid remembrance of it. After a space of thirty years one of them[2] declared that this retreat made a deep impression on him. "It was for me," he says, "the revelation of the meaning of the interior life of which I had had no exact idea. Although limited to three days, the explanation of the subject, all founded on doctrine, was complete, and I gathered from it some very solid sustenance for my soul, which has served me for spiritual food ever since without its coming to an end."[3]

A curious thing! A decade of years later, in 1907, at a time when he had won esteem and sympathy in that same university centre by his talents and goodness, Dom Marmion again felt a similar sense of timidity. At Cardinal Mercier's request he was to preach the monthly retreat to the priests of the parishes and ecclesiastical institutes of the capital. The day following the first conferences he wrote to one of his nieces: "I do not feel very much at my ease; they are all unknown to me.... I have to speak from the pulpit; that intimidates me. But I do it for God, and provided He is satisfied, that is enough."[4]

His hearers, numbering more than a hundred, were quickly gained over, and surely none of them suspected that the one who was setting the highest truths before them in so masterly a manner

[1] On the subject of this retreat, he wrote some time later (8 December 1898) to his abbot, Dom Hildebrand: "Our Lord protected and helped me in quite a special way. When I began and saw before me all the members of the different faculties, I was really dismayed, but I told myself: 'I am here out of obedience, and God must help me as He did St Placid, *vidi abbatis melotem super caput meum.*'"

[2] Now canon of the metropolitan church of Mechlines.

[3] Interview of December 1928.

[4] Letter of 20 November 1907. It must be said that he succeeded some who were renowned "conferenciers" then and above all, what he found a constraint was the outward parade: "I have to go up into the pulpit," the official and necessarily rather cold character of the first contact: so many elements which fitted ill with his spontaneity.

– he had taken as his theme: "The history of the Word"[1] – experienced any timidity on coming before them.

Where he was most truly and entirely himself was in simple and impromptu talks, especially with those he knew and loved. The spontaneous words rising up from the wellspring of his inner life, becoming now serious, now familiar, humorous, fluent, picturesque, stressed with a sometimes humorous smile, with a little point of kindly irony, always bearing fruit – passing from an anecdote to lofty speculations, yet ever within the reach of all. And when his apostolic heart let the fullness of charity overflow, then it may be said he was incomparable. It is from the heart that eloquence springs: *Pectus est....* In one of his earliest private notebooks he had taken down these lines of Henri Lacordaire which perfectly apply to himself: "That which gives power to speech is love. To be eloquent is to have a heart. All the saints were eloquent; they were so without genius, because if genius is necessary to human eloquence it is not so to divine eloquence. *Faith and love have no need of genius: they speak, and the whole earth recognises them.* Happy the people who hear the eloquence redeemed by Jesus Christ." Those who heard Dom Marmion may be numbered among these happy ones, for in him they recognised faith and love.

Among so many testimonies to the deep impression produced by Dom Marmion on his hearers we will only mention two. The first is taken from a letter written by a religious belonging to a large abbey of French Benedictine nuns, to the abbess of X— in April 1919.

> To our greatest joy and our greatest good, the Right Reverend Father Abbot of Maredsous gave us all a conference, and a splendid conference. You will guess what the subject was, for I believe your Right Reverend Abbot never opens his mouth except to announce Christ and His mysteries; like the great St Paul of whom his soul and mind seem to be quite full, he knows him by heart, judging from the way he quotes him at

---

[1] "The history of the Word – in the Trinity – in the Incarnation – in the redemption – in our inner life."

every instant. At one bound the Very Reverend Father bears us away to the bosom of God, eternal love, choosing us in His Word, and making us His adopted daughters through Jesus Christ. The developments given by Father Abbot to this doctrine were wonderful, we were positively bathed in the light and warmed by the power of his words, wherein one was conscious of a soul wholly filled with God and His love. Passages from the Holy Scriptures and the Fathers crowded on the lips of the *Révérendissime,* who appeared to be absolutely composed of the very pith and marrow of the Scriptures and the holy doctors. We have spoken many times among ourselves of this beautiful conference which struck us so vividly. We were able to take it all down, and now everyone wants it so as to enter into it the better. Our lay sisters, too, on coming away from the conference, were quite enthusiastic; one of them said in the evening: 'Listen, Mother, I have not opened a book today; after what Father Abbot of Maredsous said to us one has no inclination to seek elsewhere; it is enough to think of these things and to live them in the depth of the soul.' Next day another went to find her Mother Mistress, saying to her with tears in her eyes: 'How beautiful it was, what Father Abbot said to us, we ought always to keep these things before our eyes. We were truly happy thus to make *exauditus* acquaintance with your Very Reverend Father; he is indeed a man of God, a true son of St Benedict, full of supernatural things, living, as one well sees, only in heavenly realities, in the midst of which he moves as in his element.

The second testimony is due to Mother Stuart, Superior General of the Ladies of the Sacred Heart in England. She had the opportunity of hearing Dom Columba in February 1913. She wrote:

> I must tell you now, as I promised, the impression that Abbot Marmion made on me. I was *immensely* struck by him, and have not met anyone so interesting for a long time. He seems to me exactly like what the early Irish abbots who founded

St Gall's must have been – a great-hearted and great-souled monk. And a typical Benedictine abbot, Irish Benedictine, too, brimming over with wit and pathos. He preached a sermon of rare beauty on Romans 12:1, all Scripture and the Fathers of the Church (the Latin rolled richly off his tongue), and so condensed that a word could hardly have been cut off without loss to the sense. If the taking down has been successful I shall send you a copy of the notes.... Our chaplain was struck to the depths of his spirit by the abbot's discourse.

Of another sermon of Dom Columba's, Mother Stuart wrote: "[It was] a real Benedictine sermon, large and spacious.... One thing I liked was [the abbot's] insistence that we should *love the world*, because God so loved the world; we are to love the Father first, but after Him the world, and live intensely to God, and for God to the world, to give what we receive to it...."[1]

Is there any need to lay stress on such testimonies?

If the impression produced by Dom Marmion's words in the course of a simple spiritual conference was so deep, what is to be said of the impression made on his hearers during the exercises of a retreat? No doubt the nature of these exercises contributed to strike the mind of the hearer. The beginning was marked with reserve; gradually, however, the preacher and his hearers warmed to one another from conference to conference, and soon, if the soul of the hearer was but sincere and attentive, the result was attained.

But that is not enough to account for the impression, often ineffaceable, that in such circumstances Dom Marmion produced on those who heard him. What made these retreat conferences "unforgettable," according to the expression of one of them, was the harmonious combination of qualities rarely attained: before everything the essentially supernatural character of the conference, which determined so clearly the habitual moral tonality of many of these

---

1 *Life and Letters of Janet Erskine Stuart*, ch. 24.

retreats; the teaching so luminously concentrated on the fundamental points; the unction arising from constant recourse to the Holy Scriptures; abundant illustrations of true examples obtained from long experience of souls and the ways of spirituality; noble simplicity of bearing and often smiling *bonhomie* which kept him in touch with his hearers; persuasive force springing from deep personal conviction and the intensity of the interior life; and over and above all this, fructifying it, the apostolic ardour of a soul communicating itself to other souls in view of gaining them to Christ.

To the influence of words spoken in general add his more individual contact with each soul in particular, in the confessional or in direction, a contact marked, where Dom Marmion was concerned, with comprehensive kindness, unwearied patience, self-forgetfulness and the gift of self – and you will have no difficulty in understanding the exceeding good done by his retreats.

Quite at the beginning of his residence at Louvain Dom Marmion gave a preached retreat to some English nuns. Twenty-five years afterwards a religious of the convent thus summed up her impression:

> All those who took part in this retreat realised that we had in the midst of us a great mind and a great heart. Dom Marmion positively spent himself, without counting the cost, in spiritual direction and in the confessional. The good he did us was extraordinary. Each of us felt that he was only concerned with souls and concerned with each in particular, as if that one had been the only one in the world. This retreat will ever be for us unforgettable."[1]

In an account written by the superior of a community, we read:

> All that Dom Columba did in the course of his retreats to imbue us all with notions of sound and lofty theology, is beyond calculation. Simple lay sisters understood what he said

[1] Letter of 26 June 1926, to the author.

of the mysteries of the Blessed Trinity, of the Incarnation and divine adoption, quite as well as when he spoke of the vows and religious virtues. And if anything escaped them, they asked him in private, and he lent himself with extraordinary kindness to satisfy these requests. He brought great light to their souls and taught them to live in a purely supernatural atmosphere.

In 1913 Dom Marmion preached a retreat to a large community of English-speaking monks. Fourteen years later the superior of this house wrote: "The present and unanimous opinion is that before the retreat preached by Dom Marmion no one was to be compared to him, and that since then none has equalled him."[1]

It is not to be wondered at if these retreats often had a decisive influence on souls, and that for several amongst them, according to the expression of one of his hearers, these retreats constituted a "unique experience." We may recall that it was in the course of a retreat given by Dom Columba that Dom Pie Hemptinne beheld the royal path of love open out before him and received the supreme impulsion of his soaring towards holiness.[2]

For her part, a superior of contemplative nuns writes: "The retreat preached ... by Dom Marmion produced a total transformation here. Our monastery was founded ... years ago, and we have passed through serious internal difficulties. Before the retreat we were a *group of individuals;* since, we have become a *community.*"[3]

A testimony singularly full of meaning in its expressive conciseness and which gives an idea with what abundant spiritual blessings the spirit of love confirmed the words of His servant.

If we would indeed discover the ultimate secret of the empire of this apostolic speech and action we must pass beyond the material plane and plunge into the sanctuary of his soul's union with God, the principle of all good and source of all fecundity.

---

1 Letter of 31 December 1927, to the author.
2 See p. 340.
3 Letter of 22 July 1927, to the author.

Dom Marmion was too well versed in spiritual things to imagine that the apostolate could bear fruit if union with God was lacking.

On this subject, how many times has he not commented on the verse of the Psalm: *Nisi Dominus aedificaverit domum!*[1]

"Our activity," he wrote, "is pleasing to God in the exact measure in which it is the overflow of our union with Him."[2]

"We can," he writes again,[3] "we must give ourselves, give God to souls, but this ministry must be the quite 'natural' manifestation of our inmost life in God."[4]

"The intimate union of our soul with the Word," he writes to a missionary nun, "will render your apostolate infinitely fruitful. He will be your Bridegroom, you His bride, and the manifestation through you of His Divinity will be your fecundity."[5]

This last thought of great depth could only have sprung from Dom Marmion's intense personal conviction.

Dom Columba's own union with God in his apostolate took especially two forms: suffering and prayer.

From assiduous contemplation of the divine mysteries Dom Marmion derived the abundant lights which he afterwards shared with others. And never did his words touch with more power than when they were the direct and immediate echo of his intimate communings with God. Not only was his teaching then more living, being more the result of experience, but, nearer to its source, the divine

---

[1] Unless the Lord build the house: they labour in vain that build it" (Ps. 126).
[2] Letter of 2 November 1915.
[3] In *Christ the Ideal of the Monk*.
[4] In his work *La métaphysique des saints* (T. II), Fr Brémond cites the example of a priest who scrupulously refrained from utilising in his preaching the lights received in prayer, for fear of losing recollection. "A prudent practice, observes a critic (Fr Jules Lebreton, SJ, *Études,* 20 January 1929) "and one I believe to be common enough, but which would be much less necessary if the soul were more united to God; he would not need to say to men more of his prayer than a single word, *Vidi Dominum,* and it is this word that Christians look for from it." These last lines were fully verified in Dom Marmion.
[5] Letter of 12 December 1920. He added: "Many things are contained in these lines. Meditate on them well in the presence of God."

virtue which overflowed from his heart to his lips led the mind and will of his hearers more effectually along the path of perfection.[1]

To this union with God in contemplation, suffering added the price of blood. It was a remarkable thing that it often happened during retreats that Dom Marmion was in some way attacked by suffering.

"The retreat has been blessed and the price to be paid has been that I have been ill the whole time."[2] And again: "I am feeling rather seedy. This is generally the price I have to pay for God's blessing on a retreat."[3]

So true is it that every grace flows from the cross and that every apostle only sees his work blessed if it is marked with this sign. It was in union with our Lord's Sacrifice, renewed upon the altar and shared in by patience, that the apostle in Dom Marmion found the secret of his burning zeal, and it is in the light of this Divine Sacrifice that we shall understand all his wonderful influence on souls. He thus forcibly expresses the thought that inspired him: "Every day at the altar I eat Jesus Christ immolated, in order to have the grace to let myself be eaten every day too by souls. May Jesus Christ be glorified by my destruction as He is by His Sacrifice!"

NOTE

Dom Marmion always envisaged his apostolic ministry in the purest supernatural light. The thoughts that it was customary with him to express at the opening of his retreats are from this point of view significant. We will give some of them here.

> It is a joy for me to give you this retreat, first of all because of the holy affection that unites us in the Heart of Jesus. Every morning we receive the same Christ; we are, as St Paul says, *unum corpus* (we who *de uno pane participamus*

1 See p 247.
2 Letter of 16 August 1905.
3 Letter of 28 April 1908.

(1 Cor. 10:17), and as I love you most sincerely in Christ, I much desire your progress in the spiritual life, and your holiness. It is, then, for me a great happiness to have been chosen by Divine Providence to give you the best of all gifts: the *verbum bonum*.

Secondly, I am happy to give you this retreat because I wish to give pleasure to our Lord. I have a great desire to devote myself entirely to procure His glory; I want to be eaten up with zeal for my Divine Master's service. I know that He desires your sanctification with infinite desire: holy souls who are altogether given up to Him are a compensation for those who do not love Him. It will then be a real happiness for me if I am able in some manner to contribute to give this joy to our Lord.

I feel, too, a great joy in speaking to you of Jesus and His mysteries. You see, when we love anyone very much, we would speak of that person from morning till night. For us, God is the one and only beloved of our hearts; so we love nothing so much as to speak to Him, and after that to speak of Him.

The words that I shall give you will not be my own; I say to you as Christ did: *Doctrina mea non est mea*. I shall endeavour to take what I say to you from words inspired by God Himself and set before us by His Church in the writings of the Fathers and the theologians. Accept the word of God as little children. Incline not the ear of your mind, but that of your heart, to listen to it. Christ says, in speaking of the children of God: *Et erunt docibiles Dei*. For that, we must listen *sicut parvuli*.

Let us pray together during this retreat that it may do you good. Our spiritual life is a supernatural life, our sanctification is a supernatural work; it can therefore only be the work of God. He alone can give the divine seed which, germinating in our soul, brings forth the flower and fruit of holiness. This is why every day I humbly ask the Heavenly Father from whom comes down every perfect gift, to give me the light and unction I need in order that all may come from Him, and that I may say to you what He Himself wishes me to say to you.[1]

---

[1] It is noteworthy that long before the pontifical decree on frequent and daily Communion, Dom Marmion exhorted his hearers to communicate every day during the exercises of the retreat, "because it is above all our Lord who does the work of the retreat in us."

15 HIS WRITTEN WORK

If Dom Marmion's apostolic labours frequently took him outside his abbey, and if, at these times, other hearers claimed their right to his message as eagerly as did his sons, a moment came when his teaching was to take a shape which placed it at the free disposal of all thinking minds. To study this teaching in its printed form is what now remains for us to do.

As a young monk Dom Columba had wished to take up his pen, and had done so more than once to write on some philosophical subject in a review. But he almost immediately laid it down again at a sign from his superior, who considered him to be especially gifted for direct action – the professorate or preaching; such in fact was his lot during the greater part of his career, and even, we may say, until its very end.

However, we may be allowed to ask ourselves whether he had not cherished some thought of returning to his first and very legitimate ambition and, consequently, some intention of safeguarding in this way, like many professors and preachers, the literary rights of his own theological teaching and ascetical instructions in view of future publication.

The reply must be given categorically in the negative.

During the long pre-war years, when he lavishly gave of his teaching before many and varied classes of hearers, he had no other aim than that of giving Christ to those who listened to him. "You are our epistle," he was ready to say to them, like St Paul, "the epistle of Christ, ministered by us, and written, not with ink, but with the spirit of the living God ... in the fleshly tables of the heart."[1]

He therefore delivered up unstintedly the matter of these conferences to any who cared to take it, and willingly left everyone entire liberty to turn it to any account that might suggest itself: happy even to recognise his personal ideas, occasionally his manner of

---

[1] 2 Cor. 3:2, 3.

developing them even to the very letter, expressed by the mouth or pen of others. In the abbey of which he was now the head Dom Marmion saw a somewhat extensive literary activity reigning; he encouraged his sons in these labours without allowing himself to be drawn to emulate their example. It was just at this time when he had relinquished any such ambition that urgent steps began to be taken on the part of various persons to induce him to leave a memorial of his teaching, and this decided him to do so.

The spiritual conferences of the Abbot of Maredsous are collected in three volumes: *Christ the Life of the Soul* appeared in 1918; *Christ in His Mysteries* was published in 1919, and *Christ the Ideal of the Monk* came from the press in 1922, a few months before the author's death.

The diffusion of these works was truly extraordinary; *Christ the Life of the Soul* soon reached its seventy-fifth thousand in the French edition, and, in spite of the size of the work and the difficulties inherent to the very nature of the subject, has already been translated into seven languages.

According to the expression of a competent critic, Fr Paul Doncœur, SJ, who does not write without having something to say, "the Catholic world gave this work a unanimous welcome."[1] Indeed, cordial expressions of gratitude reached the author from all sides.

This rapid diffusion and universal welcome constitutes, not only a fact forcing itself on the attention, but moreover, a first element of appreciation of which the critic cannot mistake the import. Indeed, if there was ever an occasion when the proverb, *Vox populi, vox Dei*, could be legitimately applied, it was surely now when the faithful so spontaneously and unanimously agreed upon a matter where Catholic instinct itself was fundamentally concerned. So it would be objectless to try to establish the value of a teaching which is already "in possession."

But this approbation expressed in numerical terms, here of

1 *Études*, February 1923.

high warrant, has besides been ratified almost beyond expectation; these ratifications have come from theologians and spiritual writers belonging to the most diverse schools, from souls advanced in the ways of perfection and from directors experienced in guiding souls, from heads of dioceses and princes of the Church, notably from Cardinal Mercier, Cardinal Bourne and Cardinal Logue, and from the Vicar of Jesus Christ himself. Readers will have noticed that the letter of His Holiness Benedict xv, placed at the beginning of the edition brought out in 1922 of the two first volumes of his spiritual conferences (the third had not yet appeared), was something far more than a mere august mark of honour; its tone will be better understood when we learn that, on being received in a private audience at the Vatican in the following year, Dom Marmion had the pleasurable emotion of hearing the Sovereign Pontiff say, as he showed him *Christ the Life of the Soul* on a shelf near at hand: "It is a great help to me in my spiritual life."[1] Subsequently, on receiving Msgr Andrej Szeptickij, Archbishop of Lemberg, in audience, the Vicar of Christ recommended Dom Marmion's books to him: "Read that," he said, "it is the pure doctrine of the Church."[2]

What intrinsic reasons justified such unanimous approbation?

No doubt the analysis we are about to attempt will scarcely succeed in giving a complete idea of the wealth of doctrine, the depth of thought, the fullness of devotion contained in these works, for they are something more than books condensing a system of teaching; they reveal a soul, a soul overflowing with love and zeal. For

---

[1] One of Dom Marmion's confrères who had presented the two volumes to the pope in the name of the author, wrote to him on 6 October 1919: "Msgr Aurelio Galli, *Segretario dei Brevi* begs a copy of these two volumes for himself. When the Holy Father writes a letter to an author, the *Segretario* can as a rule keep the work, but this time the Sovereign Pontiff asks to have your works returned to him, for he says he wishes to use them for his own spiritual reading." Let us add that *Christ the Life of the Soul* appears in the list of works given by His Holiness Pius xi to his niece on the occasion of her marriage (*La Croix*, 21 July 1927).

[2] This incident was reported by Msgr Szeptickij himself at the time of a visit to Maredsous.

this reason they should be read and re-read in the same spirit that animates them. Nevertheless, inadequate as any analysis of them may run the risk of being, the critic cannot evade the necessity of summarising them the better to grasp what it is that makes their true merit.

Let us add that it will be well to support our statements on outside testimony; whoever has experienced for himself the *quotidiana vilescunt* of St Augustine will not doubt that there is security in thus controlling the analysis of a "household" spirituality of which the impression produced had a certain familiarity to those who received it in the freshness of the spoken word.

What then were the reasons why the spiritual works of Dom Marmion have won such wide favour?

These reasons may be explained on divers heads: Dom Marmion's work is eminently *one*, and this unity is due to *the central role filled by the Person of Christ*; it makes the Christian life to rest on the *organic whole of Christian dogma*; it is *redolent of the fragrance of prayer*; *scriptural texts* constitute its living web; it places the soul in a *purely spiritual atmosphere*; it bears the impress of *the wisdom of experience*; finally, filling the soul with *confidence, peace and joy*, it *urges to action by the fullness of interior life*.

Do not the titles of these books convey much in themselves: *Christ the Life of the Soul; Christ in His Mysteries; Christ the Ideal of the Monk?* We cannot fail, especially on closer acquaintance, to discover one and the same idea running through them, which, gaining strength under three connected forms, makes at once for the cohesion of the series. The reader will quickly notice this fact. What will at once strike him in Dom Marmion's work, and will remain as a definite impression after having meditated on it, is the *vital and powerful unity* wherein is grounded Christian *doctrine* and to an equal degree Christian *piety*, finally, Christian *perfection, all acting in harmony* – we note the persistence of the idea – *around the Person of Christ*.[1]

---

[1] "Christ," writes Dom Marmion, "is not one of the means of the spiritual life; He is *all* our spiritual life" (*Christ the Life of the Soul*, conference IV). In his Preface to this volume, Cardinal Mercier emphasises this thought.

The first of these treatises has evidently a more fundamental character.

Starting with this text of St Paul: God chose us in Christ "before the foundation of the world, that we should be holy and unspotted in His sight in charity, who hath predestinated us unto the adoption of children through Jesus Christ,"[1] the author begins by placing the general economy of the Divine Plan in bold relief. In the designs of the Blessed Trinity the Word-made-Flesh is placed at the centre of creation, and the same design of predestination embraces at once this Incarnate Word, Jesus Christ, and all humanity. Thus Christ, our God and our brother, is simultaneously the only Model of our perfection, the Author of our redemption, the infinite Treasury of our merits, the Ransom for our sins, and the Efficient Cause of grace; finally, He is Himself the Head, and, through His Spirit, the Sanctification of His Church;[2] in a word, the *Life of the Soul*.

These theological principles once established, Dom Marmion devotes the rest of his book to showing *how the soul can and must adapt itself to the Divine Plan* in order to receive this divine life brought to it by Christ. In virtue of the initial act of faith and of the sacrament of adoption, namely baptism, there must be wrought in the soul, according to St Paul's expression and teaching, a mystery of death and a mystery of life.

But, for the soul, the whole art of dying and the whole art of living is the art of participating in the death and life of its Divine Head, and of using the supernatural and spiritual means which bring it under the sway of Christ's influence. "Death to sin" by the sacrament and virtue of penance; "life unto God" in the charity maintained by the Eucharist (sacrifice and sacrament), and by liturgical and individual prayer, that it may overflow to the neighbour in

---

[1] Eph. 1: 4–6.
[2] Of this part of the volume it might be said in the precise language of the schools, that it is "the demonstration and deduction of the Christian life by means of all the kinds of causality that the Incarnate Word exercises in the supernatural order."

zealous love, until the soul, fully united to Christ, becomes His co-heir in glory and shares in the bliss of God's own life.

Thus it is declared anew that the Christian life is a supernatural life; thus the point of view of asceticism is linked and subordinated, in a strict degree, to the point of view of revealed truth and dogma, and *Christ the Life of the Soul* is essentially a book of a single idea, happily expressed by its title and pervading it throughout: *Mihi vivere Christus est.*

The same idea is no less predominant in *Christ in His Mysteries.*

However, the manner in which it predominates is slightly different. In the former book principles are stated and considered for the most part *in themselves;* here we see them lived by the incomparable *exemplar,* we contemplate the working out of these principles in the mysteries of Christ. With the help of the teaching of the Gospel and passages of the liturgy Dom Marmion establishes the reality, both human and divine, of these mysteries, their marvellous splendour, their logical enchainment and the profound unity which binds them together; he points out their signification, and applies them to the Christian soul. As to the choice to be made among the dogmatic aspects or the divine events of the Incarnation and the redemption, he especially dwells on those which the Church, our infallible guide, particularly sets before us in the liturgical cycle. Who, he says, knows better than she does the secrets of her spouse and possesses the art of distributing the Gospel? Who better than she can lead us to the Saviour?

The mysteries are next successively unrolled before us from the "Admirable Exchange" wrought in the Incarnation to the supreme glorification of Jesus Christ in His Ascension. Four conferences on "The Mission of the Holy Spirit," "The Bread of Life," "The Heart of Christ," finally, on "Christ, the Crown of all the Saints," fittingly complete the synthesis.

But before touching on the successive states and mysteries of Christ, the moments and scenes of His career, Dom Marmion first lays down the fundamental truths which should enlighten us all along our pilgrimage. In a very telling preliminary conference he shows how "the mysteries of Jesus," inasmuch as they are His, "are also ours." They are ours because Christ, the Universal Man, makes but one with us; because it is for us that Christ lived them; and because in all of them Christ is our Model. Dom Marmion next traces out the essential characteristics of the very Person of Jesus (Eternal Word – Word-made-Flesh – Saviour and High Priest), for in these mysteries something more than the merits and example of Jesus in times past holds us under their influence; He is personally living in them, He whom our faith must ever, in each one of them, behold in "the bosom of the Father"; His divine all-powerful virtue abides in these mysteries that it may, through them, be blended with our inmost dispositions and supply for our needs.

In the school of the devout author we may thus learn the dogmatic and mystical teaching of the liturgical year; following Jesus from season to season, we may obtain that virtue which goes out from Him, one and manifold, invariable and successive, as it were a treasure coined by the recurring feasts, but ever bearing the effigy of the one and only Saviour revealed to us by the Gospel.

The author having in his first book given and explained almost *ex professo* the simple and majestic plan of spiritual life – then applied and developed it in the light of the mysteries of Jesus in the second – he next, as might be looked for, sets forth the claims and rulings of *perfection* in the third volume, *Christ the Ideal of the Monk*, and before his death he had likewise the consolation of seeing its great influence for good.

In this volume the sound teaching of the two first is extended to the religious life in its general ideal and practical detail: the state of perfection involves a work of absolute detachment, preluding a work of intimate union with God. The disciple of St Benedict understands that the supreme object of his vocation is solely to seek God, that his whole speciality is to follow Christ more closely than other Christians, and that all the real value and efficacy of the observances of the cloister only lie in their being integrated in a simple sustained and continuous effort to attain oneness with Christ: "Behold we have left all things – to follow Thee."

A spirituality reserved for monks, some may say.

On the contrary, who does not grasp its essentially Christian character? Who can fail to see the universal spirit and conditions for the sanctification of souls, spontaneously arising from the special rules of the monastic institute? Dom Marmion himself wrote, that "in the ages of the Patriarch of Monks, the religious state, in that which is essential to it, is not an institution created on the confines of Christianity; it is this selfsame Christianity lived in its fullness, in the full light of the Gospel: *Per ducatum Evangelii pergamus itinera Christi.*"

The extraordinary fecundity which the Benedictine *Rule* has given proof of throughout the centuries can only be satisfactorily explained by the fact that this *Rule* is the pure heritage of the spirituality of the first Christian generations, nourished as they were by the Scriptures, and because it is, as it were, incorporated in the tradition of the Church.[1] *Religious perfection as taught by St Benedict is essentially akin to Christian holiness.* Never has the ideal of the Gospel – precepts and counsels – been shown to be more indivisible.

This last work of Dom Marmion is in every point worthy of its predecessors. Appearing at first sight to differ from them in matter, it is in reality closely related: the same comprehensive mode of conceiving the subject, the same method of treating it, the same firm and logical design, the same characteristic note of doctrinal certitude, width of thought, clarity of expression. If dogma is brought less into evidence, if at times the Face of Christ seems to be contemplated less openly, we are all the time conscious that theology plays a vigilant part in the inner life of the ascetic, and that the Word-made-Flesh is the one ideal towards which his gaze is turned and all his efforts after virtue tend.

Such is the remarkable trilogy raised to the glory of Jesus Christ by Dom Marmion. Each volume undoubtedly forms an independent

---

1 "The *Rule of St Benedict* is not exclusively a family patrimony; it belongs to the whole Church by reason of the truly ecumenical traditions garnered up in it and the immense influence it has exerted on the most recent schools of asceticism" (*Études*, 20 February 1923).

and homogeneous whole, but all three have a common appeal, are linked together and mutually complete one another.

Whether you look at the triptych as a whole or linger at each of the panels, you become aware of a pronounced oneness of inspiration and workmanship, of a striking beauty which satisfies, charms and gives the sense of repose; you see the Divine Figure of the Incarnate Word, the fount of all life and all perfection shine out in clear light. Nothing is better calculated than this contemplation to touch and attract the soul, and to call forth the efforts needful to remain faithful to so high a vocation, one so rich in eternal promises.

Only a consummate theologian and master of all the avenues of learning could have been able to conceive and develop the vigorous synthesis we have just been considering, and which may be said to open out on wide horizons of dogma. More than twenty years chiefly spent in the study of Holy Writ, had, as we know, been preparing Abbot Marmion for this work.

Another reason which makes for the power of this work and the fecundity of this spirituality, is that of its being, as we have suggested, *theologically synthetic;* that is to say, it *expresses exactly the whole Catholic dogma.*

Firstly, in this construction all theology enters: the word being of course taken here in a limited sense – revealed truths, definitions of councils, outstanding theological certitudes, outlines of Thomism.

This would already be enough to assure a distinct place for these conferences, even among synthetical works of spirituality. But Dom Marmion's originality is shown much more in *the coherent and rigorous manner in which he worked out his plan.* Here there is no fear of coming upon beautiful promises only half fulfilled; titles to which the contents of the chapters scarcely correspond; theses followed by commentaries which deter or deviate from the point. In these volumes the *theology which dictates the premises remain the souls of the whole exposé;* the principles once laid down make their influence felt even in details. In fact, strictly speaking, "literary" development is absent, so that it follows that the unity of the work is not merely a nominal unity, vague or assumed; it is, in the strict definition of the term, an organic unity. In this lies one of the secrets of the power and simplicity of this work, and it is important that we should emphasise it.

When indeed it is studied closely and objectively in itself it clearly appears that Dom Marmion has built up – if we may be allowed the technical term – and has adequately modelled his spirituality on the whole of dogma and Catholic theology, *whilst respecting both the importance of the individual and the application of the mysteries and dogmas to ourselves.*

And this is no ordinary merit.

We may recall how Ferdinand Brunetière, on his conversion to Catholicism, wrote in a brochure: "The fundamental dogma of Christianity is the Incarnation." It was obligatory to point out to him that the fundamental dogma of Christianity is the Blessed Trinity, which is the "absolute," whilst the Incarnation, inasmuch as it is the entrance of God into His own creation is "relative." The Trinity sustains all; it dominates the whole series of dogmas; but the Incarnation, subordinate, "relative" as it is to the sole "absolute," namely the Trinity, presently becomes, *as regards ourselves,* all our way, all our perfection, all our salvation. The figure of Christ draws all to Himself; He is the centre around which all is organised; Christ is the one and only Way, the sole Truth, the true Life, and no one goes to the Father but by Him. We have but to look upon Him, to follow Him with the Church as our guide, to imitate Him, to unite ourselves to Him – although definitely, our intention passes through Christ's sacred humanity to go to the Trinity and, by this very fact, only rests at the Father.

Such is precisely Dom Marmion's point of view. To be convinced of this it suffices to see how at the beginning of *Christ the Life of the Soul,* in a conference which is the keystone of the entire proposition, he describes in broad outline the scope of supernatural endeavour. No doubt the idea of Christ informs almost the whole matter of his teaching; no doubt, too, the title of each of the three volumes is very apposite, but on condition it is rightly understood, and that, following the author's meaning, Christ is given His theological position, and it is realised that He Himself depends on the "absolute" – and leads to it.

Dom Marmion accepts just as they are the "values of truth," as "values of spirituality"; *he accepts all dogma precisely according as it is hierarchically established by God Himself in revelation, and coordinated in the teaching of the Church,*[1] *such in brief as the liturgy, which is doctrine become prayer, presents it to our belief and to our love.*[2]

In a word, he takes the dogmatic organism in as much as it is an organism, without treating any part of it as independent of the rest, or giving undue proportion to any of its components; he applies it, he traces upon it, if we may thus speak, the whole of his spirituality. This spirituality of his is truly adequate to the synthesis of the whole of theology. It is therefore too little to say simply that Dom Marmion's conferences are doctrinal; they are – and this is much more important – wholly measured by dogma.

This clear and simple adequation imprints on his whole work an intense character of fullness and unity, simplicity and strength, equilibrium and harmony: it is hence not surprising that this work should have satisfied so many thinking minds and pleased so many souls.

---

1 With the employment of the relative means fixed and proposed by the Church under the inspiration or direction of the Holy Spirit.
2 Some will say: "It is quite natural for a professor of dogma who is accustomed to make over and over again the synthetical study of theology, to apprehend the *Summa* of St Thomas." Doubtless every theologian by profession *teaches* synthesis well, but he can choose not to take as the food of his spiritual life all the elements of synthesis or not to take them according to the hierarchy of their value. Doubtless, too, when a mind is in possession of theological synthesis, there is nothing of this theology which is not more or less implicated in his way of thinking, his love, his prayer; but he can nonetheless put what is personal, subjective, in the choice of his mode of spirituality. Dom Marmion, for his part, accepted *all* dogma *such as it is proposed to us* in the teaching of the Church. And despite appearances, this adequation at once total and simple is not easy to realise. And yet, what an impression of ease it leaves upon Dom Marmion's readers! Is not this because we find ourselves in the presence of the work of a master?

In confirmation of what we have just written, we may be allowed to cite several particularly characteristic testimonies. A competent critic, Fr Joseph de Guibert, SJ, writes these lines, which exactly meet the case:

> The keynote of this book appears truly to be that 'continuity of thought' and that 'simplification' which Cardinal Mercier signals out in his preface and which have their source in a twofold intent: to bring out the broad lines and underlying principles of the spiritual life and conjoin them with the central points of Catholic dogma; and for this, to find inspiration above all in Holy Scripture and the official prayer and teaching of the Church. Thus formulated, this programme may appear rather commonplace; its realisation by Dom Marmion is not so at all.
>
> With Dom Marmion, dogma stands clearly out; the temptation may sometimes be great to give a large place in spiritual direction to side-issues of dogma, to beautiful, pious and moving thoughts, which yet lie a little beyond the confines of the great truths taught by the Church, or else to systematic views, daring and profound theories of the schools, elucidating and synthesising large groups of subjects, but linked to particular conceptions. Here, whatever be the reader's personal views, he will always feel in entire harmony with his guide; he will have the pleasant sensation of being in constant contact with the *Catholic* thought of the Church, at the same time very complete and very pure.

Not less characteristic, on account of the personality of the author, is the testimony of Msgr Martin Grabmann, professor at the *Universität München,* whose fine works on St Thomas are well known as well as his special theological attainments. In his preface to the German translation of *Christ the Life of the Soul,* he writes:

> Few recent works of religious literature have impressed me so much as this book, which shows with such depth, light

and warmth the role of the God-Man in the dawning, development and crowning of the spiritual life in each soul and in the Universal Church. Seldom does one find so beautiful a synthesis of the Christian dogmas in their relation with the spiritual life. This book must be numbered with those which reveal in a striking manner the depths of theological doctrine, in conjunction with the penetrating unction of solid and true piety.... The oneness and concordance existing between biblical theology and Thomist theology are here shown in a masterly manner; they are the outcome of a long and assiduous familiarity with the organically construed dogmatics of the Angelic Doctor.... Without being discouraged by the technical difficulties of manuals of theology, the reader who takes Dom Marmion as a guide will acquire a more perfect comprehension of the meaning and mutual connection of Catholic dogmas.

These are the approbations of theologians well able to perceive the essential character of a work by one of their compeers.

A curious fact, and one interesting to note, is that, although less prepared to explain it, lay folk have likewise grasped this quality of completeness of theological and spiritual unity. It is even found that, far from being an obstacle to the diffusion of these works, this doctrinal and synthetical character has contributed to their success. So true it is that in our day, when multitudinous causes are tending to unchristianise souls, people are more than ever hungering for solid doctrine and pure light.

Among the many spontaneous testimonies which have reached us on this subject we will only mention the following: it comes from one of the foremost doctors in the French Navy:[1] "I cannot resist the pleasure of telling you the excellent impression made on me by this real masterpiece of the *Révérendissime abbé*. One does not

---

[1] Letter of 15 April 1920. The letter is evidently signed, but its author was unknown to Dom Marmion: it is not addressed to him, but to a third person. We may add that the words in italics were underlined by the writer of the letter himself.

know which to praise the most, the pious author who has known how to condense the whole essential of theology and mysticism in so few pages or the wonderful rhapsody which so successfully conveys the impression of one unbroken harmony. It seems as if the *unity* and *concatenation* of the Catholic doctrine could not have been better brought out and at the same time with more *clearness* and *attractiveness*."[1]

This power of attraction and edification which Dom Marmion's books exerted over so many souls, resembling one another in their holy yearning for the supernatural, but on different levels on the ladder of knowledge, is not to be entirely explained by the intellectual labours alone of the theologian.

The secret of this is to be found in the *perfume of prayer emanating from it.*

In these pages another unity in fact, one of a psychological and moral nature, interiorly quickens the objective unity of doctrine; another synthesis, one of the mind and heart, enters into and gives life to the synthesis of ideas. For it is the soul of a priest – whole and entire: it is a mind and heart which to other souls – who must be whole-hearted too – sends forth light and heat, indivisibly vibrating in the same rays. *The lesson to be learnt in these pages, the apprenticeship to be made in them, have to do with the science of love.* Like all true masters, Dom Marmion subordinates all else to the one thing necessary: the love of God and of the neighbour.

---

[1] It is true that, at the beginning of *Christ the Life of the Soul,* a few chapters may appear rather arduous reading to the uninitiated. The nature of the subjects lend themselves perforce to this difficulty. Dom Marmion himself confesses it. "Our minds," he wrote, "are so made that they are easily wearied in the analysis or meditation of fundamental notions. All initiation in a science...in an art...in a doctrine such as that of the inner life, requires an attention from which the mind is prone to wander.... But it is greatly to be feared that if the mind does not carefully fathom the principles, it will lack solidity in the conclusions that it will afterwards draw from them, however brilliant these may appear to be" (*Christ the Life of the Soul,* conference 1, § 2).

It is because, as we also know, Dom Marmion's years of study had been years of prayer, and of a prayer nourished at the sources of sacred study, both prayer and study tending to one same end.

From his seminary days sacred study was for him ever a fruitful source of the mysteries of love. Later on he understood this truth still better, and daily lived it in the school of the holy liturgy, where theology becomes prayer or canticle in the feasts, the Mass, the sacramental rites and praises, and where this expression of his belief is ever being voiced by the Church, the Bride of Christ.

Doubtless, under the conditions of human life, no part of theological study can be formally taken as an act of prayer; but the rays cast from the divine focus of revelation bring the soul as much warmth as light; and in short, if these rays bathe the intellect it is in order that they may reign in the heart. Taken in itself, and in its pure and simple meaning, theology tends to invest the will by enlightening the mind, and to find its culmination in prayer; for when the soul responds to this light by the affection of its charity the movement which uplifts it to God is eminently prayer.[1]

We have seen, in studying the theologian, how Dom Marmion envisaged his mission as professor of dogma and with what piety he imbibed his theological teaching. His written work equally bears this character, and because his teaching is informed throughout by his intercourse with the spirit of love, because it is often only the pure and warm radiation of the abundant lights received in prayer, the pages in which he has condensed this teaching glow with the happiest influences; in them is to be found that of which nothing else can take the place: *contact with God*. As Cardinal Mercier said: "Dom Marmion makes one touch God." So it follows that, for many souls, the attentive reading of these pages is naturally transposed

---

[1] "Theological study represents an excellent form of contemplative prayer, on condition, of course, that in its development it is not separated from the affections, antecedents and consequences, of charity" (Antoine Lemonnyer, OP, *La vie contemplative chrétienne*, appendix 2 in the volume: "*Somme théologique de Saint-Thomas-d'Aquin, La vie humaine,*" Paris, 1926).

and prolonged without effort into mental prayer, which itself becomes a source of action.¹

It is understandable how, after having perused this work, His Holiness Benedict XV was ready to render the author the precious testimony that these pages are "singularly conducive to excite and maintain the flame of divine love in the soul, and to foster the desire to imitate Christ and to live by Him...."

Many readers have proved the truth of the Sovereign Pontiff's words for themselves. "I can so well testify to the good results wrought amongst us by your work *Christ the Life of the Soul*," a superior of the Ladies of the Sacred Heart wrote to Dom Marmion, "that I have found nothing better to offer to our houses in France and England, and you would be happy if you could see for yourself how much this spiritual treasure is appreciated. One of our mothers, an ex-mistress of novices, writes to me that she kisses the pages when she finishes reading it."²

"Your book, your teaching," writes for her part the Mother General of an institute devoted to works of charity, "has done too much good to my own soul for me not to feel an immense desire to procure for other souls, and especially for those of my daughters, the opportunity of meditating on it and being penetrated by it; it seems to me that whoever reads it can no longer have any but this one ambition, this one prayer in their heart: 'Jesus, be Thou alone the life of my soul and of all souls, be all to all, and all to me in particular.'"³

The coming into contact with God which the reader experiences

1 No doubt this was why the Archbishop Primate of Braga, on approving the Portuguese translation of *Christ the Life of the Soul* and "wishing to further propagate it," grants one hundred days' indulgence for reading a chapter.
2 Letter of 2 July 1919. Another devout person wrote in the same strain: "Is it because Dom Marmion's book does me so much good that I sometimes feel I must kiss it like Holy Scripture?" Many other like tributes might be quoted, but they are so copious they would need a whole volume.
3 Letter of 10 June 1918.

in Dom Marmion's works especially results from *the author's constant recourse to Holy Scripture.*

Open his books, especially the two first, at no matter what page, you will find sacred texts, oftentimes in abundance. In this there is nothing of pedantry in the author. More often an act of deep faith in the sanctifying value of the inspired word from which virtue goes out to illumine the mind and touch the heart.

It has been remarked elsewhere, in reference to Dom Marmion's conferences, that "spiritual authors too easily content themselves, when making use of Holy Scripture, with taking isolated texts to which they attach their own personal ideas, instead of striving to enter into and develop the entire doctrine of St John or St Paul: they place in the foreground some simple incidental remark, a word said in passing, but which easily becomes a peg on which to hang familiar present-day ideas, instead of placing in their full light the ideas which were the centre and the mainstay of the apostles."[1]

With Dom Marmion, on the contrary, we see the sacred texts almost continually furnish the soul with the doctrinal development. And the intention of giving the true meaning of these texts is so evident, the application to be deducted therefrom so sustained, the wish to keep the whole conscientious *exposé* dependent upon them, that it gains a power of singular influence; furthermore, it trains souls in the art of discovering and appreciating the supernatural strength and sweetness of the sacred words.

A most exacting critic, Ferdinand Cavallera, SJ, has stressed this character in the following terms: "The reason why *Christ the Life of the Soul* is so eminently calculated to do good is because Holy Scripture is the truly fruitful source whence arise as of themselves the most beautiful developments and most profitable applications. Nothing systematic, artificial, fantastic or far-fetched. It is the spiritual life as understood by the first Christians, when they heard St Paul speak, which harmoniously unifies our belief and action.... By this very simple method the author has known how to put fresh

---

[1] Fr de Guibert, *loc. cit.*

life into subjects of which the interest might have appeared to be completely exhausted."¹

Dom Marmion's knowledge of the inspired pages was extensive and exact; he had read and re-read them assiduously, and his extraordinary memory served him admirably in the use that he made of the sacred texts. The Old Testament was no less familiar to him than the New; for he had learnt from St Paul that Christ is "yesterday and today and the same forever"; that everything under the old law was a figure of the new Adam and of His work.² The Psalms were his delight; he liked to linger over those which, under the title "messianic," foretell events in Christ's terrestrial life and especially reveal His Heart and mind.

Of the four Gospels his favourite was that of St John, and we have seen how, when he was appointed professor of exegesis at Louvain, he chose to treat of the doctrine of the disciple "whom Jesus loved."

But the sacred author whom he particularly loved and studied was St Paul. A thorough knowledge of Greek enabled him to read the "Divine Epistles" in the original.³ He truly made his own, not only the text, but the doctrine, the inmost thought, the spirit, even to the very aspirations and affections of the apostle.⁴ It could be said that *Christ the Life of the Soul* was a rich mine of St Paul (*St Paul en barres,* according to the expression of a distinguished Dominican theologian); and that "it constituted a complete synthesis of the personality of Christ according to St Paul."⁵

This love that Dom Marmion had for St Paul is so characteristic that we cannot set aside the necessity of seeking the reason for it here. If Dom Marmion loved the Apostle of the Nations to such a degree, if he commented on him in preference to others, and before preaching a retreat sought spiritual reinforcement in the

1 *Bulletin de littérature ecclésiastique,* May–June 1920.
2 1 Cor. 10: 11.
3 Letter of 4 April 1917.
4 "We have here in *Christ the Life of the Soul* the whole of St Paul, all his knowledge of which we know the divine abridgement to have been *mihi vivere Christus est*" (*La vie et les actes liturgiques,* April 1919).
5 Fr Henri-Dominique Noble, OP.

epistles, it was because St Paul is pre-eminently the theologian of Christ, above all of the Christ in heaven; it is, secondly, because in him is personified in some measure the supernatural synthesis of nature and grace; *mihi vivere Christus est*. But there is something more. The reason for this preference is to be especially found in affinities of soul which are undeniably evident; a heart of flame, a passionate love for Christ and invincible confidence in His merits, ardent love for the neighbour, gift of sympathy, delicacy and constancy of affection, generous self-forgetfulness, patience and long-suffering, apostolic zeal: these are so many points which bring the disciple into close touch with the master. And, better than any other preparation, these spiritual affinities helped Dom Marmion to enter into the spirit of St Paul.

As to the way in which he used passages of Holy Scripture, it was, observed Fr Matthieu Barge, OP, "individual and personal. This was in every point excellent: natural and prompt, simple and direct, without seeking after literary effect and yet very attractive. Never at fault in the choice of inspired texts, nor in the theological interpretation in which he developed his teaching."[1]

This constant recourse to Holy Scripture imprints a *supernatural character* on the whole of Dom Marmion's works.

Without in any wise underestimating the necessity of apologetics, he did not stay to deal with them.[2] At the very outset of his work

---

[1] *Revue des jeunes*, 10 November 1920.
[2] Whilst keeping himself regularly *au courant* with the attacks of opponents, Dom Marmion considered that the best apologetic is always that of a simple, clear, and objective setting forth of the truth. Controversy was always distasteful to him; nothing could have been more Irenaean than was his teaching. Fr Gervasius, Dutch Capuchin, wrote: "I would like *Christ the Life of the Soul* to be distributed by the thousand among my Protestant co-citizens in order to end once for all so many false ideas held by them on the subject of Christian doctrine, and which are still prevalent in these parts. I do not know of any better work to put in the hands of Protestants at this present time" (*Ons Eigenblad*, January 1921).

he uplifts the reader into a supernatural atmosphere, and keeps him in it to the very end. Relying on the Christian perception placed in the soul by baptismal grace, he takes before all things faith for guide, and if there are works more specifically demonstrative, of finer psychological analysis, or in which a larger place is given to actuality, there are none in which the tonality is so essentially supernatural: in these pages we only listen to the Word of God, with its absolute character of eternity and universal virtue. It is the *primauté du spirituel* in the deepest sense.

It must be acknowledged that in many quarters, even in religious communities, people have long since grown unaccustomed to this style, and this is one of the reasons why the works of the Abbot of Maredsous, although they only contain the most traditional substance of Christian doctrine, have for a great number the attraction of a revelation.

But this revelation was signalised and welcomed as a singular boon by able judges. "We must joyfully hail," wrote one of them,[1] "the publication of books so rich in sane mysticism, so deeply based on dogma, so unerringly built on the teaching of Holy Scripture and of the Fathers of the Church.... The extraordinary success of these books which has brought them particularly into evidence is consoling.... Dom Marmion's work marks a new tendency. It initiates us into the very nature of Christianity: our supernatural relations with God. It graphically depicts for us the splendid efflorescence of a truly Christian life responding to the Divine Plan of our supernatural predestination."

"Thanks be to God," writes another critic whom we have already cited, "modern spirituality has ceased to be only a vague psychotherapy. We are coming back to the great Catholic tradition – to its first source, which is Holy Scripture. And this contact with the pure Truth, with the one and only Master, the Holy Spirit, assures to it a power all divine.... An immense movement is today teaching all spirituals to re-integrate dogma in asceticism, and the

---

[1] Fr Louis Lemmens in *Pastor Bonus*, February 1920. The critic associates in his eulogium the works of Cardinal Mercier and those of Dom Marmion.

most beautiful spiritual book of these latter years, *Christ the Life of the Soul,* by the Abbot of Maredsous, bears witness to the fruitfulness of this method."[1]

In this paramount work of reintegrating dogma in asceticism Dom Marmion has had an undeniable and even major share. By an apostolate of more than a quarter of a century,[2] which will be continued by his written work, he ever brings souls back to the purest doctrinal sources, and accustoms them to the atmosphere of the supernatural. A signal benefit, the extent of which we are not yet in a position to estimate; we do not yet know all we owe him. Later on the historian of the piety of the period will scarcely fail, however little he may be attentive and loyal, to record the weight of Dom Marmion's influence and to show the exceptional worth of his merit.[3]

---

[1] Fr Doncœur, *Études*, 5 November 1921. Later (*Études*, 20 June 1923), in reference to Fr Francis Vincent's work on St Francis de Sales, Fr Doncœur comes back to the same idea. "I fear lest the overweening care for the culture of the 'ego' may cause what comes first in Christianity to be overlooked.... The education of the will is certainly very opportune, but were we not first baptised in the name of the Blessed Trinity, to live by our divine life as sons, through Christ's grace in the Holy Spirit, and can all the stoicism and all the culture ever have the value of the loving glance which an old tertiary casts on his Jesus crucified?... Greater interests are involved. Too many souls are stifled in the prison of religious moralism; we have striven too painfully, for the last twenty years, to learn again from St Paul, from St John and all the great Christians, the living basis of Christianity, not to be moved when this deliverance would seem to have its cause taken up anew."

[2] From the first retreat preached in 1895 until his death in 1923.

[3] In an interesting study: *La spiritualité chrétienne ramenée à son fondement* (Paris, 1925), Fr Valentin Breton, OFM, after having spoken of "the ravages made by the invasion of naturalism in contemporary piety, of which the productions all follow the same tendency and are founded on the assumptions of a philosophical moralism," he adds: "Let us however acknowledge, so as to conclude what we have been saying with a more consoling assertion, that this era of ignorance and forgetfulness of the truth that piety in order to be *Christian* must be *Christocentric,* seems to be approaching its end. The success of Dom Marmion's works, attested by the number of editions and by imitation, shows to what a point souls hunger and thirst for a teaching essentially Christian...."

Because with gentle strength they reinstate the Christian in face of his true vocation and keep him steadfastly in the supernatural viewpoint of the Divine Plan – because they thus give him the sense of Christianity, in all its purity and plenitude by causing him to draw, not at the tributary streams, but at the fresh and abundant fountain-head – Dom Marmion's works refresh the soul and bring it at once light, security, peace and gladness.

It may have been a long time since many persons had felt the *gaudium de veritate* to such a degree as in reading these pages. Invited to rise to these heights of the pure supernatural ideal, their souls breathed a larger air – the health-giving, vivifying air of the hill tops. "When one has read *Christ the Life of the Soul*," wrote Fr Barge, OP, "that book which can only be properly appreciated in meditation, one cannot bear to be separated from it. We keep it near at hand, like a friend to whom we love to turn to ask for some special light on a subject, for authoritative and wise counsel, and for the sweet and strong impulsion that sustains the uplifting of the soul towards God and Christ."

"I cannot tell you," wrote the Reverend Mother of a convent of the Assumption to Dom Marmion, "the good that your book, *Christ the Life of the Soul,* has done me. It is a living source of grace for my soul; when I read it I end with meditating on the Epistle to the Ephesians, and *I seem to be entering, thanks to you, into a fresh path*.... Many times I have prayed for you, out of gratitude for all that I shall ever owe to you for my spiritual life."[1]

"It is great boldness," a Carmelite nun of the south of France wrote for her part to Dom Marmion, "to venture to tell you the happiness – I might say the beatitude – that you have stored up for God's children in your books; after having read them, one no longer wants to open any others, so much does one find there all that the soul needs in order to live and to love."[2]

A Poor Clare of Flanders echoes the above in a personal testimony of naïve simplicity. To someone who had made her a gift of

1 Letters of 4 April 1918 and 4 May 1918.
2 Letter of 22 July 1919.

Christ the Life of the Soul, she sent the following note: "I absolutely must thank you for Father Abbot Marmion's book. We are reading it in the evening at collation, and our sisters are so enchanted that they forget to munch their morsel of dry bread. Our Reverend Mother then says: 'Come, my children, go on eating, or we shall be too late for Compline! You can listen and eat at the same time!' This author uplifts the soul above ordinary everyday things, and yet through these things, is it not so? Thank you once more!"[1]

A strong impulsion to action goes together with this gladness and security. It could be said in all truth that "under the guidance of this master, Christian doctrines, of which the faithful think too little become sources of a more intense and active Christian life."[2] In fact, this doctrine urges to action, but through the fullness of the inner life. The soul satisfied with good things feels not only the need of living this life, whereof the abundant sources have been opened to her, but in her turn to communicate the gift received and to shed around some of the rays in which she has been so generously bathed.

Countless souls have thus been given largeness of outlook on coming in contact with this doctrine, luminous and aglow with life, lofty and fruitful, generating action and setting aflame with zeal.

Chosen out of many others, these following lines, written by one unknown to the author, must be recorded. They are entirely spontaneous and well sum up the variety and extent of the influence of this teaching.

> Will you allow one of your readers to express the gratitude she owes you since reading your books?
>
> You have gone so deeply into the mysteries of God; you lead souls thither with so much light, that your work, it seems to me, forms a mystic bond between the visible and the invisible, between matter and spirit, between man and his God. My father, I owe to you the most beautiful moments of my life! All that we feel, all that we believe, when union with God

---

1 Letter of 20 December 1920.
2 *Messager du Cœur de Jésus,* March 1920.

makes us enter a little way into the divine secrets, you have said for us. Your books are a real revelation; the happy soul at last finds expressed what she felt and knew, but so confusedly! And this sense of close connection between the intuition of the soul and what she finds expressed in the book is a clear proof of truth and inspiration.

I cannot thank you enough; one can only look to God to pay such debts; my father, probably I shall never meet you, but I may own to you that very often when reading your pages I stop, as it were dazzled, and I join your thought to that of God – and this thought is a prayer.

You lead the way to accessible heights; you attract the soul to no imaginary ideal; and one comes down from these heights athirst for love, but also with an intense desire to do good. Thank you for all you have already done for me!

Excuse the simplicity with which I am writing to you, and believe, my father, in the very respectful gratitude of a future missionary.[1]

Finally, the crowning quality of Dom Marmion's teaching is *wisdom bearing the stamp of experience*.

These works are the pleasant fruit of full maturity; having come almost to the end of his career – he had passed his sixtieth year – Dom Marmion gives, often unknown to himself, the result of his own experience, his intense inner life and long practice in directing souls. The attentive reader will feel that these books were lived before being published, so much prudence is revealed in the sublimity of his teaching and it is accompanied by such practical lessons. Dom Marmion is seen to be one commanding respect, yet easy of access; exacting, yet measured; firm, yet lenient; very supernatural, yet very human.

Whilst discovering to the soul the vast and luminous horizons of the Christian life he forewarns against illusion and temerity. He

1 Letter of 14 July 1919.

does not cut out any of the different stages, but he looks for spiritual advancement in loving fidelity, even down to the smallest things. If he abhors mediocrity and carelessness in God's service, he has an equal horror of formalism and pharisaism; what keen irony at times in his description of the "outward correctness" of certain persons! If he expects religious to be constantly attentive to their promises and vows, he yet vigorously denounces those who, starting with a false idea of perfection, hold cheaply the most elementary precepts of Christian charity and natural justice. He lays the path of love widely open before the child of God, provided that, ever conscious of his fundamental condition as creature, this child safeguards, by a sense of adoration, the outpourings of his tenderness. He would have the Christian sing in his heart for joy at being, through Christ, the child of God; but affective love is illusory unless translated into fidelity. Ever ready to stoop in pity towards infirmities, weaknesses, frailties, even grave ones, of surprise, he does not cease to warn the soul to be on the watch against voluntary infidelities, deliberate shortcomings and negligence in correcting the least faults. If he insists on the precept of self-renunciation, he yet points out the altogether relative value of material mortification. You will hear him frequently and lovingly commenting on the words of Jesus, "Without Me, you can do nothing"; but you will see him linger, with still more marked delight, to make souls understand how rich they are in Christ: "I can do all things in Him who strengtheneth me." To the deepest humility he would have them unite the most complete sincerity and absolute confidence which makes for magnanimity. He extols, and in a wonderful way, the Church's official prayer in her liturgy, and likewise seriously inculcates the indispensable necessity of regular private prayer in order to ensure progress in perfection.

And what a liberal mind, what a sense of due moderation when practices of piety are concerned! One should read, to give a single example, the conference "The Bread of Life."[1] With what height of view and depth of doctrine the author sets forth, whilst linking it to

[1] In *Christ the Life of the Soul*.

the very meaning of Communion, the duty of preparation and of thanksgiving in reception of the Eucharist! And directly afterwards, on coming to the practice of this duty, he accommodates himself to the needs and attractions of each soul with singular adaptability.

There is ever revealed in Dom Marmion, together with an elevation and fullness of doctrine occasionally verging on the sublime, that realistic sense of the supernatural life which Cardinal Mercier was so ready to remark in him, that judicious prudence in the application of principles, respect for the suggestions of grace, that extreme concern for the liberty of souls, in a word, that admirable discretion so pleasant to meet with in him and without which, especially in spiritual matters, nothing is of much avail.

So that – as has been remarked[1] – whatever be your state of life, the spiritual school to which you belong, the path by which the Holy Spirit is leading you, the degree of virtue you have attained, the reading of these pages ever remains attractive and profitable. They greatly help those, and they are many, who feel the need of simplifying their inner life by basing it more directly on the great mysteries of faith. Others, too, who, far advanced in the spiritual life, yet find what is for them an indispensable help in methods and practices, need not fear to give themselves up to this guide. By his luminous and fruitful teaching, he elucidates methods, he puts life into "practices," and removing from them anything that might run the risk of being burdensome or artificial, ensures their value and increases all they contain of good.

Dare we suppose we have succeeded in revealing in these pages the soul of Dom Marmion's spiritual conferences, in showing the origin and nature of the charm and of the fruitful action they have exerted and continue to exert on Christian souls of all sorts and conditions, but all equally in love with the things of God? A work evincing a powerful unity by reason of the central place which the Person of Christ holds in it; a work fully adequate to the whole of

[1] Fr de Guibert, *loc. cit.*

theology and Catholic doctrine; a work breathing the perfume of prayer and overflowing with the unction of the Holy Scriptures; a work steeped in the supernatural and balanced by happy discretion gained by long experience of souls; a work which is at once a feast for the mind and peaceful joy for the heart; a work which induces to contemplation and urges to action; and, giving harmony to the whole, a simple form, on pure and unstudied lines: such the structure of these conferences appears to be on attentive consideration.

That which we have attempted to put into words Dom Marmion's friends and hearers knew by experience, and his readers have understood it on coming into direct contact with his books. All have felt that, in this personality which so warmly gave itself out to them, were carried out to a high degree the supernatural unison of mind and heart and the perfection of faith in charity;[1] that in this theologian the purest learning was integrally turned to loving; that in this master of spirituality, the man was homogeneous to the doctrine he taught; in fine, that in this soul of a priest, one passion alone reigned: the passion for Christ and for souls to be won to Christ for the glory of the Father.

All agree in the judgment passed by critics of the highest authority who place the author in the foremost rank of contemporary masters of spirituality.[2]

NOTES

I

To complete what we have said as to the sources from which Dom Marmion drew his teaching, we must mention the masters of the spiritual life. He was well acquainted with the Fathers of the

---

1 To employ the phraseology of the schools: "the information of faith by charity."
2 "There is a sum-total of qualities in Dom Marmion: his conferences reveal him as liturgist, theologian, contemplative, priest and apostle." *Revue des sciences philosophiques et théologiques*, January–April 1920.

Church, although he had not made a personal study of their works; he had read and re-read St Augustine's *Tractus in Joannem,* the *Pastoral* of St Gregory the Great, and St Bernard's Homilies *Super missus est* and *Commentary on the Canticle of Canticles;* it was especially in the course of his theological lectures and in his breviary that he met and savoured them. "One is struck," wrote a critic (*Biblica,* 1920), "by the sureness and traditional character of Dom Marmion's theses in his work *Christ in His Mysteries;* it echoes the thoughts of the Fathers of the Church, although they are scarcely named; but is not he their direct heir who, following their example, is nourished on Holy Scripture?"

Another influence, less apparent to general view, was constantly brought to bear on Dom Columba: that of the *Rule of St Benedict,* from which he imbibed his very practical conception of our relations with God, as those of children with their "Father by adoption," the principle of fundamental asceticism, of which the first conference in *Christ the Life of the Soul* gives such a warm sense of strength and sweetness. Again, it was the text and the spirit of the old monastic code, at the same time as the spirit of the liturgy, which kept at such a high level his gift of discretion, further brought to a fine degree of perfection by his experience of souls.

He had a great love for St Gertrude and St Mechtilde, who so well understood the riches of the mystery of Christ; he held Blosius in high esteem, and never wearied of advising others to read his writings, especially the *Book of Spiritual Instruction.*

We know the particular esteem and affection he ever had for St Thomas. On 19 December 1919, Fr Édouard Hugon, OP, professor at the *Pontificium Collegium Internationale Angelicum* in Rome, wrote to Dom Marmion: "I was greatly charmed and edified on reading your pages full of so much pious doctrine and doctrinal piety, and of such comprehensive and complete Thomism." Of the Dominican school, Dom Columba specially appreciated St Catherine of Siena and Bl. Henry Suso.

He read closely and over and over again the works of St John of the Cross, and above all those of St Teresa; in his notes written in the first years of his monastic life are to be found whole passages taken from the works of the great Carmelite of Ávila.

In his teaching on love he comes nearest to St Francis de Sales (see p. 170). What did he exactly owe to the French school of the seventeenth century? He had read Jean-Jacques Olier, Charles de Condren, Pierre de Bérulle; certain expressions give the idea of a close spiritual filiation, but in reality he does not depend on them; if he retains certain of their formulae, it is because they are in keeping with his mentality, nothing more; he is much more human than Bérulle, and has his own personal manner. For his Christology he took St Paul as his great master to whom he ever returned because he was the first of his masters according to date.

He loved Bossuet and was specially fond of his *Méditations sur l'Évangile*. It is a custom in the Abbey of Maredsous to read in the refectory, on high festivals, one of Bossuet's sermons relating to the feast or mystery of the day; and on these occasions Dom Marmion was always particularly attentive to the reading, and afterwards made a note of the passages which had struck him.

As to modern writers, he knew Fr Frederick Faber, Msgr Cuthbert Hedley, OSB, and Msgr Charles Gay. We may add that he constantly read the lives of the saints and holy personages, and simply revelled in them; the number of biographies that he thus read was considerable.

II

As is generally known (see the preface to *Christ the Life of the Soul*) Dom Marmion did not *write* his works himself; he had neither the inclination nor, above all, the leisure. This writing was the work of one of his monks who was particularly well prepared for the task. A student of Dom Marmion in philosophy and theology, always present at his spiritual conferences at Louvain during four years, and then at Maredsous, he was familiarised with Dom Columba's doctrine and manner.

He had at his disposal considerable collections of notes of the conferences, some taken down in shorthand, others carefully noted by attentive listeners. With regard to one of these MS. collections which was to serve as source, Dom Marmion himself wrote (letter of 5 October 1906) to a person who had asked him to lend it to her: "The notes of retreat I sent were taken down almost word for word. The nun was almost scrupulously careful to reproduce *exactly* what I said. I don't think there is an expression or a thought which I had not communicated."

These words might be applied to almost all the pages consulted for the putting together of his works.

To quote Dom Marmion's own foreword to the English edition of *Christ the Life of the Soul* (15 January 1922): "It was a difficult task to put these notes together, and above all to preserve what was original and personal in them. It would seem to me, however, that the member of our community to whom this work was entrusted has taken infinite pains to respect the text, while reproducing the original as far as possible, and indeed he has succeeded beyond what I could have hoped for."

The drawing up of each conference was first submitted to another monk, long accustomed to take down Dom Marmion's conferences, and therefore singularly well qualified to make this revision with sureness and efficiency, a task which he conscientiously discharged. The text was then given to Dom Marmion to check. He read it through, pencil in hand, and at need corrected, rectified, or put in more precise terms. He sometimes worded certain particularly important passages himself, but that was rarely. More often the corrections were confined to details, and the collaborator had no greater joy than that of hearing Dom Marmion say on returning the pages for the printer: "That's just me!"

Such guarantees will more than suffice.

Indeed, those who had heard Dom Marmion's conferences found them again in his books. Let us quote a few comments on this subject: the Mother Superior of a community who had had for long years the good fortune to listen to him regularly, wrote to Dom Marmion: "Let me tell you all our joy and gratitude in possessing at last these splendid instructions, where I find you again entirely with that strong and beautiful doctrine which has shaped our souls during so many years." Another hearer wrote: "In reading these conferences I seem to be listening once more to the Right Reverend Father Abbot himself, his language full of kindliness, so supernatural and all steeped in Christ Jesus." "It is truly you, *Révérendissime père*," wrote a monk, "you whom we find again in your pages, you such as we saw and heard you during our retreat." One of Dom Marmion's hearers at Louvain, now a canon of the metropolitan church, wrote to him, after reading *Christ the Life of the Soul*: "I am regaling myself on your volume: this is because I there find what in fact I seek, namely, to revive those instructions with which in bygone days I was so often favoured and which nothing up to now has been able to make me forget, because nothing has taken their place for me, and the deprivation of them at times costs me real pain." Finally, let us quote this telling appreciation from one of high standing in the university who had likewise often had the opportunity of listening to Dom Marmion at Louvain: "I have been living over again, while reading this book, the precious hours of those religious instructions which I had the great happiness to receive from your lips at Louvain. It has happened more than once that I have forestalled your thought from what I recalled, recognising even the turns of speech and expression which were impressed on my mind so many years ago!" (Letter of 6 March 1918). These testimonies, which might be multiplied, are enough to show with what loyal fidelity Dom Marmion's collaborator acquitted himself of his delicate task.

16 TO LIVE AS A CHILD OF THE HEAVENLY FATHER

Like all true masters of the spiritual life, Dom Marmion had not two spiritualities: one for himself, another for his neighbour; one which he practised, another that he kept for his sermons and his books. The object of his spirituality was, essentially, the same as that which he preached. He had only one asceticism: *coepit facere et docere*,[1] to do and to teach. The teaching that he set before others he had already proved for himself. He believed what he said; he lived what he believed. All his soul was in his preaching and in his spirituality.

Hence it was that his conferences were marked with so deep a tone of conviction, they were so aglow with life, so inspiring, and that this rather well-worn eulogy so often fell from the lips of those who heard him: "He has lived it."

What was said of his holy friend Cardinal Mercier may be applied to him to the very letter: "What struck and attracted us in him was the intense personal truth of what he said, and of what he did. Nothing conventional, nothing studied, nothing forced, but the ever free and spontaneous communication of his inner life, his truest feelings, his sincerest thoughts; the most urgent appeal to a like sincerity, a like personal and ardent truth: such was the constant method of his teaching and of his direction."[2]

It is into this intense life arrived at its consummation[3] that we

---

[1] Action and teaching (Acts 1:1). These last words are meant, of course, for the substance of what he said, not for all the questions which he entered upon before his hearers. In fact, it is evident that every spiritual writer, every director of souls is led to speak of the experience of others, of states which he himself has not personally experienced: he speaks in accordance with the lives of the saints, and mystical theology. It remains no less true that Dom Columba, in his conferences, gave many of his own spiritual experiences.

[2] Cardinal Mercier, *Le christianisme dans la vie moderne.*

[3] Some of these quotations do not relate to his latter years; if we give them here it is because they have not found a place in the foregoing chapters, or more often because they serve the better to reveal the ascendant curve of Dom

are now about to gain some insight. It is with reverence we must do this, for the inner life of a faithful soul arrived at full maturity is a sanctuary where God dwells to complete therein the divine work of His eternal love.

At the basis of Dom Marmion's whole spiritual life must be placed *faith,* or what is commonly called the *supernatural spirit.*

There is nothing in that, some may at once say, but what is ordinary and indispensable. "Without faith it is impossible to please God," and, still more, to be His child and live intimately with Him.

That is true. But with Dom Columba faith was more deep, living and firm than can be easily expressed. In this matter, as we have said, he owed much, after God, to his race. Moreover, Dom Marmion never failed to hold in highest honour the faith he had received from his forefathers, and to cultivate and make it bear fruit in works of love.

Great was the esteem in which he held this virtue. He often liked to extol the faith of Abraham, father of believers, model of unwavering faith in the direst trials. In this, too, he was but an echo of St Paul, who has exalted in terms full of poetry the faith of the patriarch of the ancient alliance.

Dom Marmion further manifested his esteem for this virtue by the place he gave to it in his preaching and his writings. In one of his most beautiful conferences he shows how faith is the foundation of the whole spiritual life.[1] Such is the value that he attaches to this thought that, in his volume on the mysteries, there is scarcely a conference where he does not return to it. In 1916, having to give a retreat, he makes this virtue very substance of the whole theme: "I have just finished this morning preaching a retreat to the Benedictine nuns of Maredret. The theme is this: the life and whole activity of Jesus considered as flowing from the contemplation of His soul, which ceaselessly beheld the Face of the Father: Model of our

Columba's inner life.
1 In his volume *Christ the Life of the Soul.*

life *of faith*, finding everything in the habitual contemplation of God, in union with the soul of Christ."[1]

Magnificent ideal, the realisation of which he himself strove to approach as closely as possible. Was not every detail of his life steeped in this heavenly light? Was not faith truly the sun which cast its rays all along his path, enlightened all his undertakings, fructified all his labours? In him, if one may thus express it, the supernatural had become temperamental; he was "naturally" supernatural. So vivid and even so constant was this virtue, that at the end of his life the mysteries had become for him objects of conviction, objects of intuition. He often said: "Now I no longer believe, I see." Not assuredly that he penetrated into the essence of dogmas, but the divine ray in his soul shone so brightly that it gave him, as it were, the vision of the object of his faith.

Dom Marmion's faith was first of all brought to bear on the Person of Christ, Son of God, Incarnate Word.

One day, at Louvain, one of his students in theology came into his cell. Before he had time to open his mouth Dom Columba, fixing his eyes straight upon him, asked him point blank:

"Brother R—, do you believe in the divinity of Jesus Christ?"

Taken aback at this unexpected question, the disciple replied:

"Surely you do not take me for a heretic?"

"Not yet," he replied laughingly. "But have you the *conviction*" (and he emphasised this word) "that Jesus Christ is God?"

This time the student spoke with less assurance:

"I hope I have."

"Well! *if* you have," replied the master, who knew his disciple better than the disciple knew himself, "thank the Lord for it, for the conviction that Jesus is God is a great grace: it is the principle of all perfection."

With Dom Columba this was a living conviction. It was bound up with the deepest fibres of his being. Therefore, probably in consequence of a light which he had received, he loved to linger over and comment upon certain episodes of the Gospel where Christ's

[1] Letter of 16 December 1916.

divinity is especially affirmed. For example, when on Thabor, the voice of the Eternal Father declares that Jesus is His beloved Son in whom He is well pleased. At Bethsaida, when Peter, enlightened, not by natural evidence, but by revelation from on high, proclaims that Jesus is the Son of the living God. Or, again during the sorrowful days of the Passion, when Jesus Himself testifies to His divinity before the Sanhedrin. Dom Marmion often referred to these episodes; he repeated, making the solemn testimony his own: "Thou art the Christ, the Son of the living God."

With what joy he commented on certain words in which Jesus testifies to His oneness of nature, His equality of perfection with the Father: "The only-begotten who is in the bosom of the Father, He hath declared Him"; "I and the Father are one"; "He that seeth Me, seeth the Father...." He constantly came back to these words as to springs of living water where he refreshed his faith.

It was above all when the liturgical cycle brought round the mysteries of the Incarnate Word that he gave free course, in his spiritual conferences, to the outpourings of his faith. At Christmas he adored the Child lying in the manger; but only to rise at once, like St John, even to the bosom of the Father where, before all beginning, the Word eternally dwells. The eye of his faith gazed reverently into this sanctuary, there to rest in glad contemplation on the ineffable mystery of the Son begotten in the splendour of holiness, *in splendoribus sanctorum*. In glorifying the Eternal Fatherhood his accents betrayed the ardour of his faith. Or again, at the Ascension, the feast of Jesus which he most loved, because it was the summit of the glory of the Risen One. Is not the title – "And now, Father glorify Thy Son" – which he gave to his conference on this mystery significant of his thought and feeling? The pages which he has devoted to magnifying the supreme exaltation of Jesus, Son of God, may be counted among the most beautiful which he has left.

From the Person of Jesus Dom Columba's faith went out to *His words*. If Christ is God – and He is – He is also infallible Truth. Hence every word falling from His divine lips is the expression of very Truth. In what reverence Dom Marmion held the words of

Jesus; what faith he had in them! As we have said, he assiduously read the Scriptures which contain these testimonies of the Word. He was of those who "rejoice in the possession of these divine testimonies, as those who have found great spoil. They truly discover therein the hidden manna, which has a thousand different tastes, contains all sorts of delights and becomes their daily food, full of savour."[1] Thus, in his preaching he continually made appeal to the Scriptures: "It is our Lord who says it.... It is St Paul who writes this.... We find that in St John...." He often supported his doctrinal teaching on such phrases and, as we have said, it is in this habitual use of the Holy Scriptures that we find the secret of the unction which fills his works and is so eminently inspiring. The soul hungers for truth, and what truth is more adequate, more absolute, more productive of life and happiness than the truth which comes from above, from Him whose very words are spirit and life?

If all the words of Christ were for Dom Columba springs of living water, there were some over which he lingered with special delight: those turns of speech in use in His time which the Incarnate Word Himself chose to repeat: *Amen, amen, dico vobis:* "In truth, in truth, I say to you..."; or those which, because they lay down a general and absolute proposition, are singularly forcible: *Omnis...nihil...quotquot...* "*As many as* received Him, He gave the power to be made the sons of God.... *Everyone* that hath left house, or brethren, or sisters, or father, or mother, or wife, or children, or lands, for My Name's sake, shall receive an hundredfold and shall possess life everlasting.... *All* that you ask of the Father in My Name, He will give it you.... Without Me, you can do *nothing*...." In coming upon these terms and expressions, which reveal, in a special and intentional manner Christ's teaching, one would have said that Dom Marmion felt his conviction growing greater in the divinity of Jesus; raising his voice, he would then slowly lay stress on these words with such impressive accents that they could not fail to touch every right-thinking mind and simple heart.

What can now be added of the faith that he had in the *merits*

---

1 *Christ the Ideal of the Monk,* conference, "Monastic Prayer."

of Christ our Saviour? We must simply give up the attempt. Like St Paul, whose thought and whose very mind he made so much his own, Dom Marmion never wearied when he approached this subject; his voice took unaccustomed and forcible intonations; as under the apostle's pen, the word accumulated upon his lips, one expression was heaped upon another in exalting these infinite merits. He spoke of "abundance," of "superabundance," "of incomparable riches," of "inexhaustible treasures," of "unfathomable depths."

> I love to contemplate the episodes of the life of Jesus where we see His touching goodness for poor sinners, for the Samaritan woman, for Mary Magdalene.[1] The more I read and meditate on the Holy Scriptures, the more I pray, the more, too, I see that God's guidance of us is full of mercy: *non volentis neque currentis, sed miserentis est Dei.*[2] This mercy of God is infinite goodness, being poured out upon the hearts of the miserable. We everywhere find this proof of God's way of acting. Now, when I recite the Divine Office, I seem to see arise from each verse of the Psalms a light which speaks to us of the Divine Mercy.

Like the one who was pre-eminently the herald of the mystery of Jesus he, too, could say: "Gladly therefore will I glory in my infirmities that the power of Christ may dwell in me."

These thoughts were so familiar to Dom Marmion that, in his last years, he made the Divine Mercy one of the favourite subjects of his preaching. He often repeated: "I hear as it were a voice which says to me: 'Preach mercy!'" He therefore excelled in making hearts open out in confidence to the fullness of the redemption brought to the world by Jesus. Even on his deathbed, in those supreme hours when the inmost soul unconsciously reveals itself and discloses the secret of its whole life, he exalted the multitude "of the mercies of the Lord."

---

[1] See "Some Aspects of the Public Life of Jesus," in *Christ in His Mysteries*.
[2] "So then it is not of him that willeth, nor of him that runneth, but of God that sheweth mercy" (Rom. 9:16).

With no less strength and intensity Dom Columba's faith reached out to all that comes forth from Jesus, to all that prolongs and continues, reveals and gives Him: the Church, the sacramentals, the sacred hierarchy, the person of the sovereign pontiff, whose actions and directions he revered, the councils, the decisions of which he so gladly held, all that supernatural organism, the work of Jesus, wherein the believing soul finds light and life.

We now possess the secret source of Dom Marmion's inner life; we know from what deep root his great virtues sprang. He himself, following the Council of Trent, compared faith to a foundation, to a root; he liked to show how, according to the idea more than once expressed by St Paul, "the just man lives by *faith*."[1] And he here discloses, unknown to himself, at what pure and unfailing source his own life drew its vigour. Without much psychological effort it would be easy to find the connection between this fundamental virtue and the inmost life of this great soul. His life, so complex in its riches, so varied in its activity, was one and simple in the underlying motive which animated it: a hymn of faith aglow with love, practical and radiating, a hymn ever rising up to Christ and breaking forth anew in varied and manifold strains on a theme identical with that of St Paul: "I live in the faith of the Son of God, who loved me and delivered Himself for me."

The fundamental dogma that faith in Christ reveals to us is that of the Divine Fatherhood and of our supernatural adoption in Jesus through grace. "Now this is eternal life: That they may know Thee the only true God, and Jesus Christ whom Thou has sent."

"But as many as received Him, He gave the power to be made the sons of God, to them that believe in His name, who are born ... of God."

This grace of divine adoption in Jesus is particularly dear to Dom Marmion. It is the very basis of the whole of his teaching and of his interior life. In *Christ the Life of the Soul*, this fundamental thought

[1] Rom. 1:17; Gal. 3:11, and Heb. 10:38.

is thrown into bold relief in order to deduce therefrom the whole direction of the religious life:

"Holiness for us is nothing else than the complete unfolding, the full development of that first grace of our divine adoption, that grace given at baptism by which we become children of God and brethren of Christ Jesus. The substance of all holiness is to draw from this initial grace of adoption all the treasures and graces which it contains and that God causes to flow from it."[1]

He therefore approached this subject frequently and with marked satisfaction. A superior of Irish Carmelites wrote, 29 October 1925:[2] "This is the secret of our veneration for Dom Marmion and the reason why we considered him as a man chosen by God. He visited us twice, in 1919; in the course of the second visit he gave a conference to the community. The subject was his favourite theme: "The Divine Adoption." Although he did not speak at length, we felt that we were listening to something never before realised, and the impression made upon us all was something altogether unique."

It is certain that for such an impression to have lasted several years (the reader will have noticed the dates), Dom Marmion must have spoken most impressively in bringing out this subject. Those who knew him well will not be surprised at this: *he lived* – and with what intensity! – this doctrine of our "adoption."

Doubtless every baptised person is a child of God; but, as he himself remarked:

> In practice, there are souls that do not *act* as the adopted children of the Eternal Father. It would seem as if their condition of children of God had only a nominal value for them; they do not understand that it is a fundamental state which requires to be constantly manifested by acts corresponding to it, and that all spiritual life ought to be the development of the spirit of divine adoption, the spirit we receive at baptism through the virtue of Christ Jesus.[3]

1 Conference, "The Holy Spirit."
2 Letter to the author.
3 *Christ in His Mysteries,* conference "The Heart of Christ."

As for him, he lived it, and had already done so for a long time. We may recall that the first written testimony which fell from his pen was dated 1887. From that date forth we have noted many proofs of the same tonality of his inner life; this tonality went on being accentuated. We remember, too, how struck Cardinal Mercier was, from the very beginning of his relations with Dom Marmion, by the manner in which the latter spoke of the Heavenly Father, a manner which visibly betrayed his innermost sentiments.

To live as a child of the Heavenly Father; such was, without any possible doubt, his ideal. It was given to him to be filled with that filial spirit which denotes one of the highest states in the life of the saints, and supposes a rare ensemble of high virtues. In a discourse in honour of St Thérèse of Lisieux, who has, as it were, renewed in our days the doctrine on this subject, Pope Benedict xv brought out the qualities belonging to this state: "Deep humility, the conviction that supernatural perfection cannot be attained by human means, but likewise a living faith in God, a practical homage to His power and mercy, and confident recourse to His Providence."

Dom Marmion constantly practised these virtues; above all during his last years. The following passages clearly show this, and it is scarcely necessary to emphasise them, so much does the reality of these virtues shine out in them.

His faith in the Divine Paternity was always very great, but at this period of his life at which we have arrived the inner consciousness that he had of this paternity and of the supernatural filiation flowing therefrom was especially strong. He knows, he feels himself to be the child of the Heavenly Father. When this thought touches him it seems as if a kind of inward enthusiasm vibrates throughout his soul. He wrote in December 1919:

> It is such a grand thing that, being founded and rooted in Jesus,[1] we can unceasingly behold the face of the Father which

---

1 Eph. 3:17.

we shall contemplate in heaven through all eternity. And as, in heaven, *similes ei erimus quia videbimus eum sicuti est*,[1] this vision being the source of our holiness, so here upon earth this vision in faith is a fountain of life: *Quoniam apud te est fons vitae et in lumine tuo videbimus lumen*.[2] Pray much for me that in the midst of so many interruptions I may not cease to contemplate the face of the Father.[3]

Therefore his confidence in his Father in heaven was boundless. With St Paul, he loved and delighted to praise God under the title of Father of Mercies. His confidence in prayer was absolute. Many and many a time he commented on the words of Jesus: "Ask, and it shall be given you.... Which of you, if he ask his father bread, will he give him a stone?... Or if he shall ask an egg, will he reach him a scorpion?... If you then being evil, know how to give good gifts to your children, how much more will your Father from heaven give the good Spirit to them that ask Him?"

So great were this faith and confidence, that he went to God in all his needs with the simplicity of a child:

> *30 September 1908* – I have received a useful light during these days on the words of Scripture: *Revela Domino viam tuam et spera in eo, et Ipse faciet.*[4] Why 'reveal' anything to God? Because He wills that we should act towards Him like good children who go in all confidence to recount all their difficulties to their father. St Paul says the same: *In omni oratione et obsecratione cum gratiarum actione petitiones vestrae.* INNOTES-CANT *apud Deum.*[5] The Psalmist reveals all *his way*, that is to say, all his troubles, the persecutions he has to endure, and his temptations [*cf.* Ps. 37]. When we have troubles we are in-

---

1 "We shall be like to Him: because we shall see Him as He is" (1 John 3: 2).
2 "For with Thee is the fountain of life: and in Thy light we shall see light" (Ps. 35: 10).
3 Letter of 13 December 1919.
4 "Reveal thy way to the Lord, and trust in Him: and He will do it" (Ps. 36: 5).
5 "In everything, by prayer and supplication, with thanksgiving, let your petitions made known to God" (Phil. 4: 6).

clined to reveal them, to recount them to ourselves or to others: which serves for nothing, except to vex us or to wound charity. Whilst when we recount them to God *it is a prayer* which opens the heart and fills us with light and courage. Above all if, leaning upon Jesus Christ, we go to God *in the spirit of adoption,* and that notwithstanding our sins, after the example of the Prodigal Son.

Ten years later we find the same expression, still more accentuated, of this sense of the filial spirit:

Our Heavenly Father, in spite of my infidelities, heaps upon me His mercies in Jesus Christ. It seems as if our Lord is revealing to me more and more the abysses of mercy and love of our Father, and I go to Him in simple and sincere faith, like a little child. It is the property of a father to communicate his life to his child and to cure his ills and thus I often come before Him, and I feel that He does not repulse me.[1]

A childlike state of soul, but luminous and strong, and which fully carries out the *nisi efficiamini sicut parvuli ...* of the Gospel. He writes to one of his dearest spiritual children:

I will sing the Mass for us both, that the Heavenly Father may unite us more and more in His holy love and lead us to Jesus. 'No man can come to Me,' says Jesus, 'unless the Father ... draw him.' Yes, my daughter, every perfect gift (Jesus, Mary, grace, holy friendship) and best gift comes down from *the Father.* Oh! Let us love Him with ALL our heart! 'Whosoever shall do the will of My Father,' says Jesus, 'he is My brother, and sister, and mother. We can do nothing dearer to the Heart of Jesus than to unite ourselves to Him in His love for His Father and in the doing of His Holy Will.[2]

But it is only in holy self-abandonment that the life of a child of

---

1 Letter of 31 July 1917.
2 Letter of 14 August 1912.

God has its perfect unfolding. Dom Marmion considered self-abandonment as one of the purest forms of filial love. On this spirit of self-abandonment he has written admirable pages which may be numbered amongst those which came most truly from his heart. It is above all in this domain that may be applied to him what St Gregory said of St Benedict on the subject of the *Rule:* "He could not write otherwise than he lived." From the very beginning of his religious life we have seen Dom Marmion serve his crucifying apprenticeship to self-abandonment: "My Jesus, I have only You on whom I can count...."[1] All through his monastic life he had to practise this virtue; the time spent at Louvain marked an important step in this direction; but at the end of his life he appears to have felt particularly strongly on this subject.

"The filial spirit," he writes to one of his spiritual daughters in a letter of 1 March 1918, "calls for a great respect and deep reverence in face of the ways of the Heavenly Father. All His ways are mercy and truth, but often remain hidden. The Father's wisdom and power are never so much manifested as when he draws good out of evil, and when He acts in such a way that the errors or even the ill will of men serve to further His designs: *Omnia servient Tibi.*"[2]

Therefore he sought with all the strength of his faith and love to carry out to the full the will of the Father, and to yield himself up to His good pleasure. A letter addressed to the same nun and dated a few weeks later – which shows that Dom Marmion continued to find abundant food in these thoughts – expresses his feelings under an arresting and original form:

> I earnestly ask our Father on your behalf: *Sanctifica eam in veritate.*[3] We ought to wish intensely to be *just* what our Heavenly Father wishes us to be, and nothing more nor less. I said to Him some days ago, from the depths of my heart: 'Father, be my director; make me just what you want me to be: very

---

1 See p. 55.
2 See *Christ the Ideal of the Monk,* ch. 16.
3 John 17:17.

weak, very miserable in myself,[1] but very strong and very faithful in You, in Your spirit. My daughter, I BELIEVE in the Father's love for us, and I want Him in return to see my love for Him in Jesus Christ.[2]

Love and self-abandonment, which trial only make shine out the more. He writes during the last year of his life:

> I am well, *Deo Gratias*. The good God sustains me. Despite great temptations and inward trials, I keep very united to His Holy Will. He seems sometimes to reject me, and I well deserve this, but I persist in hoping in Him.... I see that the true way to go to God is often to bow down before Him in a deep sense of our unworthiness, and then, *believing* in His goodness: *nos credidimus caritati Dei,* to throw oneself into His arms, upon His paternal Heart.[3]

Do not all these beautiful passages give us some idea of the intensity with which Dom Marmion lived his life as an adoptive son of God?

"Perfect happiness, supreme joy," wrote Dom Marmion in a letter of 5 June 1913, "is found in *sinu Patris,* and Jesus is the way that leads to it. Without Him we can do nothing. No one goes to the Father but by Him."

No other truth of faith was dearer to Dom Columba nor gives us better the secret of his whole inner life.

> We are here at the central point of the Divine Plan: it is from Jesus Christ, it is through Jesus Christ that we receive the divine adoption (in order to be like to Him and to partake of

---

[1] That is to say, "being conscious of the impossibility of attaining to holiness of myself." Benedict XV says again that the childlike spirit "excludes the presumption of hoping to attain, by human means, a supernatural end and the fallacious tendency to self-sufficiency in the hour of danger and temptation."
[2] Letter of 19 March 1918.
[3] Letter of 9 March 1922.

His Divine Sonship).... We are sons, like Jesus; we, by grace; He, by nature; He, God's own Son; we, His adopted sons.[1]

All Christian life, all holiness, is being by grace what Jesus is by nature: the Son of God. It is this that makes the sublimity of our religion. The source of all the greatness of Jesus, the source of the value of all His states, of the fruitfulness of all His mysteries, is His Divine Generation and His quality of Son of God. In the same way, the saint who is the highest in heaven is the one who here below was most perfectly a child of God, who made the grace of supernatural adoption in Jesus Christ fructify the most.[2]

If this doctrine constitutes "the central point of the Divine Plan," it is likewise the central point of all Dom Marmion's preaching: the whole of his spiritual work, as the very titles of his volumes testify, comes from this.

But here again there is the same unity, and his preaching is but the echo of his inner life. The attentive reader will easily follow the influence of these truths in his spiritual conferences. We evidently cannot thus analyse them here. At the point we have reached, what we can and should heed are some of the as yet unpublished documents, which disclose in this matter the special tonality of his spiritual life during his latter years. We shall find in them, as strong as ever, the expression of the virtues of the child of God.

At Louvain the constant influx of divine grace had brought Dom Marmion's soul to a total and loving dependence on the Incarnate Word to the glory of the Father. He verified the formula of St Paul: *Omnia subjecisti sub pedibus ejus.* This grace in which he had long continued was more and more strengthened by new lights.

> Our Lord gives me a great attraction for this way: the complete and *continual* laying down of my whole self at the feet of the Incarnate Word. I want to imitate the Sacred Humanity of Jesus in its unity (with the Word), in its submission and

[1] *Christ the Life of the Soul*, conference I, v.
[2] *Christ in His Mysteries*, conference "In sinu Patris," VI.

absolute dependence on the Word. Help me, my daughter, to realise this ideal, for all lies in that. Once the Father sees a soul thus *one* with His Word, there are no graces or favours which He will not give to it.

The sacred Humanity of Jesus is the 'way.' Its power to unite us to the Word is infinite. Let us then glorify Him by being saints: *In hic clarificatus est Pater meus ut fructum plurimum afferatis.*[1]

The following note, written the day after a retreat, discloses the intensity of this life of union where Dom Marmion's deep sense of humility is harmonised with his vivid consciousness of his riches in Jesus:

God has given me a deep sense of my unworthiness, of my misery. I will glory in these weaknesses *ut inhabitet in me virtus Christi.*[2] The *virtus Christi* glorifies the Father, especially when joined to the misery we acknowledge. Jesus *in assumptae carnis* INFIRMITATE[3] *was the virtus (Christus Dei virtus et Sapientia)*[4] joined to weakness, and this gave infinite glory to the Father. This *virtus* is the life of Jesus in me. The more I inwardly abase myself by the consciousness of my unworthiness, the more this *virtus*, this life of Jesus will be manifested in me.

Communion in the states and mysteries of Jesus Christ.

The life of Jesus Christ is manifested in Him by an expansion, a more perfect expression in each mystery. Different souls are called to communicate in these divers states. It is an attraction of the Holy Spirit.

To empty the soul of the creature. To fill it with God. Death to sin and to all that is not God.

To communicate in His death by compunction and the spirit of penance. To communicate in His risen life (Jesus as

---

[1] Letter of 8 November 1910.
[2] "That the power of Christ may dwell in me" (2 Cor. 12:9).
[3] In the infirmity of the flesh which He deigned to take.
[4] "Christ the power of God, and the wisdom of God" (1 Cor. 1:24).

He now is). 1. Detachment from the world; 2. Light (illuminative way).

To communicate in the life of Jesus ascended to heaven: 1. Consummation in God; 2. Glory; 3. Power.

This private note, dated 1911, is one of the last we have of his; Dom Marmion was more and more absorbed by "business." It is to letters we must henceforward look to have revealed to us – at long intervals, for they, too, become more rare – some of the interior ascensions of his soul towards the Heavenly Father in union with Jesus.

19 February 1911 – I am much more united (now) to our Lord than at the beginning (of my abbacy) and He sensibly blesses the efforts that I make to govern His house according to His Holy Will. I feel myself especially drawn by Jesus to *dwell* with Him *in sinu Patris,* but this requires much fidelity and abnegation.

16 February 1913 – I do hope I may henceforth live for God *alone.* I feel our Lord wants me to live as He did: *propter Patrem,* and that in two senses: (1) That all my inspiration may come from Him; (2) all my activity be employed for Him.

13 December 1913 – our Lord has been drawing me very strongly for some time to a life more united with Him. My great longing is to see Jesus *reign* and *live* in such a manner in my soul that all my powers, all my faculties, all my desires, may be perfectly subject to Him. Pray for this intention.

20 July 1914 – As for me, I am very close to our Lord. He is always in my heart, and I confide to Him all my cares, all my anxieties. The thought that He is ever before the face of His Father in a twofold capacity fills me with consolation and strength. He is there (*a*) inasmuch as He is the Only-begotten Son by right, in the bosom of the Father, adoring Him, loving Him, etc....; (*b*) as Head of His mystical body, *Semper apparet vultui Dei pro nobis:*[1] He is there as Jesus, 'for us and for our salvation': *Semper vivens ad interpellandum pro nobis.*[2] He presents to His Father for us His Sacrifice once offered, but *always continued*. United with Him we enter by right into the *sanctuarium exauditionis* (the sanctuary) where all petitions are heard.

Luminous passages which comment would only weaken.

The last lines were written a few days before the declaration of war. Like everyone else, Dom Marmion was drawn into the vortex, then had to undergo the manifold tribulations of the German occupation. Letters – which had to be entrusted to private messengers, who ran the risk of encountering the enemy – become rare. They, however, give us an insight of the continuity and progress of this life hidden in God with Christ.

From this epoch one thought will often return under his pen, doubtless because he had received it by an "impression of grace": like St Paul,[3] he saw in the humanity of Jesus the *veil* which hides His divinity from us and through which it is necessary to pass to come to the very fountain-head, the infinite God, "the Father of Lights." Eucharistic Communion is the special means of this union:

> I am very happy in the holy solitude of our monastery, where it is so easy to find the one whom we seek. For some time past I think I have received a special favour from our Lord. It is a deep and habitual union with the Word through the sacred humanity of Jesus, especially through Holy Communion. I understand more and more that this humanity is the *velamen*, the sacred 'veil,' through which we attain to the Word. *In me manet*, it is the formal effect of the sacrament of the Eucharist. And in return, *Ego in eo:*[4] He abides in me by His life and merits.

---

1 "That He may appear now in the presence of God for us" (Heb. 9:24).
2 "Always living to make intercession for us" (Heb. 7:25).
3 Heb 10:20.
4 "Abideth in Me, and I in Him" (John 6:57).

The more one is little and powerless in oneself the more one glorifies Jesus Christ by faith and confidence in His merits. His Precious Blood, which does not cease to flow in the Holy Sacrifice, purifies us, and we pass through the veil (the sacred humanity) into the Holy of Holies, there to surrender oneself without reservation or preference to the action of God.[1]

On the feast day of one of his daughters, her patron being St Gabriel, he shared with her the great thoughts with which the name and mission of the archangel inspired him:

May St Gabriel enlighten our hearts that we may comprehend the abysses of love in the Incarnation. It is the union of God with our nature. The more perfect this union, the more our nature is divinised. In Jesus this union is hypostatic, without human intermediary, and therefore the divinity inundates this sacred humanity with ineffable torrents of divine life. This divine life entered into Jesus by the fine point of His spirit, ever bathed in the radiance of the Beatific Vision, whence flowed this divine life which inundated the sacred humanity. Even upon the cross, whilst all the inferior powers of the soul of Jesus were submerged in a sea of sorrow and darkness, this fine point (of His spirit) ever beheld the face of the Father.

Through Holy Communion our members and our powers are identified with those of Jesus and receive little by little the grace to live the same life *by faith – justus ex fide vivit –* and *according to the measure of our union with the God-Man.* That is the way, my dear daughter. May St Gabriel give us *strength*[2] to follow it, *fortes in fide*. I will ask for you that in the midst of your trials the fine point of your soul may remain always attached to the face (*i.e.* good pleasure) of the Heavenly Father. Do not be astonished at your weaknesses. It is in weakness that virtue is perfected. The more you feel your incapac-

1 Letter of 20 December 1916.
2 *Gabriel* means "strength of God."

ity, your weakness, the more you lean upon *Him* – the more your virtue is supernatural and pleasing to God.[1]

And some months later: "Let us keep very united to the Heart of Jesus. Let us unite our soul and our heart to His, that we may see through His eyes and love with His Heart."[2]

"To see through the eyes of Jesus, to love with His Heart," in order to be through Him and like Him, a worthy child of the Heavenly Father: that was the whole aspiration of Dom Marmion's life – an aspiration kept alive at the divine and glowing furnace of faith of which the pure rays flooded his soul particularly at this time.

In 1918, in consequence of "an important light he had received," he sets forth with nervous conciseness all the mystery of the Divine Sonship – in its eternal source – in its realisation in Jesus – and in its extension in souls.

> The Word proceeds *entirely* from the Father. This is why the Father finds in Him His glory, His infinite joy. This Word flows back into the bosom of the Father *entirely*, with infinite love.
>
> Jesus expresses this mystery in His humanity: (*a*) by His absolute dependence on the Father. He has neither doctrine, nor project, nor work, but what He sees in His Father. It is absolute divine perfection; (*b*) in doing all things out of love for the Father: *quae placita sunt Patri facio semper.*
>
> So with us. 'Of His own Will hath He begotten us by the Word.'[3] In Him and with Him we ought to flow back with love *in sinu Patris.* (*a*) Our joy should be *ut faciam voluntatem ejus qui misit me.*[4] Projects and ambitious daydreaming are opposed to this love; (*b*) we should do all for this love: *ambulate in dilectione sicut filii carissimi.*[5]

[1] Letter of 14 March 1917.
[2] Letter of 4 December 1917.
[3] Jas.I:18.
[4] "To do...the will of Him that sent Me" (John 6:38).
[5] "As most dear children...walk in love" (Eph. 5:1, 2). Dom Marmion here unites in a single phrase two ideas which St Paul expresses separately. Let us also give here these following lines of the same period: "I have understood

To these vivid lights were added the call of grace: "Our Lord," he writes from the Eternal City, in 1919, "keeps me so near to Him in the midst of all kind of distractions and preoccupations. When the soul has learnt the secret of coming to the Word through the Sacred Humanity of Jesus this holy union is consummated in the midst of noise and disturbance. One understands what depth there is in these words: *Sponsabo te mihi in fide*."[1]

Those to whom mystical questions are familiar will grasp without difficulty the fullness of life that these lines reveal.

The life of Dom Marmion may be summed up in these words of St Paul, which he often paraphrased: "Let this mind be in you which was also in Christ Jesus." He in no way understood imitation of our Lord to consist in a material and literal copying of a certain category of our Saviour's actions, or of certain verses in the Gospel, however beautiful, but as an adaptation of our inner life to that of Christ Jesus, especially in His attitude towards the Heavenly Father: *Hoc sentite.*... Hence, for example, his custom of interpreting the Psalms as mysterious utterances of our Saviour's soul, and the way in which He understood devotion to the Passion – namely, as the endeavour to live the sentiments that flowed from the soul of Christ in the midst of His sufferings.

For him, then, as for St Paul, to live was Christ, and nothing, neither trials, nor comings and goings, nor solitude, nor crowds could separate him from Christ, because it was through Him that he went to the Father, through Him that he was blessed by the Father, with Him that he entered and dwelt "in the bosom of the Father."

Therefore a few months before his death he was able to write

by these words of Jesus: *Tui erant et mihi eos dedisti,* a profound mystery. We were in the Father, so to speak, called to salvation, but our predestination as children of God is wrought through *Christ: Praedestinavit nos in adoptionem filiorum per Jesum Christum.* It is He who made us children of the Heavenly Father: *Quotquot autem receperunt eum dedit eis potestatem filios Dei fieri.* We are begotten supernaturally by the Father in Jesus Christ: *Ex Deo nati sunt.* And Jesus having made us children by His Passion, offers us to His Father hidden in Him: *Ut nos offerret Deo. Omnia vestra sunt, vos autem Christi, Christus autem Dei.*"

1 "I have espoused thee in faith" (Osee 2:20). Letter of 2 February 1919.

these few lines, almost the last that he has left on his inner life: a cry of burning faith – and in what Pauline accents! – in the One who had been the passion of his whole life: "I find Christ everywhere and in everything. He is the Alpha and the Omega of all. I am so poor, so miserable in myself, and so rich in Him. To Him be all glory forever!"[1]

"It appears to me," wrote Dom Marmion one day, "that the more closely I become united with our Divine Lord, the more He draws me towards His Father – the more He wills me to be filled with His filial Spirit. It is the whole Spirit of the new Law: *Non enim accepistis spiritum servitutis in timore, sed acceptistis Spiritum* ADOPTIONIS *filiorum in quo clamanus: Abba, Pater.*"[2]

Dom Marmion brought out this thought in a striking manner in his beautiful and characteristic conference: "The Holy Spirit, the Spirit of Jesus;"[3] he there gathered together in vigorous pages all the essential points of the doctrine on this subject. He scarcely ever preached a retreat without devoting one conference to the Holy Spirit, and he spoke with exceptional gravity when he warned souls not to "extinguish or grieve" the Divine Guest.

> Rather let us remain ... faithful to the 'Spirit of Truth' who is also the Spirit of holiness; let us be souls promptly docile to the touches of this Spirit. What deep joy and what inward liberty a soul tastes that thus gives itself up to the action of the Holy Spirit! This Divine Spirit will cause us to bear fruits of holiness ... so that by His workings we may reproduce in ourselves, to the glory of the Father, the traits of that Divine Sonship that we have in Christ Jesus.[4]

In some notes – hastily set down on the leaves of a pocketbook,

---

1 Letter of 28 June 1922.
2 Rom. 8:15. Letter of 15 November 1908.
3 In *Christ the Life of the Soul*.
4 In *Christ the Life of the Soul*.

and twenty years before the publication of his works – Dom Marmion reveals how much he felt drawn to give himself up to the guidance of the Holy Spirit.

> *3 March 1900* – When the Word espoused and endowed His humanity, the spouse being God, the dowry had to be divine. According to the Fathers and the Doctors or the Church, what the Word truly gave as dowry to His humanity was the Holy Spirit, who proceeds from Him as well as from the Father, and is substantially the plenitude of holiness. This was the living and infinite unction with which He consecrated this human nature. *Unxit te Deus, Deus tuus, oleo laetitiae prae consortibus tuis.*[1]
>
> For some time I have felt more and more a special attraction towards the Holy Spirit. I have a great desire to be guided, led, moved in all things by the Spirit of Jesus. Our Lord, as man, did nothing except under the impulsion of the Holy Spirit and under His dependence. Hence it followed that possessing in Himself and Himself alone – as to the hypostatic union – this holy humanity, the Word never operated or wrought anything in His human nature save through His Holy Spirit.

And after having quoted several texts in support of this truth, Dom Marmion continues:

> We, too, have received the same Spirit in baptism, and in the sacrament of confirmation: *Quoniam estis filii, misit Spiritum Filii sui in corda vestra.*[2] *Qui adhaeret Domino, unus Spiritus est.*[3] St Paul speaks constantly of the Spirit of Jesus who guided Him and enlightened Him in all things.
>
> All that, in our activity, comes from this Holy Spirit is holy.

---

1 "God hath anointed thee with the oil of gladness above thy fellows" (Ps. 44: 8).
2 "Because you are sons, God hath sent the spirit of His Son into your hearts" (Gal. 4: 6).
3 "He who is joined to the Lord, is one spirit (with Him)" (1 Cor. 6: 17).

> *Quod natum est ex Spiritu, spiritus est...*[1] *Spiritus est qui vivificat.*[2] He who yields himself up without reserve or resistance to this Spirit who is *Pater pauperum ... Dato munerum*[3] will be infallibly led by the same path as Jesus, and in the manner that Jesus wills for each one. This Spirit led Elizabeth to praise Mary, and Mary is led by the same Spirit of Jesus to magnify the glory of the Lord.
>
> The Holy Spirit leads us to call upon the Father in the same way as Jesus did: *Spiritus adoptionis in quo clamamus: Abba, Pater;* to glorify Jesus: *Ipse testimonium perhibebit de me*[4] to pray as is right, in offering the supplications He makes for us in our hearts: *gemitibus inenarrabilibus*[5] to humility, to compunction, *quia ipse est remissio omnium peccatorum.*[6] It is by Him that we do good to souls (the apostles did so little before Pentecost). It is He who fructifies all our activity: *Nemo potest dicere Domine Jesu nisi in Spiritu sancto.*[7]
>
> Oh, I will strive to live in this Holy Spirit!

We shall be forgiven this long quotation showing us once more, as it does, at what a pure fount of doctrine the soul of Dom Marmion drank, and throwing light on one of the deepest aspects of his spiritual life.

Of his letters on this subject we will give only one passage – how difficult to choose from amongst such riches!

> God seeks those who adore Him in *Spirit* and in truth. He (the Holy Spirit) is the Spirit of the Father and Son, and those who allow themselves to be led by Him, seek the Father and the Son in truth. He is the *Holy* Spirit, because all His inspirations

---

[1] "That which is born of the Spirit is spirit" (John 3:6).
[2] "It is the spirit that quickeneth" (John 6:64).
[3] "Father of the poor, Bestower of gifts" (*Sequence* of the Mass of Pentecost).
[4] "He shall give testimony of Me" (John 15:26).
[5] "With unspeakable groanings" (Rom. 8:26).
[6] "He is Himself the remission of sins" (Prayer to obtain the gift of tears, *Missale Romanum*).
[7] "No man can say the Lord Jesus, but by the Holy Ghost" (1 Cor. 12:5).

are infinitely holy. He is the same identical Spirit which inspires Jesus in every act and thought, and it is by union with Him that the interior of Jesus Christ is formed in our hearts. He is the *Pater pauperum,* the Father of the poor, He does not disdain to unite Himself with those who remain in *adoration and spirit of annihilation* in His presence. He is the Spirit of holy charity and being the same in all unites us in holy love.[1]

Dom Marmion ardently aspired to live in this filial and loving spirit, which was to perfect in him the state of a child of God. We have as proof of this one of his habitual practices of devotion. We have said above that he often earnestly commented on the words of Jesus to His disciples: "If you, then, being evil, know how to give good gifts to your children, how much more will your Father from heaven give the good Spirit to them that ask Him!" These words must have struck him particularly, for he had taken from them, from the first years of his novitiate, the following practice of devotion to which he remained faithful until his last days. In the Divine Office the recitation of each Psalm ends with the doxology *Gloria Patri*.... Dom Marmion mentally added to each *Gloria* this prayer: "Heavenly Father, give me the spirit of adoption."

The "Father of mercies" must have heard this prayer, inspired by His Son and repeated frequently every day during long years. Does not the unction with which Dom Marmion's spiritual works abound sufficiently reveal the constant intercourse of his soul with the Spirit of love, and the abundance in him of the gift of adoption?

---

1 Letter of 5 October 1906.

17 THE FRUITS OF THE SPIRIT OF ADOPTION

The spirit of adoption shed abroad in us by sanctifying grace makes us all one in Christ, all children of the same Heavenly Father. It must therefore necessarily blossom out into love for the neighbour. St Paul places love, goodness, and joy amongst the fruits of this spirit.[1]

Dom Columba perfectly realised this doctrine. "In meditating on the institution of the Holy Eucharist," he wrote one day, "I feel urged to unite myself to Jesus, to give, like Him, my body, my blood, all, for the salvation of my neighbour. I am the adopted son of God."[2]

We need not repeat how supernatural, intense, disinterested, multiform and far-reaching was Dom Marmion's charity. A few familiar touches will help to complete the portrayal of his soul. Dom Marmion comes before us with a goodness modelled on that of the Father in heaven, and which, ever ready to give, never exhausted its resources.

A cloistered nun learnt that he was about to leave for Rome, where he would probably be received by Pius x. "Oh! How happy she would be if the Abbot of Maredsous would consent to beg for her from the Vicar of Jesus Christ a souvenir ... *all for herself.* It was great audacity, certainly, to express such a desire, but Fr Columba would thus make an old, long-cherished dream come true." Dom Marmion promised to do his best. Although he had to treat of serious and numerous affairs, he did not forget his promise. He had the joy of seeing the request granted, and directly after his conversation with the Sovereign Pontiff he sent this note to the religious:

> Just a word to say that I had a long audience with the pope today. He was *most kind.* He wrote the enclosed for you: (*Deus te repleat omni benedictione. Pius* PP.X), and I send it as a token.

[1] Gal. 5:22.
[2] February 1899.

His words are those of Jesus Christ, who really intends to fill you with every grace and benediction.¹

There were other requests of less consequence – more humble desires. Dom Columba intuitively divined the wishes of others, sometimes almost before they were formed, and the realisation of which brought joy to the simple hearts that had fostered them. He knew, besides, that the golden ray of divine charity may touch and transform the smallest acts. On one occasion he had to be absent for rather a long time. A good old lay sister of a convent which he regularly served heard it said that he had gone to Fort Augustus.² She imagined that it was far, far away – almost as if beyond the stars – and that everything must be very different in those regions. And she asked ingenuously:

"Will he not bring us a flower from that country?"

This desire was mentioned incidentally to Dom Columba in a letter about some business. And on his return he brought back a flower, a... marigold, all crumpled up, in a little envelope. And giving it to the Mother Superior:

"For Sister X—," he said.

The good old lay sister, who held Dom Marmion in affectionate veneration, was overjoyed. She carefully smoothed out the petals and gummed the flower from the "far country" on stiff paper. Then on Dom Marmion's next visit she asked him if he would be so kind as to sign his name on it.

"Willingly," he said. And as the sister was Flemish, he wrote with as much delicacy as spontaneity: *"Vader* Columba."

Ready to seize every opportunity of giving joy to those around him, Dom Marmion tried for his own part not to be an occasion of trouble or embarrassment to anyone. When he went to Ireland the necessities of his work in a certain town obliged him to stay in the house of a friend; it happened more than once, either when he

---

1 Letter of 22 September 1912.
2 In Inverness-shire, where there is a Benedictine monastery.

preached a retreat or when other affairs detained him, that he had to prolong his stay with the family who was giving him hospitality.

"It is a strange thing," the mistress of the house – to whom we owe this detail – said to him one day, "whenever you come to us, far from having any of our arrangements upset, or feeling there is any extra work, as is usual in such cases, my husband and I, as well as the maid, find that things never go so well."

"It is a gift of the Heavenly Father," he at once replied. "I do as Jesus commanded his apostles: to ask peace for those who dwell in the house where they entered. Each time a family receives me I ask the Heavenly Father that my presence may, not only cause no worry, but be a source of peace. And I see that, in His goodness, He deigns to grant me this favour on your behalf."

Delicate foresight, all imbued with the supernatural and quite in keeping with his spirit of filial faith.

Even when it was extended to strangers the warmth of his charity made itself felt. To his kindness in material almsgiving he added kind words, of which the spontaneous cordiality was more touching than all the rest.

Several years after his death the prioress of a Carmel in the south of France paid him this testimony:

> We have not had the happiness of seeing Dom Marmion or of hearing him preach. This is how we came to write to him. A few years ago some friends of our monastery undertook to beg help for us in repairing our old convent. One of them gave us some addresses, among which appeared that of Dom Marmion, to whom we were quite unknown. I wrote therefore to Father Abbot. He was not able to reply to me himself, but he had a letter written to me, so kind, so fatherly that we were deeply touched. He insisted that we should keep him *au courant* with our troubles and difficulties, interesting himself in us as if he had always known us. An offering accompanied these proofs of affectionate interest. A short time afterwards, when we heard of his death, we were

greatly grieved, for we felt as if we had lost a father who had been full of charity to us.¹

Such was Dom Marmion: a big overflowing heart; the purest and most delicate Christian charity illuminating and transfiguring every relationship; and this charity springing from the love of God, showed itself as inexhaustible as its source.

What often doubled the merit of Dom Marmion's charity and the value of his smile was the fact that he himself, whilst spreading joy around him, was under the wine-press. The "clients" of his goodness did not even suspect this, but no doubt the angels were enraptured. Does not St Paul² give patience the first place in his enumeration of the qualities of charity? And does he not see it as flowing from mildness and benignity, from the spirit of love?³ – Dom Marmion's patience, as we have said, was remarkable.

At the end of his life, he wrote:

> Our Lord has made me understand these words of St Paul: *Christo crucifixus sum cruci, vivi ego, jam non ego,*⁴ etc. It is on the cross that Jesus is most surely found during this life. He has asked me to share this cross with Him, and I there find Paradise. When we are young we serve our Lord by activity, but when old age comes (I am sixty-three) we serve Him by patience: *Passionibus Christi per patientiam participamus.*⁵ I have come to that.

In reality he had for a long time followed Christ in patience. We may recall the rugged trials of his novitiate. Reading between the lines of the extracts we have given from his letters, we see that trials, especially inward trials, were never wanting to him. But his soul

---

1 Letter of 30 September 1927, to the author.
2 1 Cor. 13:4.
3 Gal. 5:22.
4 Gal. 2:19–20.
5 *Rule of St Benedict*, "Prologue."

generously accepted the fragments of the cross that Christ broke off from His own for him in order to make him more like to Himself. And if he was often able to exhort souls to patience with sympathetic discernment, it was because he possessed that indefinable finishing touch which is given by suffering patiently endured.

"*23 January 1909* – As for me, I am in the dark night and in great weakness of soul, but all the same very content with all that God does."

The years of the German occupation and the post-war years were particularly painful; the echo of these trials reaches us at distant intervals:

> *1 December 1916* – I have had much to suffer these days, but God is always there.

> *11 February 1917* – God sends us trials which destroy self-love, trials we should not have chosen, but which are the best for us. He knows and loves us better than we do ourselves. The acts of faith and confidence which we make on these occasions are dear to Him. I have many trials, but our Heavenly Father consoles and strengthens me.

> *14 March 1917* – I have great trials of all kinds at this moment and the poor body is very weak. I know that you pray for me.

> *14 March 1921* – I have been fastened to the cross by bodily and moral sufferings. It is a gift from our Lord, for He sees what little courage I have to mortify myself, and He provides for this Himself. He knows how to do so.

We must not be misled by this last humble avowal. With this man, sensitive nature shrank from suffering and mortification. Did not Christ in person, Model of all perfection, will that His sensitive nature should shrink before the chalice of the Passion?

Dom Marmion held resolutely for his part to the practice of renunciation and penance. Never did he fail to keep a fast of the Church or fast of the *Rule*; never, even when ill, did he spare himself the strain of a Pontifical Mass or of preaching when he celebrated a late parochial Mass. A simple detail shows what he was: when travelling, he regularly took his discipline with him, and in his later years he scourged himself several times a week.

As a simple monk, as prior at Louvain, as Abbot of Maredsous, he was constantly faithful to the common life, that "penance of penances," as he called it. In the close analysis he has given of the mortifications of the regular life one feels he is speaking from experience. We may be sure that when he spoke of the "little sacrifices" which may be multiplied in the course of one day of life in the cloister he himself had made these sacrifices; he felt, and often keenly, all the persevering self-abnegation this life demands. If he could vigorously insist upon "faithfulness, out of love, in small things," it was because he first set the example of this virtue.

A frequent source of mortification was the uncertainty of his health, aggravated in his case by increasing stoutness: "It is an excellent thing," he said – thereby revealing one of his practices – "to accept uncomplainingly from our Lord's hands the body we have received with its weaknesses, its heaviness, its sufferings, and to say as Christ did: *Corpus autem aptasti mihi:*[1] O Father, I will to have this body such as You have willed it for me, with all the trouble it may bring me."

During long years, especially at the end of his life, he suffered continually from eczema, but he bore this very painful mortification with great patience and good humour:

"It is my hair shirt," he said, in laughing to the Father Infirmarian, "and so much the better in that I did not choose it for myself!"

"When Father Abbot arrived at our house," we read in one account, "through pouring rain or under a burning sun, he never allowed us to condole with him about the heat or cold, and I have seen him with the drops of perspiration on his brow, say gaily: 'It is the sun of the Heavenly Father[2].... It is the good God who made the sun.'"

1 "A body Thou has fitted to Me" (Heb. 10:5).
2 Allusion to the words of Jesus: "Your Father who is in Heaven...maketh His

THE FRUITS OF THE SPIRIT OF ADOPTION

"I try," he often said, "to meet all vexations with a smile."

There might well be heroism in that smile. Opposition from men, adverse happenings, inclemency of the weather, uncertain health, fatigues of the apostolate, daily and harassing trials of government, constantly recurring anxieties in an administration which we know was too heavy for his shoulders – he strove to welcome all these things with love.

The result of Dom Marmion's constant and daily self-abnegation was great detachment of soul and that inward liberty of the children of God which is one of its most precious fruits.

We have said enough of his detachment as regards people. In the use of creatures, for example, food – as in many other things besides – Dom Marmion had no difficulty in remaining faithful to the high principles which inspired him: in this matter to live according to the Gospel and to keep simply to the very precept of Jesus: *Manducate quae apponuntur vobis*,[1] and he showed neither preference nor aversion in regard to food.

This simplicity – as, moreover, his jovial manner and his face and figure, in which so little of the ascetic was outwardly visible – sometimes gave a wrong impression; appearances were against him, but a close observer could not be deceived. "When he was on the way to X—," relates one of his friends, "it was, for the whole family, a joy to receive him. At table he always, with perfect courtesy, did honour to all that was offered him. And yet we had clearly the impression that his soul was elsewhere. In the midst of the conversation and the sallies of his wit, all at once a remark, a single word, a simple gesture, such as that of raising his eyes to heaven, made the 'man' suddenly give place to the servant of God. But this was done so naturally, without a shadow of affectation, it rose so spontaneously from the depth of his soul, that the contrast was simply delightful. And very often it was for us a living object-lesson worth a whole instruction."

---

sun to rise upon the good and bad" (Matt. 5: 45).
1 Luke 10: 8.

In all the details of his life, the least as well as the most important, but especially in the most difficult, Dom Marmion had accustomed himself to see God's hand; he felt the nearness of the Heavenly Father's heart and ever strove to respond with a loving *fiat*.

On the occasion of a visit to Rome in 1912, he was received in audience by the Sovereign Pontiff, Pius x. These two great hearts, both so supernatural, were well made to understand one another. At the end of the interview Dom Columba begged the Holy Father to deign to give him, as he said, "a text for his own soul." Pius x reflected an instant, took a holy picture and wrote on the back these lines: *In cunctis rerum angustiis, hoc cogita: Dominus est. Et Dominus tibi erit adjutor fortis.* "In all difficult circumstances think of this: it is the Lord. And the Lord will be to you a strong helper." These lines from Christ's vicar were too much in accordance with Dom Columba's own thoughts and feelings to fail to strike him particularly. He saw in them, as it were, a confirmation of the way of self-abandonment which he had made his own. He often meditated on these words. We find the direct echo of them in a note written a few years later.

> 24 *June 1917 (Feast of the Precursor)* – I have understood why St John the Baptist, whose mission was to announce Christ, announces Him under the figure of the Lamb of God. Jeremiah had already said: *Ego quasi agnus mansuetus qui ducitur ad victimam.*[1] Isaias also: *Sicut ovis coram tondente se obmutescet.*[2] St Peter tells us that we are 'redeemed with ... the precious blood of Christ, as of a lamb unspotted and undefiled.' In the Apocalypse, Christ is represented like a lamb, as it were, slain. The lamb is then one of the scriptural figures of Christ as Victim. Now, what characterises the lamb is that it is immolated and keeps silence: *Non aperiens os suum.* Christ was immolated in yielding Himself up to the whole will of His Father, to all the sufferings of His Passion: *Faciem meam non averti....*[3]

1 "I was as a meek lamb that is carried to be a victim" (Jer. 11:19).
2 "He shall be dumb as a lamb before his shearers" (Isa. 53:7).
3 I have not turned away My face from them that rebuked Me and spit upon Me" (Isa. 50:6).

It is a *great* perfection to unite ourselves to the Lamb in this offering and to accept, with Him, without murmuring, all the sufferings and all the trials that our Heavenly Father permits, in saying: *Dominus est*. Hence the beauty of the fourth degree of humility (heroic patience)[1] and the bane of murmuring.

He wrote in a letter of 17 June 1922: "Blosius, a *great* Benedictine mystic, says that the best form of mortification is to accept with all our heart, in spite of our repugnance, all that God sends or permits, good and evil, joy and suffering. I try to do this. Let us try to do it together and to help one another to reach that absolute abandonment into the hands of God."

In this abandoning of himself at every moment to God's good pleasure Dom Columba rightly saw – because he had experienced it – one of the most crucifying forms of abnegation.

"I see that the great penance which surpasses every other is *self-abandonment carried to its furthest limits,*[2] the abdication of our personality[3] in favour of the Word, who then often leads us by the way of Calvary. This is true wisdom, and we shall be treated as was eternal wisdom."[4]

Often did he go in spirit to Calvary to learn the secret of patience in the contemplation of the sufferings of Jesus: "In making my Way of the Cross this morning I saw that Jesus has done for us *all* that His Father's justice and holiness demand, but that He invites us, like Simon the Cyrenean, to take our little share. That is why I carry my cross with joy."[5]

---

1 *Rule of St Benedict*, ch. 7.
2 Here is a curious coincidence: it was likewise on the feast of St John the Baptist twenty years before, that Dom Marmion expressed – but this time in reference to the Precursor himself – one of the most forcible thoughts on this subject of self-abandonment. See p. 123.
3 "Personality" should be taken here, as often under Dom Marmion's pen, in the order of *activity* (knowledge, love, deeds), for, in the order of *being*, the human creature keeps its personality; Dom Marmion has more than once pointed out this distinction. *Cf. Sponsa Verbi*.
4 Letter of 22 September 1918.
5 Letter of 13 December 1919.

He carried it with so much the more joy that he had within him that strength of Christ which flows from the cross and manifests to the world the triumph of tried virtue:

"Jesus has made me understand that when He said: *Corpus autem aptasti mihi*,[1] His Father had not given Him a glorious body or one exempt from weakness. He had, says St John Damascene, all the infirmities that were not unworthy of His Divine Person: *Vere languores nostros ipse tulit*.[2] This is why He asks us to share them. He *assumes* them, *divinises* them, and they become the fount of that *virtus Christi* of which St Paul speaks."[3]

To a generous soul marked with the divine seal of trial, that came to seek light and help from him at Maredsous, he sent this prayer which surely betrays his own feelings:

"Eternal Father, even as Your Divine Son, our Lord Jesus Christ, offers Himself to Your Majesty as holocaust and Victim for the human race, even so do I offer myself body and soul to You; do with me what You will; to this end I accept all the troubles, mortifications, afflictions, which it shall please You to send me this day. I accept all from Your Divine Will; O my God, may my will ever be conformed to Yours!"[4]

Such were the thoughts and feelings of Dom Marmion in the midst of adversities and vicissitudes of every kind: this serene constancy in an impressionable temperament proves the loyal endeavour which had won for him the virtue of patience.

"Won," we say, and by a long struggle. For it would be a great mistake to suppose that patience was with him the spontaneous outcome of a happy nature, or that he arrived without effort at such a degree of abnegation. On the contrary, his sensibility, far from being blunted, went on growing more acute with the years, but he struggled courageously to possess his soul in patience. To one of his intimate disciples who had spoken to him of his abandonment

---

[1] Heb. 10: 5.
[2] Isa. 53: 4.
[3] Letter of 1 November 1921.
[4] Letter of 21 December 1913.

to God he wrote a short time before his death: "The little virtues you have noticed in me – accepting events as sent or permitted by God, devoting myself to others – have been the object of my efforts for years past. This has now become natural to me."[1]

"Natural," because his virtue had attained that high degree of which St Benedict speaks, where the soul is brought by perfect love to the summit of perfection.[2]

Patience and abandonment to God's Will go together with humility. We know that St Benedict makes this last virtue to lead to heroic patience. With Dom Marmion, ever a faithful disciple of the Great Patriarch, constancy of soul was closely linked to humility and compunction.

We have from the beginning pointed out his twofold sense of humility and compunction: we find it expressed in the first pages of his notes as a novice. These begin with the Litany of Humility and a prayer to obtain compunction. Had he not, moreover, wished never to cease the cry of *Miserere,* even as the *Sanctus* of the angels never ceases?[3]

It may be said that both his prayer and his wish were heard.

It was to a rare degree, a degree that makes saints, that Dom Columba possessed compunction of heart. In his volume *Christ the Ideal of the Monk,* he devotes a whole chapter to this subject, judged so important by the old ascetical writers. A moralist who explains so well the nature of a virtue and analyses its elements with so much penetration, justice and exact shade of expression, could only speak from experience.

For long years past he had chosen as one of his most usual ejaculatory prayers the cry of the penitent David: "Cast me not away from Thy face!" and never did this cry burst forth with more vehemence than when he contemplated the sufferings of Jesus; he had

---

1 Letter of 7 June 1922.
2 *Rule of St Benedict,* ch. 7, on "Humility."
3 See p. 78.

therefore fastened this text at the foot of the crucifix on his prie-dieu. We may imagine how Dom Marmion's soul was steeped in this sense of compunction. A very vivid sense, which sometimes brought tears to his eyes when he made the Way of the Cross; which moved him when at Mass he repeated the *Confiteor* or the *Kyrie eleison*; and it was not without a catch at the heart that he could read the episode of the Samaritan woman, the conversion of the Magdalene, the parable of the Prodigal Son, or the account of the conversion of St Paul.

When he speaks of those who possess the spirit of compunction he is evidently, all unawares, describing his own state:

> Listen to St John in his divinely-inspired Epistle: 'If we say that we have no sin, we deceive ourselves, and the truth is not in us.' As regards great and holy souls, this assertion is luminous. The nearer they come to God, the Sun of Justice, and spotless Holiness, the better they perceive the stains that disfigure them; the brilliance of the divine light in which they move makes their least faults and failings appear in more striking contrast. Their inner gaze, purified by faith and love, penetrates more deeply into the Divine Perfections; they have a clearer view of their own nothingness; they are better able to measure the abyss that separates them from the infinite. Their more intimate union with Christ causes the sufferings endured by Him for the expiation of sin to touch them to the quick. Having a higher notion of the life of grace, they better grasp all that is horrible in offence committed against the Heavenly Father, in despising the Saviour's Passion, in injurious resistance to the spirit of love.[1]

We must bear these lines in mind: with Dom Marmion compunction was closely allied to his state of supernatural adoption:[2]

---

1 *Christ the Ideal of the Monk.*
2 The two ideas, far from being opposed to one another, are on the contrary bound up together: those whom God adopts are, in fact, those who have offended Him, or who at least were at first stained with Original Sin; so that His

conscious of his weakness, the son throws himself at his Father's feet to beg forgiveness; with him perfect compunction is "by its very nature ... one of the purest forms of love." That is why it was so habitual, so peaceful even in its vehemence, for it was joined to absolute confidence: "In saying at Holy Mass: *ab aeterna damnatione nos eripi*,[1] this thought often comes to me: what may particularly increase our hope of salvation is the grace of being called by God to say everyday this prayer at the moment when we are about to substitute the Victim infinitely worthy and perfect for our misery and our unworthiness."[2]

We see by these lines that Dom Marmion's compunction was joined to intense humility.

Assuredly – as we have already noted – there were, in this rich and complex nature, disconcerting contrasts. His ardour and exuberance of life, his expansive temperament, his cheerfulness, might give a wrong idea to those who only knew him superficially; but those who were in close contact with him saw and spoke of his deep humility. One of Cardinal Mercier's secretaries who was in frequent and continued communication with Dom Marmion wrote the day after the latter's death: "I think I have never known a man more really humble than Dom Columba; and this was, it seems to me, his great strength and the secret of the victories over so many souls eaten up with pride and other miseries."[3] A testimony which Cardinal Mercier himself (as we shall presently see) was later to confirm.

Dom Marmion had a very lowly opinion of himself.[4] On this

adopted children ought to be in this world repentant children.
1 "That we may be delivered from eternal damnation." From the *Hanc igitur* of the *Canon* of the Mass before the consecration.
2 Letter of 31 January 1923.
3 *Ibid.*
4 We have said (see p 247) in what sense we must take the confidences he made to his intimate disciples relating to his own soul. To those amongst them who came to open out their hearts or speak familiarly with him of their soul, Dom Marmion in return often communicated his own spiritual experiences. In the-

point may be applied to him the remark of St Francis de Sales: "As vanity is the opposite of humility, so artifice, affectation, and dissimulation are contrary to plain dealing and sincerity." And the holy bishop says again: "We should either not accustom ourselves to words of humility, or else use them with a sincere interior sentiment conformable to what we pronounce outwardly."[1] Such was Dom Columba's form of spirituality; he had that "sincere interior sentiment" of humility; the simplicity and straightforwardness warranted the sincerity of what he said.

He had, he said, "the habitual view of his misery";[2] he spoke of himself as being "like a leper with the sun on him,"[3] and "a leper is not beautiful to look at."

One of his spiritual daughters sent him for approbation an act of consecration to Jesus, and asked him to associate himself with it by saying how he would like to have it signed. He replied:

"As for me, I sign *mercy!* I have so much need of it!"

An altogether spontaneous cry coming from the depths of his soul. We must not be surprised to hear such words spoken by the servants of God. "Holiness is above all things lucidity. In the measure that the saints advance in the twofold knowledge of God and of their own heart they have so clear a view of their unworthiness that they humble themselves, realising their own nothingness, as it were, instinctively."[4]

To one who complained to him of finding so much evil in herself he wrote:

> ory, the wisdom of such a proceeding is open to discussion. In practice, those to whom it applied felt and showed its beneficial influence. "When charity requires it, we must freely and unobtrusively communicate to our neighbour, not only what is necessary for his instruction, but also what is profitable for his consolation; since humility, which conceals virtues, in order to preserve them, discovers them nevertheless, when charity requires it, in order that we may enlarge, increase and perfect them" (*The Devout Life*, III, ch. 5).

1 *The Devout Life*, III, ch. 5.
2 Letter of 9 May 1917.
3 Letter of 9 June 1917.
4 See p. 60. See also in *Christ the Ideal of the Monk*, ch. "Humility," § 3.

THE FRUITS OF THE SPIRIT OF ADOPTION

There is something in us all in league with evil, and it gives an echo when we come in contact with it. Some time ago we were reading the life of Luther. I was distressed at finding in my heart an echo to all his crimes, of which I feel myself perfectly capable. So don't be astonished to feel this at times.[1]

Pray for me, for *in all sooth*, to you, my child, I say it from my heart, I feel *such* a distance between what I preach and what I practise that I really tremble lest I become like a signpost showing the way to others and remaining stationary myself.[2]

An echo of the saying of St Paul, "lest, perhaps, when I have preached to others, I myself should become a castaway."

He therefore often begged the prayers of his spiritual children that there should be no obstacle to grace in his soul: "Pray hard for me. I am a very unfaithful soul whom our Lord inundates with lights, and yet does scarcely anything for Him."[3]

And to another: "Pray for me that in spite of my unworthiness and my *great* cowardice I may submit my whole being to Jesus living in me.[4] I count upon your prayers; it is not enough to preach to others – we must ourselves do what we preach."

There is, moreover, one very tangible criterion by which we may judge of the degree of detachment – the fruit of humility – reached by this man of intellectual authority, whose talent, joined to the circumstances and the relations of his life, seemed to point to literary and scientific production. What hold had self-love over him when it concerned the publication of his works, his rightful claim to the expression of his thoughts, or criticisms to be encountered?

[1] Letter of 10 January 1907. "When a priest hears confessions in a spirit of faith," he said, "he remains united to our Lord, he enters into His sentiments, and then whilst yet having a keen horror of sin, he feels no indignation or contempt for sinners, however great they be; he feels instead deep humility and fear, saying to himself that he is capable of doing as much, for there is no sin committed by one man that another might not commit."
[2] Letter of 8 January 1908.
[3] Letter of 1 November 1908.
[4] Letter of 31 August 1909.

465

Those who knew Dom Marmion intimately knew that vanity had no place among his motives as a writer, that the spirit of proprietorship never caused him a shadow of jealousy, and that some not altogether favourable comments did not arouse any susceptibility on his part. The *irritabile genus* never appeared in him.

We have seen how generously he gave of his doctrine without reserving to himself the bare ownership of what was original in his ascetical teaching. One of his spiritual daughters begged him to lend her some manuscript notes of his retreats. Dom Columba gave them over to her and, the occasion presenting itself, he asked her to say, after reading them, what she thought of the eventual publication of these notes, a publication asked for more than once already.[1] He received a reply in the negative. It may be said in the sister's excuse that the collected notes lent to her did not bear that character of logical unity or doctrinal synthesis which is one of the master qualities of his published works. Dom Marmion himself agreed with what his correspondent said in her letter: "I can't tell you how pleased I am at your honest way of speaking to me of my notes of retreat. If people only would, or could treat with each other thus, how agreeable life would be! Most people flatter me, either knowingly or because affection cozens them. What you say is just what I think myself."

This letter was written in 1906; it was not until nearly twelve years later – when Dom Marmion had passed his sixtieth year – that after urgent and repeated entreaties, the publication of his first volume at last appeared.

"They are beginning the printing of my conferences," he then

---

[1] Notably by the Carmelites of Louvain. "About 1902," writes one of them (letter to the author), "I naïvely put before him the question of the publication of his retreats; I even made him see that this publication was possible, for I had kept notes of these treasures. But he cut me short: 'Leave all that to the good God; for my part I do not think so.' After an interval of more than twelve years he recalled the matter (for he had an excellent memory) and at the time of a visit, in 1914, he said to me: 'Just imagine! One of my monks wants to collect and publish my conferences. As for me I should never have thought of it. I believe that he is going to ask for your notes."

wrote; "they are acting almost in spite of me. But they assure me that these volumes will make Jesus known and loved. That is a great consolation."[1]

Could detachment go farther?

When, after this publication, it was pointed out to him that imitations, sometimes very servile and scarcely veiled, were being made of his works, or that passages not even given as quotations were being taken from them, far from his evincing any astonishment, one only heard from his lips an expression of joy, that of St Paul which he could truly appropriate to himself: "So that by all means... Christ be preached: in this also I rejoice, yea, and will rejoice."

The extraordinary success of his works found him equally detached. Certainly he rejoiced at this success, but only at the thought that Christ Jesus would be better known and loved. And he added: "May He in return, forgive me my sins!"

However, some discordant voices – rare, unjustifiable, but harsh – were mingled in this chorus of praise and certain circumstances of proximity made them the more mortifying. The one at whom they were aimed contented himself with observing with perfect serenity of mind that "since the doctrine was irreproachable and his books were doing good to a great number of souls, he could wish for nothing more."

The same humble detachment with the apostle.

To a superior who thanked and congratulated him on the particularly marked success of a retreat preached in his house, he answered:

"Blessed be God for using such poor creatures as instruments!"

Was he not, as he wrote one day, "like the jawbone of an ass in the hands of the divine Samson?"[2]

He was even surprised that souls should have recourse to his lights. At the time of a general chapter of his congregation, he wrote to one of his disciples:

[1] Letter of 9 June 1917.
[2] See p. 380.

"I am quite surprised, and even embarrassed, to see the importance that people attach to all that I say."[1]

At the end of his life one of his nun sisters asked him:

"Joe, don't you feel some self-complacency at seeing so many souls come to you?"

"Oh, no," he at once replied. "I don't know that feeling, but I can tell you that I feel extreme joy at being able to help souls to love Him whom we desire to make loved and love so much ourselves."

But the infallible touchstone whereby to recognise genuine humility is invincible patience in trial and the serene and gentle acceptation of humiliations. No other criterion equals this: it is that of the saints. We have already spoken of Dom Columba's patience and constancy in the midst of adversities.

As to his acceptation of humiliations, those who came in close contact with him can attest that it was a total acceptation. The noviatiate had already provided him with hard humiliations; we may recall the harsh words spoken to him by the abbot on the evening of his religious profession. It was especially during the latter years of his life that he was to meet with this kind of trial.

"I have, as it were, the presentiment," he wrote in September 1918 "(a presentiment to which I do not attach much importance) that I shall have much to suffer and shall be greatly humiliated towards the end of my life."

This presentiment was, however, to be realised. Providence, to complete the purification of his soul and to adorn his crown, plunged him in the crucible of bitter opposition of a kind which was particularly wounding to his affections.

On these occasions he constantly kept that humble and meek patience that St Benedict requires of his disciple when beset by hard and contrary things.

More than once this meekness struck those who witnessed it. A religious – it is to her we owe this incident – rather sharply reproached him one day on the subject of some step he had thought

---

[1] Letter of 14 July 1912.

it his duty to take. After having listened to the end in silence, he responded:

"I was wrong; I acknowledge before the good God that I was mistaken."

"This response was made so humbly," recounted the religious, "that I was silenced." And she added: "I had never felt so much as I did that day what a saint Dom Columba was."

And as ever, he found this humble serenity in the remembrance of the sufferings of Jesus. A person who was not under his jurisdiction forgot himself one day to the point of saying some particularly cutting words to him. He made no reply. One of his monks,[1] a witness of the scene, afterwards expressed his astonishment:

"Why! you did not even reply. Do you mean to say you didn't feel it?"

"Oh!" he returned, "I felt it keenly enough, but I remembered our Lord in His Passion: *Jesus autem tacebat.*[2] I pictured Him in the midst of the executioners whom I had deputed by my sins to treat Him ignominiously as one would not treat the last of men. Then instead of being angry I kept my soul in peace."

He was the better able to keep this peace because under such circumstances he confided himself to God with perfect trust. He wrote in a letter of 28 March 1918:

> God is very good to me. He shows me that our strength lies in silence and in having recourse to Him. During His Passion Jesus kept His gaze fixed on the face of His Father: *Ideo non sum confusus.*[3] O my dear daughter, let us hide ourselves in Jesus: *Vita vestra abscondita est cum Christo in Deo....*[4] I saw today (Good Friday) how PERFECT Mary was in her sublime faith at the foot of the cross. Oh, may she obtain us this signal grace of a perfect faith, even in the nakedness of trial!

---

1 The details were given by himself.
2 "Jesus held His peace" (Matt. 26: 23).
3 "Therefore I am not confounded" (Isa. 50: 7).
4 "Your life is hidden with Christ in God" (Col. 3: 3).

Nothing glorifies the Father as does this unwavering faith in Christ in the midst of Calvary.[1]

And again, about the same time: "I have been meditating during these days on these words from the office of the Passion: *Faciem meam non averti ab increpantibus et conspuentibus in me. Domine Deus auxiliator meus,* IDEO NON SUM CONFUSUS. That is the secret of the silence, of the peace of Jesus's soul in His Passion: *the beholding of His Father.* I try to imitate Him by finding in this *beholding* all my strength."

So to a person who was passing through trials similar to his own he was able to write:

> Enter more and more into the *great silence.* Silence: (*a*) of the tongue; (*b*) of the movements of the passions; (*c*) of reasons and reflections on the manner in which others act. Leave that to our Heavenly Father. I am finding great peace of soul now that I do not allow myself to be concerned with the doings of others, as far as my duty as abbot permits. *I speak of these things to the Heavenly Father,* as the Psalmist constantly does. Then that becomes a prayer which makes peace and silence only the more profound.[2]

One who can let such accents escape him in the midst of trial gives undoubted proof of humility.

Great as was the virtue of humility in Dom Marmion, it almost seemed to yield to his confidence in God, or rather, to be more exact, his confidence and humility went together, and the measure of his confidence was that of his humility. Often, in the course of the preceding pages, we have heard him express the thought so dear to him that the poorer we are in ourselves the richer we may be in Christ. In Dom Columba was to be found that humility which,

[1] Letter of 28 March 1918.
[2] Letter of 3 June 1918.

recalling our misery, bows us down in lowliness before God, and that magnanimity which makes us aspire to great things, to the Divine Intimacy which God offers us.[1]

It seems even as if, with him, magnanimity was only fully brought out in its immediate contrast with humility. If he has shown in some remarkable pages the necessity and greatness of this last virtue, he has extolled trust in God in words of striking intensity. It is, above all, when he speaks of the merits of Jesus Christ that he gives free course to these sentiments.

After having declared the greatness of Christ's infinite merits he concludes with great forcibility:

> Why, then, is it that pusillanimous souls are to be found who say that holiness is not for them, that perfection is something beyond their power, who say, when one speaks to them of perfection: 'It is not for me: I could never arrive at sanctity.' Do you know what makes them speak thus? It is their lack of faith in the efficacy of Christ's merits. For it is the Will of God that all should be holy: *Haec est voluntas Dei, sanctificatio vestra.* It is our Lord's precept: 'Be ye therefore perfect, as also your Heavenly Father is perfect.'
>
> But we too often forget the Divine Plan; we forget that holiness for us is a supernatural holiness, of which the source is only in Jesus Christ, our Chief and our Head; we do a wrong to the infinite merits and inexhaustible satisfactions of Christ. Doubtless, by ourselves, we can do nothing in the way of grace or perfection; our Lord expressly tells us so. *Sine me* NIHIL *potestis facere,* and St Augustine, commenting on this text, adds: *Sive parum, sive multum, sine illo fieri non potest sine quo nihil fieri potest.* That is so true! Whether it concerns great things or small, we can do nothing without Christ. But by dying for us Christ has given us free and confident access to

---

[1] *Cf.* St Thomas Aquinas, I–II, v. 129, a. 3 and 4. *Cf.* Fr Garrigou-Lagrange, *Perfection chrétienne et contemplation.*

the Father, and through Him there is no grace for which we cannot hope.

Souls of little faith! Why do we doubt of God, of our God?[1]

Dom Marmion's living faith prepared the way for the most absolute confidence: "God gives me light and grace to understand that the creature can do nothing greater than give itself unreservedly to the good pleasure of the Creator. He shows me more and more my misery and my littleness, but He shows me at the same time His boundless mercy."[2]

Although in this "divine light" he saw himself "very miserable," he ardently aspired to holiness. Explaining one day this doctrine to one of his disciples, he confided to him that in prayer he often spoke in this way to God: "You are powerful enough, O my God, to make a saint of me, in spite of my faults and weaknesses. I believe this, because Your mercy is infinite." And he cited this trait in the life of the Bishop of Geneva to whom someone said:

"You will be a saint."

"'Yes,' he replied, 'God can work that miracle.' I say the same," added Dom Marmion, "and that would be above all a miracle of mercy."

That was why, for him as for St Francis de Sales,[3] the sight of his misery was a claim to confidence. Not that he confused misery with tepidity, infirmities with infidelities, shortcomings with negligences. He knew, and often repeated, that generosity in all things is indispensable to safeguard the treasure that the soul carries in a fragile vessel. But the sight of his frailty, far from discouraging him, kept his watchfulness on the alert, whilst above all it aroused his confidence in God:

[1] *Christ the Life of the Soul*, conference III, end of § IV.
[2] Letter of 6 February 1912. See Dom Marmion's beautiful article, *"Les voies de la miséricorde,"* published in the *Revue Liturgique*, 192.
[3] "Although I am conscious of my misery, I do not trouble myself about it, and sometimes am even joyous, thinking that I am a real good piece of work for God's mercy" (Quoted by Dom Armand Castel: *"St François de Sales d'après ses lettres,"* in *La vie spirituelle*, January 1927).

THE FRUITS OF THE SPIRIT OF ADOPTION

"I feel like you more and more," he wrote to one of his spiritual daughters, "that I can do NOTHING except in God. I love this poverty, and I fearlessly lean on the goodness of our Heavenly Father, convinced that He will never fail me so long as I only seek His good pleasure."[1]

And again, a few months later, to the same: "As for me, my daughter, I have the feeling that my soul must be an object of *horror* for God, and yet I go to Him with great confidence, for God is to me *the best of Fathers*."[2]

He made this confidence to one of his disciples: "I often say to the good God: "Father, I do not deserve to be allowed to give You this name, for I have wandered far from You, I Your child! And yet, strong in the word of Your Son Jesus, I dare to appear before You and to hide myself in Your bosom!"

This theme of mercy stooping down to the relief of misery was always dear to him, particularly at the end of his life. He writes in 1919: "our Lord sends me little splinters of His cross, but He also gives me of His *virtus,* and this so much the more because I come before Him owning my weakness."

And he at once goes on to disclose the inmost and habitual source of his spirituality – the example of Jesus: "The human weaknesses assumed by the Word were a sublime and continual prayer to His Father."[3]

The same deep tone of humility and confidence in another letter:

> The holy liturgy tells us that God manifests His almighty power *maxime miserando et parcendo.*[4] Be for Him a monument

---

[1] Letter, 14 July 1909. Sister Elizabeth of the Trinity also says: "The weakest, even the most sinful person has the greatest right to hope. By forgetting self and casting herself into the arms of God, she glorifies Him more than by any self-examination and self-reproach, which keep her attention fixed on her own defects though she possesses a Saviour within her who is always willing to purify her." *Life* (the "Praise of Glory") translated by the Benedictines of Stanbrook.

[2] Letter of 6 September 1909.

[3] Letter of 30 December 1919.

[4] "Above all, in showing pity and pardon" (Collect for the Tenth Sunday after

of His mercy during all eternity. The deeper our misery and unworthiness, the greater and more adorable His mercy: *Abyssus abyssum invocat:* the abyss of our misery calls to the abyss of His mercy.[1] It is a great consolation to me to see that you are walking in this way, which is so sure, which leads so high and glorifies the Precious Blood of Jesus Christ and the mercy of our God. It is my way too. Help me with your prayers.[2]

He loved this way, and it was for him an inexhaustible wellspring of inward peace: "I am sixty years old today. The abyss of my sins and ingratitude has been swallowed up in another abyss, *infinite,* of the mercy of the Heavenly Father."[3]

Having reached the end of his course, Dom Marmion wrote the following lines. They do more than sum up all his inner life at that period – and likewise all we have attempted to say about it: they contain a lofty concept of life which should be reverently gathered up, as the spiritual will and testament of a master and of a saint.

> From souls fixed in Jesus Christ a subconscious, unfelt prayer rises up unceasingly to the Father. It is the voice of their misery, of their weakness; and these miseries assumed by the Spouse are unceasingly offered by Him to the Father. There, my daughter, that is my inner life. Every morning I place you with myself in the Divine Heart, that His riches may cover our misery, His strength sustain our weakness: *Libenter gloriabimur in infirmitatibus nostris ut in habitet in nobis virtus Christi....*
>
> This state demands: (*a*) complete self-surrender to His goodness, to His faithfulness, to His love; (*b*) submission, uncalculating patience in all that opposes us. I try to meet with a smile all that goes against me. This state does not exclude faults and weaknesses. We ought neither to be astonished nor to vex ourselves, but deplore them in so far as they

---

Pentecost).
1 Ps. 41: 8.
2 Letter undated, but between July and November 1920.
3 Letter of 1 April 1918.

offend our God; (*c*) very great detachment from all creatures; (*d*) great self-contempt, referring all to God. That is my way.

A royal way, a divine way. We are about to see, at least to some small extent, with what generous love and constant fidelity Dom Marmion followed this way.

Death, which is the crowning point of all and lays bare the most secret depths and the ruling passion of the soul, was to place its insuperable seal on these high virtues. At that moving and supreme hour at which man's destiny is at stake one of Dom Marmion's sons began to encourage him; he recalled to him all the good done by his preaching and works, the numerous conversions effected; but he with a shake of the head at once protested and let these words escape him, which showed what were the feelings most deeply anchored in his soul: *Deus meus, misericordia mea!*[1]

---

[1] "My God, my mercy!" (Ps. 58:18).

18 SPIRITUS PRECUM

In his conferences Dom Marmion was fond of paraphrasing the words of the prophet Zacharias, where he says that, under the new covenant, God would pour out upon souls "the spirit of grace and of prayers" – that spirit which is the Holy Spirit, the spirit of adoption whom the Father sends into the hearts of those He predestines to be His children in Christ Jesus.

We have seen how abundantly this spirit of adoption was poured out in Dom Columba's soul and what virtues resulted from this. Is it possible, is it even permissible, to enter further into this sanctuary, there to discover what is greatest and most intimate – namely, his life of prayer? It is surely possible, for Dom Marmion has left some records, too rare unfortunately, but sufficiently explicit, of his life of prayer. So it may be equally permissible to linger here. To reveal the work of the spirit of love in the soul of this "adoptive son of God" is not to betray "the secret of the King."

This work of the Holy Spirit offers a twofold aspect, according as to whether we consider Dom Marmion's liturgical life or catch the aspirations of his soul in the intimacies of private prayer. But we are under no delusion: this is only a logical division accepted for the sake of better stating our point – for, in reality, the different workings of his soul interpenetrated, his thoughts and affections were harmoniously blended into one.

If Dom Marmion went to the Father through Jesus, He went to Jesus through the Church: that was one of the most clearly-marked characteristics of his spiritual life.

"Our Lord," he wrote in May 1917, "invites me more and more to keep united to Him, and more and more, too, I see it is through the Church that we draw near to Him."

An essential doctrine which he has explained too well for us to need to say more here. He has shown how the Church is inseparable from the mystery of Christ; how she perpetuates His mission here on earth. In her is contained the doctrine and jurisdiction of Jesus; she dispenses His sacraments, continues His work of religion. Dom Marmion has spoken in glorious terms of the mystical union of Christ with His Bride.[1]

What is important to notice here is that – both for his own personal spirituality and for the preaching which interpreted it – in the same way in which he accepted this dogma as hierarchically established by God in revelation, so he accepted this doctrine transmuted into prayer by the liturgy as proposed to us by the Church.

In the same letter of May 1917, he expresses his thought in an illuminating manner. We shall be forgiven for not abridging these lines which further reveal certain aspects of his hidden life.

> Jesus is the Way, the Truth and the Life. During His mortal life He was all this by His immediate action.
>
> Since His Ascension, the Church takes His place and is for us the way, the truth and the life. She is the way, above all, by *her sacraments*. By baptism she engrafts us on the vine, she brings us into fellowship with the Person of Jesus as His members, and she unites us to Him as Head; the Holy Eucharist accentuates and perfects this union.
>
> The sacramental liturgy, under the guardianship of the Holy Spirit, presides over this sacramental action of the Church, and her rites and ceremonies explain and interpret, in an *authentic* manner *adapted to the understanding of the faithful*, the true doctrine on this main point. This is why the Council of Trent wishes that the pastors of the Church should often explain these rites to their flocks.
>
> The Church is the truth, for *lex orandi, lex credendi*: liturgical prayer is the law of our faith. No other instruction is so luminous, so authentic, so perfectly adapted to the intelligence of the *simple* faithful than that contained in the prayers,

---

[1] *Christ the Life of the Soul*, conference v, "The Church the Mystical Body of Christ."

the lessons, the rites of the liturgy. During the ages of faith, although the vast majority of the faithful were uneducated, not knowing how to read and possessing no books, they were yet much better instructed in the mysteries of the faith, the mystery of Christ, than are the men and women of our days. The prayers and ceremonies of the Mass, the lessons of the Divine Office were explained to them; in a word, the Church, our Mother, instructed her children herself in an authentic manner: *Erunt docibiles Dei.*

The liturgy, under the inspiration of the Holy Spirit, draws from the Scriptures, from tradition, and from the symbolism of the Church, a pure doctrine perfectly adapted to the spiritual understanding of the faithful. It was in the liturgy I learnt to know St Paul and the Gospel.

The wording and form of the liturgy, for example the Masses *de tempore,* are masterpieces of *doctrinal* composition. There the New Testament is explained by the Old. *The right attitude of the soul* towards God is indicated in the collects. Little by little the soul is imbued with them and finds its prayer already prepared by our Mother the Church, as Jacob found the feast prepared by his mother for his father Isaac.

The great difficulty which so many persons experience in prayer comes in large part from the divorce established between individual prayer and the prayer of the Church; shut up alone in themselves, they attempt by reasoning to find out the meaning of the Scriptures and no longer go to our Lord through the Church.

The liturgy thus understood as being the authentic organ whereby the Church prays and teaches her children to pray, belongs to *the whole Church,* and Pius x strongly urged all priests, bishops and religious orders to co-operate with him to restore it to vigour. This was a part of his great plan: *Instaurare omnia in Christo.* St Teresa understood this so well that she said she would give her life for the least liturgical rubric. Understood in this sense, the liturgy is not the appanage or speciality of any religious order whatsoever, it belongs to the Church.

If by liturgy you understand the *splendour* of the offices or liturgical *erudition*, then I suppose that the Order of St Benedict is especially called upon to study and practise it, thus serving the others as *fount* and *model* of liturgical knowledge.

The good I have been enabled to do to souls – men, women, children, rich and poor – by revealing to them the treasures of spiritual life, of light and facility in their relations with God, which are contained in the liturgy, show me how greatly important it is for every priest, vicar, curate, everyone, to work at making known this wellspring, so sure and so *ecclesiastical,* of the spiritual life.

We may gather from these lines in what great esteem Dom Marmion held the official prayer of the Church. The glowing pages he has devoted to the subject of this prayer, in his spiritual works, count amongst the best he has written. This is because the supernatural conviction from which they sprang was of the intensest. He said one day to the nuns of Maredret:

I am convinced from the depths of my soul that the more we advance in life and the more we come into relation with God, the better do we understand the greatness of the Divine Praise in the choir office. There is no other work that comes anywhere near this praise: encircling the Holy Sacrifice which is its centre, it constitutes the purest glory that man can give to God, because it is the closest share the soul can have in the canticle that the Incarnate Word renders to the adorable Trinity.

He therefore prepared himself with extreme care for the accomplishment of this work. He said to one of his sons who questioned him on this point:

Before the Divine Office, after having made an act of faith in Christ present in my heart by grace, I unite myself to Him in the praise He gives to His Father; I ask Him to glorify His Blessed Mother and the saints, particularly those of the day and my holy patrons. Then I unite myself to Him as Head of the Church, as supreme High Priest in order to plead the cause of the whole Church. To this end I cast a glance over all that this earth holds of misery and need; the sick, the dying, the tempted, the despairing, sinners, the afflicted; I take into my heart all the sorrows, the anguish, the hopes of each soul.... I also direct my intention towards the works of zeal undertaken to glorify God and save the world: missions, sermons... finally, I take the intentions of those who have recommended themselves to my prayers, of those I love, the souls who are united to me, and thus I prepare myself to intercede for all with Christ *qui est semper vivens ad interpellandum pro nobis*.[1] Then I say to the Heavenly Father: 'Father, I am unworthy to appear before You, but I have absolute confidence in the sacred humanity of Your Son united to His divinity. Resting on Your Son, I dare to come before You, to penetrate into the splendours of Your bosom and, united with the Word, to sing Your praises.'[2]

On another occasion he said:

One thought which helps me in the recitation of the office is this: the Holy Spirit is the supreme Instructor whom the Father and the Son give us; He is the Master of perfection. Often I experience great joy during the Divine Office, in feeling

---

[1] "Always living to make intercession for us" (Heb. 7:25).

[2] He has particularly – and admirably – developed these thoughts in *Christ the Ideal of the Monk* in the conference, "The *Opus Dei*, means of union with God," § 4 and 5. "When the monk, united to Christ Jesus, enters the oratory, bearing in his soul the deepest and most precious interests of Jesus's Mystical Body, when his heart is filled, and then overflows with the varied affections which the Holy Spirit successively causes to rise by means of the words uttered by the lips – he gives to God an extremely pleasing homage, while torrents of light and love, flowing at his prayer from God's munificence, are poured out upon the world of souls."

that the Holy Spirit is praying in us 'with unspeakable groanings,' and that through the Psalms I have the consolation of saying to the Heavenly Father all that I have to say to Him. The Psalms contain so much! When we recite them under the direction of the Holy Spirit, who composed them, we truly tell God all our troubles, our needs, our joys, our praise, our love. So I have taken the habit of saying at each Psalm: *Pater caelestis, da mihi Spiritum tuum.*[1]

During Divine Office his attitude was most remarkably devout. He brought to the "Work of God" a particular enthusiasm, allied to that reverence on which St Benedict so much insists in those who sing God's praises. This reverence in everything that referred to his relations with God formed one of the salient characteristics of his spiritual personality. To explain this we must carry our minds back to that light on God's infinity which struck him so vividly while yet a seminarist.[2]

This reverence was continual, and modulated, so to speak, his whole outward bearing, without anything being able to disturb it. Human nature is so made that it happens sometimes, even in the most solemn assemblies, that an unforeseen concurrence of circumstances, an unexpected contrast, the awkwardness of a movement causes a sudden fit of laughter. Choirs of monks are not always proof against these accidents. Now – a noteworthy fact in a temperament like his – in such cases never did Dom Marmion let himself be taken by surprise, so strong and deep was his reverence towards God.

What are we now to say about his devotion to the Eucharistic Sacrifice, the centre of the liturgy? Some private notes, far too few, will show us.

Retreat of September 1910 – I have discovered better than ever:

[1] See p. 450.
[2] See p. 23.

1. That the Church is *Israel quem coaequasti Unigenito tuo*,[1] and when we make ourselves one with her we benefit by all the merits of Jesus Christ, despite our miseries and unworthiness.

2. On Calvary Jesus merited and even applied all. On the altar, He no longer merits, but applies all, according to our faith and union with Him.

3. The substitution of a pure Victim (for me impure), holy (for me unholy), spotless (for me all covered with the corruption of my sins), ought to fill me with joy. For this Victim perfectly fulfils *in my place* all my duties. The prayer *Hanc igitur*[2] is the substitution; the prayer *Quam oblationem*[3] is the petition to see this substitution accepted.

4. A man may die of thirst at the side of a spring of pure water. He must take the trouble to put himself into touch with it. The same at the altar: *Sicut credidisti, fiat tibi*.[4]

During the conventual Mass which we sing every day I have leisure to meditate on the great action which is accomplished at the altar and I may say that, most often, I feel my heart overflow with joy and gratitude to think that in Jesus present on the altar I possess the wherewithal to offer to the Father a reparation worthy of Him, a satisfaction of infinite price. What graces are contained in the Mass! No saint, not even the Blessed Virgin Mary, has been able to draw from it all the treasure it holds.

[1] "Israel, whom Thou has raised up to be Thy Firstborn" (Eccles. 36:12).
[2] Prayer of the *Canon* of the Mass, during which the priest extends his hands over the bread and wine which is the next moment to be changed into the Body and Blood of Christ. The gesture is symbolical. Under the Old Law, the priest extended his hand over the victim as a sign that he substituted it for himself and the guilty for whom it was offered. In the Eucharistic Sacrifice, the priest signifies by this gesture that Jesus Christ, the God-Man, is substituted for us sinners in order to redeem us.
[3] *Quam oblationem*. Prayer which immediately follows the foregoing and wherein the priest beseeches that the oblation offered to God may produce all its effects and that the miracle of Transubstantiation may be wrought.
[4] "As thou has believed, so be it done to thee" (Matt. 8:13).

If such was his faith when he assisted at the Holy Sacrifice, how are we to describe his devotion when he himself celebrated the Holy Mysteries? It is difficult to express it.

Let us say to begin with that on extremely rare occasions, when travelling, it had happened – by force of circumstances – that he had been unable to celebrate. He said afterwards that on those days "he had been unhappy until evening."

He celebrated admirably, with minute and religious respect for the rubrics. It may be said that he "lived" his Mass with a perfect "sincerity" and conviction. Few priests assisted him, few of the faithful saw him at the altar or at the pontifical offices, without being struck by his recollected air or without carrying away with them the impression that he fathomed the very depths of the meaning of the ceremonies and fully "realised" the liturgy. With what a supernatural gaze he looked upon Christ in the Host, with what ineffable respect he surrounded Him!

We recall the reflection of some simple souls who saw and heard him, while yet a young man, celebrate Christmas in a small parish in the vicinity of the abbey: "One would have said that he saw the Infant Jesus on the altar as in the manger." Indeed, his living faith made Christ's presence visible, as it were, in the Eucharist.

And yet, during the last years of his life, this faith in the Real Presence had to undergo frequent and violent assaults.[1] These temptations were so much the more painful, in that it was at the very moment of the Consecration that the spirit of darkness strove to extinguish or obscure the divine light that burnt in his soul. But the more his faith was put to the proof, with so much the more love he bowed down before Christ veiled under the Sacred Species: *Et ego credidi quia tu es Christus Filius Dei vivi. Et procidens adoravit eum.*[2]

Here and there, in letters of this period and in confidences to his disciples, are revealed some of the thoughts and affections most habitual to him in the celebration of the sacred mysteries. We may

---

[1] See p. 295.
[2] "Dost thou believe in the Son of God?... And he said: I believe, Lord. And falling down he adored Him" (John 9: 36, 38).

see once more the intensity of his faith, the depth of his piety and the ardour of his zeal.

He ordinarily celebrated Mass after the recitation of Matins[1] in choir: his soul filled with the quintessence of the psalms and other sacred texts, could not have desired a better preparation for the offering of the Divine Victim; the Holy Oblation thus "concluded" the sacrifice of praise in a perfect manner.

When, in consequence of his state of health, he did not assist at the office of Matins, his preparation for Holy Mass lasted half an hour. These were moments of union with Christ: "My usual preparation for Mass is an intimate union with Jesus, Priest and Victim.[2] While vesting before celebrating Mass I feel that, by the Church, I am entering into intimate union with the great High Priest Jesus, and with her and by her I am participating in the dispositions of Jesus Christ."[3]

Divine dispositions into which he truly entered by a lively faith and which made his priestly work so fervent and effectual:

> At the Holy Sacrifice of the Mass the priest gives to the Word His humanity. When I am celebrating Mass I often think of this with great joy, and I say to the Word: O infinite Word, I am about, in uttering in Your Name the words of the consecration: *This is My Body*... to give You Your humanity that You have espoused, and united to this humanity, I offer myself to You with all those who are united to me and whom I bear in my heart.
>
> When I am saying Holy Mass it seems to me that the Heavenly Father is before me, and that the weaknesses of my soul and of the souls for whom I pray become the weaknesses and miseries of Christ, because He identifies Himself with His members: *Vere languores nostros ipse tulit.*

Therefore his heart overflowed at these moments with zeal and

---

1 Matins (followed by Lauds) is said at 4 AM at Maredsous.
2 Letter of 4 September 1918.
3 Letter of 4 April 1917.

love: "Every day at Holy Mass I think of all those who are in misery and affliction, and I ask Christ to pray through my lips for all these miseries; in this way the priest is truly *os totius Ecclesiae.*"

But most often his thoughts rise up to the Father, saying to one of his sons:

> I have meditated a great deal upon the degree of love that God has for us in giving us His Son: *Sic Deus dilexit mundum ut Filium suum unigenitum daret.* I ask myself what I can render Him in return, and He makes me understand that I give Him this same Son. At the moment of consecration I adore this Son in whom He is well pleased, and I offer Him to the Father, and all day I try to keep in this attitude of adoration and of offering our Lord to His Father. Do this, and so you will lose yourself in Him.
>
> If God the Father is offended by many, He is also the object of a love than which there can be no greater: *Majorem hac dilectionem...*[1] our Lord said this above all of the love He had for His Father; He died above all for the glory of His Father: *Sicut mandatum dedit mihi Pater.*[2] This is why I feel great consolation to think that I hold within my hands and offer to the Heavenly Father this Son whom He infinitely loves.

If Christ is immolated upon the altar it is in order to give Himself as food to souls: sacramental Communion concludes the Eucharistic Sacrifice.

It is an aspect of Communion which Dom Columba has particularly thrown into relief and which, after his example, it is important to note: besides, the fact of its being usually passed over in silence by many ascetical authors, and those some of the best, it stresses once again the fundamental unison of his spiritual life: "Each Communion well made brings us nearer and nearer to our

---

1 John 15:13.
2 "As the Father hath given Me commandment, so do I" (John 14:31).

model; above all, it makes us penetrate more intimately into the knowledge, the love, and the practice of the mystery of our predestination and adoption in Christ Jesus, our elder brother. It perfects the grace of Divine Sonship in us."

And after having set forth this "very important" doctrine, he continues:

> To receive Christ in the Eucharist is, then, to participate in the greatest possible measure in the Divine Sonship of Jesus. And that is why every Communion well made is so vivifying and fruitful for us. Eucharistic Communion is the *most perfect act of our divine adoption*. There is no moment when we are more justly entitled to say to our Father in heaven, 'O Heavenly Father, I abide in Thy Son Jesus, and He abides in me. Thy Son, proceeding from Thee, receives the communication of Thy divine life in its fullness. I have received Thy Son with faith; faith tells me that at this moment I am with Him, and since I share in His life, behold me in Him, through Him, with Him as the son in whom Thou art well pleased.' What graces, what light, what strength does not such a prayer bring to the child of God! What superabundance of divine life, what closeness of union, what depth of adoption does not such a faith communicate to us! We here touch the culminating point, on earth, of this divine adoption.[1]

Therefore he took particular care in his preparation for this great act. Regarding a custom which went back to the early days of his monastic life,[2] he said:

> I have the custom of going every day at noon to make a short visit to the Blessed Sacrament, and there, putting everything else out of my mind, I say to our Lord: 'My Jesus, tomorrow I am to receive You into my heart, and I wish to receive You perfectly. But I am altogether incapable of this. You have

---

1 "*Panis Vitae*," end of § 6, in *Christ the Life of the Soul*.
2 See p. 85.

> Yourself said: "Without Me you can do nothing." O eternal Wisdom, do You Yourself prepare my soul to become Your temple. I offer You, with this intention, my actions and sufferings of this day, in order that You may render them pleasing in Your Divine Eyes and that You may verify Your words: *Sanctificavit tabernaculum suum Altissimus.'*[1]
>
> Such a prayer is excellent; the day is thus directed towards union with Christ; love, principle of union, envelops our actions; far from murmuring at anything disagreeable or troublesome that happens to us, we offer it to Jesus with a feeling of dilection, and the soul thus finds itself, as it were quite naturally, prepared when the moment comes to receive its God.

As to his thanksgiving, it was regularly prolonged to a full half hour. Kneeling on his prie-dieu, his head bent over his joined hands, in an attitude of great reverence, the ineffable colloquy was carried on in his soul.

He has left to one of his sons, who asked it of him in 1918, the scheme of his usual thanksgiving after Mass. We here find again, under the diversity of affections, the whole essential of his inner life as a child of God through Jesus and in Jesus:

> To sing, united to the Word, the canticle of the universe to the Father. In the *Benedicite*, each creature receives life in our intelligence, in the same way as it exists in the archetypal idea in the intelligence of the Word *in quo omnia constant, per quem omnia facta sunt.*[2] The man becomes thus the eye of all that which does not see, the ear of all that which does not hear, the heart of all that which does not love. It is for this reason that the Church places after Mass this canticle on the lips of the priest who holds the place of Christ.
>
> *Verbum caro factum est, et habitavit in nobis.*[3]

---

[1] The Most High hath sanctified His own tabernacle" (Ps. 45:5).
[2] "By Him all things consist" (Col. 1:17). "All things were made by Him" (John 1:3).
[3] "The Word was made flesh and dwelt among us" (John 1:14).

The God of revelation is 'the Father of our Lord Jesus Christ, the Father of mercies, and the God of all comfort.'[1]

Adoration, in silence, of the Divine Majesty hidden in Christ. (This varies according to the liturgy of the day and the movement of grace).

Existimate vos mortuos esse peccato, viventes autem Deo in Christo Jesu. To die to every creature in order that Christ may live in me.[2]

Consecration to Mary, to St Joseph. Prayer to the guardian angel, to our blessed father St Benedict.

This scheme is given in rather general terms. Other, more intimate, confidences help us better to enter into this "holy of holies" of the soul united to its God, there to catch, and silently to listen to, some echoes of these more than human communings.

Sometimes, after Holy Communion, having our Lord within me, I follow in spirit His life, His successive states; I adore Him in the Father's bosom, in the pure bosom of the Virgin that He chose as His abode; I go to Bethlehem, to Nazareth, to the desert, to Calvary.... I unite myself in this way to Jesus in each of His states, and in this contact with Him I receive the grace of all His mysteries.

Holy Communion makes us abide in Christ and He in us: *In me manet et Ego in eo.* You know the story of St Teresa of Ávila and of the Infant Jesus. Well! after Holy Communion I say to our Lord: 'I am Columba of Jesus! And He could say to me: 'I am Jesus of Columba!'

Cleaving to Christ, his soul rose on the wings of faith and love to the adorable Trinity. He said one day (in 1904) to the nuns of Maredret:

Holy Communion unites us through Jesus to the Three Persons. When I possess Jesus in my heart I say to the Father:

1 2 Cor. 1:3.
2 Rom. 6:11.

'Heavenly Father, I adore You, I thank You, I unite myself to Your Divine Son and I acknowledge with Him that all that I have, all that I am, comes from You: *Omne datum optimum... Manus tuae fecerunt me....*[1] I next unite myself to the Word and say to Him: 'Eternal Word, of myself I know nothing, I am nothing; but I know by faith all that You know, and I can do all things in You!' Lastly I unite myself to the Holy Spirit: 'Substantial love of the Father and of the Son, I unite myself to You; I wish to love as You love; I am good for nothing, but deign to permit me to unite myself to You with all my heart and transport me even to the bosom of God.

Most often, following the bent of his special grace, Dom Columba's soul loved "to pass through the veil of the sacred humanity of Christ," only to rest on reaching the Father:

> After Mass, I seem to hear Jesus say to me: '*Ego et Pater unum sumus.*[2] Then I lay down at His feet my soul, my heart, all my powers, and I say to Him: 'My Jesus, You are one with the Father, I am one with You, I desire only one thing: to act in all things for You, with You and in You.'
>
> I love, too, to think after Communion that the Eternal Word who is *in sinu Patris* is likewise in me *in sinu peccatoris.*[3] And this thought throws me into adoration and thanksgiving.
>
> When I possess Jesus in my heart after the Mass, I am united to Jesus. Faith tells me that He is in Me and I in Him. Jesus is in the bosom of the Father, and I, poor sinner, am there with Him. Then I say to the Father: 'I am the *Amen* of Jesus. Amen! that Your Beloved Son, the Word, say for me all that ought to be said; He knows me, He knows all my miseries, my needs, my aspirations, my desires. What confidence this thought begets!

"I cannot tell you," he writes in 1920 to one of his spiritual

[1] "Every best gift.... Thy hands have made me... ."
[2] "I and the Father are one" (John. 10:30).
[3] In the bosom of the sinner.

daughters, "the divine delight of the Heavenly Father, above all after Holy Communion, when He sees a soul all plunged in His Word, living by His life and gazing in His Face with humility and love. It is the moment of the day when I find peace and when I see God in the *darkness*."[1]

Truly, had he not the right to say: "My thanksgiving, it is Jesus Himself!"[2]

And in one of his last letters (21 April 1922) he thus reveals the whole secret of his inner life: "God is *so* good to me. I live now on my daily Communion. All the morning 'I walk in the strength of that divine food,' and from the afternoon I live on the thought of the following Communion, for It strengthens us according to our desires and preparation. Our Lord has promised that 'he who eateth Me shall live by Me.' His life becomes ours, the Source of all our activity."

One day Dom Marmion was asked if he made the Way of the Cross during Paschal time.

"Yes, to be sure I do," he replied. "And why not? One says the Mass, and the Mass is the Last Supper and Calvary; now, did not Jesus make *His* way of the cross from the Cenacle to Golgotha? Easter Sunday is the only day of the year when I do not make it, the triumph of Jesus then absorbing all my devotion. And yet I should not hesitate to make it. Was it not on the very evening of His resurrection that Jesus in person explained to the disciples of Emmaus that the Christ ought to suffer His Passion and so enter into His glory?"

By these words Dom Marmion expressed one of his most familiar thoughts and revealed the great esteem he had for meditation on the sufferings of Jesus under the form of the Way of the Cross.

He linked this practice of devotion to the central act of the liturgy, although it does not belong to the official public worship organised by the Church.

1 Letter of 8 October 1920.
2 Letter of 4 September 1918.

This devotion is the one that is most closely linked to the Eucharistic Sacrifice; like the Mass, it continues to recall to us the death of Jesus: *Mortem Domini annuntiabitis donec veniat.*[1]

In order to have the Blood of Jesus applied to us as fully as possible, this is what must be done: Every morning unite yourself to Jesus, that with Him you may offer to the Father the Blood of Christ to be offered in every Mass that day. But make this act with great intensity of faith and love: in this way you will partake as fully as possible in the chalice of Jesus, for His Blood is offered in every Mass *pro nostra omniumque salute.*

Then, when you make the Way of the Cross, offer anew to the Heavenly Father at each Station the Precious Blood that it may be applied to your soul.

Faithful to this thought, he therefore habitually made the Way of the Cross after his thanksgiving.

We may remember it was when he first entered Holy Cross College that Fr Gowan had inspired him with this devotion.[2] Since then he had remained always faithful to the suggestion of this holy religious; it may be said that he never failed a single day to practise this devotion. During his last years, even when travelling and when most absorbed in the work of preaching, he took care to spare a few minutes to do so. During his last years he made this practice the object of a vow.[3] He devoted a whole conference to it in his spiritual works,[4] and when preaching a retreat he never failed to speak of it. And with what accents! The last retreat that he preached was given at *Le grand séminaire* of Tournai, in August 1922. Several amongst his hearers have declared that his discourse on devotion to the Passion of Jesus Christ in the Way of the Cross was the most impressive. On his deathbed he still endeavoured to make the Stations of the Cross, thus uniting his last sufferings to those which marked the supreme hours of the earthly life of Jesus.

1 1 Cor. 11:26.
2 See p. 20.
3 "2 November 1920. *Hoc anno vovi viam crucis.*"
4 In his volume *Christ in His Mysteries.*

He has himself made known to us why he held this practice in such special esteem.

This contemplation of the sufferings of Jesus is very fruitful. After the sacraments and liturgical worship I am convinced there is no practice more useful for our souls than the Way of the Cross made with devotion. Its supernatural efficacy is sovereign. The Passion is the 'holy of holies' among the mysteries of Jesus, the pre-eminent work of our supreme High Priest; it is there above all that His virtues shine forth, and when we contemplate Him in His sufferings He gives us, according to the measure of our faith, the grace to practise the virtues that He manifested during these holy hours.

At each station our Divine Saviour presents Himself to us in this triple character: as the mediator who saves us by His merits, the perfect Model of sublime virtues, and the efficacious Cause who can, through His Divine Omnipotence, produce in our souls the virtues of which He gives us the example.[1]

It is above all in this exercise that we must carry out St Paul's precept: 'Let this mind be in you, which was also in Christ Jesus... who being in the form of God humbled Himself... even to the death of the cross.'

Therefore he began this devotion with this prayer: "My Jesus, I wish to make this Way of the Cross in union with You; with that same love You had for Your Father and for souls, I wish to enter into your thoughts and affections, to offer myself to the Father like You and with You."

These pages which he has devoted to the Way of the Cross must be read in order to see how deeply he entered into these thoughts and affections; the short prayer with which, at each station, he ended the meditation on Christ's sufferings is particularly

---

[1] See the development of these thoughts in *Christ in His Mysteries* in the conference, "In the Footsteps of Jesus, from the Praetorium to Calvary."

characteristic of his piety as a child of God. He lingered above all at the fourteenth Station, which spoke to him of baptism.

> The sacramental virtue of our baptism forever endures. In uniting ourselves by faith and love to Christ laid in the tomb we renew this grace of dying to sin in order to live only for God. 'Lord Jesus, may I bury in Your tomb all my sins, all my failings, all my infidelities; by the virtue of Your death and burial, give me grace to renounce more and more all that separates me from You; to renounce Satan, the world's maxims, my self-love. By the virtue of Your resurrection grant that, like You, I may no longer live save for the glory of Your Father!'

Neither shall we be surprised that after this contemplation he showed himself so patient, so humble, so ready to forgive, so zealous for the salvation of souls. He found in it, moreover, light and strength for his own soul. He said some months before his death: "When I have worries, when things go wrong with me, when I endure aridity and dryness, it is enough for me to meditate on the Passion of Jesus in making the Way of the Cross in order to feel strengthened; it is like a bath in which my soul is plunged; it never comes away without its vigour and joy being renewed; it acts upon my soul like a sacrament."[1]

However, one important remark which the attentive reader will already have foreseen is here necessary. For Dom Marmion this practice of the Way of the Cross had not the material character which certain souls attach to it; for his past, he put all the emphasis on the most essential point: meditation on the sufferings of Jesus Christ, union with Him in the midst of His sufferings, and sharing by patience in these sufferings themselves.

There is still more. Dom Marmion, as we have said, had a sense

---

[1] "I too," he wrote one day, "have many miseries: every morning after my thanksgiving, I make the Way of the Cross, and, at the Seventh Station, when I see our Lord fall to the ground, I cast myself down with Him before the Eternal Father, and I say to Him: "Father, I am full of miseries, but my miseries are those of Thy Son Jesus, for He has fellowship with us, and like Him I fall beneath the weight. But *quod infirmum est Dei fortius est hominibus.*"

of values, and his piety, like his preaching, was traced upon dogma and the liturgy, the nursing mother of both. We cannot on this subject speak of "special" devotion in the narrow meaning of the word, to such or such mystery. Not that he dissuaded others from these particular devotions; such exclusiveness would have been repugnant to his wide views, and above all to his religious mentality; rarely has anyone shown more careful discretion in respecting the movements of the Spirit in the Church, and the attractions placed by this Spirit in each soul. But Dom Columba's distinctive gift, the grace proper to him – a grace corresponding, moreover, to his love of synthesis in theology – was to cleave to Christ Himself, to the Incarnate Word, considered in the oneness of His Divine Person in the integrity of His commandment, in the totality of His "mystery," in the plenitude of His work; to the Eternal Word who became a child of man that He might make us like unto Him through grace, children of the Father. With Dom Marmion the gaze of faith – the supreme rule of his spirituality – reached from eternity to eternity.

If he loved to dwell on the Passion it was because for him what Jesus tells us it was for His own soul: *Hora ejus.* "His hour," the paramount hour, the hour which was "to baptise Him," the hour to which from the time of His coming into the world He had tended with all the energy of His Divine Being, as to the summit, if not to the crowning-point of His work here below; the hour when He finished doing His Father's commandment, when He confessed His infinite rights and restored to us, by reopening Heaven's gates, the inheritance of adoptive children.

In the same way as Calvary is the culminating point of the earthly history of the God-Man, in the same way as the cross dominates the altar of which it is the centre, and as the sign of the cross is the special sign of the liturgy and the Christian profession, so in his devotion to the Passion of Jesus Dom Marmion gave it the correlative place that it holds in the mind of the Church and in that of her Divine Spouse.

The same sense of equilibrium, which gives to each devotion the place it ought to hold in spirituality taken as a whole, characterises Dom Columba's piety towards the Blessed Virgin Mary.

"No piety would be truly Christian if it did not include in its object the Mother of the Incarnate Word.... In the same way as the quality of 'Son of Man' cannot be separated in Christ from that of 'Son of God,' so is Mary united to Jesus; indeed, the Blessed Virgin Mary enters into the mystery of the Incarnation by a title belonging to the very nature of the mystery."[1]

As we see, it is ever the thought of Christ, the Incarnate Word which here, as elsewhere, directs his devotion. "We must," he would sometimes say, "imitate Jesus in all things; He, the Eternal Word, *chose* Mary for His Mother; so we should *choose* her for our Mother and have for her a childlike devotion."

How could this "childlike devotion" fail to be his? He confided to one of his spiritual sons:

> In the morning, after Mass, when I possess Jesus in my heart I consecrate myself to the Blessed Virgin and say to her: '*Ecce Filius tuus* – Behold thy Son. O Virgin Mary, I am your child; still more I share in the Priesthood of Jesus; accept me for your son as you accepted Jesus. I am unworthy of your gifts, but a member of the Mystical Body of your Divine Son. And He Himself has said: All that you do to the least of those who believe in Me, you do it unto Me; I am one of these *minimis meis*; to refuse me would be to refuse Jesus Himself.'

He insisted on persons fixing for themselves some practices of piety in manifestation of honour, love and confidence towards the Mother of Jesus. He added that it is not necessary to overburden oneself with practices, but to remain faithful, very faithful, to those once determined upon. As for himself, besides the consecration made in the morning after Mass and the recitation of the *Angelus*, he was especially attached to the Rosary:

---

[1] "The Mother of the Incarnate Word," in *Christ the Life of the Soul*.

In it, we praise Mary, ever united to her Son; we unceasingly and lovingly repeat the praise with which the heavenly messenger of the Incarnate Word saluted her; we contemplate Christ in the series of His mysteries, in order to unite ourselves with Him; we congratulate the Blessed Virgin on having been so closely associated with these mysteries and return thanks to the Holy Trinity, through the *Gloria,* for all the privileges of the Mother of Jesus.[1]

I confess that should I happen to reach the end of the day without having said my Rosary I should be very discontented with myself. There are some who say: 'The Rosary is all very well for women and children.' Let us admit it. But what does our Lord say? – and here his tone would become very impressive – 'Unless you… become as little children you shall not enter into the Kingdom of heaven.' And I wish to enter there!

As to his devotion to the saints, it was habitually in accordance with the liturgy. Nevertheless, besides the devotion he had to his guardian angel which he had learnt from his mother, he was drawn by a special attraction of grace to honour above all his patron St Joseph, "the shadow of the Eternal Father"; St Paul; St Benedict; St Thomas Aquinas; St Francis de Sales, whom he called "the eminent doctor of the inner life"; St Mary Magdalene, whom he invoked several times a day; St Gertrude and St Mechtilde, "because they so well understood the riches and the mystery of Jesus"; St Teresa of Ávila, "on account," he said, "of her love for the Incarnation."

In this way all Dom Marmion's spiritual life came from Christ or converged to Him by one of those innermost movements which irresistibly drew the whole man. And in him, impressionability of soul found a sure support in the firmness of his convictions, and the vividness of his faith took away nothing from the warmth of his spontaneity.

---

1 *Cf.* "The Mother of the Incarnate Word," in *Christ the Life of the Soul.*

Dom Marmion wrote one day:

The means we have of ever tending to God and remaining united to Him – the sacraments, Mass, Divine Office, the life of obedience and labour – only attain the *summum* of their efficacy if we lead a life of prayer. All these means are valuable and fruitful only if we do not put any obstacle in the way of their action, but bring to it the interior dispositions of faith, confidence, love, compunction, humility and abandonment to God's Will. Now it is above all by the life of prayer, by habitual union with God in prayer, that we gather strength to thrust obstacles aside and keep ourselves in dispositions favourable to grace. A soul that does not live this habitual life of prayer needs great effort each time it wants to be recollected and to arouse the affections upon which, generally speaking, depend the fruitfulness of the supernatural means that we have for sanctifying ourselves. On the other hand, a soul that leads a life of prayer never lets the divine fire go out, but keeps it ever smouldering; and when the regular hours of prayer or moments of inspiration arrive where this fire is put more directly or more exclusively in contact with grace – as occurs in the sacraments, the Holy Sacrifice, the *Opus Dei*, the orders of obedience, the trials sent or permitted by God – these smouldering embers burst into flame and become a glowing furnace, wherein the soul sees its love for God and the neighbour increased and transformed, sometimes in a very high degree. Love of God being the only source, and its intensity being the only measure of the fruitfulness of our acts, even of the most ordinary ones, the life of prayer which maintains and increases this within us becomes the secret of holiness for us.[1]

In this page Dom Marmion reveals *the secret* of *his* holiness; at the close of this study it is the contemplative whom we have to consider.

It would take too long to point out, even in a very succinct

---

[1] *Christ the Ideal of the Monk,* ch. "Monastic Prayer."

summary, Dom Marmion's ideas on this vital subject; we must necessarily refer the reader to the pages where he has developed his teaching – pages which have been praised by the highest critics for justness of view and supernatural and sympathetic penetration. He has put himself in these pages, and their purposely didactic character does not succeed in veiling the personal experiences on which they are based.

Here it is above all he himself, speaking of himself in all transparency, to whom we shall find ourselves listening, and the teaching will not on this account be less profitable.

Dom Marmion had the highest estimation of mental prayer: "The frequent contact of the soul with God, through the prayer of faith and the life of prayer, is a powerful aid towards the supernatural transformation of our souls. If prayer is well made the life of prayer is transforming...."

From the fact that our sanctification is of an essential supernatural order, and God the principal author of this sanctification, Dom Marmion deduced that, "according to ordinary ways, our progress in divine love practically depends on our life of prayer."[1] The extracts that will one day be given from his letters – for they are too numerous to be cited here – will show how much he insisted on this idea and how zealously he acted on it.

Such was his esteem for prayer that he looked upon it as man's highest activity. In a letter dated 29 May 1915, he reminds one of his spiritual children that God created us for Himself and we can do nothing greater than to surrender ourselves to Him in order to fulfil His designs. To allow God to act in us in prayer is neither idleness nor inaction. In such moments there imperceptibly passes into the uttermost depths of our soul a divine activity, worth far more than our own human activity. The nearer a soul draws to God, the simpler she becomes, and no word, no formula can express nor render what she would say, but the Church says it for her in the liturgy: "O

---

[1] See "Prayer" in the volume *Christ the Life of the Soul*, and "Monastic Prayer," in *Christ the Ideal of the Monk*. In both these conferences Dom Marmion has revealed many of his personal experiences.

FACSIMILE OF AUTOGRAPH PAGE FROM
DOM MARMION'S WRITINGS

God, before whom every heart lieth open and to whom *every wish* speaketh, and from whom nothing is hidden, purify our hearts by the inpouring of the Holy Ghost, so that we may be able to love Thee perfectly and to praise Thee worthily."

For lack of documents it is impossible for us to follow in detail and with precision the "curve" of Dom Marmion's spiritual ascensions in prayer.

At the seminary he made his meditation according to the discursive method applied in the works *ad hoc* which abounded in the last centuries; he remained faithful to this during the first years of his priesthood, although according to certain confidences he made this way of praying did not appeal to his intuitive and responsive temperament.

What is quite certain is that from the beginning of his novitiate he was well aware of one of the most essential, if not the most essential, character of prayer: *the loving intercourse of the child of God with his Heavenly Father.*

He had written in his *Notes*, feast of the Sacred Heart (1887): "I felt today that we are pleasing to God in proportion as we are conformable to Jesus Christ, especially in His interior dispositions. This is why a *childlike* confidence in prayer, in spite of our sins, is so pleasing to God. 'I know that Thou always hearest me,' said Jesus (to His Father). We are the adopted children of God and should always in all humility and simplicity treat Him in the same manner."

And several months later (September 25th), after reading the life of St Joseph Cupertino: "[This saint's] manner of praying was 'as it were to identify himself with the Persons of the Holy Trinity.' As I am the adopted son of God, I should try to *imitate Jesus Christ perfectly* in His relations with the Holy Trinity."

Convincing and enlightening traits. We hence grasp that from the first days of Dom Marmion's religious life, his prayer, and his state of prayer had but one aspect – but one of great intensity – of the grace which was his: to live as a child of the Heavenly Father.

It is above all through Jesus, by uniting oneself with Jesus in trusting to His merits, that, according to him, prayer becomes fruitful.[1]

The abundance and vividness of the lights which he received whilst at Louvain, on the Blessed Trinity, on the Incarnate Word and His mysteries, show that already at that period his soul had attained the state of contemplation. We know that at that time he exchanged views with the late much-regretted Augustin Poulain, SJ, on the subject of prayer. What has become of this correspondence? Failing these letters, some confidences, unhappily too rare, show us certain aspects of his prayer at this time.

> In prayer I spend nearly all the time in contemplating, in adoring God's Will, seen in the wisdom of His Word, in whom I lose myself in oneness of love for the Father.[2]

When one is united by faith to Jesus Christ and when in the dimness of faith one lays down his understanding at Christ's feet, accepting with love all that he does in our name in the full vision of His Father, that prayer is of a high order, and

---

[1] At that period his soul was already drawn towards contemplation. In a diary of 1899, he notes in February these lines of Francisco Suárez, SJ which responded to what was in his mind: "*In hoc statu (contemplativo seu unitivo) jam non est necessarius multarum meditationum usus, nec morosi discursus, sed simplex Dei et attributorum vel beneficiorum ejus memoria, cum aliqua ponderatione, majori vel minori, juxta dispositiones personae; quantum sufficiat ad affectus illos excitandos, in quibus praecipue haec via ejusque perfectio consistit*" (*De religione*, T. 11). In the same diary under the date of February 13th he writes: "Contemplation is a gaze fixed on God or on a divine truth to which one is urged by love" (St Thomas Aquinas). "It comes from the light of faith, made clear to us by the gifts of understanding, wisdom and knowledge. And as faith and these gifts are to be found in every soul in a state of grace, St Thomas teaches that everyone may reach this contemplation. From this the *importance of devotion to the Holy Spirit.*" And for the study of these gifts he goes back to Giovanni Scaramelli, SJ, *Il direttorio mistico*. He adds: "Another definition of *ordinary* contemplation: 'The uplifting of the soul to God by a simple affective intuition.'" And again at the same date: "My prayer may be defined in these words: *Hoc enim sentite in vobis quod et in Christo Jesu.*"

[2] Letter of 28 February 1902.

made in spirit and in truth. At these moments sometimes the Spirit of Christ inclines us to rest in silence and adoration at the feet of Jesus; at other times he urges us to unite ourselves to His oblation, to His submission towards His Father. We must follow these movements.

And finally,[1] this beautiful passage full of significance:

One with Jesus, we love Him *in sinu Patris*. It is the life of *pure love* which supposes the effort to do always that which is most pleasing to the Father.... It supposes, too, a deep contempt of ourselves and realisation of our nothingness, so much the greater in that we are so near to this infinite holiness ... it supposes still further that we rest upon Jesus ... it supposes, in fine, the absence of all deliberate sin and of all refusal to follow the inspirations of the Holy Spirit. All that one does *in the bosom of the Father, in a filial spirit of adoption,* is of immense value. In this sanctuary one receives graces, and often the repose of contemplation.

At the end of his life, summing up and condensing the result of prolonged experience, he wrote (1918): "Prayer, then, is like the expression of our intimate life as children of God, like the outcome of our divine sonship in Christ, the spontaneous blossoming of the gifts of the Holy Ghost."[2]

And again (1922):

Prayer is the normal outcome, under the Holy Spirit's action, of the affections resulting from our divine adoption.... It will bear the impress both of a high degree of piety and of a deep reverence. Indeed, for the child of God, for the brother of Christ Jesus, no tenderness, no intimacy is too great but on condition that it be always accompanied and sustained by a sense of unutterable reverence before the immense majesty

---

[1] April 1906.
[2] *Christ the Life of the Soul.*

of the Father: *Patrem immensae majestatis.* This is to adore the Father in spirit and in truth.[1]

Nature and grace had well prepared Dom Marmion for this life of prayer. Why must we always find these curious contrasts in him? This temperament so genial, so sociable, so expansive, so happy to give itself out in action, was at the same time very meditative. You would see him at the hour of recreation full of enthusiasm and gaiety – and immediately afterwards, when this exercise came to an end, you would see him again in the oratory, his head bowed over his joined hands, in the recollected attitude of most humble reverence, his soul plunged, this time utterly, in close intercourse with God alone *in sinu Patris.* It is because he had equally the taste for solitude, for interior silence, for reflection, or rather – for he was above all *intuitive* – the taste for contemplation itself: to see, to gaze, to let himself be bathed in light, to savour and, in consequence – for his heart was as generous as his mind was deep – to give, to surrender himself.

Dom Columba was inclined by grace even more than by nature to mystical union in contemplation. All we have recorded of his inner life gives us sufficiently to understand his detachment from self and creatures;[2] his simplicity which saw and judged all things in the supernatural light alone; his generous constancy in seeking to know the divine good pleasure in all vicissitudes; his spirit of compunction, his docility to the inspirations of the Holy Spirit, the fervour of his charity: all these virtues largely opened the way to the abundance of the gifts of the Spirit.

[1] *Christ the Ideal of the Monk,* ch. "Monastic Prayer," § 2.
[2] He had already written in February 1899 (diary), "The great obstacle to contemplation is attachment to creatures which sullies the soul: *Beati mundo quoniam ipsi Deum videbunt.*" Such was his desire for detachment and purity that he made his confession at that time every evening, and during the conventual Mass he prepared himself for this confession by asking God to grant him *gratiam et donum poenitentiae.* On the theological basis of this last practice see *Christ the Life of the Soul,* ch. "The Sacrament and Virtue of Penance," § 2.

His humility especially prepared him to receive the gifts of God's mercy. "If there are few contemplatives," says the author of the *Imitation*, "it is above all because there are few souls that are deeply humble." Grave words which Bossuet echoed when he wrote: "The humble of heart enter into the deep things of God without being moved, and, far from the world and its way of thinking, they find life in the height of God's works."[1] Truths of which Fr Columba was convinced to the very depth of his soul; how many times has he not commented in this sense on the words of Scripture: "God resisteth the proud and giveth grace to the humble," and above all on these words of Jesus: "I confess to Thee, O Father, because Thou hast hid these things from the wise and prudent and hast revealed them to little ones!" And this is why, faithful to St Benedict's teaching, he did not cease to show that in humility lies the surest way of learning the secrets of God.[2]

However, there is one virtue belonging so essentially to the very nature of contemplation that it seems, if we may thus speak, as if the degree of contemplation may be measured by it. This virtue is faith. One of the most learned theologians of our day, Fr Garrigou-Lagrange, has thus described "the perfect contemplative: one who goes even to the heights of his faith, and while believing in the supernatural mysteries, probes them, sounds their depths, savours them, assimilates them, or rather allows himself to be assimilated by them; he is one who is not content with believing alone, but lives fully by his faith (*justus ex fide vivit*) and judges of everything accordingly; that is to say, according to the very thoughts of God, as if he saw with the eye of God."[3]

---

1 *Élévations sur les mystères*, 18ᵉ semaine, 12ᵉ élévation.
2 And by one of those "exchanges of causality," well known to philosophers, the habit of prayer produces in the soul an increase of virtue, and notably, in Dom Marmion's case, an increase of humility; he gained this much more from contemplation of the Divine Perfections than from the sight of his miseries, never so vivid as in the rays of God's light.
3 *Perfection chrétienne et contemplation*, T. I. "Faith is the sole proximate and proportionate means of the soul's union with God, seeing that there is no other alternative, but that God is either seen, or believed in. For as God is infinite, so

Out of all these traits there is not one which does not perfectly apply to Dom Marmion; he might truly have served as the model for this description. His spiritual works testify, in fact, to the living faith wherewith his whole life was imbued, and the impressive eloquence which, as it were, breathes forth from each page attests to his habitual contact with the spirit of wisdom and love. He has, moreover, himself left a portrait of the contemplative which is like the anticipated commentary on the lines we have just quoted:

> Christ lives in the soul of the just; under the infallible direction of this inner Master the soul... penetrates into the divine light; Christ gives it His Spirit, the first Author of Holy Writ, that it may there search into the very depths of the infinite: *Omnia scrutatur etiam profunda Dei;* it contemplates God's marvels in respect to men; it measures, by faith, the divine proportions of the mystery of Jesus, and this wonderful spectacle, whereof the splendours enlighten and illuminate it, touches, draws, enraptures, uplifts, transports and transforms the soul. It experiences in its turn what the disciples of Emmaus felt when Christ Jesus Himself vouchsafed to interpret to them the Sacred Books: 'Was not our heart burning within us, whilst He spoke in the way, and opened to us the Scriptures': *Nonne cor nostrum ardens erat in nobis – dum loqueretur in via et aperiret nobis Scripturas?*
>
> What is there astonishing, then, in the fact that the soul, charmed and won by this living word 'which penetrates even to the marrow,' makes the prayer of these disciples its own: *Mane nobiscum,* 'Stay with us!' O Thou, the incomparable Master, indefectible light, infallible truth, the only true life of our

---

faith proposes Him as infinite, and as He is Three and One, so faith proposes Him to us as Three and One. And thus by this means alone that is faith, God manifests Himself to the soul in the divine light, which surpasses all understanding, and therefore the greater the faith of the soul the more is that soul united to God.... For in this darkness God unites Himself to the understanding, being Himself hidden in it." "St John of the Cross," *Ascent of Mount Carmel,* Book II, ch. 9, translated by David Lewis.

souls! Forestalling these holy desires, 'the Holy Spirit Himself asketh for us with unspeakable groanings,' which constitute true prayer; these vehement desires to possess God, to live no longer save for the Father's glory and for that of His Son Jesus. Love, become great and burning by contact with God, takes possession of all the powers of the soul, renders it strong and generous to do perfectly all the Father's Will, to give itself up fully to the divine good pleasure.

What better or more fruitful prayer than this? What contemplation can be comparable to it?[1]

This beautiful page surely tells of personal experience. Nevertheless, in this important matter it is interesting to glean in the unpublished collection of Dom Columba's notes and letters explicit evidences, rare though they be, of his life of prayer. Out of such a rich treasury is not anything we can extract of high value? And is not any experience of such a master a light for us? Certain of his words are like sparks which could only come from the furnace of divine union, and if they throw a light on one moment of the inner life of a soul it is enough to enable us to judge of the depth of this life.

Dom Marmion's prayer was nourished above all by the revealed word of God. This is not astonishing. Is it not in the Scriptures that God makes Himself known? Dom Marmion used to recall St Gregory's beautiful saying: "Would you enter into the innermost things of God? Listen to His words. *Disce cor Dei in verbis Dei.*" Dom Marmion's impressive pages on the Scriptures as source of prayer should be read;[2] when he speaks of persons who have obtained the gift of understanding from Holy Writ through great humility and persevering prayer be sure that all unwittingly he is speaking of himself. He wrote in 1918: "I read the Holy Scriptures while praying. Many of Christ's contemporaries who saw Him considered only the man

[1] *Christ the Ideal of the Monk*, ch. "Monastic Prayer."
[2] *Christ the Ideal of the Monk*, ch. "Monastic Prayer," § 7.

in Him; yet He was the Divine Word. Many Christians, priests, professors of Holy Scripture see in the Scriptures only the written text without being convinced that this text is *Verbum divinum*. Neither one nor the other receives any profit for the soul which remains insensible."[1]

Therefore he concluded on another occasion: "The principal source of prayer is to be found in Holy Scripture read with devotion and reverence and laid up in the heart."[2]

In the Scriptures he found above all the ever-living figure of Christ. And faithful in this to St Teresa's counsel, of which he had himself proved the value, it was through the sacred humanity of Jesus he united Himself to God in prayer:

> As for my prayer, I unite myself to the Word through the sacred humanity, and generally the Word draws me to speak with Him on some incident in one of the mysteries of His life, or on some text of Holy Scripture. For the rest my inner life is most simple: *Mihi vivere Christus est.*[3]
>
> One form of prayer which helps me much in the midst of my weaknesses and my cares is to cast myself at the feet of the Eternal Father *in the name* of Jesus Christ, saying to Him: 'Father, Jesus has said that all that is done to the least of His, is done to Himself; and I am one of the members of Thy Son, *concorporei et consanguinei Christi,*[4] and all that Thou doest for me Thou doest it for Him. He has never refused Thee anything; my miseries are His: *vere languores nostros ipse tulit.*'[5] I feel that this prayer touches the Father of mercies.[6]

And again: "My prayer consists in falling down at Christ's feet like the poor lepers in the Gospel; I come before God like the poor man

---

[1] Letter of June 1918.
[2] Letter of 9 August 1920.
[3] Letter of 4 September 1918.
[4] "Made partakers of the Body and Blood of Christ," St Cyril of Jerusalem.
[5] "Surely he hath...carried our sorrows" (Isa. 53: 4).
[6] Letter of 10 December 1911.

who lay on the road to Jericho, wounded and stripped; I say nothing, I only show God my misery and await help from His mercy."[1]

How could it be otherwise than that Dom Marmion should often have contemplated Christ on the cross?

> As for me, I must say with St Jean Perboyre: My crucifix takes the place of all books for my mental prayer, for Christ is the 'way' and it is through Him that God wills to reveal Himself to us: *Illuxit nobis in facie Christi Jesu:* He enlightens us 'in the face of Christ Jesus.'[2] When I contemplate Christ upon the cross, I pass, through the veil (His humanity), into the Holy of Holies of the Divine Secrets.[3]

And in a more concise form: "*Christo confixus sum cruci ... vivit in me Christus.* That has been all my prayer for some time past."[4]

We have seen above that it was in the liturgy that Dom Marmion gained such thorough knowledge of St Paul and the Gospels. The liturgical cycle and the sacred texts enshrined in it frequently supplied the frame and matter of his prayer.

It was one of his favourite maxims that those who recite the Divine Office with generosity and recollection easily arrive at contemplation.[5]

One of the souls dear to him had told him she was about to make a retreat, and asked him to join with her in order to obtain from above the outpouring of divine gifts. He replied:

> During this Paschaltide the Church invites us to *stir up* within us the grace of our baptism (as St Paul exhorts Timothy to 'stir up the grace' of his priestly ordination). The three

[1] Without exact date, but at the end of his life.
[2] 2 Cor. 4:6.
[3] Letter of 12 December 1916.
[4] Letter of 12 March 1921.
[5] He said in 1919: "At the beginning of my monastic life, the abbot, Dom Placide, said that when one goes to the choir detached from everything and absorbed in the presence of God, one arrives, almost without suspecting it, at contemplation: at that time I could hardly believe it: now I know that it is true" (Conference to the Benedictine nuns of Maredret).

sacraments: baptism, confirmation, holy orders, leave within us the *pignus spiritus* 'the pledge of the Spirit,' a pledge which always calls down the grace of the sacrament. Baptism contains *in germ all holiness.*

(*a*) Grace: Participation in the *Divine Nature,* dwelling in the essence of the soul; (*b*) Theological virtues: faith, hope, charity, in the *powers of the soul;* (*c*) gifts of the Holy Spirit; (*d*) infused moral virtues. All these gifts are the appanage, the portion of the child of the Heavenly Father, redeemed by Jesus Christ.

Confirmation fortifies and perfects this germ; the Eucharist nourishes it. Faith is its root and its life: *Justus* EX *fide vivit.* All the rites and prayers used in the administration of these sacraments have *lasting* effects which we can stir up by faith and in the Holy Spirit.

I often make my prayer looking at the Heavenly Father in Jesus Christ, begging Him to renew in me all that the Church has asked and wrought in me at the time of the reception of these sacraments. That is my retreat, unless the spirit of Christ draws me to other operations.[1]

There was nothing in creation that did not serve as a ladder for the uplifting of his soul. The saints have not disdained these helps. "Do you think," wrote St Teresa to the Prioress of the Carmelites of Seville, who from the windows of their convent amused themselves in looking at the flag-bedecked galleys on the Guadalquivir, "do you think it is a small matter to be in a monastery where you can see these galleys of which you tell me! The sisters at Castilla are quite envious of you, for that is a great help in praising our Lord." Dom Marmion, who had read and re-read the works of the saint must have known this passage. In him the contemplative found a

---

[1] Letter of 9 April 1917. This attraction of the Spirit must have lasted a long time: we find it echoed again in a letter of 4 September 1918: "I am often urged by our Lord to revive within myself the grace of my baptism, of my confirmation and of my ordination to the priesthood." In September 1919, he made of this thought the whole programme of the spiritual exercises of a retreat.

SPIRITUS PRECUM

happy auxiliary in that precious gift with which his Celtic temperament had endowed him, namely, the faculty of wonder and admiration, a faculty which he kept intact until his last days.[1] Wide plains, golden harvest fields, the solitude of forests, the restless immensity of the sea, a fair-haired child with innocent eyes, a delicate thought, an eloquent page, a noble deed, a trait of kindness, an act of virtue; all that is great and beautiful and bears the seal or the vestige of its divine origin, was for him a cause of admiration.

And this wonder and admiration in his heart grew into love. In presence of the great spectacles of nature his soul lent its own voice to all creation;[2] that was why he so much loved to recite, united to the Word, the *Benedicite;* everything served him as a ladder to mount up to the Heavenly Father near whom his childlike soul rested full of faith and love.

All the passages we have cited show us to what a degree of Divine Intimacy his great soul had attained: with him, prayer had become a state:

> Never forget that prayer is a *state,* and that with souls who seek God prayer becomes continuous, often in an unconscious manner, in the *spiritual depths* of the soul. It is there, in this sanctuary, that the Word espouses the soul *in pure faith, Sponsabo te mihi in fide.* These silent longings, these sighings

[1] In a letter of 12 March 1912, sent from Tivoli, where he had gone during a stay in Rome, he wrote: "We have been a long walk of several hours: it brought back to me some very touching memories, The Irish College has its country house at Tivoli and with great happiness I have been looking again on those sights I used to admire so much more than thirty years ago. Those magnificent waterfalls gushing out of the rock by many apertures and falling into the ravine six hundred feet below, those mountains, the immense Roman *campagna* and St Peter's in the distance form a picture most difficult to describe." "Often," he said to the Benedictine nuns of Maredret (conference in 1917), "when I am alone in the country, I like to think that our Lord, He, too, went about the countrysides of Judea and of Galilee, and I like to think of the emotions that the sight of nature aroused in Him. Christ appreciated these beauties; in the universe He saw the reflection of the Divine Perfection, and He praised His Father in the name of all creation."

[2] See *Christ the Ideal of the Monk,* ch. "The *Opus Dei,* Divine Praise," § 4.

are the true voice of the Holy Spirit within us which touches the heart of God: *Desiderium pauperum exaudivit auris tua.*[1] You should do like St Catherine of Siena: she made for herself a tabernacle in the midst of her heart, and there she ever found her Bridegroom, without anyone being able to hinder her from visiting this tabernacle.[2]

That we may finish studying the aspects of his prayer and inner life towards the end of his life we will note some traits here and there in his letters:

28 February 1916 – Our Lord draws me more and more to a *life of prayer in bare faith,* without consolation, but in the truth.

22 August 1916 – *Caro et sanguis non revelavit tibi sed Pater meus qui in coelis est.*[3] I am trying myself to live in this *light* from on high, for it is, according to [Jan van] Ruysbroeck, the point of contact where the soul meets the Word. *Erat* LUX VERA *quae illuminat omnem hominem venientem in hunc mundum.*[4] The *oratio fidei* alone leads us to this light. It purifies, it divinises, it transforms from light to light.

20 November 1916 – I feel that our Lord is drawing me more and more to the prayer of faith.

---

[1] "Thy ear, O Lord, hath heard the desire of the poor" (*Cf.* Ps. 9:17). How may we resist quoting here the beautiful passages from St Gregory, another contemplative, commenting on the words of Scripture, "the Lord heareth my desire." "Remark this word," says the great pope, "my desire. True prayer is not in the voice but in the heart. It is not our words, it is our desires that make, in the mysterious ears of God, the strength of our cries. If with our mouth we ask for eternal life, without desiring it from the bottom of our hearts, our cry is a silence. If, without speaking, we desire it from the bottom of our heart, our silence cries out" (*Moralia in Job, Patrologia Latina,* 36, col. 258.

[2] Letter of 24 February 1921.

[3] "Flesh and blood bath not revealed it (My divinity) to thee, but My Father who is in heaven" (Matt. 16:17).

[4] "The true light, which enlighteneth every man that cometh into this world" (John 1:9).

Dom Marmion greatly esteemed this "prayer of faith." "Very simple," he said, "but very fruitful"; when he spoke of it, it was in impressive tones betraying long experience.

A curious thing – the form of his prayer is at times, even during the last years of his life, singularly imaginative:

4 April 1917 – One thought which is very profitable for my soul and helps me to keep united with God is this. The temple of Jerusalem was a figure of Jesus, and in this temple were three porches or courts, and finally the Holy of Holies where the High Priest was alone with God. This Holy of Holies in Jesus Christ was the fine point of His soul where He contemplated the Face of the Father. United with Jesus, it seems to me that there is in myself, too, this Holy of Holies, where I adore the Father in presence of the mercy seat which is the sacred humanity of Jesus.

Apart from these moments, it seems to me that my soul stays always at the same point; that is to say, much light and facility, when I have to speak of God or exercise any function of my ministry, but in the ordinary course of life a confused sense of cleaving to Christ, and through Him of *resting under the eye* of God – that eye which is ordinarily hidden in darkness: *Nubes et caligo in circuitu ejus.*[1]

And a few weeks later,[2] to the same:

Every perfect gift, every grace and heavenly favour comes down from the Father, but, by a law of His wisdom, He wills that His Christ and the Church, the Mystical Body of His Christ, should be the channel of His favours.

For myself, I feel the power of grace and great light in the depth of my soul; it seems to me that Christ not only abides in me, but that I am, as it were, buried in Him, *spiritually encompassed* with His holy presence. I adore Him, in answer

---

[1] "Clouds and darkness around about Him" (Ps. 96: 2).
[2] Letter of 9 May 1917.

to the Father who reveals to me His Godhead, and all this, gently, without effort and more and more habitually. Hence great faith and boundless confidence in the goodness of the Heavenly Father, in spite of the constant view He gives me of my misery, my sins, my unworthiness.

Yet two other testimonies, particularly characteristic and taken from his letters of 1918, admit us into his soul's most secret sanctuary and yield to us some last confidences; we shall see that his prayer corresponded to the special and singular grace which truly seems to have been his in the Divine Predestination – namely, the very vivid and deep sense of being, in Jesus, the child of the Heavenly Father. We shall notice once more, to say it in passing, the nervous and condensed style in which this master knew how to sum up a dogmatic question with a stroke of the pen, and how in him the theologian was at the service of the ascetic.

It seems to me that, habitually, if not actually, the point of my spirit seeks the face of the Father in faith: *Quaerite faciem ejus semper.*[1] I have never received an extraordinary grace that I know of. Never any interior voice, never any vision, ecstasy, any capture of the powers of the soul binding their activity. Nothing of that kind; I have no attraction for it. But it seems to me that the grace of adoption (that *germ* received in baptism, fortified at confirmation, nourished by the Holy Eucharist) is developed more and more in me through the strength of Christ.

As St Thomas's doctrine on the knowledge of Christ has helped me much to comprehend this grace and to cooperate in it, I am going to tell it to you in a few words. St Thomas distinguishes between three kinds of knowledge or notions in Christ:

(*a*) *Beatific* knowledge, whereby the fine point of His blessed mind contemplated unceasingly the Face of the Father (or the Word). In this vision His soul beheld the Divine

---

[1] "Seek His face evermore" (Ps. 104: 4)

Essence and in it all things in a divine manner. This knowledge began at the moment of the Incarnation and never ceased even in the midst of the darkness of Calvary.

(b) *Infused* knowledge. The angels, by nature, do not perceive directly things in themselves, but in the ideas which are infused in them. This notion – infinitely inferior to the beatific notion – is much superior to our own. Simultaneously with the beatific knowledge the soul of Christ possessed this infused knowledge to a degree which infinitely surpasses angelic knowledge. In this knowledge He perfectly knew all that regards the universe whereof He is the Head.

(c) His *experimental* knowledge. A man like unto us, in all excepting sin, Jesus acquired, like us, notions by experience, in employing His natural faculties like us. This knowledge increased daily in Him by reason of each new perception.

These three kinds of knowledge existed simultaneously, but *without confusion* in Christ's blessed soul. The higher kind cast their lights, their radiations on the inferior: *Illuminans tu mirabiliter a montibus aeternis*,[1] as happens in contemplatives. This Christ is our exemplar. In heaven we shall have three kinds of knowledge. Here below the fine point of our understanding attains to God in the obscure light of faith, and when this view becomes habitual it is a great gift – as precious as those of a more extraordinary order. 'God,' says St [Jeanne de] Chantal, 'had shed on the summit of [St Francis de Sales'] understanding a light so clear that he saw at a simple view the truths of faith and their excellence... and he submitted to these truths which were shown to him by a simple acquiescence of his will. He called the place where these lights were brought forth God's sanctuary, where nothing enters save the soul alone with God.' It is the normal development of the grace of our baptism: *Peccatis mortui, viventes autem Deo in Christo Jesu.*[2] This fine point of the spirit the di-

---

1 "Thou enlightenest wonderfully from the everlasting hills" (Ps. 75:5).
2 "Dead to sin, but alive unto God, in Christ Jesus" (Rom. 6:11).

vine life penetrates within us, and, by redundancy, divinises the rest of our being.¹

The other passage, taken from a letter written a few months later, is not less significant. At this epoch his medical advisers had insisted on Dom Marmion going for a rest to Luxembourg; he was the guest of the Redemptorist Fathers at Beauplateau. In his solitary walks he read the commentaries of St Bernard and of St Teresa on the Canticle of Canticles, and the works of Bl. Henry Suso.² In a letter written at that time he took up again, but in a more concise way, the thought of the threefold knowledge of Christ, as frame of prayer.

> My attraction is to find ALL *in* Jesus and *through* Him. He is the way that the Father gives us; it is by Him that we must go to the Father. When in prayer I try to empty my mind completely, putting on one side all the beautiful words, figures, comparisons that Jesus used in His teaching, I am paralysed.
>
> This is how I understand mental prayer for myself.
>
> In Jesus there were three kinds of prayer:
>
> (*a*) That which corresponded to His beatific knowledge, continual contemplation of the Face of the Father. This prayer was made in the summit of His soul, in pure and spiritual understanding. *It never ceased.*
>
> (*b*) That which corresponded to infused knowledge. By that prayer He beheld the whole plan of the universe, of redemption, etc... and by these notions His soul was raised to the Father. In this manner everything in the prophets, the Psalms, etc... was matter of prayer for Him.
>
> (*c*) That which corresponded to His acquired knowledge. All around Him was matter for prayer: 'Behold the lilies, the vine, the little birds who do not fall to the ground without the Father's permission.'
>
> Now I like in my union with Jesus and through Him to pray sometimes according to one, sometimes according to

---

1 Letter of 9 April 1918.
2 Letter of 22 July 1918.

another of these kind of knowledge. Only, for myself, the two last raise me to the first, and when I am there I seek nothing more.

Two passages have furnished me with matter for reflection and prayer during these days. I will transcribe them for you. I think you will see all their depths. The next time we meet I will speak to you about them. The first is from St Bernard, on the Canticle of Canticles: *Quaesivi dilectum in lectulo suo*. 'When you shall see a soul leave all things to adhere to the Word with all her strength, live by Him, allow herself to be guided by Him, conceive what she should bring forth by Him ... then you can indubitably recognise her for a spouse of the Word.'[1]

The second passage is from Albert the Great.[2] He explains how a soul arrives at perfect union with the Word: 'Let that soul never have anything before her eyes except Christ marked with His five wounds. Let her strive continually and diligently to go by Him to Him: by the Man to God, through the wounds of His manhood to the Godhead.'

I like to unite in faith my soul and my powers to the members of Christ. I annihilate my human personality[3] in presence of the Divine Person. I strive to live in Him and by Him for the Father. At the beginning of my prayer and during my walks I renew this union; then the Spirit of Jesus often suggests to me the text or incident in the life of Christ, the attribute of the Father, upon which He wills me to speak to Him. There is my prayer.

For the rest, my inner life is very simple. During my stay here at Beauplateau (September 1918) our Lord has united me closely to Himself, but in *simple faith*. I have the conviction

---

1 Dom Marmion was later to comment on this passage with rare elevation of thought and great delicacy of sentiment. See his opuscule *Sponsa Verbi*, "The Virgin consecrated to Christ."
2 The passage is not that of Bl. Albert the Great, but of Jean de Castel.
3 On the meaning of this phrase see p. 459, note 3.

ABBOT MARMION
(In his last years)

that it is by this way that He wishes to lead me. I never have sensible consolations. I do not desire them. I have lights, sudden glimpses of the depths of revealed truths. I have a special attraction for compunction: The Father of the Prodigal Son, the Good Samaritan, Jesus with Magdalene at His feet, fill me with compunction and confidence.[1]

Out of all these passages it is possible to gather some characteristic traits of Dom Marmion's prayer.

Prayer with him ordinarily took the form, the attitude, the habitual style, of a loving intercourse of a child of God with his Father in heaven.

This prayer is first of all "illumined"; that is to say, often accompanied with a most vivid, most clear understanding of such or such truths of faith.

And then it was with very great liberty of soul that, in order to unite himself to God, he used either representations or symbols surprisingly tangible, imaginative or scenic, or intellectual concepts, such as the great theological ideas concerning the plan of redemption, our identification with Christ, etc.[2]

But above the pictured scenes on which his mind rested, beyond the concepts of his understanding, there existed in him a close union with God, surpassing all the operations of the natural faculties. In this union the supernatural action of the gifts of the Holy Spirit appear particularly manifest; it was the ineffable access, through Jesus Christ, and with Jesus Christ, under the breathing of the Spirit, *in sinu Patris*....

At the end of his life Dom Marmion let fall these words which reveal to what happy summits his contemplative soul attained: "Oh! It is good to live beyond the precious veil of the sacred humanity

---

[1] Letter of 25 September 1918.
[2] It was by reason of this liberty" that he wrote at the same date in reference to prayer: "I have been reading St John of the Cross attentively. This reading is not in accord with my soul. It makes me lose my liberty with God."

of Jesus, under the *direct* gaze of the Father. It is the *sanctuarium exauditionis.*"[1]

His soul was soon to penetrate into this sanctuary of the Trinity and contemplate forever, openly, in the eternal splendours, the face of the Father, so long and eagerly sought: *In lumine tuo videbimus lumen!*[2]

---

[1] Letter of May 1922. On this expression "the sanctuary where our prayers are heard," see p. 275, note 3.
[2] "In Thy light we shall see light" (Ps. 35:10).

19 TO THE FATHER'S HOUSE

Since 1915 Dom Marmion's health had been considerably shattered. It was evident he had not recovered from the attacks which ever since the beginning of the war had continued to tell on a constitution strong only in appearance.

Early in 1918 a serious affection of the throat compelled him to relax his apostolic labours and to take absolute rest. He wrote to one of his sons on 17 March 1918:

> The goodness and the paternal and maternal tenderness of our Heavenly Father has given me both a grace and a rest. It is good to put oneself in His hands for everything. I have been suffering a good deal, not having been able to shake off the influenza. Latterly this has taken the form of violent inflammation of the throat, deafness in both ears, and bronchitis. The Bishop of Namur on coming to see me absolutely insisted on bringing me away with him.... Here I have long hours of solitude and prayer.... I have really suffered, and I am keeping Lent, which is a great grace. Thank the Heavenly Father with me for all His goodness.

In spite of every care, the cure remained incomplete.[3] Two months later he wrote:

> As you know, I have had an attack of pharyngitis and laryngitis, which has kept me secluded since Easter. I am better, but have to spare my vocal chords, which are still tender. It is for me a time of recollection and rest for body, heart and soul. Silence is a great grace: *In silentio et spe erit fortitudo vestra*. There is a threefold silence: that of the tongue, that of the passions, and that of earthly thoughts; when one reaches

---

[3] "My throat is very bad: laryngitis, pharyngitis, inflammation of the vocal chords. The doctors condemn me to a rigorous seclusion and to absolute silence for several weeks" (Letter of 1 May 1918).

this degree of silence God speaks to the soul: *Ducam eam in solitudinem et loquar ad cor ejus.* Let us try to reach this state which is a source of great graces and of light.[1]

In face of the persistence of the malady his medical advisers then ordered him some weeks of rest, which he spent in Luxembourg, at the Convent of the Redemptorist Fathers of Beauplateau.[2] The brotherly hospitality of the sons of St Alphonsus, the solitude of these regions of which he intensely appreciated the tranquil almost wild beauty, brought some relief, but could not stay the malady.[3]

The continual fatigues of an apostolate in which he never spared himself, the great and heavy burden of administration, the very keen sense he had of being answerable to God for the many souls entrusted to his care, had gradually undermined his constitution. Then, endowed as he was "with that depth and wealth of sensibility to which life spares no shock, he was prematurely worn out by the force of hidden sufferings and silent reactions."[4] General toxaemia caused chronic somnolency which frequently overtook him and became for him a real mortification.[5]

His still earnest glance was often overshadowed by melancholy. Dom Marmion's strength was henceforward to go on declining,

---

[1] Letter of 12 May 1918.
[2] "Here I am at Beauplateau since the 16th. I am in absolute solitude: the Redemptorist Fathers received me with great charity. This was the only means of securing this absolute silence without which my poor throat could never be cured. It is already better, and I have good hopes of a perfect cure. I know I may count on your prayers.... I am not able yet to go about in this delightful country among the pines, for I am so laid by the heels that I can only walk with difficulty. This is a little cross to begin with" (Letter of 22 July 1918).
[3] "Here I am at the end of my stay in this place. I have the conviction that this rest of soul and body has been willed and arranged by the Heavenly Father's goodness. My throat is not yet completely cured: the mischief has become chronic, and will still need time" (Letter of 2 September 1918).
[4] Renée Zeller, *La vie dominicaine.*
[5] "*I know* that you pray for me. I need it. Physically I feel so feeble, so overcome with sleep that prayer is often impossible. But I abandon myself to God's Holy Will" (Letter of 4 September 1920).

and death, which had brushed him with its wings, was preparing to strike the last blow.

For long years past Dom Marmion had familiarised himself with the thought of death and the last ends: "Every morning," he had already written in 1908, "I offer myself to the good God and accept the kind of death that He wills to send me and when He wills."[1]

The supreme visitant was not to take him unawares. Dom Columba's soul sought more and more to draw near to God that it might be united with Him on the day of the eternal meeting.

These thoughts gave rise in him to the most diverse feelings. Let us look at the saints as they are. It is their greatness to become saints. It is their charm, too, that the end of a long life spent in seeking after God they yet remain so near to ourselves, being like us of flesh and blood, subject to the shrinkings of sensitive nature in face of the tremendous problem of human destiny.

A few confidences, gleaned here and there, reveal what Dom Marmion was feeling: fear and confidence followed in alternate succession in his soul, blending during his last days in a peaceful sense of utter dependence on God. He wrote in March 1914: "I could wish sometimes to flee into solitude, there to live alone with God, but this is not His Will. And certainly the adorable Creator has every right to do as He wills with His creature. I hope, however, not to go to Purgatory. I intend to be so united with His Divine Will in life and in death that nothing may separate me from my God."[2]

When he was staying in England, in 1916, he knew himself to be on the very brink of death: "I cannot tell you what it is to come to such a moment; experience alone can make one understand what one feels on seeing oneself about to appear before God. When I thus saw myself on the threshold of eternity I felt possessed by fear, and I resolved, if God left me longer to live, to be such at the moment of death that I could no longer have this fear."

1 Letter of 14 January 1908.
2 Letter of 14 March 1914.

This fact must have left a deep impression on him: more and more he lived on familiar terms with death.

"Death is a great thing," he said in 1917;[1] "it is a solemn hour. Our blessed father St Benedict tells us to have it ever before our eyes: *Mortem quotidie ante oculos suspectam habere.* As for me, I confess to you that I have it continually present to me."

On 1 April 1917, he said to his sons: "By God's grace I am entering today on my sixtieth year; that is to say, the eternal hills begin to cast their shadow over my life. I ask your prayers that I may worthily spend for God the years that remain to me, if years there are."

The letters of this period likewise bear the trace of the alternations by which his soul was tossed about:

> *9 May 1917* – We are journeying together towards that eternity where all will be consummated in the love of God.

> *Beginning of 1919* – God is very good to me. He tries me in every way, but at the same time unites me more and more to Himself. The thought of God, of eternity, of death, hardly ever leaves me, but it keeps me in joy and in great peace. I have a great fear of God's majesty, of His holiness, and justice, and at the same time a certainty based on love that our Heavenly Father will arrange all *for the best.*

> *1 January 1920* – I, too, have a great fear of death. It is the *divine* punishment of sin: *merces peccati mors,* and this fear of death honours God; and if it is accompanied by hope it honours God very much. Often those who have most dreaded death during their life have no longer this fear when death comes. For myself, when making my Way of the Cross each day, I recommend myself to Jesus and to Mary for the moment of my agony and the judgment, and I have the conviction that they will be there to help me.

> *20 February 1920* – I feel a great longing for heaven. Yet I don't feel as if my work was done. I fear the judgment, and yet I

---

[1] Without exact date.

cast myself on God's bosom with all my miseries and my responsibilities and hope in His mercy. Nothing else can save us, for our poor little works are not fit to be presented, and only His fatherly affection deigns to accept them. *Non aestimator meriti sed veniae quaesumus largitor admitte,* as we pray at Mass.

At times the thought of the vision of God after death stirred his whole being. In the retreat of 1921 he said to the Benedictine nuns of Maredret:

> Let us think what will happen to us when we enter into eternity, what will then be granted to us. There are some words in Holy Scripture which have much struck me these days: *Denudabit absconsa sua illi.*[1] We should meditate on these words. We should meditate on these words. God will show Himself to the souls 'without secret,' as He is: *denudabit.* He will disclose to her, will 'unveil' to her, the *absconsa,* the depths of His divinity, He will be all open to her, He will show Himself in the light, in the full day of His essential truth.[2]

That is why in the midst of all the sufferings which then weighed upon him he yearned for that happy moment: "our Lord has taught me," he writes in a letter of 16 September 1922, "that the great sacrifice is the offering of Jesus bearing His cross and ours, our miseries,

---

[1] Eccles. 4:21.

[2] It was to the same nuns that he spoke these words, likewise at this time: "For several days, during Holy Mass, one thought has greatly encouraged me. Reciting the *nobis quoque peccatoribus,* prostrate in spirit before God and trusting in His infinite mercies, I have expressed the hope of being one day in the fellowship of Agatha, Cecily, Agnes, Lucy, and of all those saints whose names we repeat each day. And I have thought with joy: our union with all these saints in heaven will one day become a reality.... We are at times tempted to say: 'Yes, one day it is true...but it is still so far away!' Oh, no, it is not so far away; on the contrary, we shall be there so soon! The few years that still separate us from eternal life are like a drop of water in the infinite ocean. Then we shall see, we shall know St Peter, St Paul, all those saints whom we have loved and invoked here below without seeing them; and they will say to us: 'I have known you well; I have helped and aided you.' And they will be our brothers, and we shall love them with a love henceforth perfect."

our weaknesses, and which He offers with Himself to the Father. I am *overwhelmed* with business and fatigue. I begin to look forward to the Heavenly Father's home, but I fear the terrible and problematic passing through death."

Thus as he drew nearer and nearer to eternity that twofold sense of humble compunction and confident love which never ceased to set the rhythmical measure to his whole spiritual life became manifestly yet more clear and forcible.

At the same period (September 1922) Providence arranged for him the joy of a pilgrimage to Lourdes. Msgr Thomas Heylen, Bishop of Namur, had given him the charge of conducting, in his name, the diocesan pilgrimage.

"I set out on Monday for Lourdes. It is my first visit to this sanctuary. I have to preside, preach, etc. Pray that I may have the strength, for my sixty-four years begin to weigh upon me."[1]

He has not left us any record of what were his impressions at the feet of the Blessed Virgin. But on his return he said to one of his sons who had accompanied him: "Several years ago I went to Paray, and that was a great grace for my soul. Shortly afterwards I was elected Abbot of Maredsous. Now I have returned from Lourdes, and that visit also was a great favour. I am henceforth going to withdraw into solitude, or else our Lord is going to call me to Himself."

This thought of death became more and more familiar to him. It was at times betrayed in a striking manner.

On the third Sunday of Advent (17 December 1922), he gave the Benedictines of Maredret a spiritual conference which was to be the last he ever gave them. He took as subject of his conference the Introit of the Mass of the day, of which the text is taken from St Paul: "Rejoice in the Lord always: again I say, rejoice. Let your modesty be known to all men. The Lord is nigh."[2]

---

[1] Letter of 16 September 1922.
[2] Philip. 4: 4–5.

We ought to keep ourselves in continual joy, in modesty and humility. (*a*) Our joy ought to be great because of all the graces we have received through Christ Jesus. He has given Himself for us, He has redeemed us, has offered us to His Father, has filled us with His life: *Christus pro peccatis nostris mortuus est, justus pro injustis, ut nos offerret Deo, mortificatus quidem carne, vivificatus spiritu.*[1] (*b*) *Justus pro injustis*. We are sinners, unjust. This is why we ought to be modest, humble. We are filled with miseries, with weaknesses, but Christ has willed to take upon Himself all these infirmities, in order to bestow upon us His strength. In the measure in which we acknowledge our miseries, in which we accept to share in the Passion of Jesus and in the weakness with which He deigned to clothe Himself, in that same measure we shall share in His divine strength: *Gloriabor in infirmitatibus meis.... Dum infirmor tunc potens sum.*[2] We then become the object of the Divine Mercy and of the delight of the Heavenly Father who beholds us in His Son.

And this is the deep – and touching – conclusion of that last conference:

> It is at the hour of death above all that we experience this mystery and benefit by it. Christ has destroyed the penalty of death; our death has been swallowed up in His. Henceforward His death cries for mercy on us, and the Father sees in our death the image of the death of His Son. This is why the death of the just is precious in the sight of the Lord. *Pretiosa in conspectu Domini mors sanctorum ejus.* For some time past I have been imploring Christ each morning at Holy Mass and asking Him to lend His own death to all the dying. In offering this prayer we can be sure that Christ will do for us, at

---

[1] "Christ also died once for our sins, the just for the unjust: that He might offer us to God, being put to death indeed in the flesh, but enlivened in the spirit" (1 Pet. 3:18).

[2] 2 Cor. 12:5, 9, 10.

the moment of our agony and death, what we have asked Him to do for others.

In the measure that he approached the end, without, however, knowing that this end was imminent, the remembrance of the sufferings of Jesus, which had ever been so dear to him, made a still deeper impression upon him. We have had the good fortune to find some of his last letters: nothing could better disclose the thoughts and feelings that filled his soul. In one dated 21 December 1922, he returns to the stupendous truth that Jesus is our strength for in taking upon Himself our weakness it becomes *divine weakness;* "the weakness of God is stronger than men" (1 Cor. 1: 25), and our Lord's Passion is the very triumph of divine weakness over all human strength and weakness.

Replying to his dear Poor Clares of Cork,[1] for whom he felt a true fatherly tenderness – that tenderness which flows out from the letters of St John and St Paul – he writes, on 30 December 1922, a month before his death:

> My dear little children, the Irish have great faith, and even when God seems to forget them they cry after Him until He is forced to turn to them and, like the Canaanean woman, I have often thought lately that you might be tempted to think I have forgotten you. Quite the contrary, I daily think of you, and place you in *His* Heart, which is in the centre of mine while I celebrate. I beg Him to take us all together through the mystic veil of the Holy of Holies, which St Paul

---

[1] These Irish nuns bore Dom Columba a particular affection; they had written, about Christmas time, a letter expressing their great longing to have news of him; so on December 28th Dom Columba had sent them a card to re-assure them. "I was deeply touched by your remembering me so faithfully. I have had to keep my room and I have been incapable of doing anything, I will write you a long letter soon. May God bless you and love you all as I do from the bottom of my heart. I said the second Mass of Christmas for you." He wrote the promised letter two days later. The beginning of this letter alludes to the entreaties of his dear Poor Clares.

tells us is His mangled Body, and then to present us before the throne of God.

You have no idea of how I am taken up at every moment while I am ill and suffering and everybody expects me to be ready. Our Lord helps me, for He has taken all our sufferings and weakness on Him. At present I am *really* crushed with work and anxiety and suffering pain – the flu.... So, my darling little children, you see it is not want of affection but overwork which keeps me from sending you what my heart would say to you at present.

I am *most grateful* to you for the two lovely Irish books....

May God bless and love you all as I do from my heart of hearts.

This underlying thought of the "passing through the veil," scarcely touched upon in the letter we have just read, he develops in another letter written on the eve of the same date[1] to one of his spiritual daughters. Ultimate confidences which yield to us the secret of his inner life, on the eve of being consummated – without, however, his foreseeing it – in the eternal union.

(After a few words of excuse for his delay in replying, he continues):

Every morning at Holy Mass I place you in our dear Lord's Heart and I beg Him, as He enters into the 'Holy of Holies' (His Father's bosom) through the veil, which St Paul tells us is His crucified humanity, to take us with Him and present us to the Father. 'Christ has died for all,' says St Peter, 'in order to present us to His Father. He, the just one, for us sinners, having died in His Flesh to be filled with the force and strength of His Spirit for us.'[2] What *He* presents to the Father is ever most acceptable, however miserable we may be. You have this every morning....

I see our dear Lord is just introducing you into the last

[1] December 29th.
[2] *Cf.* 1 Pet. 3:18.

stage, through which your soul has need to pass before going to Him. Our Lord has taken all our sins on Him and has fully [expiated] them and this expiation is applied to us by *compunction* and absolution. But besides this He has taken on Him all the infirmities and incapacity of His Spouse. Before going to Him, she must *see* and *feel* and *know* that all come to her from Him, and that it is our misery, poverty, and imperfection which having been *assumed* by His Sacred Humanity, are raised to a divine value in Him. This is a great secret which few understand. St Paul expresses it in these words: 'Willingly do I glory in my infirmities, in order that it be Christ's virtue and strength which dwells in me. This is why I take pleasure in my infirmities.' When I make my Stations daily and contemplate God the *infinite,* the *all powerful* crushed by weakness and trembling in Gethsemane, I see that instead of taking on Himself a glorified body, He has assumed a body like unto that of us sinners *in order to render our weakness divine in Him.*

This is what you are passing through at present, in order to destroy and eradicate entirely from your soul the last traces of confidence in yourself, or the talents or qualities which He gave you, and on which you have perhaps leaned just a little up to this. 'His left hand supports your head and His right hand encircles you in your weakness.'

He has been showing me this in my soul for some time, and I am never so happy as when prostrate before His infinite mercy, and showing Him my misery, weakness and unworthiness, but I keep looking all the time, not at my misery so much as at His infinite mercy. Just like a little girl who having fallen into a pool of dirty mud, runs to her mother showing her pinafore and crying until it is cleaned.

I am laid up at present with a kind of flu, but it is getting better.

In one passage of this letter Dom Columba alludes to a journey that he was presently to undertake in response to a long-expressed wish of his monks who had been urging him to have his portrait painted in accordance with their monastic tradition. This work was entrusted to the celebrated painter Abraham Janssens, a friend of the abbey, and to whom they already owed the portrait of one of the former abbots. Dom Marmion went then to Antwerp. In a few days the work was sketched out in a masterly manner.

On leaving Antwerp Dom Columba stayed at the Convent of the Ladies of the Sacred Heart of Linthout; then he paid a visit to his dear Carmel of Louvain.

He had not visited them for a year and a half. He only went now after earnest entreaties and moved by his apostolic zeal, that zeal which always wished to be all to all. There was in this monastery a young professed nun of English parentage who being seriously ill was now slowly sinking. Often in the course of her illness the mistress of novices had spoken to her of Dom Columba of the great good done by his teaching, of his love for Christ and for souls. A strong desire to see and hear him was enkindled in the heart of the sick nun: she wanted to speak to Dom Marmion in her own language, and above all to confide to him the care of a soul of a compatriot in whose well-being she was particularly interested.

This desire, which the whole community eagerly shared, was transmitted by letter to Father Abbot. He replied by return of post: "*8 January 1923* – Influenza has left me very pulled down, but I will do everything that my fatherly affection and zeal for your souls prompts me to do, so as to see you as soon as possible: this week or the week after, 'for you have ten thousand instructors,' but Christ has only given you *one father.*"[1]

By January 13th he was able to have a talk with the young suffering nun. Out of the abundance of his heart he spoke of death and the tender mercy of God. It was a spiritual feast for the one who had only a few more weeks to live and was awaiting eternity.

After this Dom Columba went to the parlour to give the

---

1 1 Cor. 4:15.

conference to the community. In the midst of those souls whom he had known and guided so long in the paths of perfection he let his fatherly heart go out in one of those simple and intimate talks of which he held the secret. Only now he spoke with more touching impressiveness than ever. It made one think of a lamp that had been lowered; if the light was less bright its radiance was the softer and more penetrating. The summary of this conference has been kept: it contains thoughts of concentrated power only to be found with master-thinkers, and under the dry brevity of the scheme the ardent yearning of his spirit makes itself felt:

In heaven, two choirs: the angels: *sanctus, sanctus sanctus.* We the redeemed: *Misericordias Domini* IN AETERNUM *cantabo.*[1] Our heaven: praise, thanksgiving for God's infinite mercy.

1. To enter into the bosom of the Father, there to comprehend that longing, that, as it were, irresistible inclination that He has to show mercy. The proof: the message of infinite mercy to misery: *Jesus,* come to establish upon earth the reign of mercy by making Himself like unto the miserable.

Beatus qui intelligit super egenum et pauperem.[2] Blessed is he who understands the mystery of this 'poor one,' this 'needy one' who is Jesus: who while He was rich became poor for our sakes,[3] *Cum esset dives, propter nos egenus factus est.* He who understands this mystery has entered into the secret of God's designs; he understands that God truly has our misery in His Heart: (*misericors, miserum cor*).

The plan of the redemption based on mercy. God loved us 'when as *yet we were sinners.*'[4] He willed that His Son should become one of us and *should be made sin,*[5] to blot out our sins and regenerate us from our misery.

He placed at the head of the Church a sinner (story of

---

1 "The mercies of the Lord: I will sing for evermore" (Ps. 80: 2).
2 Ps. 40: 2.
3 2 Cor. 8: 9.
4 Rom. 5: 8.
5 2 Cor. 5: 21.

St Peter's fall), one who had learnt by experience to grant to others the mercy that he had himself received.

2. The attitude of misery in face of this Divine Mercy: utter confidence (*a*) *in the merits* of Jesus, to raise us from our falls; (*b*) *in the friendship* of Jesus; surrendering ourselves to His love He will take care of us.

For myself at this moment, my whole spiritual life is to display my misery before Him.

The conference ended, he rose and, standing in the middle of the parlour, said: "My dear daughters, let us meet again *in sinu Patris*."

Then without another word he went out. Many had the impression that it was a farewell.

After he had gone, the dying nun, a keen observer, said to her mother mistress:

"Fr Columba is a saint... but he is going to die. A fortnight from now you will hear that he is ill; he is so already... but that will be the end...."

These words were to be fulfilled to the letter; on January 30th God called Dom Marmion to Himself, and on February 3rd, the little Carmelite went in her turn to heaven; their next meeting was to be amidst the unceasing joys of paradise.

Dom Marmion returned to the abbey on Saturday, January 20th, with a heavy cold; he found a number of his monks down with influenza.

In spite of his ailing state, he devoted himself to his usual occupations, visited his sons who were ill, and nothing gave reason to foresee that the epidemic was reserving its most fatal attack for the head of the monastery and in a few days was to bear him away.[1]

---

[1] For this account of Dom Marmion's last days we have largely drawn on the article in *Le messager de Saint-Benoît* for February 1923, on the same subject, an article due to the pen of one of his infirmarians, Dom Eucher Foccroulle. With a persevering zeal, to which we are happy to give this expression of our gratitude, the same confrère has helped us gather together documents relating

On the morning of 25th he was so weak and exhausted as to be scarcely able to stand.

"I got up," he said during the day to his confessor, "so as to be able to celebrate the Mass of St Paul."

We knew what love Dom Columba bore to the great apostle and to what a degree he had made his own the teaching, the thought, and even the mind, of the herald of Jesus; we know, too, with what facility he took home to himself the inmost meaning of the words of the liturgy. We may therefore imagine how the apostle's very words, chosen by the Church for the composition of the proper of this Mass, found an echo in his soul. "I know whom I have believed, and I am certain that He is able to keep that which I have committed to Him, against that day, being a just judge." Then Dom Columba read once again that wonderful account of the conversion of St Paul on which he had commented so many times and which the words of the Gradual emphasised: "The grace of God in me hath not been void; but His grace always remaineth in me." The Tract placed upon his lips fervent invocations to the saint with whom he had so much affinity of soul: "Thou art a vessel of election, holy Paul the Apostle; truly thou art worthy to be glorified. The preacher of truth, and doctor of the Gentiles, in faith and in truth, intercede for us to God, who chose thee."

Long ago, on the day when the title of child of God was conferred on him by the grace of baptism in a church dedicated to the apostle, the spirit of Paul had rested on his infancy; for many years in his childhood and youth his eyes had contemplated the picture representing the conversion of St Paul. In the course of a long life, he had placed himself in the school of Christ's herald; now that his course was finished, God granted that he should not descend from the altar for the last time until he had once more celebrated the marvels of Divine Mercy in Saul's conversion. God's Providence at times links together by such coincidences the stages in the path of his chosen ones.

to several other periods of Dom Columba's life.

After the Mass the father infirmarian came to speak to him about the monks down with the *grippe*.

"The *grippe!*" said Dom Columba. "I believe I have caught it too."

The doctor, being at once summoned, ordered him to bed.

Dom Marmion wished first of all to write a promised letter; it was a petition to the Holy Father, asking for the introduction at Rome of the cause of Mother d'Hoogvorts, foundress of the *Société de Marie réparatrice*.[1] So the last lines which fell from his pen were again to be inspired by that passion which was his for the glory of Christ's Mystical Body.[2] After this he made arrangements for some Mass intentions that had been given to him and still remained to be said. Then he put himself into the doctors' hands.

In the evening, when the Father Prior came to see him, he appeared very exhausted. Looking at the prior, he said, in answer to some words of his:

"Father Prior, I can tell you that for years past an hour has not gone by without my thinking of death."

Death might now come.

Next day, Friday the 26th, his state was aggravated to such a point that in the evening the doctor diagnosed the case as congestion of the lungs and liver, with other complications. The Father Prior therefore decided to suggest without delay to the revered abbot that he should receive the last sacraments.

Dom Marmion, with perfect calm, at once accepted the suggestion. He asked for his confessor and carefully prepared himself. The hour was already advanced; many of his sons were laid up with the epidemic, which had taken a violent turn; only a few witnessed and assisted at the ceremony so deeply touching in its simplicity.

The Father Prior entered, bearing the Blessed Sacrament. In

---

1 Mother Marie de Jésus, who died 22 February 1878.
2 On the previous day he had finished drawing up the report to send to the Holy See in which the nuns of Tyburn asked their canonical affiliation to the Order of St Benedict.

accordance with monastic ritual, the dying man was invited to renew his baptismal promises and religious vows. Dom Columba recited the formulas by heart and in a steady voice. After the usual prayers he received the Holy Viaticum.

The rite of extreme unction followed.

"Révérendissime Père," the prior asked him, "do you accept the Will of God?"

"Oh! absolutely," was the immediate reply, made in a tone of deep and touching conviction.

The sacred anointing was then administered and the last prayers were said.

When he had prayed in silence for some time Dom Marmion called his secretary and arranged some private affairs with him.

The following day the exhaustion remained extreme; all medical science was powerless to arrest the progress of the disease.

Dom Marmion showed gratitude for the least services rendered him, expressing his thanks each time with a touching humility. He was never exacting; he went so far as to refuse the mattress urged upon him, preferring to keep the ordinary *palliasse*; but when the infirmarian insisted he gave way, and further submitted with the simplicity of a child to all that was prescribed for him.

Although his malady caused a certain lethargy of his outward senses, inwardly he remained fully conscious, in spite of his exhaustion. One of his sons said to him that his presence amongst them was still necessary. Dom Columba replied:

"I leave myself in the hands of the good God."

Shortly afterwards, another having asked him if he was content to go to heaven, he made the same reply. All was summed up for him in that sense of trust in the Divine Mercy.

This was sometimes betrayed in a singular manner. In order to encourage him, someone thought it a duty to remind him of the good he had done by his works, and especially by the conversions he had made.... But he immediately protested with a shake of the head and murmured: *Deus meus, misericordia mea!*

This utter trust had its source especially in the thought of Christ's sufferings.

"Give me my Way of the Cross," he often said. He meant by this a little pocket Way of the Cross, composed of fourteen metal plaques, folding one over the other, and on which were engraved the scenes of the Passion; it had been indulgenced by Benedict XV. Several times Dom Marmion contemplated Christ at each station of the sorrowful way, and thus united his own sufferings to those which had marked the supreme moments of the Divine Master. In the cross alone, which hallows everything, is salvation indeed to be found.

At one moment he cried out:

"Some holy water!" His strong faith had always made him place great confidence in the Church's blessings. Never had he entered a monastic cell or left it without devoutly making the sign of the cross and taking holy water from the little stoup near the door. Holy water was thereupon brought to him, and with a quick gesture he threw some of it in three different directions. During this action a marked expression of indignation and contempt was seen on his countenance, which led it to be supposed that he was intent on driving away the Evil Spirit. The next moment he had regained his composure. There is nothing in this that need surprise us. Have not the greater number of saints experienced, in like circumstances, the onslaughts of the spirit of darkness?[1] Must not "the prince of this world" have borne a special hatred towards that apostolic soul who had displayed so much zeal in snatching from him other souls?

Mass was celebrated every morning in the abbey chapel, near the cell of the abbot, who joined in it with great devotion and then received Holy Communion. His face was illumined with inward

---

[1] We know that a few weeks before her death, St Thérèse of Lisieux had the clear impression of an onslaught of the devil and was conscious of feeling his sensible action. She said in an anguished tone: "Oh, how we ought to pray for the dying! If one knew what it is...I believe that the devil has asked the good God for permission to tempt me by extreme suffering so as to make me lose patience and confidence."

joy each time that the small table on which the ciborium was to be placed was brought near his bed.

On Monday the 29th, feast of St Francis de Sales, a picture of that saint was brought to him; during many years he had had it on the table in the room where he worked; he kissed it reverently, then asked to have the collect of the day read to him: "O God, who, in order that souls may be saved, didst will that Blessed Francis should become all things to all men, fill our hearts, we beseech Thee, with that charity which is sweet, so that, guided by his teaching and having a share in his merits, we may come to everlasting happiness."

Had not Dom Marmion learnt in the writings of the holy doctor the secret of the love of God and, after his example, had he not, whereby to win souls, endeavoured to make himself all to all? Nevertheless, such was his state of suffering that he let these words escape him:

"One has not much devotion when one is ill."

His devotion was all contained in the spirit of self-surrender. However, he did not cease to pray. During the night between the 29th and 30th, which was his last, his prayer was intensified. He often said his Rosary. Did he recall what he had written in *Christ the Life of the Soul?* "If each day we have often said to the Blessed Virgin: 'Mother of God, pray for us ... *now* and *at the hour of our death*,' we may be sure that, when the moment comes at which *nunc* and the *hora mortis nostrae* will be one and the same, the Blessed Virgin will not forsake us."

To the Rosary succeeded the *Magnificat* and, following his usual bent, he lingered over and repeated several times the verses which exalt the divine loving kindness: "And His mercy is from generation to generation to them that fear Him: He hath received (Israel) his servant being mindful of His mercy."

Often, too, he was heard to murmur the *Benedicite omnia opera Domini Domino*, one of his accustomed prayers; he felt the need of calling upon all creatures to magnify the glory of the Lord which he was so soon to contemplate. To these sacred canticles and psalms he joined the liturgical collects so familiar to him.[1]

Thus all that had served him habitually during life as food for his private prayer again rose to his lips at the approach of death to prepare his soul for the Divine Meeting.

This meeting was very near. Earthly things, even the greatest and most sacred – the symbols of worship, the outward forms of God's service – were slipping away from him and, in the nearing splendour of eternity, the soul withdrew within itself. Dom Marmion's numerous friends and religious communities who had been informed of his illness at once began to respond to the request for prayers. Almost every moment arrived testimonies of interest and veneration. He was told of them as far as his state allowed. The telegram sent by Her Majesty the Queen of Belgium was read to him, and that of Cardinal Mercier recalling the close bonds of old friendship and asking to be kept *au courant* with the situation. He was visibly touched by these tokens of sympathy, but he offered no word. Was it owing to weakness and difficulty in speaking? Doubtless; but also because he was becoming more and more absorbed in God.

After the reading of a note announcing a wedding in a family in which he was particularly interested he repeated those simple words of the Psalmist: *Omnis caro faenum*. A touching response, if we place the words in their context and stay to consider the integral thought of the sacred writer: "*All flesh is grass,* and all the glory thereof as the flower of the field. The grass is withered and the flower is fallen, because the spirit of the Lord is blown upon it."[2] Did he not himself at that moment exemplify this striking image? But if the mortal

---

[1] No doubt it is hard to say when he left off praying and when prayer became, as it were, automatic; but difficult as it is to make this distinction, this unconscious automatism deserves to be noticed: it shows how far prayer had become habitual to Dom Marmion and fixed in his psychological subconsciousness.

[2] Isa. 40: 6–7.

frame was about to be dissolved, according to St Paul's expression, the soul was soon to be forever with Christ.

He was touched by the arrival of Dom Robert de Kerchove, Abbot of Mont-César at Louvain and president of the Belgian Congregation. It was Dom de Kerchove who in times past as prior had, with Dom Placide, welcomed the young Irish priest to Maredsous; since then, during many years, he had had him as confrère, then as subordinate, and always as friend. He brought to the dying man a last testimony of brotherly esteem and the affectionate consolation of his presence.

Every morning, too, a good number of his sons came to learn news of him, although bulletins of his health were regularly issued to the community. The last two days his sons came in greater numbers, because it was known that he was worse. They were eager to receive a last blessing and a last fatherly glance from those eyes soon to be closed in death. Dom Marmion still easily recognised them; to some he spoke a few words of affection, to others he recalled the graces God had granted them, to all he gave a sign of interest.

Tuesday the 30th was to be the last day of his earthly life. As on other days, he was able to receive the Bread of Life. On this *feria* in Septuagesima week the Mass was that of the preceding Sunday, *Circumdederunt me genitus mortis.* "The sorrows of death," thus begins the Introit, "encompassed me; in my affliction I called upon the Lord, and He heard my voice from His holy temple... I will love Thee, O Lord, my strength: the Lord is my firmament, my refuge and my deliverer."

For him it was that all his sons repeated the liturgical words of the Gradual, so applicable to that hour: "Thou art, O Lord, a helper in due time in tribulation: let them trust in Thee who know Thee: for Thou hast not forsaken them that seek Thee."

Dom Columba had "sought" the Lord; he had made that "sincere seeking after God" required by St Benedict the law of his whole life. Had he not been of those who, according to the words of St Paul in the epistle of the Mass, had run in the race that he might receive the prize? Or again, according to our Saviour's own parable repeated in the Gospel of the day, was he not among those labourers whom the Father of the household sent to his vineyard, there to work unremittingly for the glory of their Master? Now "evening was come," and the faithful servant, after having "borne the burden of the day and the heats," was about to receive his wages.

His strength continued to ebb, and it was clear that the end was near. In the afternoon Dom Marmion's confessor came to comfort him with these words:

"*Mon Révérendissime Père*, you are soon going to appear before our Lord Jesus Christ; show him now that unshaken confidence that you have preached so often."

The dying monk was no longer able to articulate a distinct reply. But no words could have been more fitting at that moment than those just spoken to that soul ready to vibrate at every word of faith. His prayer, moreover, responded to this suggestion; he was many times heard to repeat that verse of the *Magnificat*: "He hath received Israel His servant, being mindful of His mercy," *Recordatus misericordiae suae*.

In the evening, about five o'clock, the community assembled for the recommendation of the departing soul, while the dying abbot held the blessed candle in his hand. Dom de Kerchove, Father Abbot, president of the Congregation, recited the prayers to which the community responded. A touching sight was this crown of sons encircling a venerated father with their prayers, and inviting all the heavenly court to come to aid and meet a soul on its passing to eternity. And how striking were certain of the invocations, considering the circumstances:

"O God most merciful, O God most loving and kind, look favourably upon Thy servant Columba, and deign to hear him. Lord, have pity on his sighs, have pity on his tears, and since his only hope is in Thy mercy, grant him the grace to enter into peace with Thee. Through Jesus Christ our Lord...."

The prayers being ended, the community withdrew; only a few privileged ones remained. Supplications for the dying man were continuous and grew ever more earnest; in low tones those near him repeated the Litany of Our Lady, the Psalms most appropriate for the occasion: *Qui habitat in adjutorio Altissimi*; the *Benedictus*. From time to time those texts on which his soul had been nourished were suggested to him: "O Jesus, Thou art the Christ, the Son of the living God.... No man cometh to the Father but by Me.... Gladly will I glory in my infirmities that the power of Christ may dwell in me.... Lord, cast me not away from Thy face!"

The last prayer proved to be the Litany of the Sacred Heart, where are summed up all the acts of confidence of a believing loving soul: "Heart of Jesus, salvation of them that hope in Thee.... Hope of them that die in Thee...." And then: "Jesus, Mary, Joseph"; and finally, the supreme invocation, "Jesus, Jesus, Jesus...!"

About half-past nine his breathing became sensibly fainter, his face grew pallid, the moment of eternity had come. The dying abbot's brow was aspersed with holy water, the crucifix was held for him to kiss. Shortly before ten o'clock one last effort, a contraction of the lips: the soul had escaped from its mortal frame to appear before its judge....

The prior at once recited the *Subvenite:* "Come ye saints of God... come forth to meet him, ye angels of the Lord!... May Christ who hath called thee, receive thee forever into His Kingdom...."

As soon as the tidings were spread abroad of Dom Columba's death, touching tributes arrived from every side. We will not linger over them; we need only recall the general feeling expressed by them: grateful veneration for one who had gone about doing good by the wide influence of his apostolic words and writings and the constant example of his high virtues.

Neither will we stay to give an account of Dom Columba's funeral, which took place at Maredsous three days after his death. Despite the rigour of the weather and the difficulty in travelling, friends hastened in great numbers to pay their last homage to the head of the abbey. The Bishop of Namur, Msgr Heylen, had it at heart to preside at the funeral ceremony; he was assisted by Msgr Amédée

Crooy, Bishop of Tournai, and around him were several abbots of the Order of St Benedict and of St Norbert, and numerous eminent ecclesiastics. In the first rank of notabilities were General Doutrepont, representing His Majesty King Albert of Belgium, and Baron Edmond de Gaiffier d'Hestroy, Governor of the Province of Namur.

In the panegyric preached by one of Dom Marmion's sons it was eloquently pointed out how during his whole life, and above all during his abbacy, Dom Columba had carried out his motto: *Magis prodesse quam praeesse.* "To be useful rather than to command."

The memory of this great monk, the example of his holy life spent entirely in the service of Christ and of souls, possessed the thoughts of all; at the close of the obsequies two lay persons who had long been at bitter enmity were reconciled: invisibly, beyond the tomb, Christ's apostle was continuing his good work of peace and love.

Dom Marmion rests in the abbots' vault, at the end of the little monastic cemetery in the shadow of that church wherein he had vowed himself to God thirty-five years before, and where during thirteen years he had presided, in the midst of his sons, at the sacrifice of praise.

Cardinal Mercier's absence from the funeral had been the more remarked, in that some time previously, at the celebration of the abbey's golden jubilee in October 1922, the great prelate had spoken of the intimate and unfaltering friendship existing between himself and the Abbot of Maredsous. This absence was caused by the indisposition of the cardinal. A letter written by him to a nun two months afterwards, on 9 April 1923, reveals what his feelings were on this occasion. A page of great and noble simplicity, honouring the one who wrote it as much as the one who inspired it:

> You were so good as to tell me about the dear *Révérendissime* Abbot Columba. Can you believe how much I suffer on hearing again what you tell me of his last moments? And this is why: as soon as I was informed of the gravity of his state I wanted, as it was my duty and my heart's desire, to set out

for Maredsous. Those around me (vicars general and secretary) made such opposition to my taking the journey that I gave in. I had in fact committed an imprudence. Believing myself cured of an attack of influenza, I had risked taking the return journey from Brussels and had a relapse which became a cause of anxiety. Hence the solicitude, reasonable I grant, of those around me, but which, it seems to me, I ought to have stood out against; friendship has its rights, gratitude has its duties, and I thought – I still think – that was the moment to apply to myself the saying: the heart has its reasons which reason does not understand.

"But as it was I gave in. I have suffered more than I can tell you, the dear and venerated abbot passed to eternity without having been able to understand or explain to himself my absence.

"After his death, at the time of the funeral, the same conflict, the same distress. For the public, too, for the fathers especially, the fact that, without being confined to my bed and in serious danger, I was not there to render my last duties to an old friend, to a faithful confessor, was naturally disconcerting. This has made me suffer, and the memory of it humiliates me still when I think of it again. More than once I have taken up my pen, meaning to send an explanation, but the idea that there might be difficulty in accepting it paralysed me, and I have had to content myself to wait for the good God to show His chosen one that I did not fail in friendship.

"I am trying to think what I can say to you about the dear *Révérendissime*. My impression as a whole is that he possessed a great heart and was sensibility personified; he was never known to feel bitterness towards anyone, but welcomed, sought every occasion of devoting himself to others. He was very sensitive, suffered much morally, but always bore outwardly a countenance of good humour and accepted all his trials with filial and supernatural submission. He knew how to be compassionate because he had suffered, and suffered even in things that others might have loftily regarded with stoical disdain. As for him, he was at the antipodes of stoicism: he was loving, humble, I was going to say a 'good fellow.' He told me – not long ago – that he thought every day of death, and, in anticipation, made a point of committing his soul into the hands of the good God. His soul is in the divine hands, and I cannot doubt that the divine tender mercy, in which his faith was so deep, has already forgiven his human imperfections and made him enter *in gaudium Domini sui.*

We will supplement this letter by some words of Cardinal Mercier spoken in the course of a conversation he had, more than two years later, with a mutual friend. At the time of this interview Dom Columba's name having been mentioned, the other ventured to ask the cardinal:

"Eminence, may I know what remembrance you have kept of Fr Columba?"

"What remembrance I have kept of him? An ineffable remembrance. You know that we were very intimate; I had for him the affection of a friend ever since the time when I was at Louvain; I bore him a real veneration.

"Certainly, as you also know, Fr Columba, like all men, had his limitations; he lacked certain of the qualities of a man of administration; at times impulsive in action, easily exuberant, but these were, with him, defects of his race and temperament.

"But what a man of God! And above all what an interior soul! On this point he must be praised unreservedly. He was an admirable religious, a truly priestly soul, full of zeal. He was, too, of a beautiful simplicity in his manners and words; extremely kind and good-natured and ready to do anyone a service. What always struck me in him was his living faith and deep humility...."

At that moment the cardinal, being urgently called away, had to interrupt the conversation and take leave of his interlocutor.

Concise as is this testimony, it is all the more significant, and assuredly those of our readers who have followed us thus far will ratify it.

He comes before us as an original personality, rich and ardent; we see him constantly tending to the seeking after God and wonderfully faithful to grace; this faithfulness shines forth throughout the whole course of his existence like a luminous track, which, as it ever grows brighter, attracts and captivates us. God's possessive power over him made Dom Marmion an interior man, a great mystic, a spiritual director after Jesus Christ's own Heart, an apostle utterly detached from himself and full of holy zest for the perfection of his neighbour. The divine light bathed him in its splendour and the ardour of his faith radiated upon souls. Dom Marmion was great, with the greatness which confers on a human life the unflagging and undeviating continuity of its ascent towards the summits of God; he was great by reason of the width of his charity, as he was by the depth of his contemplation.

The man in Dom Columba has passed away with his human limitations;[1] but his personality survives upon this earth, in the manner wherein those survive who, consecrated to God, have generously served both Him and His Church by virtue, action and the pen.

He survives, in the first place, in a way unknown to all – known to God alone – by the hidden power that his merits have exerted upon others, and by the graces that his prayers and sacrifices, like

---

[1] "It is possible to be a great saint and yet to be imperfect in many respects," writes Msgr Alban Goodier, SJ, who likewise honoured Dom Marmion with his friendship and whose writings contain teaching very similar to that of Dom Columba. "Ask the saints themselves and they will all tell you of their many failures and shortcomings. But one thing is not possible; it is not possible to grow in the knowledge, and love, and imitation of Jesus Christ, without at the same time growing in the perfection of every virtue and becoming more a saint every day.... Truth, sanctity, only begins when the core of the creature is affected. And this is done, almost alone, by love; when the creature loves, then it is changed, until then scarcely at all. Thus it is that the knowledge and love of Jesus Christ grows deeper down than any Stoic striving after virtue:... it gives life and substance" (*A More Excellent Way*).

so much divine seed destined to bring forth a perennial harvest, have in silence and secret brought down upon souls.[1]

He survives in souls who, without having had with him any other relations beyond those of a penitent to an occasional confessor or of a listener to a passing preacher, have felt the warmth of his zeal and the exceptional good wrought by his counsel or his words. We may recall what a young Canadian girl wrote long months after Dom Columba's death: "I only spoke once with Dom Marmion, but he left upon me such an impression of supernatural goodness that all that I recall of him brings me nearer to the good God. It is as if the grace that accompanied his presence still clings to his memory."

He survives, too, and more particularly, in the memory and affections of many. With those who knew and loved him, either through having direct relations with him or through the intercourse of spiritual correspondence, there remains the ineffaceable remembrance of a noble mind, a great heart, uplifted, upheld and possessed by one great passion: the passion for Christ, and for souls to be brought and given to Christ to the glory of the Father. And is it not because he gave himself up – that was the term he loved to use – and gave himself up entirely to the Lord Jesus, that the most diverse gifts and energies of a rich nature were so remarkably developed in him under the breath of the Spirit of God? Was it not in Christ's service that in him the natural and the supernatural, thought and action, preaching and the inner life, formed together a harmony of which the sincerity was one of the most attractive charms of his extraordinary personality?... It is the beauty, the greatness and the strength of this inner life as well as its incomparable radiant unity.

[1] More than one favour has been already obtained through Dom Columba's intercession; let us quote only these lines, dated 21 September 1925, from an Irish Carmelite nun: "On three different occasions this year, I have obtained very special favours through the intercession of your holy father, Abbot Columba. I have absolute confidence in his power with God. Each time that I have invoked him I have been answered before the end of the novena, and I asked him personal spiritual favours which have had a great influence on my spiritual life as regards my interior progress."

In short, if he has thus a posthumous existence in the far-reaching good effected by his virtues and action and in the faithful remembrance kept of him by those who particularly appreciated and had recourse to him, he still lives on in an enduring and indestructible manner in his spiritual writings, which continue and will indefinitely continue to extend his apostolate.

Soon after Dom Marmion's death one well-qualified to judge[1] wrote: "For thousands of Christian souls his [image] will always be connected with the Saviour's light and love that they have found in the three volumes which perpetuate his apostolic action in the bosom of the Church. Few works of spirituality have known the same success among every variety of soul: a success which will be maintained, for these books, while having their own special character, are of those which endure."

An appreciation confirmed as well as explained by another critic of the same school, and one not less competent, Fr Paul Doncœur: "Solid theology, knowledge and understanding of souls, genuine limpidity of expression, give to such books more than ephemeral success. Human equilibrium and the unction of the Holy Spirit are the guarantee and secret of their lasting fruitfulness."[2]

Death indeed does not extinguish such torches.

We have so often left Dom Marmion to speak for himself that we shall be allowed once more to gather from his own lips, by way of conclusion, his last teaching. *Ultima verba*, in fact, or if preferred *ultima scripta*, for it contains his past spiritual letter written only seven days before his death. It is addressed to an Irish novice in whose spiritual progress he was particularly interested; she was about to make her private retreat before consecrating herself to God by the vows of religion. As ever, his warm charity and zeal for souls shine out in this characteristic page. We are already familiar with some of the ideas contained in these lines, but here all that is best and highest

1 Fr de Guibert, *Revue d'ascétique*, April 1923.
2 Fr Doncœur, *Études, loc. cit.*

in Dom Marmion's teaching is summed up under a concise form. But above all these lines disclose what were his own most habitual feelings and aspirations on the eve of leaving this world. Lines so much the more touching in that at the hour when they were written he was himself unaware of the imminence of his departure for heaven, for he speaks of a retreat he was to preach some weeks later. Some echo of eternity, however, reverberates through these lines, recalling, as they do, the farewell prayer that Jesus offered for "His own" to His Father at the moment of consummating His supreme Sacrifice. For all these reasons they are to be read with reverence.

> *Maredsous, 23 January 1923* – My dear child, just a little word straight from my heart to tell you I am with you in your offering. St Paul says: '*Christus pro omnibus crucifixus est; justus pro injustus, ut nos offerret Deo.*' What the crucified Jesus offers His Father is ever acceptable, however miserable we are.
>
> I am offering Mass for you on the 25th, asking Jesus to take you with Him through the veil, that is His crucified humanity, into the Holy of Holies.
>
> During our little retreat I hope to show you what this 'Holy of Holies' is. I want it to be *our* home. 'Father,' says Jesus, 'I will that where I am My servant also may be.' I want us to pass through the veil, and to dwell there with Jesus in love. This program is high, but it is our destiny, it is God's wish, it is the fruit and object of the Passion of Jesus.
>
> I am really sorry not to be at ... for your profession, but there is no distance for those united in Christ. I want you to make this little retreat with great fervour, as it contains the program of that journey which I am to guide you by during your life.
>
> I know you pray for me, as I do *daily* for you.
>
> Your father in J.C.

A worthy spiritual will and testament of a master of asceticism and of a great monk into whose wonderful life we have gained some insight – however little – throughout the pages of this volume.

May we not have the sure hope that this holy soul has "passed forever through the veil" and abides henceforward "in the eternal bosom of the Father – with Jesus – in love…"?

This life so rich and of such oneness is full of manifold and precious teaching, but it seems above all to repeat to us that saying of St Paul which applies so well to Dom Marmion: "By the grace of God, I am what I am, and His grace in me hath not been void.…"

In leaving him have we not a prayer on out lips rather than a farewell – a prayer that we may be, like him, generously "unflaggingly faithful in love"?

About The Cenacle Press at Silverstream Priory

An apostolate of the Benedictine monastery of Silverstream Priory in Ireland, the mission of The Cenacle Press can be summed up in four words: *Quis ostendit nobis bona*—who will show us good things (Psalm 4:6)? In an age of confusion, ugliness, and sin, our aim is to show something of the Highest Good to every reader who picks up our books. More specifically, we believe that the treasury of the centuries-old Benedictine tradition and the beauty of holiness which has characterized so many of its followers through the ages has something beneficial, worthwhile, and encouraging in it for every believer.

www.cenaclepress.com

Also Available:

Robert Hugh Benson
The Friendship of Christ

Robert Hugh Benson
Confessions of a Convert

Fr Willie Doyle, SJ
Pamphlets for the Faithful

Dom Pius de Hemptinne, OSB
A Benedictine Soul: Biography, Letters, and Spiritual Writings of Dom Pius de Hemptinne

Blessed Columba Marmion, OSB
Christ the Ideal of the Monk

Blessed Columba Marmion, OSB
Words of Life on the Margin of the Missal

St John Henry Newman (*ed.* Melinda Nielsen)
Festivals of Faith: Sermons for the Liturgical Year

Fr Ryan T. Sliwa
New Nazareths in Us

Dom Hubert van Zeller, OSB
Approach to Prayer

Dom Hubert van Zeller, OSB
Sanctity in Other Words

Visit www.cenaclepress.com for our full catalogue.

www.ingramcontent.com/pod-product-compliance
Lightning Source LLC
Chambersburg PA
CBHW030031100526
44590CB00011B/154